D1064717

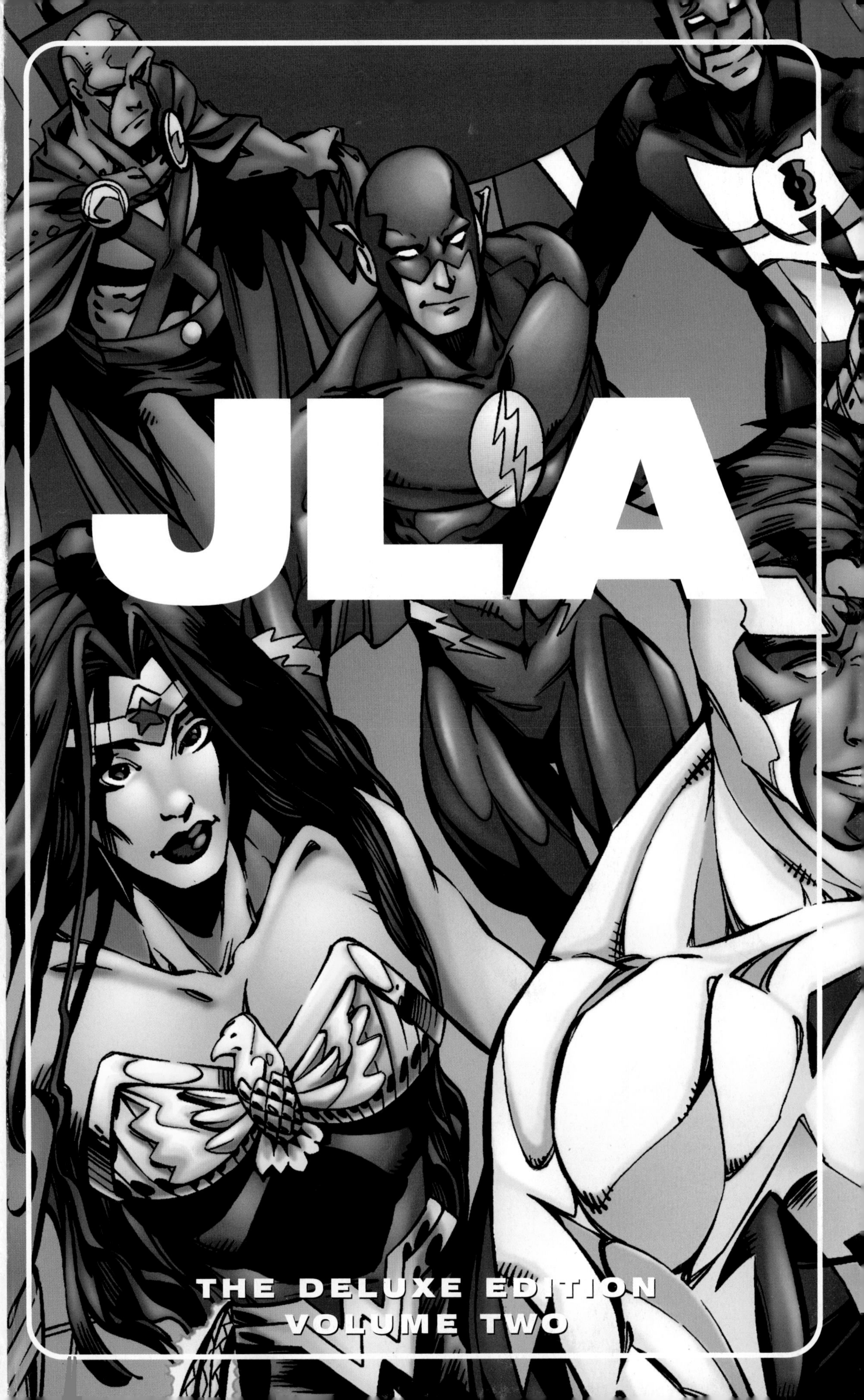
JLA
THE DELUXE EDITION
VOLUME TWO

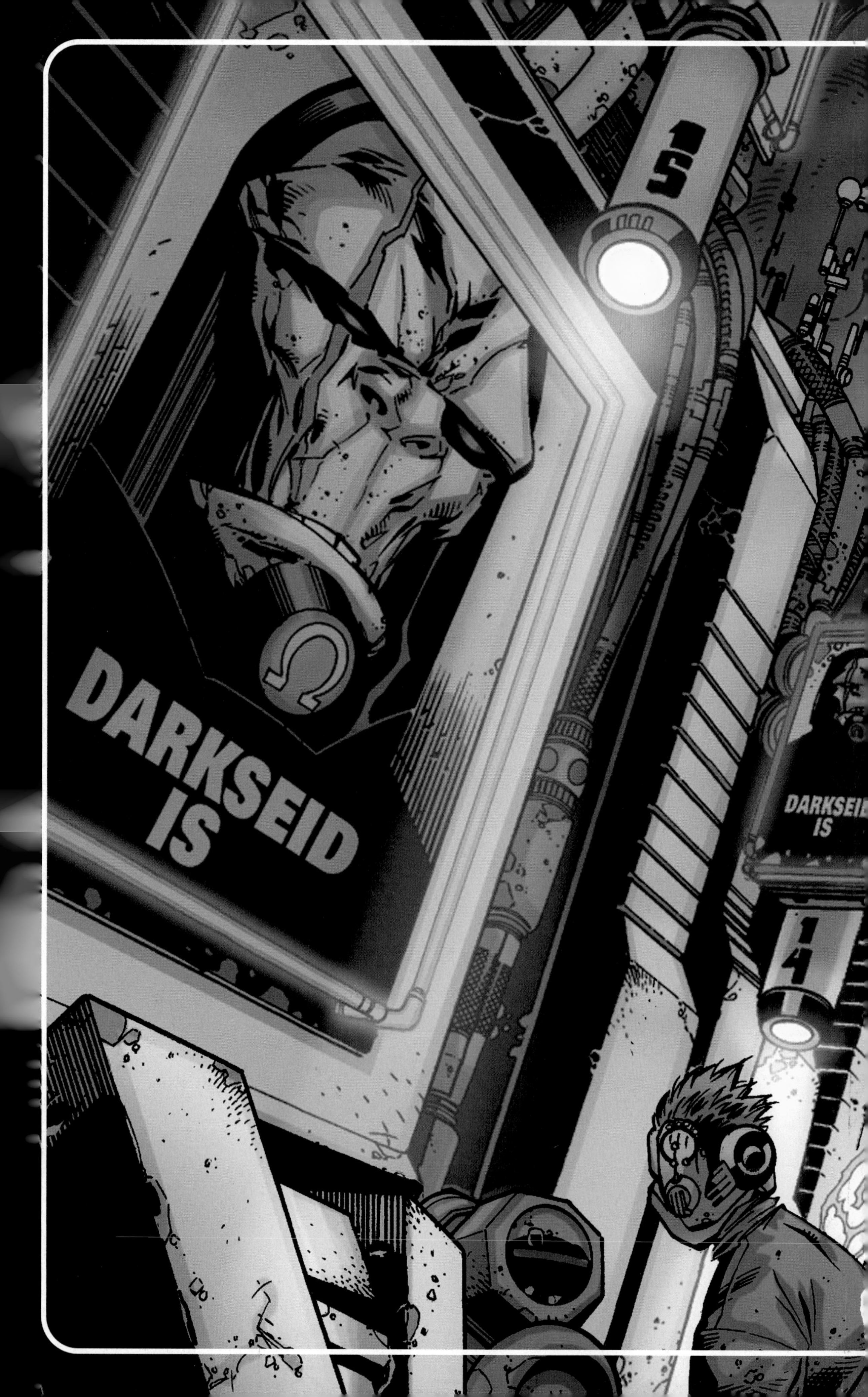

15
DARKSEID IS
DARKSEI IS
14

JLA

THE DELUXE EDITION
VOLUME TWO

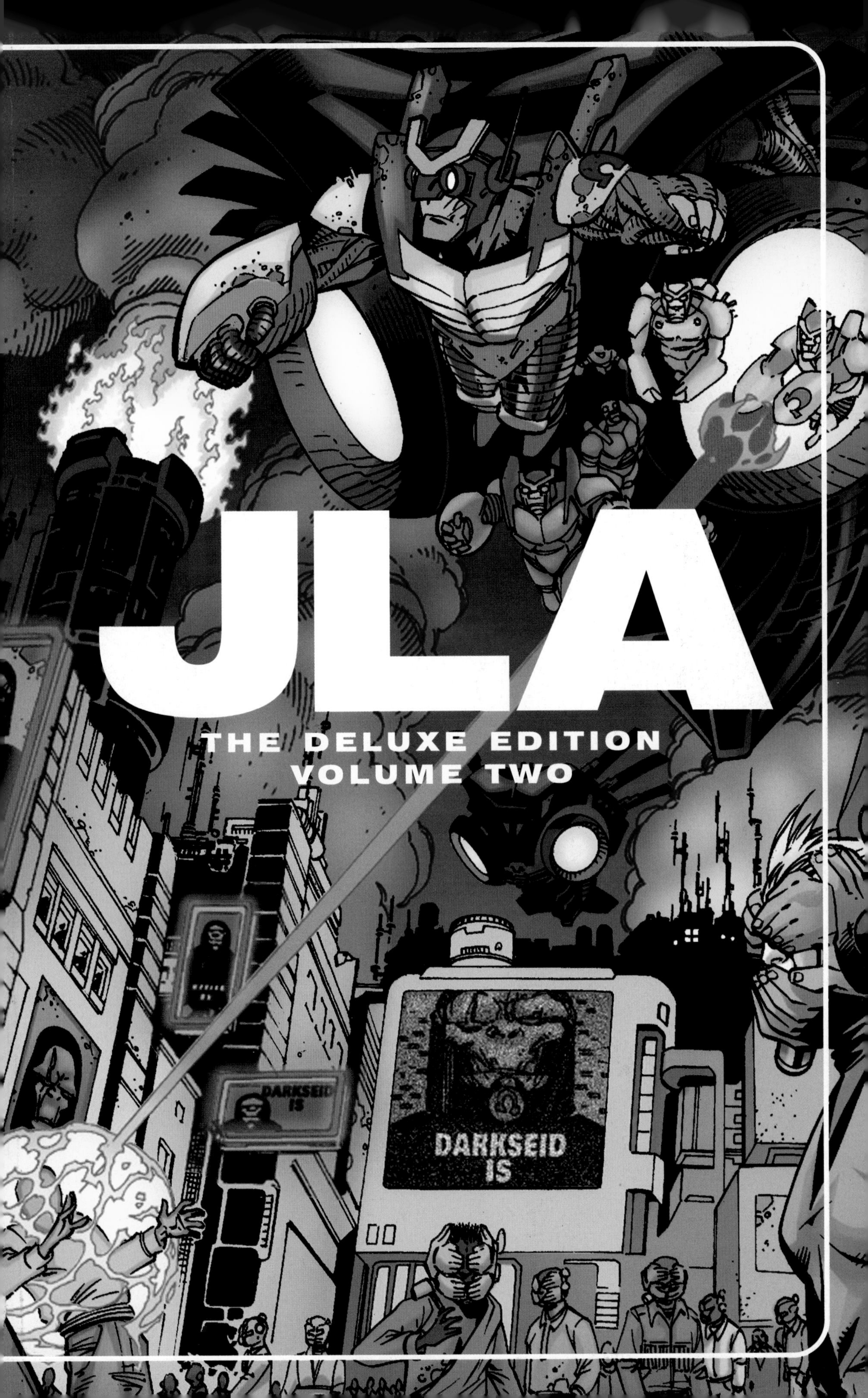
DARKSEID IS
DARKSEID IS

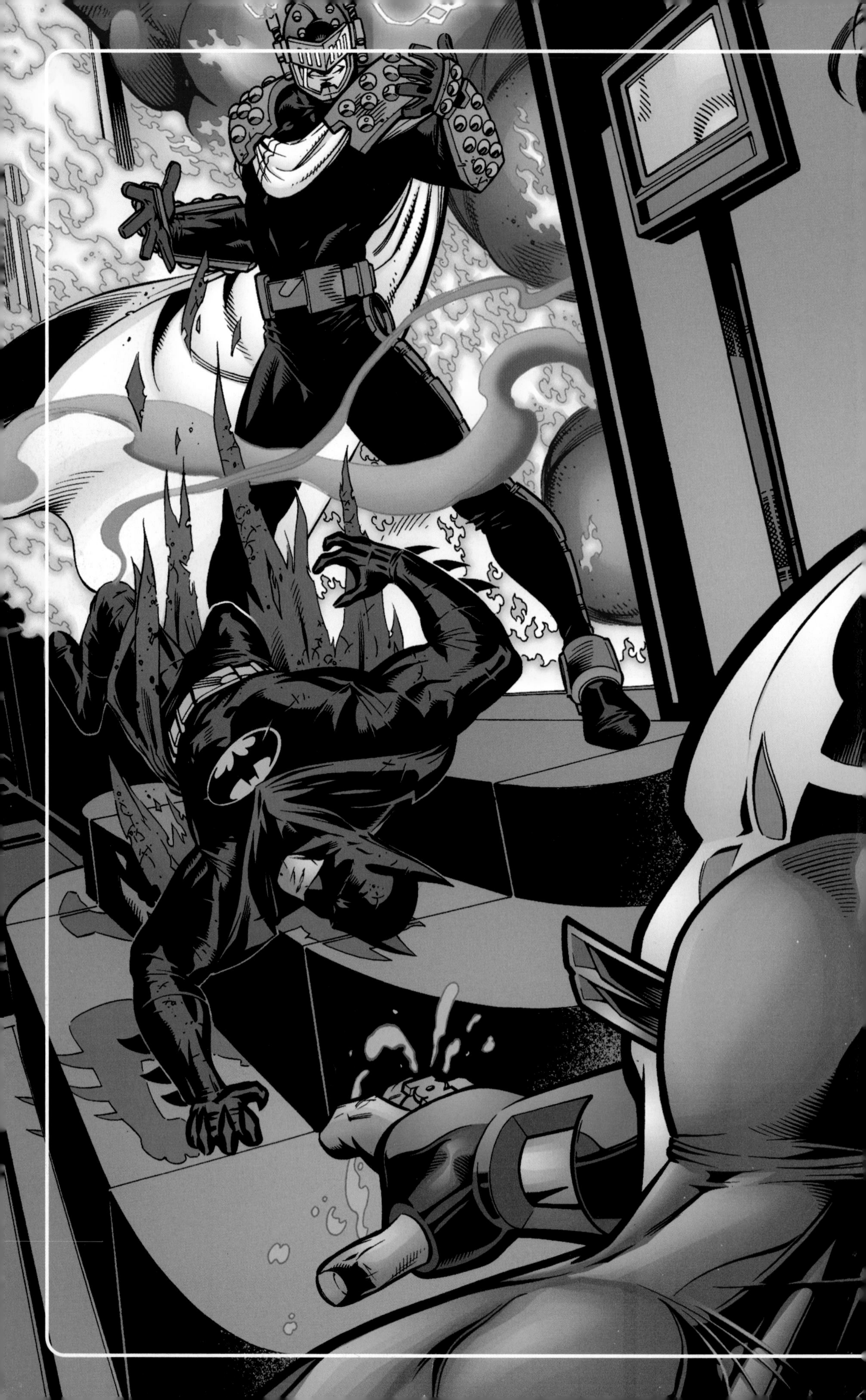

GRANT MORRISON
writer

HOWARD PORTER
penciller

JOHN DELL
inker

..

VAL SEMEIKS
Penciller on JLA/WILDC.A.T.S.

ARNIE JORGENSEN
Penciller on "There Was a Crooked Man"
and "Prometheus Unbound"

GARY FRANK
GREG LAND
Additonal pencillers on "Stone of Destiny"

KEVIN CONRAD
DAVID MEIKIS
RAY KRYSSING
BOB MCLEOD
MARK PENNINGTON
Additional Inkers

PAT GARRAHY
JAMES SINCLAIR
Colorists

KEN LOPEZ
JANICE CHIANG
Letterers

..

Superman created by
JERRY SIEGEL & JOE SHUSTER

Batman created by
BOB KANE

Wonder Woman created by
WILLIAM MOULTON MARSTON

Aquaman created by
PAUL NORRIS

DAN DIDIO Senior VP-Executive Editor :: DAN RASPLER Editor-original series :: L.A. WILLIAMS Associate Editor-original series
ANTON KAWASAKI Editor-collected edition :: ROBBIN BROSTERMAN Design Director-Books :: PAUL LEVITZ President & Publisher
GEORG BREWER VP-Design & DC Direct Creative :: RICHARD BRUNING Senior VP-Creative Director
PATRICK CALDON Executive VP-Finance & Operations :: CHRIS CARAMALIS VP-Finance :: JOHN CUNNINGHAM VP-Marketing
TERRI CUNNINGHAM VP-Managing Editor :: AMY GENKINS Senior VP-Business & Legal Affairs :: ALISON GILL VP-Manufacturing
DAVID HYDE VP-Publicity :: HANK KANALZ VP-General Manager, WildStorm :: JIM LEE Editorial Director-WildStorm
GREGORY NOVECK Senior VP-Creative Affairs :: SUE POHJA VP-Book Trade Sales :: STEVE ROTTERDAM Senior VP-Sales & Marketing
CHERYL RUBIN Senior VP-Brand Management :: ALYSSE SOLL VP-Advertising & Custom Publishing
JEFF TROJAN VP-Business Development, DC Direct :: BOB WAYNE VP-Sales

Cover by Howard Porter with Edgar Delgado. Interior color separations by Heroic Age & Digital Chameleon.

JLA: THE DELUXE EDITION Volume Two
Published by DC Comics. Cover and compilation Copyright © 2009 DC Comics. All Rights Reserved. Originally
published in single magazine form in JLA #1-9, JLA SECRET FILES #1. Copyright © 1997 DC Comics. All Rights
Reserved. All characters, their distinctive likenesses and related elements featured in this publication are trademarks of
DC Comics. The stories, characters and incidents featured in this publication are entirely fictional. DC Comics does
not read or accept unsolicited submissions of ideas, stories or artwork.

DC Comics. 1700 Broadway, New York, NY 10019. A Warner Bros. Entertainment Company
Printed in USA. First Printing. ISBN: 978-1-4012-2265-9

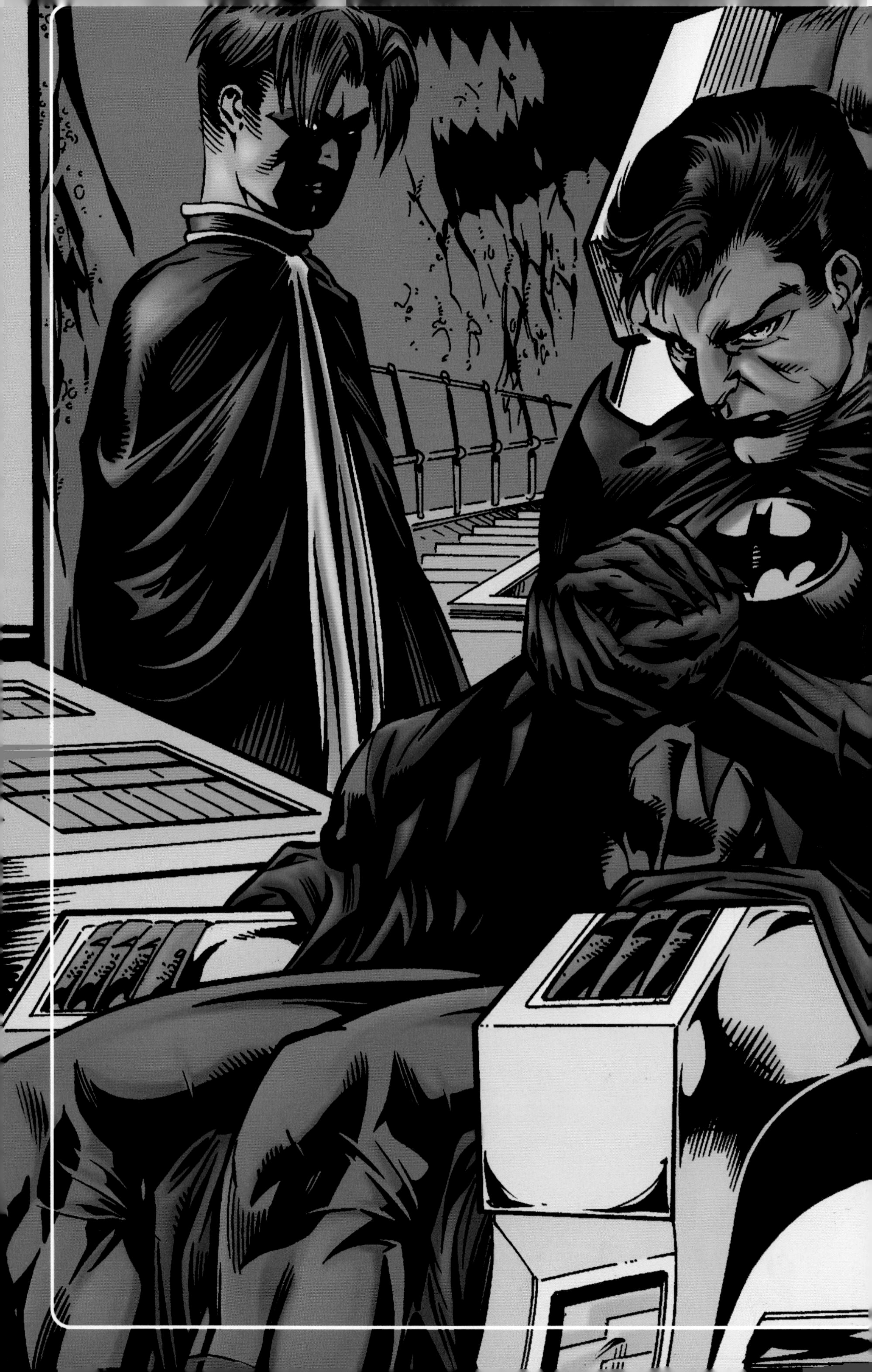

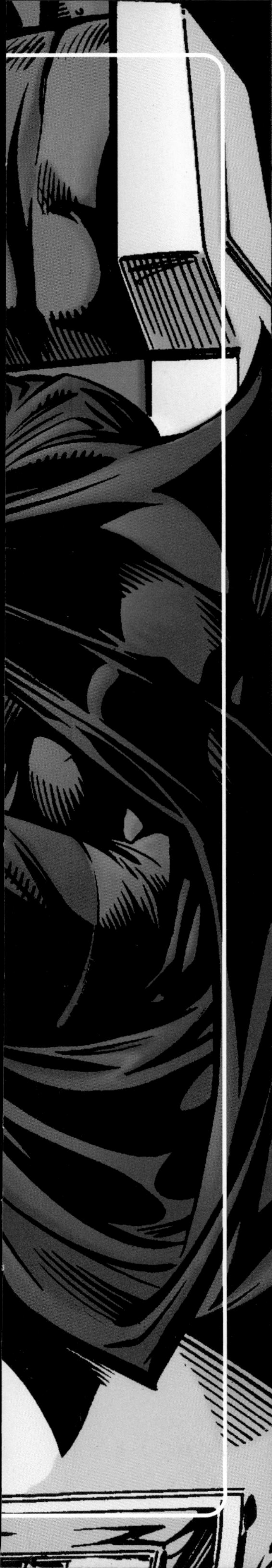

CURRENT MEMBERSHIP:

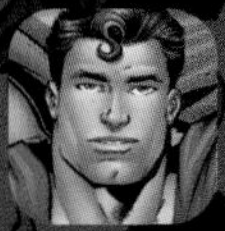

SUPERMAN

The last son of the doomed planet Krypton, Kal-El uses his incredible powers of flight, super-strength, and invulnerability to fight for truth and justice on his adopted planet, Earth. When not protecting the planet, he is Daily Planet reporter Clark Kent, married to fellow journalist Lois Lane.

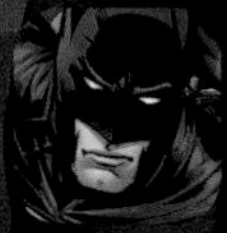

BATMAN

Dedicated to ridding the world of crime since the brutal murder of his parents, billionaire Bruce Wayne dons the cape and cowl of the Dark Knight to battle evil from the shadows of Gotham City.

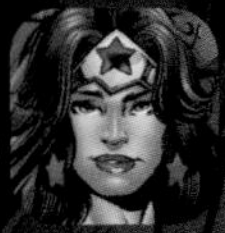

WONDER WOMAN

Born an Amazonian princess, Diana was chosen to serve as her people's ambassador of peace in the World of Man. Armed with the Lasso of Truth and indestructible bracelets, she directs her gods-given abilities of strength and speed toward the betterment of mankind. Her mother, Queen Hippolyta, was the first Wonder Woman — and will temporarily take Diana's place in the League.

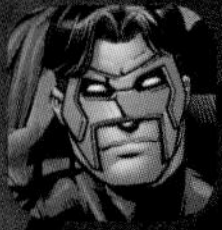

GREEN LANTERN

After the destruction of the Green Lantern Corps, Kyle Rayner was chosen to be the one true Green Lantern. The powers of his ring are limited only by the imagination of its bearer — a strong suit of Kyle, who toils by day as a commercial artist.

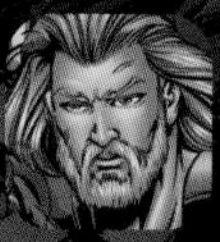

AQUAMAN

A founding member of the Justice League, Arthur is the royal ruler of a kingdom that covers over two-thirds of the planet. His abilities to withstand the awesome pressure of the deep and to communicate with all the ocean's inhabitants help to make him the undersea world's greatest protector.

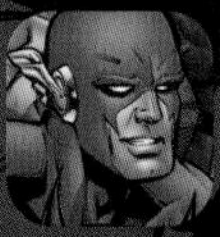

THE FLASH

A member of the Teen Titans when he was known as Kid Flash, Wally West now takes the place of the fallen Flash, Barry Allen, as the speedster of the Justice League.

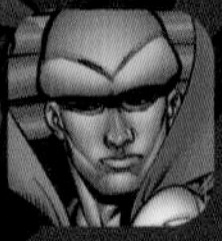

MARTIAN MANHUNTER

J'onn J'onzz has been a member of the JLA for every one of the team's many incarnations. His strength rivals that of Earth's mightiest heroes, and his shape-shifting abilities allow him to pass anonymously among our planet's populace. His awesome mental powers serve to link the entire League in thought.

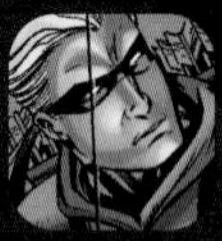

GREEN ARROW

The only known son of the original Green Arrow, Connor Hawke is the complete antithesis to his volatile, womanizing father. An earnest young man with a mature and thoughtful nature, Green Arrow is far more than a guy with a bow and arrow — he is also an expert in martial arts.

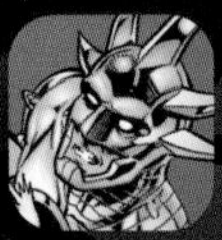

AZTEK

Uno was raised by the secret Q Society to become the human vessel for the Aztec god Quetzalcoatl's power. Donned with a magical suit of armor that bestows many super-human abilities (including strength, flight, invisibility and intangibility), Aztek serves as the JLA's newest recruit.

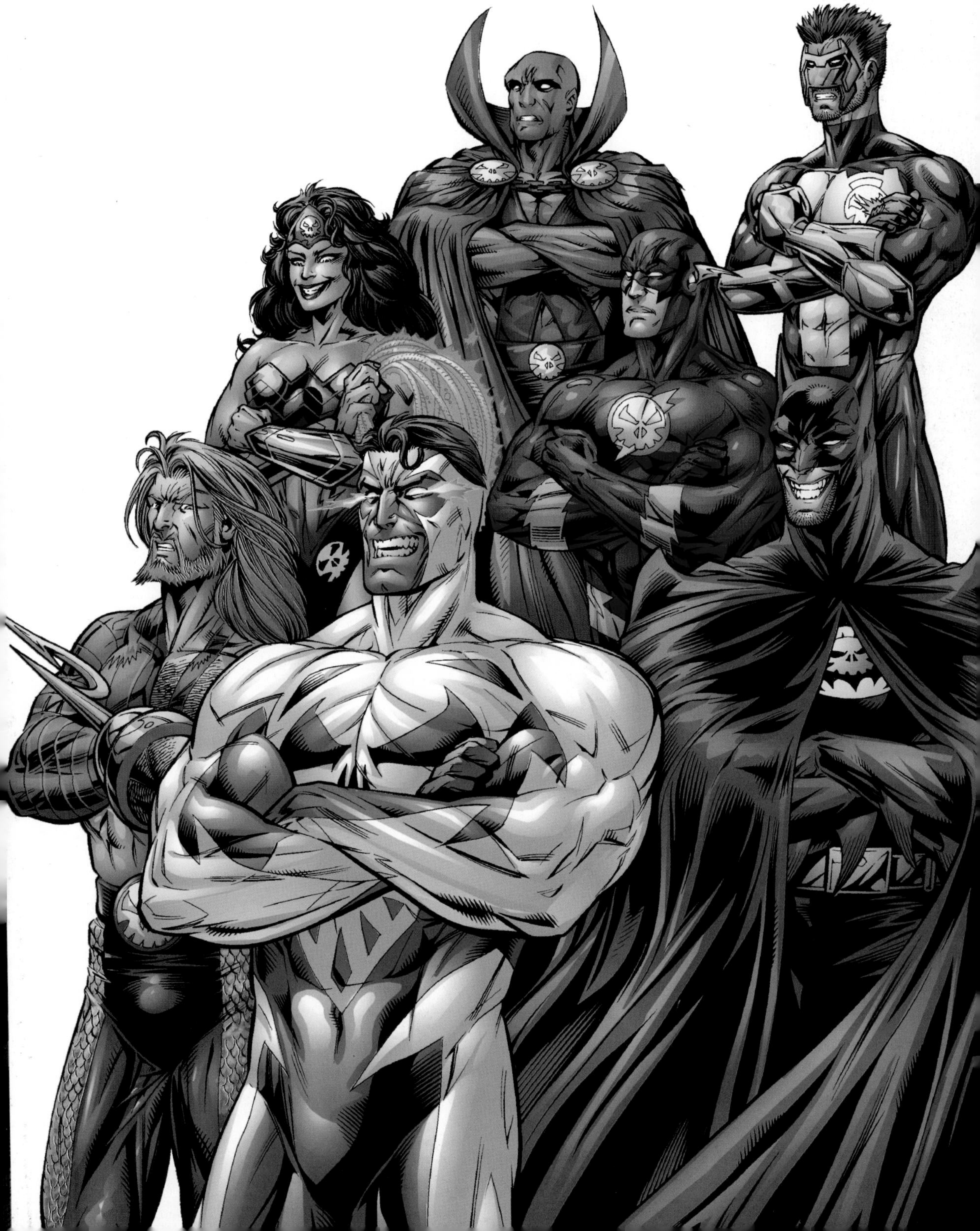

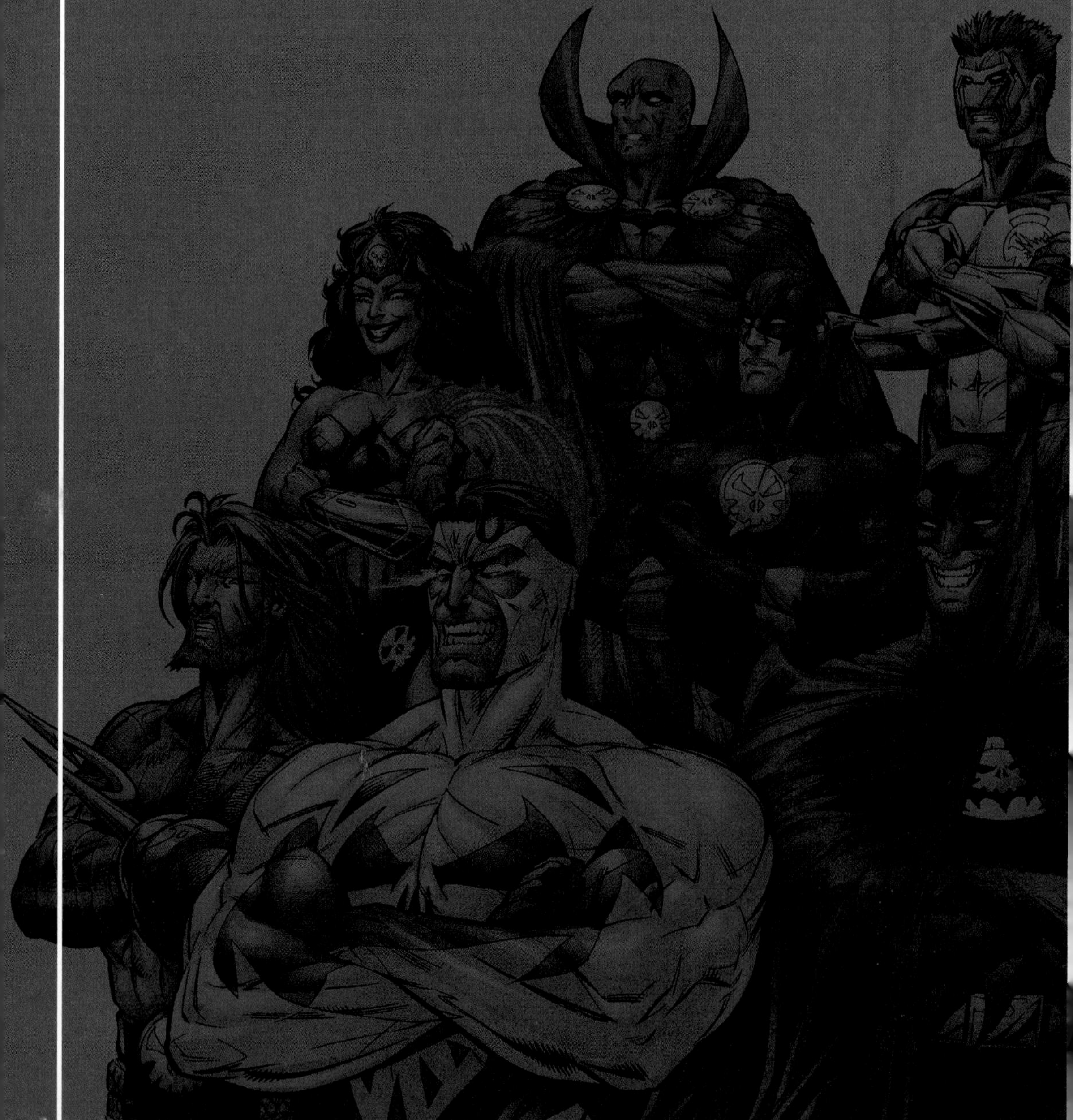

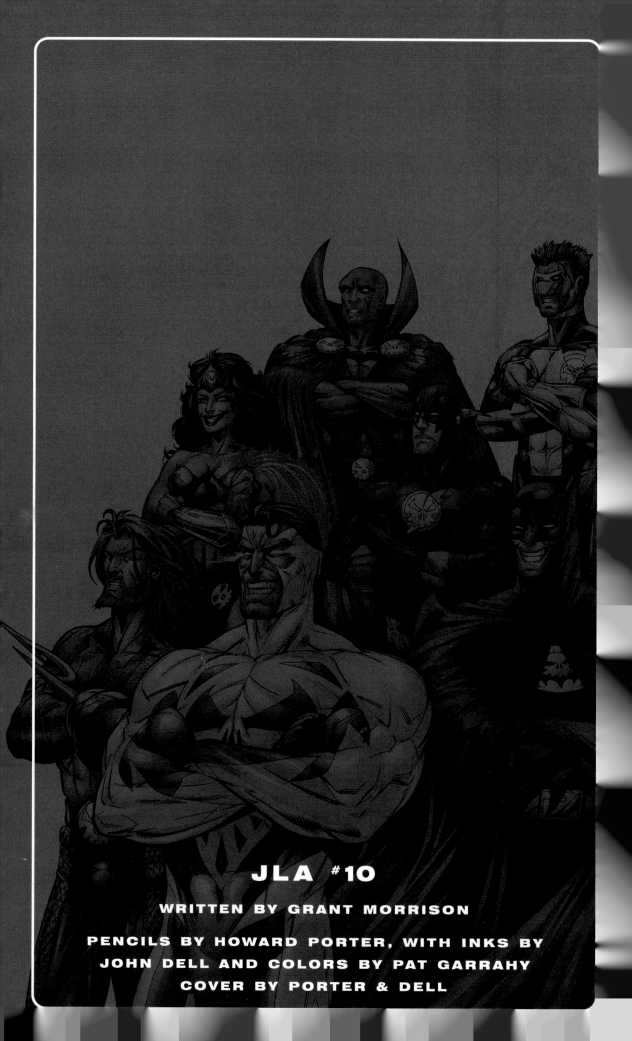

JLA #10

WRITTEN BY GRANT MORRISON

PENCILS BY HOWARD PORTER, WITH INKS BY JOHN DELL AND COLORS BY PAT GARRAHY
COVER BY PORTER & DELL

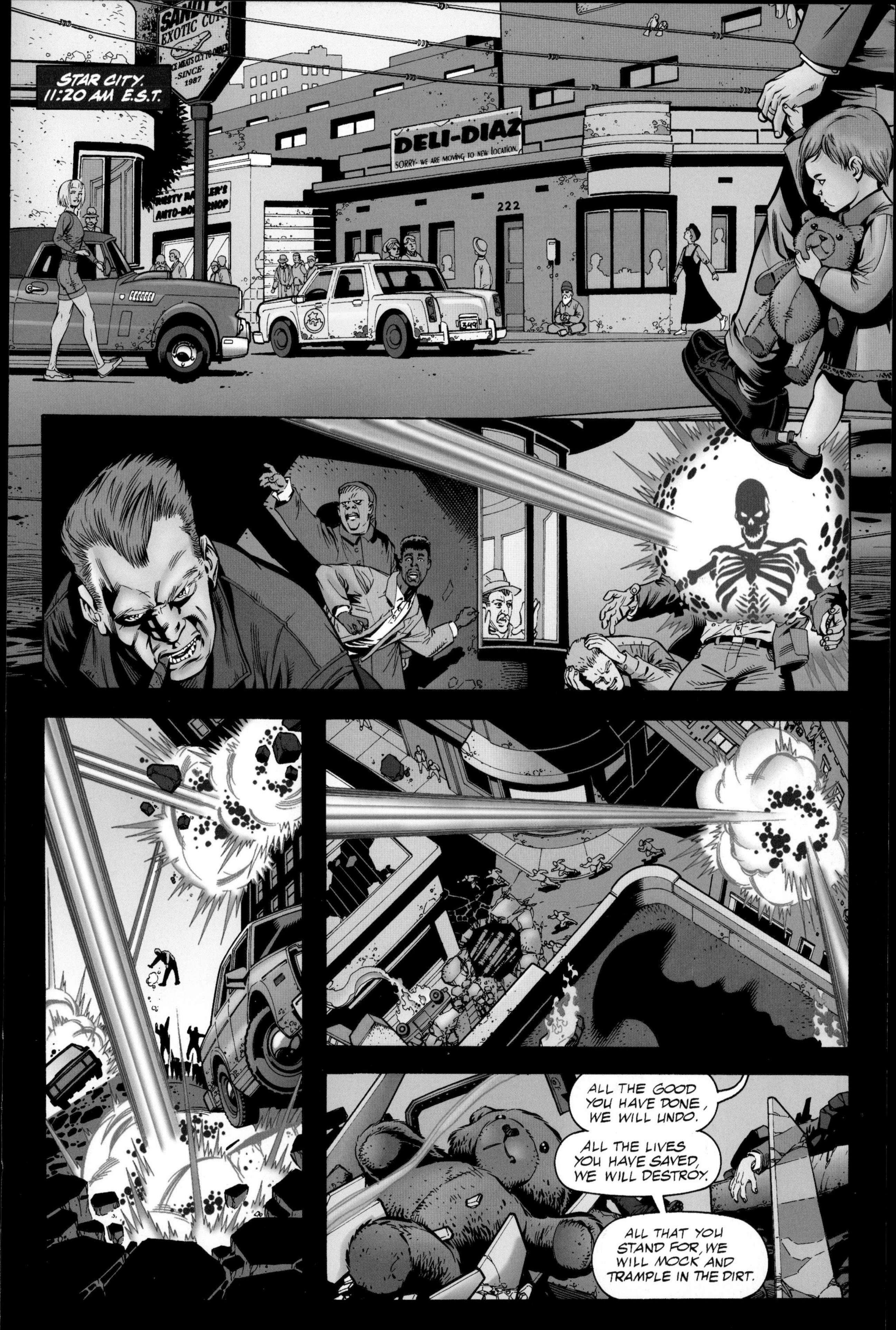
STAR CITY.
11:20 AM E.S.T.
SANDY'S
EXOTIC CUTS
SINCE 1987
DELI-DIAZ
SORRY- WE ARE MOVING TO NEW LOCATION.
AUTO-BODY SHOP
222
ALL THE GOOD YOU HAVE DONE, WE WILL UNDO.
ALL THE LIVES YOU HAVE SAVED, WE WILL DESTROY.
ALL THAT YOU STAND FOR, WE WILL MOCK AND TRAMPLE IN THE DIRT.

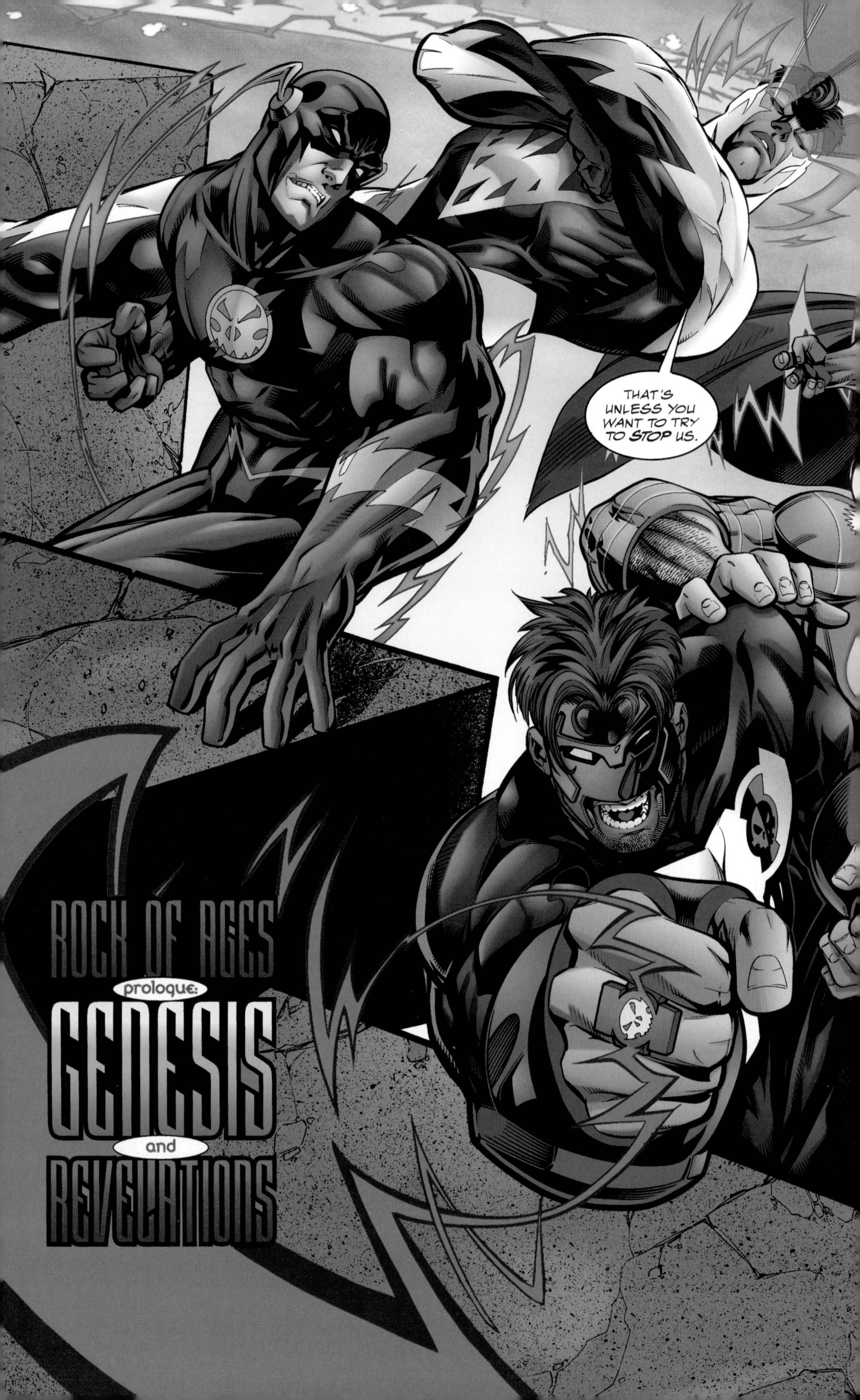
THAT'S UNLESS YOU WANT TO TRY TO STOP US.
ROCK OF AGES
prologue:
GENESIS
and
REVELATIONS

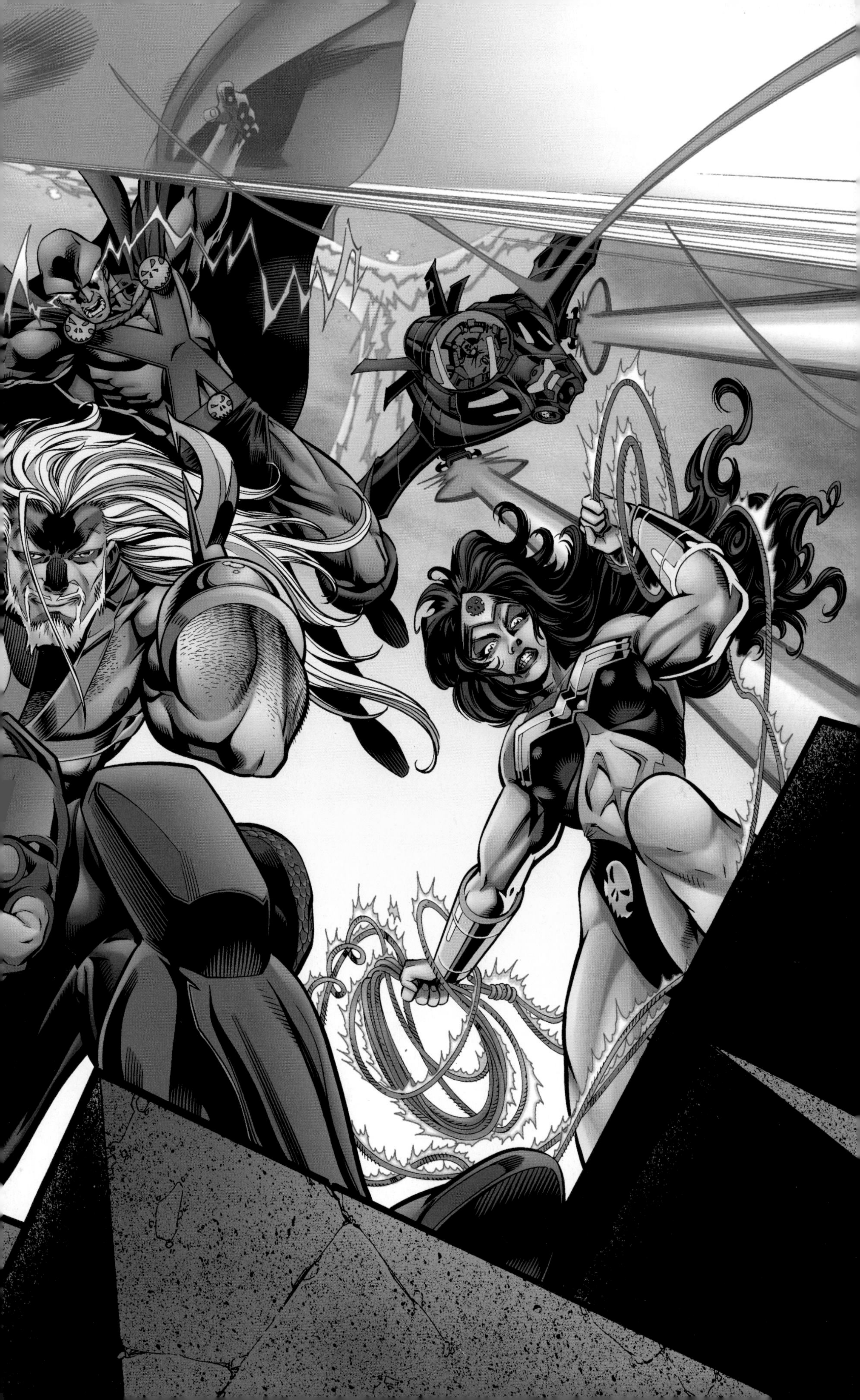

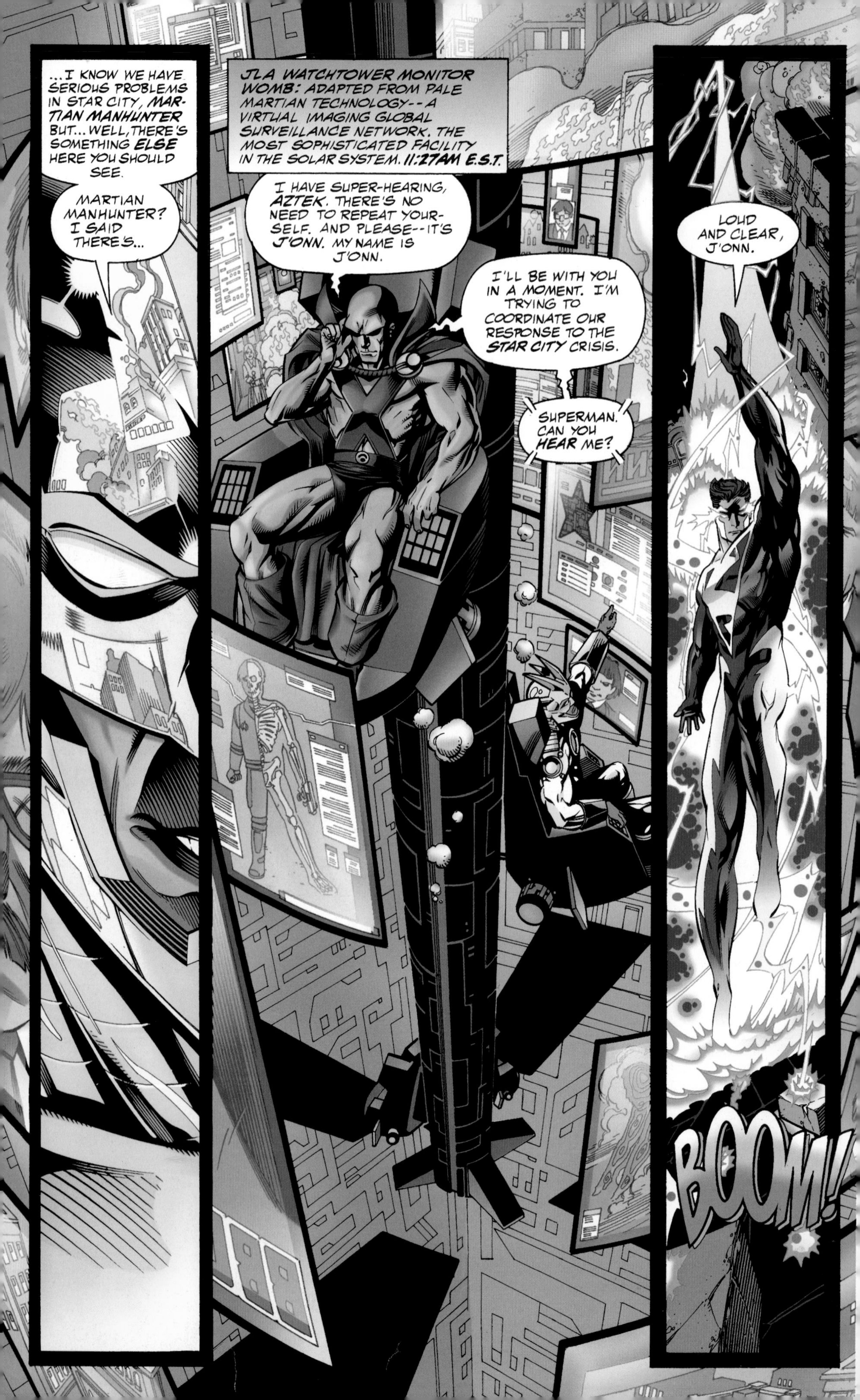
...I KNOW WE HAVE SERIOUS PROBLEMS IN STAR CITY, MARTIAN MANHUNTER BUT...WELL, THERE'S SOMETHING ELSE HERE YOU SHOULD SEE.
MARTIAN MANHUNTER? I SAID THERE'S...
JLA WATCHTOWER MONITOR WOMB: ADAPTED FROM PALE MARTIAN TECHNOLOGY--A VIRTUAL IMAGING GLOBAL SURVEILLANCE NETWORK, THE MOST SOPHISTICATED FACILITY IN THE SOLAR SYSTEM. 11:27AM E.S.T.
I HAVE SUPER-HEARING, AZTEK. THERE'S NO NEED TO REPEAT YOURSELF. AND PLEASE--IT'S J'ONN. MY NAME IS J'ONN.
I'LL BE WITH YOU IN A MOMENT. I'M TRYING TO COORDINATE OUR RESPONSE TO THE STAR CITY CRISIS.
SUPERMAN. CAN YOU HEAR ME?
LOUD AND CLEAR, J'ONN.
BOOM!

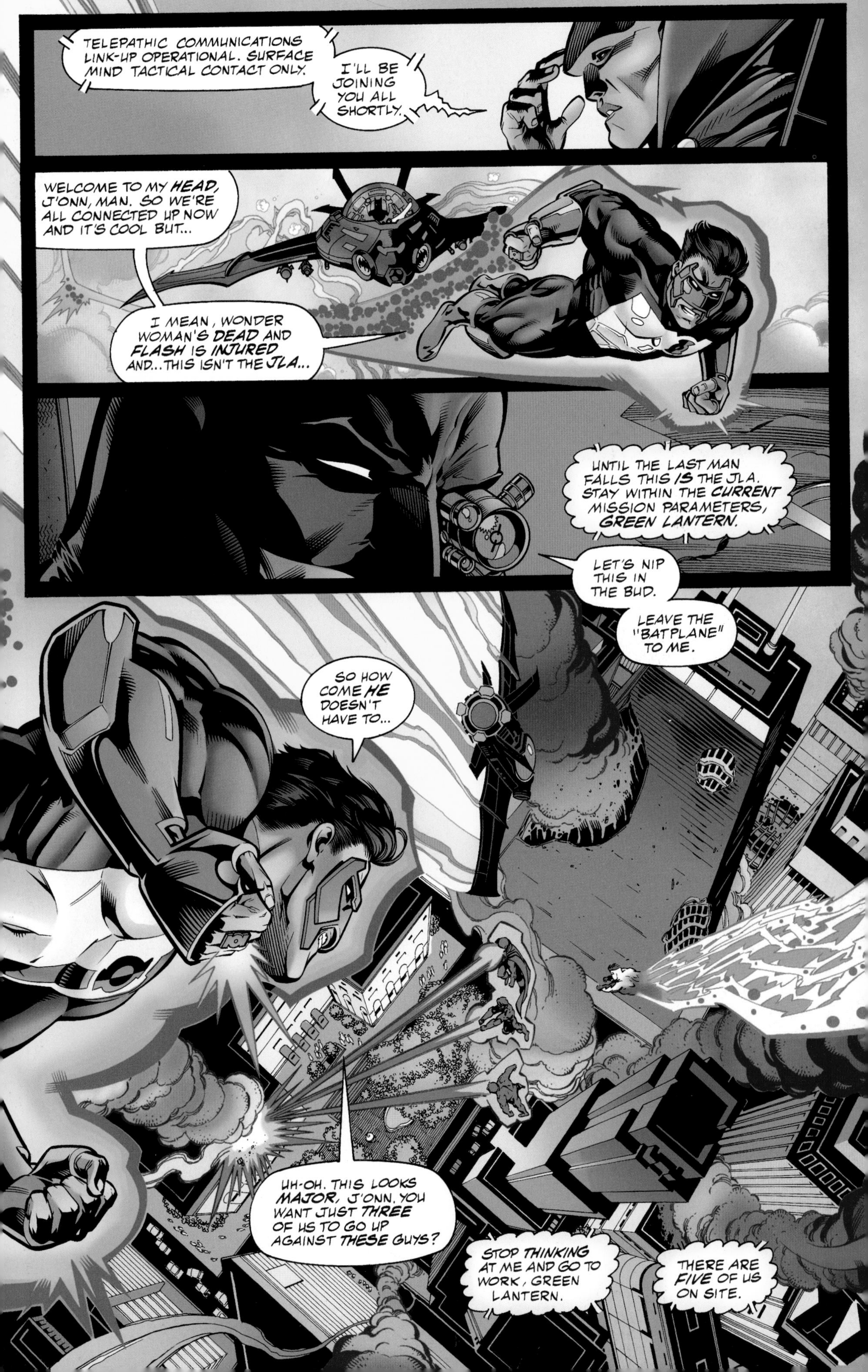

TELEPATHIC COMMUNICATIONS LINK-UP OPERATIONAL. SURFACE MIND TACTICAL CONTACT ONLY.
I'LL BE JOINING YOU ALL SHORTLY.
WELCOME TO MY HEAD, J'ONN, MAN. SO WE'RE ALL CONNECTED UP NOW AND IT'S COOL BUT...
I MEAN, WONDER WOMAN'S DEAD AND FLASH IS INJURED AND...THIS ISN'T THE JLA...
UNTIL THE LAST MAN FALLS THIS IS THE JLA. STAY WITHIN THE CURRENT MISSION PARAMETERS, GREEN LANTERN.
LET'S NIP THIS IN THE BUD.
LEAVE THE "BATPLANE" TO ME.
SO HOW COME HE DOESN'T HAVE TO...
UH-OH. THIS LOOKS MAJOR, J'ONN. YOU WANT JUST THREE OF US TO GO UP AGAINST THESE GUYS?
STOP THINKING AT ME AND GO TO WORK, GREEN LANTERN.
THERE ARE FIVE OF US ON SITE.

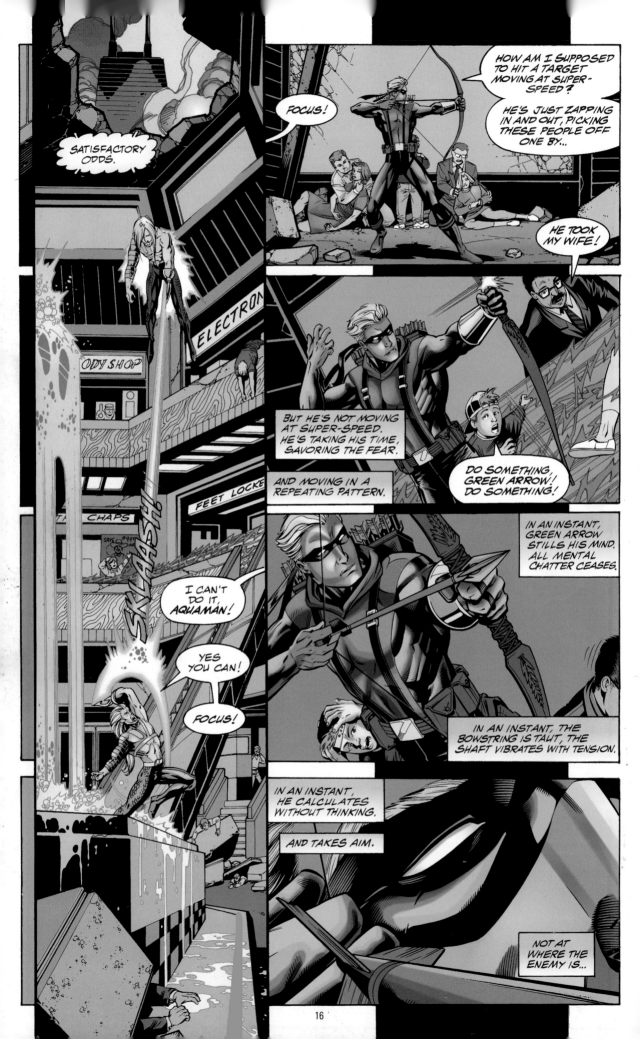

SATISFACTORY ODDS.

ELECTRON

ODY SHOP

FEET LOCKER

THE CHAPS

SAVE #99

SKLASSH!

I CAN'T DO IT, AQUAMAN!

YES YOU CAN!

FOCUS!

HOW AM I SUPPOSED TO HIT A TARGET MOVING AT SUPER-SPEED?

HE'S JUST ZAPPING IN AND OUT, PICKING THESE PEOPLE OFF ONE BY...

FOCUS!

HE TOOK MY WIFE!

BUT HE'S NOT MOVING AT SUPER-SPEED. HE'S TAKING HIS TIME, SAVORING THE FEAR.

AND MOVING IN A REPEATING PATTERN.

DO SOMETHING, GREEN ARROW! DO SOMETHING!

IN AN INSTANT, GREEN ARROW STILLS HIS MIND. ALL MENTAL CHATTER CEASES.

IN AN INSTANT, THE BOWSTRING IS TAUT, THE SHAFT VIBRATES WITH TENSION.

IN AN INSTANT, HE CALCULATES WITHOUT THINKING.

AND TAKES AIM.

NOT AT WHERE THE ENEMY IS...

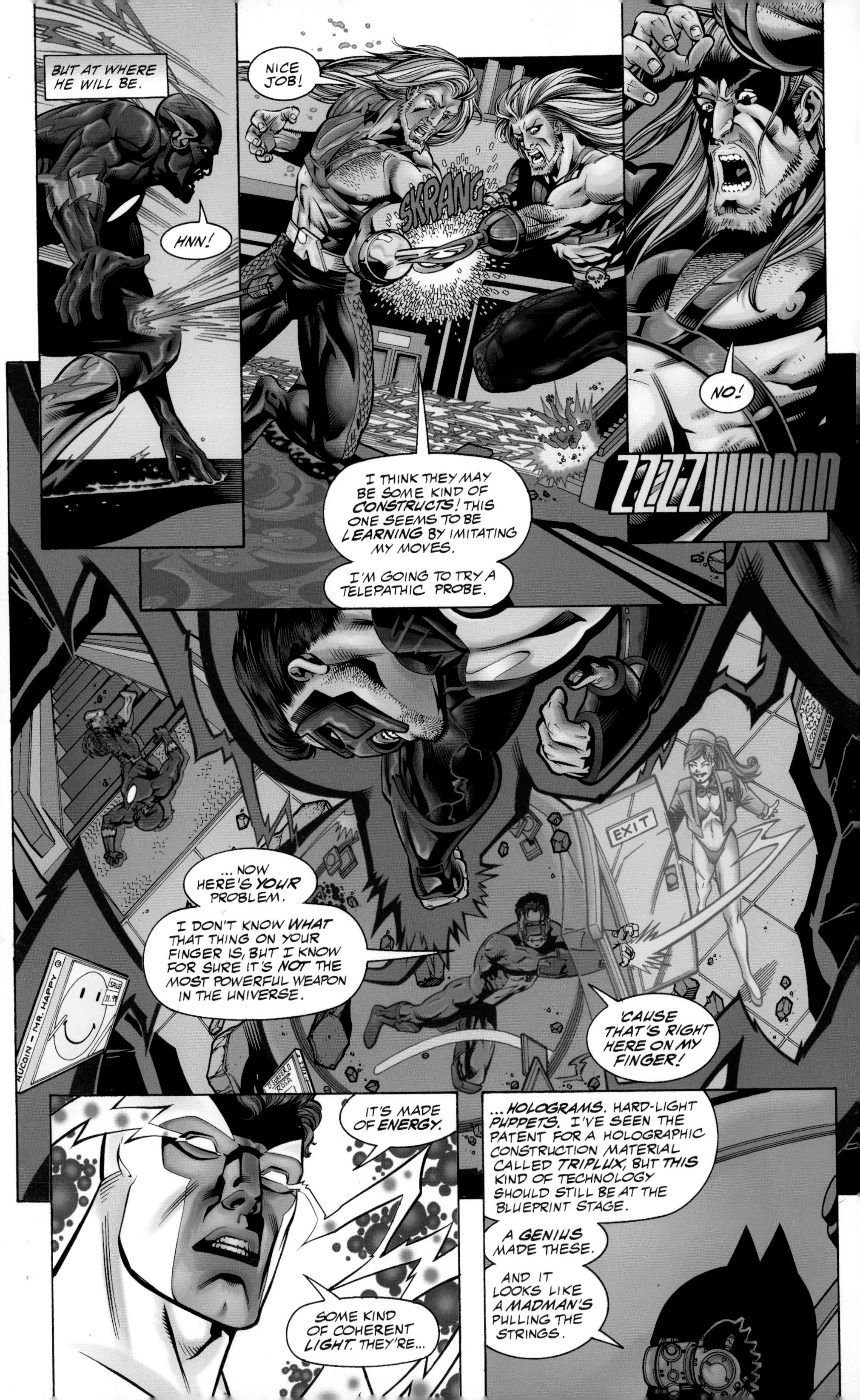
BUT AT WHERE HE WILL BE.
HNN!
NICE JOB!
SKRANG
NO!
ZZZZIIIIINNNN
I THINK THEY MAY BE SOME KIND OF CONSTRUCTS! THIS ONE SEEMS TO BE LEARNING BY IMITATING MY MOVES.
I'M GOING TO TRY A TELEPATHIC PROBE.
EXIT
... NOW HERE'S YOUR PROBLEM.
I DON'T KNOW WHAT THAT THING ON YOUR FINGER IS, BUT I KNOW FOR SURE IT'S NOT THE MOST POWERFUL WEAPON IN THE UNIVERSE.
'CAUSE THAT'S RIGHT HERE ON MY FINGER!
AUCOIN - MR. HAPPY
IT'S MADE OF ENERGY.
SOME KIND OF COHERENT LIGHT. THEY'RE...
...HOLOGRAMS. HARD-LIGHT PUPPETS. I'VE SEEN THE PATENT FOR A HOLOGRAPHIC CONSTRUCTION MATERIAL CALLED TRIPLUX, BUT THIS KIND OF TECHNOLOGY SHOULD STILL BE AT THE BLUEPRINT STAGE.
A GENIUS MADE THESE.
AND IT LOOKS LIKE A MADMAN'S PULLING THE STRINGS.

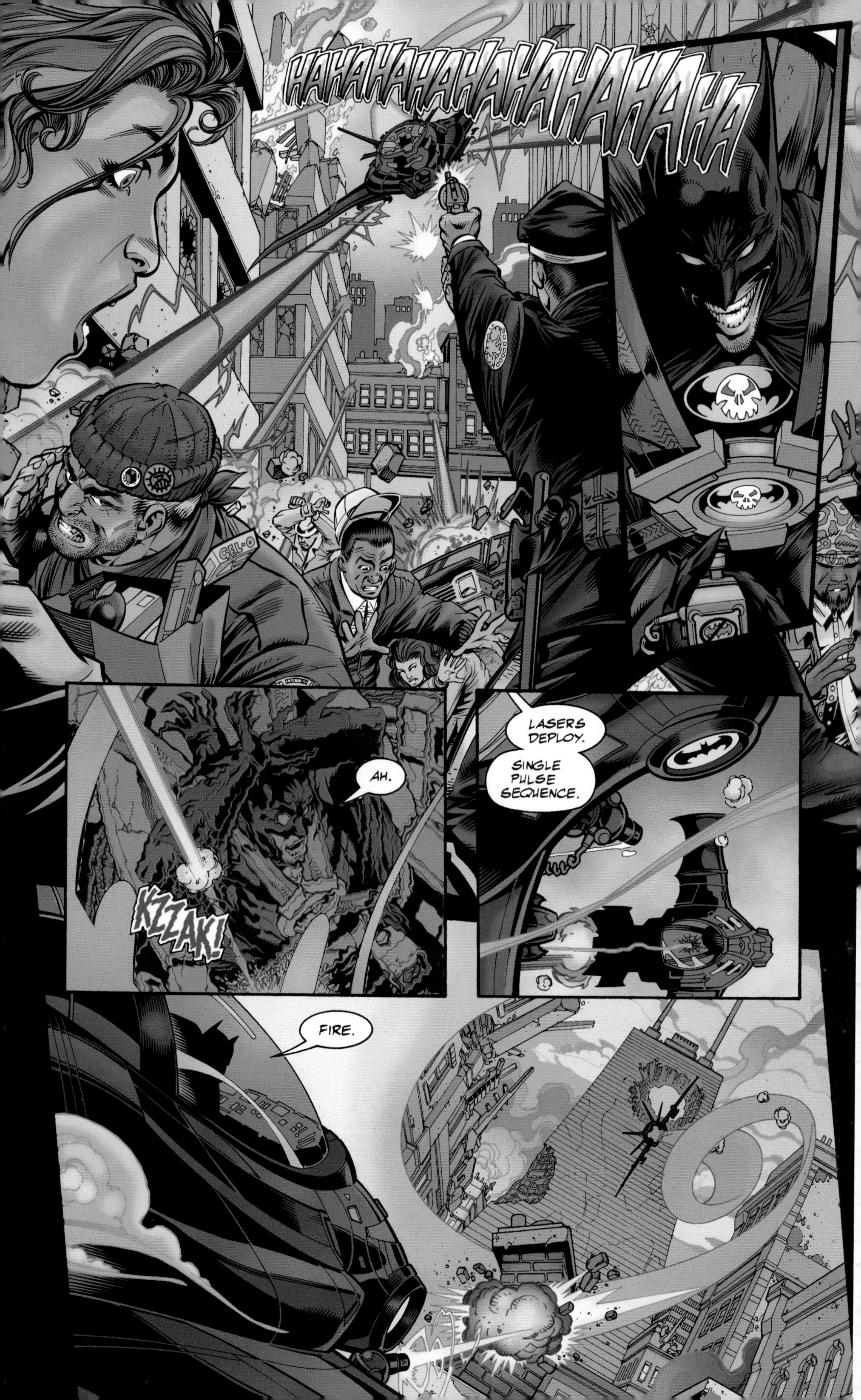
HAHAHAHAHAHAHAHAHAHAHA
GEL-O
AH.
KZZAK!
LASERS DEPLOY.
SINGLE PULSE SEQUENCE.
FIRE.

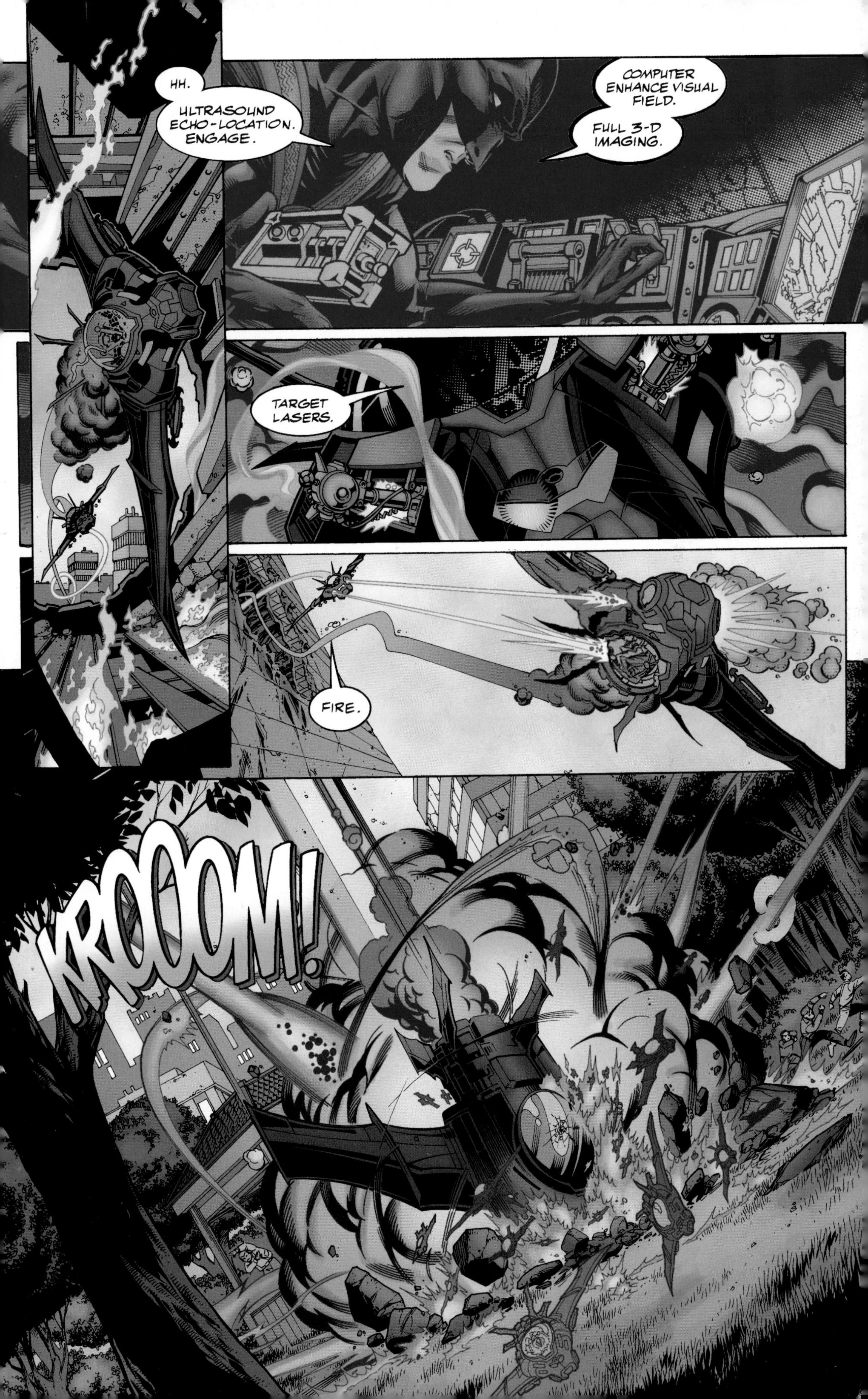
HH.
ULTRASOUND ECHO-LOCATION. ENGAGE.
COMPUTER ENHANCE VISUAL FIELD.
FULL 3-D IMAGING.
TARGET LASERS.
FIRE.
KROOOM!

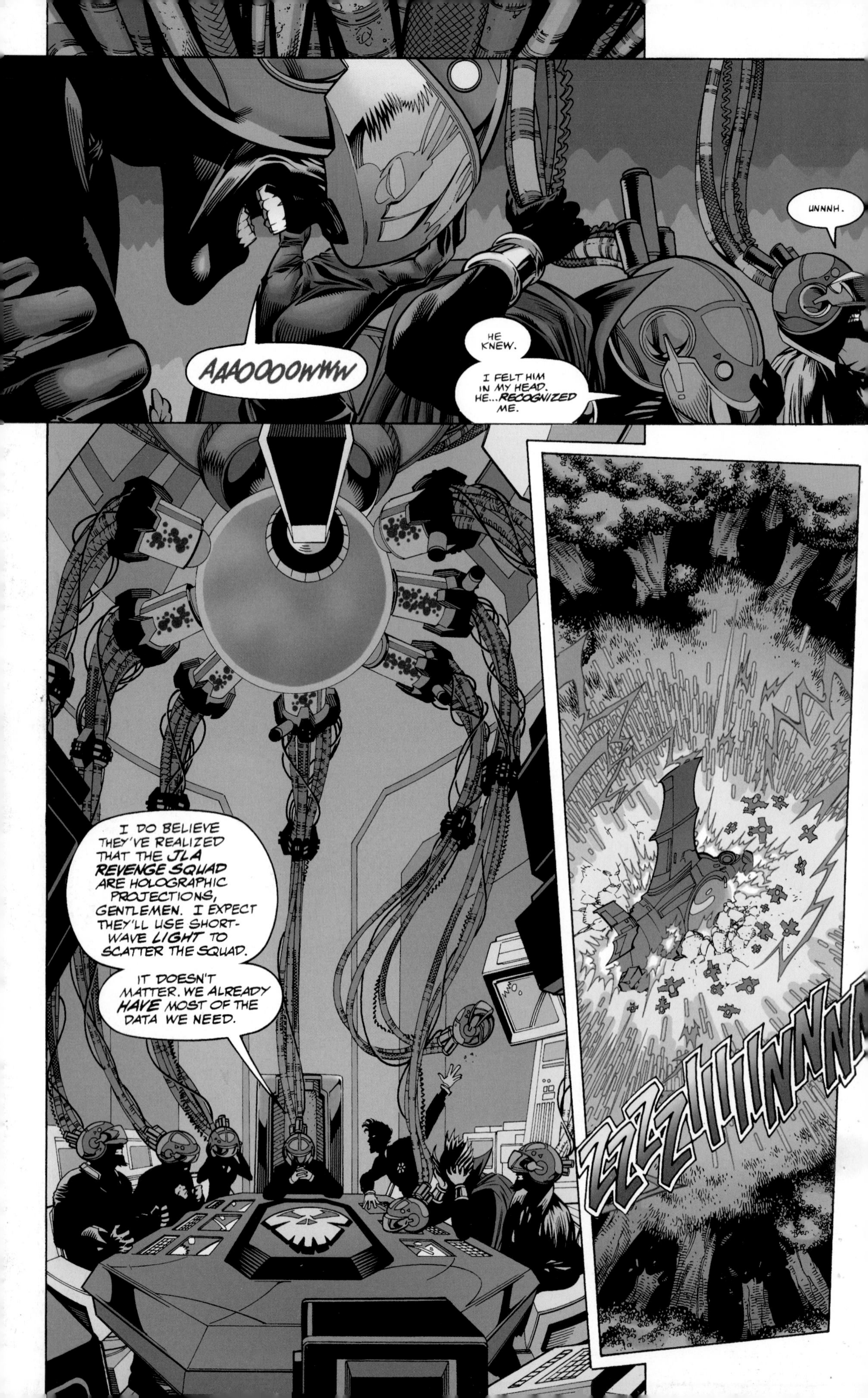
UNNNH.
AAAOOOOWWW
HE KNEW.
I FELT HIM IN MY HEAD. HE...RECOGNIZED ME.
I DO BELIEVE THEY'VE REALIZED THAT THE JLA REVENGE SQUAD ARE HOLOGRAPHIC PROJECTIONS, GENTLEMEN. I EXPECT THEY'LL USE SHORT-WAVE LIGHT TO SCATTER THE SQUAD.
IT DOESN'T MATTER. WE ALREADY HAVE MOST OF THE DATA WE NEED.
ZZZIIIIINNNA

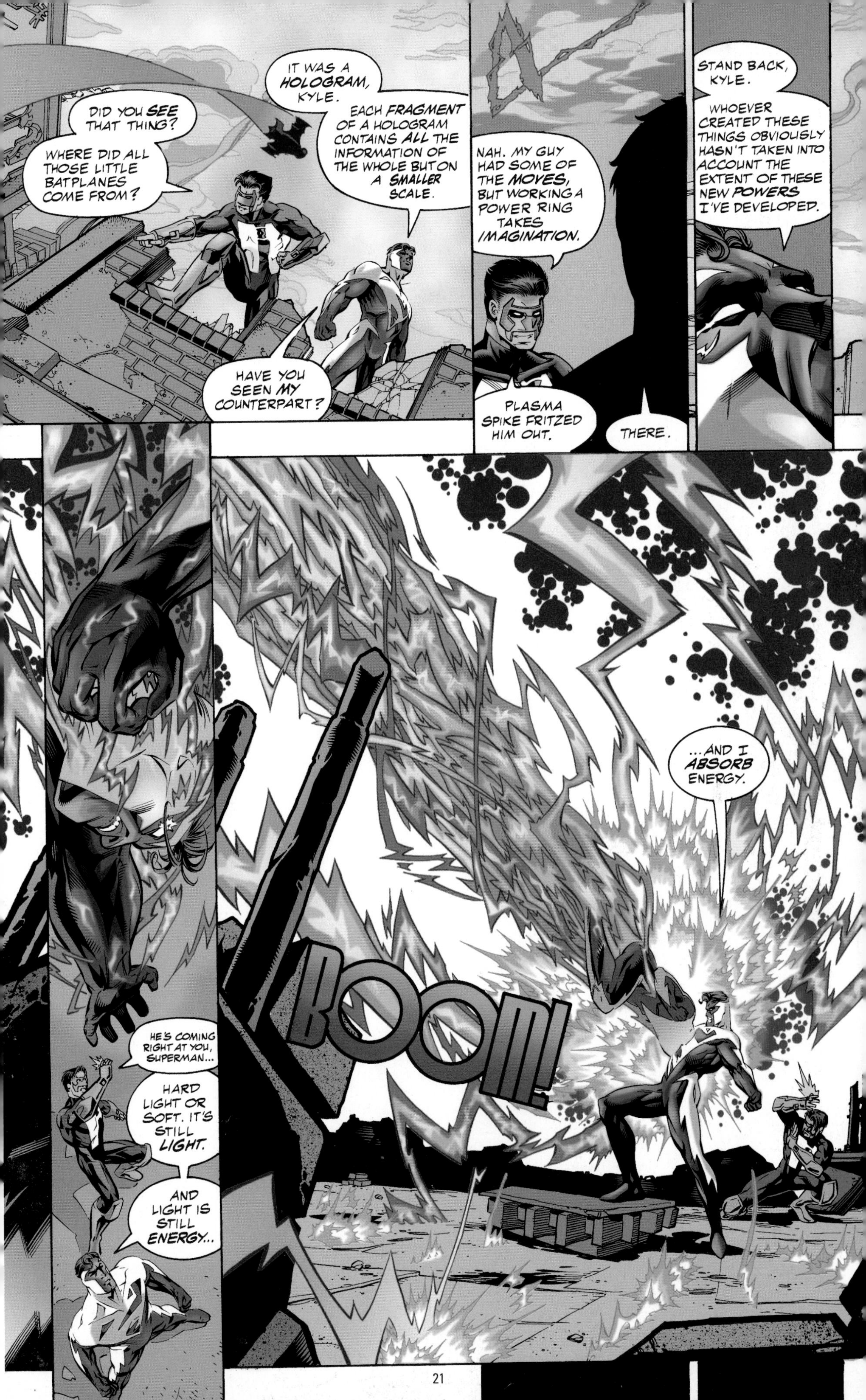
DID YOU SEE THAT THING?
WHERE DID ALL THOSE LITTLE BATPLANES COME FROM?
IT WAS A HOLOGRAM, KYLE.
EACH FRAGMENT OF A HOLOGRAM CONTAINS ALL THE INFORMATION OF THE WHOLE BUT ON A SMALLER SCALE.
HAVE YOU SEEN MY COUNTERPART?
NAH. MY GUY HAD SOME OF THE MOVES, BUT WORKING A POWER RING TAKES IMAGINATION.
PLASMA SPIKE FRITZED HIM OUT.
THERE.
STAND BACK, KYLE.
WHOEVER CREATED THESE THINGS OBVIOUSLY HASN'T TAKEN INTO ACCOUNT THE EXTENT OF THESE NEW POWERS I'VE DEVELOPED.
HE'S COMING RIGHT AT YOU, SUPERMAN...
HARD LIGHT OR SOFT. IT'S STILL LIGHT.
AND LIGHT IS STILL ENERGY...
...AND I ABSORB ENERGY.
BOOM!

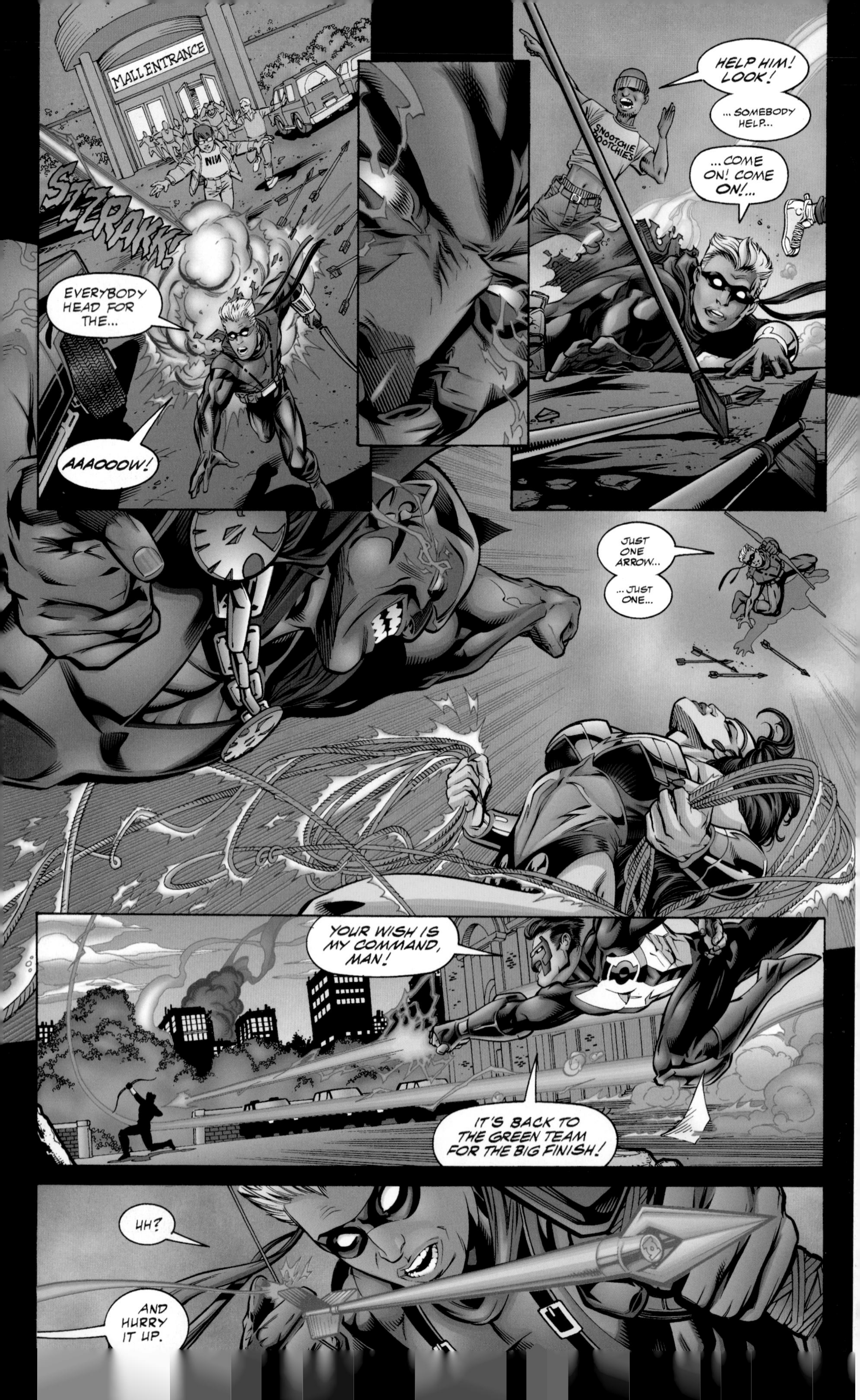
MALL ENTRANCE
NIN
SZZRAKK!
EVERYBODY HEAD FOR THE...
AAAOOOW!
SNOOTCHIE BOOTCHIES
HELP HIM! LOOK!
... SOMEBODY HELP...
...COME ON! COME ON!...
JUST ONE ARROW...
...JUST ONE...
YOUR WISH IS MY COMMAND, MAN!
IT'S BACK TO THE GREEN TEAM FOR THE BIG FINISH!
UH?
AND HURRY IT UP.

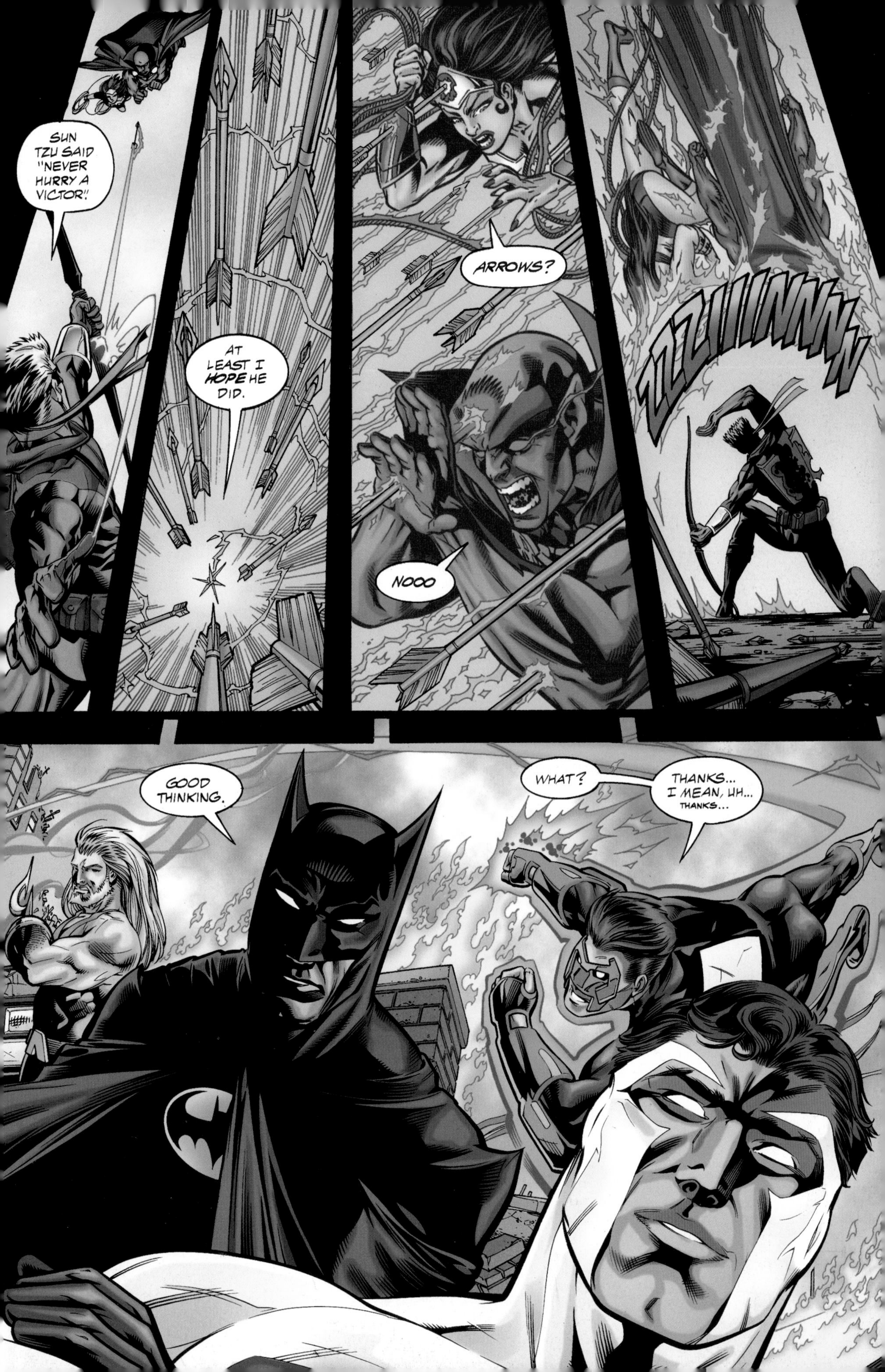
SUN TZU SAID "NEVER HURRY A VICTOR."
AT LEAST I HOPE HE DID.
ARROWS?
NOOO
ZZZIIIINNNNN
GOOD THINKING.
WHAT?
THANKS... I MEAN, UH... THANKS...

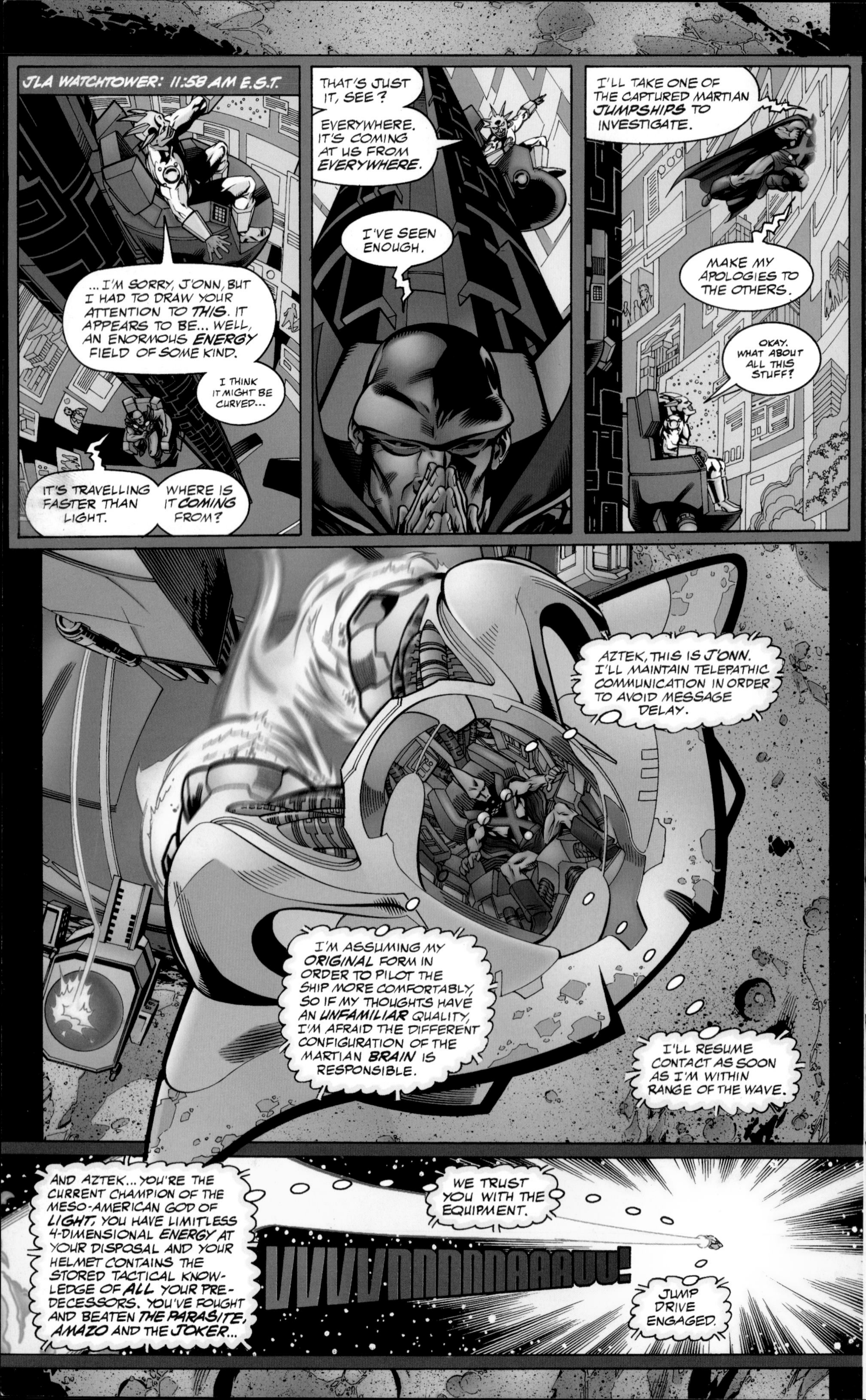
JLA WATCHTOWER: 11:58 AM E.S.T.
...I'M SORRY, J'ONN, BUT I HAD TO DRAW YOUR ATTENTION TO THIS. IT APPEARS TO BE... WELL, AN ENORMOUS ENERGY FIELD OF SOME KIND.
I THINK IT MIGHT BE CURVED...
IT'S TRAVELLING FASTER THAN LIGHT.
WHERE IS IT COMING FROM?
THAT'S JUST IT, SEE?
EVERYWHERE. IT'S COMING AT US FROM EVERYWHERE.
I'VE SEEN ENOUGH.
I'LL TAKE ONE OF THE CAPTURED MARTIAN JUMPSHIPS TO INVESTIGATE.
MAKE MY APOLOGIES TO THE OTHERS.
OKAY. WHAT ABOUT ALL THIS STUFF?
AZTEK, THIS IS J'ONN. I'LL MAINTAIN TELEPATHIC COMMUNICATION IN ORDER TO AVOID MESSAGE DELAY.
I'M ASSUMING MY ORIGINAL FORM IN ORDER TO PILOT THE SHIP MORE COMFORTABLY, SO IF MY THOUGHTS HAVE AN UNFAMILIAR QUALITY, I'M AFRAID THE DIFFERENT CONFIGURATION OF THE MARTIAN BRAIN IS RESPONSIBLE.
I'LL RESUME CONTACT AS SOON AS I'M WITHIN RANGE OF THE WAVE.
AND AZTEK... YOU'RE THE CURRENT CHAMPION OF THE MESO-AMERICAN GOD OF LIGHT, YOU HAVE LIMITLESS 4-DIMENSIONAL ENERGY AT YOUR DISPOSAL AND YOUR HELMET CONTAINS THE STORED TACTICAL KNOWLEDGE OF ALL YOUR PREDECESSORS. YOU'VE FOUGHT AND BEATEN THE PARASITE, AMAZO AND THE JOKER...
WE TRUST YOU WITH THE EQUIPMENT.
VVVVNNNNNAAAUU!
JUMP DRIVE ENGAGED.

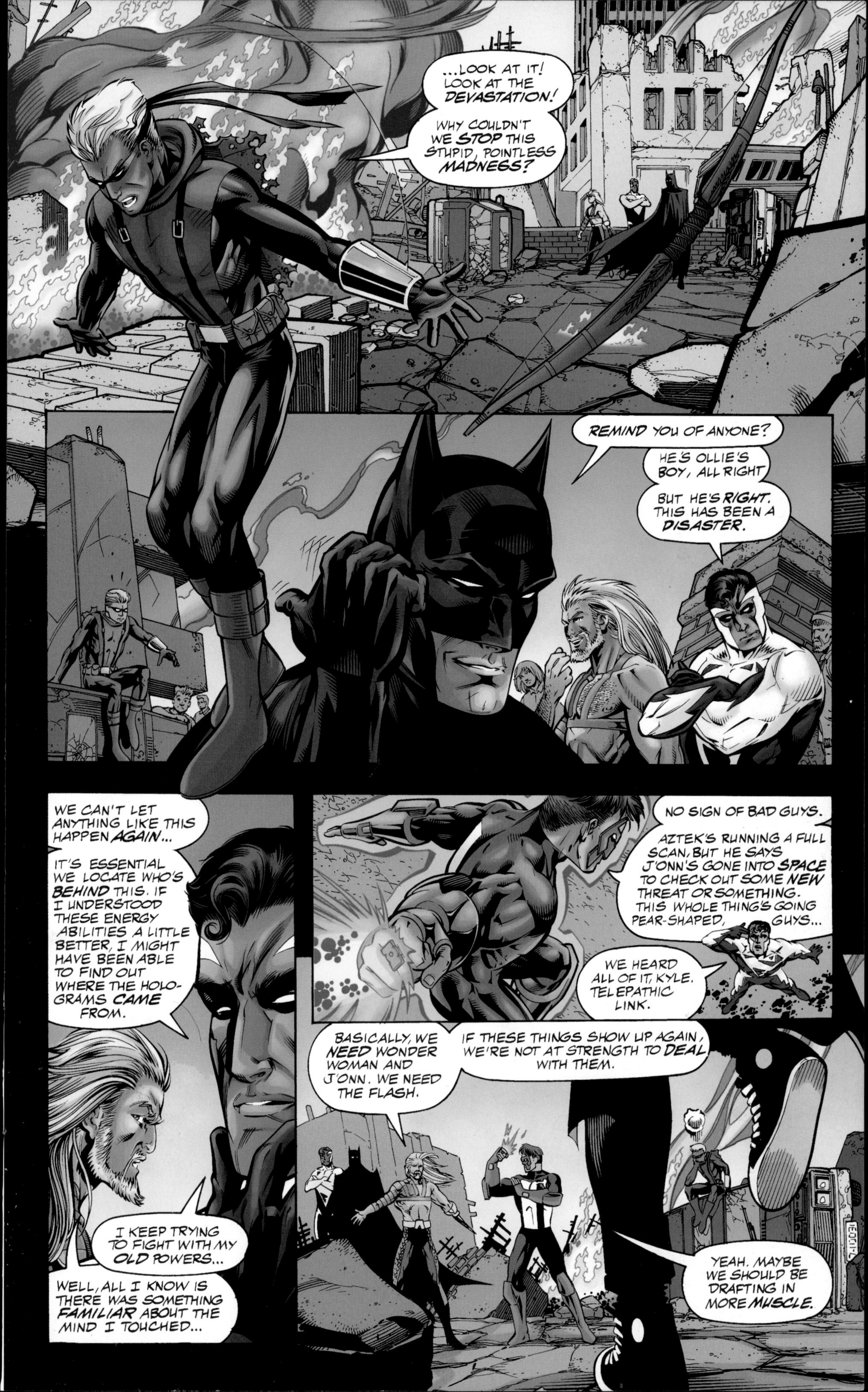
...LOOK AT IT! LOOK AT THE DEVASTATION!
WHY COULDN'T WE STOP THIS STUPID, POINTLESS MADNESS?
REMIND YOU OF ANYONE?
HE'S OLLIE'S BOY, ALL RIGHT.
BUT HE'S RIGHT. THIS HAS BEEN A DISASTER.
WE CAN'T LET ANYTHING LIKE THIS HAPPEN AGAIN...
IT'S ESSENTIAL WE LOCATE WHO'S BEHIND THIS. IF I UNDERSTOOD THESE ENERGY ABILITIES A LITTLE BETTER, I MIGHT HAVE BEEN ABLE TO FIND OUT WHERE THE HOLOGRAMS CAME FROM.
I KEEP TRYING TO FIGHT WITH MY OLD POWERS...
WELL, ALL I KNOW IS THERE WAS SOMETHING FAMILIAR ABOUT THE MIND I TOUCHED...
NO SIGN OF BAD GUYS.
AZTEK'S RUNNING A FULL SCAN, BUT HE SAYS J'ONN'S GONE INTO SPACE TO CHECK OUT SOME NEW THREAT OR SOMETHING. THIS WHOLE THING'S GOING PEAR-SHAPED, GUYS...
WE HEARD ALL OF IT, KYLE. TELEPATHIC LINK.
BASICALLY, WE NEED WONDER WOMAN AND J'ONN. WE NEED THE FLASH.
IF THESE THINGS SHOW UP AGAIN, WE'RE NOT AT STRENGTH TO DEAL WITH THEM.
YEAH. MAYBE WE SHOULD BE DRAFTING IN MORE MUSCLE.

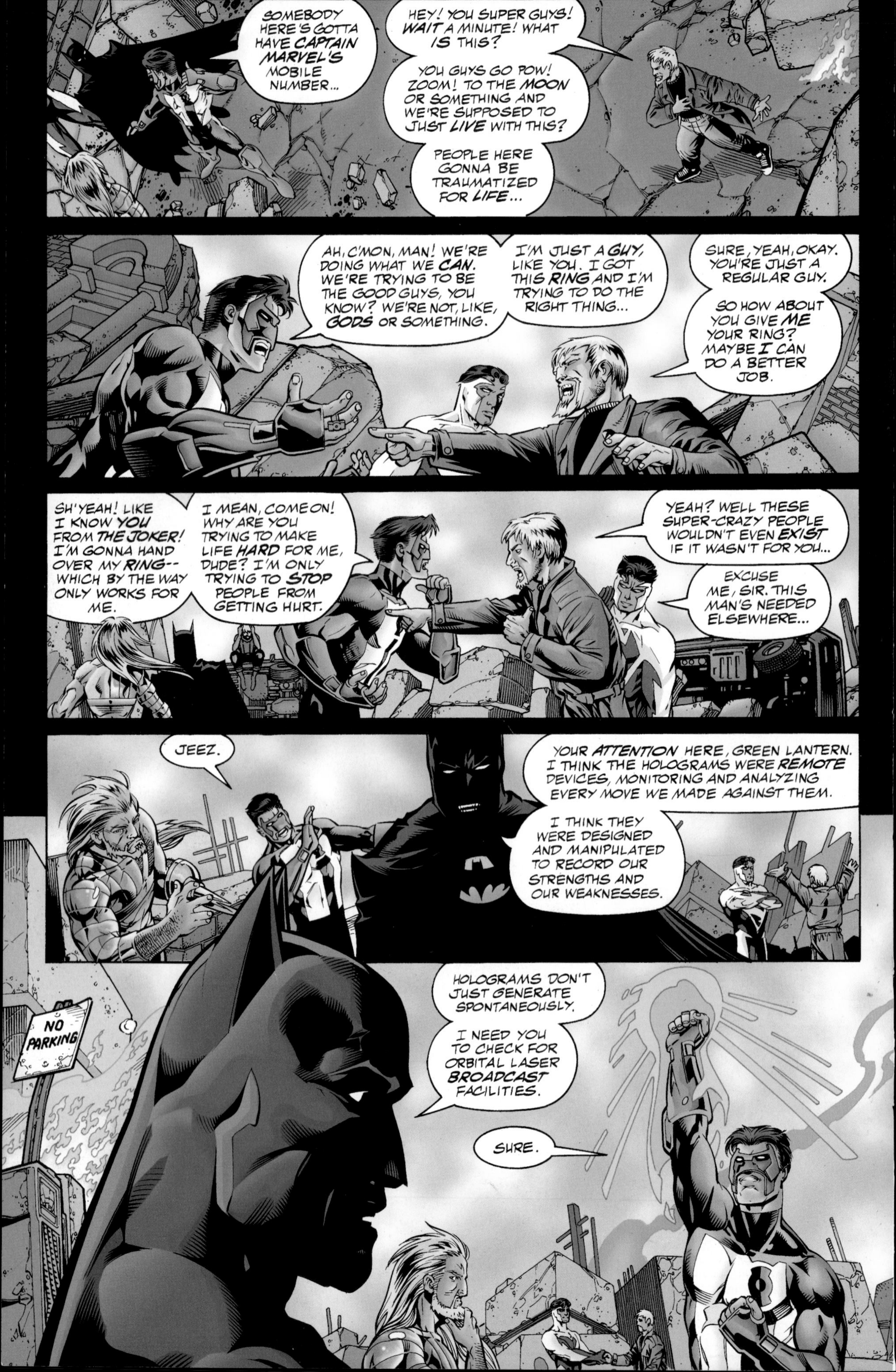
SOMEBODY HERE'S GOTTA HAVE CAPTAIN MARVEL'S MOBILE NUMBER...
HEY! YOU SUPER GUYS! WAIT A MINUTE! WHAT IS THIS?
YOU GUYS GO POW! ZOOM! TO THE MOON OR SOMETHING AND WE'RE SUPPOSED TO JUST LIVE WITH THIS?
PEOPLE HERE GONNA BE TRAUMATIZED FOR LIFE...
AH, C'MON, MAN! WE'RE DOING WHAT WE CAN. WE'RE TRYING TO BE THE GOOD GUYS, YOU KNOW? WE'RE NOT, LIKE, GODS OR SOMETHING.
I'M JUST A GUY, LIKE YOU. I GOT THIS RING AND I'M TRYING TO DO THE RIGHT THING...
SURE, YEAH, OKAY. YOU'RE JUST A REGULAR GUY.
SO HOW ABOUT YOU GIVE ME YOUR RING? MAYBE I CAN DO A BETTER JOB.
SH'YEAH! LIKE I KNOW YOU FROM THE JOKER! I'M GONNA HAND OVER MY RING-- WHICH BY THE WAY ONLY WORKS FOR ME.
I MEAN, COME ON! WHY ARE YOU TRYING TO MAKE LIFE HARD FOR ME, DUDE? I'M ONLY TRYING TO STOP PEOPLE FROM GETTING HURT.
YEAH? WELL THESE SUPER-CRAZY PEOPLE WOULDN'T EVEN EXIST IF IT WASN'T FOR YOU...
EXCUSE ME, SIR. THIS MAN'S NEEDED ELSEWHERE...
JEEZ.
YOUR ATTENTION HERE, GREEN LANTERN. I THINK THE HOLOGRAMS WERE REMOTE DEVICES, MONITORING AND ANALYZING EVERY MOVE WE MADE AGAINST THEM.
I THINK THEY WERE DESIGNED AND MANIPULATED TO RECORD OUR STRENGTHS AND OUR WEAKNESSES.
NO PARKING
HOLOGRAMS DON'T JUST GENERATE SPONTANEOUSLY.
I NEED YOU TO CHECK FOR ORBITAL LASER BROADCAST FACILITIES.
SURE.

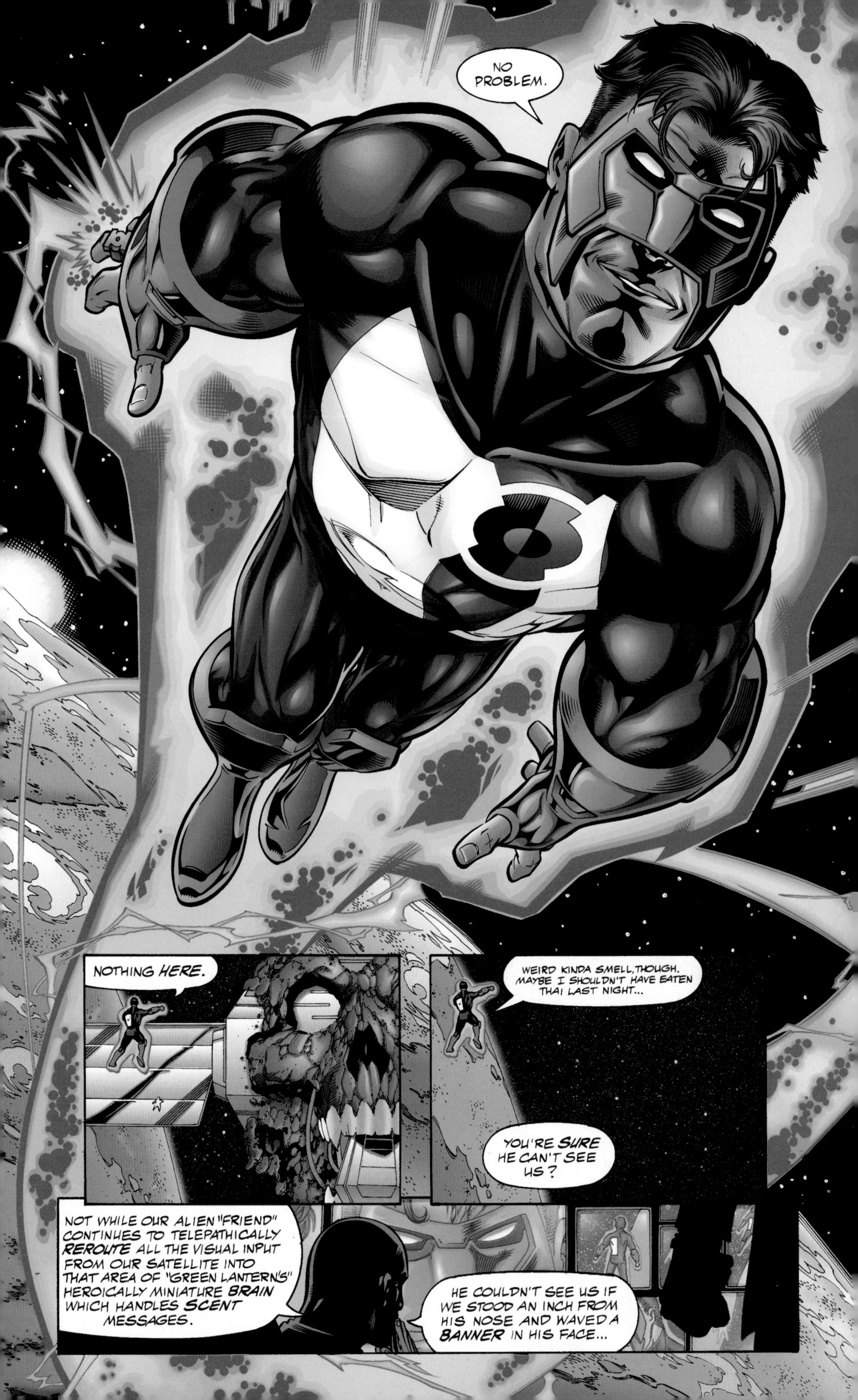
NO PROBLEM.
NOTHING HERE.
WEIRD KINDA SMELL, THOUGH. MAYBE I SHOULDN'T HAVE EATEN THAI LAST NIGHT...
YOU'RE SURE HE CAN'T SEE US?
NOT WHILE OUR ALIEN "FRIEND" CONTINUES TO TELEPATHICALLY REROUTE ALL THE VISUAL INPUT FROM OUR SATELLITE INTO THAT AREA OF "GREEN LANTERN'S" HEROICALLY MINIATURE BRAIN WHICH HANDLES SCENT MESSAGES.
HE COULDN'T SEE US IF WE STOOD AN INCH FROM HIS NOSE AND WAVED A BANNER IN HIS FACE...

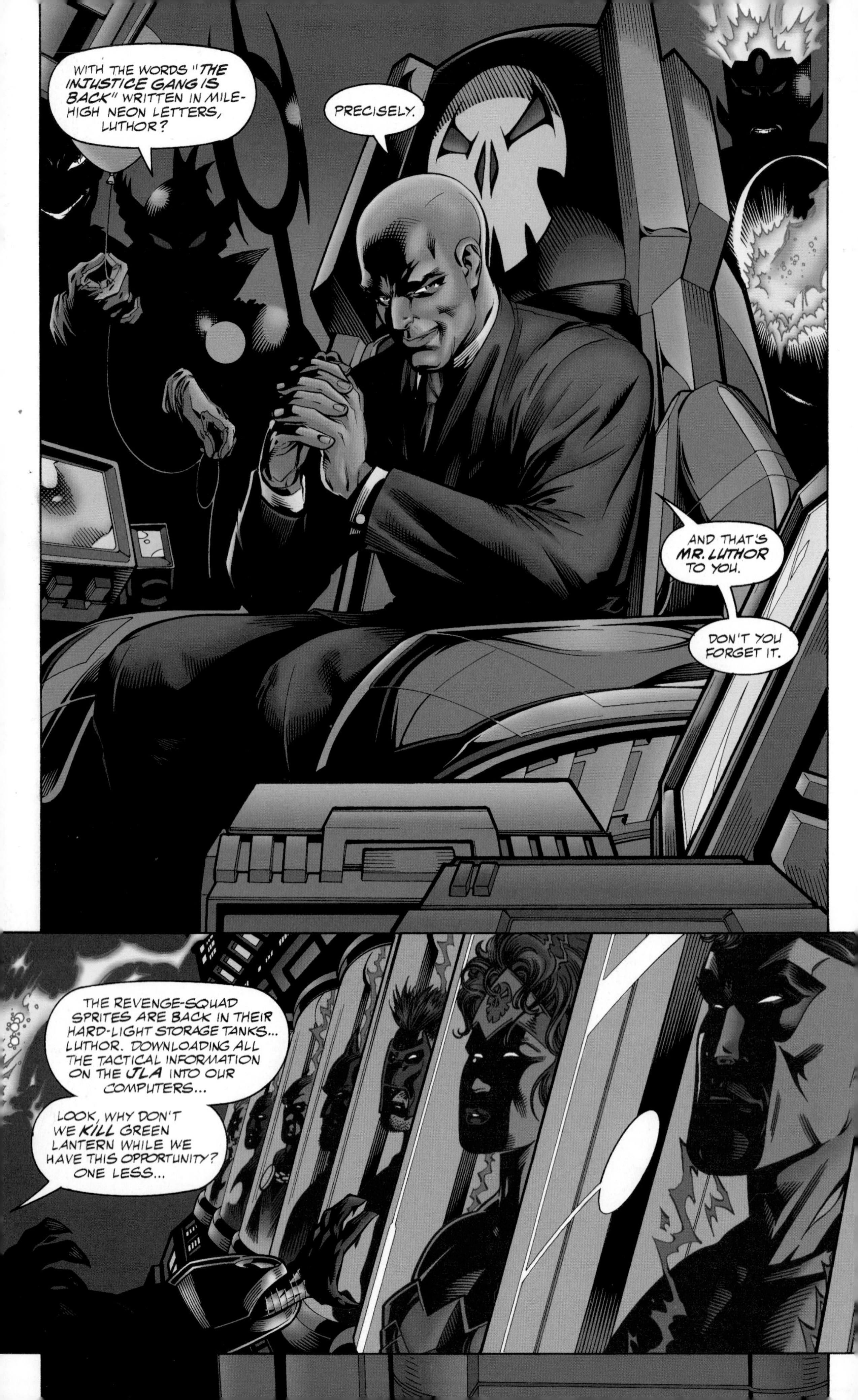
WITH THE WORDS "THE INJUSTICE GANG IS BACK" WRITTEN IN MILE-HIGH NEON LETTERS, LUTHOR?
PRECISELY.
AND THAT'S MR. LUTHOR TO YOU.
DON'T YOU FORGET IT.
THE REVENGE-SQUAD SPRITES ARE BACK IN THEIR HARD-LIGHT STORAGE TANKS... LUTHOR. DOWNLOADING ALL THE TACTICAL INFORMATION ON THE JLA INTO OUR COMPUTERS...
LOOK, WHY DON'T WE KILL GREEN LANTERN WHILE WE HAVE THIS OPPORTUNITY? ONE LESS...

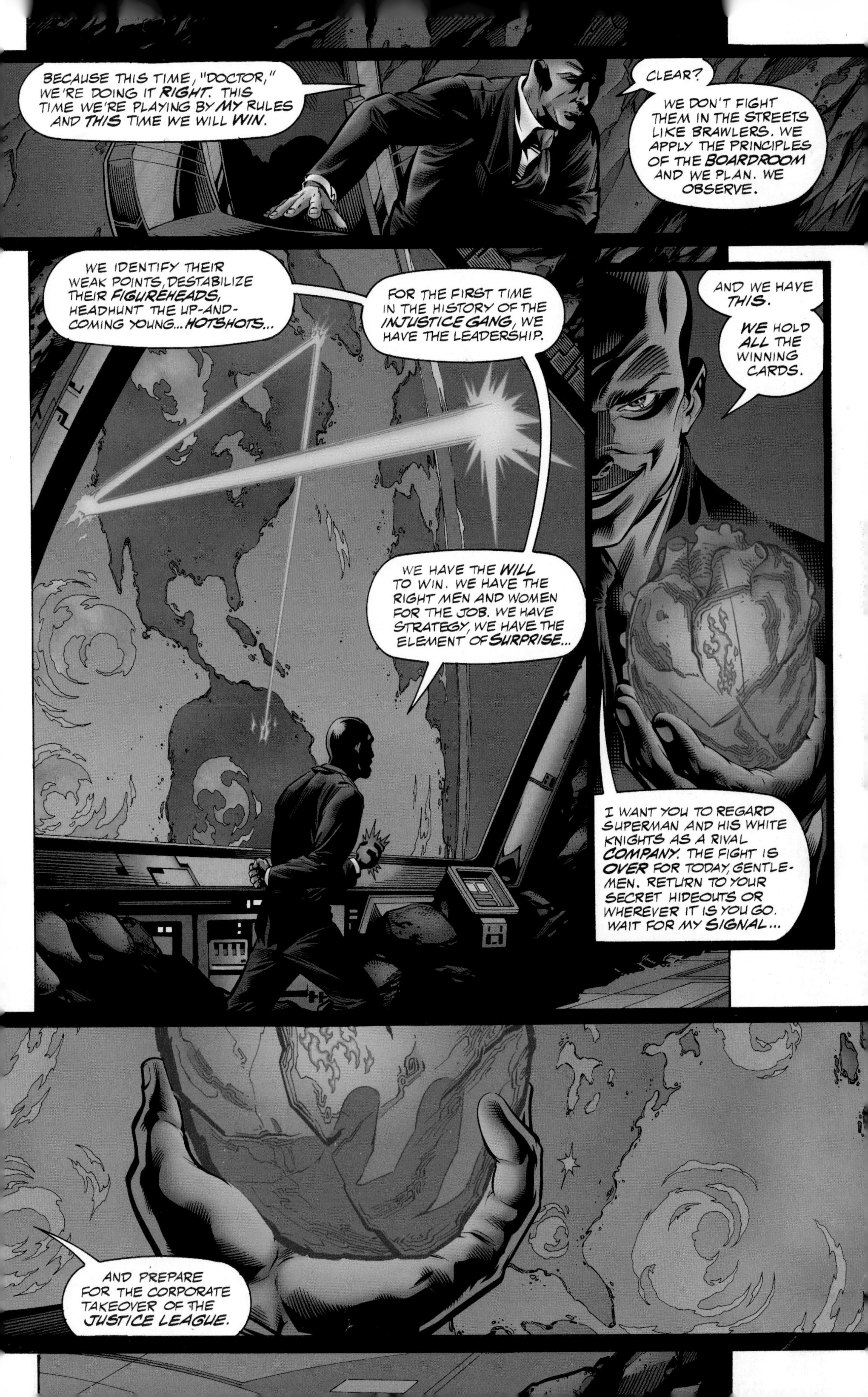
BECAUSE THIS TIME, "DOCTOR," WE'RE DOING IT RIGHT. THIS TIME WE'RE PLAYING BY MY RULES AND THIS TIME WE WILL WIN.
CLEAR?
WE DON'T FIGHT THEM IN THE STREETS LIKE BRAWLERS. WE APPLY THE PRINCIPLES OF THE BOARDROOM AND WE PLAN. WE OBSERVE.
WE IDENTIFY THEIR WEAK POINTS, DESTABILIZE THEIR FIGUREHEADS, HEADHUNT THE UP-AND-COMING YOUNG... HOTSHOTS...
FOR THE FIRST TIME IN THE HISTORY OF THE INJUSTICE GANG, WE HAVE THE LEADERSHIP.
WE HAVE THE WILL TO WIN. WE HAVE THE RIGHT MEN AND WOMEN FOR THE JOB. WE HAVE STRATEGY, WE HAVE THE ELEMENT OF SURPRISE...
AND WE HAVE THIS.
WE HOLD ALL THE WINNING CARDS.
I WANT YOU TO REGARD SUPERMAN AND HIS WHITE KNIGHTS AS A RIVAL COMPANY. THE FIGHT IS OVER FOR TODAY, GENTLE-MEN. RETURN TO YOUR SECRET HIDEOUTS OR WHEREVER IT IS YOU GO. WAIT FOR MY SIGNAL...
AND PREPARE FOR THE CORPORATE TAKEOVER OF THE JUSTICE LEAGUE.

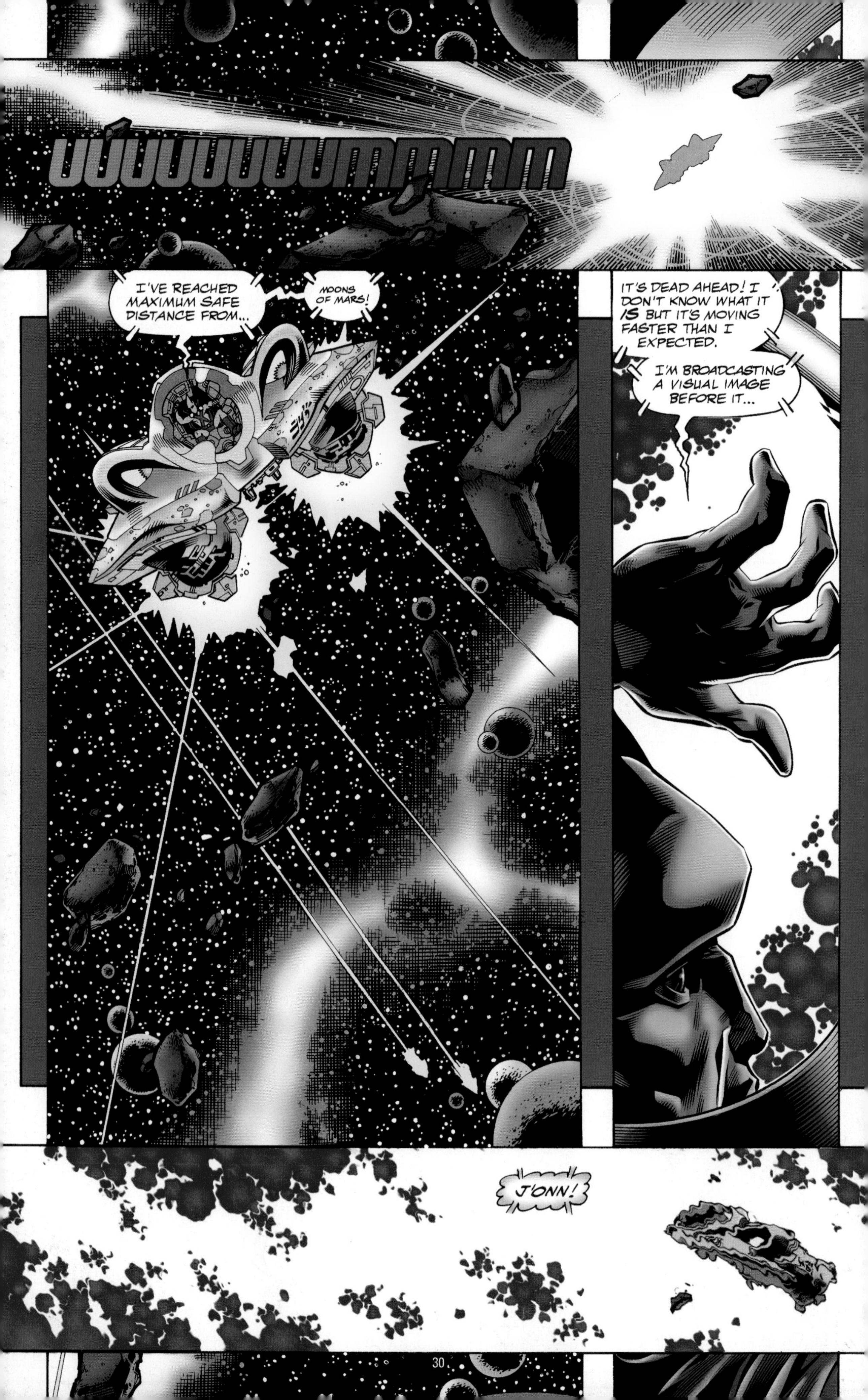
UUUUUUUUMMMMM
I'VE REACHED MAXIMUM SAFE DISTANCE FROM...
MOONS OF MARS!
IT'S DEAD AHEAD! I DON'T KNOW WHAT IT IS BUT IT'S MOVING FASTER THAN I EXPECTED.
I'M BROADCASTING A VISUAL IMAGE BEFORE IT...
J'ONN!

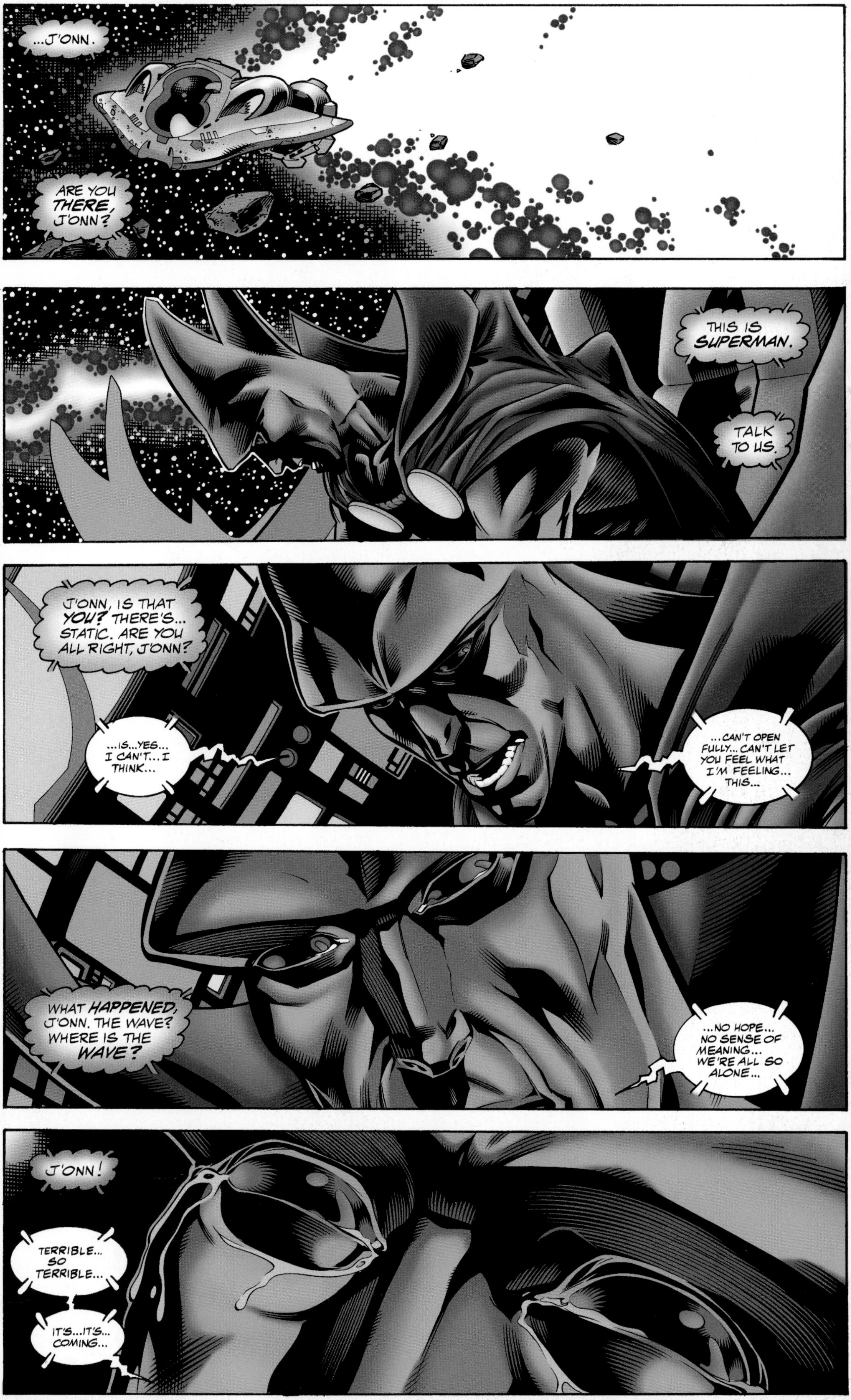
...J'ONN.
ARE YOU THERE, J'ONN?
THIS IS SUPERMAN.
TALK TO US.
J'ONN, IS THAT YOU? THERE'S... STATIC. ARE YOU ALL RIGHT, J'ONN?
...IS...YES... I CAN'T... I THINK...
...CAN'T OPEN FULLY... CAN'T LET YOU FEEL WHAT I'M FEELING... THIS...
WHAT HAPPENED, J'ONN. THE WAVE? WHERE IS THE WAVE?
...NO HOPE... NO SENSE OF MEANING... WE'RE ALL SO ALONE...
J'ONN!
TERRIBLE... SO TERRIBLE...
IT'S...IT'S... COMING...

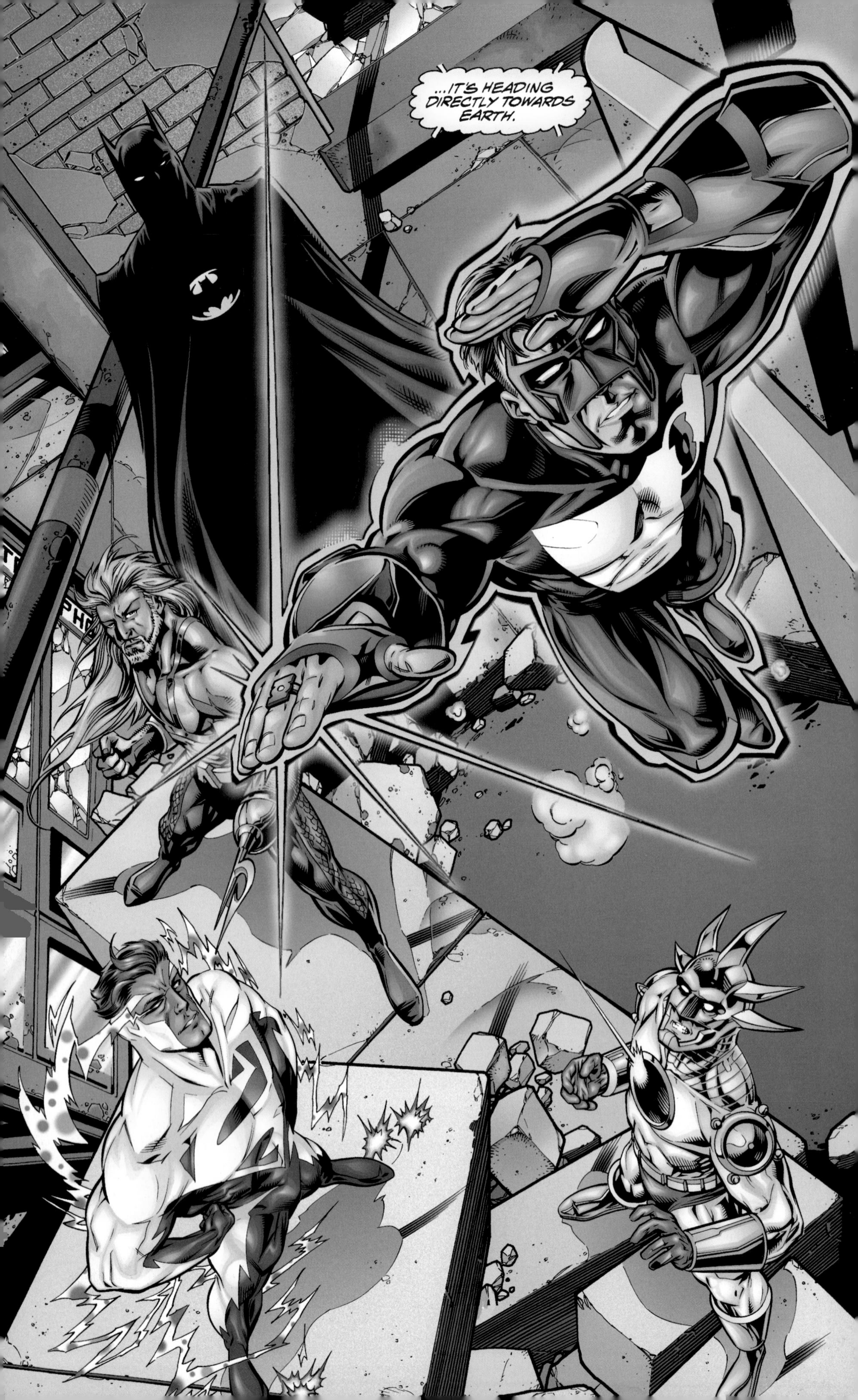
...IT'S HEADING DIRECTLY TOWARDS EARTH.

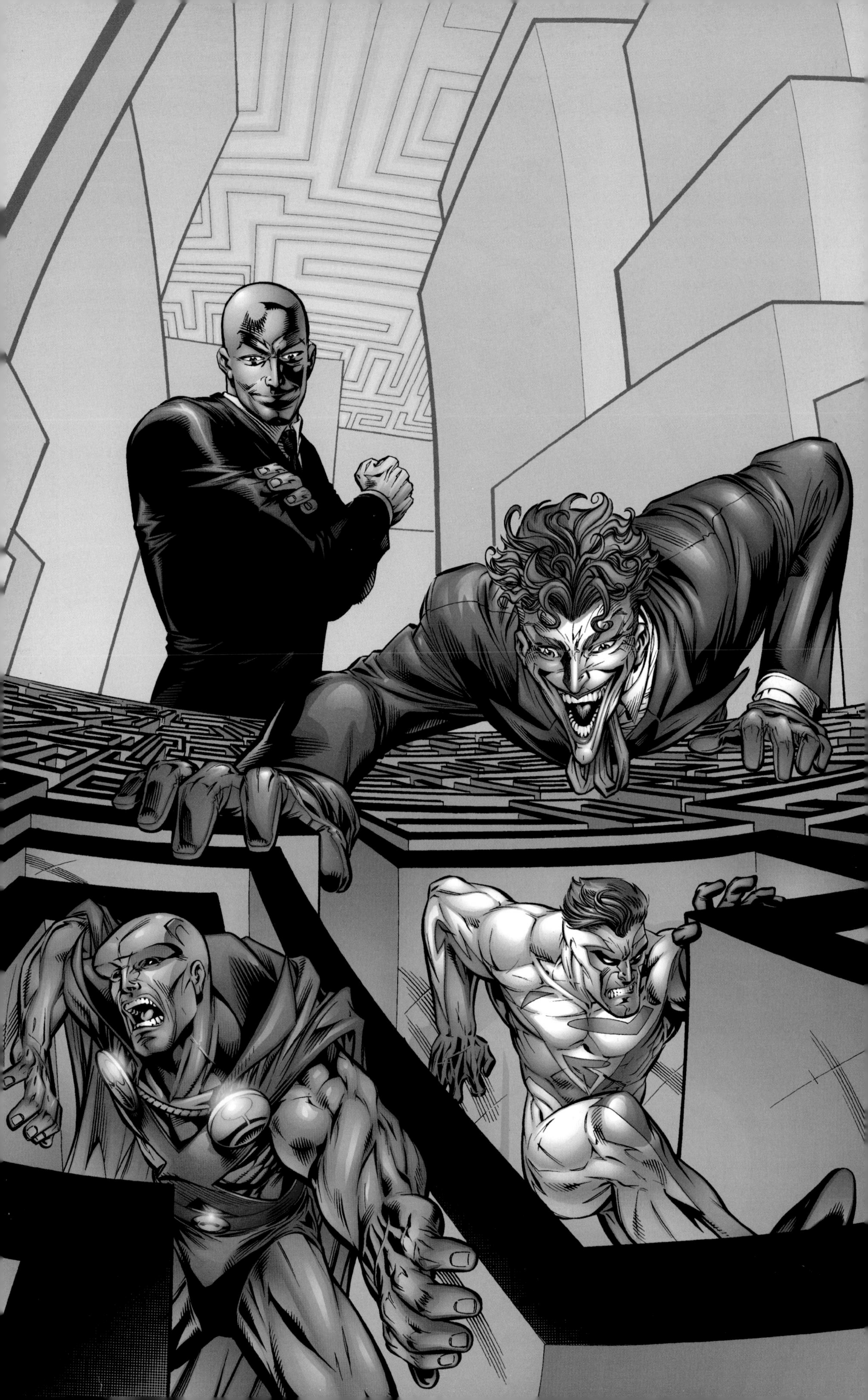

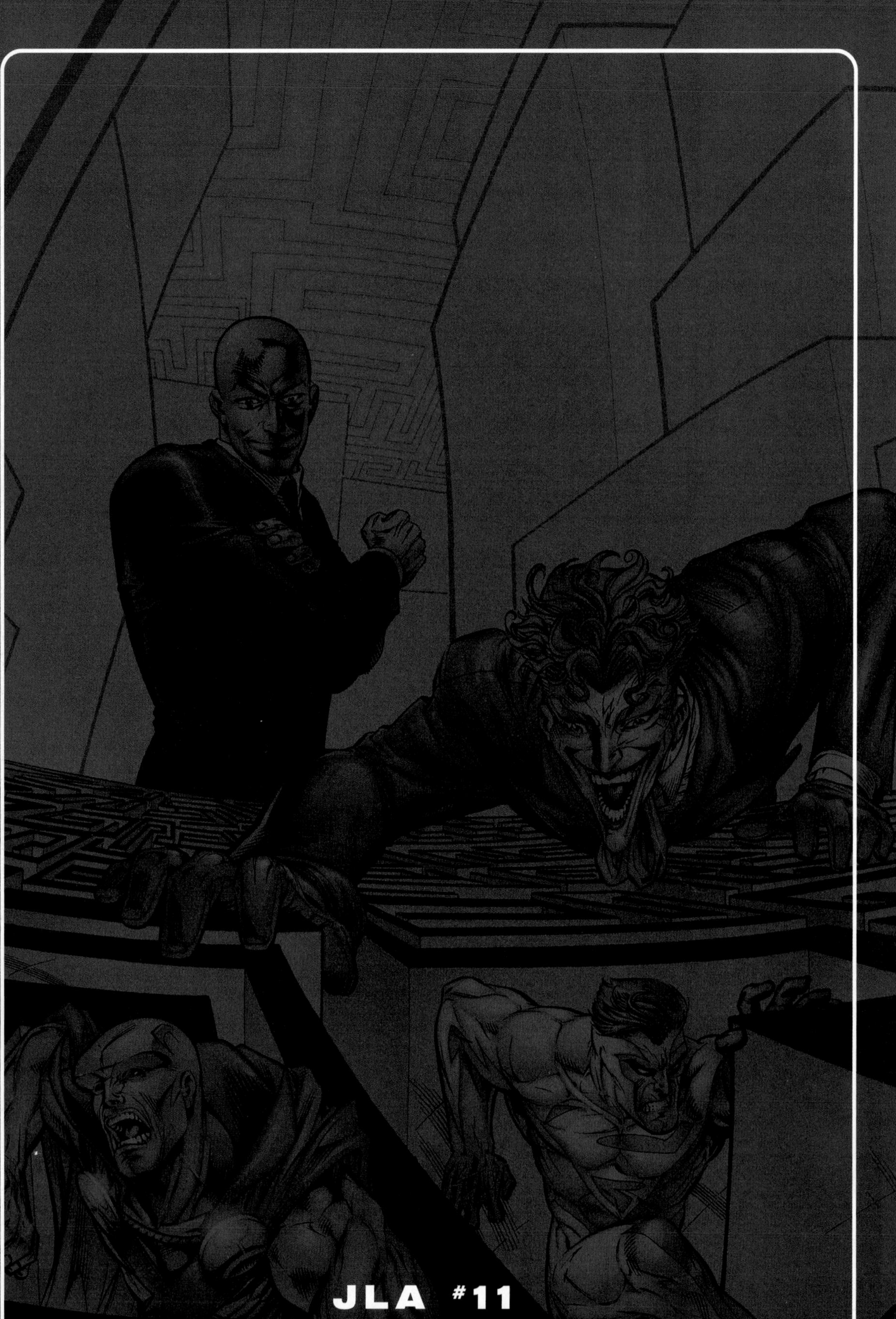

JLA #11

WRITTEN BY GRANT MORRISON

PENCILS BY HOWARD PORTER, WITH INKS BY JOHN DELL AND COLORS BY PAT GARRAHY

COVER BY PORTER & DELL

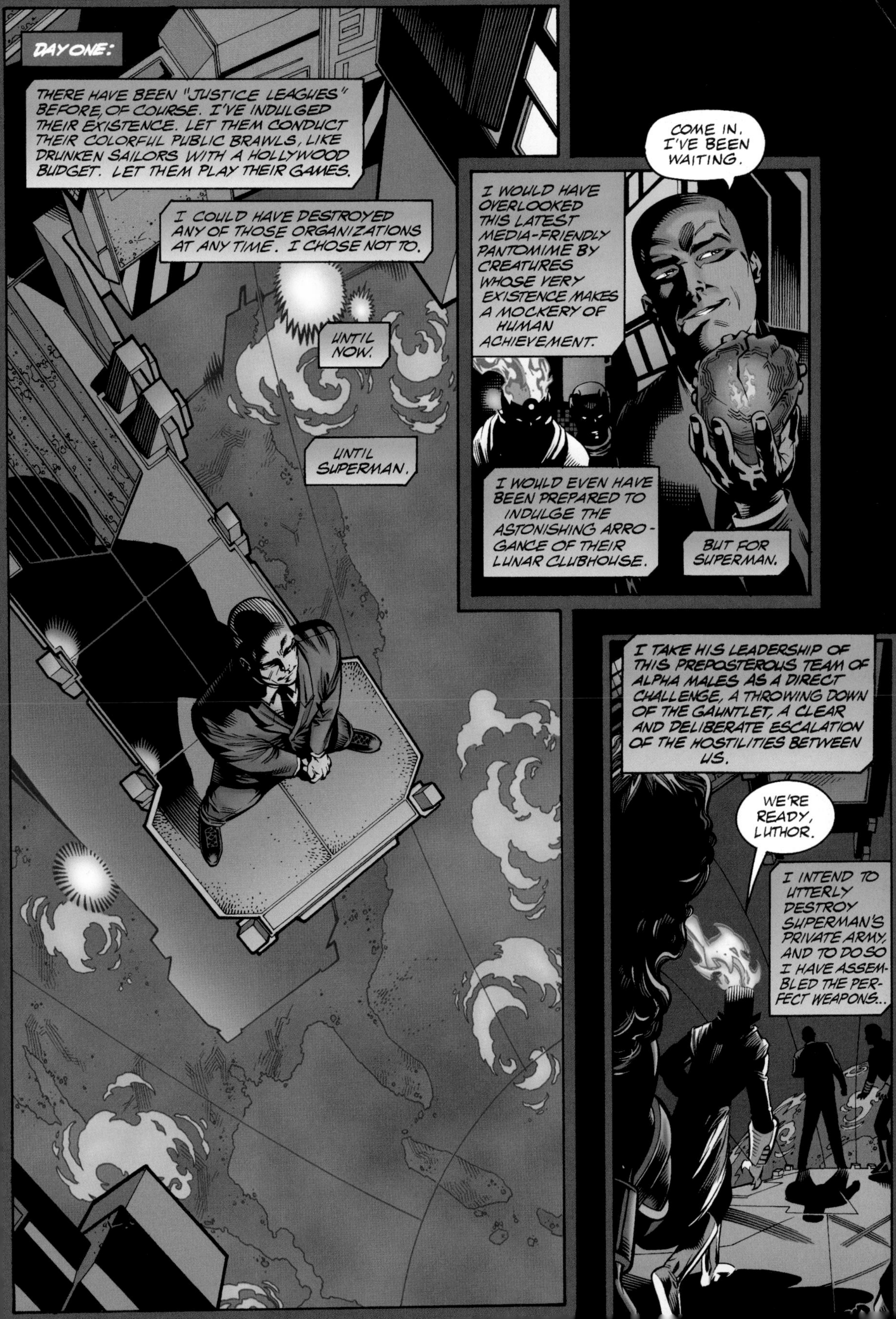
DAY ONE:
THERE HAVE BEEN "JUSTICE LEAGUES" BEFORE, OF COURSE. I'VE INDULGED THEIR EXISTENCE. LET THEM CONDUCT THEIR COLORFUL PUBLIC BRAWLS, LIKE DRUNKEN SAILORS WITH A HOLLYWOOD BUDGET. LET THEM PLAY THEIR GAMES.
I COULD HAVE DESTROYED ANY OF THOSE ORGANIZATIONS AT ANY TIME. I CHOSE NOT TO.
UNTIL NOW.
UNTIL SUPERMAN.
COME IN. I'VE BEEN WAITING.
I WOULD HAVE OVERLOOKED THIS LATEST MEDIA-FRIENDLY PANTOMIME BY CREATURES WHOSE VERY EXISTENCE MAKES A MOCKERY OF HUMAN ACHIEVEMENT.
I WOULD EVEN HAVE BEEN PREPARED TO INDULGE THE ASTONISHING ARROGANCE OF THEIR LUNAR CLUBHOUSE.
BUT FOR SUPERMAN.
I TAKE HIS LEADERSHIP OF THIS PREPOSTEROUS TEAM OF ALPHA MALES AS A DIRECT CHALLENGE, A THROWING DOWN OF THE GAUNTLET, A CLEAR AND DELIBERATE ESCALATION OF THE HOSTILITIES BETWEEN US.
WE'RE READY, LUTHOR.
I INTEND TO UTTERLY DESTROY SUPERMAN'S PRIVATE ARMY, AND TO DO SO I HAVE ASSEMBLED THE PERFECT WEAPONS...

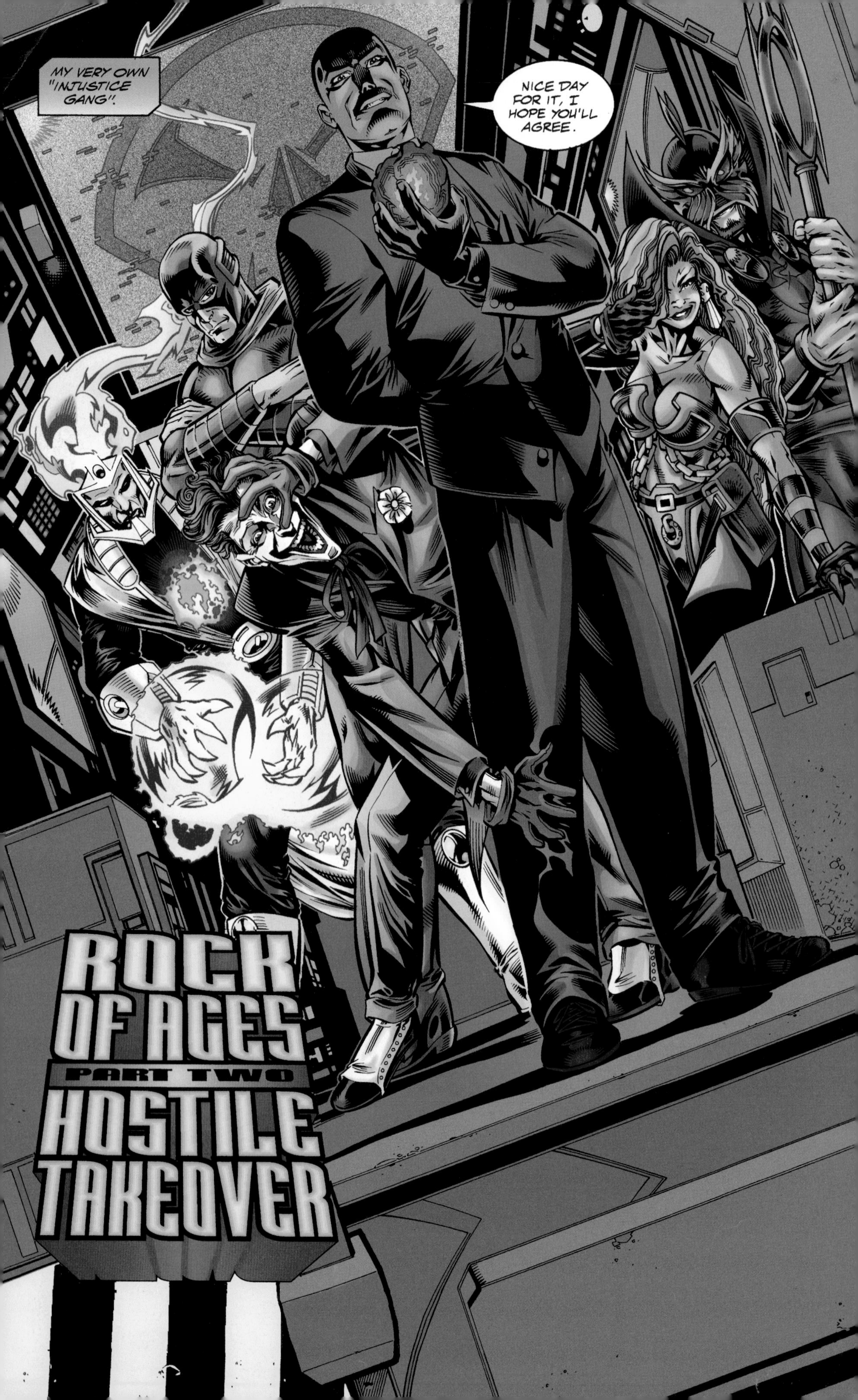

MY VERY OWN "INJUSTICE GANG".
NICE DAY FOR IT, I HOPE YOU'LL AGREE.
ROCK OF AGES
PART TWO
HOSTILE TAKEOVER

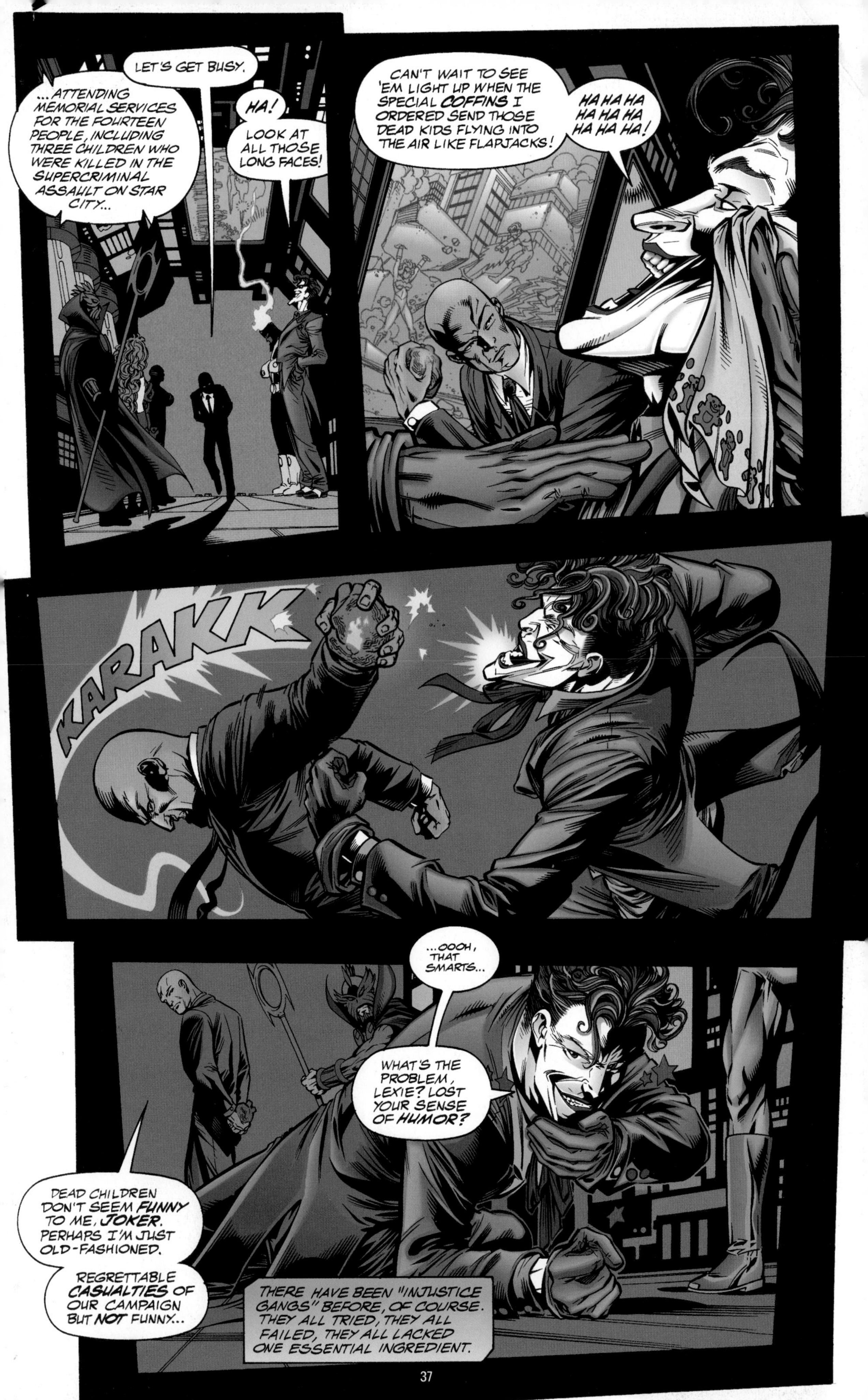
...ATTENDING MEMORIAL SERVICES FOR THE FOURTEEN PEOPLE, INCLUDING THREE CHILDREN WHO WERE KILLED IN THE SUPERCRIMINAL ASSAULT ON STAR CITY...
LET'S GET BUSY.
HA!
LOOK AT ALL THOSE LONG FACES!
CAN'T WAIT TO SEE 'EM LIGHT UP WHEN THE SPECIAL COFFINS I ORDERED SEND THOSE DEAD KIDS FLYING INTO THE AIR LIKE FLAPJACKS!
HA HA HA HA HA HA HA HA HA!
KARAKK
...OOOH, THAT SMARTS...
WHAT'S THE PROBLEM, LEXIE? LOST YOUR SENSE OF HUMOR?
DEAD CHILDREN DON'T SEEM FUNNY TO ME, JOKER. PERHAPS I'M JUST OLD-FASHIONED.
REGRETTABLE CASUALTIES OF OUR CAMPAIGN BUT NOT FUNNY...
THERE HAVE BEEN "INJUSTICE GANGS" BEFORE, OF COURSE. THEY ALL TRIED, THEY ALL FAILED, THEY ALL LACKED ONE ESSENTIAL INGREDIENT.

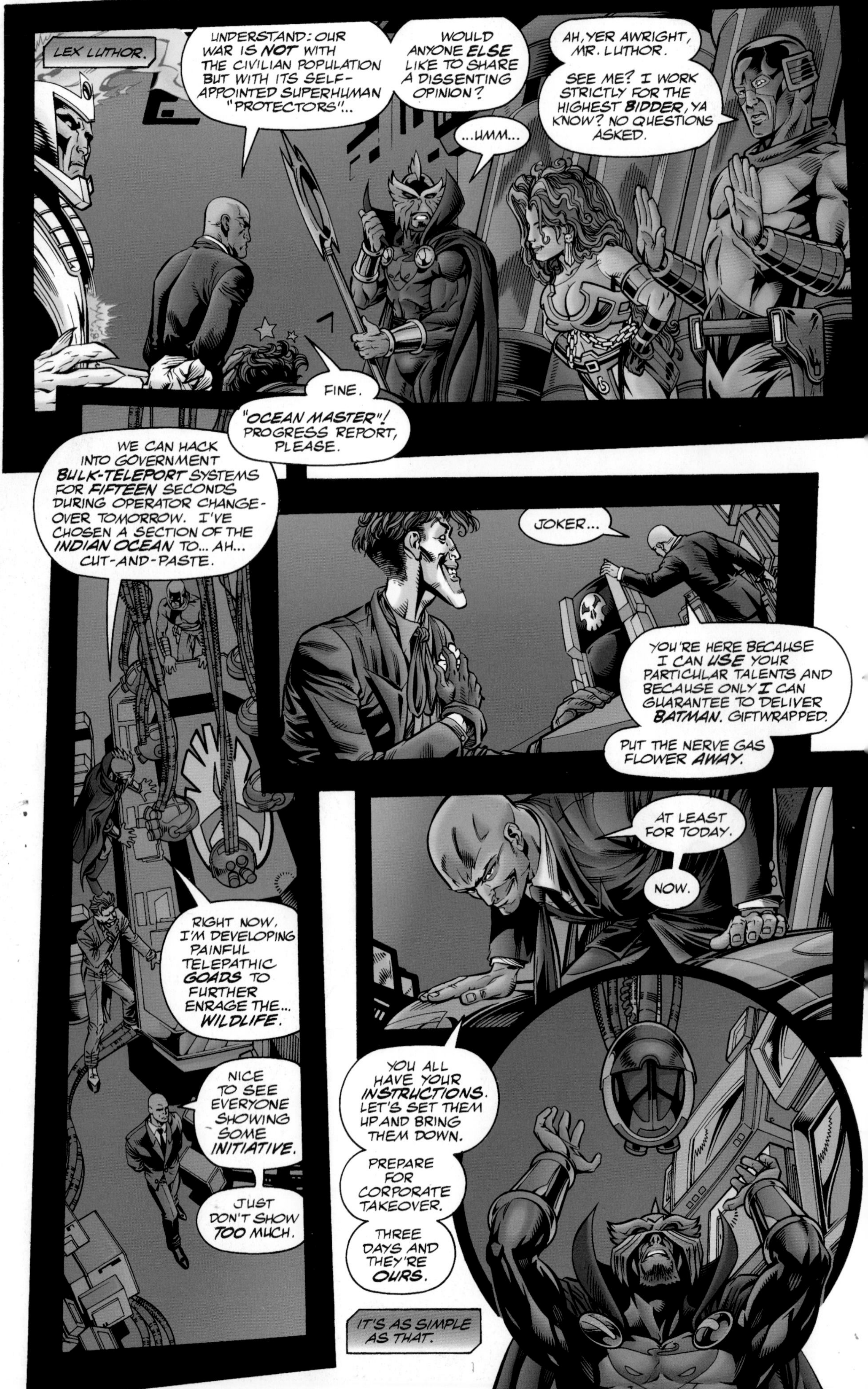

LEX LUTHOR.
UNDERSTAND: OUR WAR IS NOT WITH THE CIVILIAN POPULATION BUT WITH ITS SELF-APPOINTED SUPERHUMAN "PROTECTORS"...
WOULD ANYONE ELSE LIKE TO SHARE A DISSENTING OPINION?
...UMM...
AH, YER AWRIGHT, MR. LUTHOR.
SEE ME? I WORK STRICTLY FOR THE HIGHEST BIDDER, YA KNOW? NO QUESTIONS ASKED.
FINE.
"OCEAN MASTER"! PROGRESS REPORT, PLEASE.
WE CAN HACK INTO GOVERNMENT BULK-TELEPORT SYSTEMS FOR FIFTEEN SECONDS DURING OPERATOR CHANGE-OVER TOMORROW. I'VE CHOSEN A SECTION OF THE INDIAN OCEAN TO... AH... CUT-AND-PASTE.
JOKER...
YOU'RE HERE BECAUSE I CAN USE YOUR PARTICULAR TALENTS AND BECAUSE ONLY I CAN GUARANTEE TO DELIVER BATMAN. GIFTWRAPPED.
PUT THE NERVE GAS FLOWER AWAY.
AT LEAST FOR TODAY.
NOW.
RIGHT NOW, I'M DEVELOPING PAINFUL TELEPATHIC GOADS TO FURTHER ENRAGE THE... WILDLIFE.
NICE TO SEE EVERYONE SHOWING SOME INITIATIVE.
JUST DON'T SHOW TOO MUCH.
YOU ALL HAVE YOUR INSTRUCTIONS. LET'S SET THEM UP AND BRING THEM DOWN.
PREPARE FOR CORPORATE TAKEOVER.
THREE DAYS AND THEY'RE OURS.
IT'S AS SIMPLE AS THAT.

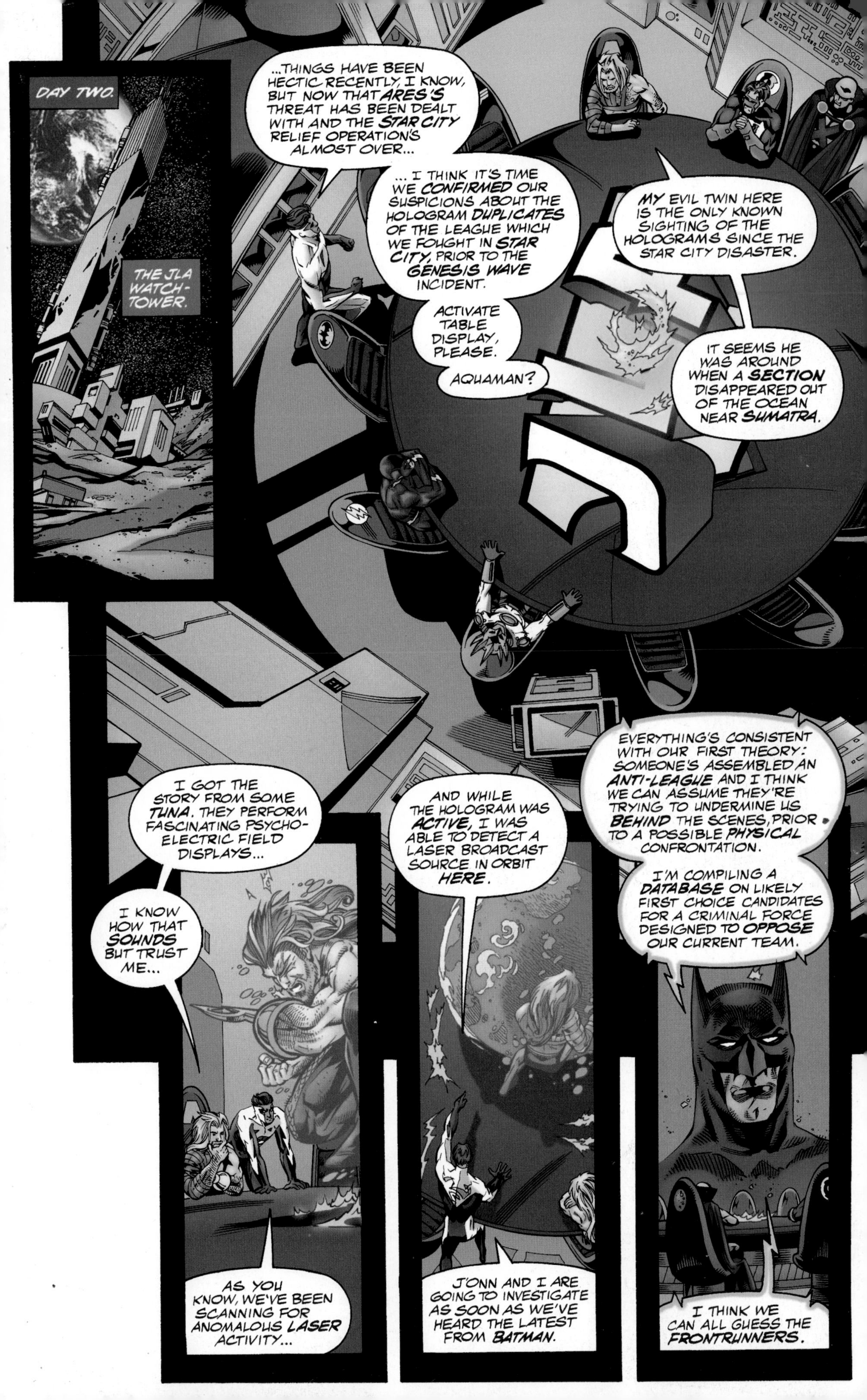
DAY TWO.
THE JLA WATCH-TOWER.
...THINGS HAVE BEEN HECTIC RECENTLY, I KNOW, BUT NOW THAT ARES'S THREAT HAS BEEN DEALT WITH AND THE STAR CITY RELIEF OPERATION'S ALMOST OVER...
... I THINK IT'S TIME WE CONFIRMED OUR SUSPICIONS ABOUT THE HOLOGRAM DUPLICATES OF THE LEAGUE WHICH WE FOUGHT IN STAR CITY, PRIOR TO THE GENESIS WAVE INCIDENT.
ACTIVATE TABLE DISPLAY, PLEASE.
AQUAMAN?
MY EVIL TWIN HERE IS THE ONLY KNOWN SIGHTING OF THE HOLOGRAMS SINCE THE STAR CITY DISASTER.
IT SEEMS HE WAS AROUND WHEN A SECTION DISAPPEARED OUT OF THE OCEAN NEAR SUMATRA.
I GOT THE STORY FROM SOME TUNA. THEY PERFORM FASCINATING PSYCHO-ELECTRIC FIELD DISPLAYS...
I KNOW HOW THAT SOUNDS BUT TRUST ME...
AS YOU KNOW, WE'VE BEEN SCANNING FOR ANOMALOUS LASER ACTIVITY...
AND WHILE THE HOLOGRAM WAS ACTIVE, I WAS ABLE TO DETECT A LASER BROADCAST SOURCE IN ORBIT HERE.
J'ONN AND I ARE GOING TO INVESTIGATE AS SOON AS WE'VE HEARD THE LATEST FROM BATMAN.
EVERYTHING'S CONSISTENT WITH OUR FIRST THEORY: SOMEONE'S ASSEMBLED AN ANTI-LEAGUE AND I THINK WE CAN ASSUME THEY'RE TRYING TO UNDERMINE US BEHIND THE SCENES, PRIOR TO A POSSIBLE PHYSICAL CONFRONTATION.
I'M COMPILING A DATABASE ON LIKELY FIRST CHOICE CANDIDATES FOR A CRIMINAL FORCE DESIGNED TO OPPOSE OUR CURRENT TEAM.
I THINK WE CAN ALL GUESS THE FRONTRUNNERS.

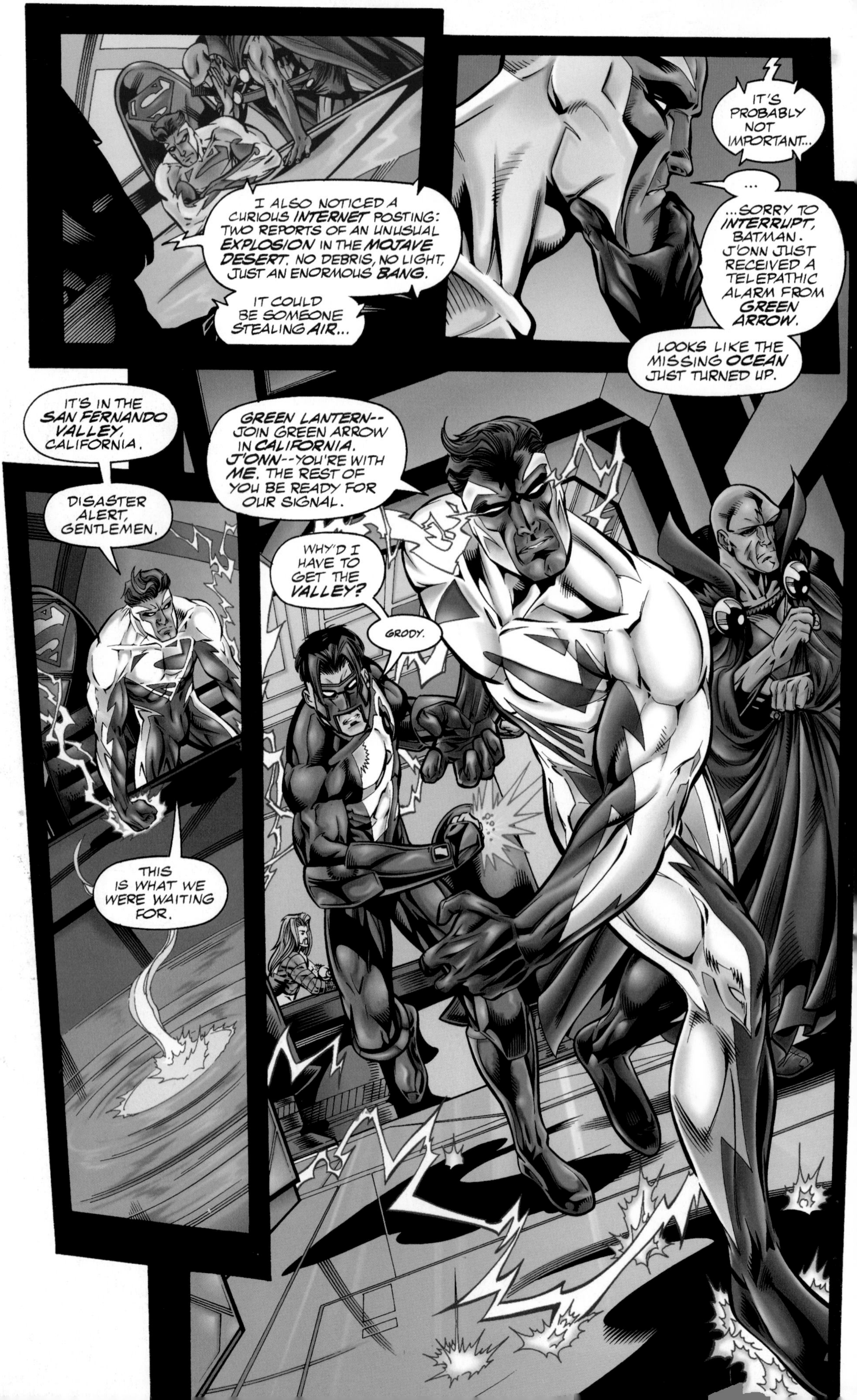
I ALSO NOTICED A CURIOUS INTERNET POSTING: TWO REPORTS OF AN UNUSUAL EXPLOSION IN THE MOJAVE DESERT. NO DEBRIS, NO LIGHT, JUST AN ENORMOUS BANG.
IT COULD BE SOMEONE STEALING AIR...
IT'S PROBABLY NOT IMPORTANT...
...
...SORRY TO INTERRUPT, BATMAN. J'ONN JUST RECEIVED A TELEPATHIC ALARM FROM GREEN ARROW.
LOOKS LIKE THE MISSING OCEAN JUST TURNED UP.
IT'S IN THE SAN FERNANDO VALLEY, CALIFORNIA.
DISASTER ALERT, GENTLEMEN.
THIS IS WHAT WE WERE WAITING FOR.
GREEN LANTERN--JOIN GREEN ARROW IN CALIFORNIA. J'ONN--YOU'RE WITH ME. THE REST OF YOU BE READY FOR OUR SIGNAL.
WHY'D I HAVE TO GET THE VALLEY?
GRODY.

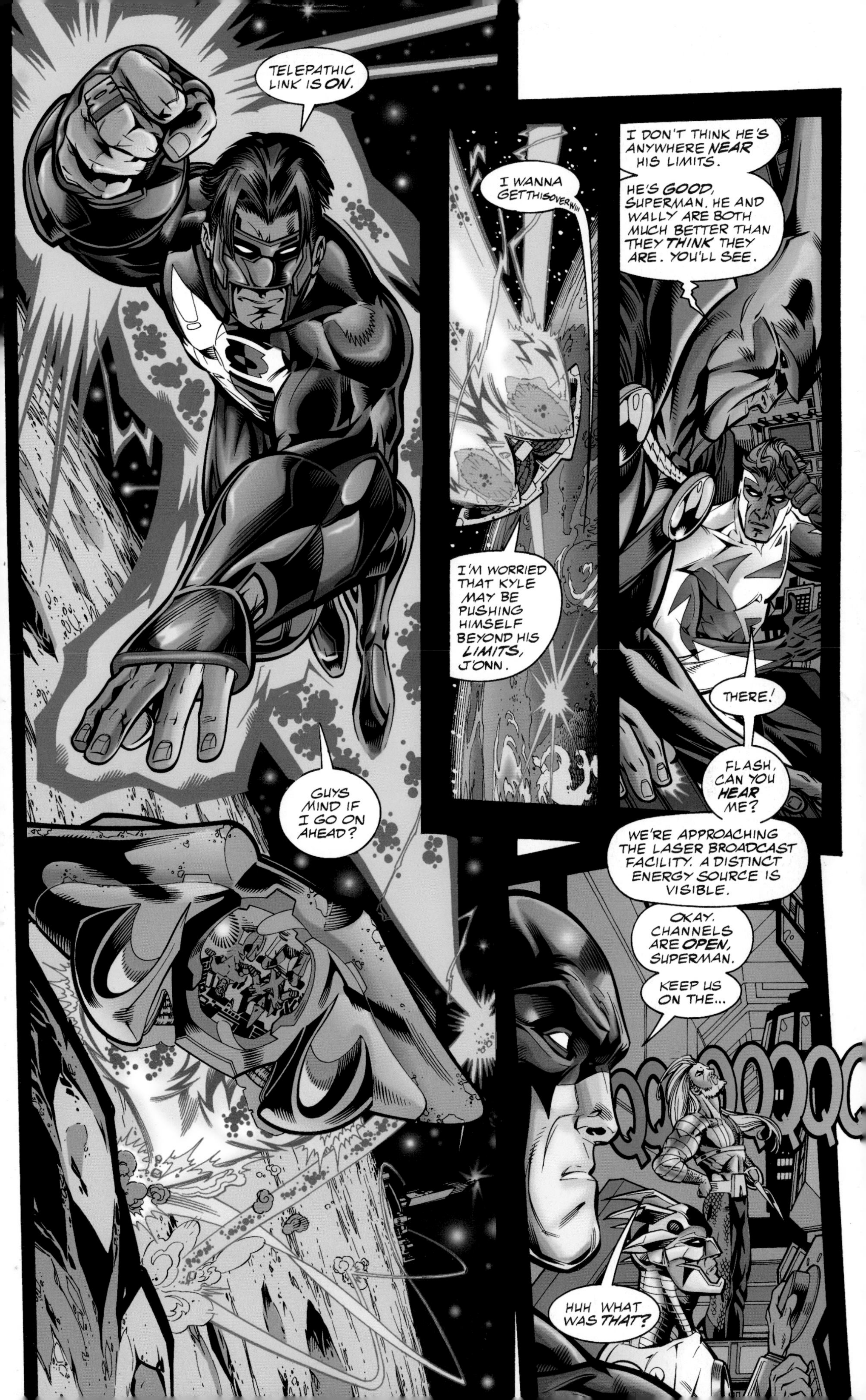
TELEPATHIC LINK IS ON.
I WANNA GET THIS OVER WIII
I'M WORRIED THAT KYLE MAY BE PUSHING HIMSELF BEYOND HIS LIMITS, J'ONN.
I DON'T THINK HE'S ANYWHERE NEAR HIS LIMITS.
HE'S GOOD, SUPERMAN. HE AND WALLY ARE BOTH MUCH BETTER THAN THEY THINK THEY ARE. YOU'LL SEE.
THERE!
FLASH, CAN YOU HEAR ME?
GUYS MIND IF I GO ON AHEAD?
WE'RE APPROACHING THE LASER BROADCAST FACILITY. A DISTINCT ENERGY SOURCE IS VISIBLE.
OKAY. CHANNELS ARE OPEN, SUPERMAN.
KEEP US ON THE...
QQQQQQQ
HUH WHAT WAS THAT?

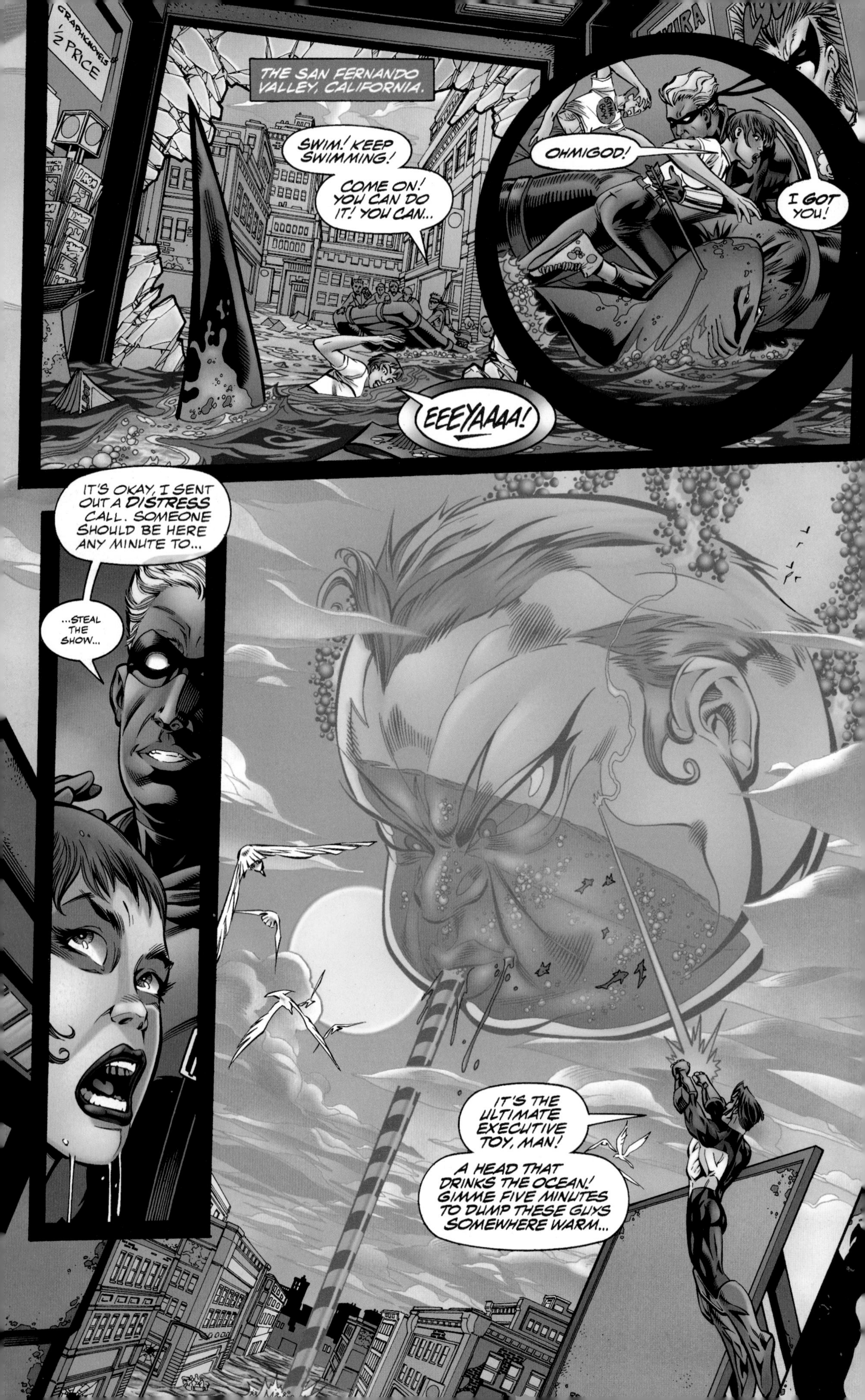
GRAPHIC NOVELS ½ PRICE
THE SAN FERNANDO VALLEY, CALIFORNIA.
SWIM! KEEP SWIMMING!
COME ON! YOU CAN DO IT! YOU CAN...
EEEYAAAA!
OHMIGOD!
I GOT YOU!
IT'S OKAY, I SENT OUT A DISTRESS CALL. SOMEONE SHOULD BE HERE ANY MINUTE TO...
...STEAL THE SHOW...
IT'S THE ULTIMATE EXECUTIVE TOY, MAN!
A HEAD THAT DRINKS THE OCEAN! GIMME FIVE MINUTES TO DUMP THESE GUYS SOMEWHERE WARM...

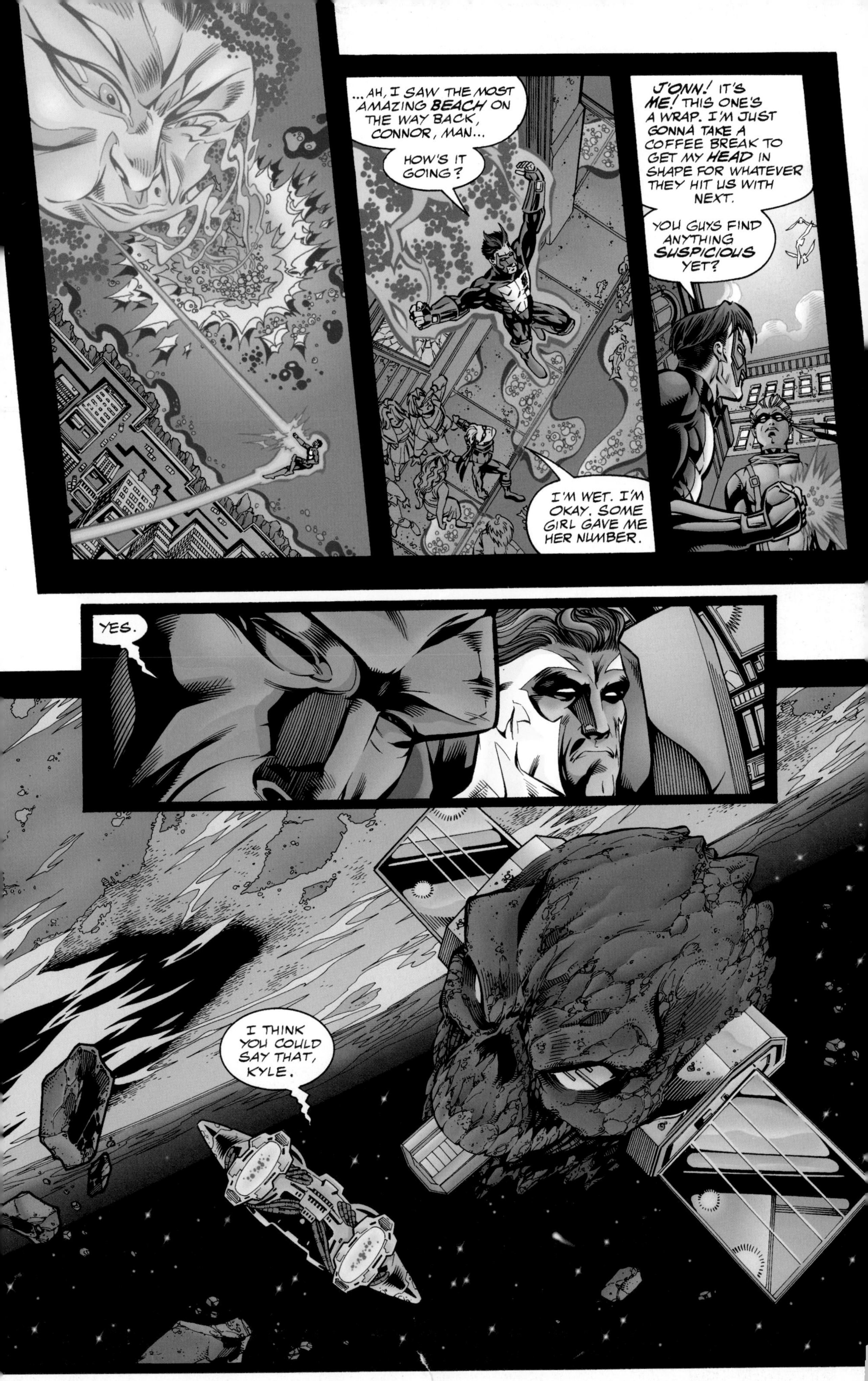
...AH, I SAW THE MOST AMAZING BEACH ON THE WAY BACK, CONNOR, MAN...
HOW'S IT GOING?
I'M WET. I'M OKAY. SOME GIRL GAVE ME HER NUMBER.
J'ONN! IT'S ME! THIS ONE'S A WRAP. I'M JUST GONNA TAKE A COFFEE BREAK TO GET MY HEAD IN SHAPE FOR WHATEVER THEY HIT US WITH NEXT.
YOU GUYS FIND ANYTHING SUSPICIOUS YET?
YES.
I THINK YOU COULD SAY THAT, KYLE.

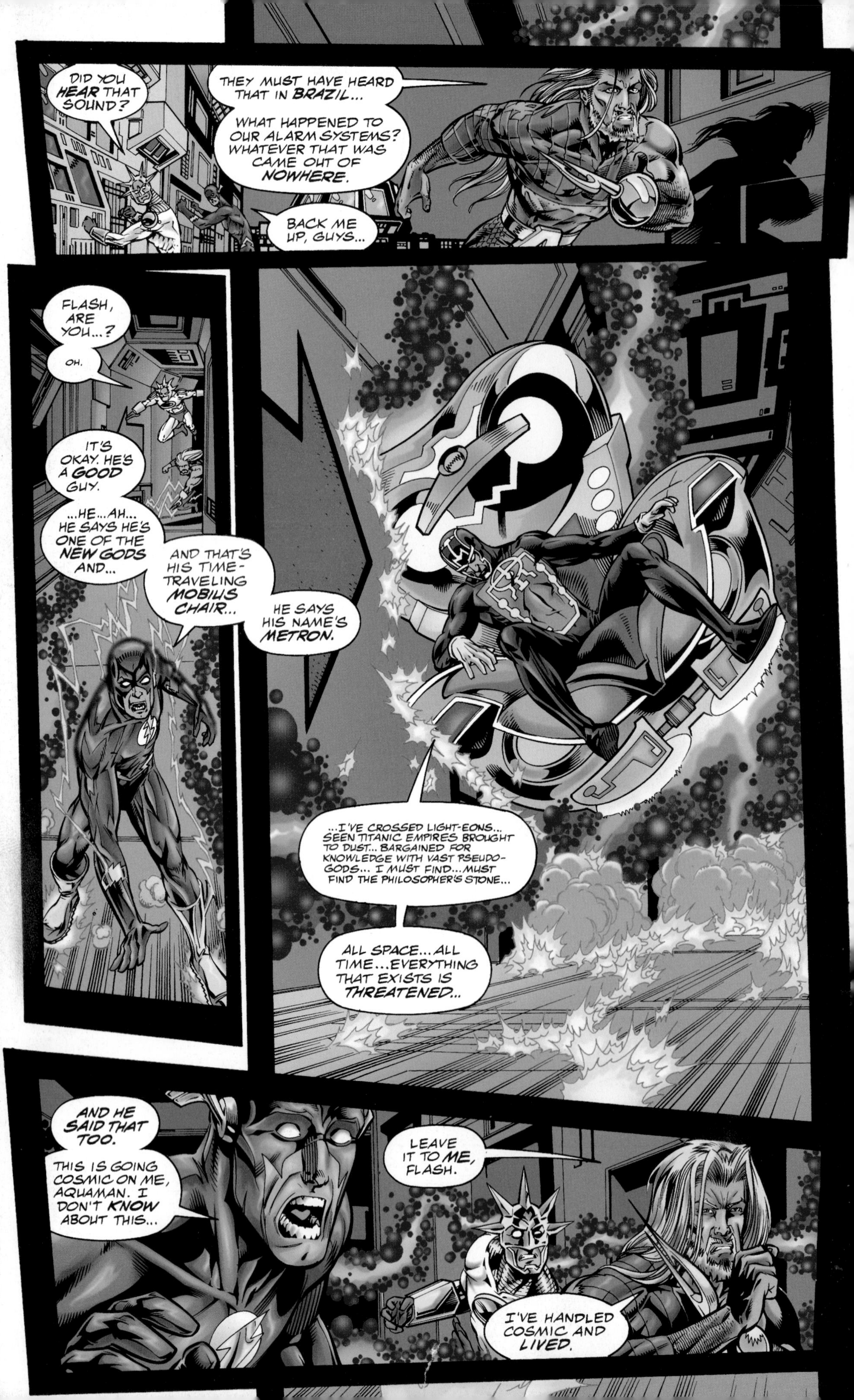
DID YOU HEAR THAT SOUND?
THEY MUST HAVE HEARD THAT IN BRAZIL...
WHAT HAPPENED TO OUR ALARM SYSTEMS? WHATEVER THAT WAS CAME OUT OF NOWHERE.
BACK ME UP, GUYS...
FLASH, ARE YOU...?
OH.
IT'S OKAY. HE'S A GOOD GUY.
...HE...AH... HE SAYS HE'S ONE OF THE NEW GODS AND...
AND THAT'S HIS TIME-TRAVELING MOBIUS CHAIR...
HE SAYS HIS NAME'S METRON.
...I'VE CROSSED LIGHT-EONS... SEEN TITANIC EMPIRES BROUGHT TO DUST... BARGAINED FOR KNOWLEDGE WITH VAST PSEUDO-GODS... I MUST FIND...MUST FIND THE PHILOSOPHER'S STONE...
ALL SPACE...ALL TIME...EVERYTHING THAT EXISTS IS THREATENED...
AND HE SAID THAT TOO.
THIS IS GOING COSMIC ON ME, AQUAMAN. I DON'T KNOW ABOUT THIS...
LEAVE IT TO ME, FLASH.
I'VE HANDLED COSMIC AND LIVED.

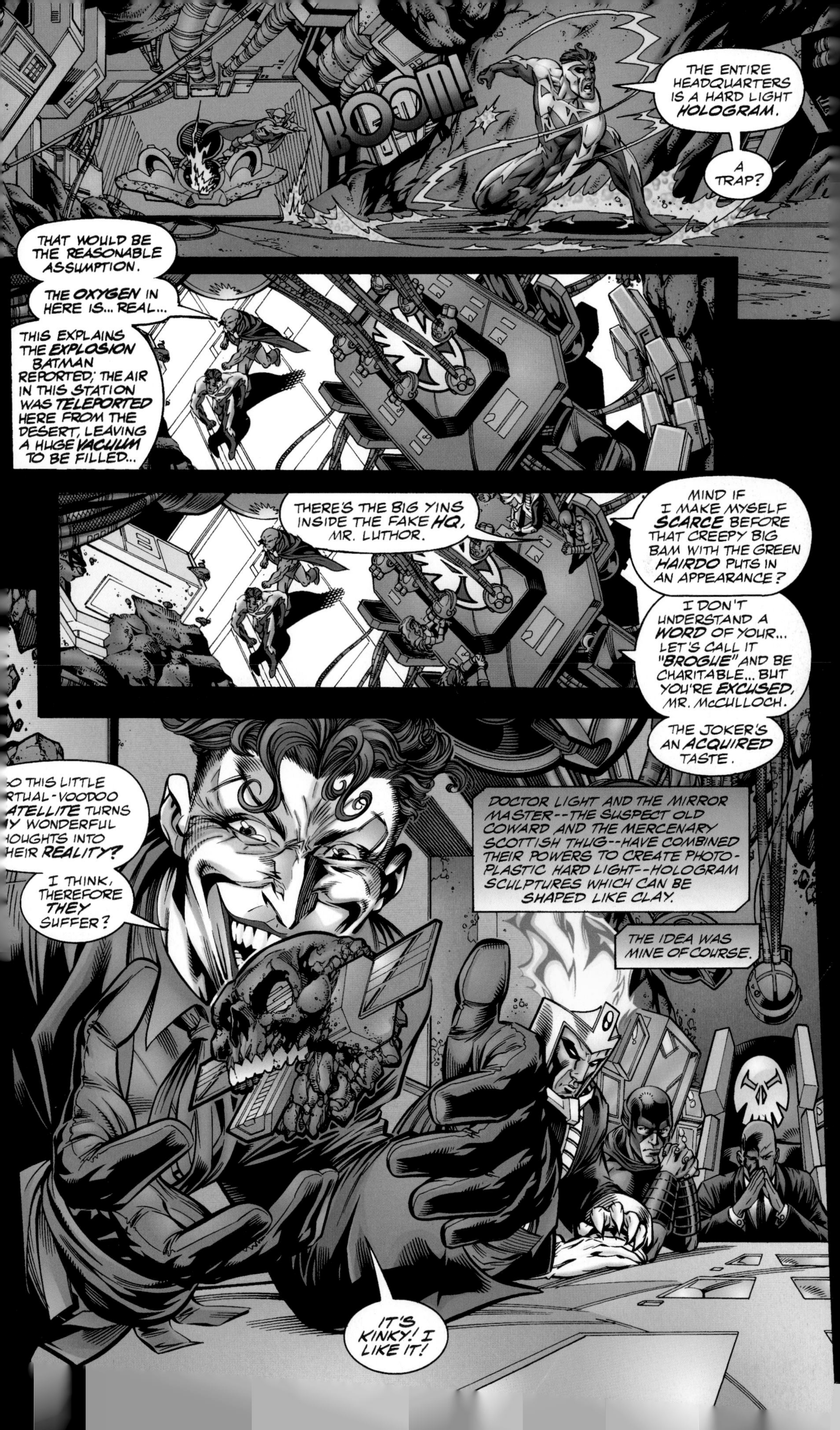
BOOM!
THE ENTIRE HEADQUARTERS IS A HARD LIGHT HOLOGRAM.
A TRAP?
THAT WOULD BE THE REASONABLE ASSUMPTION.
THE OXYGEN IN HERE IS... REAL...
THIS EXPLAINS THE EXPLOSION BATMAN REPORTED; THE AIR IN THIS STATION WAS TELEPORTED HERE FROM THE DESERT, LEAVING A HUGE VACUUM TO BE FILLED...
THERE'S THE BIG YINS INSIDE THE FAKE HQ, MR. LUTHOR.
MIND IF I MAKE MYSELF SCARCE BEFORE THAT CREEPY BIG BAM WITH THE GREEN HAIRDO PUTS IN AN APPEARANCE?
I DON'T UNDERSTAND A WORD OF YOUR... LET'S CALL IT "BROGUE" AND BE CHARITABLE... BUT YOU'RE EXCUSED, MR. McCULLOCH.
THE JOKER'S AN ACQUIRED TASTE.
DOCTOR LIGHT AND THE MIRROR MASTER--THE SUSPECT OLD COWARD AND THE MERCENARY SCOTTISH THUG--HAVE COMBINED THEIR POWERS TO CREATE PHOTO-PLASTIC HARD LIGHT--HOLOGRAM SCULPTURES WHICH CAN BE SHAPED LIKE CLAY.
THE IDEA WAS MINE OF COURSE.
THIS LITTLE RTUAL-VOODOO ATELLITE TURNS Y WONDERFUL HOUGHTS INTO HEIR REALITY?
I THINK, THEREFORE THEY SUFFER?
IT'S KINKY! I LIKE IT!

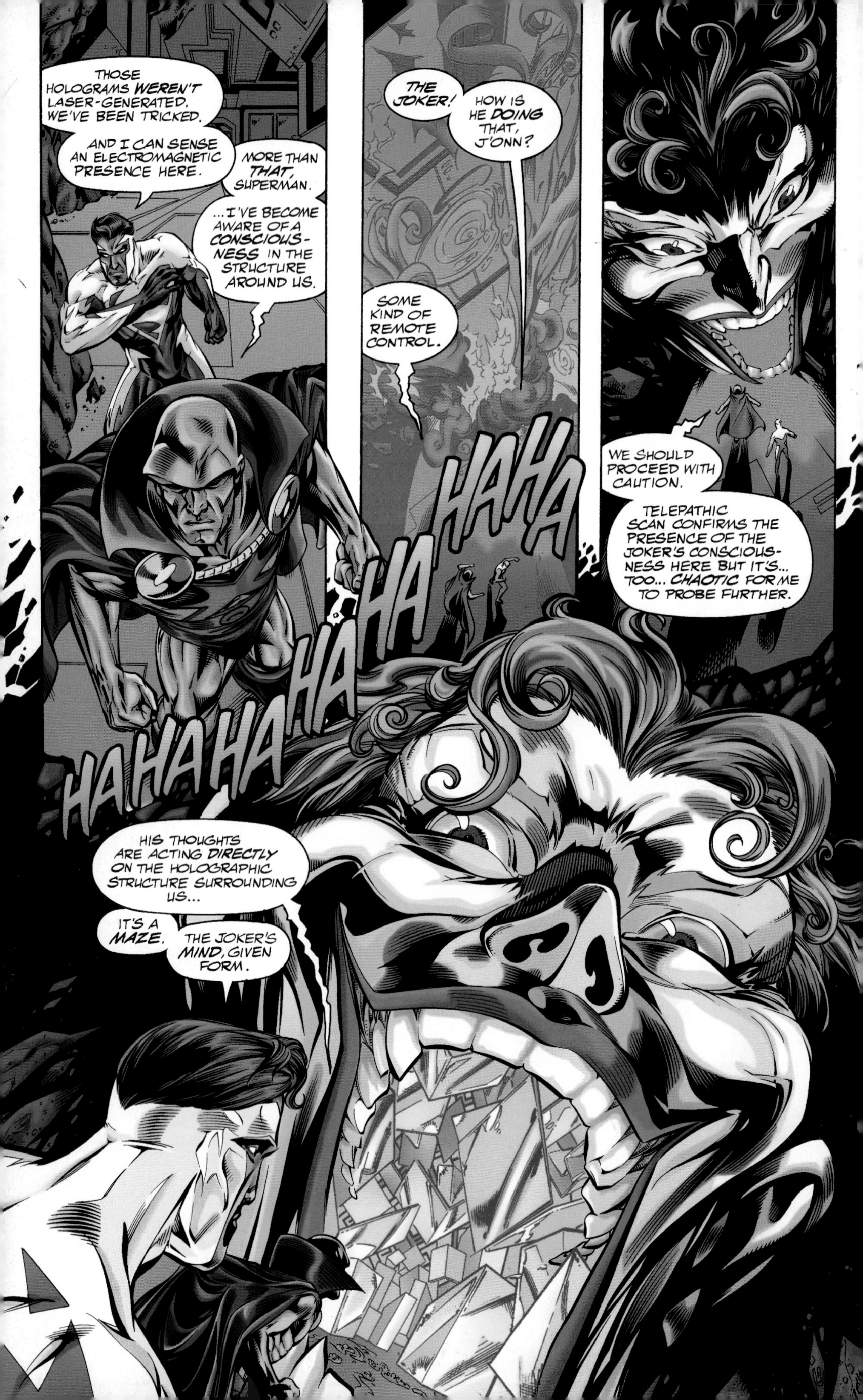
THOSE HOLOGRAMS WEREN'T LASER-GENERATED. WE'VE BEEN TRICKED.
AND I CAN SENSE AN ELECTROMAGNETIC PRESENCE HERE.
MORE THAN THAT, SUPERMAN.
...I'VE BECOME AWARE OF A CONSCIOUSNESS IN THE STRUCTURE AROUND US.
THE JOKER!
HOW IS HE DOING THAT, J'ONN?
SOME KIND OF REMOTE CONTROL.
WE SHOULD PROCEED WITH CAUTION.
TELEPATHIC SCAN CONFIRMS THE PRESENCE OF THE JOKER'S CONSCIOUSNESS HERE BUT IT'S... TOO... CHAOTIC FOR ME TO PROBE FURTHER.
HAHAHAHAHAHAHAHAHAHA
HIS THOUGHTS ARE ACTING DIRECTLY ON THE HOLOGRAPHIC STRUCTURE SURROUNDING US...
IT'S A MAZE.
THE JOKER'S MIND, GIVEN FORM.

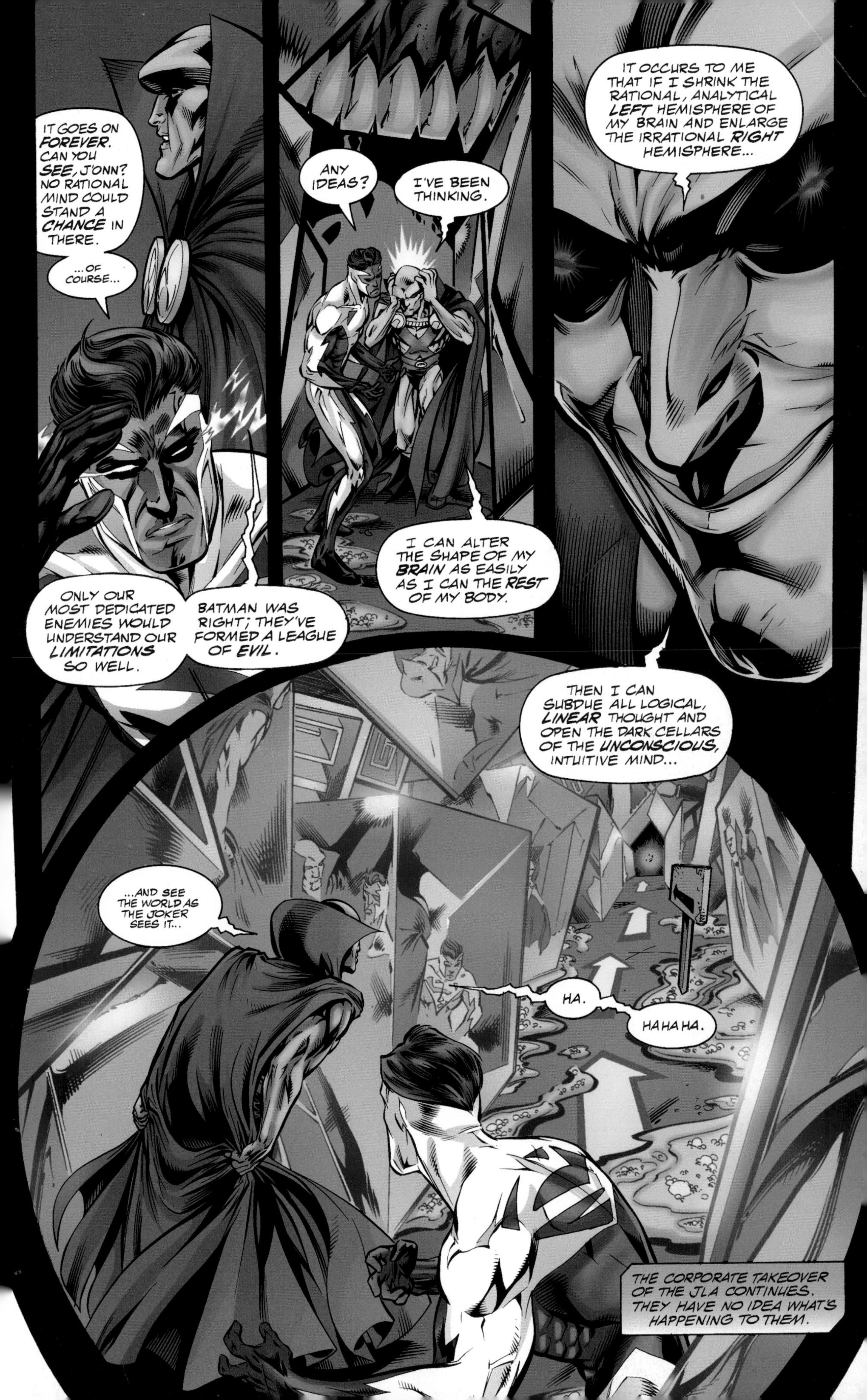
IT GOES ON FOREVER. CAN YOU SEE, J'ONN? NO RATIONAL MIND COULD STAND A CHANCE IN THERE.
...OF COURSE...
ONLY OUR MOST DEDICATED ENEMIES WOULD UNDERSTAND OUR LIMITATIONS SO WELL.
BATMAN WAS RIGHT; THEY'VE FORMED A LEAGUE OF EVIL.
ANY IDEAS?
I'VE BEEN THINKING.
I CAN ALTER THE SHAPE OF MY BRAIN AS EASILY AS I CAN THE REST OF MY BODY.
IT OCCURS TO ME THAT IF I SHRINK THE RATIONAL, ANALYTICAL LEFT HEMISPHERE OF MY BRAIN AND ENLARGE THE IRRATIONAL RIGHT HEMISPHERE...
THEN I CAN SUBDUE ALL LOGICAL, LINEAR THOUGHT AND OPEN THE DARK CELLARS OF THE UNCONSCIOUS, INTUITIVE MIND...
...AND SEE THE WORLD AS THE JOKER SEES IT...
HA.
HAHAHA.
THE CORPORATE TAKEOVER OF THE JLA CONTINUES. THEY HAVE NO IDEA WHAT'S HAPPENING TO THEM.

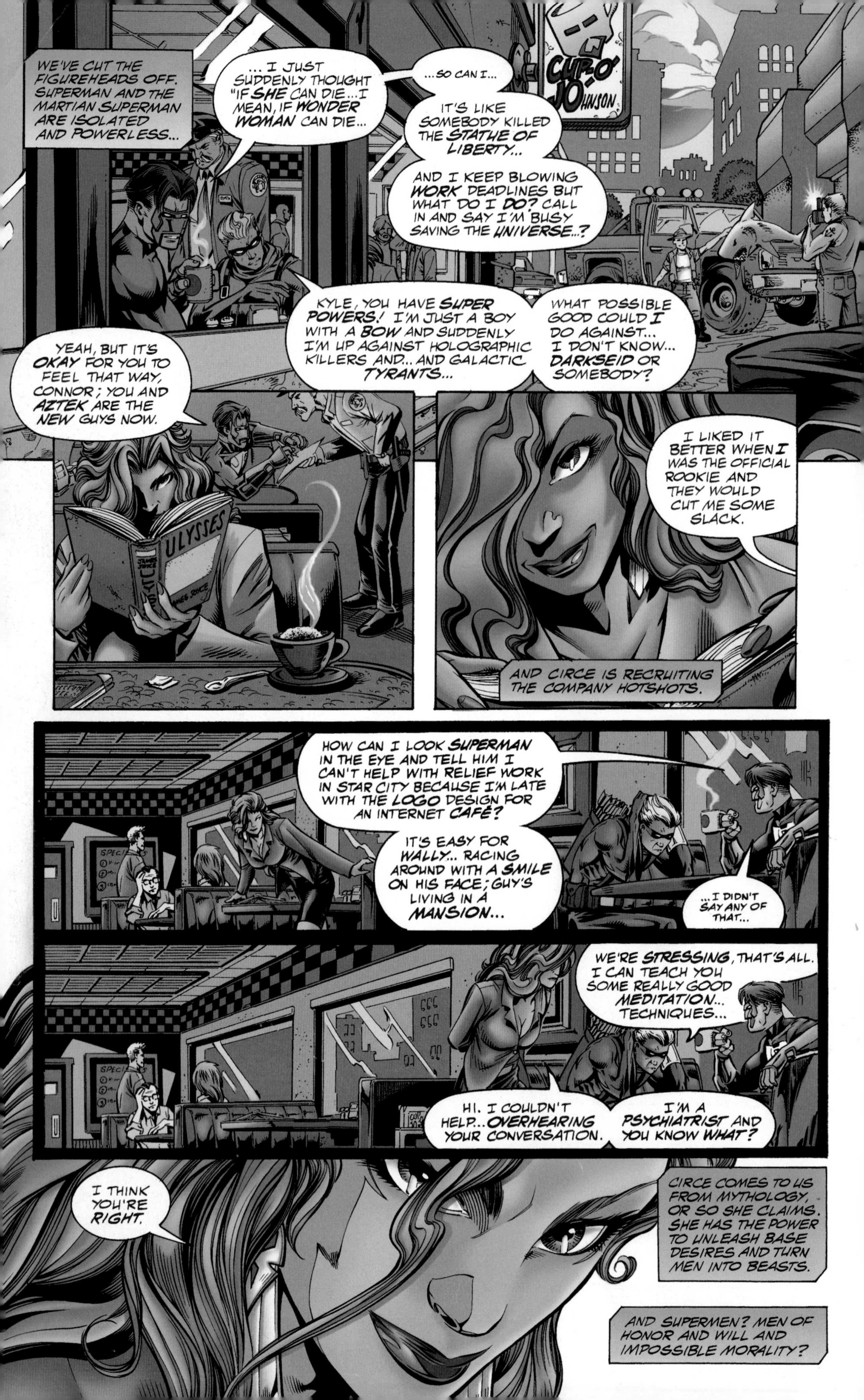

WE'VE CUT THE FIGUREHEADS OFF. SUPERMAN AND THE MARTIAN SUPERMAN ARE ISOLATED AND POWERLESS...
... I JUST SUDDENLY THOUGHT "IF SHE CAN DIE... I MEAN, IF WONDER WOMAN CAN DIE...
...SO CAN I...
IT'S LIKE SOMEBODY KILLED THE STATUE OF LIBERTY...
AND I KEEP BLOWING WORK DEADLINES BUT WHAT DO I DO? CALL IN AND SAY I'M BUSY SAVING THE UNIVERSE..?
CUP-O' JOHNSON
KYLE, YOU HAVE SUPER POWERS! I'M JUST A BOY WITH A BOW AND SUDDENLY I'M UP AGAINST HOLOGRAPHIC KILLERS AND... AND GALACTIC TYRANTS...
WHAT POSSIBLE GOOD COULD I DO AGAINST... I DON'T KNOW... DARKSEID OR SOMEBODY?
YEAH, BUT IT'S OKAY FOR YOU TO FEEL THAT WAY, CONNOR; YOU AND AZTEK ARE THE NEW GUYS NOW.
ULYSSES
JAMES JOYCE
I LIKED IT BETTER WHEN I WAS THE OFFICIAL ROOKIE AND THEY WOULD CUT ME SOME SLACK.
AND CIRCE IS RECRUITING THE COMPANY HOTSHOTS.
HOW CAN I LOOK SUPERMAN IN THE EYE AND TELL HIM I CAN'T HELP WITH RELIEF WORK IN STAR CITY BECAUSE I'M LATE WITH THE LOGO DESIGN FOR AN INTERNET CAFÉ?
IT'S EASY FOR WALLY... RACING AROUND WITH A SMILE ON HIS FACE; GUY'S LIVING IN A MANSION...
...I DIDN'T SAY ANY OF THAT...
WE'RE STRESSING, THAT'S ALL. I CAN TEACH YOU SOME REALLY GOOD MEDITATION... TECHNIQUES...
HI. I COULDN'T HELP... OVERHEARING YOUR CONVERSATION.
I'M A PSYCHIATRIST AND YOU KNOW WHAT?
I THINK YOU'RE RIGHT.
CIRCE COMES TO US FROM MYTHOLOGY, OR SO SHE CLAIMS. SHE HAS THE POWER TO UNLEASH BASE DESIRES AND TURN MEN INTO BEASTS.
AND SUPERMEN? MEN OF HONOR AND WILL AND IMPOSSIBLE MORALITY?

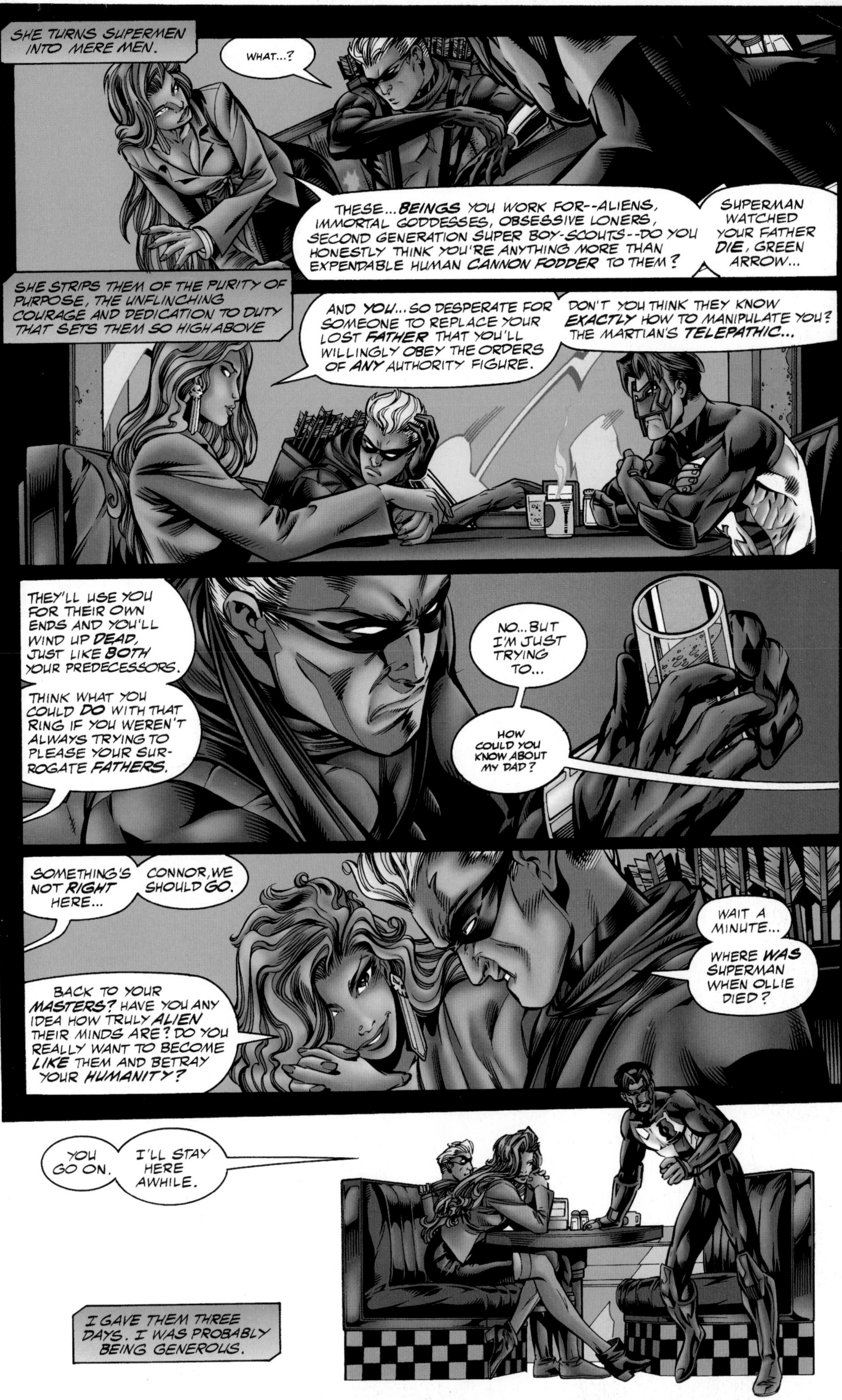
SHE TURNS SUPERMEN INTO MERE MEN.
WHAT...?
THESE... BEINGS YOU WORK FOR--ALIENS, IMMORTAL GODDESSES, OBSESSIVE LONERS, SECOND GENERATION SUPER BOY-SCOUTS--DO YOU HONESTLY THINK YOU'RE ANYTHING MORE THAN EXPENDABLE HUMAN CANNON FODDER TO THEM?
SUPERMAN WATCHED YOUR FATHER DIE, GREEN ARROW...
SHE STRIPS THEM OF THE PURITY OF PURPOSE, THE UNFLINCHING COURAGE AND DEDICATION TO DUTY THAT SETS THEM SO HIGH ABOVE
AND YOU... SO DESPERATE FOR SOMEONE TO REPLACE YOUR LOST FATHER THAT YOU'LL WILLINGLY OBEY THE ORDERS OF ANY AUTHORITY FIGURE.
DON'T YOU THINK THEY KNOW EXACTLY HOW TO MANIPULATE YOU? THE MARTIAN'S TELEPATHIC...
THEY'LL USE YOU FOR THEIR OWN ENDS AND YOU'LL WIND UP DEAD, JUST LIKE BOTH YOUR PREDECESSORS.
THINK WHAT YOU COULD DO WITH THAT RING IF YOU WEREN'T ALWAYS TRYING TO PLEASE YOUR SURROGATE FATHERS.
NO... BUT I'M JUST TRYING TO...
HOW COULD YOU KNOW ABOUT MY DAD?
SOMETHING'S NOT RIGHT HERE...
CONNOR, WE SHOULD GO.
BACK TO YOUR MASTERS? HAVE YOU ANY IDEA HOW TRULY ALIEN THEIR MINDS ARE? DO YOU REALLY WANT TO BECOME LIKE THEM AND BETRAY YOUR HUMANITY?
WAIT A MINUTE...
WHERE WAS SUPERMAN WHEN OLLIE DIED?
YOU GO ON.
I'LL STAY HERE AWHILE.
I GAVE THEM THREE DAYS. I WAS PROBABLY BEING GENEROUS.

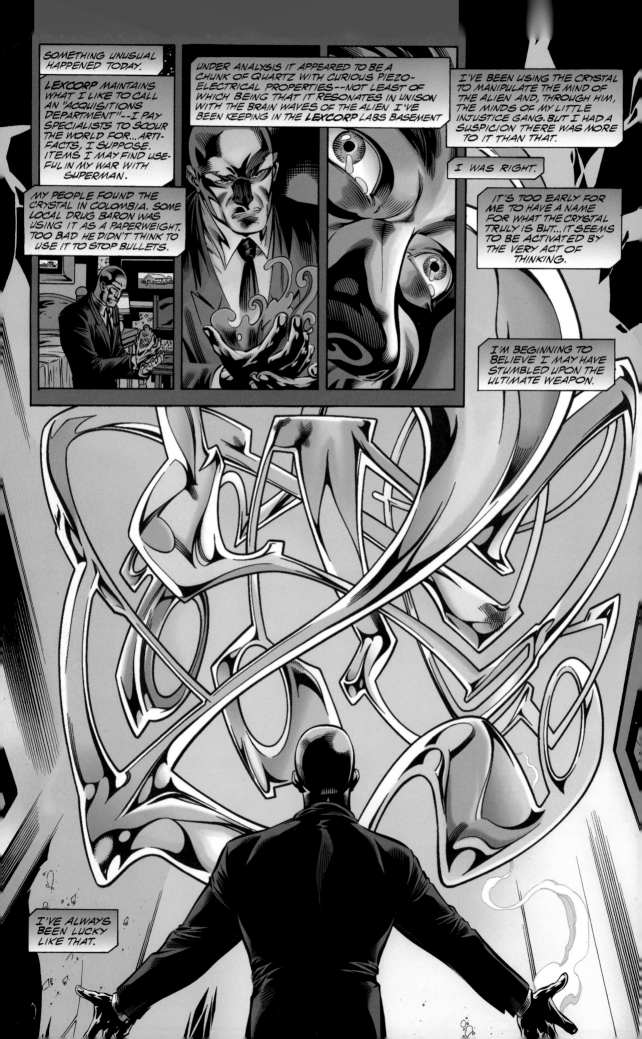

SOMETHING UNUSUAL HAPPENED TODAY.

LEXCORP MAINTAINS WHAT I LIKE TO CALL AN "ACQUISITIONS DEPARTMENT"--I PAY SPECIALISTS TO SCOUR THE WORLD FOR...ARTI-FACTS, I SUPPOSE. ITEMS I MAY FIND USE-FUL IN MY WAR WITH SUPERMAN.

MY PEOPLE FOUND THE CRYSTAL IN COLOMBIA. SOME LOCAL DRUG BARON WAS USING IT AS A PAPERWEIGHT. TOO BAD HE DIDN'T THINK TO USE IT TO STOP BULLETS.

UNDER ANALYSIS IT APPEARED TO BE A CHUNK OF QUARTZ WITH CURIOUS PIEZO-ELECTRICAL PROPERTIES--NOT LEAST OF WHICH BEING THAT IT RESONATES IN UNISON WITH THE BRAIN WAVES OF THE ALIEN I'VE BEEN KEEPING IN THE **LEXCORP** LABS BASEMENT

I'VE BEEN USING THE CRYSTAL TO MANIPULATE THE MIND OF THE ALIEN AND, THROUGH HIM, THE MINDS OF MY LITTLE INJUSTICE GANG. BUT I HAD A SUSPICION THERE WAS MORE TO IT THAN THAT.

I WAS RIGHT.

IT'S TOO EARLY FOR ME TO HAVE A NAME FOR WHAT THE CRYSTAL TRULY IS BUT...IT SEEMS TO BE ACTIVATED BY THE VERY ACT OF THINKING.

I'M BEGINNING TO BELIEVE I MAY HAVE STUMBLED UPON THE ULTIMATE WEAPON.

I'VE ALWAYS BEEN LUCKY LIKE THAT.

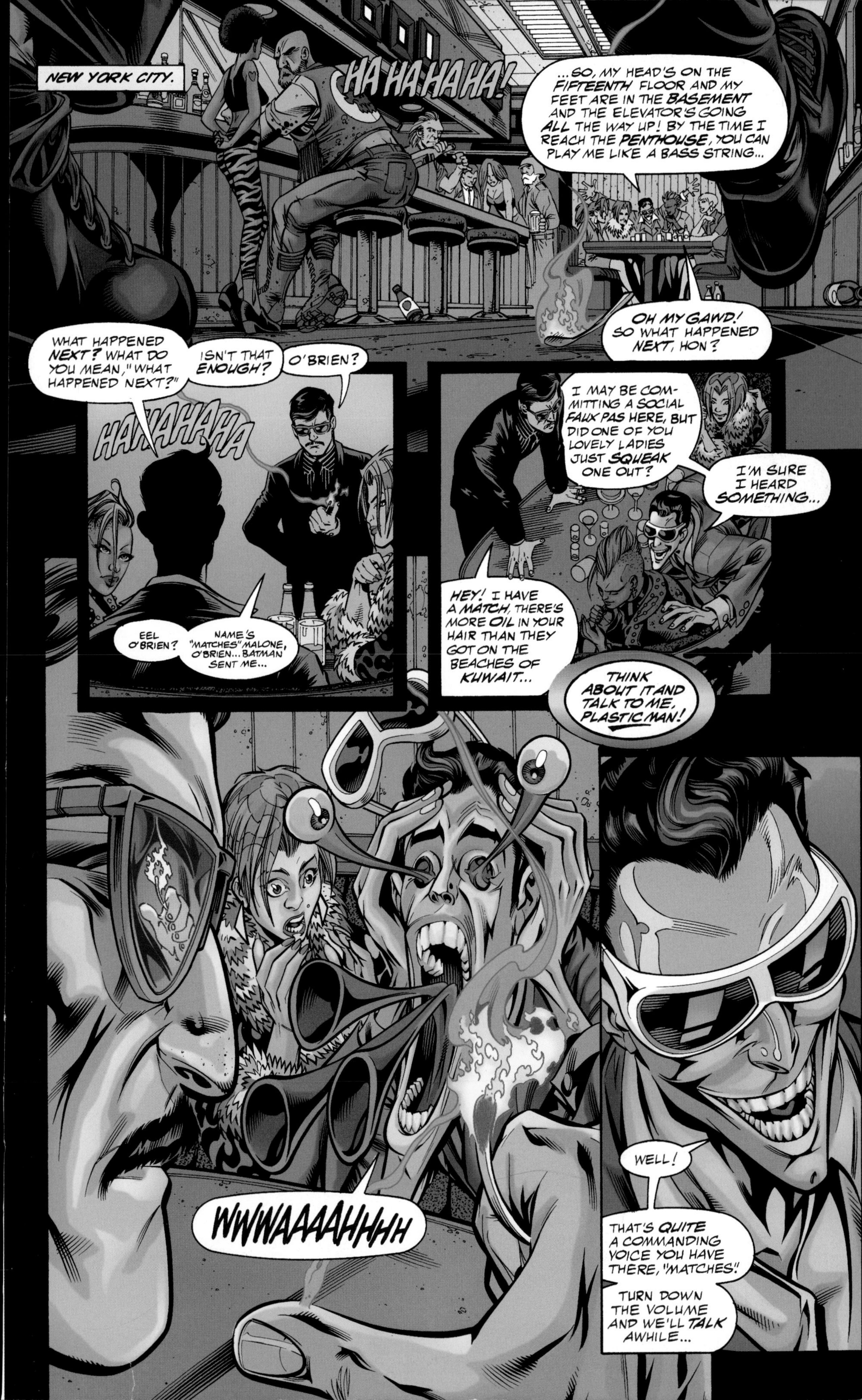
NEW YORK CITY.
HA HA HA HA HA!
...SO, MY HEAD'S ON THE FIFTEENTH FLOOR AND MY FEET ARE IN THE BASEMENT AND THE ELEVATOR'S GOING ALL THE WAY UP! BY THE TIME I REACH THE PENTHOUSE, YOU CAN PLAY ME LIKE A BASS STRING...
OH MY GAWD! SO WHAT HAPPENED NEXT, HON?
WHAT HAPPENED NEXT? WHAT DO YOU MEAN, "WHAT HAPPENED NEXT?"
ISN'T THAT ENOUGH?
O'BRIEN?
HAHAHAHA
EEL O'BRIEN?
NAME'S "MATCHES" MALONE, O'BRIEN... BATMAN SENT ME...
I MAY BE COMMITTING A SOCIAL FAUX PAS HERE, BUT DID ONE OF YOU LOVELY LADIES JUST SQUEAK ONE OUT?
I'M SURE I HEARD SOMETHING...
HEY! I HAVE A MATCH, THERE'S MORE OIL IN YOUR HAIR THAN THEY GOT ON THE BEACHES OF KUWAIT...
THINK ABOUT IT AND TALK TO ME, PLASTIC MAN!
WWWAAAAHHHH
WELL!
THAT'S QUITE A COMMANDING VOICE YOU HAVE THERE, "MATCHES."
TURN DOWN THE VOLUME AND WE'LL TALK AWHILE...

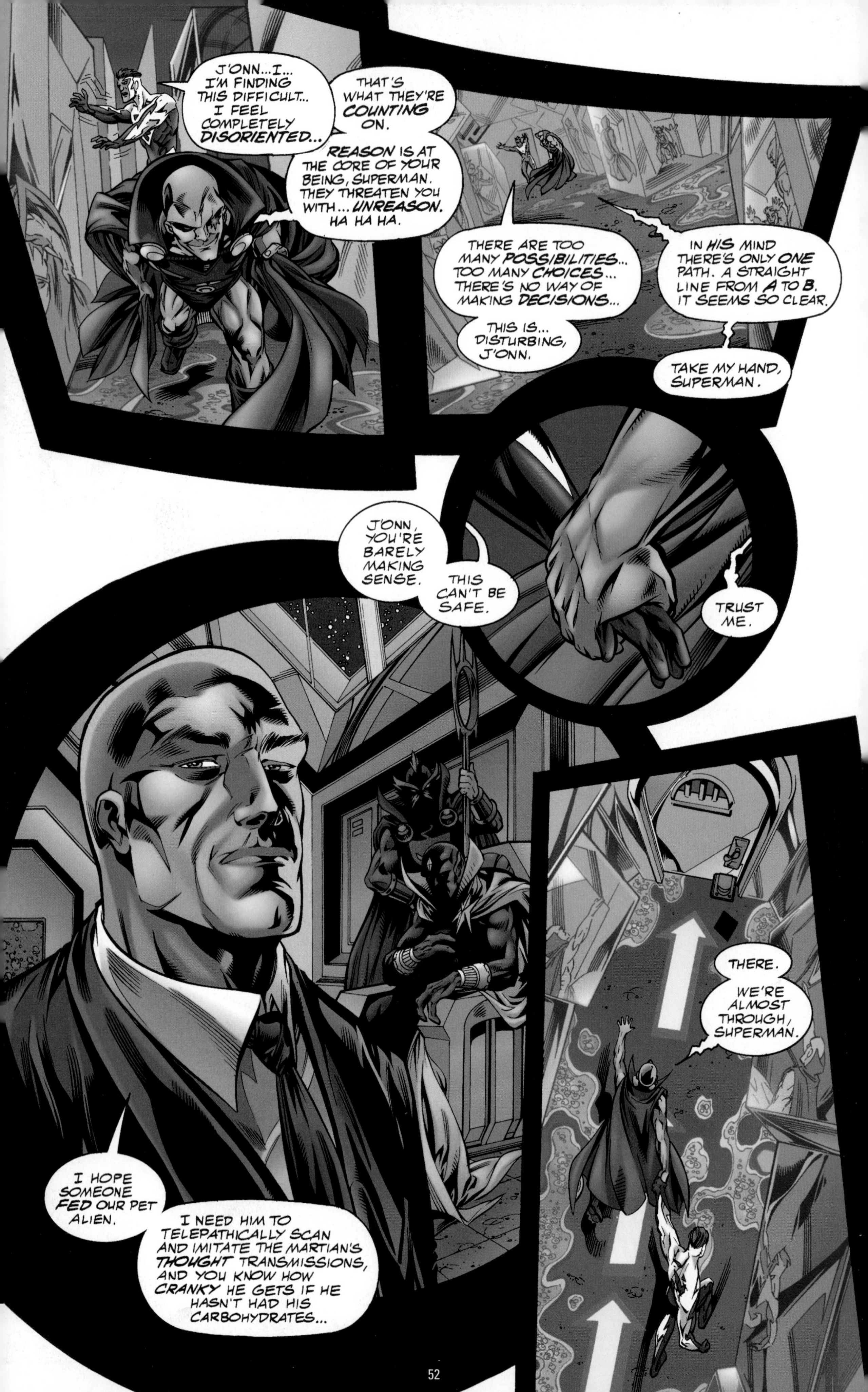
J'ONN...I... I'M FINDING THIS DIFFICULT... I FEEL COMPLETELY DISORIENTED...
THAT'S WHAT THEY'RE COUNTING ON.
REASON IS AT THE CORE OF YOUR BEING, SUPERMAN. THEY THREATEN YOU WITH... UNREASON. HA HA HA.
THERE ARE TOO MANY POSSIBILITIES... TOO MANY CHOICES... THERE'S NO WAY OF MAKING DECISIONS...
THIS IS... DISTURBING, J'ONN.
IN HIS MIND THERE'S ONLY ONE PATH. A STRAIGHT LINE FROM A TO B. IT SEEMS SO CLEAR.
TAKE MY HAND, SUPERMAN.
J'ONN, YOU'RE BARELY MAKING SENSE.
THIS CAN'T BE SAFE.
TRUST ME.
I HOPE SOMEONE FED OUR PET ALIEN.
I NEED HIM TO TELEPATHICALLY SCAN AND IMITATE THE MARTIAN'S THOUGHT TRANSMISSIONS, AND YOU KNOW HOW CRANKY HE GETS IF HE HASN'T HAD HIS CARBOHYDRATES...
THERE.
WE'RE ALMOST THROUGH, SUPERMAN.

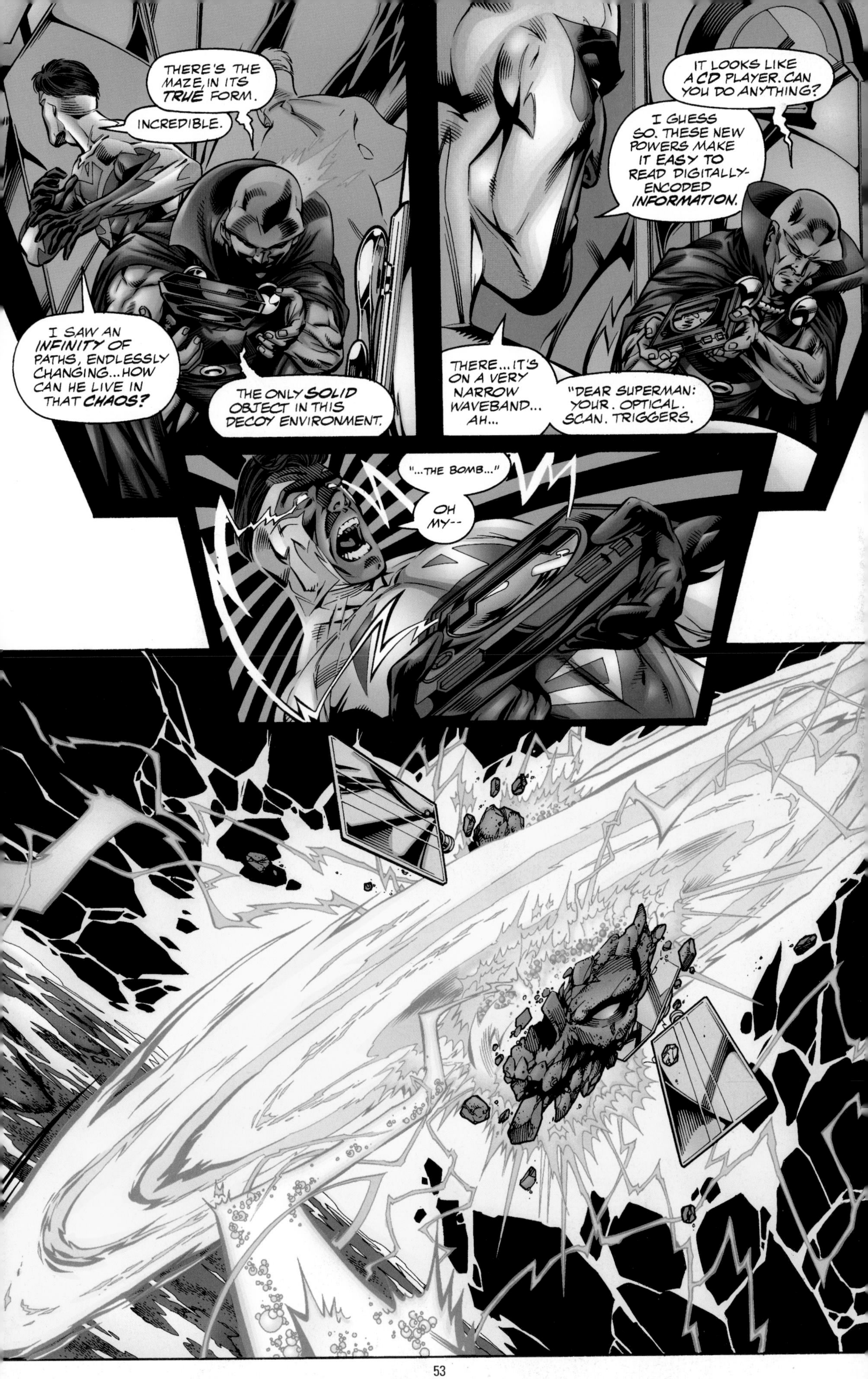
THERE'S THE MAZE, IN ITS TRUE FORM.
INCREDIBLE.
I SAW AN INFINITY OF PATHS, ENDLESSLY CHANGING...HOW CAN HE LIVE IN THAT CHAOS?
THE ONLY SOLID OBJECT IN THIS DECOY ENVIRONMENT.
IT LOOKS LIKE A CD PLAYER. CAN YOU DO ANYTHING?
I GUESS SO. THESE NEW POWERS MAKE IT EASY TO READ DIGITALLY-ENCODED INFORMATION.
THERE... IT'S ON A VERY NARROW WAVEBAND... AH...
"DEAR SUPERMAN: YOUR. OPTICAL. SCAN. TRIGGERS.
"...THE BOMB..."
OH MY--

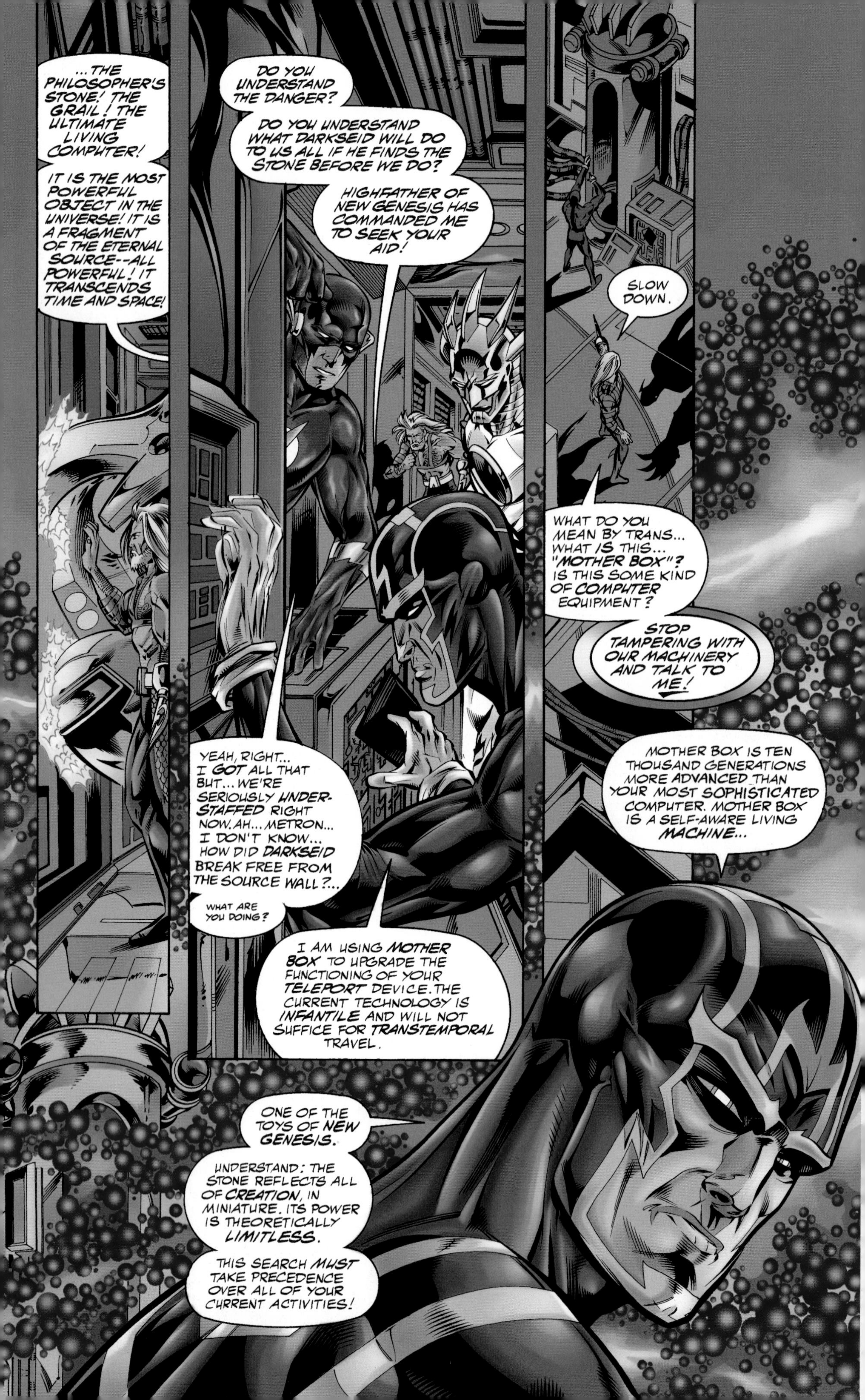
...THE PHILOSOPHER'S STONE! THE GRAIL! THE ULTIMATE LIVING COMPUTER!
IT IS THE MOST POWERFUL OBJECT IN THE UNIVERSE! IT IS A FRAGMENT OF THE ETERNAL SOURCE--ALL POWERFUL! IT TRANSCENDS TIME AND SPACE!
DO YOU UNDERSTAND THE DANGER?
DO YOU UNDERSTAND WHAT DARKSEID WILL DO TO US ALL IF HE FINDS THE STONE BEFORE WE DO?
HIGHFATHER OF NEW GENESIS HAS COMMANDED ME TO SEEK YOUR AID!
SLOW DOWN.
WHAT DO YOU MEAN BY TRANS... WHAT IS THIS... "MOTHER BOX"? IS THIS SOME KIND OF COMPUTER EQUIPMENT?
STOP TAMPERING WITH OUR MACHINERY AND TALK TO ME!
YEAH, RIGHT... I GOT ALL THAT BUT... WE'RE SERIOUSLY UNDER-STAFFED RIGHT NOW. AH... METRON... I DON'T KNOW... HOW DID DARKSEID BREAK FREE FROM THE SOURCE WALL?...
WHAT ARE YOU DOING?
I AM USING MOTHER BOX TO UPGRADE THE FUNCTIONING OF YOUR TELEPORT DEVICE. THE CURRENT TECHNOLOGY IS INFANTILE AND WILL NOT SUFFICE FOR TRANSTEMPORAL TRAVEL.
MOTHER BOX IS TEN THOUSAND GENERATIONS MORE ADVANCED THAN YOUR MOST SOPHISTICATED COMPUTER. MOTHER BOX IS A SELF-AWARE LIVING MACHINE...
ONE OF THE TOYS OF NEW GENESIS.
UNDERSTAND: THE STONE REFLECTS ALL OF CREATION, IN MINIATURE. ITS POWER IS THEORETICALLY LIMITLESS.
THIS SEARCH MUST TAKE PRECEDENCE OVER ALL OF YOUR CURRENT ACTIVITIES!

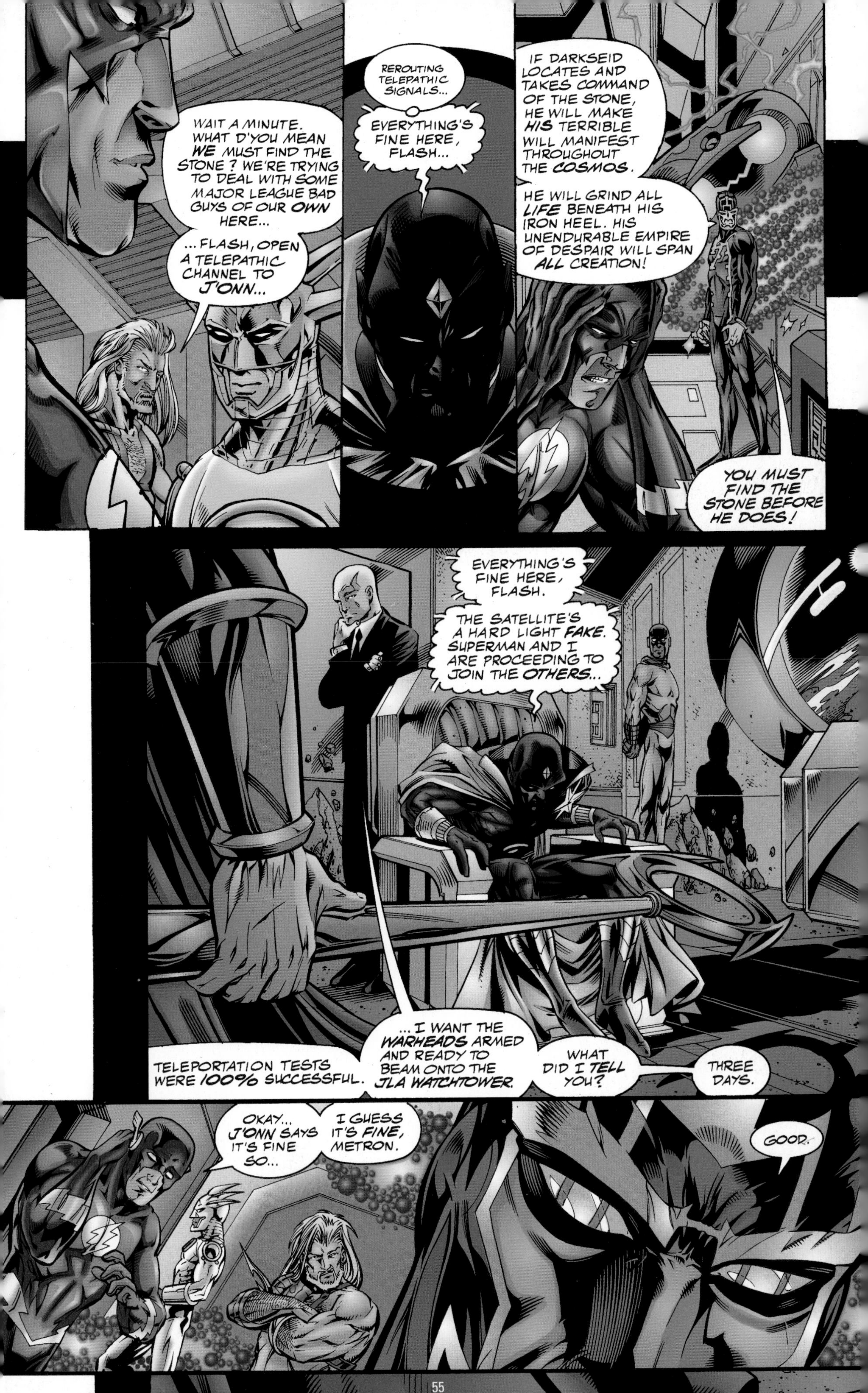
WAIT A MINUTE. WHAT D'YOU MEAN WE MUST FIND THE STONE? WE'RE TRYING TO DEAL WITH SOME MAJOR LEAGUE BAD GUYS OF OUR OWN HERE...
...FLASH, OPEN A TELEPATHIC CHANNEL TO J'ONN...
REROUTING TELEPATHIC SIGNALS...
EVERYTHING'S FINE HERE, FLASH...
IF DARKSEID LOCATES AND TAKES COMMAND OF THE STONE, HE WILL MAKE HIS TERRIBLE WILL MANIFEST THROUGHOUT THE COSMOS.
HE WILL GRIND ALL LIFE BENEATH HIS IRON HEEL. HIS UNENDURABLE EMPIRE OF DESPAIR WILL SPAN ALL CREATION!
YOU MUST FIND THE STONE BEFORE HE DOES!
EVERYTHING'S FINE HERE, FLASH.
THE SATELLITE'S A HARD LIGHT FAKE. SUPERMAN AND I ARE PROCEEDING TO JOIN THE OTHERS...
TELEPORTATION TESTS WERE 100% SUCCESSFUL.
...I WANT THE WARHEADS ARMED AND READY TO BEAM ONTO THE JLA WATCHTOWER.
WHAT DID I TELL YOU?
THREE DAYS.
OKAY... J'ONN SAYS IT'S FINE SO...
I GUESS IT'S FINE, METRON.
GOOD.

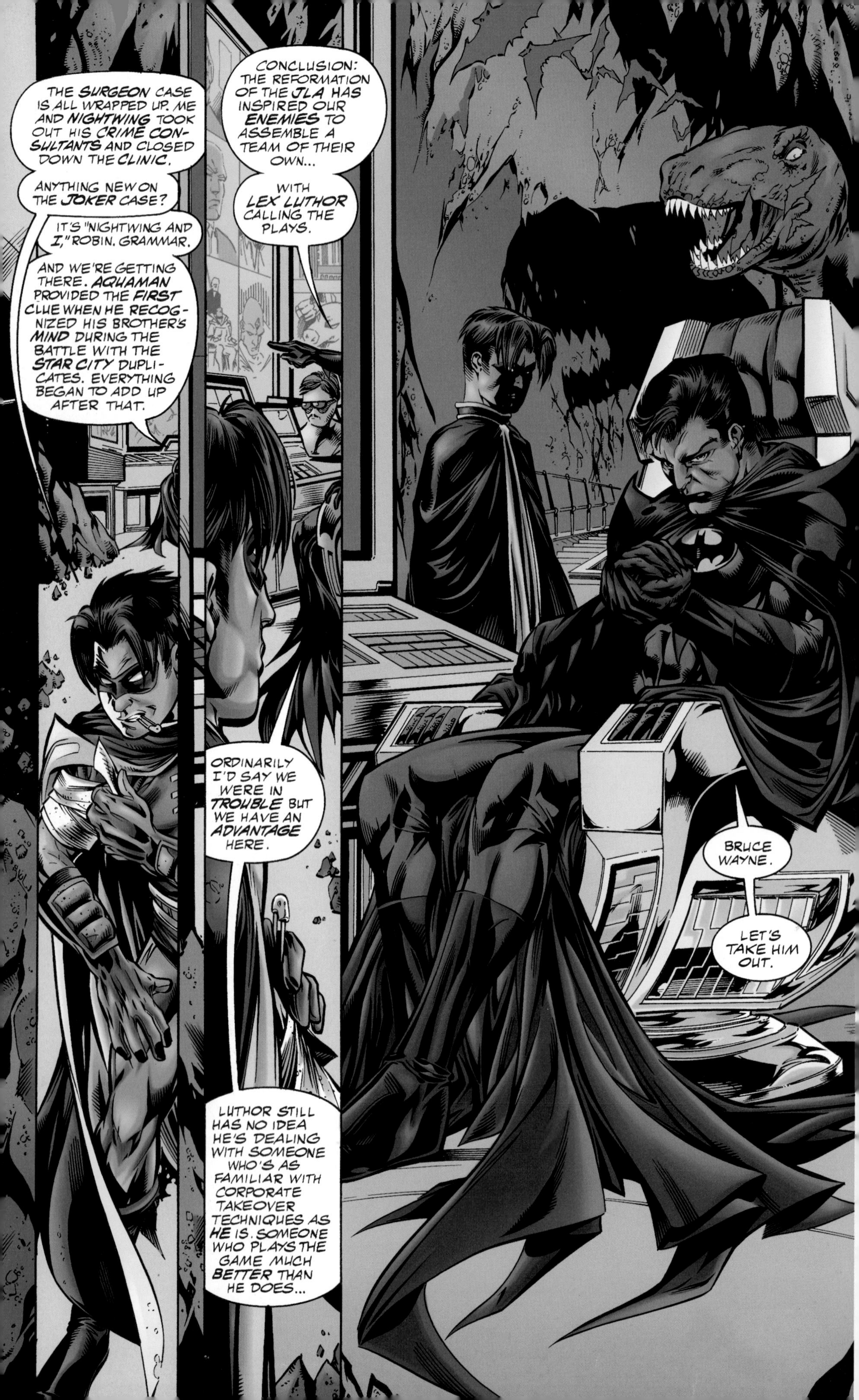
THE SURGEON CASE IS ALL WRAPPED UP. ME AND NIGHTWING TOOK OUT HIS CRIME CONSULTANTS AND CLOSED DOWN THE CLINIC.
ANYTHING NEW ON THE JOKER CASE?
IT'S "NIGHTWING AND I," ROBIN. GRAMMAR.
AND WE'RE GETTING THERE. AQUAMAN PROVIDED THE FIRST CLUE WHEN HE RECOGNIZED HIS BROTHER'S MIND DURING THE BATTLE WITH THE STAR CITY DUPLICATES. EVERYTHING BEGAN TO ADD UP AFTER THAT.
CONCLUSION: THE REFORMATION OF THE JLA HAS INSPIRED OUR ENEMIES TO ASSEMBLE A TEAM OF THEIR OWN...
WITH LEX LUTHOR CALLING THE PLAYS.
ORDINARILY I'D SAY WE WERE IN TROUBLE BUT WE HAVE AN ADVANTAGE HERE.
LUTHOR STILL HAS NO IDEA HE'S DEALING WITH SOMEONE WHO'S AS FAMILIAR WITH CORPORATE TAKEOVER TECHNIQUES AS HE IS. SOMEONE WHO PLAYS THE GAME MUCH BETTER THAN HE DOES...
BRUCE WAYNE.
LET'S TAKE HIM OUT.

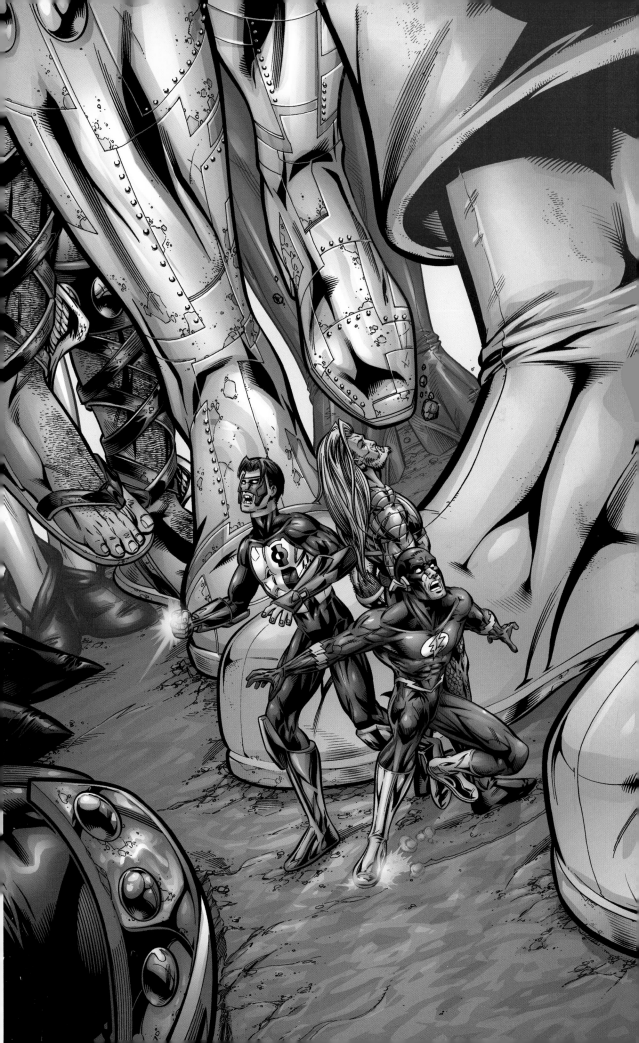

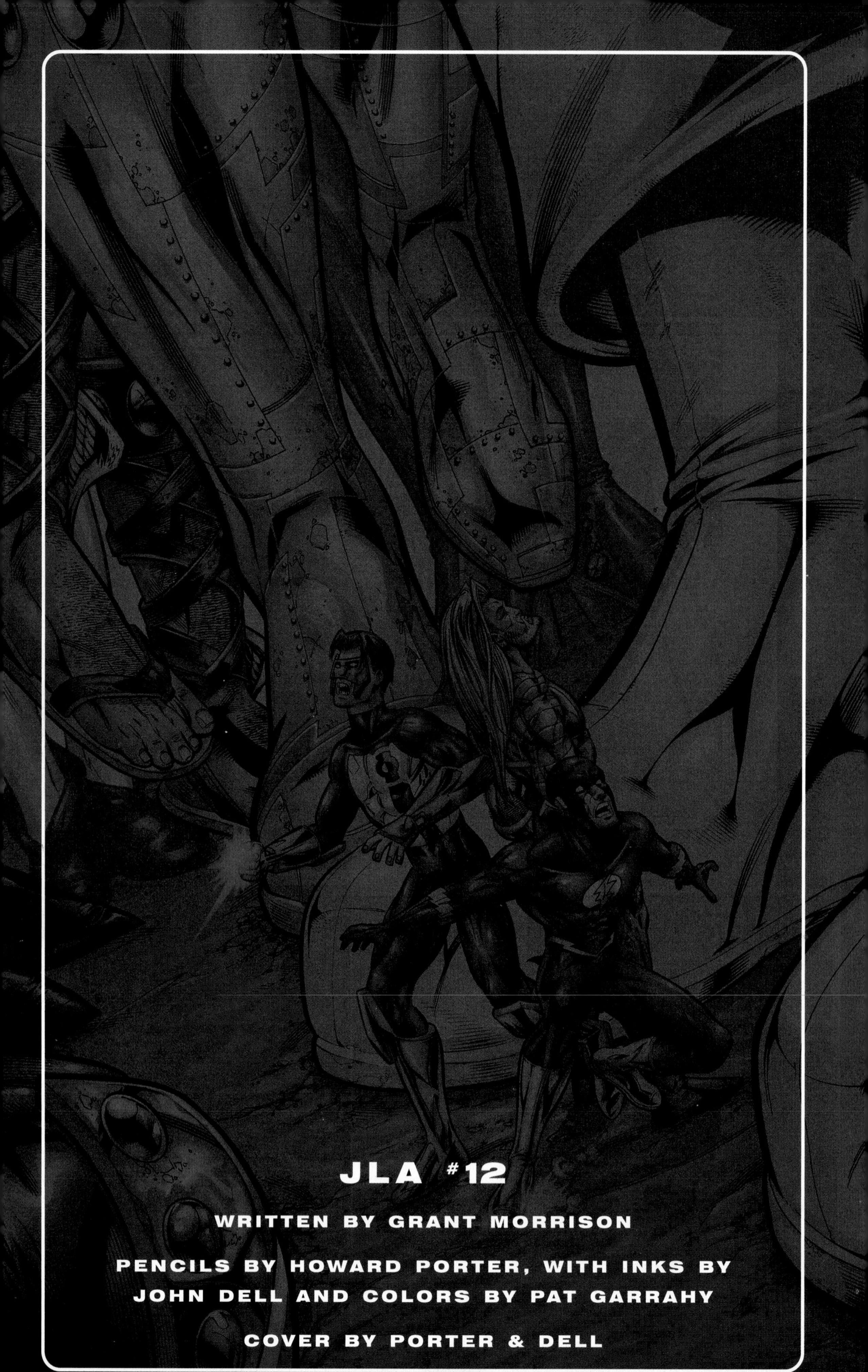

JLA #12

WRITTEN BY GRANT MORRISON

PENCILS BY HOWARD PORTER, WITH INKS BY JOHN DELL AND COLORS BY PAT GARRAHY

COVER BY PORTER & DELL

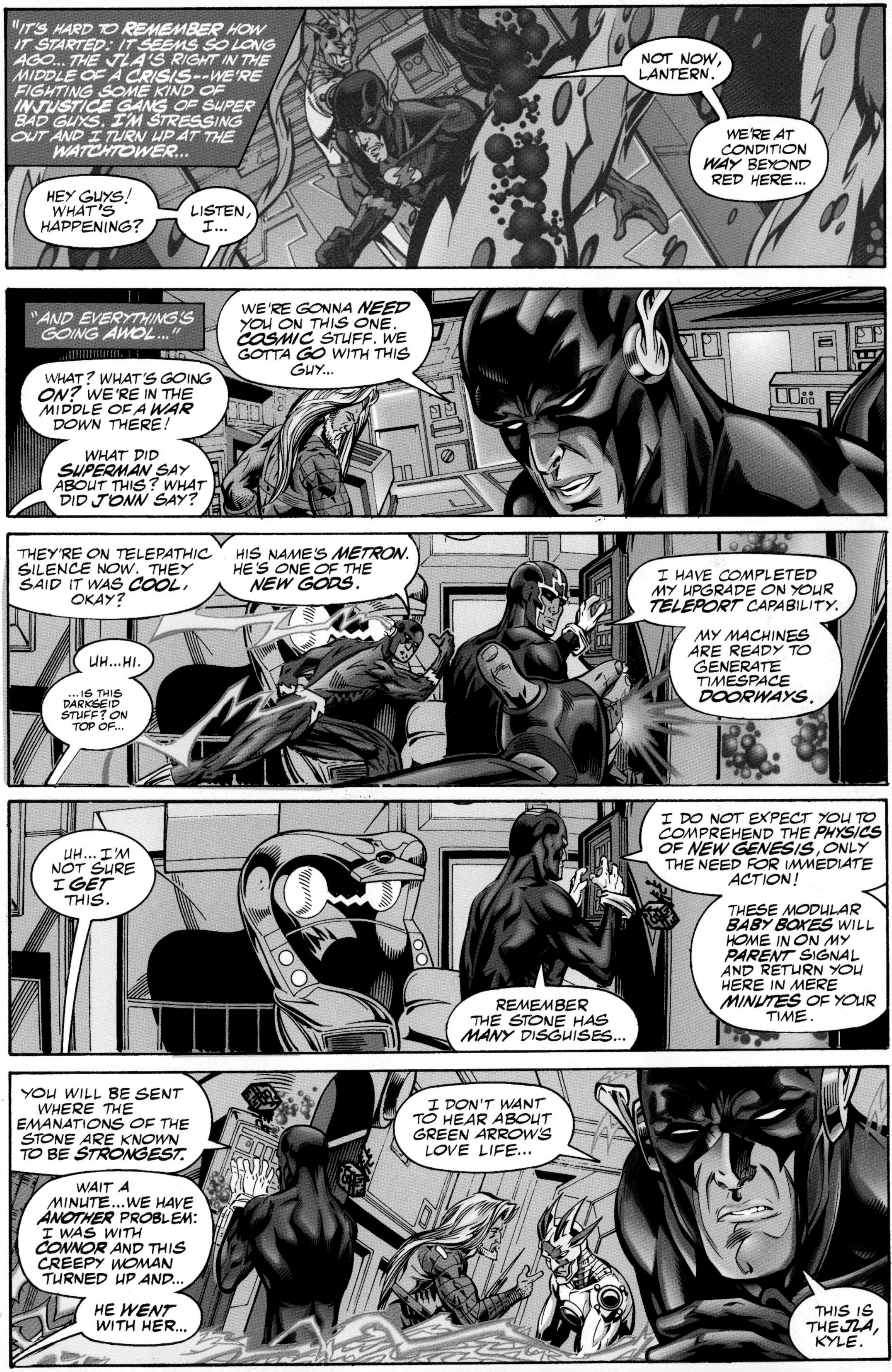
"IT'S HARD TO REMEMBER HOW IT STARTED: IT SEEMS SO LONG AGO... THE JLA'S RIGHT IN THE MIDDLE OF A CRISIS--WE'RE FIGHTING SOME KIND OF INJUSTICE GANG OF SUPER BAD GUYS. I'M STRESSING OUT AND I TURN UP AT THE WATCHTOWER...
NOT NOW, LANTERN.
WE'RE AT CONDITION WAY BEYOND RED HERE...
HEY GUYS! WHAT'S HAPPENING?
LISTEN, I...
"AND EVERYTHING'S GOING AWOL..."
WE'RE GONNA NEED YOU ON THIS ONE. COSMIC STUFF. WE GOTTA GO WITH THIS GUY...
WHAT? WHAT'S GOING ON? WE'RE IN THE MIDDLE OF A WAR DOWN THERE!
WHAT DID SUPERMAN SAY ABOUT THIS? WHAT DID J'ONN SAY?
THEY'RE ON TELEPATHIC SILENCE NOW. THEY SAID IT WAS COOL, OKAY?
HIS NAME'S METRON. HE'S ONE OF THE NEW GODS.
I HAVE COMPLETED MY UPGRADE ON YOUR TELEPORT CAPABILITY.
MY MACHINES ARE READY TO GENERATE TIMESPACE DOORWAYS.
UH...HI.
...IS THIS DARKSEID STUFF? ON TOP OF...
UH... I'M NOT SURE I GET THIS.
I DO NOT EXPECT YOU TO COMPREHEND THE PHYSICS OF NEW GENESIS, ONLY THE NEED FOR IMMEDIATE ACTION!
THESE MODULAR BABY BOXES WILL HOME IN ON MY PARENT SIGNAL AND RETURN YOU HERE IN MERE MINUTES OF YOUR TIME.
REMEMBER THE STONE HAS MANY DISGUISES...
YOU WILL BE SENT WHERE THE EMANATIONS OF THE STONE ARE KNOWN TO BE STRONGEST.
I DON'T WANT TO HEAR ABOUT GREEN ARROW'S LOVE LIFE...
WAIT A MINUTE...WE HAVE ANOTHER PROBLEM: I WAS WITH CONNOR AND THIS CREEPY WOMAN TURNED UP AND...
HE WENT WITH HER...
THIS IS THE JLA, KYLE.

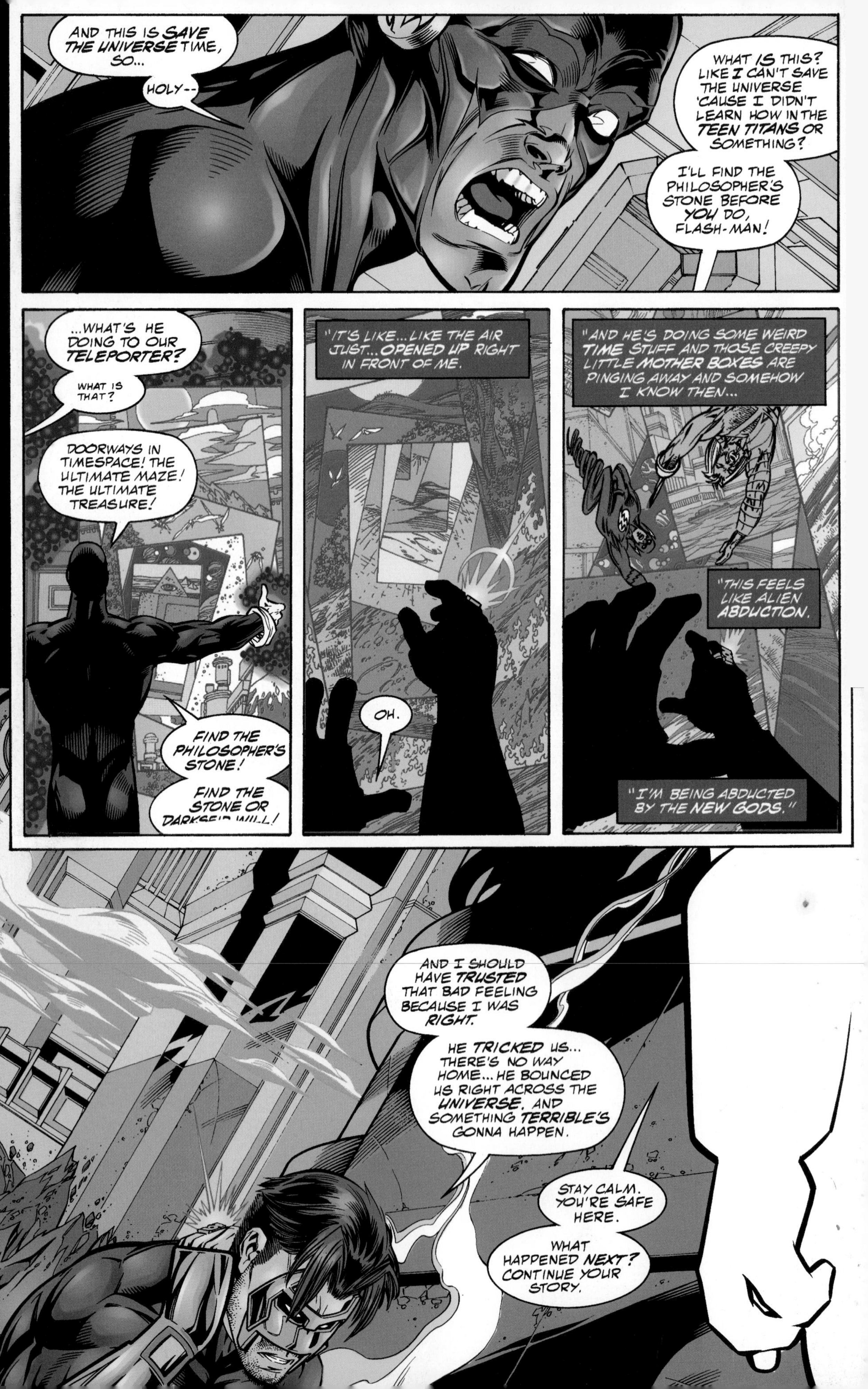
AND THIS IS SAVE THE UNIVERSE TIME, SO...
HOLY--
WHAT IS THIS? LIKE I CAN'T SAVE THE UNIVERSE 'CAUSE I DIDN'T LEARN HOW IN THE TEEN TITANS OR SOMETHING?
I'LL FIND THE PHILOSOPHER'S STONE BEFORE YOU DO, FLASH-MAN!
...WHAT'S HE DOING TO OUR TELEPORTER?
WHAT IS THAT?
DOORWAYS IN TIMESPACE! THE ULTIMATE MAZE! THE ULTIMATE TREASURE!
FIND THE PHILOSOPHER'S STONE!
FIND THE STONE OR DARKSEID WILL!
"IT'S LIKE... LIKE THE AIR JUST... OPENED UP RIGHT IN FRONT OF ME.
OH.
"AND HE'S DOING SOME WEIRD TIME STUFF AND THOSE CREEPY LITTLE MOTHER BOXES ARE PINGING AWAY AND SOMEHOW I KNOW THEN...
"THIS FEELS LIKE ALIEN ABDUCTION.
"I'M BEING ABDUCTED BY THE NEW GODS."
AND I SHOULD HAVE TRUSTED THAT BAD FEELING BECAUSE I WAS RIGHT.
HE TRICKED US... THERE'S NO WAY HOME... HE BOUNCED US RIGHT ACROSS THE UNIVERSE. AND SOMETHING TERRIBLE'S GONNA HAPPEN.
STAY CALM. YOU'RE SAFE HERE.
WHAT HAPPENED NEXT? CONTINUE YOUR STORY.

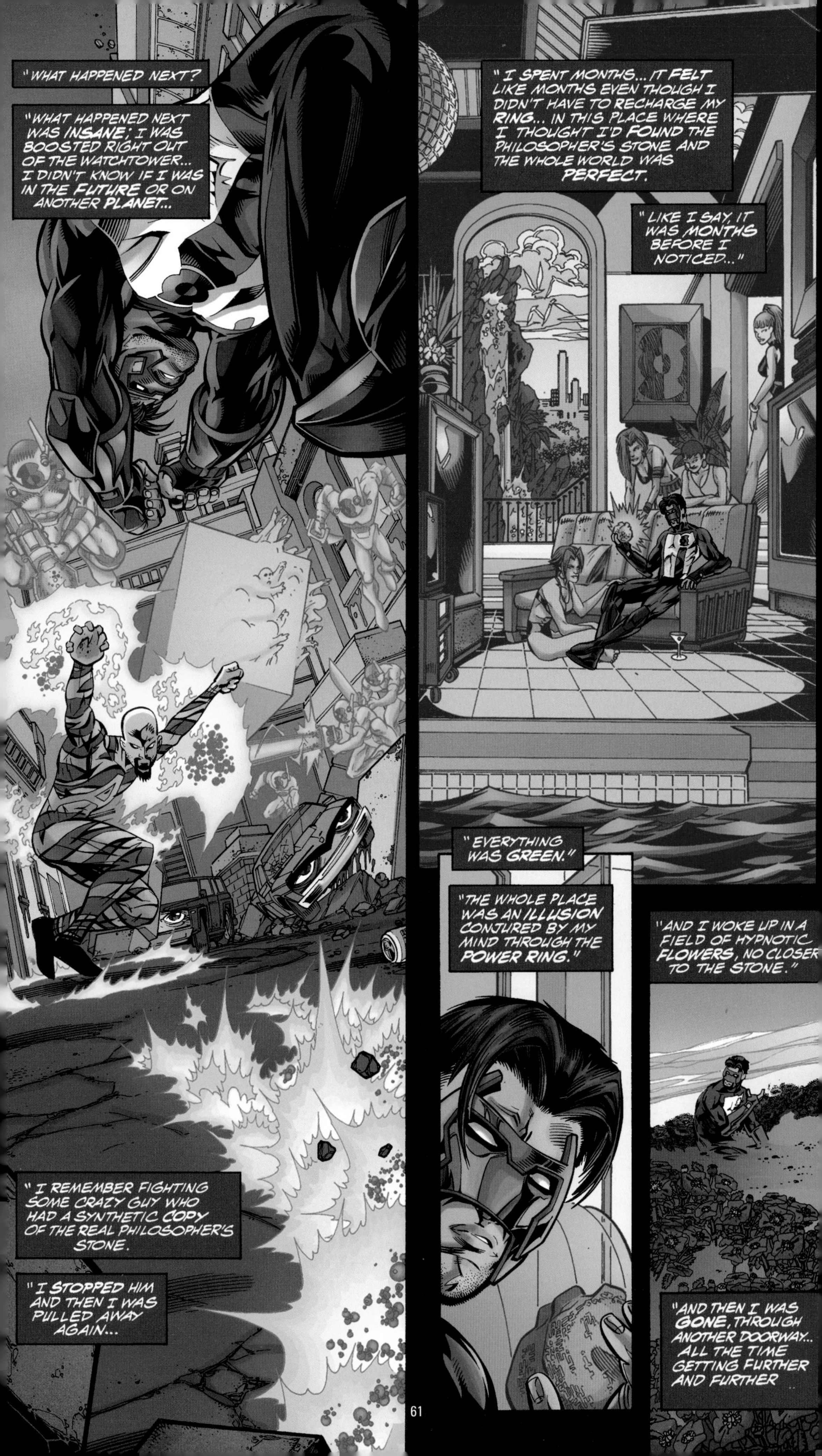
"WHAT HAPPENED NEXT?
"WHAT HAPPENED NEXT WAS INSANE; I WAS BOOSTED RIGHT OUT OF THE WATCHTOWER... I DIDN'T KNOW IF I WAS IN THE FUTURE OR ON ANOTHER PLANET...
"I REMEMBER FIGHTING SOME CRAZY GUY WHO HAD A SYNTHETIC COPY OF THE REAL PHILOSOPHER'S STONE.
"I STOPPED HIM AND THEN I WAS PULLED AWAY AGAIN...
"I SPENT MONTHS... IT FELT LIKE MONTHS EVEN THOUGH I DIDN'T HAVE TO RECHARGE MY RING... IN THIS PLACE WHERE I THOUGHT I'D FOUND THE PHILOSOPHER'S STONE AND THE WHOLE WORLD WAS PERFECT.
"LIKE I SAY, IT WAS MONTHS BEFORE I NOTICED..."
"EVERYTHING WAS GREEN."
"THE WHOLE PLACE WAS AN ILLUSION CONJURED BY MY MIND THROUGH THE POWER RING."
"AND I WOKE UP IN A FIELD OF HYPNOTIC FLOWERS, NO CLOSER TO THE STONE."
"AND THEN I WAS GONE, THROUGH ANOTHER DOORWAY... ALL THE TIME GETTING FURTHER AND FURTHER

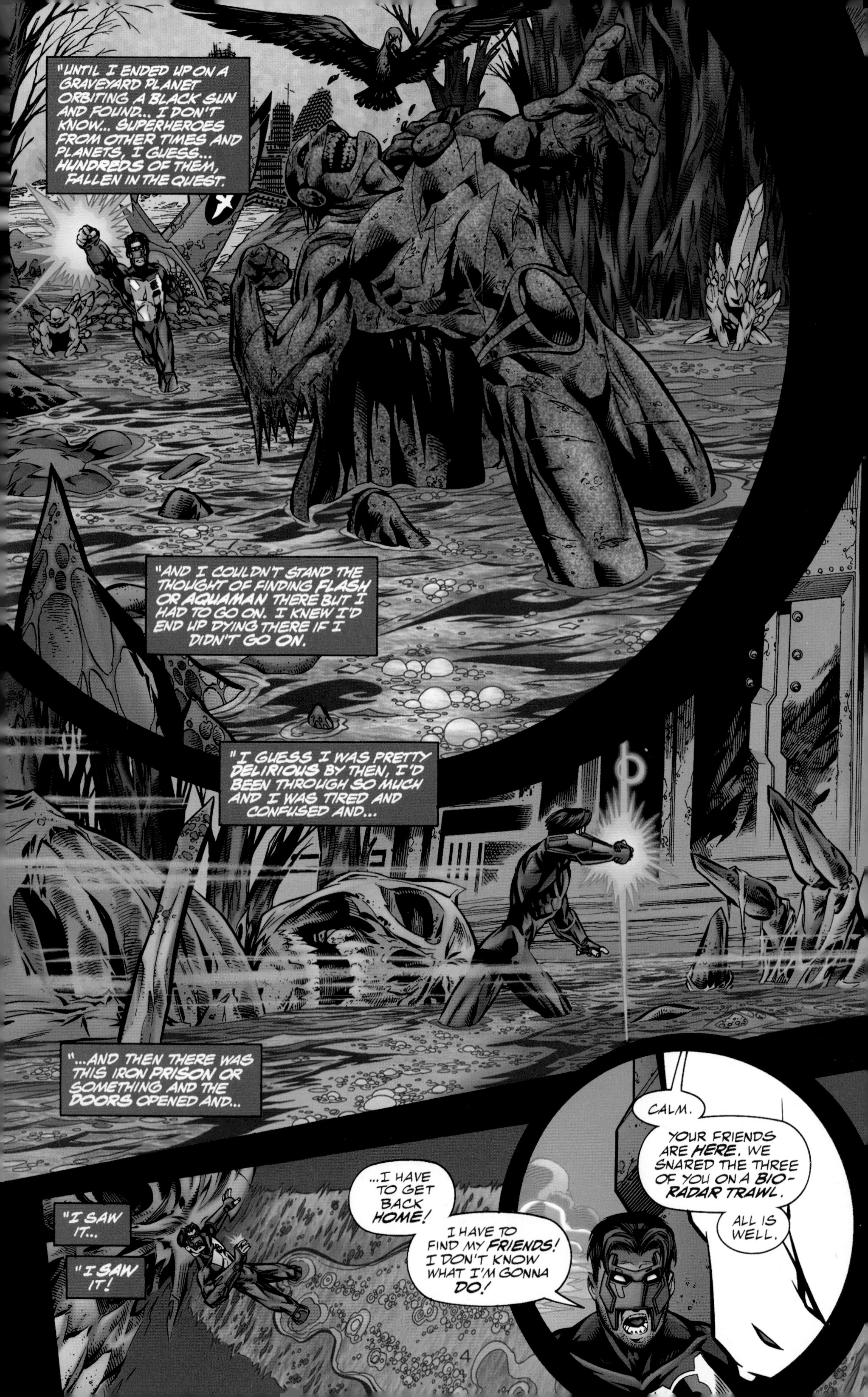
"UNTIL I ENDED UP ON A GRAVEYARD PLANET ORBITING A BLACK SUN AND FOUND... I DON'T KNOW... SUPERHEROES FROM OTHER TIMES AND PLANETS, I GUESS... HUNDREDS OF THEM, FALLEN IN THE QUEST.
"AND I COULDN'T STAND THE THOUGHT OF FINDING FLASH OR AQUAMAN THERE BUT I HAD TO GO ON. I KNEW I'D END UP DYING THERE IF I DIDN'T GO ON.
"I GUESS I WAS PRETTY DELIRIOUS BY THEN, I'D BEEN THROUGH SO MUCH AND I WAS TIRED AND CONFUSED AND...
"...AND THEN THERE WAS THIS IRON PRISON OR SOMETHING AND THE DOORS OPENED AND...
"I SAW IT...
"I SAW IT!
...I HAVE TO GET BACK HOME!
I HAVE TO FIND MY FRIENDS! I DON'T KNOW WHAT I'M GONNA DO!
CALM.
YOUR FRIENDS ARE HERE. WE SNARED THE THREE OF YOU ON A BIO-RADAR TRAWL.
ALL IS WELL.

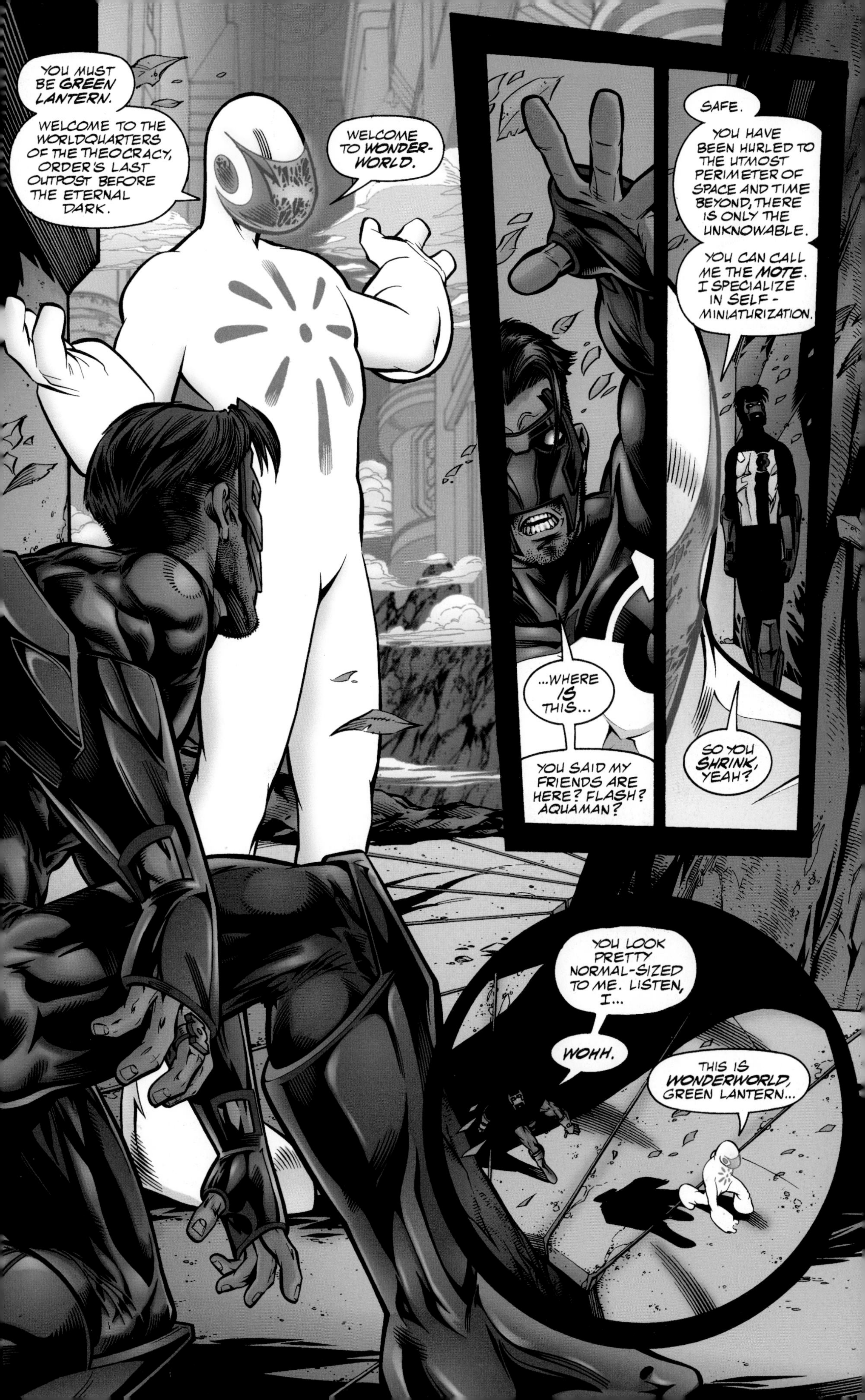
YOU MUST BE GREEN LANTERN.
WELCOME TO THE WORLDQUARTERS OF THE THEOCRACY, ORDER'S LAST OUTPOST BEFORE THE ETERNAL DARK.
WELCOME TO WONDER-WORLD.
...WHERE IS THIS...
SAFE.
YOU HAVE BEEN HURLED TO THE UTMOST PERIMETER OF SPACE AND TIME BEYOND, THERE IS ONLY THE UNKNOWABLE.
YOU CAN CALL ME THE MOTE. I SPECIALIZE IN SELF-MINIATURIZATION.
YOU SAID MY FRIENDS ARE HERE? FLASH? AQUAMAN?
SO YOU SHRINK, YEAH?
YOU LOOK PRETTY NORMAL-SIZED TO ME. LISTEN, I...
WOHH.
THIS IS WONDERWORLD, GREEN LANTERN...

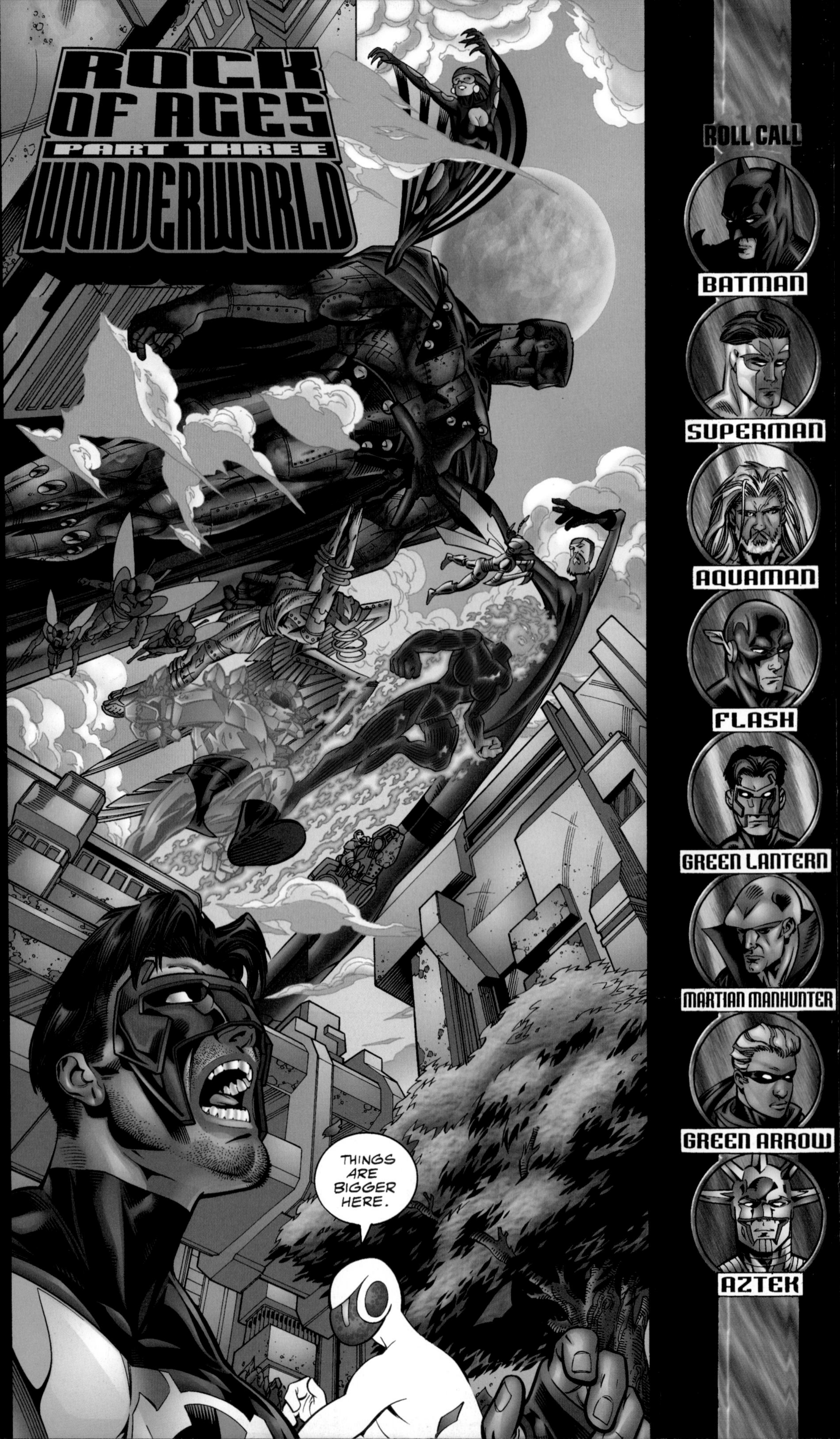
ROCK OF AGES
PART THREE
WONDERWORLD
ROLL CALL
BATMAN
SUPERMAN
AQUAMAN
FLASH
GREEN LANTERN
MARTIAN MANHUNTER
GREEN ARROW
AZTEK
THINGS ARE BIGGER HERE.

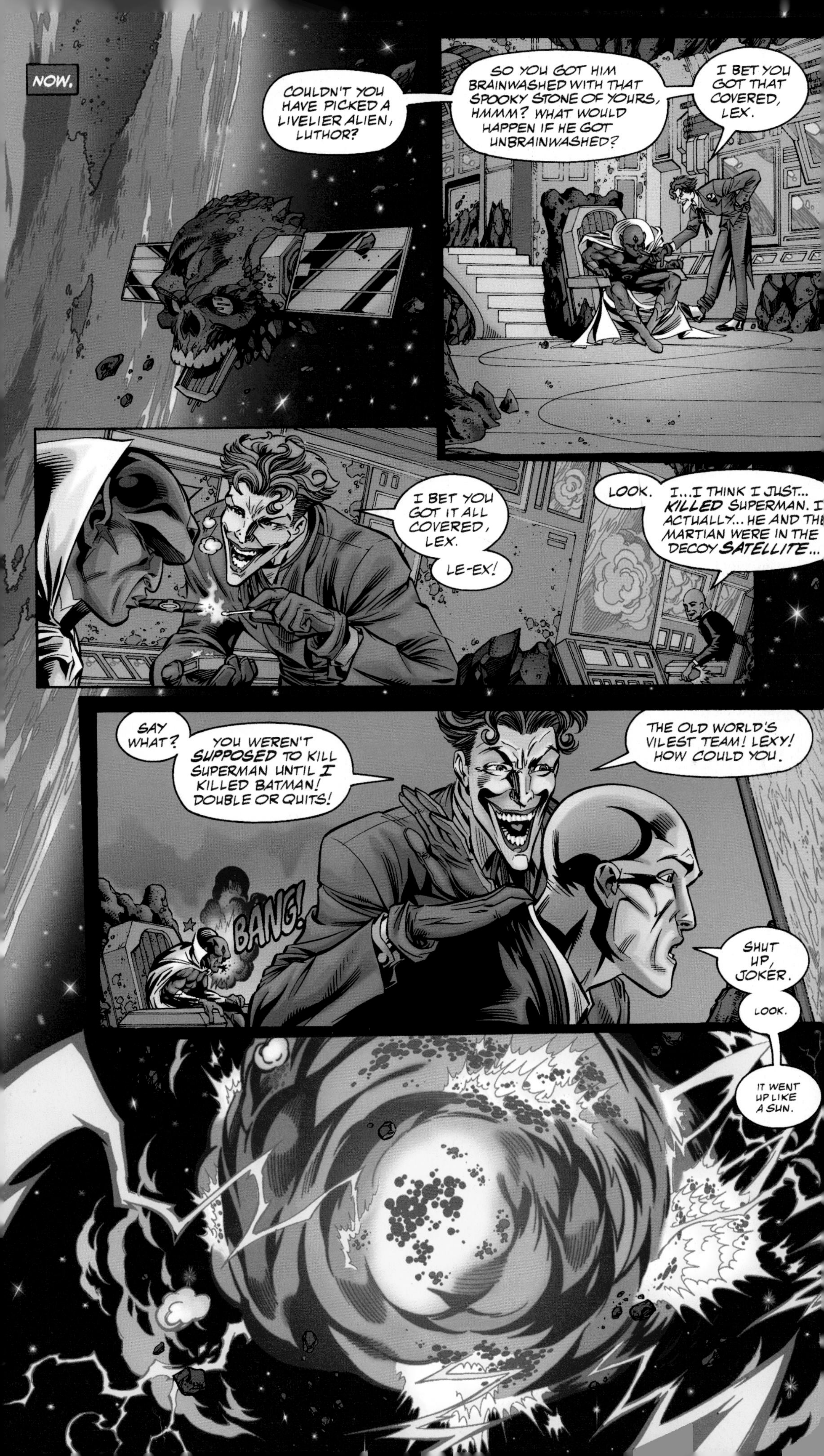
NOW.
COULDN'T YOU HAVE PICKED A LIVELIER ALIEN, LUTHOR?
SO YOU GOT HIM BRAINWASHED WITH THAT SPOOKY STONE OF YOURS, HMMM? WHAT WOULD HAPPEN IF HE GOT UNBRAINWASHED?
I BET YOU GOT THAT COVERED, LEX.
I BET YOU GOT IT ALL COVERED, LEX.
LE-EX!
LOOK.
I...I THINK I JUST... KILLED SUPERMAN. I ACTUALLY... HE AND THE MARTIAN WERE IN THE DECOY SATELLITE...
SAY WHAT?
YOU WEREN'T SUPPOSED TO KILL SUPERMAN UNTIL I KILLED BATMAN! DOUBLE OR QUITS!
THE OLD WORLD'S VILEST TEAM! LEXY! HOW COULD YOU.
BANG!
SHUT UP, JOKER.
LOOK.
IT WENT UP LIKE A SUN.

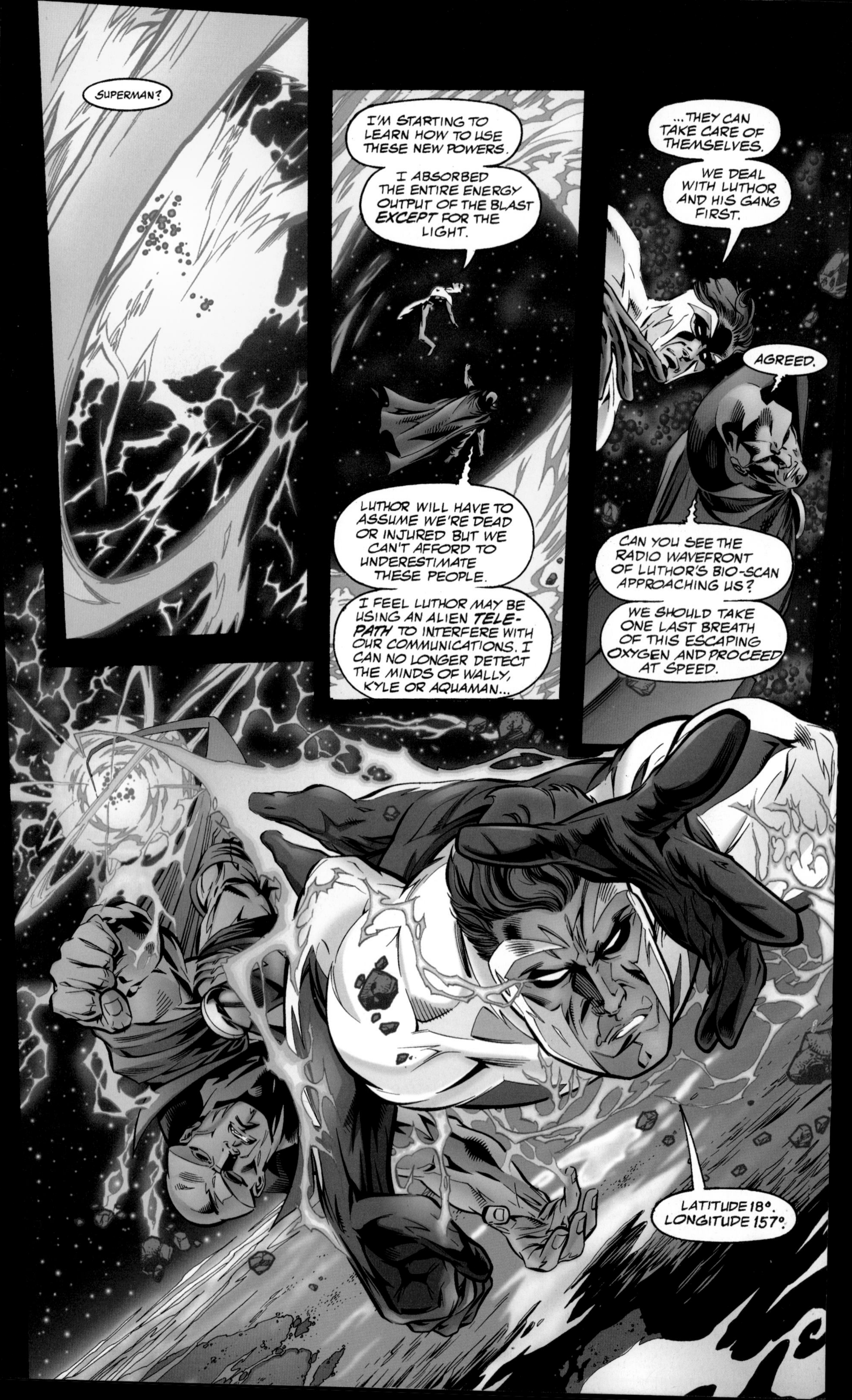
SUPERMAN?
I'M STARTING TO LEARN HOW TO USE THESE NEW POWERS.
I ABSORBED THE ENTIRE ENERGY OUTPUT OF THE BLAST EXCEPT FOR THE LIGHT.
LUTHOR WILL HAVE TO ASSUME WE'RE DEAD OR INJURED BUT WE CAN'T AFFORD TO UNDERESTIMATE THESE PEOPLE.
I FEEL LUTHOR MAY BE USING AN ALIEN TELEPATH TO INTERFERE WITH OUR COMMUNICATIONS. I CAN NO LONGER DETECT THE MINDS OF WALLY, KYLE OR AQUAMAN...
...THEY CAN TAKE CARE OF THEMSELVES.
WE DEAL WITH LUTHOR AND HIS GANG FIRST.
AGREED.
CAN YOU SEE THE RADIO WAVEFRONT OF LUTHOR'S BIO-SCAN APPROACHING US?
WE SHOULD TAKE ONE LAST BREATH OF THIS ESCAPING OXYGEN AND PROCEED AT SPEED.
LATITUDE 18°. LONGITUDE 157°.

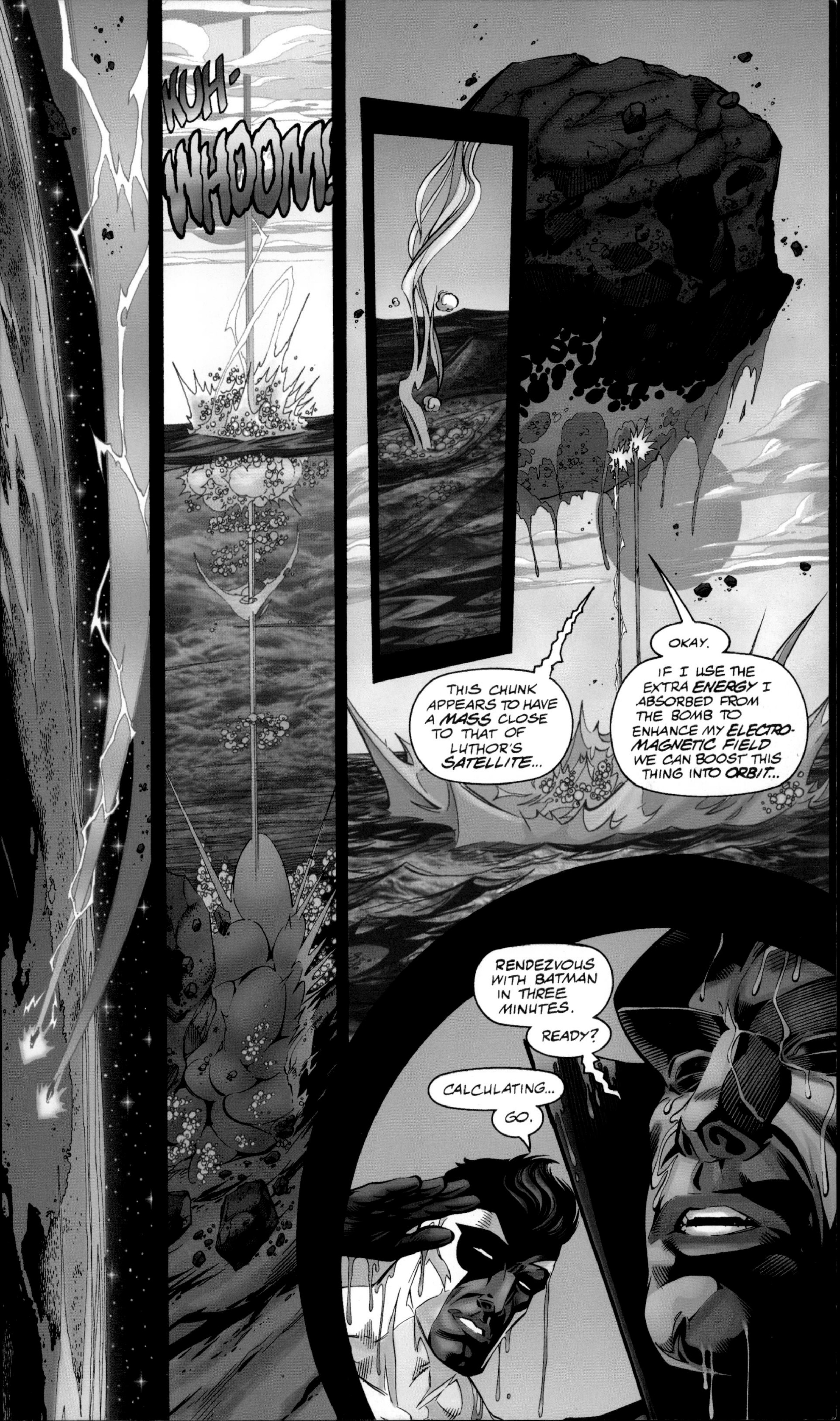
KUH-WHOOM!
THIS CHUNK APPEARS TO HAVE A MASS CLOSE TO THAT OF LUTHOR'S SATELLITE...
OKAY.
IF I USE THE EXTRA ENERGY I ABSORBED FROM THE BOMB TO ENHANCE MY ELECTRO-MAGNETIC FIELD WE CAN BOOST THIS THING INTO ORBIT...
RENDEZVOUS WITH BATMAN IN THREE MINUTES.
READY?
CALCULATING...
GO.

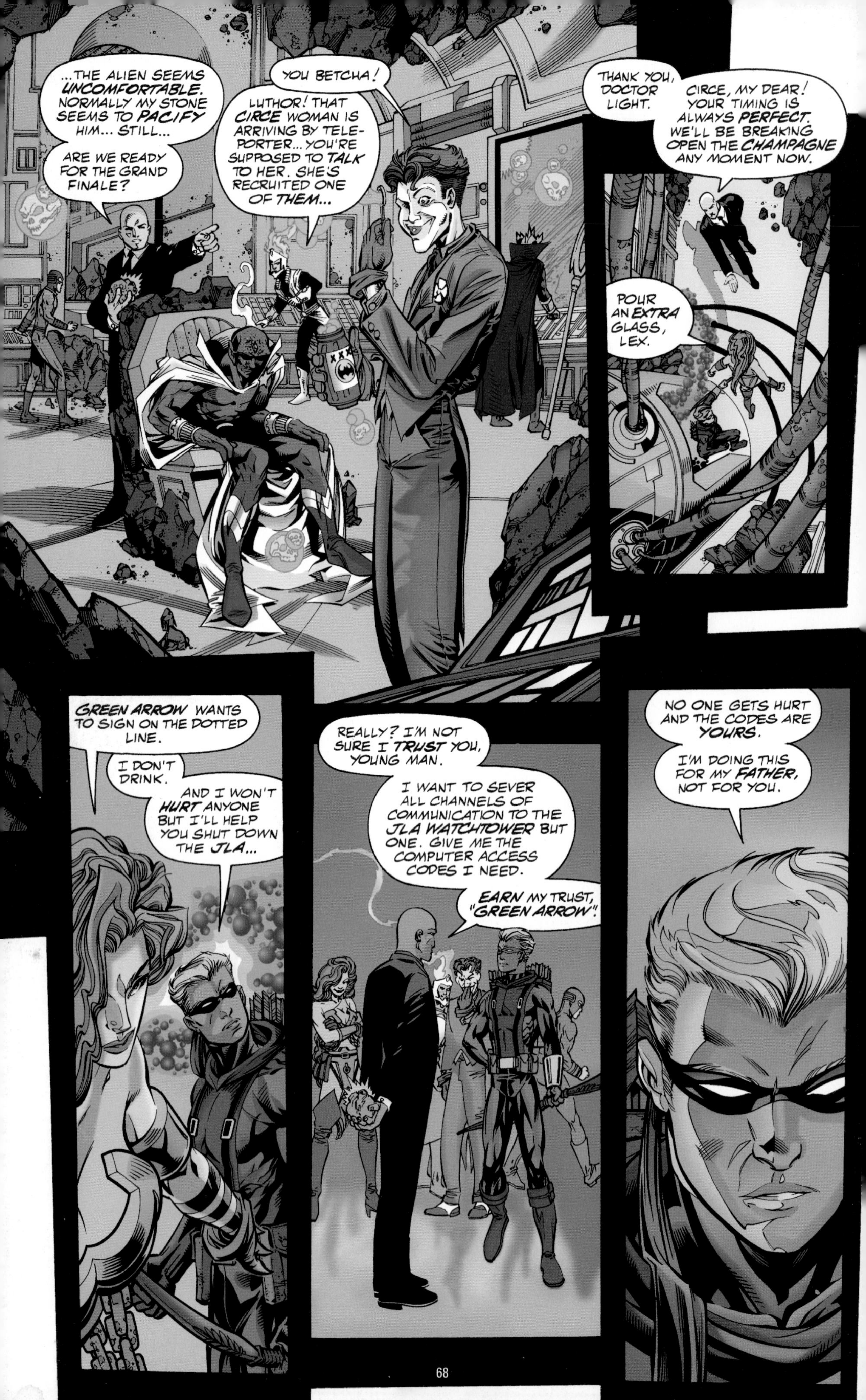
...THE ALIEN SEEMS UNCOMFORTABLE. NORMALLY MY STONE SEEMS TO PACIFY HIM... STILL...
ARE WE READY FOR THE GRAND FINALE?
YOU BETCHA!
LUTHOR! THAT CIRCE WOMAN IS ARRIVING BY TELE-PORTER... YOU'RE SUPPOSED TO TALK TO HER. SHE'S RECRUITED ONE OF THEM...
THANK YOU, DOCTOR LIGHT.
CIRCE, MY DEAR! YOUR TIMING IS ALWAYS PERFECT. WE'LL BE BREAKING OPEN THE CHAMPAGNE ANY MOMENT NOW.
POUR AN EXTRA GLASS, LEX.
GREEN ARROW WANTS TO SIGN ON THE DOTTED LINE.
I DON'T DRINK.
AND I WON'T HURT ANYONE BUT I'LL HELP YOU SHUT DOWN THE JLA...
REALLY? I'M NOT SURE I TRUST YOU, YOUNG MAN.
I WANT TO SEVER ALL CHANNELS OF COMMUNICATION TO THE JLA WATCHTOWER BUT ONE. GIVE ME THE COMPUTER ACCESS CODES I NEED.
EARN MY TRUST, "GREEN ARROW".
NO ONE GETS HURT AND THE CODES ARE YOURS.
I'M DOING THIS FOR MY FATHER, NOT FOR YOU.

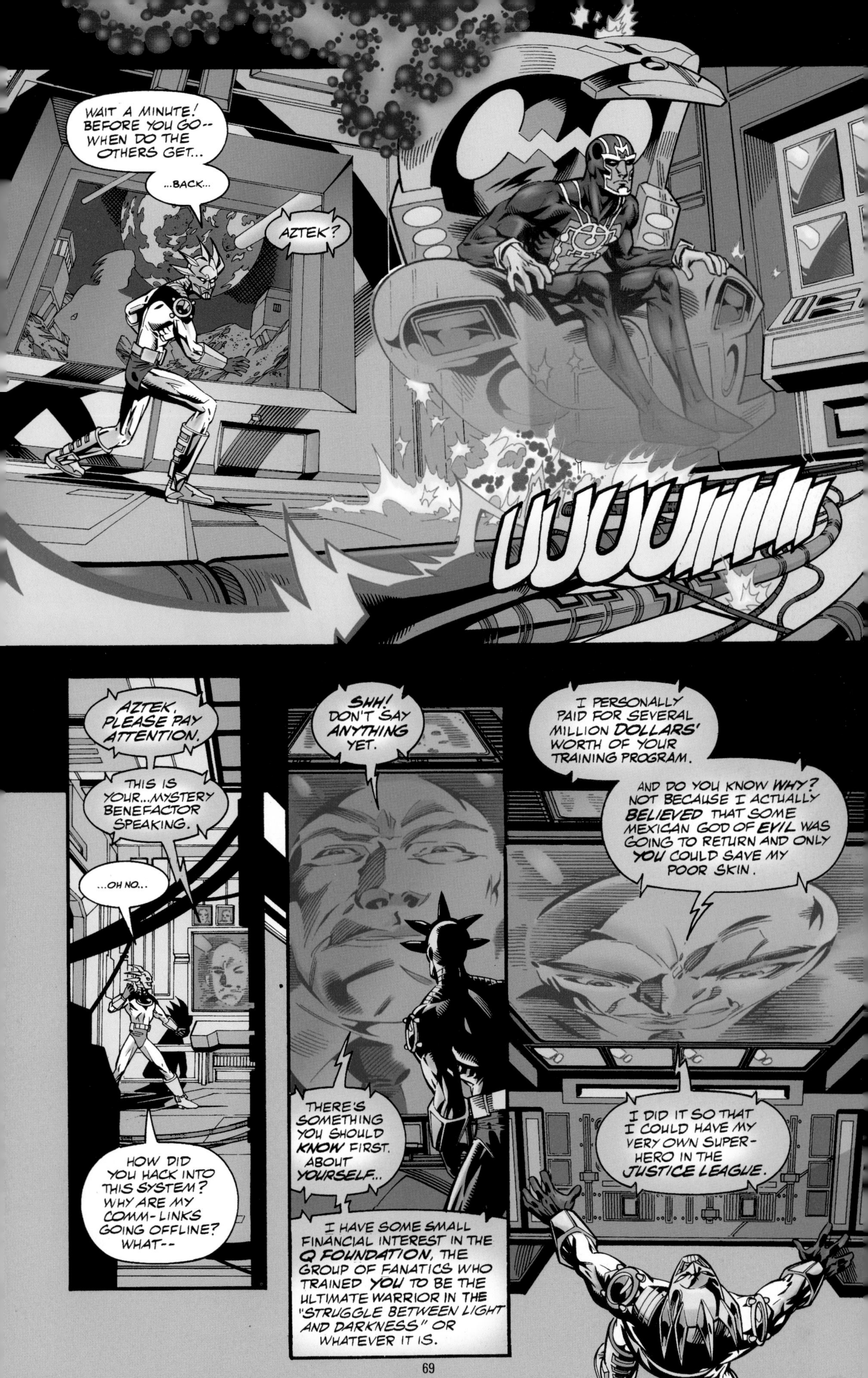
WAIT A MINUTE! BEFORE YOU GO-- WHEN DO THE OTHERS GET...
...BACK...
AZTEK?
UUUUrrr!!!
AZTEK, PLEASE PAY ATTENTION.
THIS IS YOUR...MYSTERY BENEFACTOR SPEAKING.
...OH NO...
HOW DID YOU HACK INTO THIS SYSTEM? WHY ARE MY COMM-LINKS GOING OFFLINE? WHAT--
SHH! DON'T SAY ANYTHING YET.
THERE'S SOMETHING YOU SHOULD KNOW FIRST. ABOUT YOURSELF...
I HAVE SOME SMALL FINANCIAL INTEREST IN THE Q FOUNDATION, THE GROUP OF FANATICS WHO TRAINED YOU TO BE THE ULTIMATE WARRIOR IN THE "STRUGGLE BETWEEN LIGHT AND DARKNESS" OR WHATEVER IT IS.
I PERSONALLY PAID FOR SEVERAL MILLION DOLLARS' WORTH OF YOUR TRAINING PROGRAM.
AND DO YOU KNOW WHY? NOT BECAUSE I ACTUALLY BELIEVED THAT SOME MEXICAN GOD OF EVIL WAS GOING TO RETURN AND ONLY YOU COULD SAVE MY POOR SKIN.
I DID IT SO THAT I COULD HAVE MY VERY OWN SUPER-HERO IN THE JUSTICE LEAGUE.

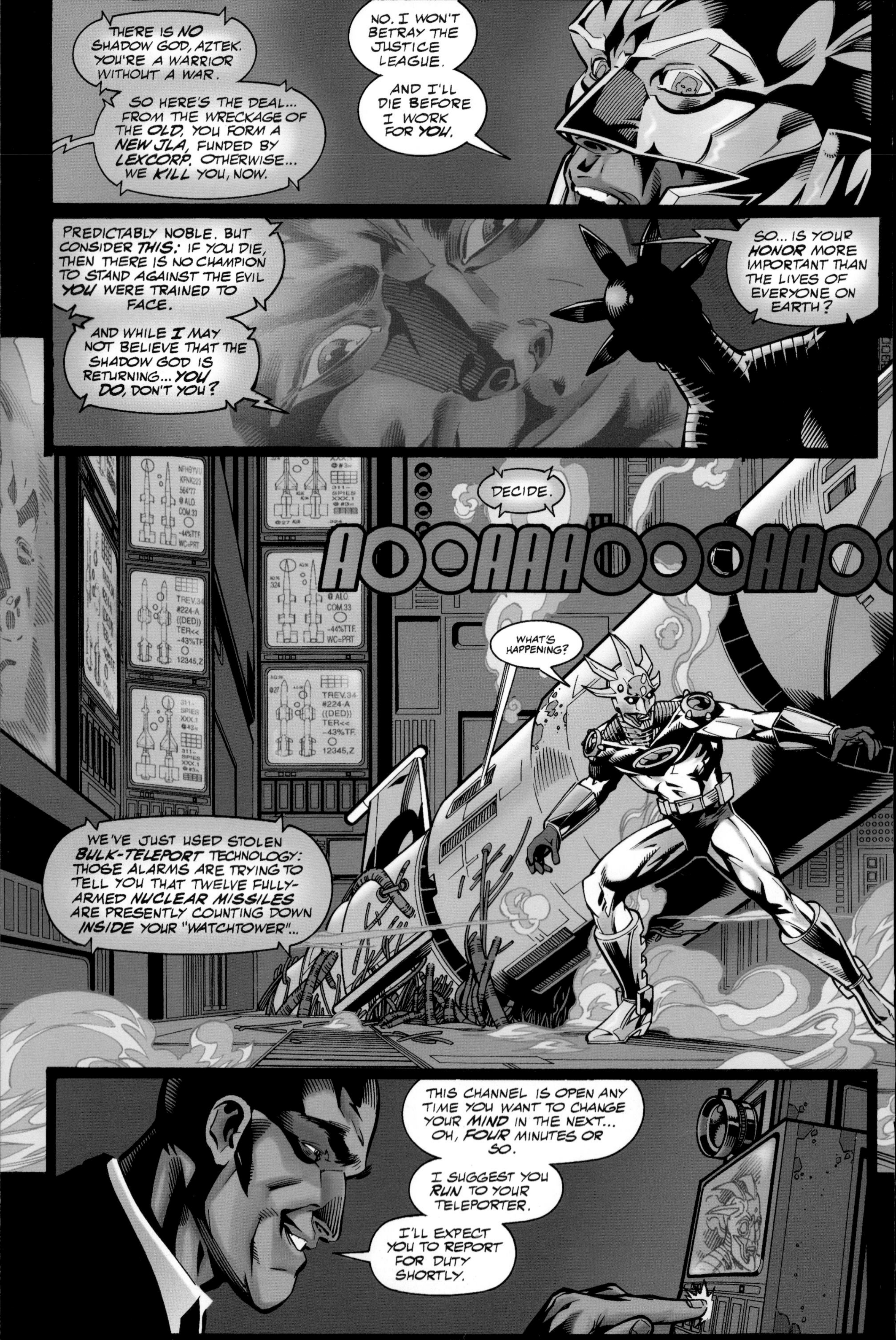
THERE IS NO SHADOW GOD, AZTEK. YOU'RE A WARRIOR WITHOUT A WAR.
SO HERE'S THE DEAL... FROM THE WRECKAGE OF THE OLD, YOU FORM A NEW JLA, FUNDED BY LEXCORP. OTHERWISE... WE KILL YOU, NOW.
NO. I WON'T BETRAY THE JUSTICE LEAGUE.
AND I'LL DIE BEFORE I WORK FOR YOU.
PREDICTABLY NOBLE. BUT CONSIDER THIS: IF YOU DIE, THEN THERE IS NO CHAMPION TO STAND AGAINST THE EVIL YOU WERE TRAINED TO FACE.
AND WHILE I MAY NOT BELIEVE THAT THE SHADOW GOD IS RETURNING... YOU DO, DON'T YOU?
SO... IS YOUR HONOR MORE IMPORTANT THAN THE LIVES OF EVERYONE ON EARTH?
DECIDE.
AOOAAAOOOOAAO
WHAT'S HAPPENING?
WE'VE JUST USED STOLEN BULK-TELEPORT TECHNOLOGY: THOSE ALARMS ARE TRYING TO TELL YOU THAT TWELVE FULLY-ARMED NUCLEAR MISSILES ARE PRESENTLY COUNTING DOWN INSIDE YOUR "WATCHTOWER"...
THIS CHANNEL IS OPEN ANY TIME YOU WANT TO CHANGE YOUR MIND IN THE NEXT... OH, FOUR MINUTES OR SO.
I SUGGEST YOU RUN TO YOUR TELEPORTER.
I'LL EXPECT YOU TO REPORT FOR DUTY SHORTLY.

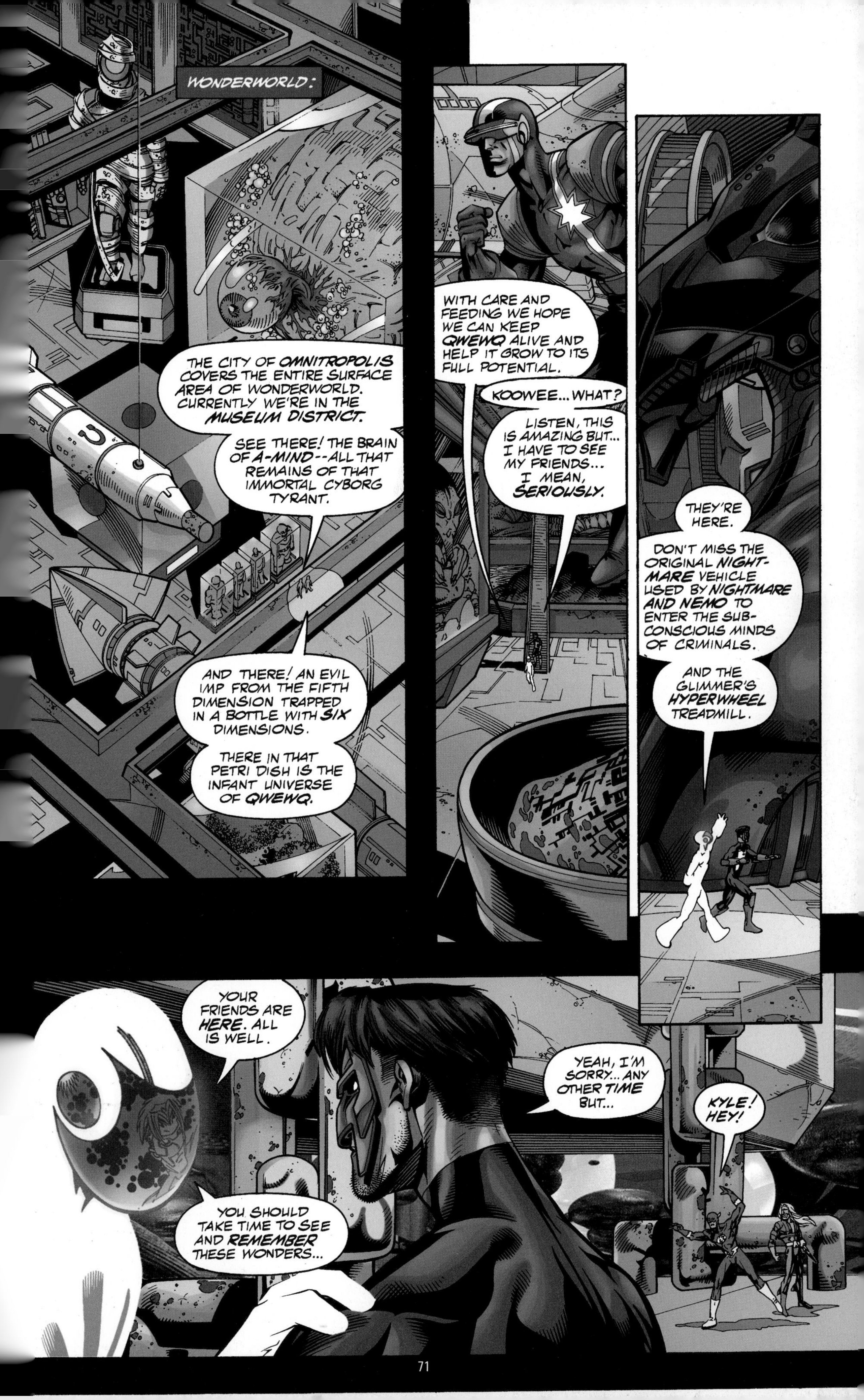
WONDERWORLD:
THE CITY OF OMNITROPOLIS COVERS THE ENTIRE SURFACE AREA OF WONDERWORLD. CURRENTLY WE'RE IN THE MUSEUM DISTRICT.
SEE THERE! THE BRAIN OF A-MIND--ALL THAT REMAINS OF THAT IMMORTAL CYBORG TYRANT.
AND THERE! AN EVIL IMP FROM THE FIFTH DIMENSION TRAPPED IN A BOTTLE WITH SIX DIMENSIONS.
THERE IN THAT PETRI DISH IS THE INFANT UNIVERSE OF QWEWQ.
WITH CARE AND FEEDING WE HOPE WE CAN KEEP QWEWQ ALIVE AND HELP IT GROW TO ITS FULL POTENTIAL.
KOOWEE... WHAT?
LISTEN, THIS IS AMAZING BUT... I HAVE TO SEE MY FRIENDS... I MEAN, SERIOUSLY.
THEY'RE HERE.
DON'T MISS THE ORIGINAL NIGHT-MARE VEHICLE USED BY NIGHTMARE AND NEMO TO ENTER THE SUB-CONSCIOUS MINDS OF CRIMINALS.
AND THE GLIMMER'S HYPERWHEEL TREADMILL.
YOUR FRIENDS ARE HERE. ALL IS WELL.
YOU SHOULD TAKE TIME TO SEE AND REMEMBER THESE WONDERS...
YEAH, I'M SORRY... ANY OTHER TIME BUT...
KYLE! HEY!

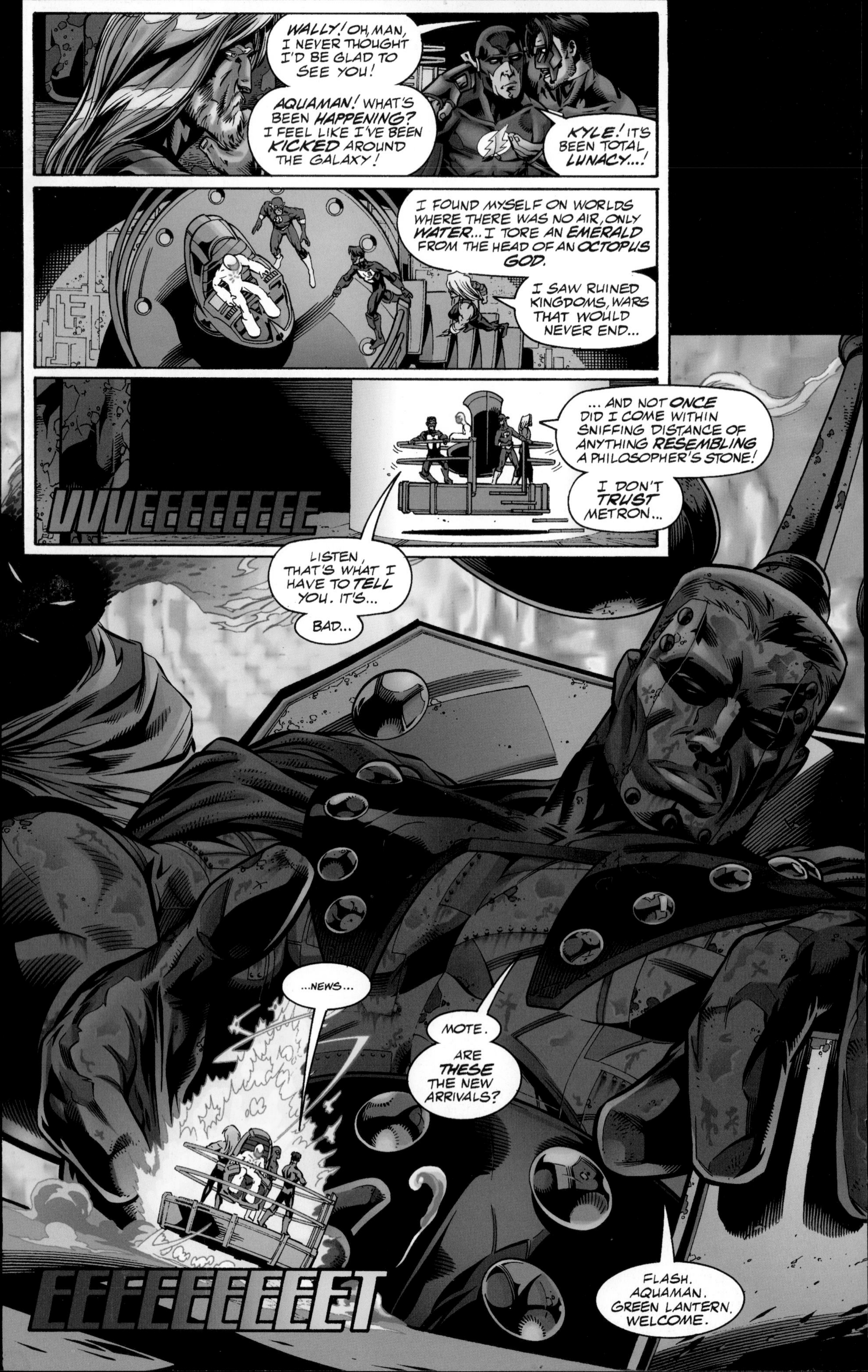
WALLY! OH, MAN, I NEVER THOUGHT I'D BE GLAD TO SEE YOU!
AQUAMAN! WHAT'S BEEN HAPPENING? I FEEL LIKE I'VE BEEN KICKED AROUND THE GALAXY!
KYLE! IT'S BEEN TOTAL LUNACY...!
I FOUND MYSELF ON WORLDS WHERE THERE WAS NO AIR, ONLY WATER... I TORE AN EMERALD FROM THE HEAD OF AN OCTOPUS GOD.
I SAW RUINED KINGDOMS, WARS THAT WOULD NEVER END...
VVVEEEEEEEEE
... AND NOT ONCE DID I COME WITHIN SNIFFING DISTANCE OF ANYTHING RESEMBLING A PHILOSOPHER'S STONE!
I DON'T TRUST METRON...
LISTEN, THAT'S WHAT I HAVE TO TELL YOU. IT'S...
BAD...
...NEWS...
MOTE.
ARE THESE THE NEW ARRIVALS?
EEEEEEEEEEET
FLASH. AQUAMAN. GREEN LANTERN. WELCOME.

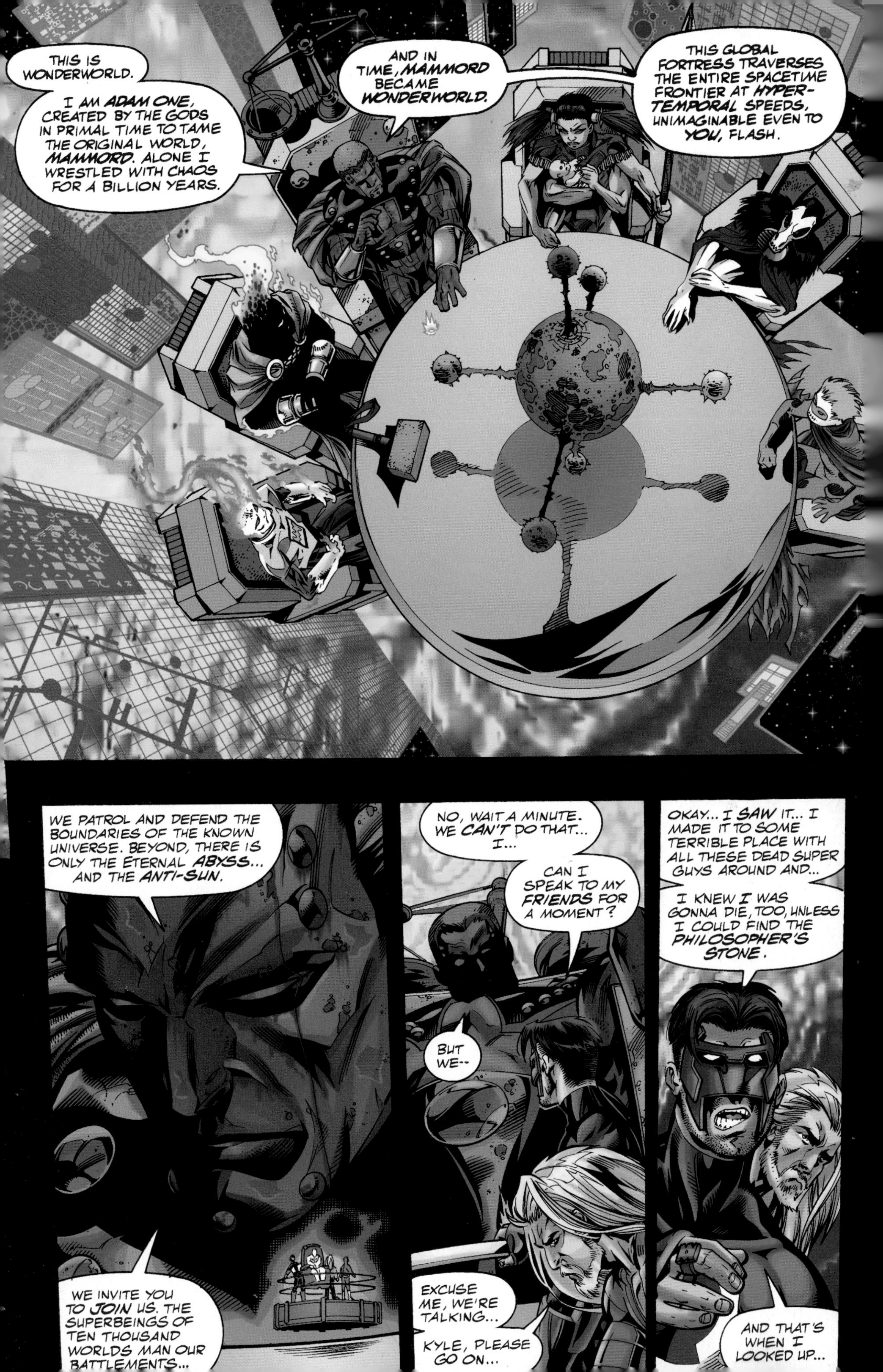
THIS IS WONDERWORLD.
I AM ADAM ONE, CREATED BY THE GODS IN PRIMAL TIME TO TAME THE ORIGINAL WORLD, MAMMORD. ALONE I WRESTLED WITH CHAOS FOR A BILLION YEARS.
AND IN TIME, MAMMORD BECAME WONDERWORLD.
THIS GLOBAL FORTRESS TRAVERSES THE ENTIRE SPACETIME FRONTIER AT HYPER-TEMPORAL SPEEDS, UNIMAGINABLE EVEN TO YOU, FLASH.
WE PATROL AND DEFEND THE BOUNDARIES OF THE KNOWN UNIVERSE. BEYOND, THERE IS ONLY THE ETERNAL ABYSS... AND THE ANTI-SUN.
WE INVITE YOU TO JOIN US. THE SUPERBEINGS OF TEN THOUSAND WORLDS MAN OUR BATTLEMENTS...
NO, WAIT A MINUTE. WE CAN'T DO THAT... I...
CAN I SPEAK TO MY FRIENDS FOR A MOMENT?
BUT WE--
EXCUSE ME, WE'RE TALKING...
KYLE, PLEASE GO ON...
OKAY... I SAW IT... I MADE IT TO SOME TERRIBLE PLACE WITH ALL THESE DEAD SUPER GUYS AROUND AND...
I KNEW I WAS GONNA DIE, TOO, UNLESS I COULD FIND THE PHILOSOPHER'S STONE.
AND THAT'S WHEN I LOOKED UP...

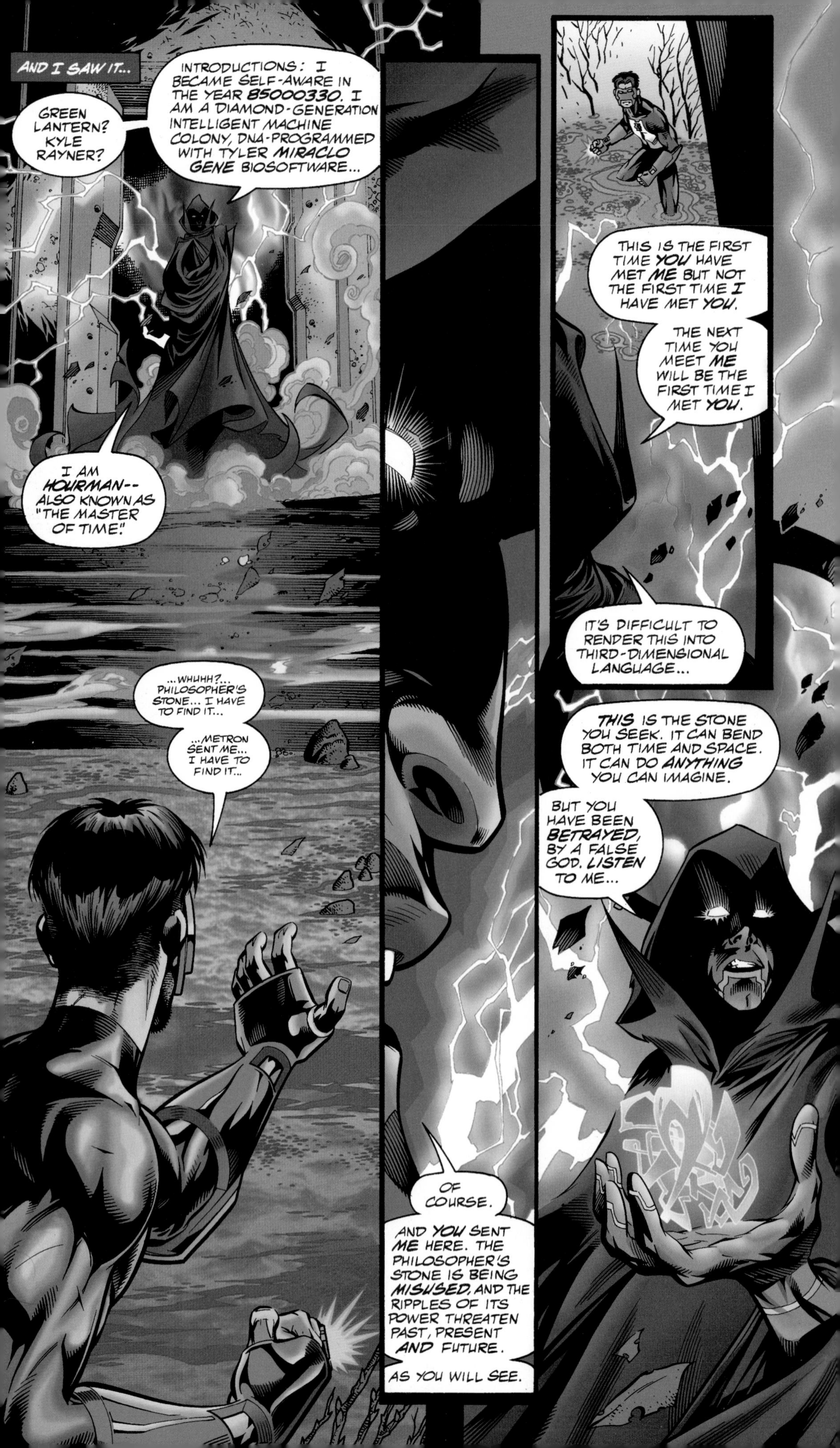
AND I SAW IT...
GREEN LANTERN? KYLE RAYNER?
INTRODUCTIONS: I BECAME SELF-AWARE IN THE YEAR 85000330. I AM A DIAMOND-GENERATION INTELLIGENT MACHINE COLONY, DNA-PROGRAMMED WITH TYLER MIRACLO GENE BIOSOFTWARE...
I AM HOURMAN-- ALSO KNOWN AS "THE MASTER OF TIME."
...WHUHH?... PHILOSOPHER'S STONE... I HAVE TO FIND IT...
...METRON SENT ME... I HAVE TO FIND IT...
OF COURSE.
AND YOU SENT ME HERE. THE PHILOSOPHER'S STONE IS BEING MISUSED, AND THE RIPPLES OF ITS POWER THREATEN PAST, PRESENT AND FUTURE.
AS YOU WILL SEE.
THIS IS THE FIRST TIME YOU HAVE MET ME BUT NOT THE FIRST TIME I HAVE MET YOU.
THE NEXT TIME YOU MEET ME WILL BE THE FIRST TIME I MET YOU.
IT'S DIFFICULT TO RENDER THIS INTO THIRD-DIMENSIONAL LANGUAGE...
THIS IS THE STONE YOU SEEK. IT CAN BEND BOTH TIME AND SPACE. IT CAN DO ANYTHING YOU CAN IMAGINE.
BUT YOU HAVE BEEN BETRAYED, BY A FALSE GOD. LISTEN TO ME...

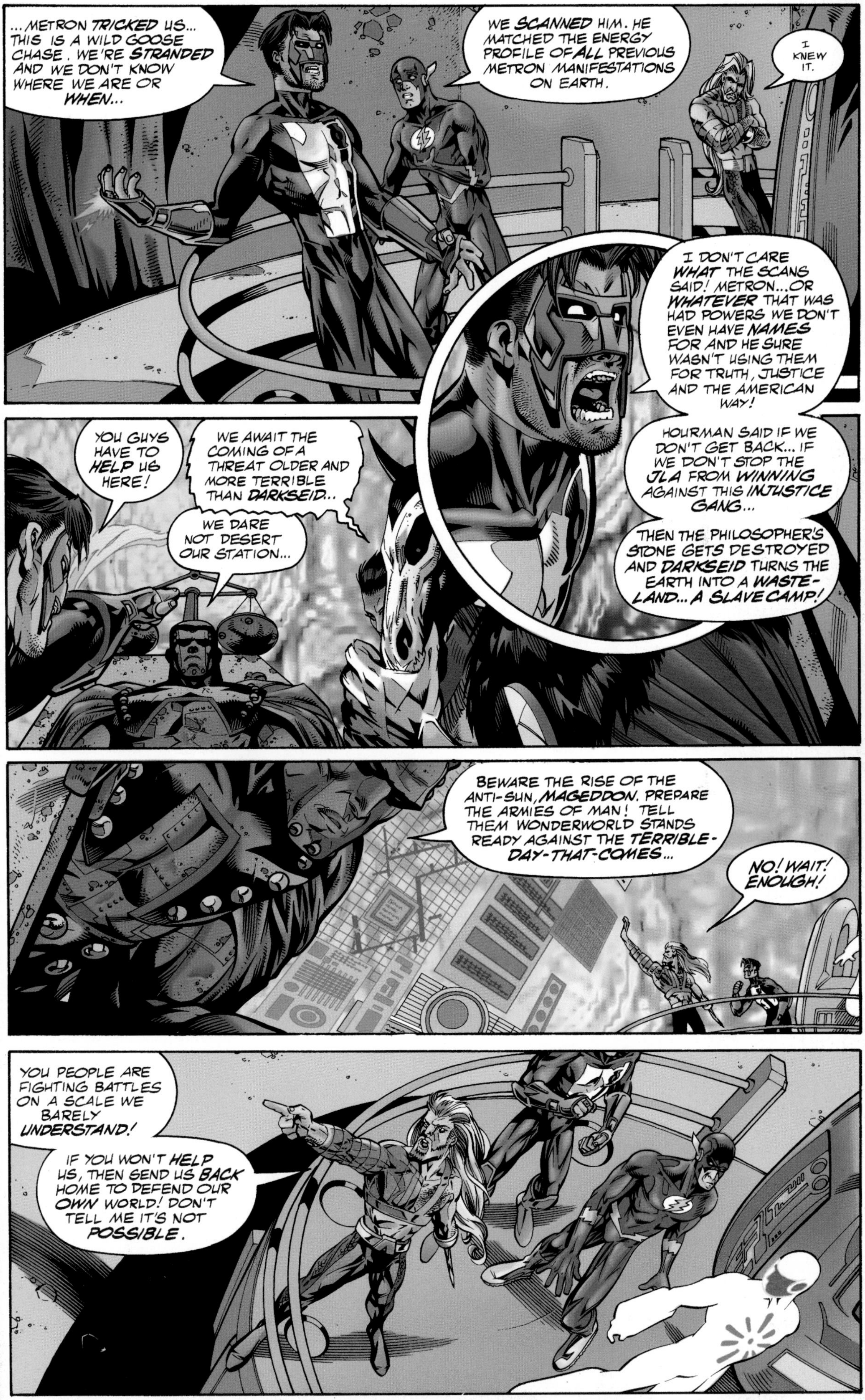
...METRON TRICKED US... THIS IS A WILD GOOSE CHASE. WE'RE STRANDED AND WE DON'T KNOW WHERE WE ARE OR WHEN...
WE SCANNED HIM. HE MATCHED THE ENERGY PROFILE OF ALL PREVIOUS METRON MANIFESTATIONS ON EARTH.
I KNEW IT.
I DON'T CARE WHAT THE SCANS SAID! METRON...OR WHATEVER THAT WAS HAD POWERS WE DON'T EVEN HAVE NAMES FOR AND HE SURE WASN'T USING THEM FOR TRUTH, JUSTICE AND THE AMERICAN WAY!
YOU GUYS HAVE TO HELP US HERE!
WE AWAIT THE COMING OF A THREAT OLDER AND MORE TERRIBLE THAN DARKSEID...
WE DARE NOT DESERT OUR STATION...
HOURMAN SAID IF WE DON'T GET BACK... IF WE DON'T STOP THE JLA FROM WINNING AGAINST THIS INJUSTICE GANG...
THEN THE PHILOSOPHER'S STONE GETS DESTROYED AND DARKSEID TURNS THE EARTH INTO A WASTE-LAND... A SLAVE CAMP!
BEWARE THE RISE OF THE ANTI-SUN, MAGEDDON. PREPARE THE ARMIES OF MAN! TELL THEM WONDERWORLD STANDS READY AGAINST THE TERRIBLE-DAY-THAT-COMES...
NO! WAIT! ENOUGH!
YOU PEOPLE ARE FIGHTING BATTLES ON A SCALE WE BARELY UNDERSTAND!
IF YOU WON'T HELP US, THEN SEND US BACK HOME TO DEFEND OUR OWN WORLD! DON'T TELL ME IT'S NOT POSSIBLE.

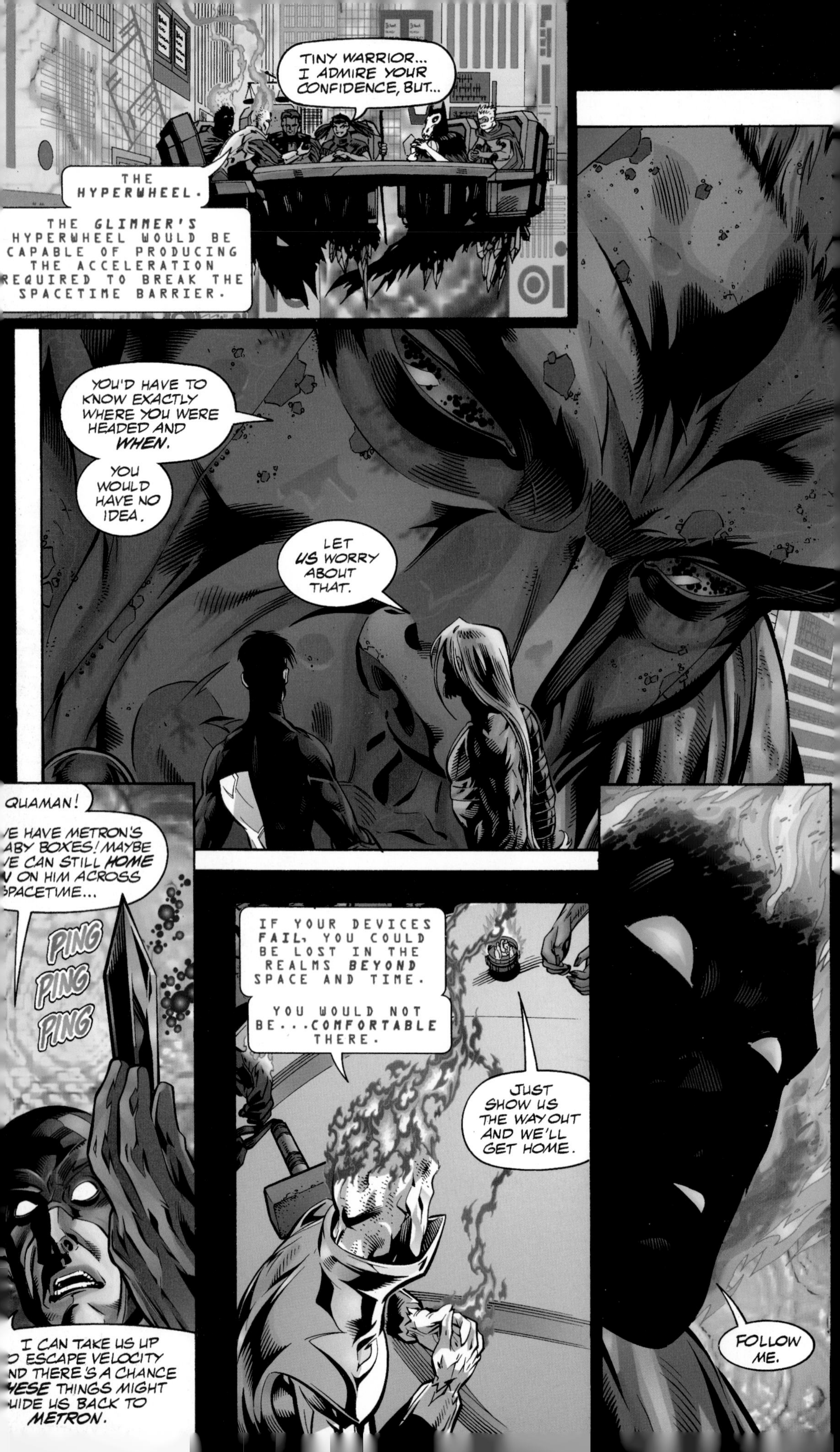

TINY WARRIOR... I ADMIRE YOUR CONFIDENCE, BUT...
THE HYPERWHEEL.
THE GLIMMER'S HYPERWHEEL WOULD BE CAPABLE OF PRODUCING THE ACCELERATION REQUIRED TO BREAK THE SPACETIME BARRIER.
YOU'D HAVE TO KNOW EXACTLY WHERE YOU WERE HEADED AND WHEN.
YOU WOULD HAVE NO IDEA.
LET US WORRY ABOUT THAT.
QUAMAN!
VE HAVE METRON'S ABY BOXES! MAYBE VE CAN STILL HOME N ON HIM ACROSS SPACETIME...
PING PING PING
I CAN TAKE US UP O ESCAPE VELOCITY ND THERE'S A CHANCE HESE THINGS MIGHT UIDE US BACK TO METRON.
IF YOUR DEVICES FAIL, YOU COULD BE LOST IN THE REALMS BEYOND SPACE AND TIME.
YOU WOULD NOT BE...COMFORTABLE THERE.
JUST SHOW US THE WAY OUT AND WE'LL GET HOME.
FOLLOW ME.

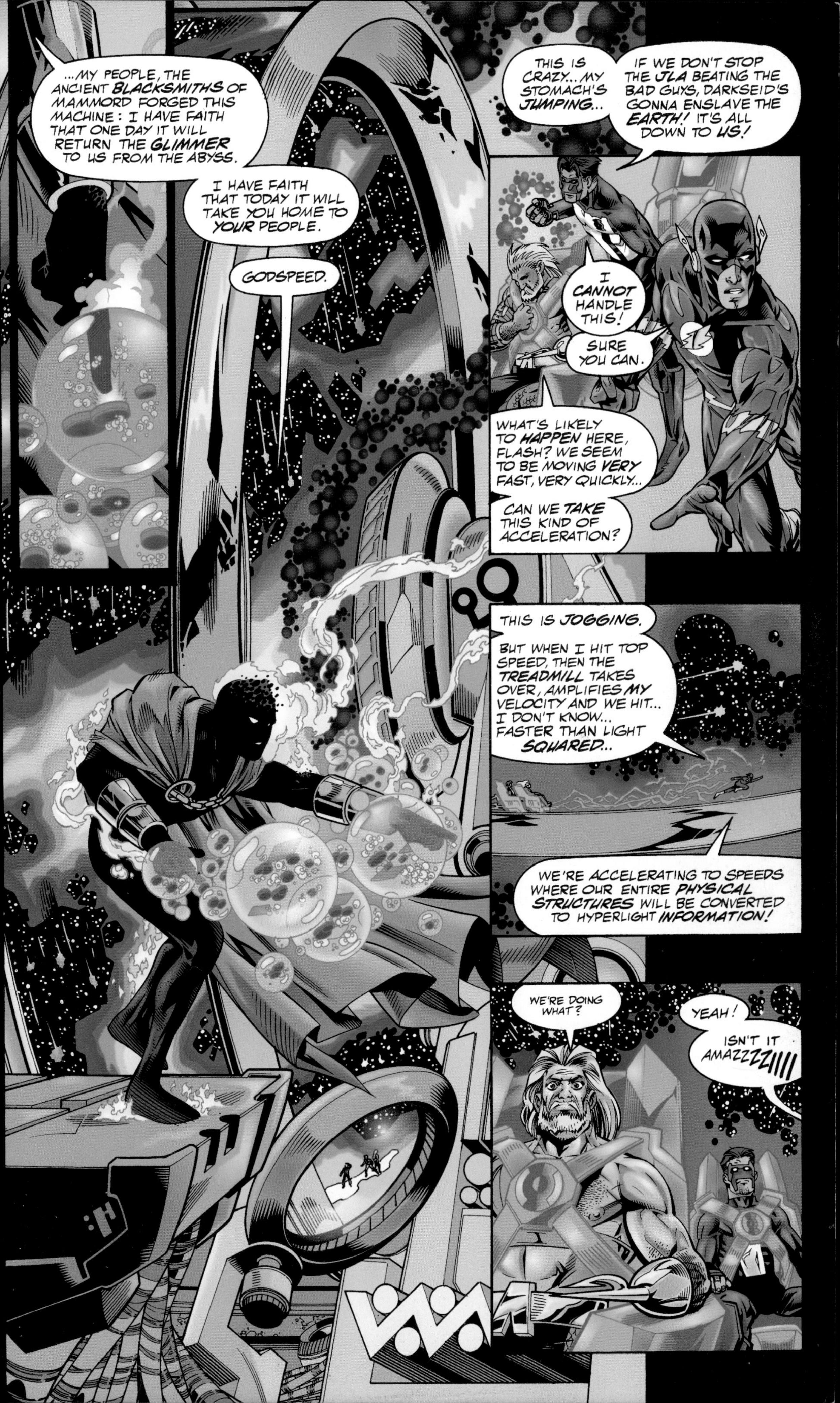

...MY PEOPLE, THE ANCIENT BLACKSMITHS OF MAMMORD FORGED THIS MACHINE : I HAVE FAITH THAT ONE DAY IT WILL RETURN THE GLIMMER TO US FROM THE ABYSS.
I HAVE FAITH THAT TODAY IT WILL TAKE YOU HOME TO YOUR PEOPLE.
GODSPEED.
THIS IS CRAZY... MY STOMACH'S JUMPING...
IF WE DON'T STOP THE JLA BEATING THE BAD GUYS, DARKSEID'S GONNA ENSLAVE THE EARTH! IT'S ALL DOWN TO US!
I CANNOT HANDLE THIS!
SURE YOU CAN.
WHAT'S LIKELY TO HAPPEN HERE, FLASH? WE SEEM TO BE MOVING VERY FAST, VERY QUICKLY...
CAN WE TAKE THIS KIND OF ACCELERATION?
THIS IS JOGGING.
BUT WHEN I HIT TOP SPEED, THEN THE TREADMILL TAKES OVER, AMPLIFIES MY VELOCITY AND WE HIT... I DON'T KNOW... FASTER THAN LIGHT SQUARED...
WE'RE ACCELERATING TO SPEEDS WHERE OUR ENTIRE PHYSICAL STRUCTURES WILL BE CONVERTED TO HYPERLIGHT INFORMATION!
WE'RE DOING WHAT?
YEAH!
ISN'T IT AMAZZZZIIIII

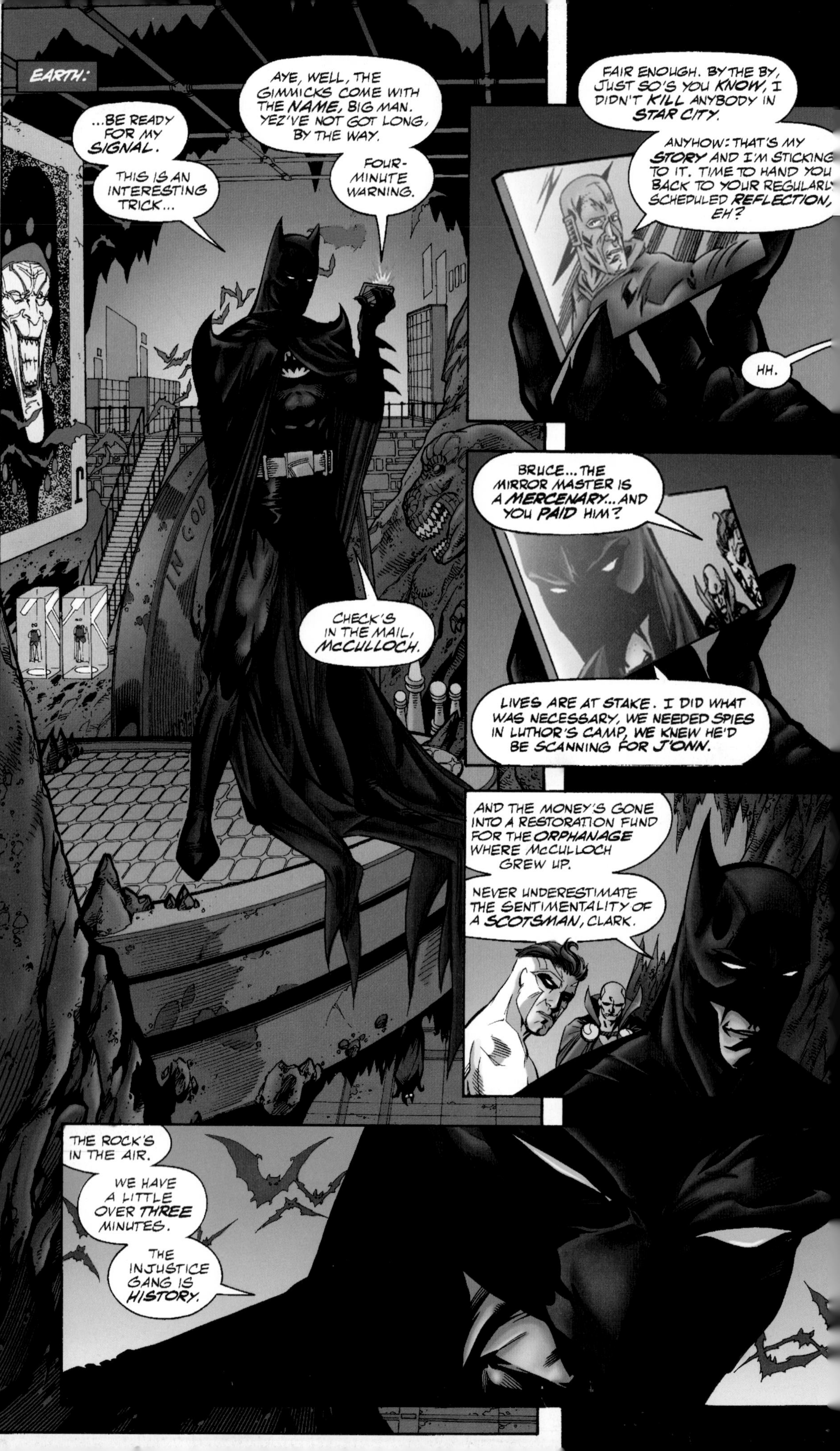
EARTH:
...BE READY FOR MY SIGNAL.
THIS IS AN INTERESTING TRICK...
AYE, WELL, THE GIMMICKS COME WITH THE NAME, BIG MAN. YEZ'VE NOT GOT LONG, BY THE WAY.
FOUR-MINUTE WARNING.
CHECK'S IN THE MAIL, McCULLOCH.
FAIR ENOUGH. BY THE BY, JUST SO'S YOU KNOW, I DIDN'T KILL ANYBODY IN STAR CITY.
ANYHOW: THAT'S MY STORY AND I'M STICKING TO IT. TIME TO HAND YOU BACK TO YOUR REGULARLY SCHEDULED REFLECTION, EH?
HH.
BRUCE... THE MIRROR MASTER IS A MERCENARY... AND YOU PAID HIM?
LIVES ARE AT STAKE. I DID WHAT WAS NECESSARY, WE NEEDED SPIES IN LUTHOR'S CAMP, WE KNEW HE'D BE SCANNING FOR J'ONN.
AND THE MONEY'S GONE INTO A RESTORATION FUND FOR THE ORPHANAGE WHERE McCULLOCH GREW UP.
NEVER UNDERESTIMATE THE SENTIMENTALITY OF A SCOTSMAN, CLARK.
THE ROCK'S IN THE AIR.
WE HAVE A LITTLE OVER THREE MINUTES.
THE INJUSTICE GANG IS HISTORY.

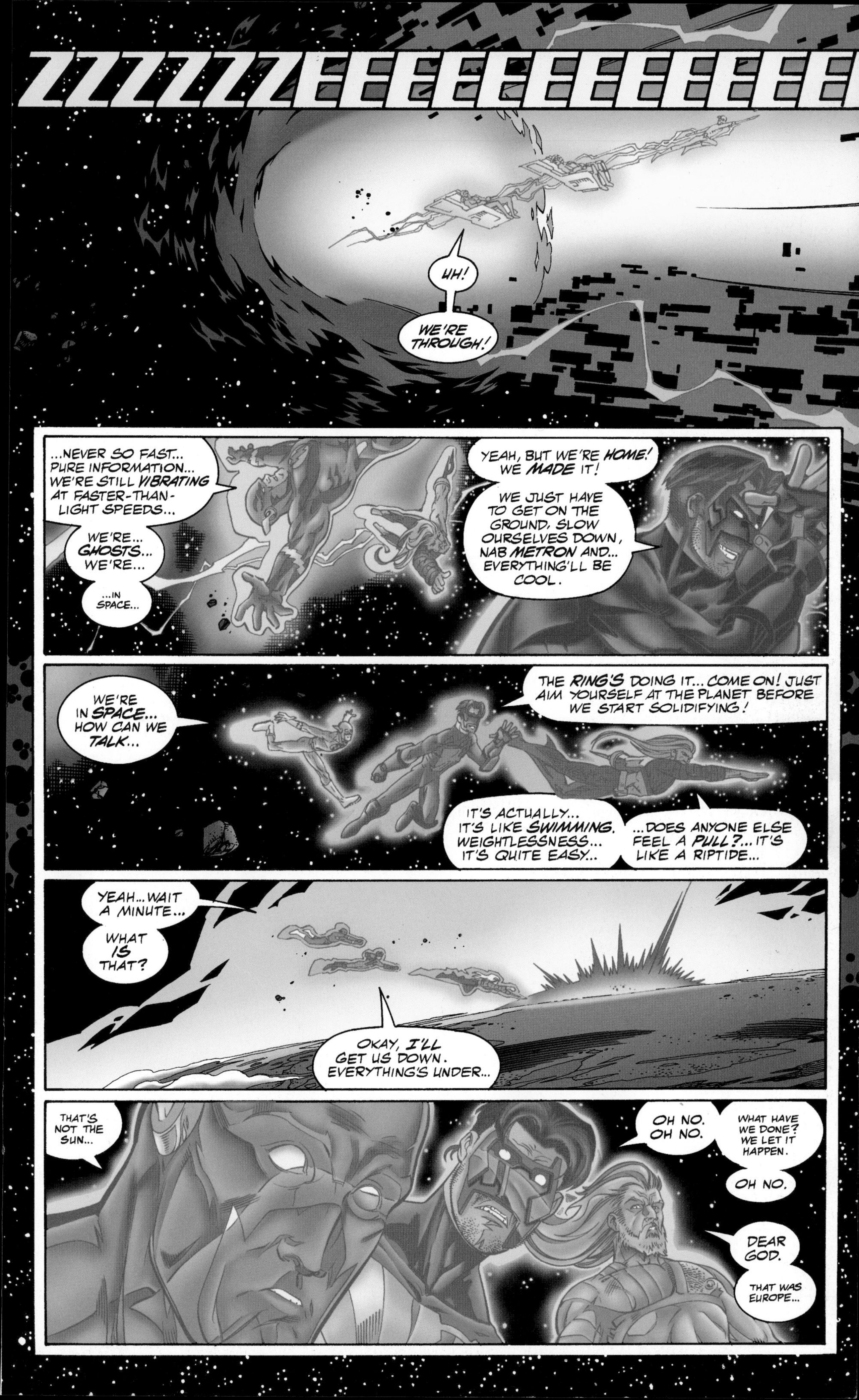
ZZZZZZEEEEEEEEEEEEEE
UH!
WE'RE THROUGH!
...NEVER SO FAST... PURE INFORMATION... WE'RE STILL VIBRATING AT FASTER-THAN-LIGHT SPEEDS...
WE'RE... GHOSTS... WE'RE...
...IN SPACE...
YEAH, BUT WE'RE HOME! WE MADE IT!
WE JUST HAVE TO GET ON THE GROUND, SLOW OURSELVES DOWN, NAB METRON AND... EVERYTHING'LL BE COOL.
WE'RE IN SPACE... HOW CAN WE TALK...
THE RING'S DOING IT... COME ON! JUST AIM YOURSELF AT THE PLANET BEFORE WE START SOLIDIFYING!
IT'S ACTUALLY... IT'S LIKE SWIMMING. WEIGHTLESSNESS... IT'S QUITE EASY...
...DOES ANYONE ELSE FEEL A PULL?... IT'S LIKE A RIPTIDE...
YEAH... WAIT A MINUTE...
WHAT IS THAT?
OKAY, I'LL GET US DOWN. EVERYTHING'S UNDER...
THAT'S NOT THE SUN...
OH NO. OH NO.
WHAT HAVE WE DONE? WE LET IT HAPPEN.
OH NO.
DEAR GOD.
THAT WAS EUROPE...

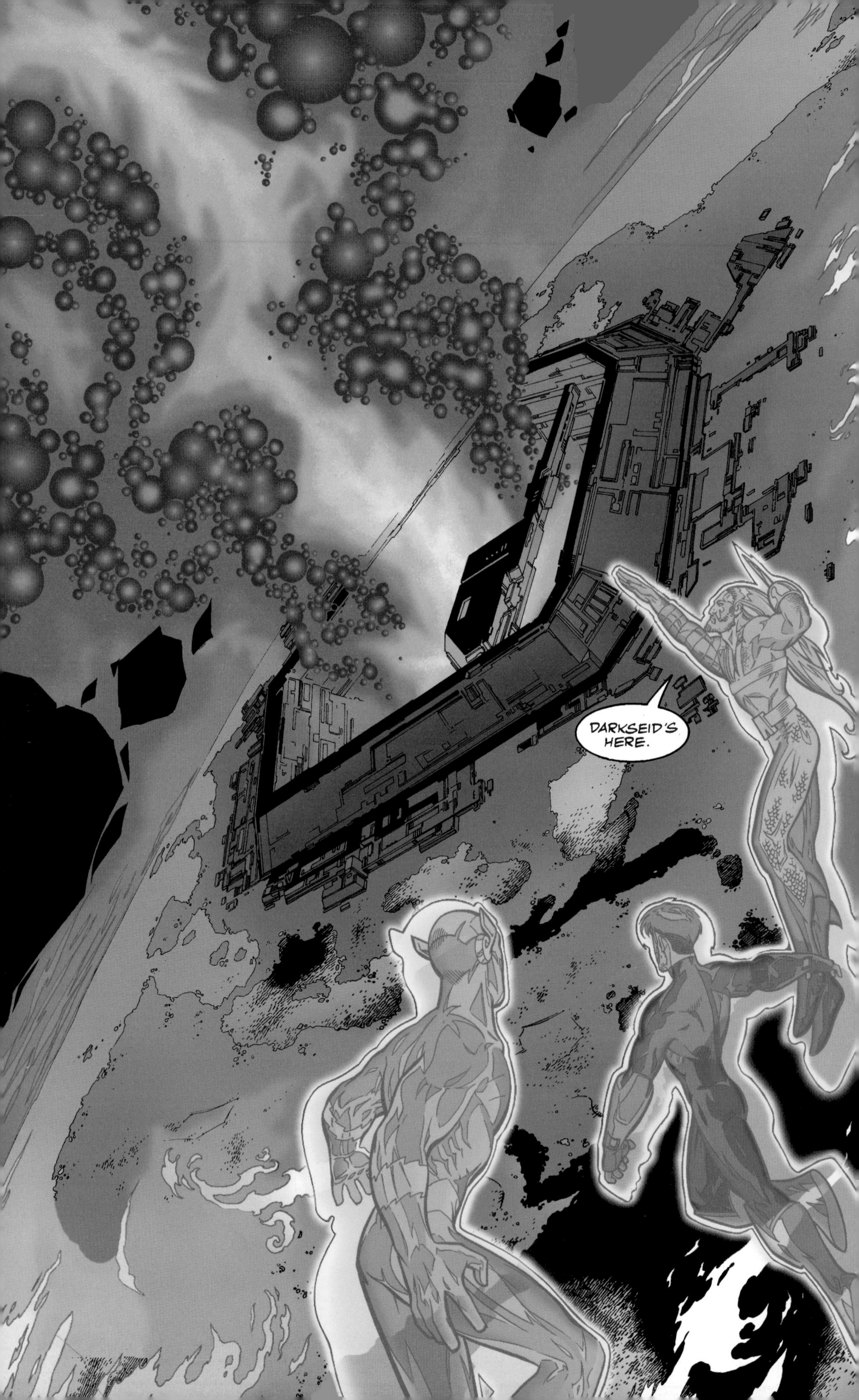
DARKSEID'S HERE.

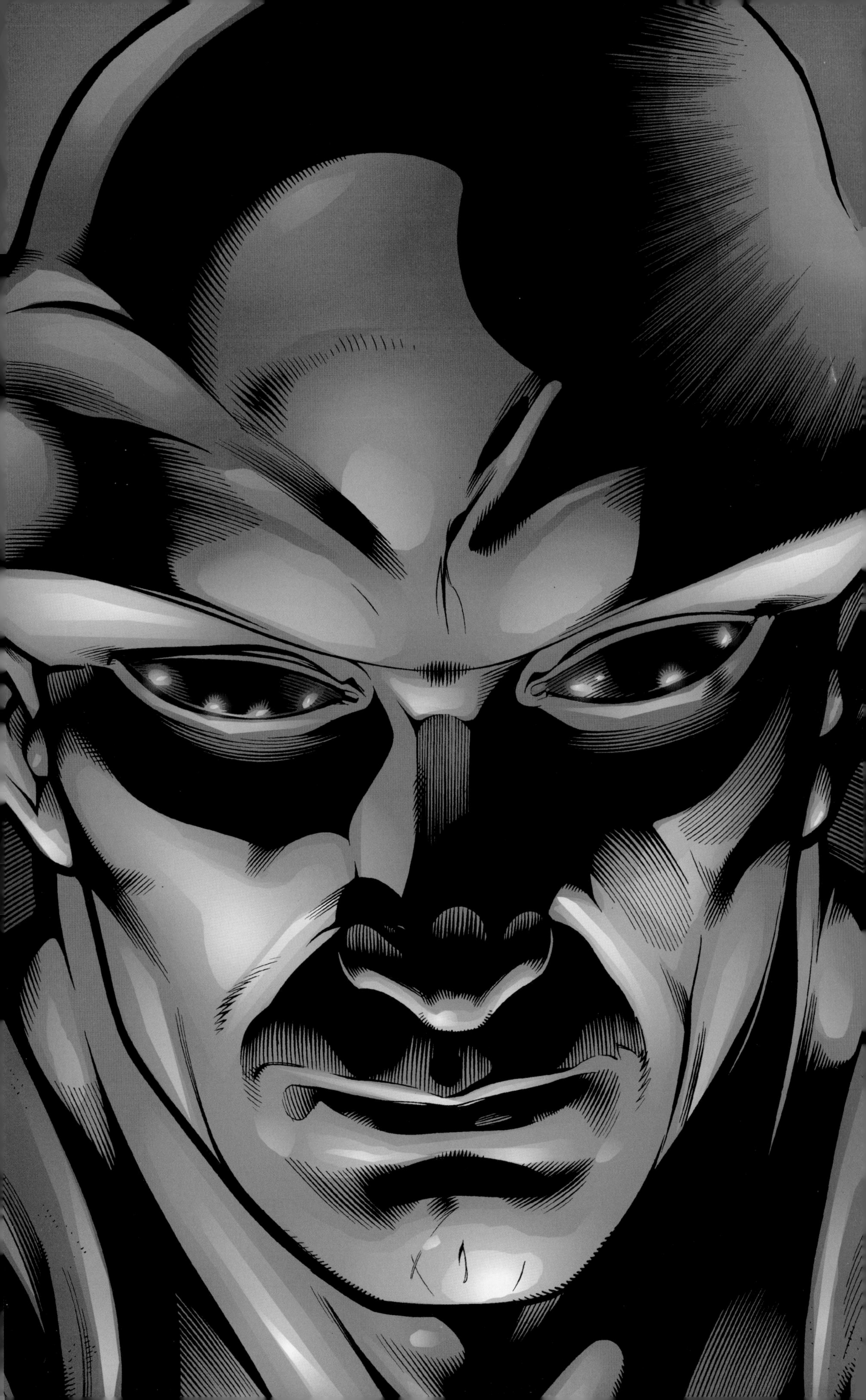

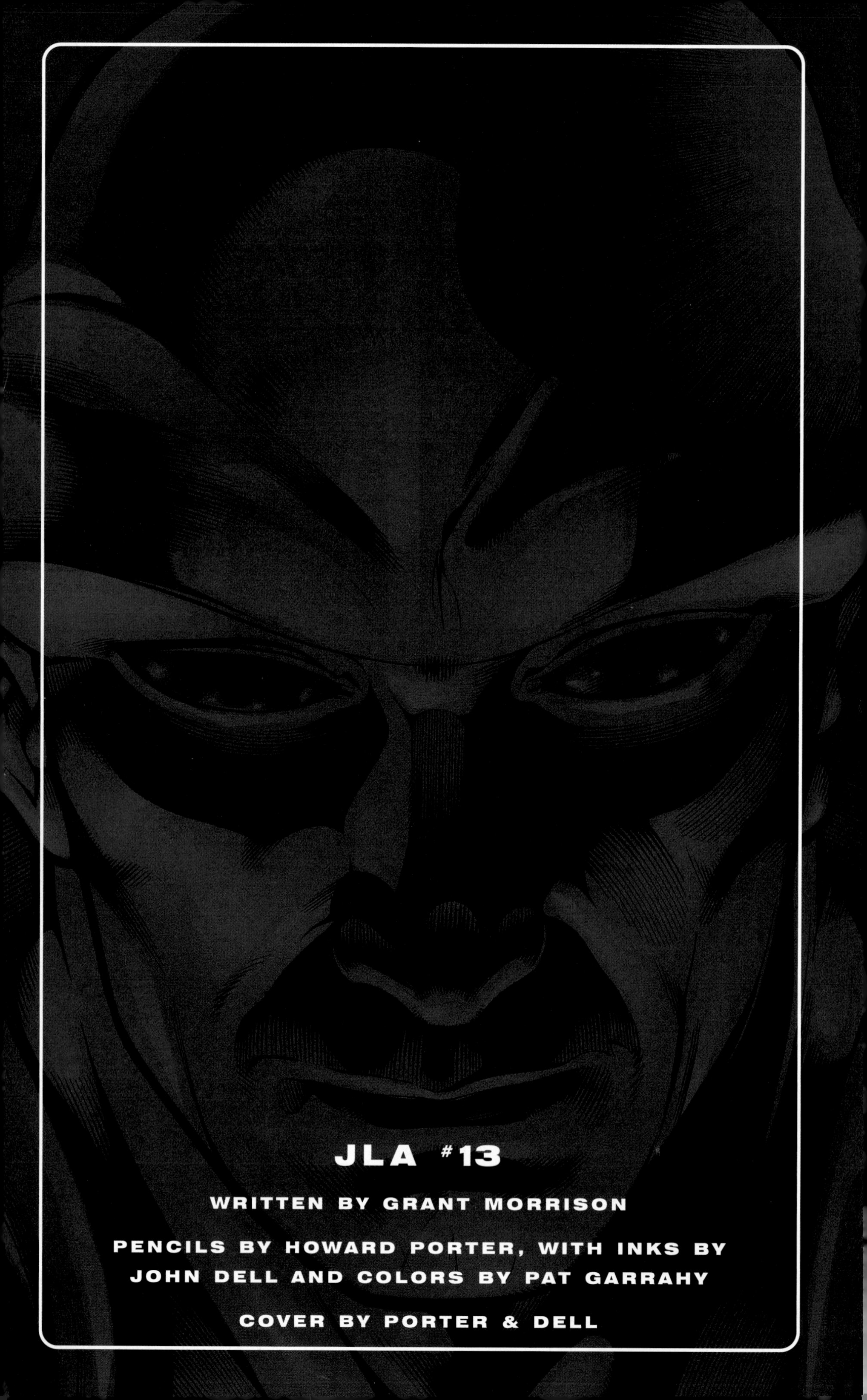

JLA #13

WRITTEN BY GRANT MORRISON

PENCILS BY HOWARD PORTER, WITH INKS BY JOHN DELL AND COLORS BY PAT GARRAHY

COVER BY PORTER & DELL

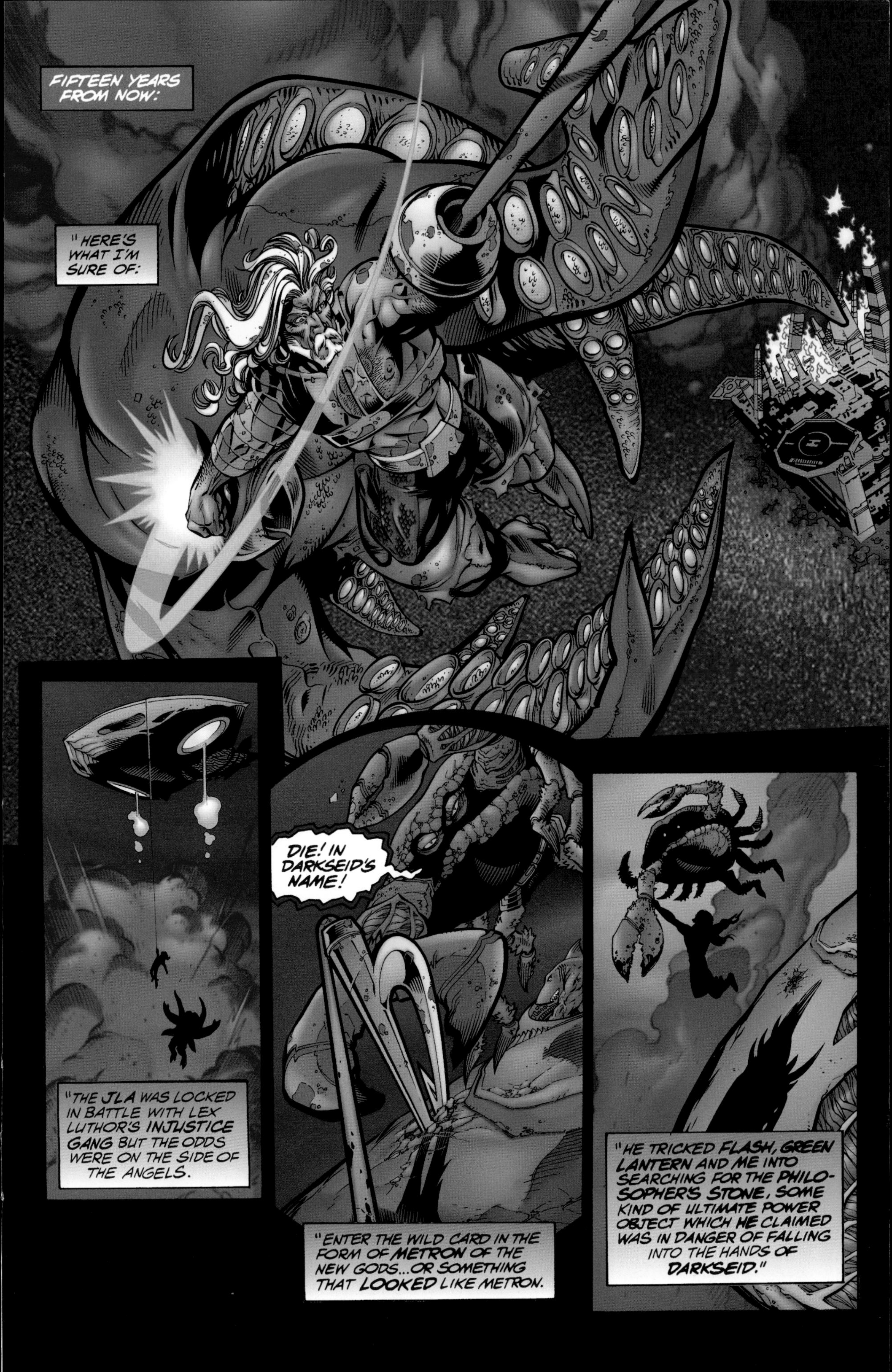
FIFTEEN YEARS FROM NOW:
"HERE'S WHAT I'M SURE OF:
"THE JLA WAS LOCKED IN BATTLE WITH LEX LUTHOR'S INJUSTICE GANG BUT THE ODDS WERE ON THE SIDE OF THE ANGELS.
DIE! IN DARKSEID'S NAME!
"ENTER THE WILD CARD IN THE FORM OF METRON OF THE NEW GODS...OR SOMETHING THAT LOOKED LIKE METRON.
"HE TRICKED FLASH, GREEN LANTERN AND ME INTO SEARCHING FOR THE PHILOSOPHER'S STONE, SOME KIND OF ULTIMATE POWER OBJECT WHICH HE CLAIMED WAS IN DANGER OF FALLING INTO THE HANDS OF DARKSEID."

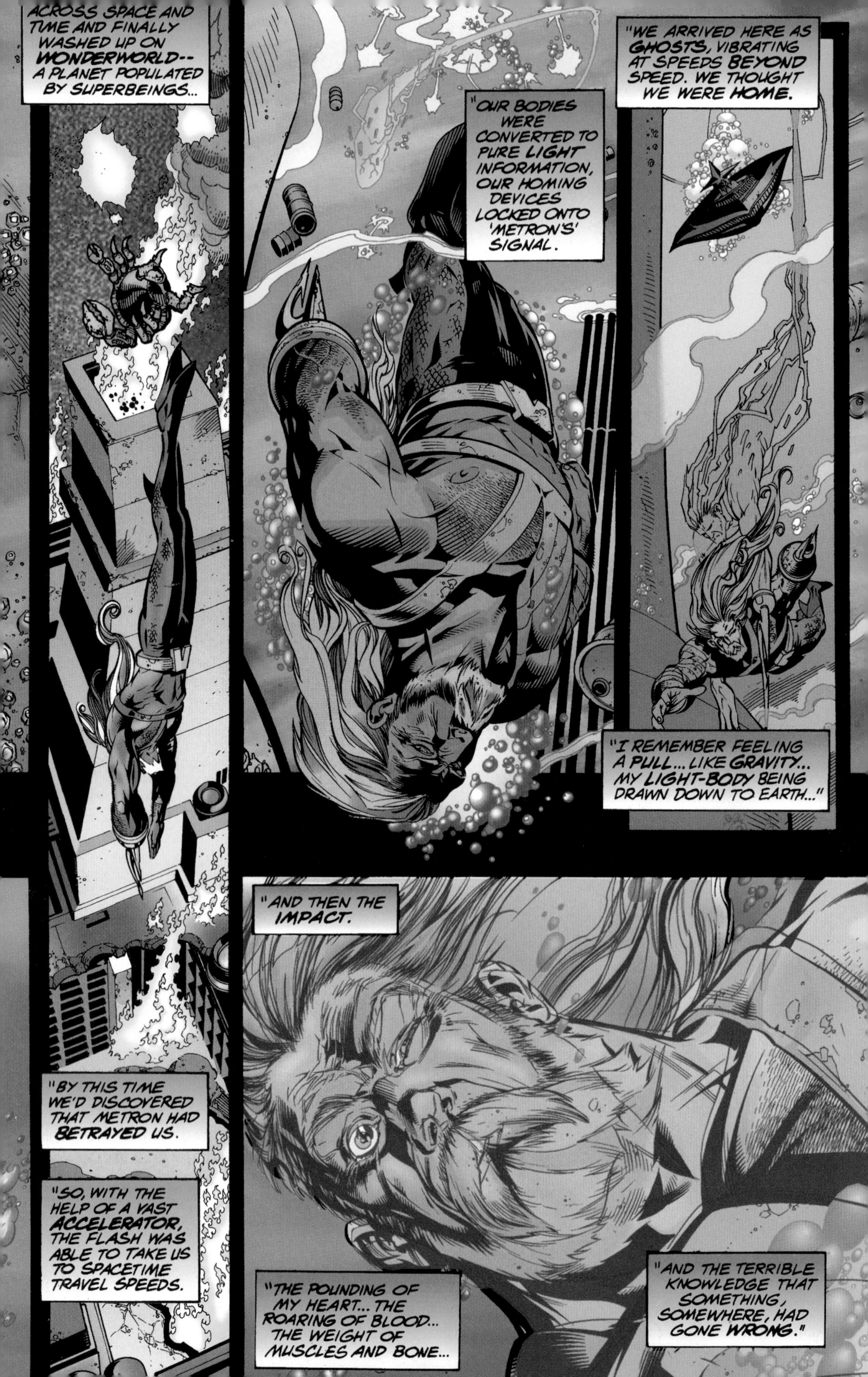
ACROSS SPACE AND TIME AND FINALLY WASHED UP ON WONDERWORLD-- A PLANET POPULATED BY SUPERBEINGS...
"OUR BODIES WERE CONVERTED TO PURE LIGHT INFORMATION, OUR HOMING DEVICES LOCKED ONTO 'METRON'S' SIGNAL.
"WE ARRIVED HERE AS GHOSTS, VIBRATING AT SPEEDS BEYOND SPEED. WE THOUGHT WE WERE HOME.
"I REMEMBER FEELING A PULL... LIKE GRAVITY... MY LIGHT-BODY BEING DRAWN DOWN TO EARTH..."
"BY THIS TIME WE'D DISCOVERED THAT METRON HAD BETRAYED US.
"SO, WITH THE HELP OF A VAST ACCELERATOR, THE FLASH WAS ABLE TO TAKE US TO SPACETIME TRAVEL SPEEDS.
"AND THEN THE IMPACT.
"THE POUNDING OF MY HEART... THE ROARING OF BLOOD... THE WEIGHT OF MUSCLES AND BONE...
"AND THE TERRIBLE KNOWLEDGE THAT SOMETHING, SOMEWHERE, HAD GONE WRONG."

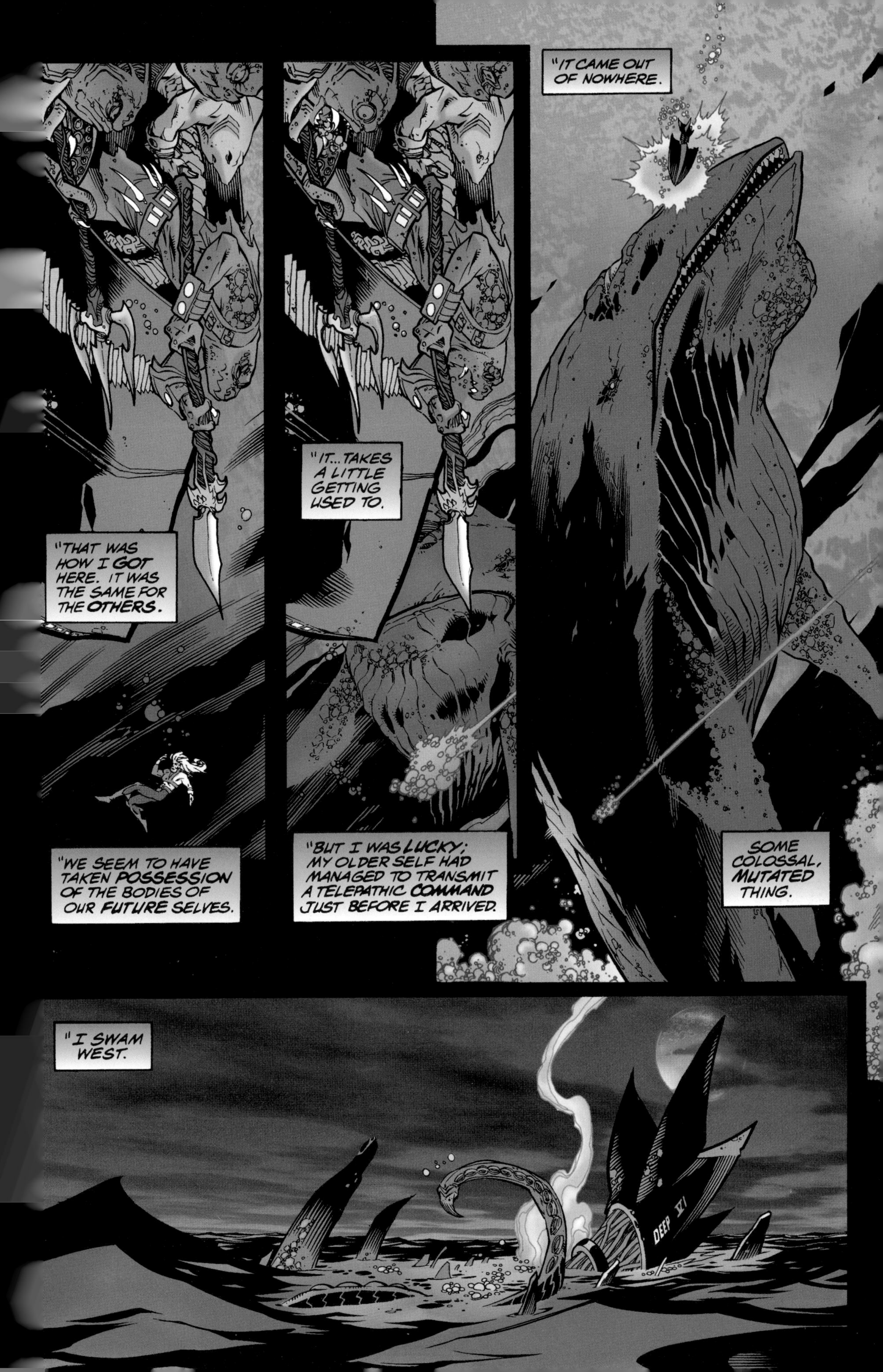
"THAT WAS HOW I GOT HERE. IT WAS THE SAME FOR THE OTHERS.
"WE SEEM TO HAVE TAKEN POSSESSION OF THE BODIES OF OUR FUTURE SELVES.
"IT...TAKES A LITTLE GETTING USED TO.
"BUT I WAS LUCKY; MY OLDER SELF HAD MANAGED TO TRANSMIT A TELEPATHIC COMMAND JUST BEFORE I ARRIVED.
"IT CAME OUT OF NOWHERE.
SOME COLOSSAL, MUTATED THING.
"I SWAM WEST.
DEEP VI

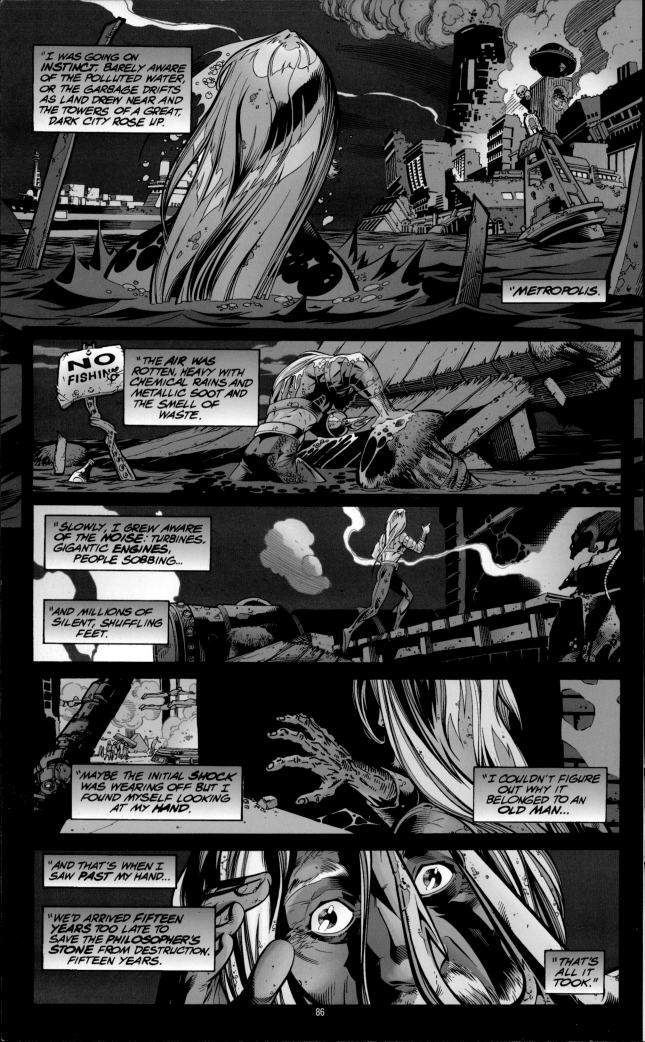

"I WAS GOING ON INSTINCT, BARELY AWARE OF THE POLLUTED WATER, OR THE GARBAGE DRIFTS AS LAND DREW NEAR AND THE TOWERS OF A GREAT, DARK CITY ROSE UP.

"METROPOLIS.

NO FISHING

"THE AIR WAS ROTTEN, HEAVY WITH CHEMICAL RAINS AND METALLIC SOOT AND THE SMELL OF WASTE.

"SLOWLY, I GREW AWARE OF THE NOISE: TURBINES, GIGANTIC ENGINES, PEOPLE SOBBING...

"AND MILLIONS OF SILENT, SHUFFLING FEET.

"MAYBE THE INITIAL SHOCK WAS WEARING OFF BUT I FOUND MYSELF LOOKING AT MY HAND.

"I COULDN'T FIGURE OUT WHY IT BELONGED TO AN OLD MAN...

"AND THAT'S WHEN I SAW PAST MY HAND...

"WE'D ARRIVED FIFTEEN YEARS TOO LATE TO SAVE THE PHILOSOPHER'S STONE FROM DESTRUCTION. FIFTEEN YEARS.

"THAT'S ALL IT TOOK."

86

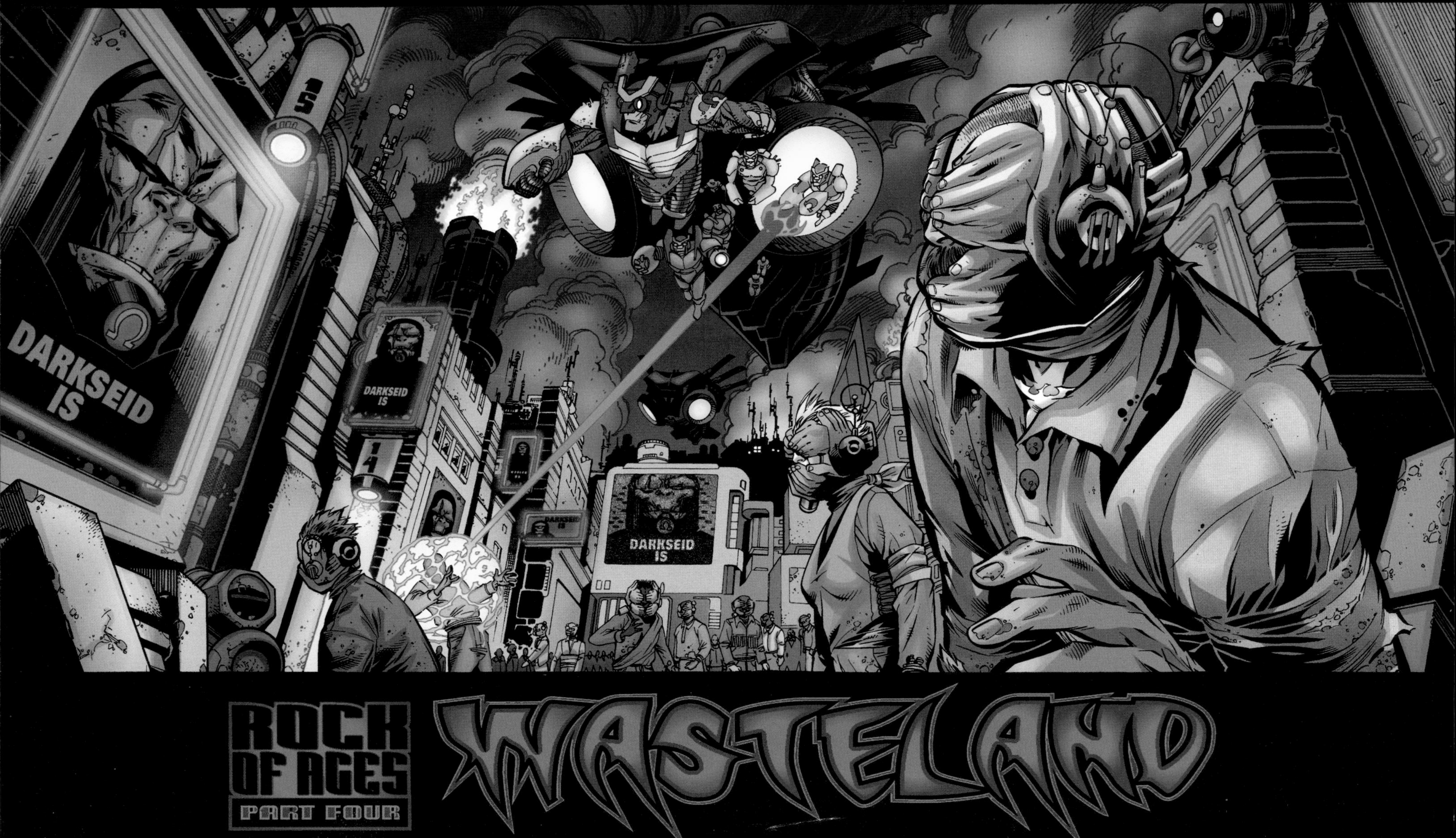

DARKSEID IS
15
DARKSEID IS
14
DARKSEID IS
DARKSEID IS
ROCK OF AGES
PART FOUR
WASTELAND

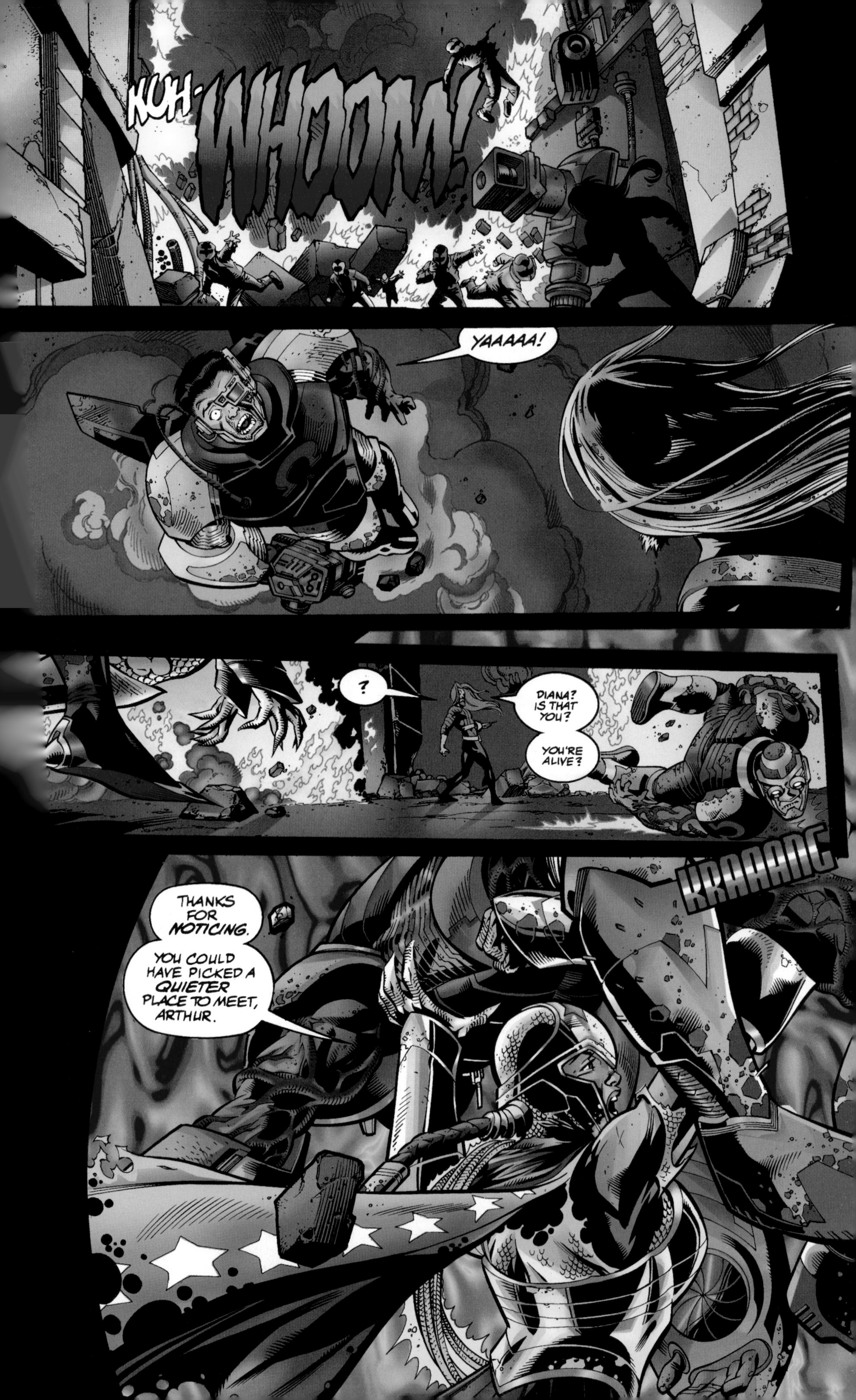
KUH-WHOOM!
YAAAAA!
?
DIANA? IS THAT YOU?
YOU'RE ALIVE?
KRAAANG
THANKS FOR NOTICING.
YOU COULD HAVE PICKED A QUIETER PLACE TO MEET, ARTHUR.

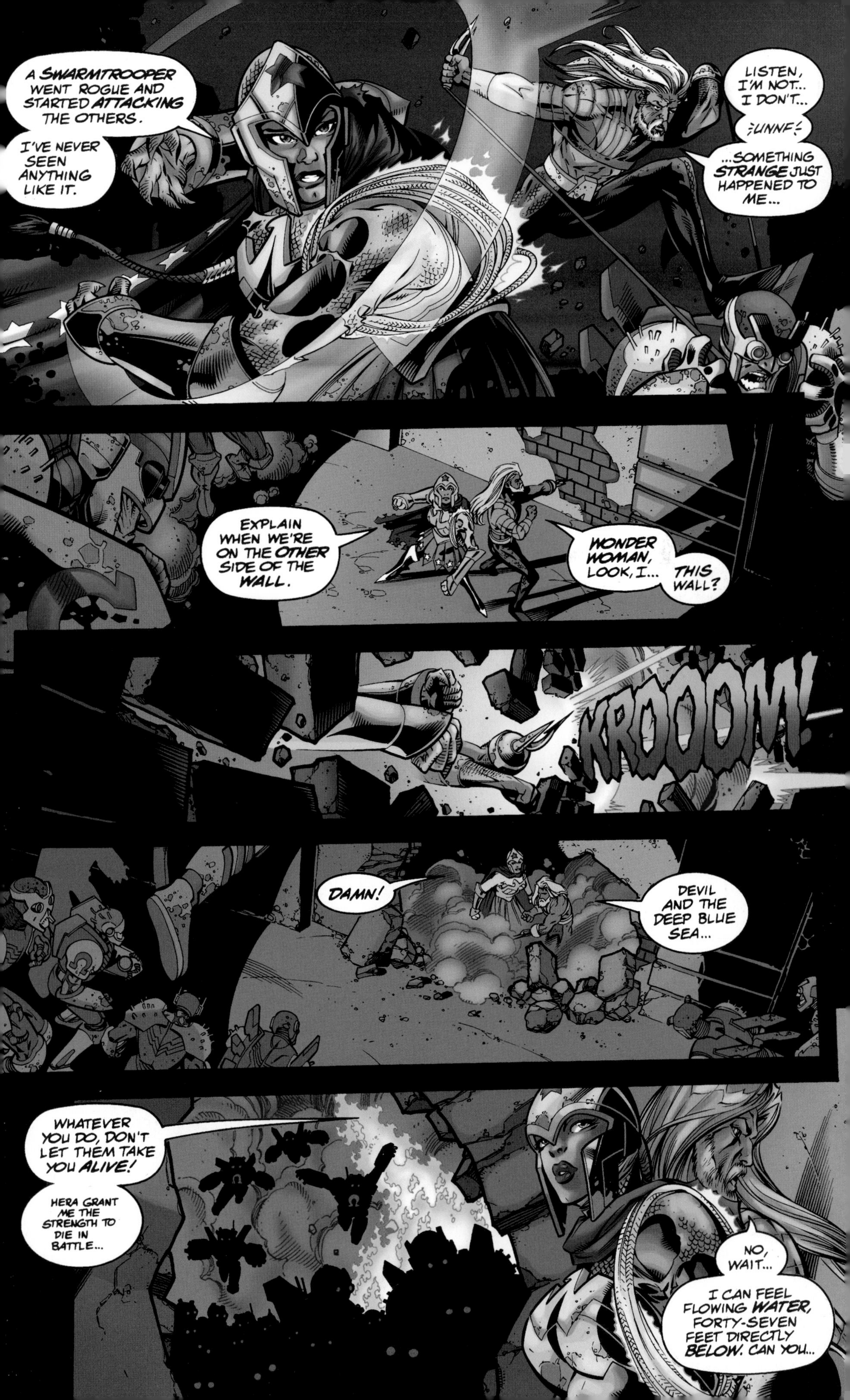
A SWARMTROOPER WENT ROGUE AND STARTED ATTACKING THE OTHERS.
I'VE NEVER SEEN ANYTHING LIKE IT.
LISTEN, I'M NOT... I DON'T...
UNNF
...SOMETHING STRANGE JUST HAPPENED TO ME...
EXPLAIN WHEN WE'RE ON THE OTHER SIDE OF THE WALL.
WONDER WOMAN, LOOK, I...
THIS WALL?
KROOOM!
DAMN!
DEVIL AND THE DEEP BLUE SEA...
WHATEVER YOU DO, DON'T LET THEM TAKE YOU ALIVE!
HERA GRANT ME THE STRENGTH TO DIE IN BATTLE...
NO, WAIT...
I CAN FEEL FLOWING WATER, FORTY-SEVEN FEET DIRECTLY BELOW. CAN YOU...

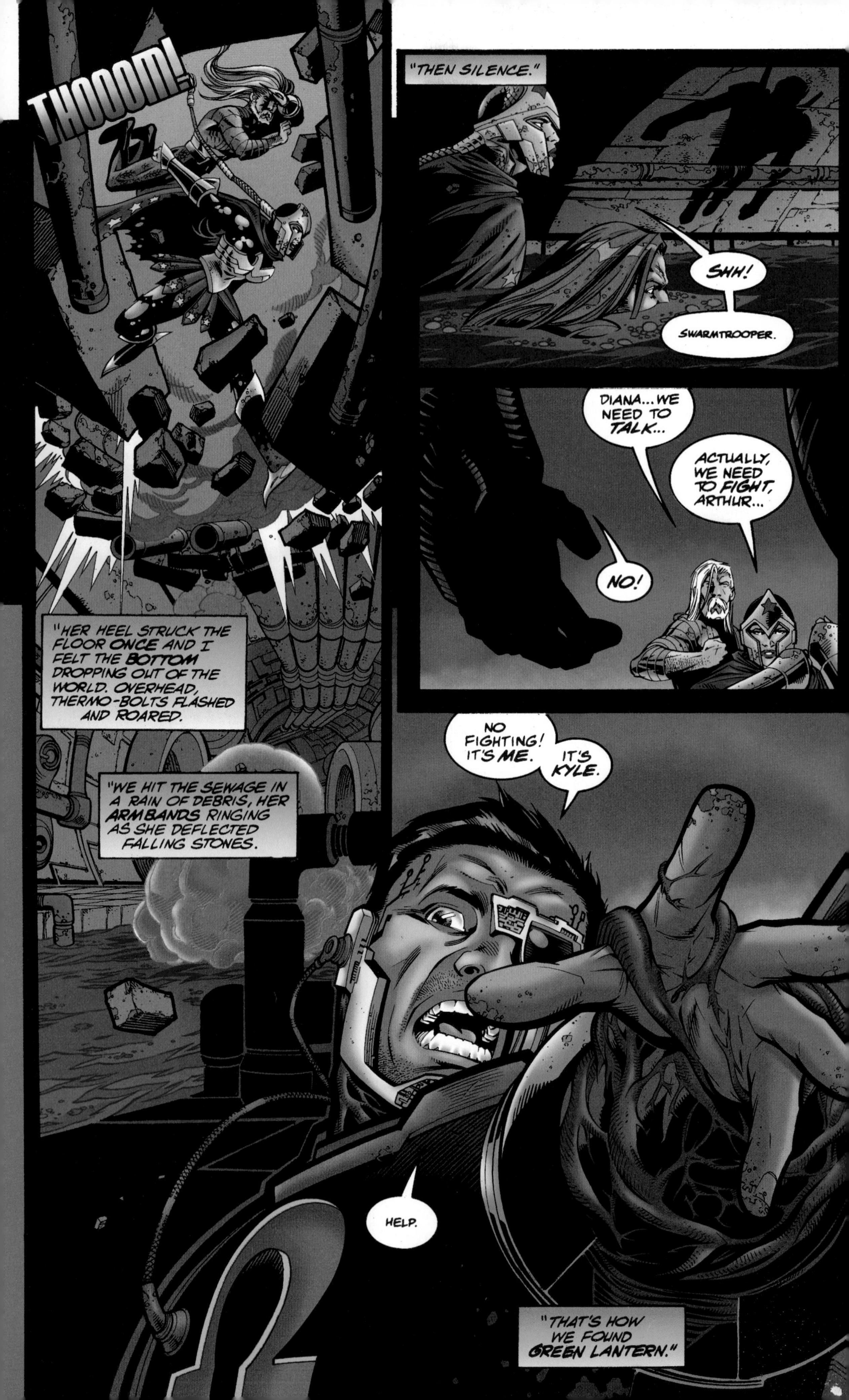
THOOOM!
"THEN SILENCE."
SHH!
SWARMTROOPER.
DIANA... WE NEED TO TALK...
ACTUALLY, WE NEED TO FIGHT, ARTHUR...
NO!
"HER HEEL STRUCK THE FLOOR ONCE AND I FELT THE BOTTOM DROPPING OUT OF THE WORLD. OVERHEAD, THERMO-BOLTS FLASHED AND ROARED.
"WE HIT THE SEWAGE IN A RAIN OF DEBRIS, HER ARMBANDS RINGING AS SHE DEFLECTED FALLING STONES.
NO FIGHTING! IT'S ME.
IT'S KYLE.
HELP.
"THAT'S HOW WE FOUND GREEN LANTERN."

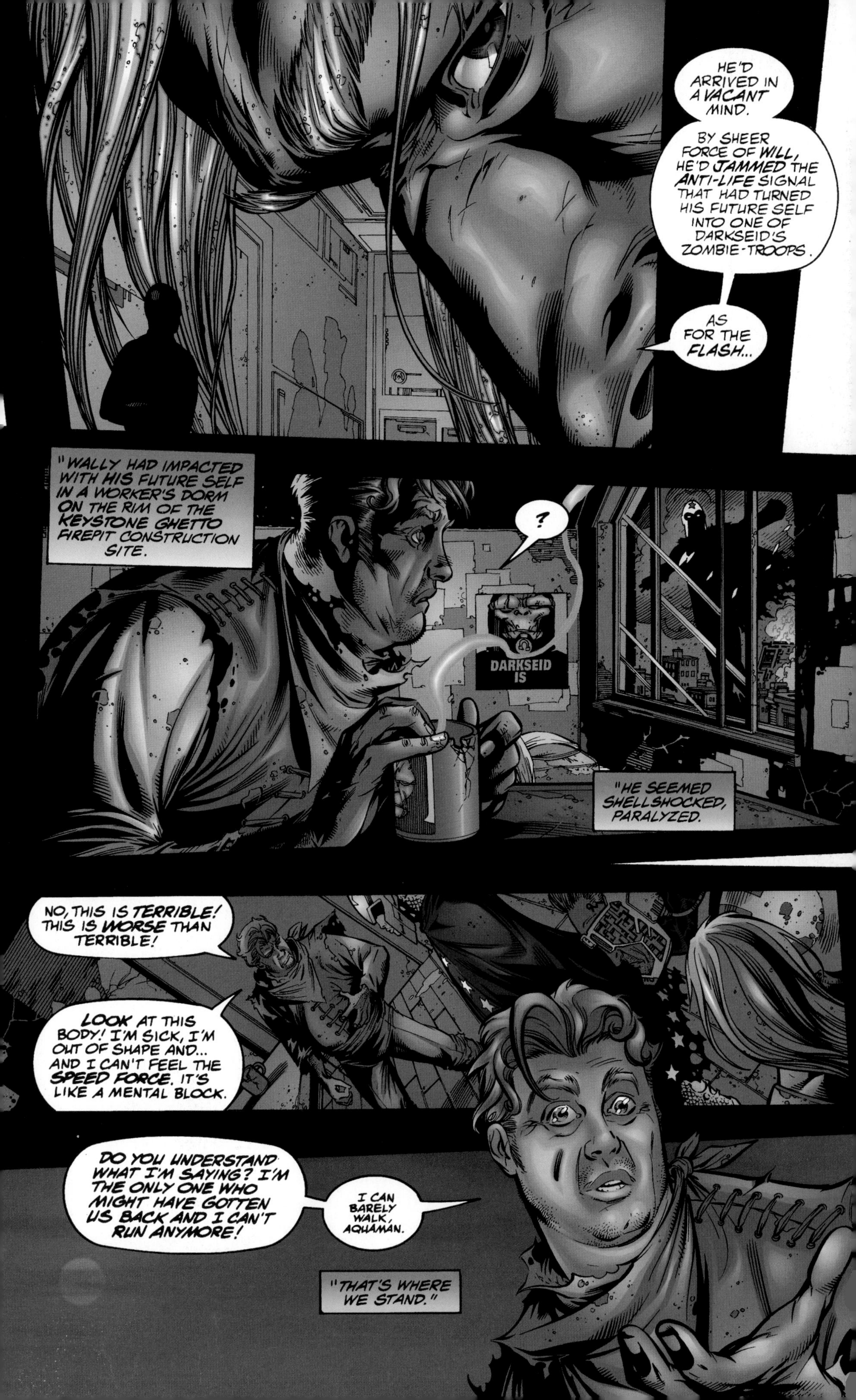
HE'D ARRIVED IN A VACANT MIND.
BY SHEER FORCE OF WILL, HE'D JAMMED THE ANTI-LIFE SIGNAL THAT HAD TURNED HIS FUTURE SELF INTO ONE OF DARKSEID'S ZOMBIE-TROOPS.
AS FOR THE FLASH...
"WALLY HAD IMPACTED WITH HIS FUTURE SELF IN A WORKER'S DORM ON THE RIM OF THE KEYSTONE GHETTO FIREPIT CONSTRUCTION SITE.
?
DARKSEID IS
"HE SEEMED SHELLSHOCKED, PARALYZED.
NO, THIS IS TERRIBLE! THIS IS WORSE THAN TERRIBLE!
LOOK AT THIS BODY! I'M SICK, I'M OUT OF SHAPE AND... AND I CAN'T FEEL THE SPEED FORCE. IT'S LIKE A MENTAL BLOCK.
DO YOU UNDERSTAND WHAT I'M SAYING? I'M THE ONLY ONE WHO MIGHT HAVE GOTTEN US BACK AND I CAN'T RUN ANYMORE!
I CAN BARELY WALK, AQUAMAN.
"THAT'S WHERE WE STAND."

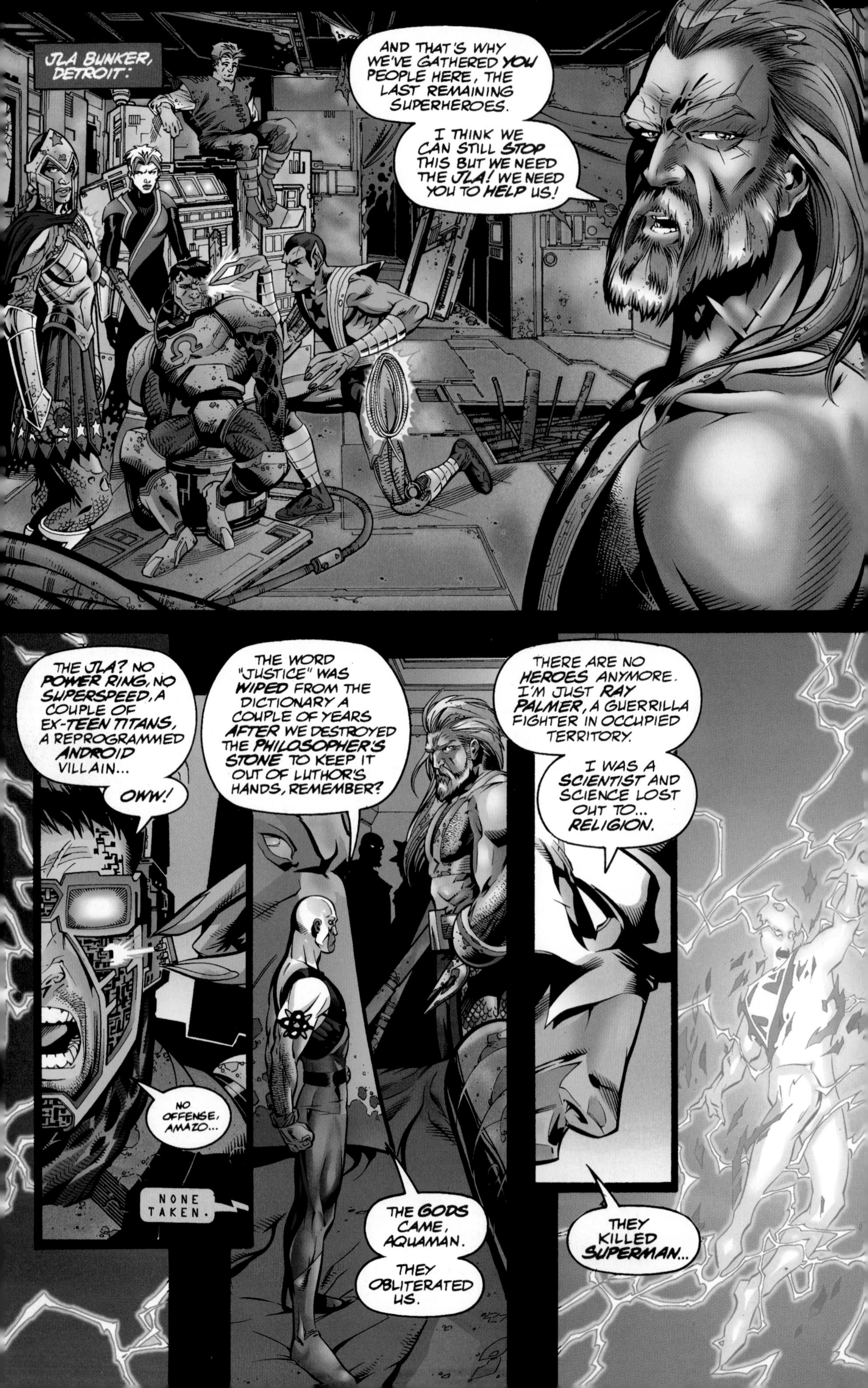

JLA BUNKER, DETROIT:
AND THAT'S WHY WE'VE GATHERED YOU PEOPLE HERE, THE LAST REMAINING SUPERHEROES.
I THINK WE CAN STILL STOP THIS BUT WE NEED THE JLA! WE NEED YOU TO HELP US!
THE JLA? NO POWER RING, NO SUPERSPEED, A COUPLE OF EX-TEEN TITANS, A REPROGRAMMED ANDROID VILLAIN...
OWW!
NO OFFENSE, AMAZO...
NONE TAKEN.
THE WORD "JUSTICE" WAS WIPED FROM THE DICTIONARY A COUPLE OF YEARS AFTER WE DESTROYED THE PHILOSOPHER'S STONE TO KEEP IT OUT OF LUTHOR'S HANDS, REMEMBER?
THE GODS CAME, AQUAMAN.
THEY OBLITERATED US.
THERE ARE NO HEROES ANYMORE. I'M JUST RAY PALMER, A GUERRILLA FIGHTER IN OCCUPIED TERRITORY.
I WAS A SCIENTIST AND SCIENCE LOST OUT TO... RELIGION.
THEY KILLED SUPERMAN...

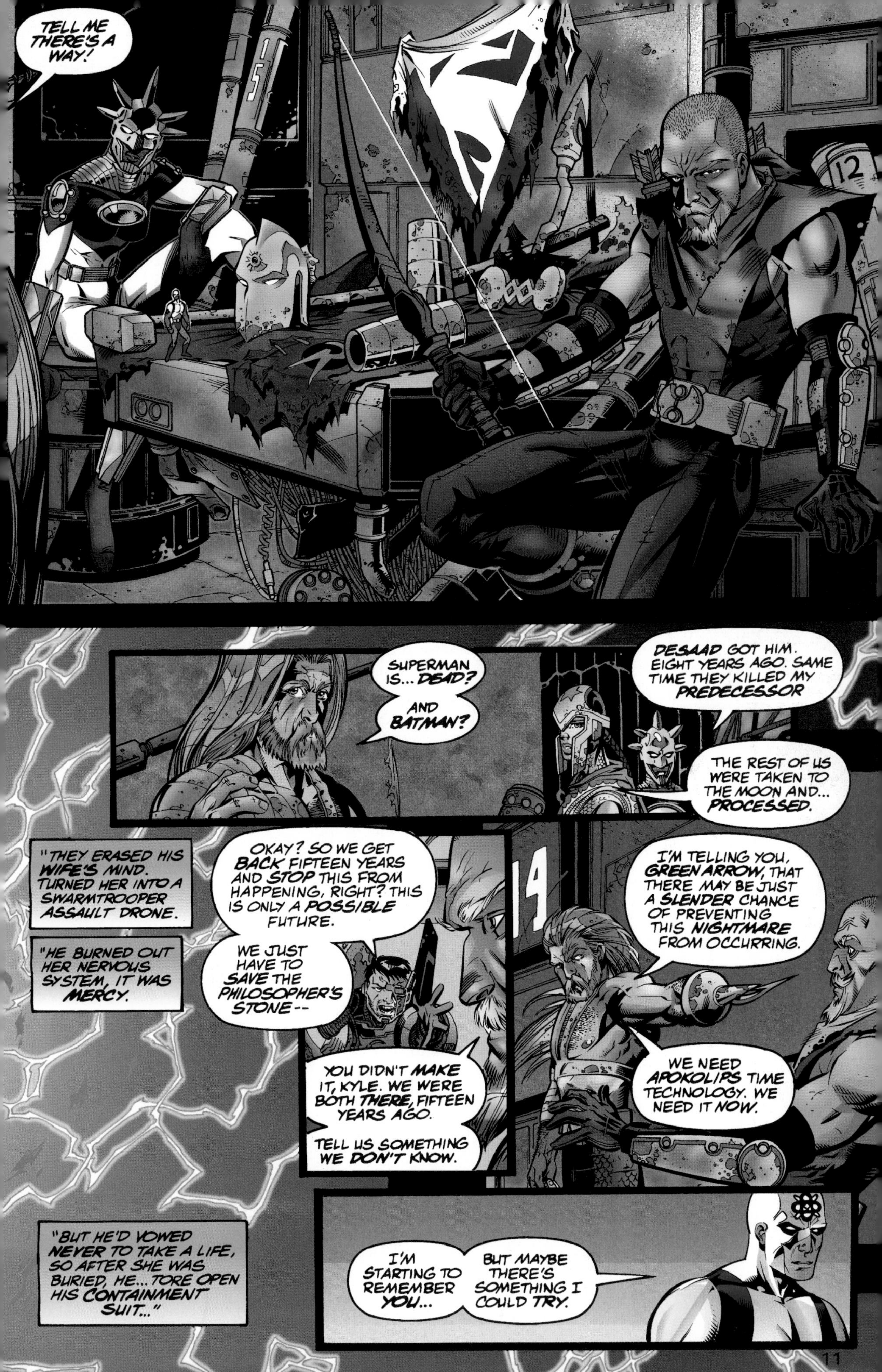

TELL ME THERE'S A WAY!
SUPERMAN IS... DEAD?
AND BATMAN?
DESAAD GOT HIM. EIGHT YEARS AGO. SAME TIME THEY KILLED MY PREDECESSOR
THE REST OF US WERE TAKEN TO THE MOON AND... PROCESSED.
"THEY ERASED HIS WIFE'S MIND. TURNED HER INTO A SWARMTROOPER ASSAULT DRONE.
"HE BURNED OUT HER NERVOUS SYSTEM, IT WAS MERCY.
OKAY? SO WE GET BACK FIFTEEN YEARS AND STOP THIS FROM HAPPENING, RIGHT? THIS IS ONLY A POSSIBLE FUTURE.
WE JUST HAVE TO SAVE THE PHILOSOPHER'S STONE--
YOU DIDN'T MAKE IT, KYLE. WE WERE BOTH THERE, FIFTEEN YEARS AGO.
TELL US SOMETHING WE DON'T KNOW.
I'M TELLING YOU, GREEN ARROW, THAT THERE MAY BE JUST A SLENDER CHANCE OF PREVENTING THIS NIGHTMARE FROM OCCURRING.
WE NEED APOKOLIPS TIME TECHNOLOGY. WE NEED IT NOW.
"BUT HE'D VOWED NEVER TO TAKE A LIFE, SO AFTER SHE WAS BURIED, HE...TORE OPEN HIS CONTAINMENT SUIT..."
I'M STARTING TO REMEMBER YOU...
BUT MAYBE THERE'S SOMETHING I COULD TRY.

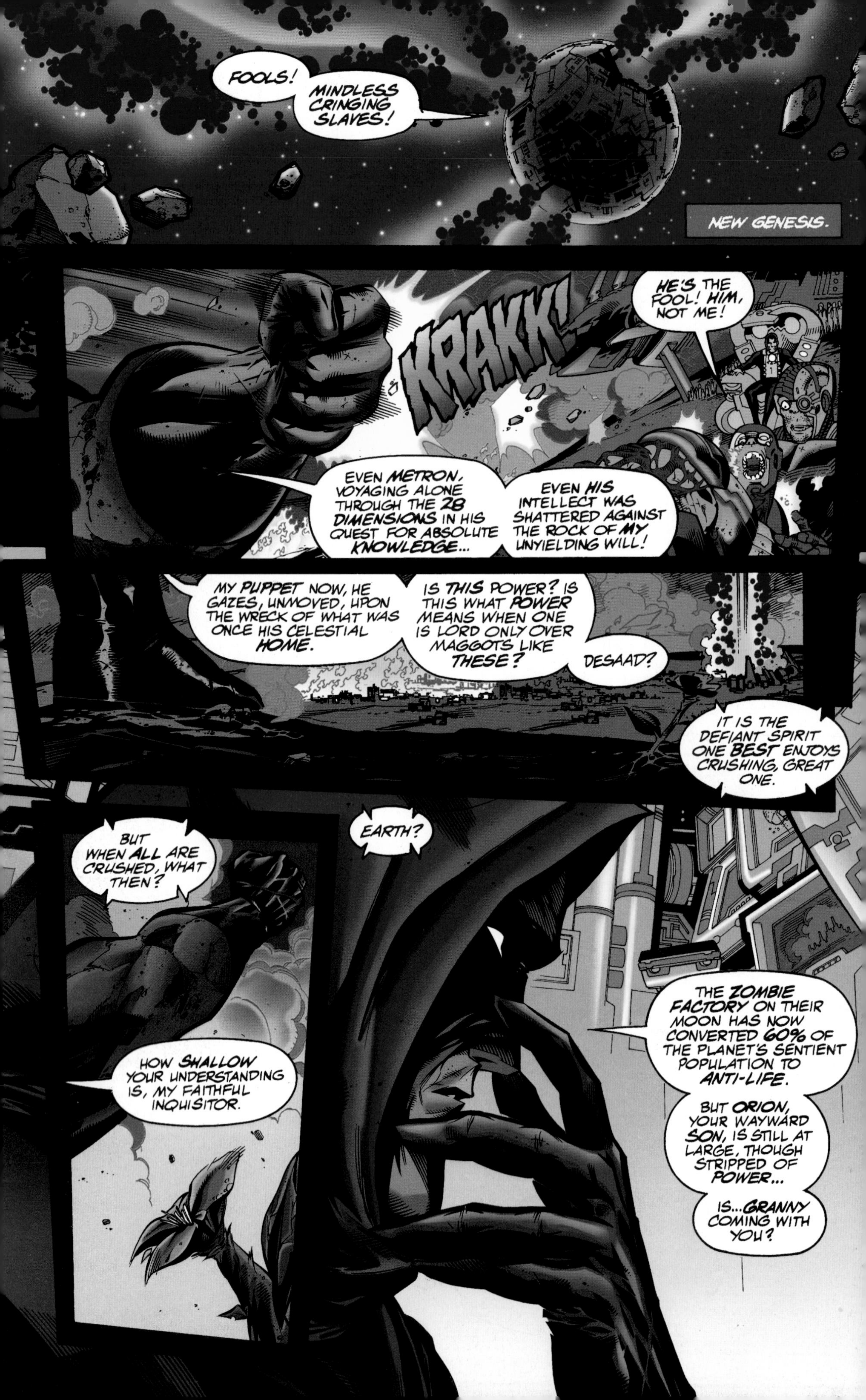
FOOLS!
MINDLESS CRINGING SLAVES!
NEW GENESIS.
KRAKK!
HE'S THE FOOL! HIM, NOT ME!
EVEN METRON, VOYAGING ALONE THROUGH THE 28 DIMENSIONS IN HIS QUEST FOR ABSOLUTE KNOWLEDGE...
EVEN HIS INTELLECT WAS SHATTERED AGAINST THE ROCK OF MY UNYIELDING WILL!
MY PUPPET NOW, HE GAZES, UNMOVED, UPON THE WRECK OF WHAT WAS ONCE HIS CELESTIAL HOME.
IS THIS POWER? IS THIS WHAT POWER MEANS WHEN ONE IS LORD ONLY OVER MAGGOTS LIKE THESE?
DESAAD?
IT IS THE DEFIANT SPIRIT ONE BEST ENJOYS CRUSHING, GREAT ONE.
BUT WHEN ALL ARE CRUSHED, WHAT THEN?
EARTH?
HOW SHALLOW YOUR UNDERSTANDING IS, MY FAITHFUL INQUISITOR.
THE ZOMBIE FACTORY ON THEIR MOON HAS NOW CONVERTED 60% OF THE PLANET'S SENTIENT POPULATION TO ANTI-LIFE.
BUT ORION, YOUR WAYWARD SON, IS STILL AT LARGE, THOUGH STRIPPED OF POWER...
IS...GRANNY COMING WITH YOU?

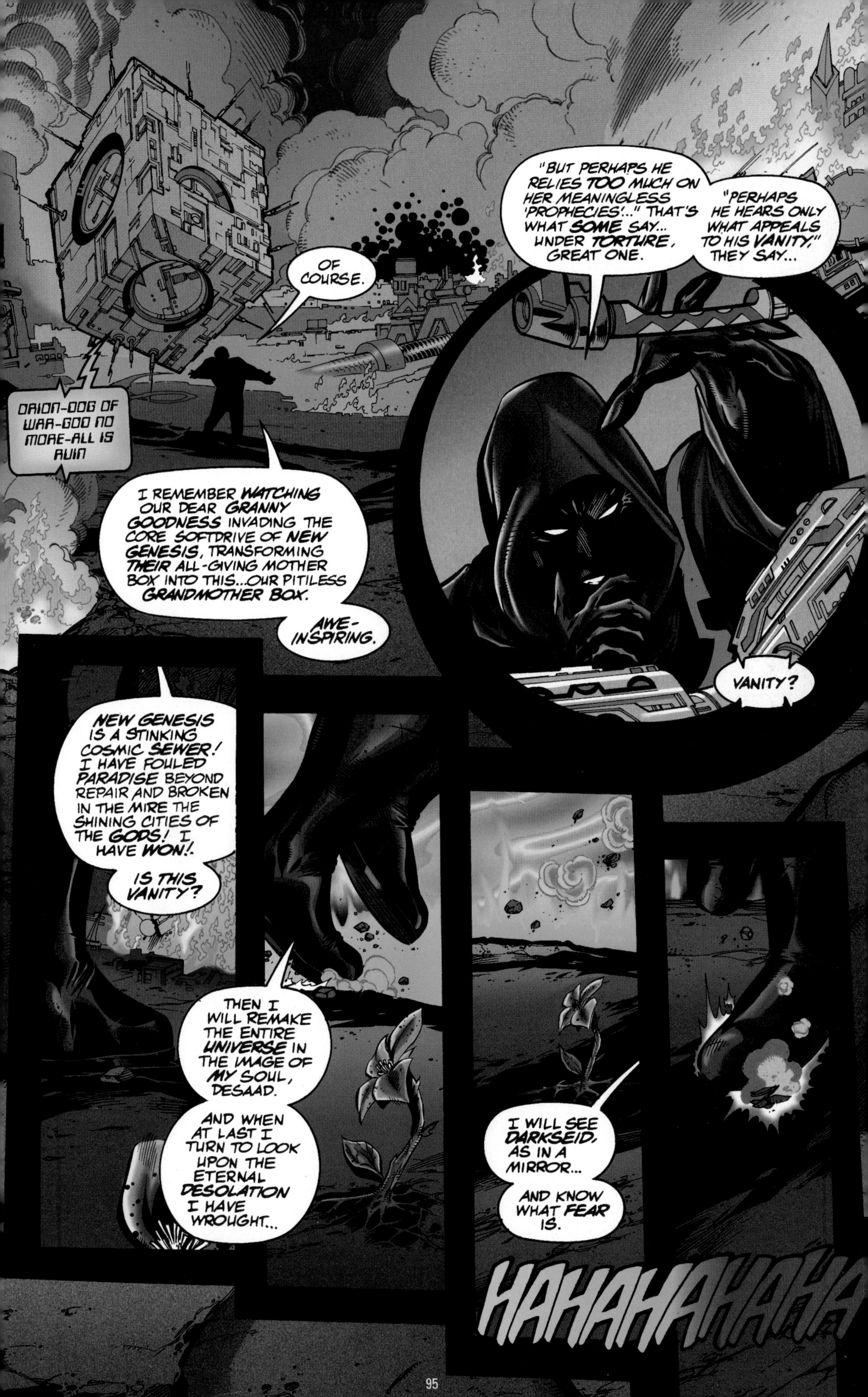

OF COURSE.
"BUT PERHAPS HE RELIES TOO MUCH ON HER MEANINGLESS 'PROPHECIES'..." THAT'S WHAT SOME SAY... UNDER TORTURE, GREAT ONE.
"PERHAPS HE HEARS ONLY WHAT APPEALS TO HIS VANITY," THEY SAY...
ORION-DOG OF WAR-GOD NO MORE-ALL IS RUIN
I REMEMBER WATCHING OUR DEAR GRANNY GOODNESS INVADING THE CORE SOFTDRIVE OF NEW GENESIS, TRANSFORMING THEIR ALL-GIVING MOTHER BOX INTO THIS...OUR PITILESS GRANDMOTHER BOX.
AWE-INSPIRING.
VANITY?
NEW GENESIS IS A STINKING COSMIC SEWER! I HAVE FOULED PARADISE BEYOND REPAIR AND BROKEN IN THE MIRE THE SHINING CITIES OF THE GODS! I HAVE WON!.
IS THIS VANITY?
THEN I WILL REMAKE THE ENTIRE UNIVERSE IN THE IMAGE OF MY SOUL, DESAAD.
AND WHEN AT LAST I TURN TO LOOK UPON THE ETERNAL DESOLATION I HAVE WROUGHT...
I WILL SEE DARKSEID, AS IN A MIRROR...
AND KNOW WHAT FEAR IS.
HAHAHAHAHAHA

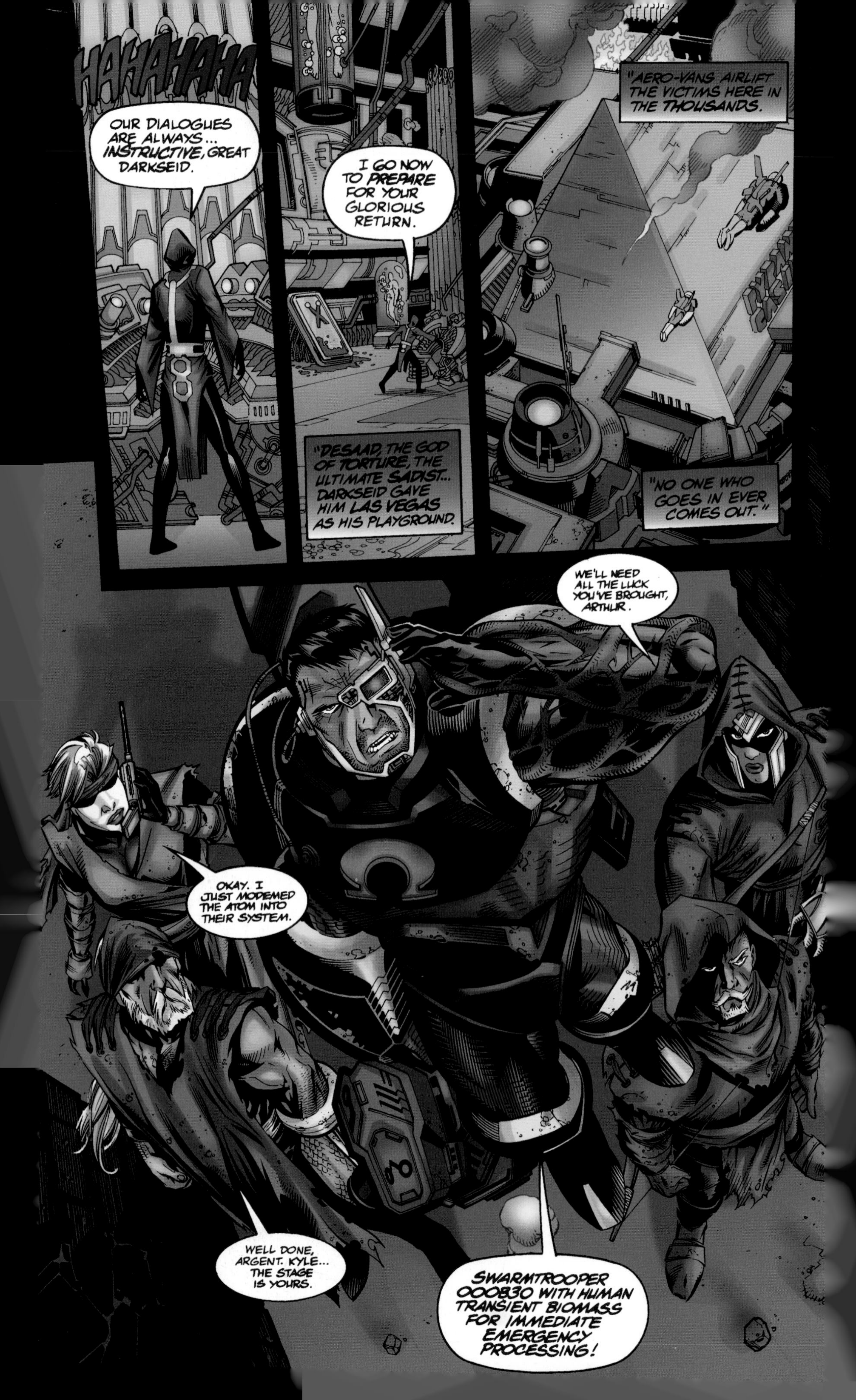
HAHAHAHA
OUR DIALOGUES ARE ALWAYS... INSTRUCTIVE, GREAT DARKSEID.
I GO NOW TO PREPARE FOR YOUR GLORIOUS RETURN.
"DESAAD, THE GOD OF TORTURE, THE ULTIMATE SADIST... DARKSEID GAVE HIM LAS VEGAS AS HIS PLAYGROUND.
"AERO-VANS AIRLIFT THE VICTIMS HERE IN THE THOUSANDS.
"NO ONE WHO GOES IN EVER COMES OUT."
WE'LL NEED ALL THE LUCK YOU'VE BROUGHT, ARTHUR.
OKAY. I JUST MODEMED THE ATOM INTO THEIR SYSTEM.
WELL DONE, ARGENT. KYLE... THE STAGE IS YOURS.
SWARMTROOPER 000830 WITH HUMAN TRANSIENT BIOMASS FOR IMMEDIATE EMERGENCY PROCESSING!

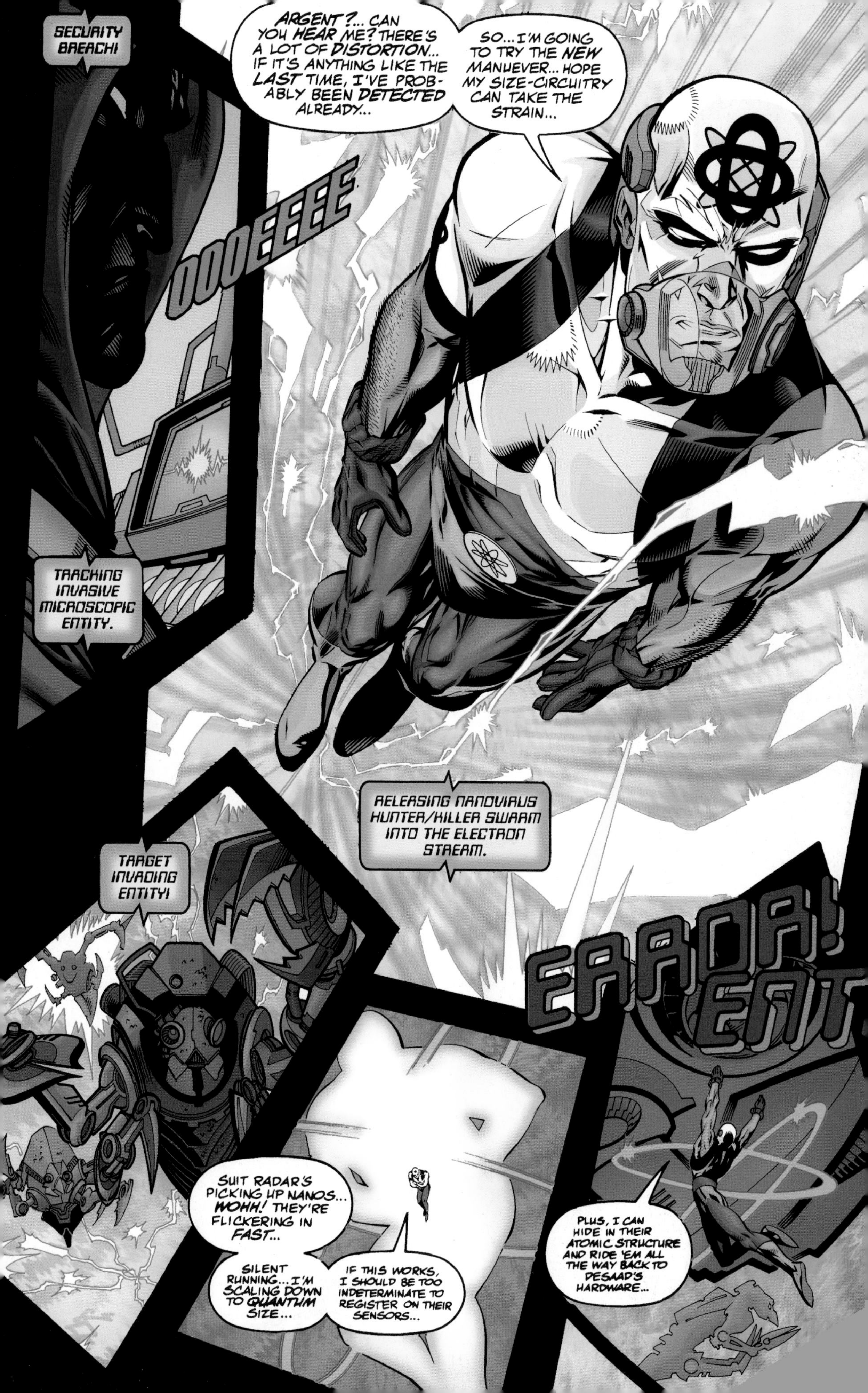
SECURITY BREACH!
ARGENT?... CAN YOU HEAR ME? THERE'S A LOT OF DISTORTION... IF IT'S ANYTHING LIKE THE LAST TIME, I'VE PROBABLY BEEN DETECTED ALREADY...
SO... I'M GOING TO TRY THE NEW MANUEVER... HOPE MY SIZE-CIRCUITRY CAN TAKE THE STRAIN...
OOOEEEEE
TRACKING INVASIVE MICROSCOPIC ENTITY.
RELEASING NANOVIRUS HUNTER/KILLER SWARM INTO THE ELECTRON STREAM.
TARGET INVADING ENTITY!
SUIT RADAR'S PICKING UP NANOS... WOHH! THEY'RE FLICKERING IN FAST...
SILENT RUNNING... I'M SCALING DOWN TO QUANTUM SIZE...
IF THIS WORKS, I SHOULD BE TOO INDETERMINATE TO REGISTER ON THEIR SENSORS...
PLUS, I CAN HIDE IN THEIR ATOMIC STRUCTURE AND RIDE 'EM ALL THE WAY BACK TO DESAAD'S HARDWARE...

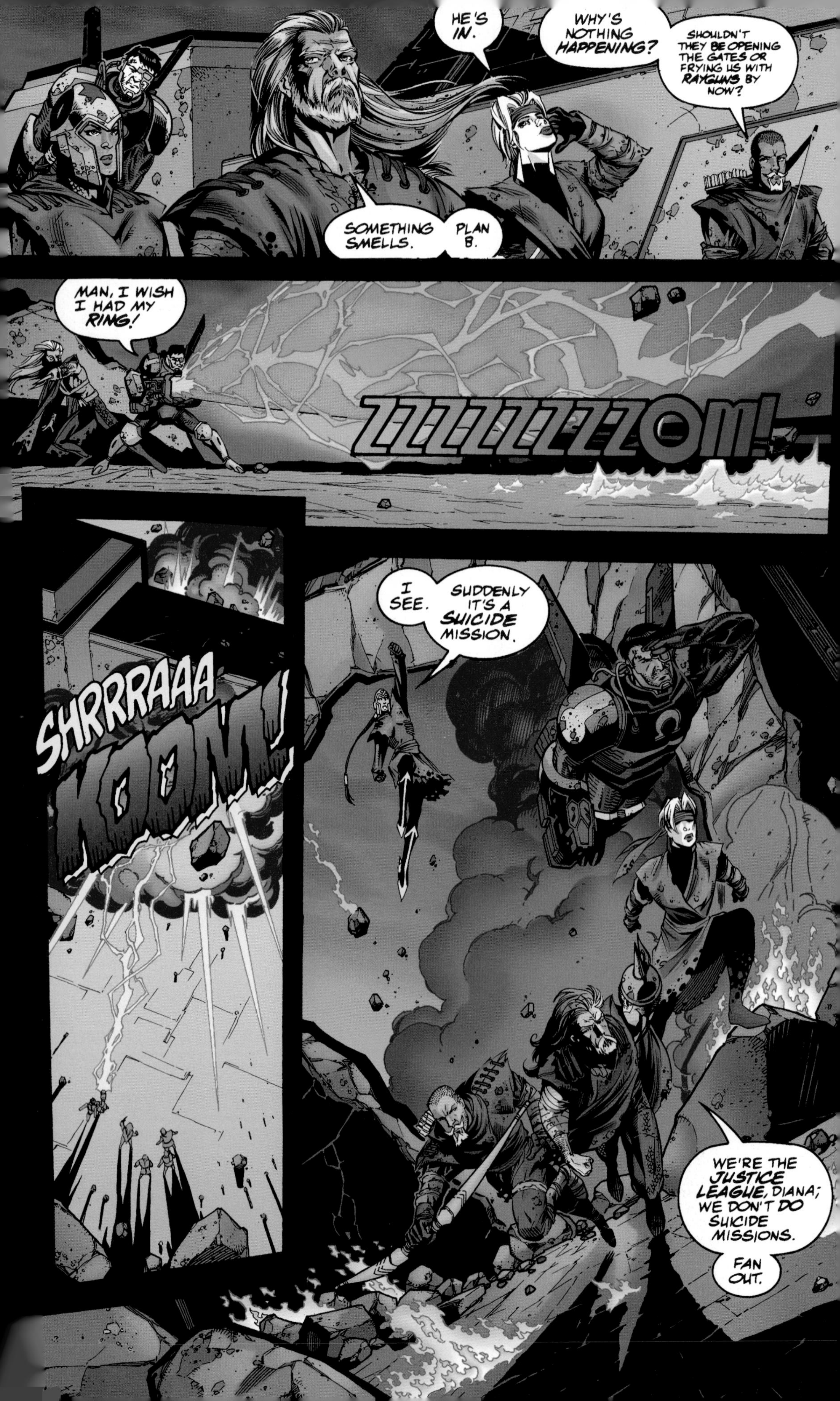
HE'S IN.
WHY'S NOTHING HAPPENING?
SHOULDN'T THEY BE OPENING THE GATES OR FRYING US WITH RAYGUNS BY NOW?
SOMETHING SMELLS.
PLAN B.
MAN, I WISH I HAD MY RING!
ZZZZZZZZZZOM!
SHRRRAAA KOOM!
I SEE.
SUDDENLY IT'S A SUICIDE MISSION.
WE'RE THE JUSTICE LEAGUE, DIANA; WE DON'T DO SUICIDE MISSIONS.
FAN OUT.

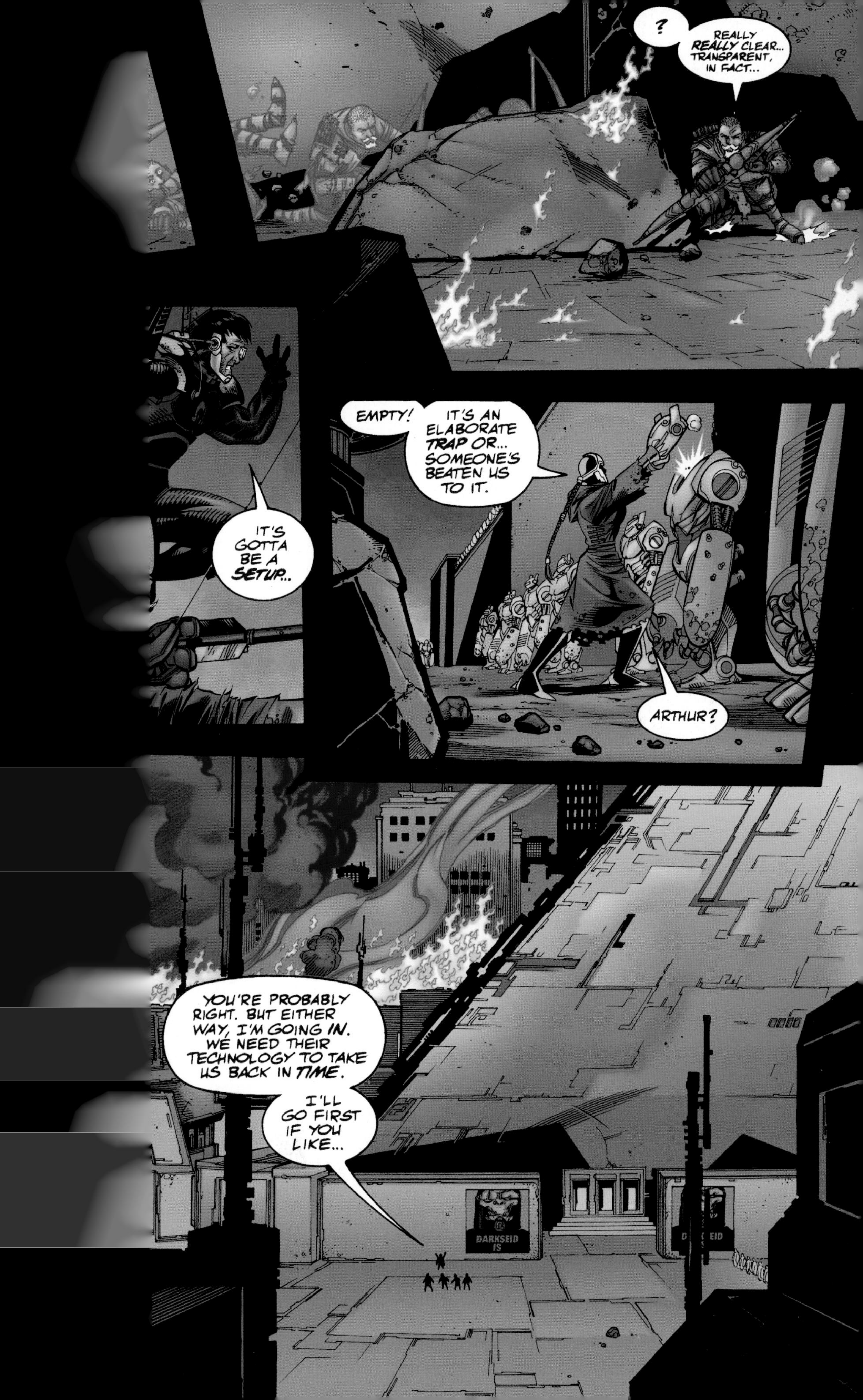
?
REALLY REALLY CLEAR... TRANSPARENT, IN FACT...
IT'S GOTTA BE A SETUP...
EMPTY!
IT'S AN ELABORATE TRAP OR... SOMEONE'S BEATEN US TO IT.
ARTHUR?
YOU'RE PROBABLY RIGHT. BUT EITHER WAY, I'M GOING IN. WE NEED THEIR TECHNOLOGY TO TAKE US BACK IN TIME.
I'LL GO FIRST IF YOU LIKE...
DARKSEID IS

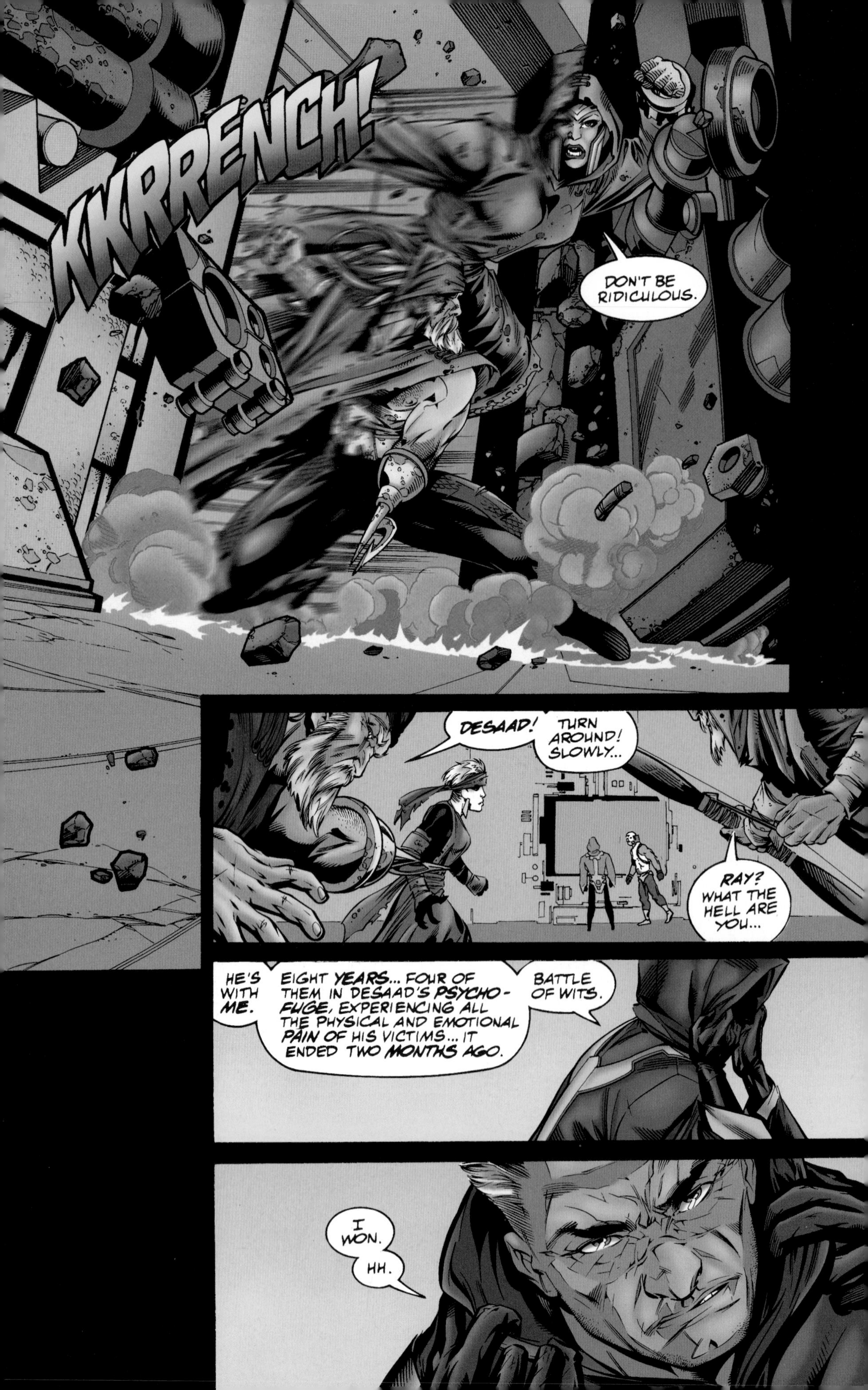
KKRRENCH!
DON'T BE RIDICULOUS.
DESAAD!
TURN AROUND! SLOWLY...
RAY? WHAT THE HELL ARE YOU...
HE'S WITH ME.
EIGHT YEARS... FOUR OF THEM IN DESAAD'S PSYCHO-FUGE, EXPERIENCING ALL THE PHYSICAL AND EMOTIONAL PAIN OF HIS VICTIMS... IT ENDED TWO MONTHS AGO.
BATTLE OF WITS.
I WON.
HH.

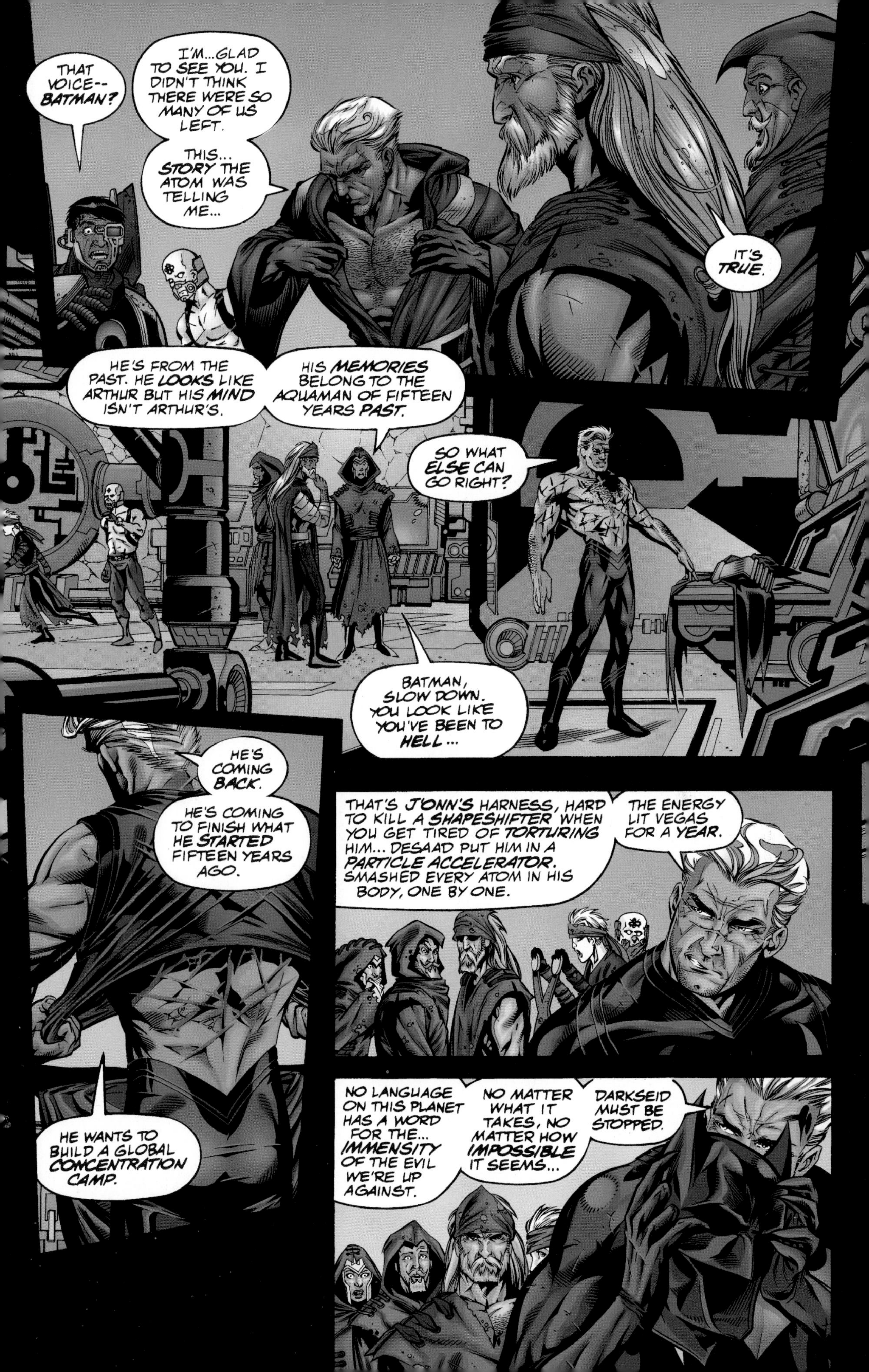
THAT VOICE-- BATMAN?
I'M...GLAD TO SEE YOU. I DIDN'T THINK THERE WERE SO MANY OF US LEFT.
THIS... STORY THE ATOM WAS TELLING ME...
IT'S TRUE.
HE'S FROM THE PAST. HE LOOKS LIKE ARTHUR BUT HIS MIND ISN'T ARTHUR'S.
HIS MEMORIES BELONG TO THE AQUAMAN OF FIFTEEN YEARS PAST.
SO WHAT ELSE CAN GO RIGHT?
BATMAN, SLOW DOWN. YOU LOOK LIKE YOU'VE BEEN TO HELL...
HE'S COMING BACK.
HE'S COMING TO FINISH WHAT HE STARTED FIFTEEN YEARS AGO.
HE WANTS TO BUILD A GLOBAL CONCENTRATION CAMP.
THAT'S J'ONN'S HARNESS, HARD TO KILL A SHAPESHIFTER WHEN YOU GET TIRED OF TORTURING HIM... DESAAD PUT HIM IN A PARTICLE ACCELERATOR. SMASHED EVERY ATOM IN HIS BODY, ONE BY ONE.
THE ENERGY LIT VEGAS FOR A YEAR.
NO LANGUAGE ON THIS PLANET HAS A WORD FOR THE... IMMENSITY OF THE EVIL WE'RE UP AGAINST.
NO MATTER WHAT IT TAKES, NO MATTER HOW IMPOSSIBLE IT SEEMS...
DARKSEID MUST BE STOPPED.

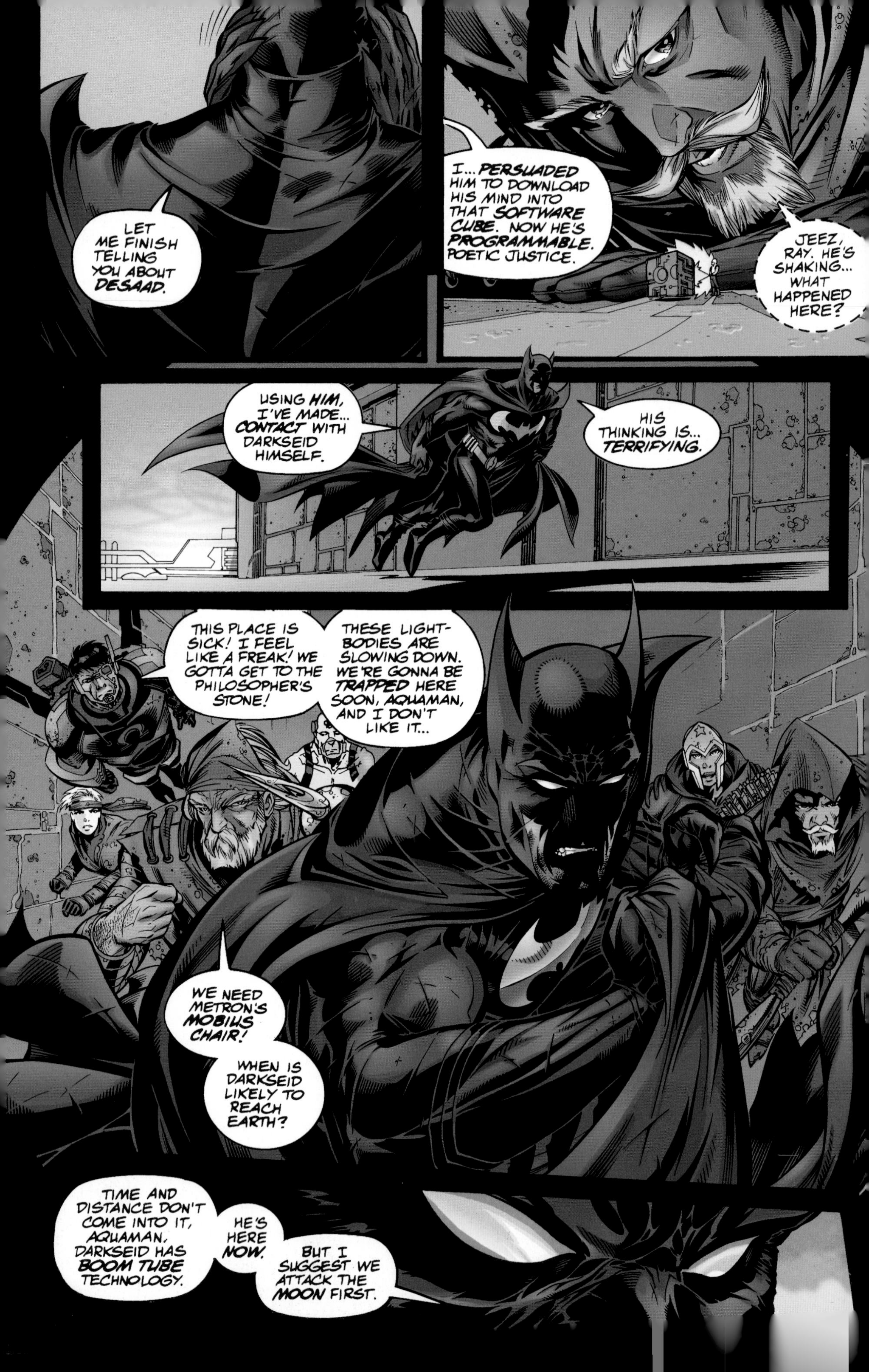
LET ME FINISH TELLING YOU ABOUT DESAAD.
I... PERSUADED HIM TO DOWNLOAD HIS MIND INTO THAT SOFTWARE CUBE. NOW HE'S PROGRAMMABLE. POETIC JUSTICE.
JEEZ, RAY. HE'S SHAKING... WHAT HAPPENED HERE?
USING HIM, I'VE MADE... CONTACT WITH DARKSEID HIMSELF.
HIS THINKING IS... TERRIFYING.
THIS PLACE IS SICK! I FEEL LIKE A FREAK! WE GOTTA GET TO THE PHILOSOPHER'S STONE!
THESE LIGHT-BODIES ARE SLOWING DOWN. WE'RE GONNA BE TRAPPED HERE SOON, AQUAMAN, AND I DON'T LIKE IT...
WE NEED METRON'S MOBIUS CHAIR!
WHEN IS DARKSEID LIKELY TO REACH EARTH?
TIME AND DISTANCE DON'T COME INTO IT, AQUAMAN. DARKSEID HAS BOOM TUBE TECHNOLOGY.
HE'S HERE NOW.
BUT I SUGGEST WE ATTACK THE MOON FIRST.

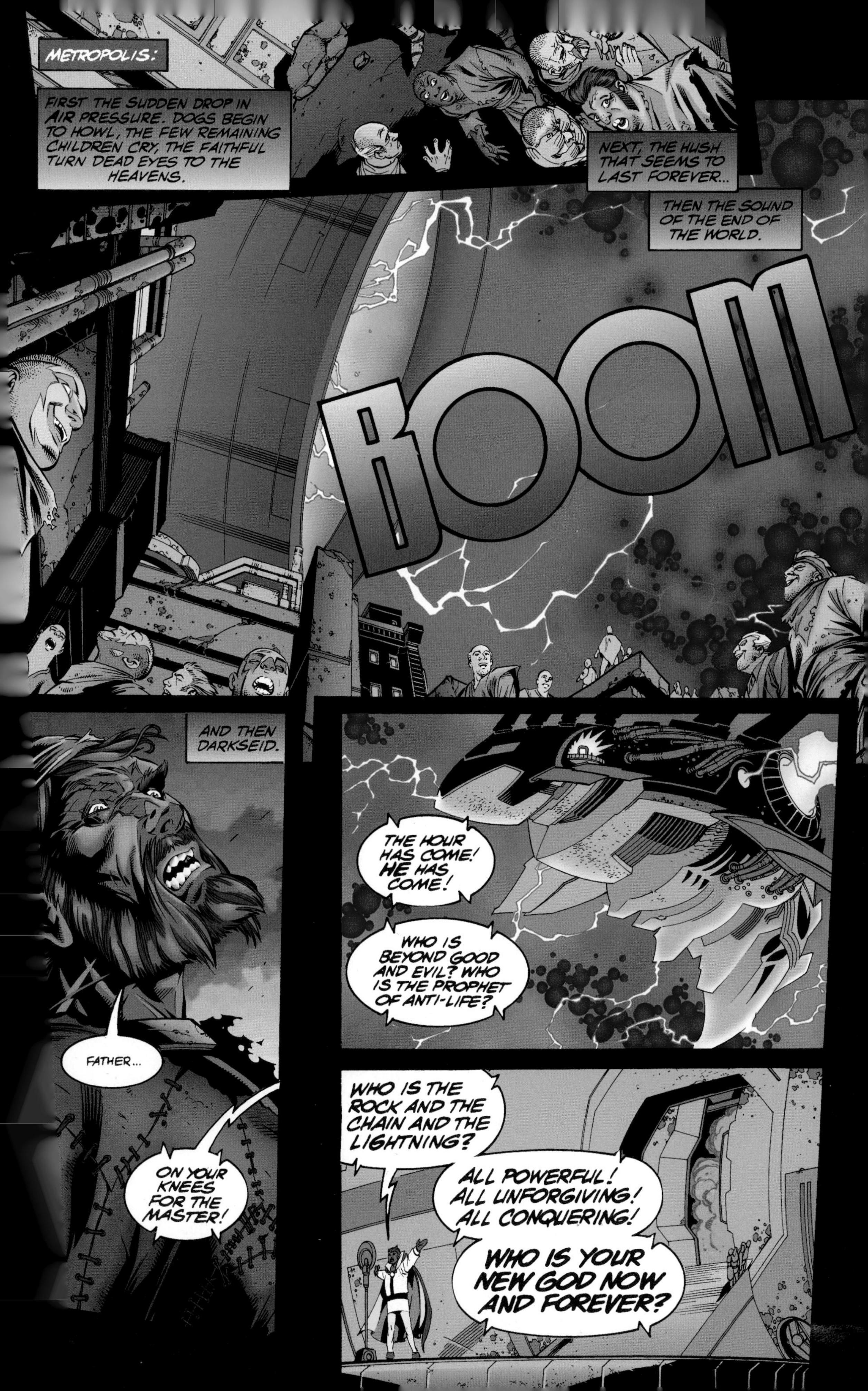
METROPOLIS:
FIRST THE SUDDEN DROP IN AIR PRESSURE. DOGS BEGIN TO HOWL, THE FEW REMAINING CHILDREN CRY, THE FAITHFUL TURN DEAD EYES TO THE HEAVENS.
NEXT, THE HUSH THAT SEEMS TO LAST FOREVER...
THEN THE SOUND OF THE END OF THE WORLD.
BOOM
AND THEN DARKSEID.
THE HOUR HAS COME! HE HAS COME!
WHO IS BEYOND GOOD AND EVIL? WHO IS THE PROPHET OF ANTI-LIFE?
FATHER...
ON YOUR KNEES FOR THE MASTER!
WHO IS THE ROCK AND THE CHAIN AND THE LIGHTNING?
ALL POWERFUL! ALL UNFORGIVING! ALL CONQUERING!
WHO IS YOUR NEW GOD NOW AND FOREVER?

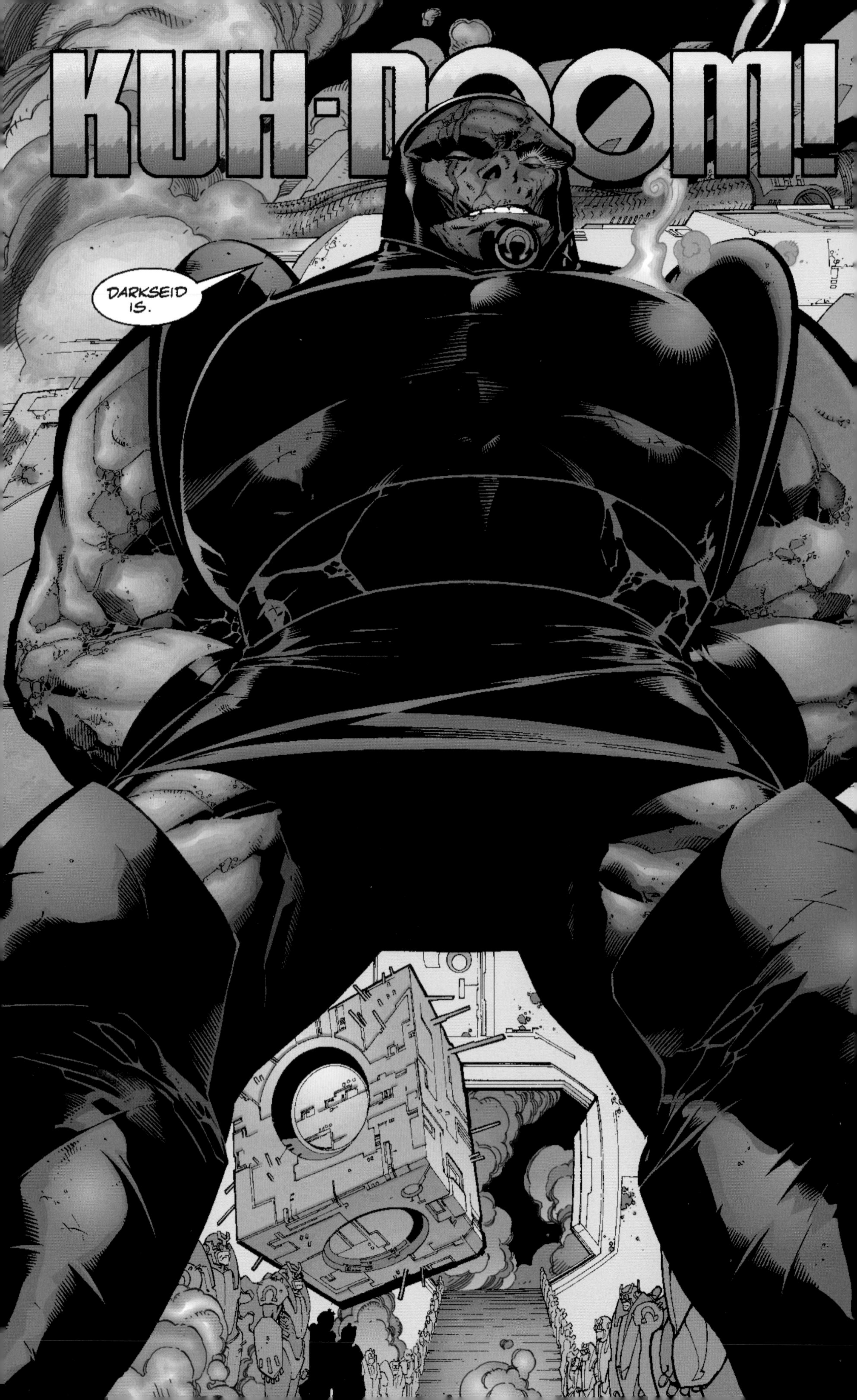
KUH-DOOM!
DARKSEID IS.

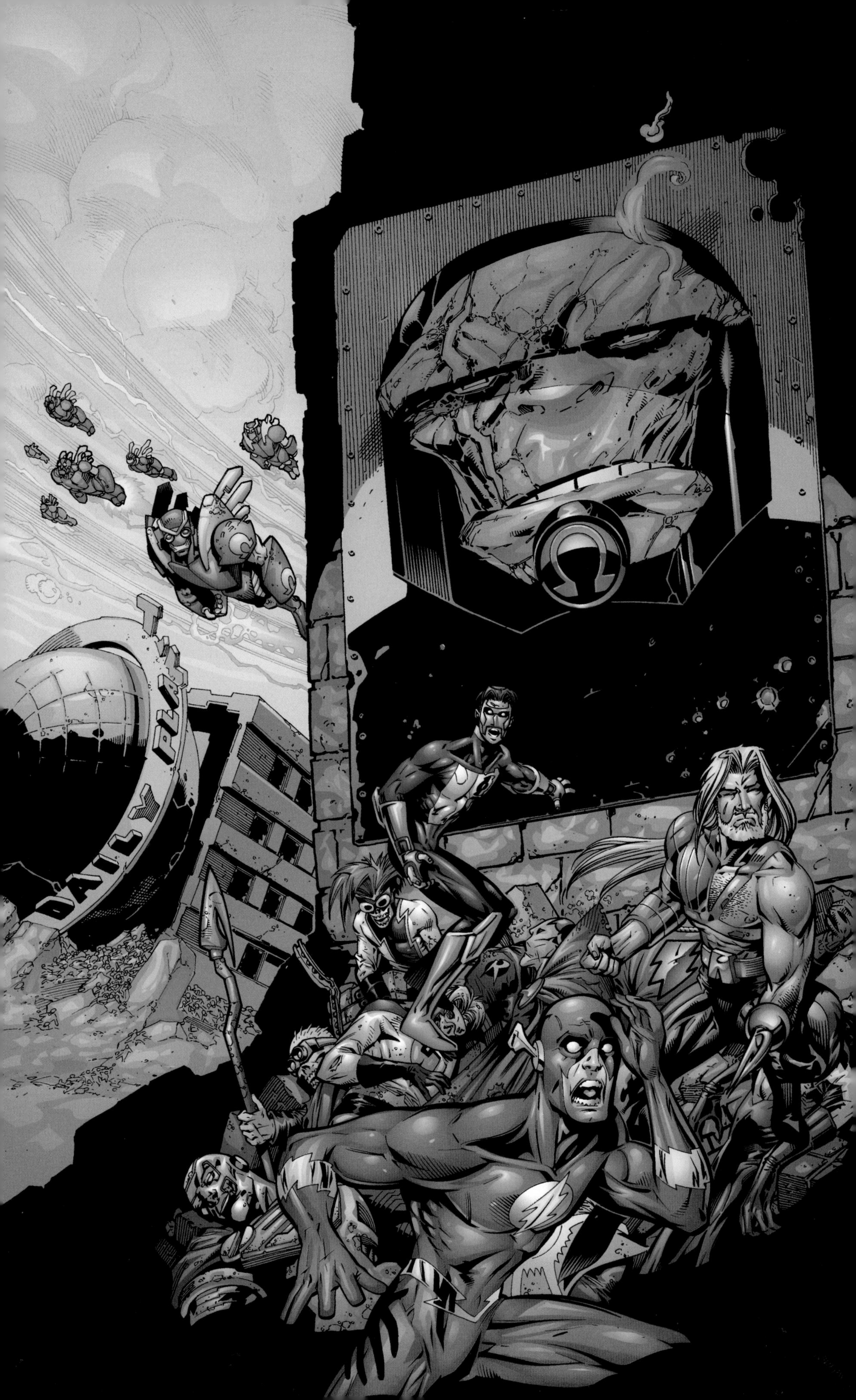

DAILY

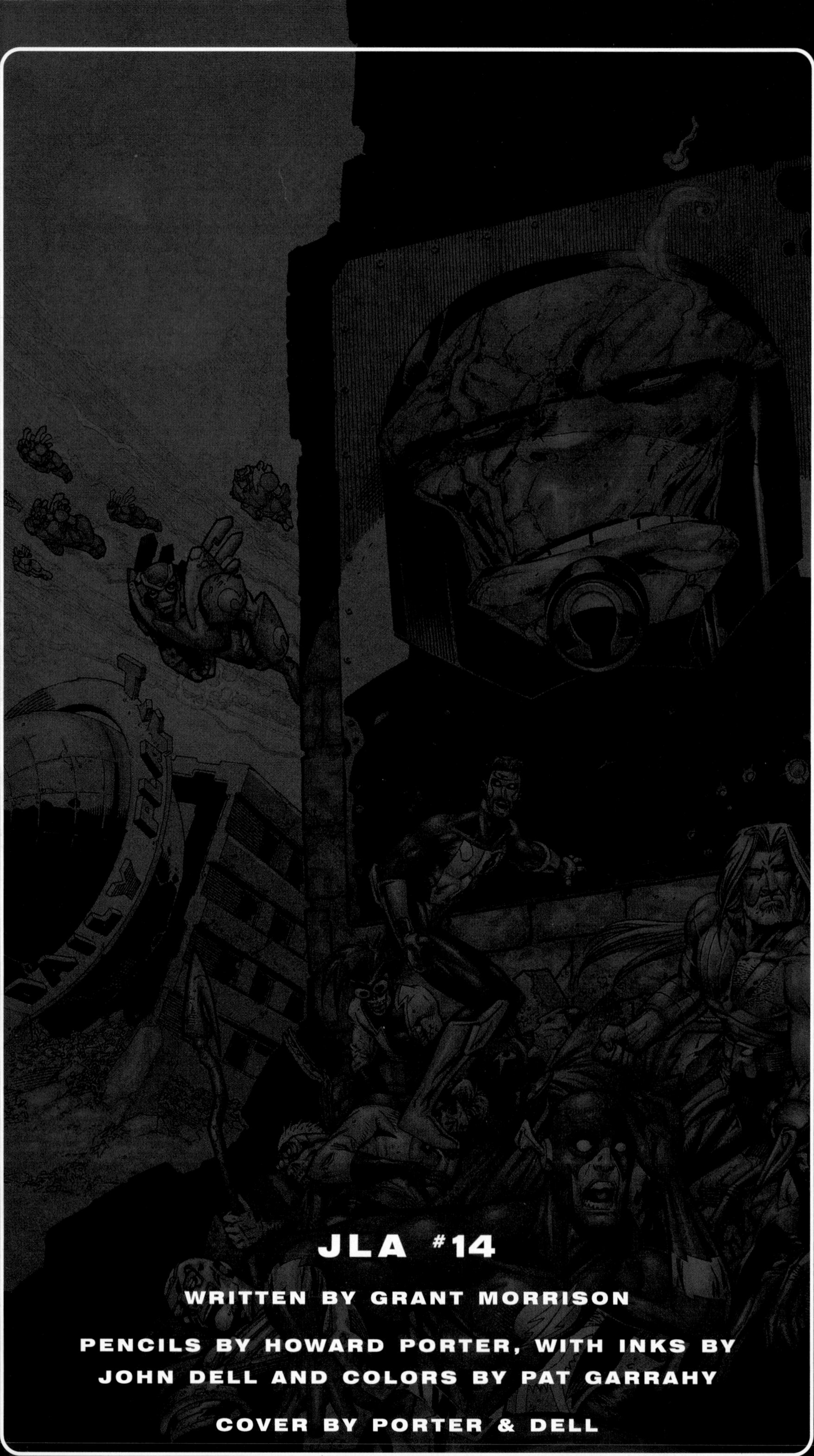

JLA #14

WRITTEN BY GRANT MORRISON

PENCILS BY HOWARD PORTER, WITH INKS BY JOHN DELL AND COLORS BY PAT GARRAHY

COVER BY PORTER & DELL

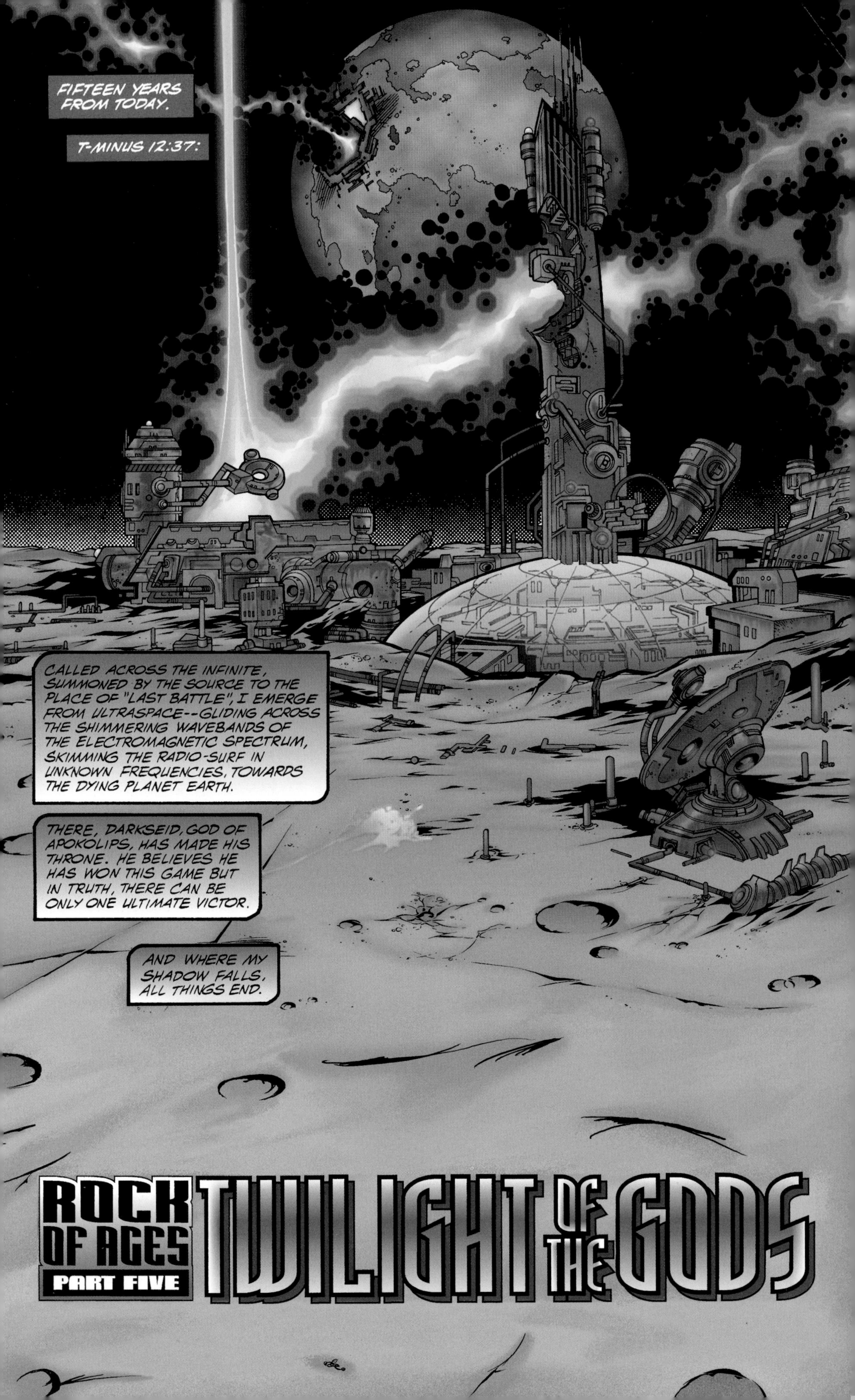
FIFTEEN YEARS FROM TODAY.
T-MINUS 12:37:
CALLED ACROSS THE INFINITE, SUMMONED BY THE SOURCE TO THE PLACE OF "LAST BATTLE", I EMERGE FROM ULTRASPACE--GLIDING ACROSS THE SHIMMERING WAVEBANDS OF THE ELECTROMAGNETIC SPECTRUM, SKIMMING THE RADIO-SURF IN UNKNOWN FREQUENCIES, TOWARDS THE DYING PLANET EARTH.
THERE, DARKSEID, GOD OF APOKOLIPS, HAS MADE HIS THRONE. HE BELIEVES HE HAS WON THIS GAME BUT IN TRUTH, THERE CAN BE ONLY ONE ULTIMATE VICTOR.
AND WHERE MY SHADOW FALLS, ALL THINGS END.
ROCK OF AGES
PART FIVE
TWILIGHT OF THE GODS

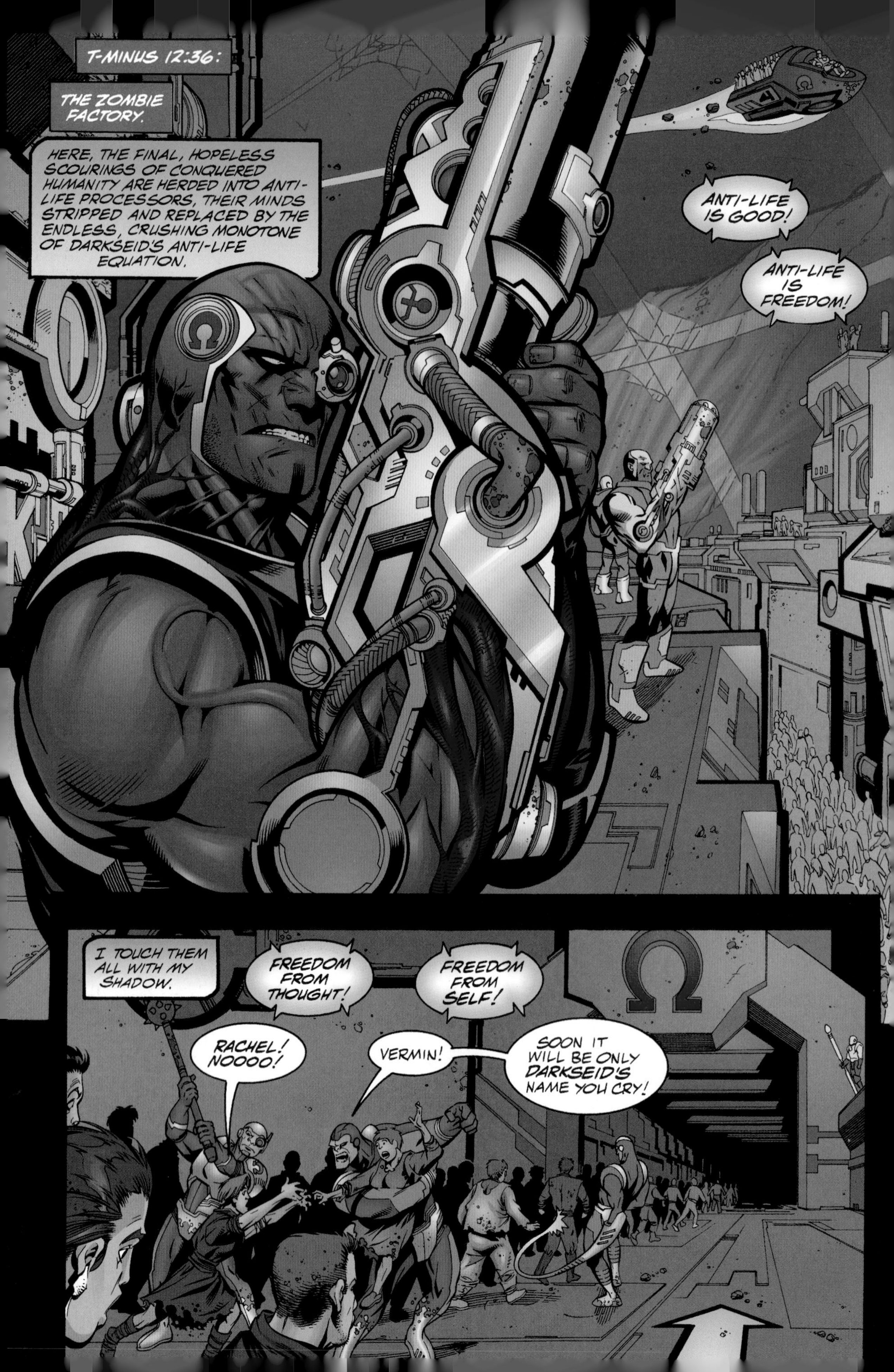
T-MINUS 12:36:
THE ZOMBIE FACTORY.
HERE, THE FINAL, HOPELESS SCOURINGS OF CONQUERED HUMANITY ARE HERDED INTO ANTI-LIFE PROCESSORS, THEIR MINDS STRIPPED AND REPLACED BY THE ENDLESS, CRUSHING MONOTONE OF DARKSEID'S ANTI-LIFE EQUATION.
ANTI-LIFE IS GOOD!
ANTI-LIFE IS FREEDOM!
I TOUCH THEM ALL WITH MY SHADOW.
FREEDOM FROM THOUGHT!
FREEDOM FROM SELF!
RACHEL! NOOOO!
VERMIN!
SOON IT WILL BE ONLY DARKSEID'S NAME YOU CRY!

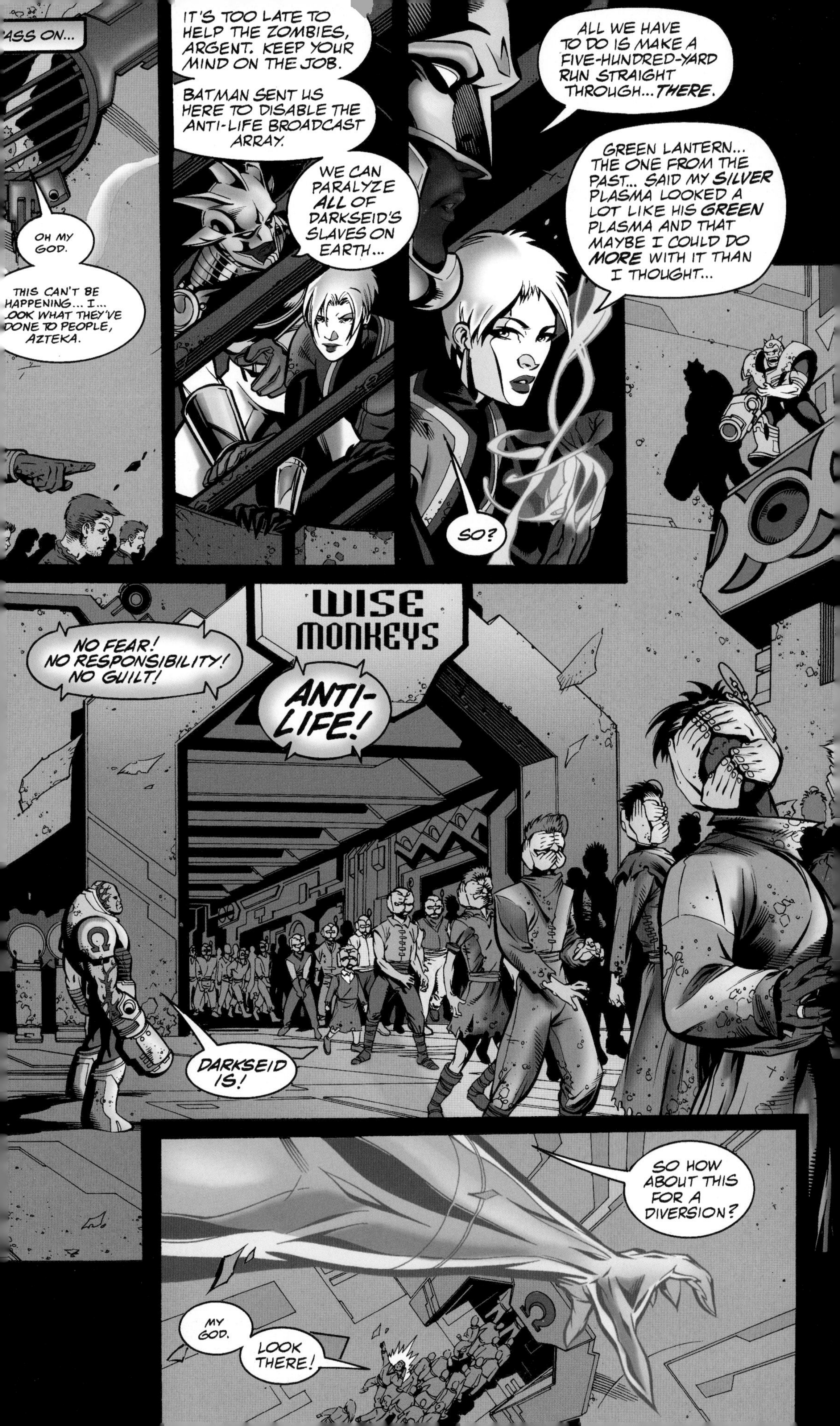

ASS ON...
IT'S TOO LATE TO HELP THE ZOMBIES, ARGENT. KEEP YOUR MIND ON THE JOB.
BATMAN SENT US HERE TO DISABLE THE ANTI-LIFE BROADCAST ARRAY.
ALL WE HAVE TO DO IS MAKE A FIVE-HUNDRED-YARD RUN STRAIGHT THROUGH... THERE.
OH MY GOD.
THIS CAN'T BE HAPPENING... I... LOOK WHAT THEY'VE DONE TO PEOPLE, AZTEKA.
WE CAN PARALYZE ALL OF DARKSEID'S SLAVES ON EARTH...
GREEN LANTERN... THE ONE FROM THE PAST... SAID MY SILVER PLASMA LOOKED A LOT LIKE HIS GREEN PLASMA AND THAT MAYBE I COULD DO MORE WITH IT THAN I THOUGHT...
SO?
WISE MONKEYS
NO FEAR! NO RESPONSIBILITY! NO GUILT!
ANTI-LIFE!
DARKSEID IS!
SO HOW ABOUT THIS FOR A DIVERSION?
MY GOD.
LOOK THERE!

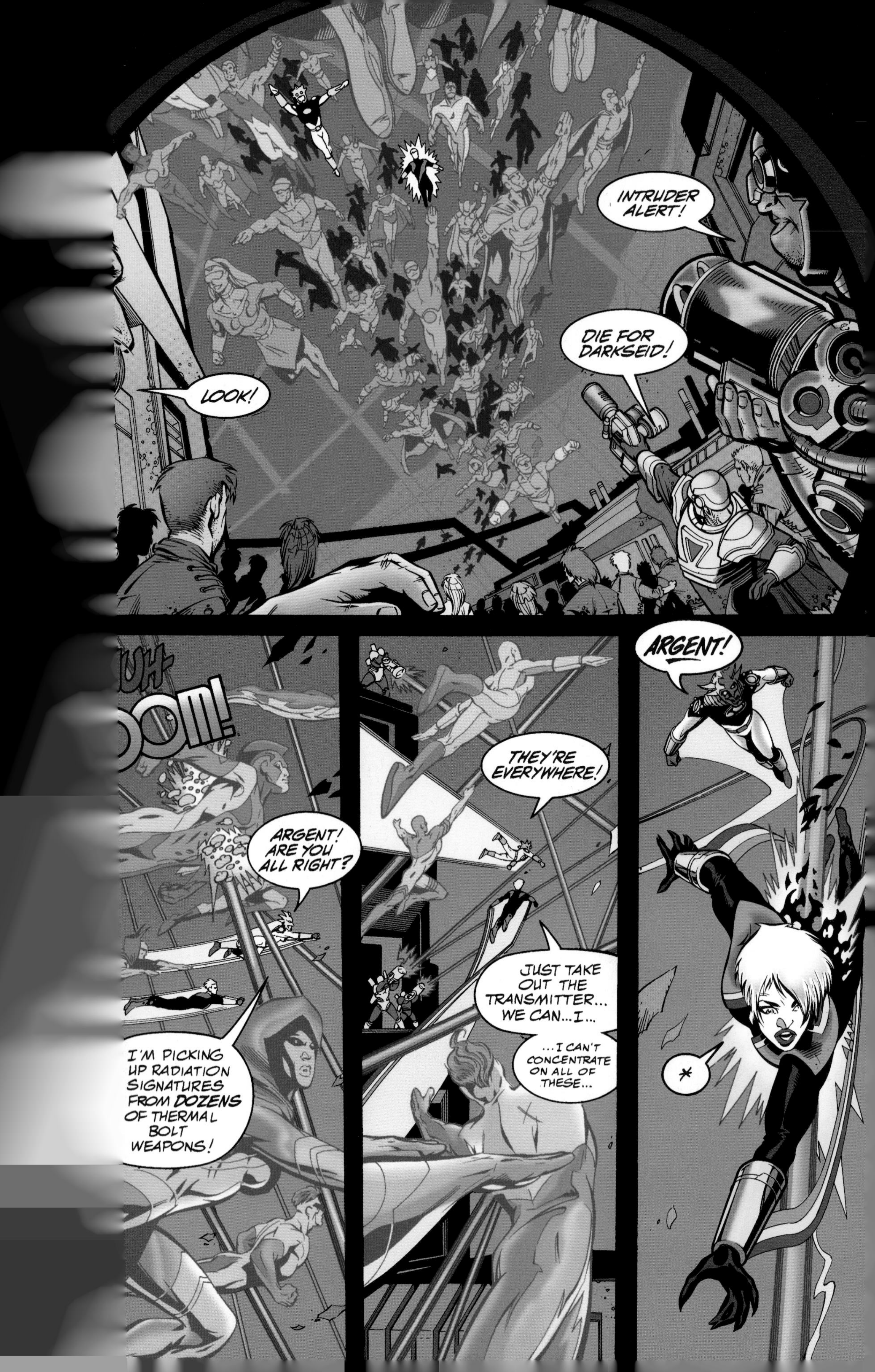

INTRUDER ALERT!
DIE FOR DARKSEID!
LOOK!
UH
OOM!
ARGENT! ARE YOU ALL RIGHT?
I'M PICKING UP RADIATION SIGNATURES FROM DOZENS OF THERMAL BOLT WEAPONS!
THEY'RE EVERYWHERE!
JUST TAKE OUT THE TRANSMITTER... WE CAN...I...
...I CAN'T CONCENTRATE ON ALL OF THESE...
ARGENT!
*

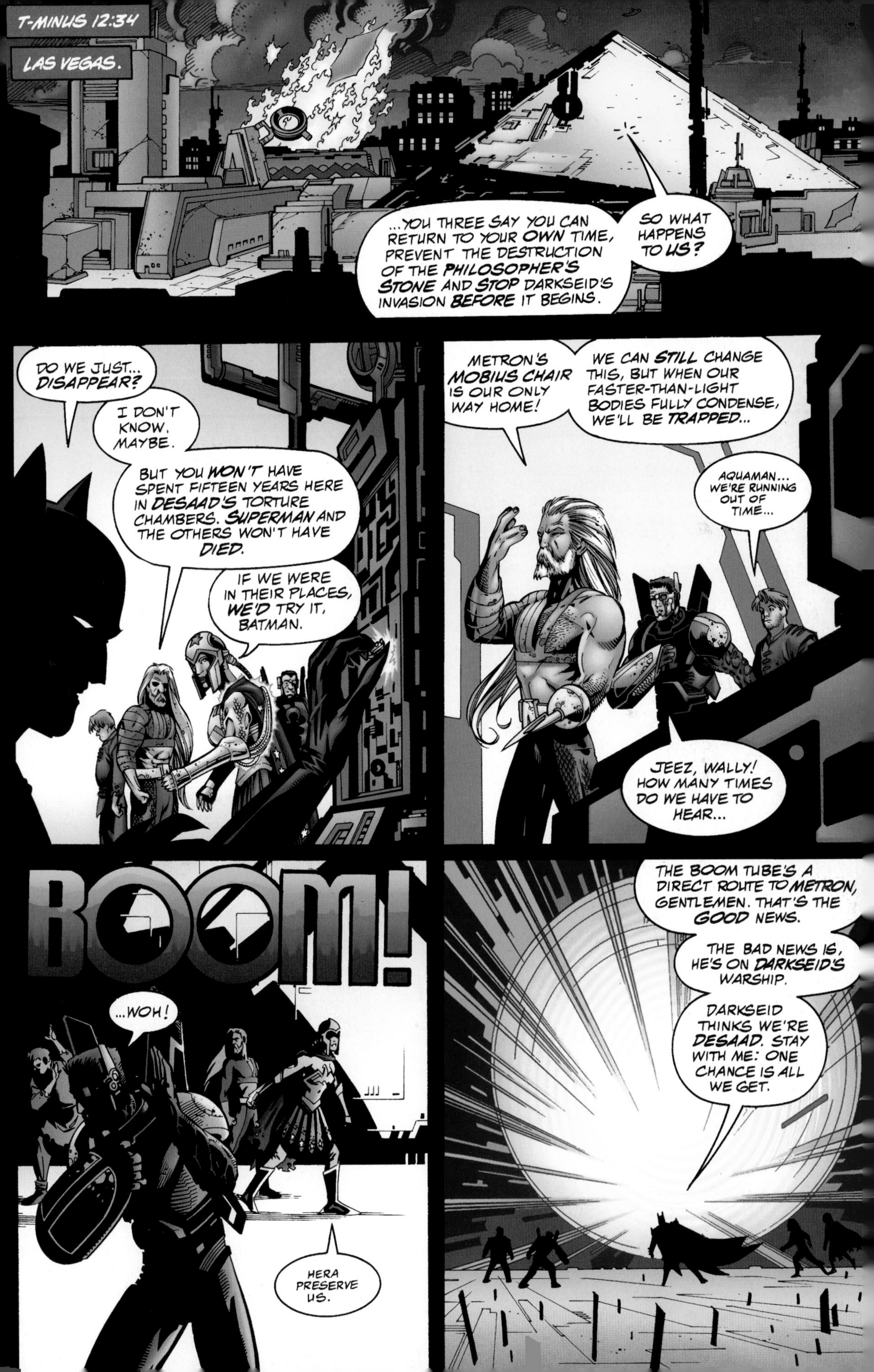
T-MINUS 12:34
LAS VEGAS.
...YOU THREE SAY YOU CAN RETURN TO YOUR OWN TIME, PREVENT THE DESTRUCTION OF THE PHILOSOPHER'S STONE AND STOP DARKSEID'S INVASION BEFORE IT BEGINS.
SO WHAT HAPPENS TO US?
DO WE JUST... DISAPPEAR?
I DON'T KNOW. MAYBE.
BUT YOU WON'T HAVE SPENT FIFTEEN YEARS HERE IN DESAAD'S TORTURE CHAMBERS. SUPERMAN AND THE OTHERS WON'T HAVE DIED.
IF WE WERE IN THEIR PLACES, WE'D TRY IT, BATMAN.
METRON'S MOBIUS CHAIR IS OUR ONLY WAY HOME!
WE CAN STILL CHANGE THIS, BUT WHEN OUR FASTER-THAN-LIGHT BODIES FULLY CONDENSE, WE'LL BE TRAPPED...
AQUAMAN... WE'RE RUNNING OUT OF TIME...
JEEZ, WALLY! HOW MANY TIMES DO WE HAVE TO HEAR...
BOOM!
...WOH!
HERA PRESERVE US.
THE BOOM TUBE'S A DIRECT ROUTE TO METRON, GENTLEMEN. THAT'S THE GOOD NEWS.
THE BAD NEWS IS, HE'S ON DARKSEID'S WARSHIP.
DARKSEID THINKS WE'RE DESAAD. STAY WITH ME: ONE CHANCE IS ALL WE GET.

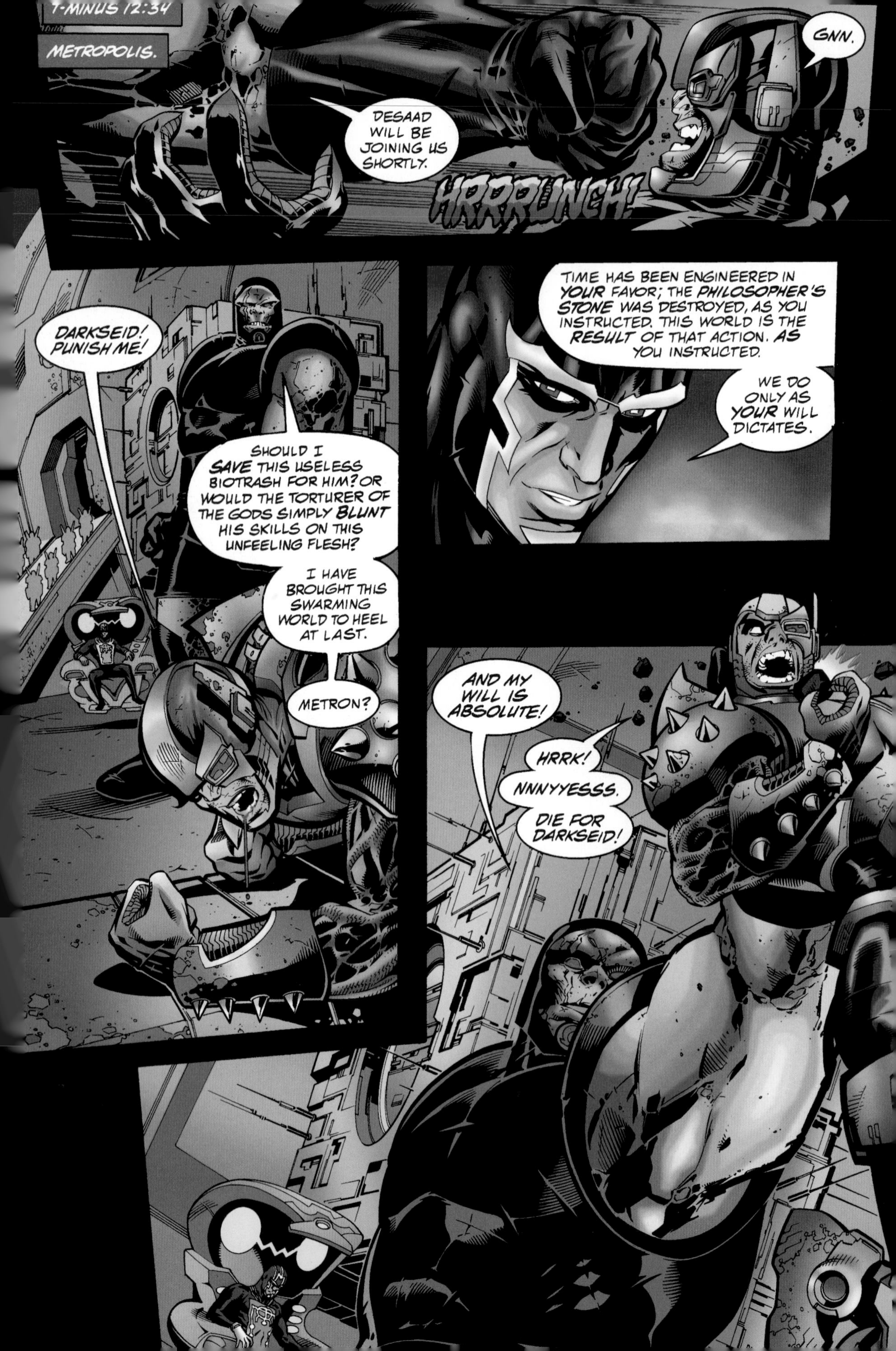
T-MINUS 12:34
METROPOLIS.
DESAAD WILL BE JOINING US SHORTLY.
GNN.
HRRRUNCH!
DARKSEID! PUNISH ME!
SHOULD I SAVE THIS USELESS BIOTRASH FOR HIM? OR WOULD THE TORTURER OF THE GODS SIMPLY BLUNT HIS SKILLS ON THIS UNFEELING FLESH?
I HAVE BROUGHT THIS SWARMING WORLD TO HEEL AT LAST.
METRON?
TIME HAS BEEN ENGINEERED IN YOUR FAVOR; THE PHILOSOPHER'S STONE WAS DESTROYED, AS YOU INSTRUCTED. THIS WORLD IS THE RESULT OF THAT ACTION. AS YOU INSTRUCTED.
WE DO ONLY AS YOUR WILL DICTATES.
AND MY WILL IS ABSOLUTE!
HRRK!
NNNYYESSS.
DIE FOR DARKSEID!

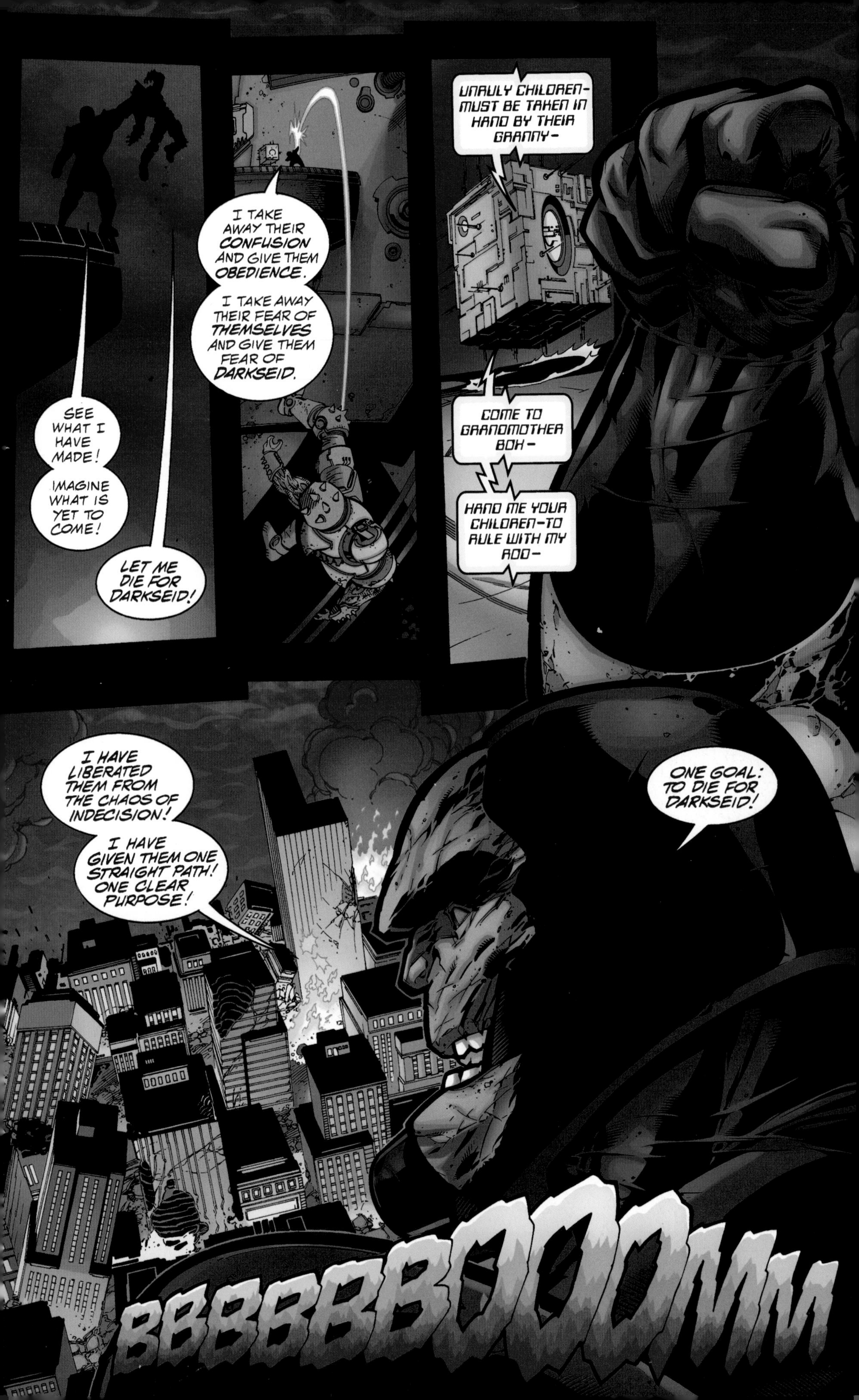
SEE WHAT I HAVE MADE!
IMAGINE WHAT IS YET TO COME!
LET ME DIE FOR DARKSEID!
I TAKE AWAY THEIR CONFUSION AND GIVE THEM OBEDIENCE.
I TAKE AWAY THEIR FEAR OF THEMSELVES AND GIVE THEM FEAR OF DARKSEID.
UNRULY CHILDREN- MUST BE TAKEN IN HAND BY THEIR GRANNY-
COME TO GRANDMOTHER BOX-
HAND ME YOUR CHILDREN-TO RULE WITH MY ROD-
I HAVE LIBERATED THEM FROM THE CHAOS OF INDECISION!
I HAVE GIVEN THEM ONE STRAIGHT PATH! ONE CLEAR PURPOSE!
ONE GOAL: TO DIE FOR DARKSEID!
BBBBBBOOOMM

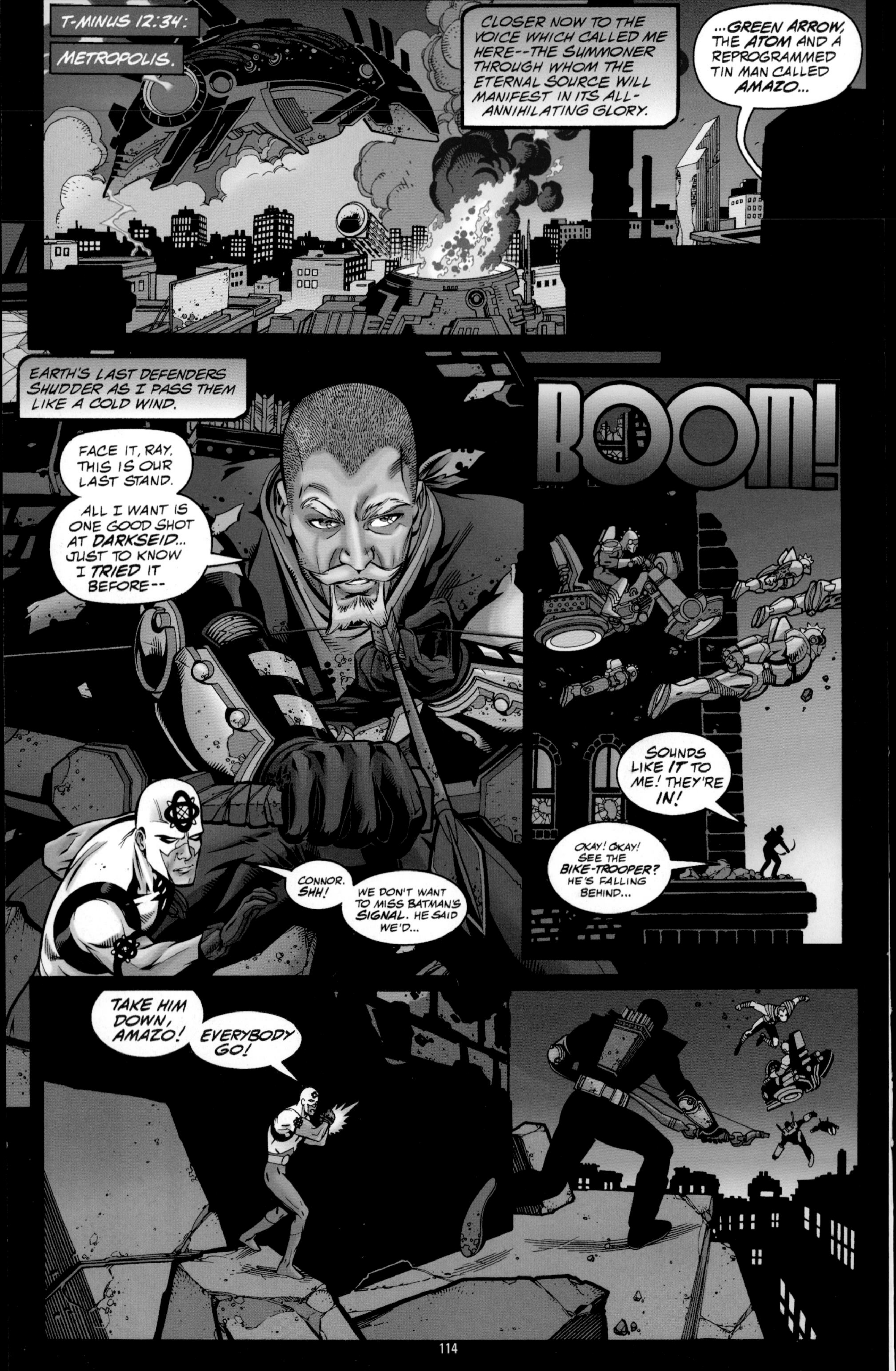
T-MINUS 12:34:
METROPOLIS.
CLOSER NOW TO THE VOICE WHICH CALLED ME HERE--THE SUMMONER THROUGH WHOM THE ETERNAL SOURCE WILL MANIFEST IN ITS ALL-ANNIHILATING GLORY.
...GREEN ARROW, THE ATOM AND A REPROGRAMMED TIN MAN CALLED AMAZO...
EARTH'S LAST DEFENDERS SHUDDER AS I PASS THEM LIKE A COLD WIND.
FACE IT, RAY. THIS IS OUR LAST STAND.
ALL I WANT IS ONE GOOD SHOT AT DARKSEID... JUST TO KNOW I TRIED IT BEFORE--
CONNOR. SHH!
WE DON'T WANT TO MISS BATMAN'S SIGNAL. HE SAID WE'D...
BOOM!
SOUNDS LIKE IT TO ME! THEY'RE IN!
OKAY! OKAY! SEE THE BIKE-TROOPER? HE'S FALLING BEHIND...
TAKE HIM DOWN, AMAZO!
EVERYBODY GO!

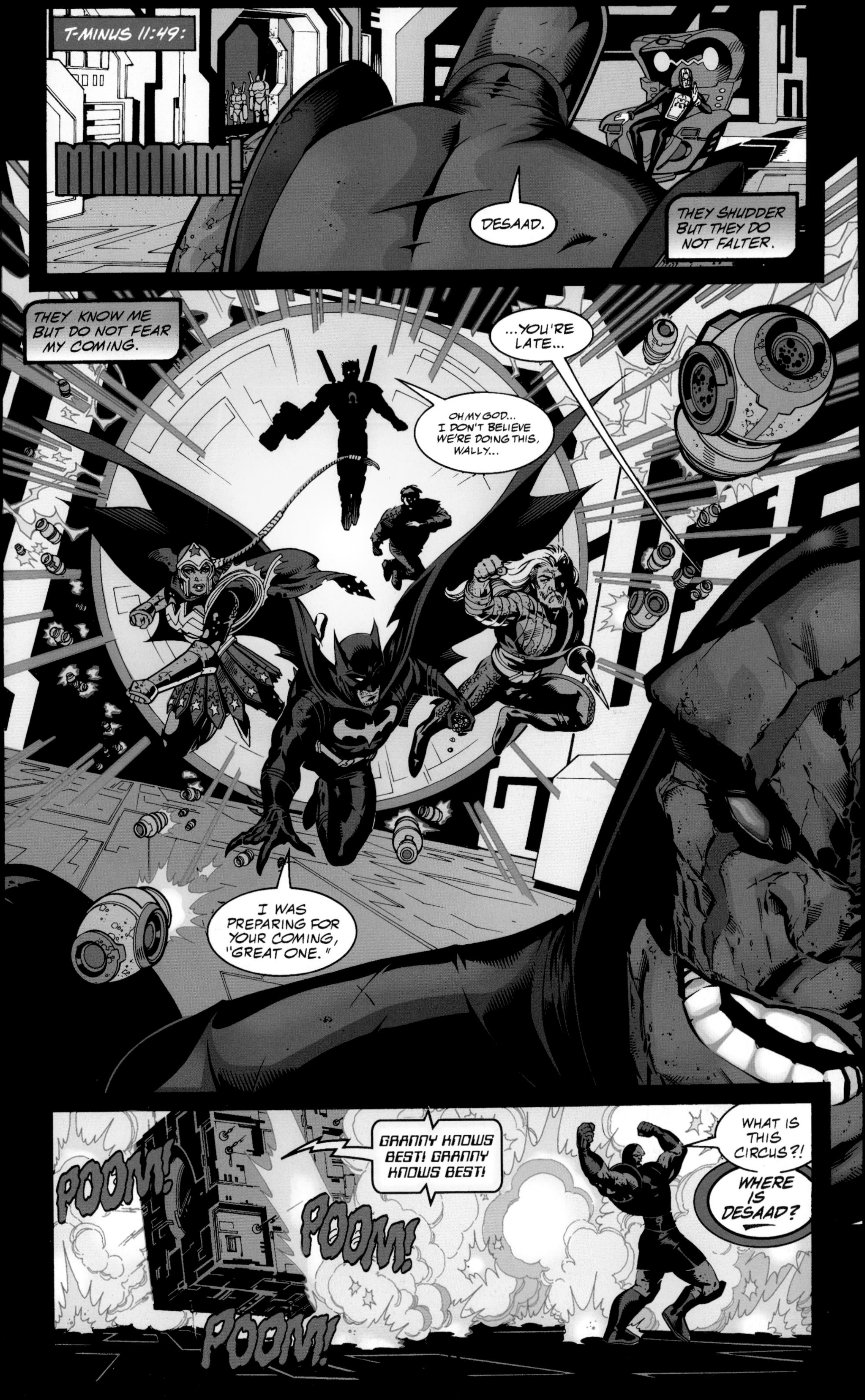
T-MINUS 11:49:
MMMMMM!
DESAAD.
THEY SHUDDER BUT THEY DO NOT FALTER.
THEY KNOW ME BUT DO NOT FEAR MY COMING.
...YOU'RE LATE...
OH MY GOD... I DON'T BELIEVE WE'RE DOING THIS, WALLY...
I WAS PREPARING FOR YOUR COMING, "GREAT ONE."
POOM!
GRANNY KNOWS BEST! GRANNY KNOWS BEST!
POOM!
POOM!
WHAT IS THIS CIRCUS?!
WHERE IS DESAAD?

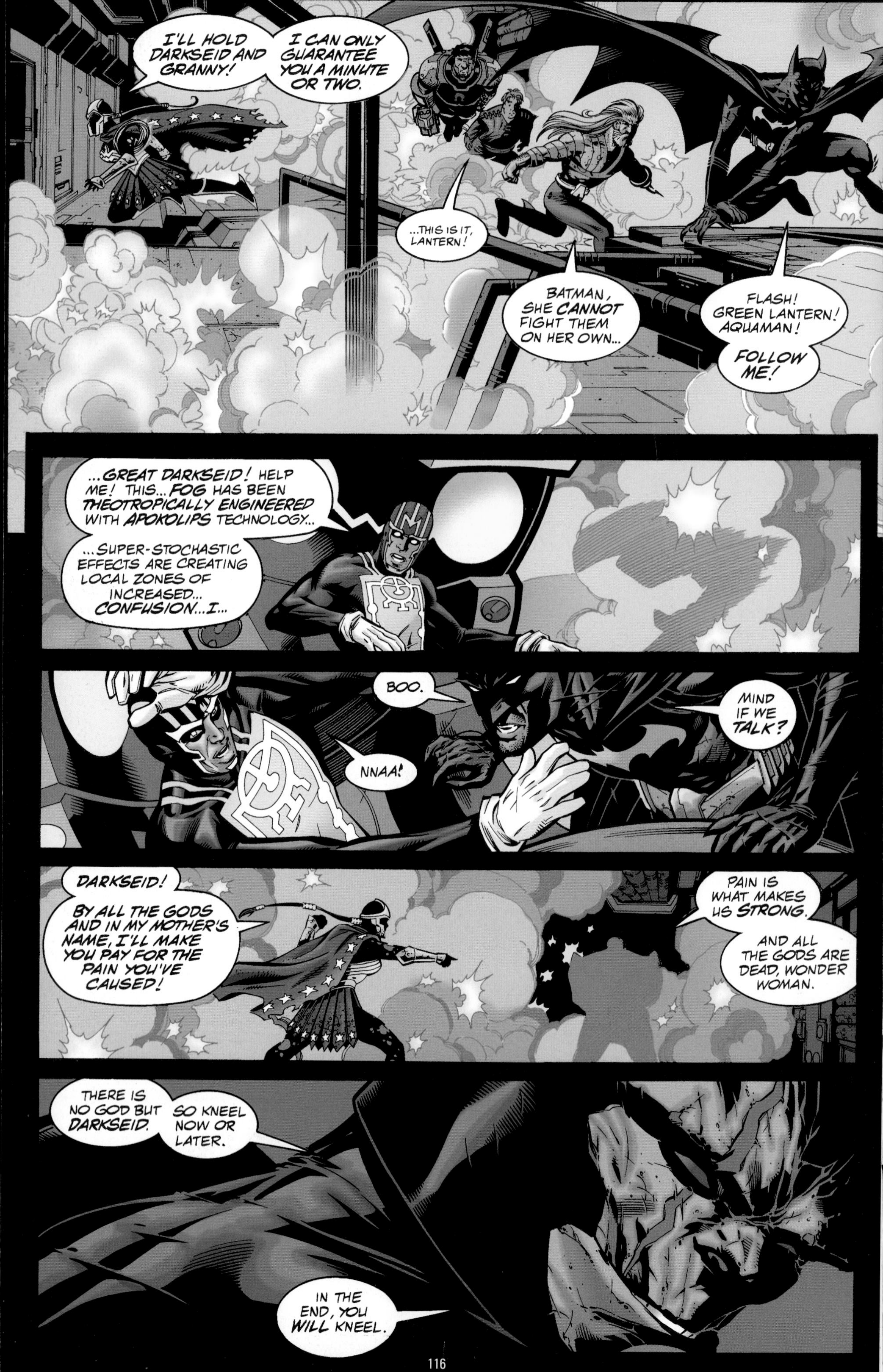
I'LL HOLD DARKSEID AND GRANNY!
I CAN ONLY GUARANTEE YOU A MINUTE OR TWO.
...THIS IS IT, LANTERN!
BATMAN, SHE CANNOT FIGHT THEM ON HER OWN...
FLASH! GREEN LANTERN! AQUAMAN!
FOLLOW ME!
...GREAT DARKSEID! HELP ME! THIS... FOG HAS BEEN THEOTROPICALLY ENGINEERED WITH APOKOLIPS TECHNOLOGY...
...SUPER-STOCHASTIC EFFECTS ARE CREATING LOCAL ZONES OF INCREASED... CONFUSION...I...
BOO.
MIND IF WE TALK?
NNAA!
DARKSEID!
BY ALL THE GODS AND IN MY MOTHER'S NAME, I'LL MAKE YOU PAY FOR THE PAIN YOU'VE CAUSED!
PAIN IS WHAT MAKES US STRONG.
AND ALL THE GODS ARE DEAD, WONDER WOMAN.
THERE IS NO GOD BUT DARKSEID.
SO KNEEL NOW OR LATER.
IN THE END, YOU WILL KNEEL.

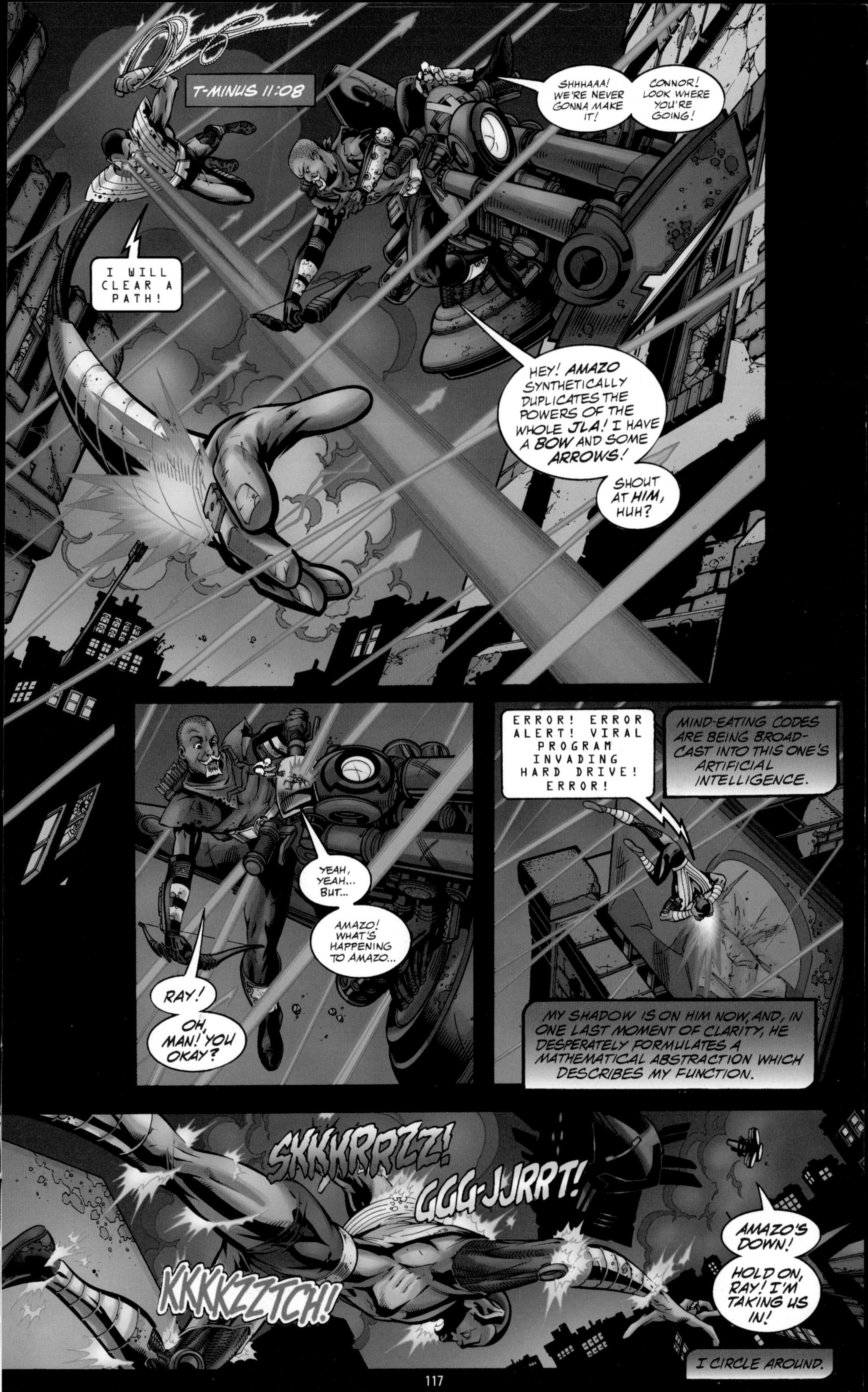

T-MINUS 11:08
SHHHAAA! WE'RE NEVER GONNA MAKE IT!
CONNOR! LOOK WHERE YOU'RE GOING!
I WILL CLEAR A PATH!
HEY! AMAZO SYNTHETICALLY DUPLICATES THE POWERS OF THE WHOLE JLA! I HAVE A BOW AND SOME ARROWS!
SHOUT AT HIM, HUH?
YEAH, YEAH... BUT...
AMAZO! WHAT'S HAPPENING TO AMAZO...
RAY!
OH, MAN! YOU OKAY?
ERROR! ERROR ALERT! VIRAL PROGRAM INVADING HARD DRIVE! ERROR!
MIND-EATING CODES ARE BEING BROADCAST INTO THIS ONE'S ARTIFICIAL INTELLIGENCE.
MY SHADOW IS ON HIM NOW, AND, IN ONE LAST MOMENT OF CLARITY, HE DESPERATELY FORMULATES A MATHEMATICAL ABSTRACTION WHICH DESCRIBES MY FUNCTION.
SKKKRRZZ!
GGG-JJRRT!
KKKKZZZTCH!
AMAZO'S DOWN!
HOLD ON, RAY! I'M TAKING US IN!
I CIRCLE AROUND.

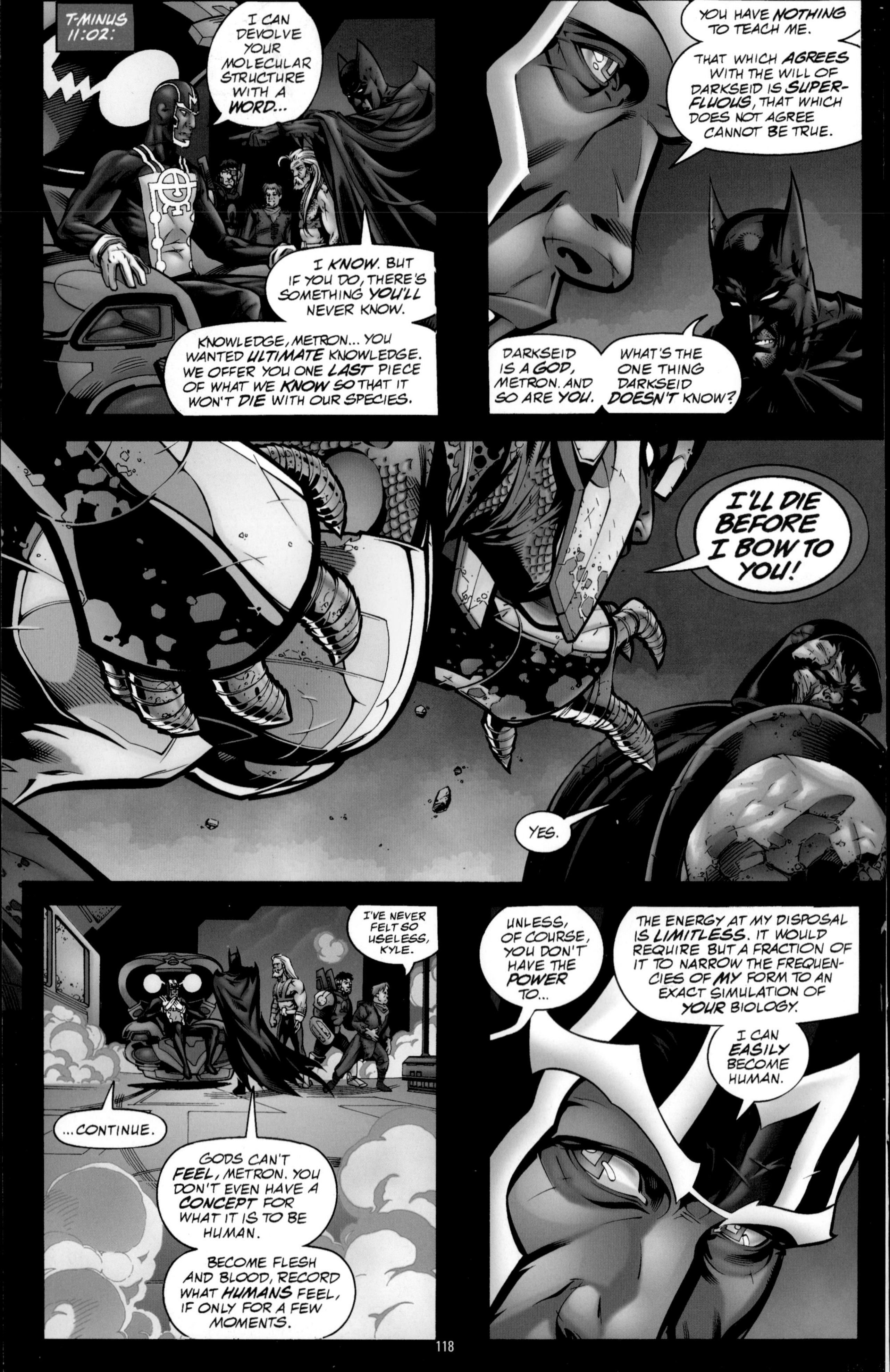

T-MINUS 11:02:
I CAN DEVOLVE YOUR MOLECULAR STRUCTURE WITH A WORD...
I KNOW. BUT IF YOU DO, THERE'S SOMETHING YOU'LL NEVER KNOW.
KNOWLEDGE, METRON... YOU WANTED ULTIMATE KNOWLEDGE. WE OFFER YOU ONE LAST PIECE OF WHAT WE KNOW SO THAT IT WON'T DIE WITH OUR SPECIES.
YOU HAVE NOTHING TO TEACH ME.
THAT WHICH AGREES WITH THE WILL OF DARKSEID IS SUPERFLUOUS, THAT WHICH DOES NOT AGREE CANNOT BE TRUE.
DARKSEID IS A GOD, METRON. AND SO ARE YOU.
WHAT'S THE ONE THING DARKSEID DOESN'T KNOW?
I'LL DIE BEFORE I BOW TO YOU!
YES.
I'VE NEVER FELT SO USELESS, KYLE.
...CONTINUE.
GODS CAN'T FEEL, METRON. YOU DON'T EVEN HAVE A CONCEPT FOR WHAT IT IS TO BE HUMAN.
BECOME FLESH AND BLOOD, RECORD WHAT HUMANS FEEL, IF ONLY FOR A FEW MOMENTS.
UNLESS, OF COURSE, YOU DON'T HAVE THE POWER TO...
THE ENERGY AT MY DISPOSAL IS LIMITLESS. IT WOULD REQUIRE BUT A FRACTION OF IT TO NARROW THE FREQUENCIES OF MY FORM TO AN EXACT SIMULATION OF YOUR BIOLOGY.
I CAN EASILY BECOME HUMAN.

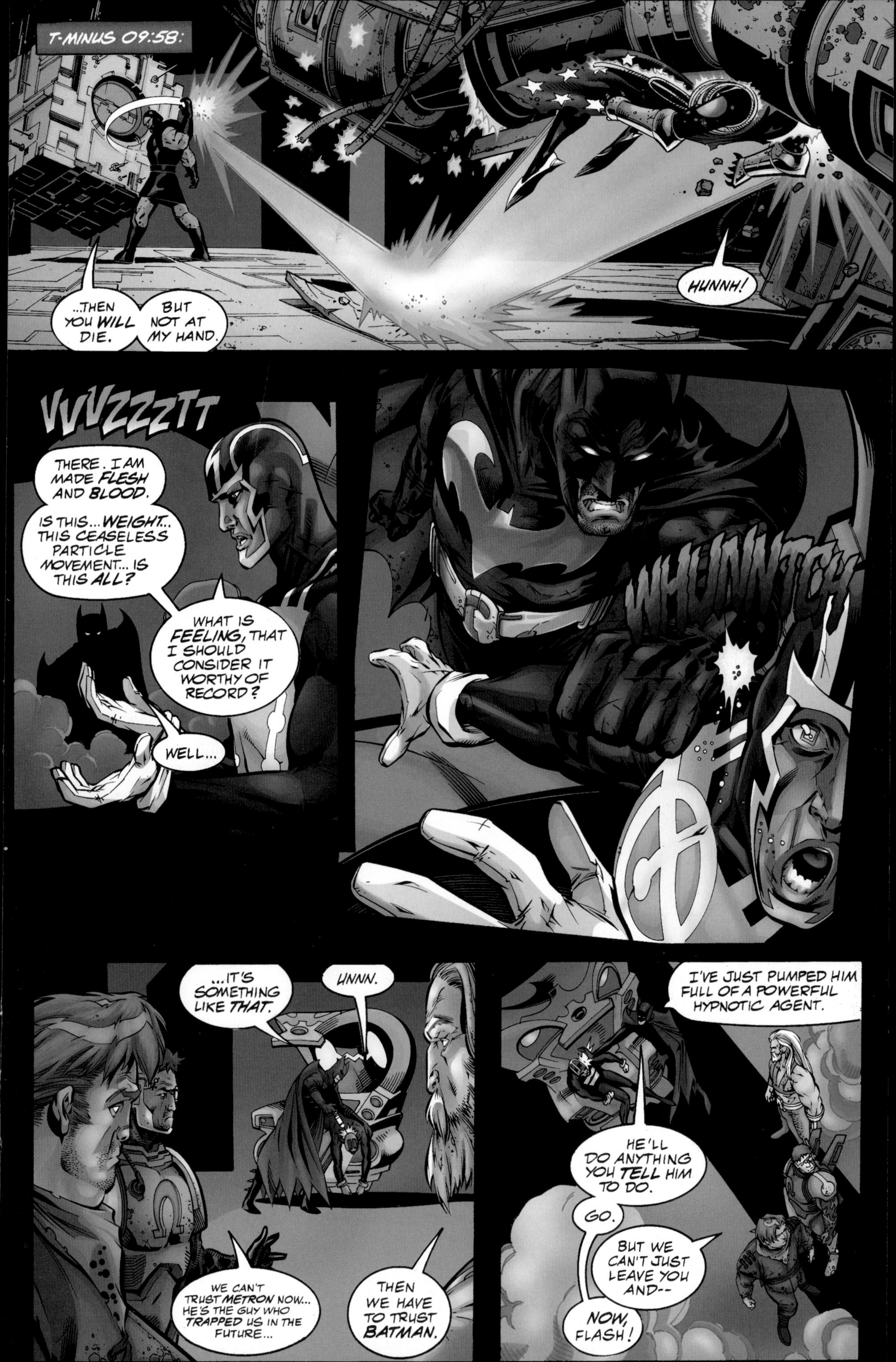
T-MINUS 09:58:
...THEN YOU WILL DIE.
BUT NOT AT MY HAND.
HUNNH!
VVVZZZZTT
THERE. I AM MADE FLESH AND BLOOD.
IS THIS... WEIGHT... THIS CEASELESS PARTICLE MOVEMENT... IS THIS ALL?
WHAT IS FEELING, THAT I SHOULD CONSIDER IT WORTHY OF RECORD?
WELL...
WHUNNTCH
...IT'S SOMETHING LIKE THAT.
UNNN.
WE CAN'T TRUST METRON NOW... HE'S THE GUY WHO TRAPPED US IN THE FUTURE...
THEN WE HAVE TO TRUST BATMAN.
I'VE JUST PUMPED HIM FULL OF A POWERFUL HYPNOTIC AGENT.
HE'LL DO ANYTHING YOU TELL HIM TO DO.
GO.
BUT WE CAN'T JUST LEAVE YOU AND--
NOW, FLASH!

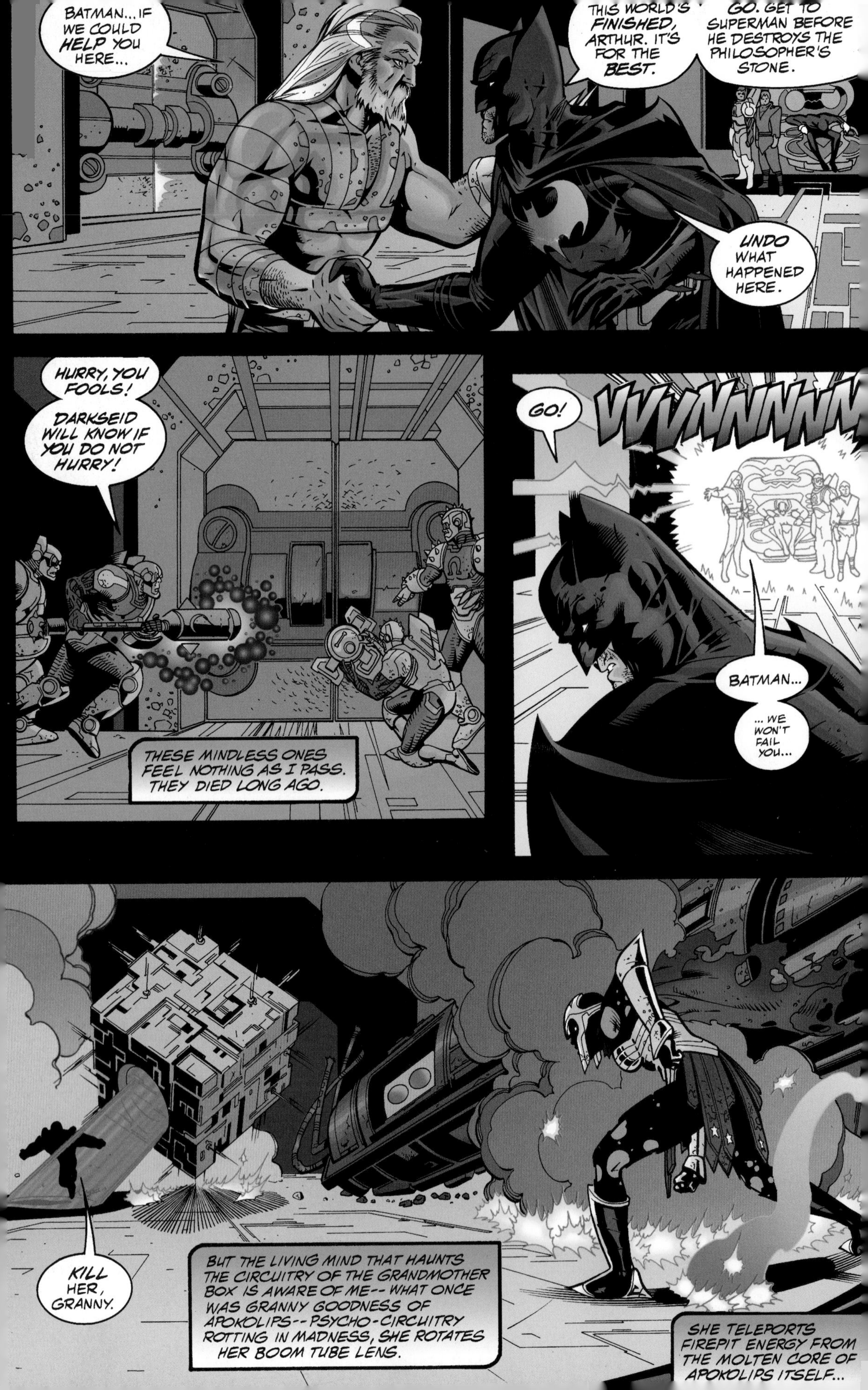
BATMAN... IF WE COULD HELP YOU HERE...
THIS WORLD'S FINISHED, ARTHUR. IT'S FOR THE BEST.
GO. GET TO SUPERMAN BEFORE HE DESTROYS THE PHILOSOPHER'S STONE.
UNDO WHAT HAPPENED HERE.
HURRY, YOU FOOLS!
DARKSEID WILL KNOW IF YOU DO NOT HURRY!
THESE MINDLESS ONES FEEL NOTHING AS I PASS. THEY DIED LONG AGO.
GO!
VVVNNNNNN
BATMAN...
... WE WON'T FAIL YOU...
KILL HER, GRANNY.
BUT THE LIVING MIND THAT HAUNTS THE CIRCUITRY OF THE GRANDMOTHER BOX IS AWARE OF ME-- WHAT ONCE WAS GRANNY GOODNESS OF APOKOLIPS-- PSYCHO-CIRCUITRY ROTTING IN MADNESS, SHE ROTATES HER BOOM TUBE LENS.
SHE TELEPORTS FIREPIT ENERGY FROM THE MOLTEN CORE OF APOKOLIPS ITSELF...

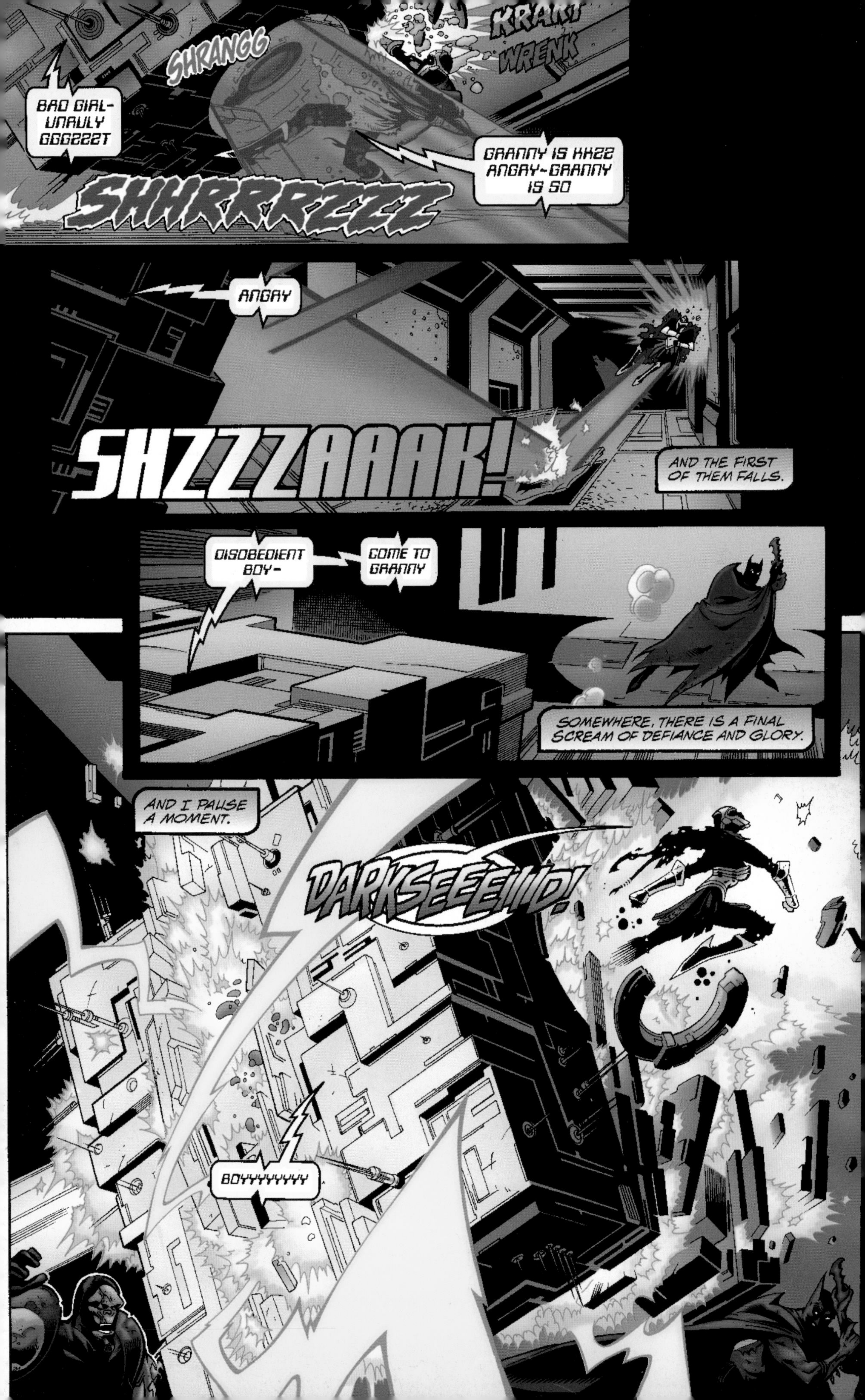
SHRANGG
KRAKT
WRENK
BAD GIRL-
UNRULY
GGGZZZT
GRANNY IS KKZZ
ANGRY-GRANNY
IS SO
SHHRRRZZZZ
ANGRY
SHZZZAAAK!
AND THE FIRST
OF THEM FALLS.
DISOBEDIENT
BOY-
COME TO
GRANNY
SOMEWHERE, THERE IS A FINAL
SCREAM OF DEFIANCE AND GLORY.
AND I PAUSE
A MOMENT.
DARKSEEEIIID!
BOYYYYYYYY

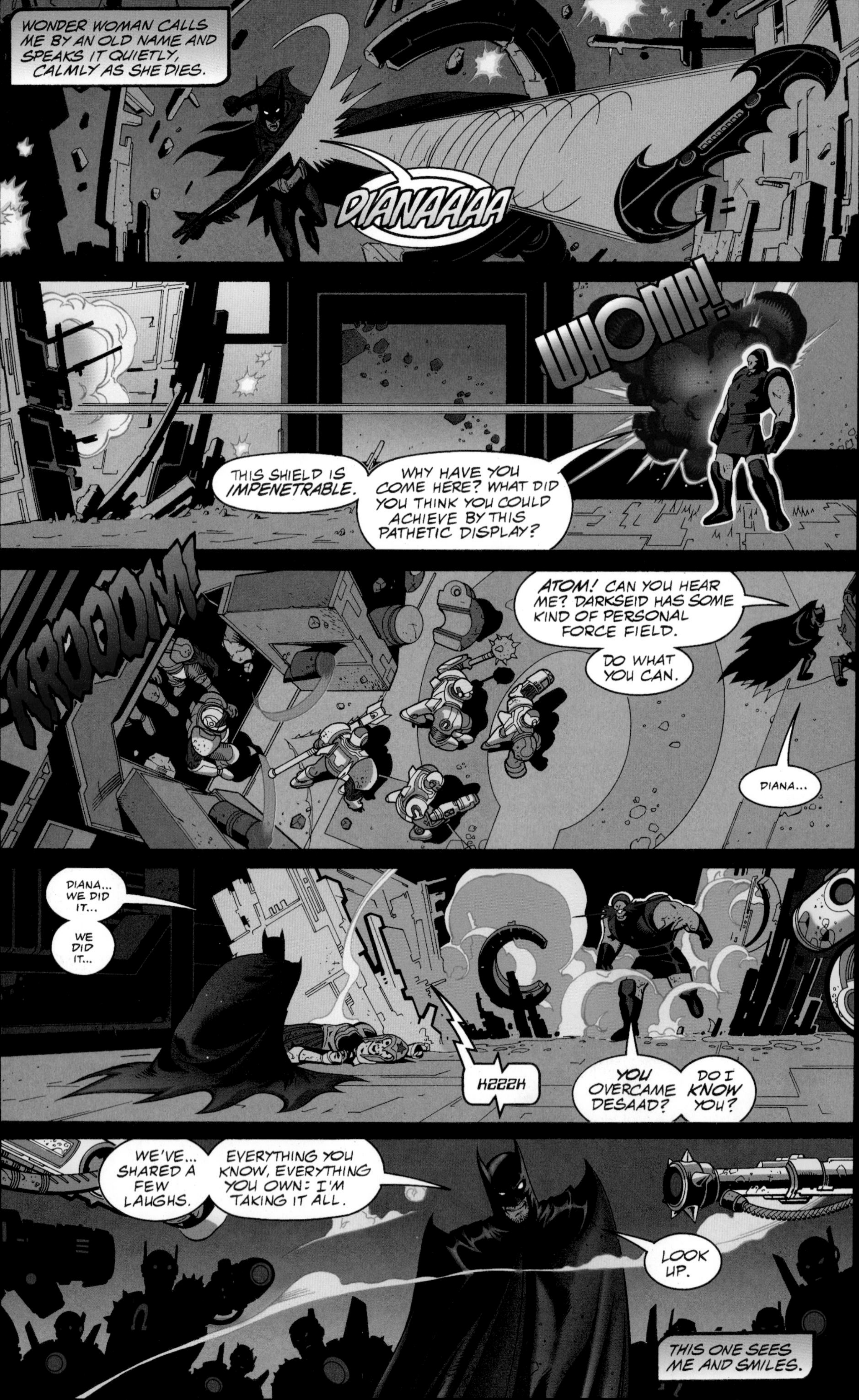
WONDER WOMAN CALLS ME BY AN OLD NAME AND SPEAKS IT QUIETLY, CALMLY AS SHE DIES.
DIANAAAA
WHOMP!
THIS SHIELD IS IMPENETRABLE.
WHY HAVE YOU COME HERE? WHAT DID YOU THINK YOU COULD ACHIEVE BY THIS PATHETIC DISPLAY?
KRROOOM!
ATOM! CAN YOU HEAR ME? DARKSEID HAS SOME KIND OF PERSONAL FORCE FIELD.
DO WHAT YOU CAN.
DIANA...
DIANA... WE DID IT...
WE DID IT...
HZZZH
YOU OVERCAME DESAAD?
DO I KNOW YOU?
WE'VE... SHARED A FEW LAUGHS.
EVERYTHING YOU KNOW, EVERYTHING YOU OWN: I'M TAKING IT ALL.
LOOK UP.
THIS ONE SEES ME AND SMILES.

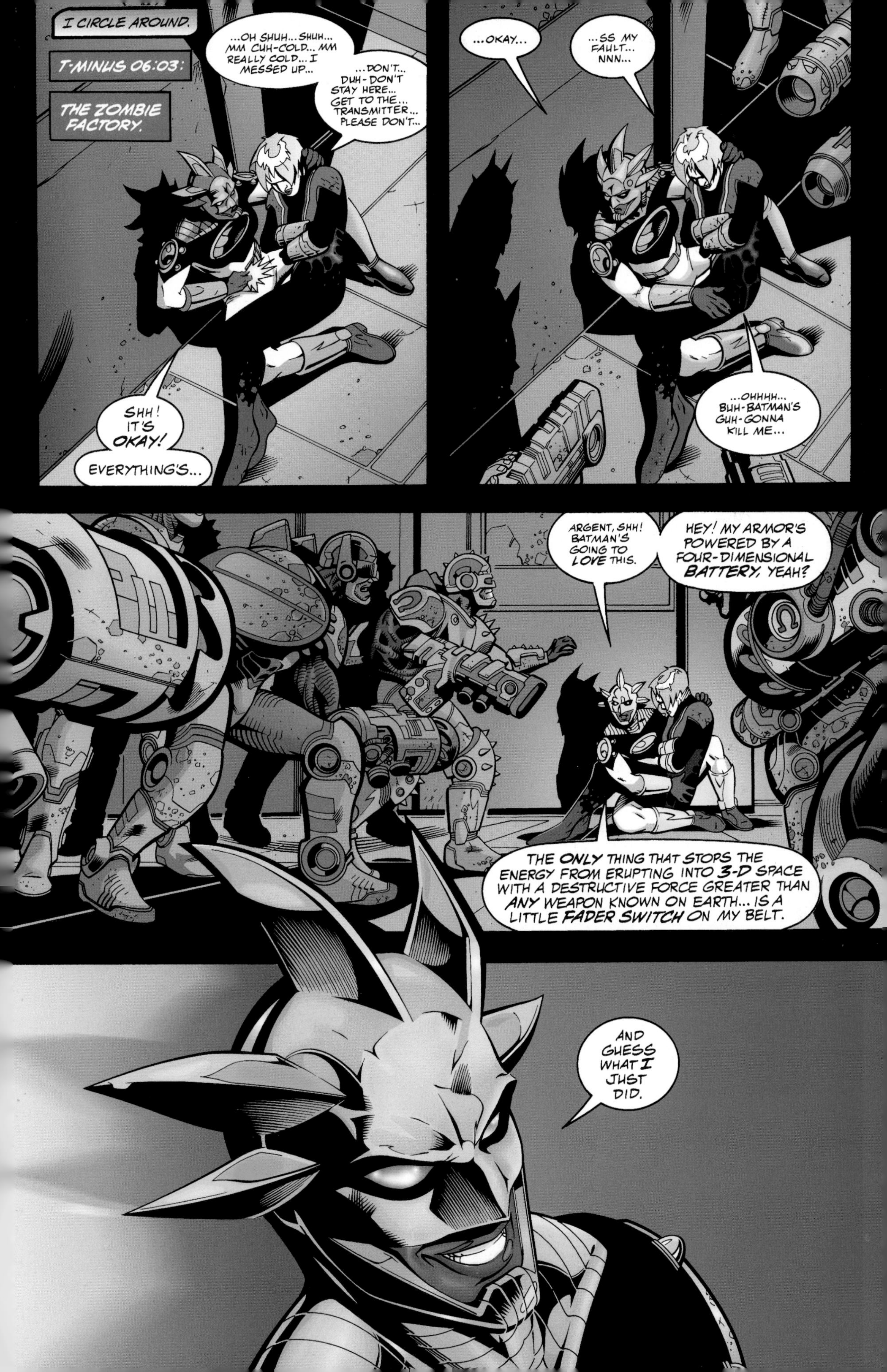

I CIRCLE AROUND.
T-MINUS 06:03:
THE ZOMBIE FACTORY.
...OH SHUH...SHUH... MM CUH-COLD... MM REALLY COLD... I MESSED UP...
...DON'T... DUH-DON'T STAY HERE... GET TO THE... TRANSMITTER... PLEASE DON'T...
SHH! IT'S OKAY!
EVERYTHING'S...
...OKAY...
...SS MY FAULT... NNN...
...OHHHH... BUH-BATMAN'S GUH-GONNA KILL ME...
ARGENT, SHH! BATMAN'S GOING TO LOVE THIS.
HEY! MY ARMOR'S POWERED BY A FOUR-DIMENSIONAL BATTERY, YEAH?
THE ONLY THING THAT STOPS THE ENERGY FROM ERUPTING INTO 3-D SPACE WITH A DESTRUCTIVE FORCE GREATER THAN ANY WEAPON KNOWN ON EARTH... IS A LITTLE FADER SWITCH ON MY BELT.
AND GUESS WHAT I JUST DID.

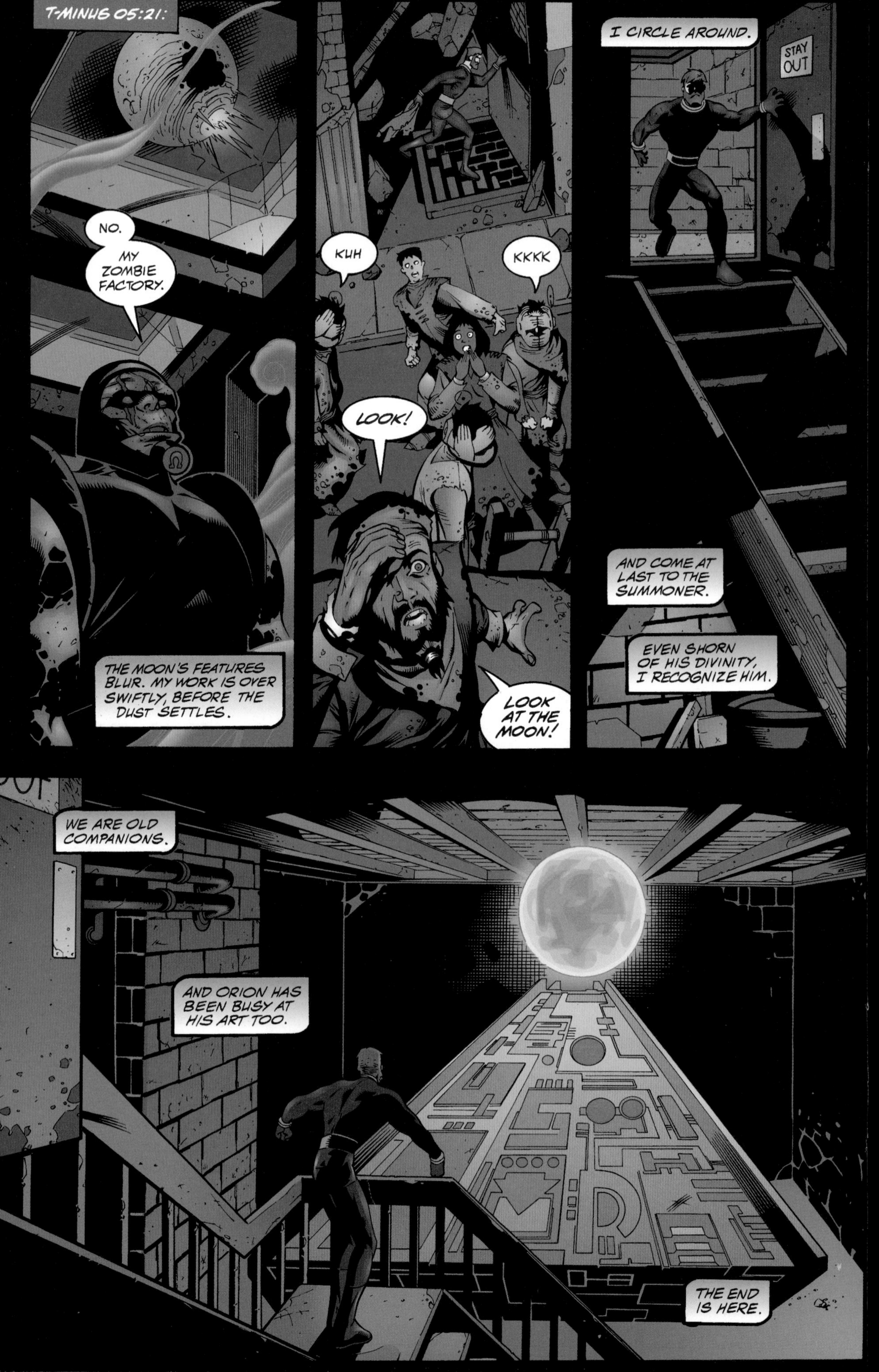
T-MINUS 05:21:
NO.
MY ZOMBIE FACTORY.
THE MOON'S FEATURES BLUR. MY WORK IS OVER SWIFTLY, BEFORE THE DUST SETTLES.
KUH
KKKK
LOOK!
LOOK AT THE MOON!
I CIRCLE AROUND.
STAY OUT
AND COME AT LAST TO THE SUMMONER.
EVEN SHORN OF HIS DIVINITY, I RECOGNIZE HIM.
WE ARE OLD COMPANIONS.
AND ORION HAS BEEN BUSY AT HIS ART TOO.
THE END IS HERE.

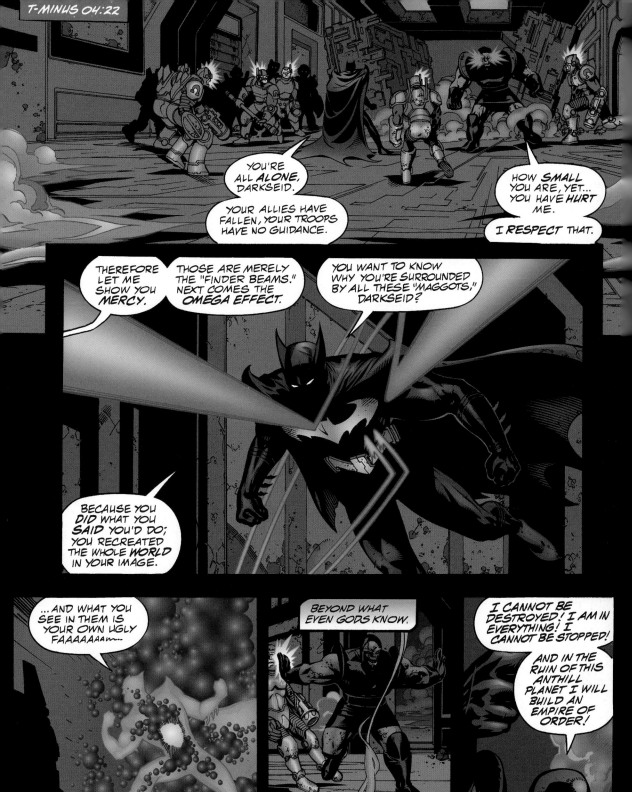

YOU'RE ALL *ALONE,* DARKSEID.

YOUR ALLIES HAVE FALLEN, YOUR TROOPS HAVE NO GUIDANCE.

HOW *SMALL* YOU ARE, YET... YOU HAVE *HURT* ME.

I *RESPECT* THAT.

THEREFORE LET ME SHOW YOU *MERCY.*

THOSE ARE MERELY THE "FINDER BEAMS." NEXT COMES THE *OMEGA EFFECT.*

YOU WANT TO KNOW WHY YOU'RE SURROUNDED BY ALL THESE "MAGGOTS," DARKSEID?

BECAUSE YOU *DID* WHAT YOU *SAID* YOU'D DO; YOU RECREATED THE WHOLE *WORLD* IN YOUR IMAGE.

...AND WHAT YOU SEE IN THEM IS YOUR OWN UGLY *FAAAAAAA*—

BEYOND WHAT EVEN GODS KNOW.

I CANNOT BE *DESTROYED!* I AM IN *EVERYTHING!* I CANNOT BE *STOPPED!*

AND IN THE *RUIN* OF THIS *ANTHILL* PLANET I WILL BUILD AN *EMPIRE* OF *ORDER!*

THEN HE IS *GONE,* OUT OF *TIME,* OUT OF *SPACE.*

MINDLESS SLAVES! PITIFUL MANNEQUINS! WHERE IS *METRON?*

WHY WAS THIS ALLOWED TO *OCCUR?*

THAT IS MY *WILL!* THAT IS THE WILL OF *DARKSEID!*

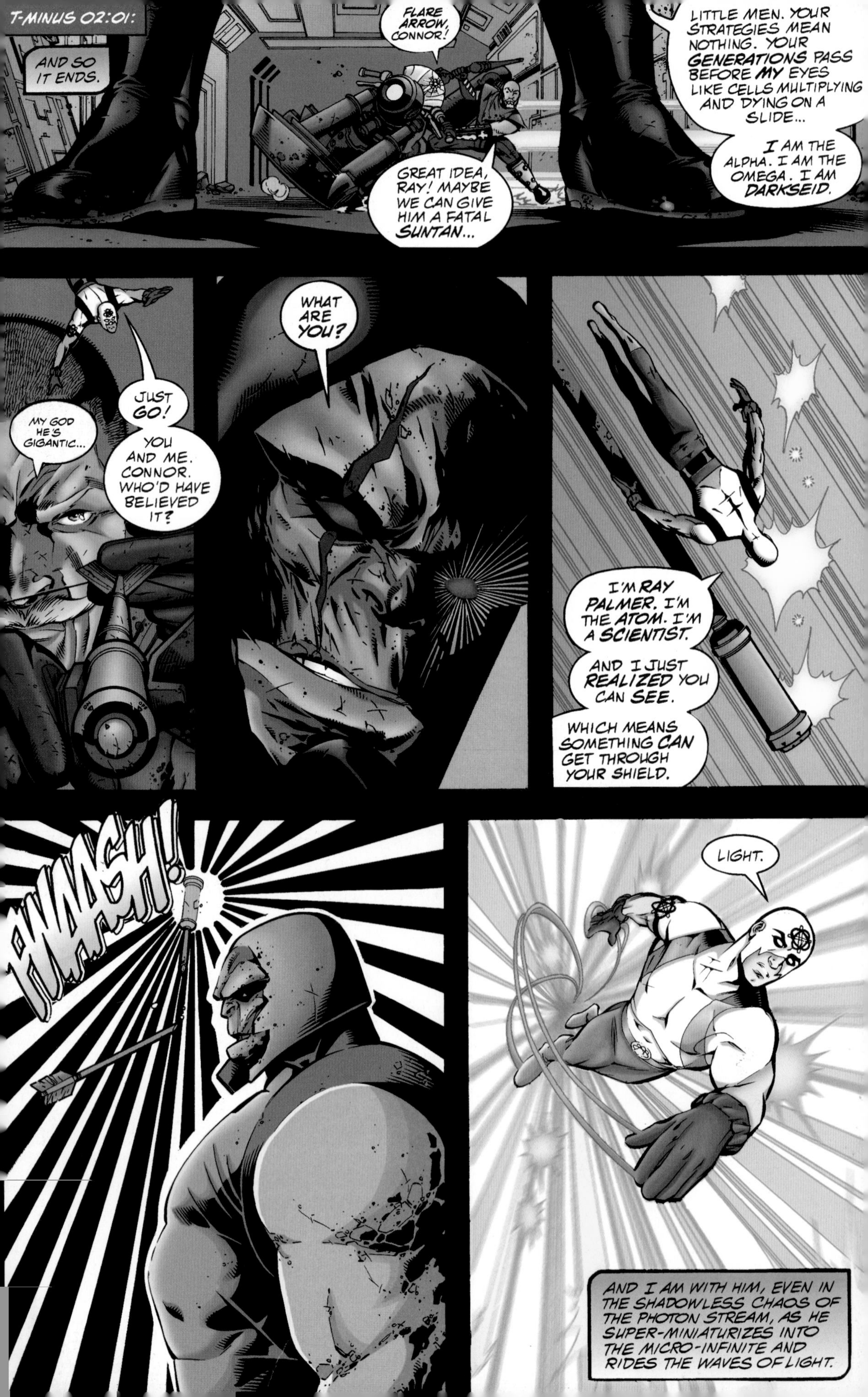
T-MINUS 02:01:
AND SO IT ENDS.
FLARE ARROW, CONNOR!
GREAT IDEA, RAY! MAYBE WE CAN GIVE HIM A FATAL SUNTAN...
LITTLE MEN. YOUR STRATEGIES MEAN NOTHING. YOUR GENERATIONS PASS BEFORE MY EYES LIKE CELLS MULTIPLYING AND DYING ON A SLIDE...
I AM THE ALPHA. I AM THE OMEGA. I AM DARKSEID.
MY GOD HE'S GIGANTIC...
JUST GO!
YOU AND ME. CONNOR. WHO'D HAVE BELIEVED IT?
WHAT ARE YOU?
I'M RAY PALMER. I'M THE ATOM. I'M A SCIENTIST.
AND I JUST REALIZED YOU CAN SEE.
WHICH MEANS SOMETHING CAN GET THROUGH YOUR SHIELD.
FWAASH!
LIGHT.
AND I AM WITH HIM, EVEN IN THE SHADOWLESS CHAOS OF THE PHOTON STREAM, AS HE SUPER-MINIATURIZES INTO THE MICRO-INFINITE AND RIDES THE WAVES OF LIGHT.

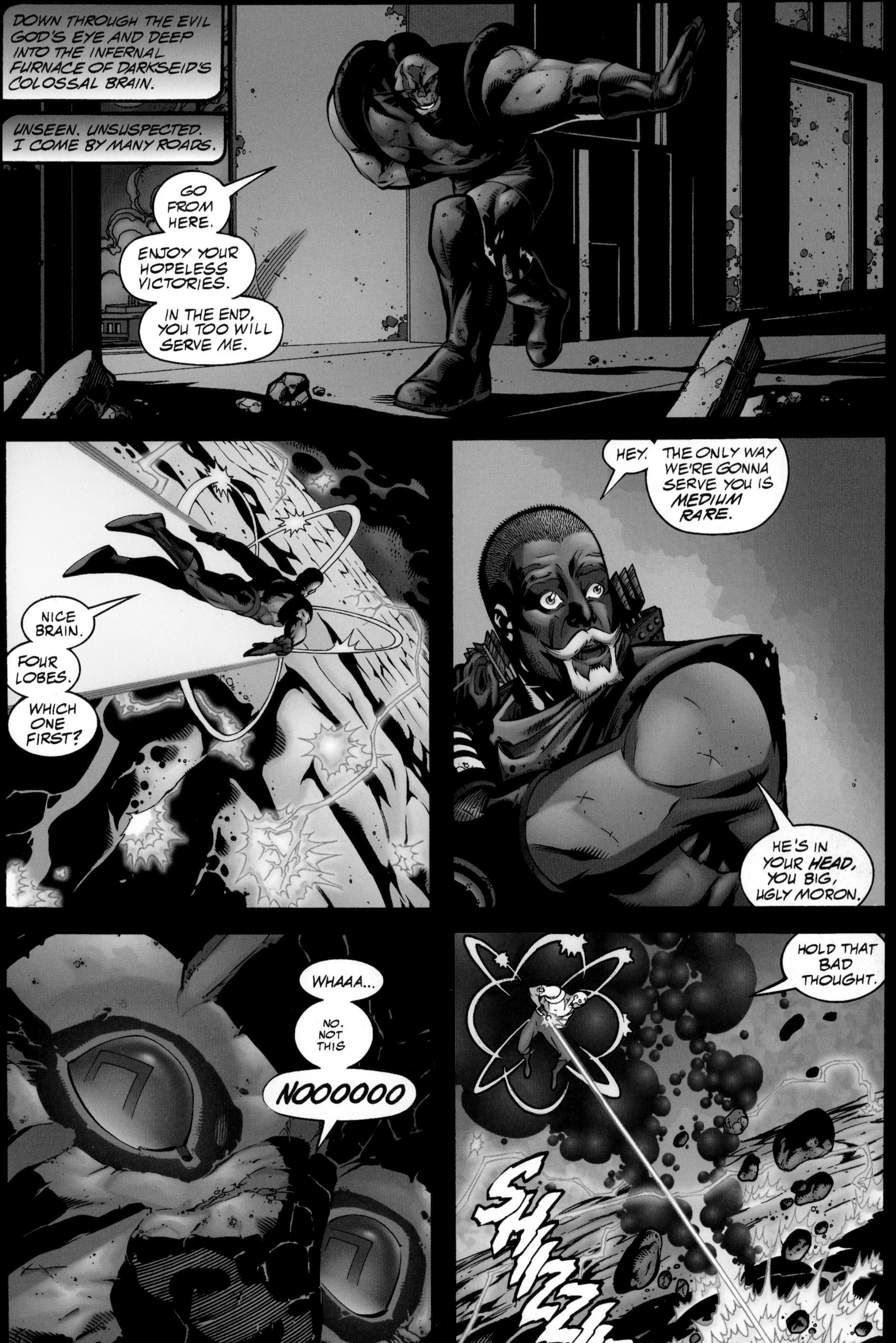
DOWN THROUGH THE EVIL GOD'S EYE AND DEEP INTO THE INFERNAL FURNACE OF DARKSEID'S COLOSSAL BRAIN.
UNSEEN. UNSUSPECTED. I COME BY MANY ROADS.
GO FROM HERE.
ENJOY YOUR HOPELESS VICTORIES.
IN THE END, YOU TOO WILL SERVE ME.
NICE BRAIN.
FOUR LOBES.
WHICH ONE FIRST?
HEY.
THE ONLY WAY WE'RE GONNA SERVE YOU IS MEDIUM RARE.
HE'S IN YOUR HEAD, YOU BIG, UGLY MORON.
WHAAA...
NO. NOT THIS
NOOOOOO
HOLD THAT BAD THOUGHT.
SHIZZZIT!

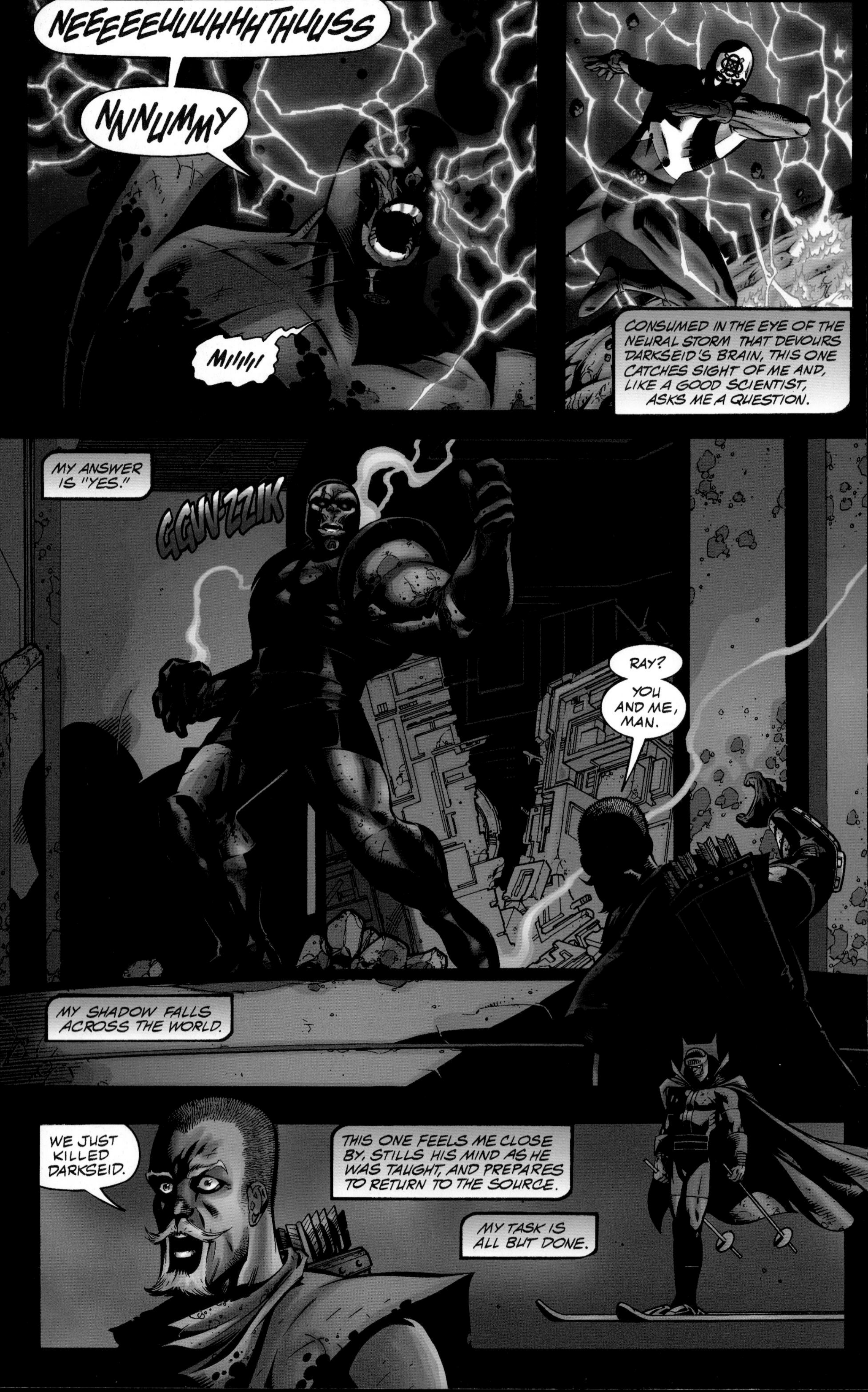

NEEEEEUUUHHHTHUUSS
NNNUMMY
MIIIII
CONSUMED IN THE EYE OF THE NEURAL STORM THAT DEVOURS DARKSEID'S BRAIN, THIS ONE CATCHES SIGHT OF ME AND, LIKE A GOOD SCIENTIST, ASKS ME A QUESTION.
MY ANSWER IS "YES."
GGVVZZIK
RAY?
YOU AND ME, MAN.
MY SHADOW FALLS ACROSS THE WORLD.
WE JUST KILLED DARKSEID.
THIS ONE FEELS ME CLOSE BY, STILLS HIS MIND AS HE WAS TAUGHT, AND PREPARES TO RETURN TO THE SOURCE.
MY TASK IS ALL BUT DONE.

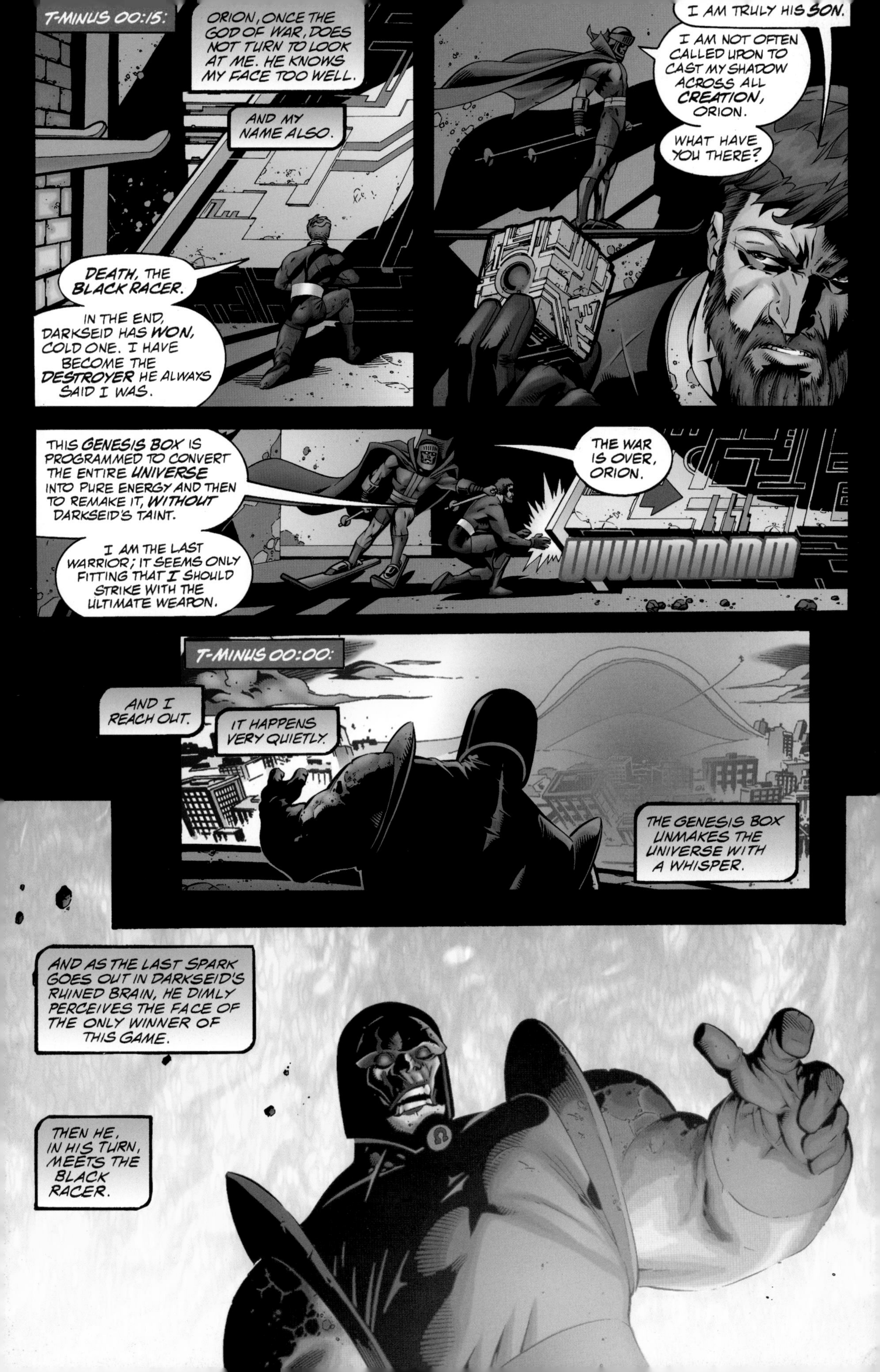
T-MINUS 00:15:
ORION, ONCE THE GOD OF WAR, DOES NOT TURN TO LOOK AT ME. HE KNOWS MY FACE TOO WELL.
AND MY NAME ALSO.
DEATH, THE BLACK RACER.
IN THE END, DARKSEID HAS WON, COLD ONE. I HAVE BECOME THE DESTROYER HE ALWAYS SAID I WAS.
I AM TRULY HIS SON.
I AM NOT OFTEN CALLED UPON TO CAST MY SHADOW ACROSS ALL CREATION, ORION.
WHAT HAVE YOU THERE?
THIS GENESIS BOX IS PROGRAMMED TO CONVERT THE ENTIRE UNIVERSE INTO PURE ENERGY AND THEN TO REMAKE IT, WITHOUT DARKSEID'S TAINT.
I AM THE LAST WARRIOR; IT SEEMS ONLY FITTING THAT I SHOULD STRIKE WITH THE ULTIMATE WEAPON.
THE WAR IS OVER, ORION.
VUUUMMMM
T-MINUS 00:00:
AND I REACH OUT.
IT HAPPENS VERY QUIETLY.
THE GENESIS BOX UNMAKES THE UNIVERSE WITH A WHISPER.
AND AS THE LAST SPARK GOES OUT IN DARKSEID'S RUINED BRAIN, HE DIMLY PERCEIVES THE FACE OF THE ONLY WINNER OF THIS GAME.
THEN HE, IN HIS TURN, MEETS THE BLACK RACER.

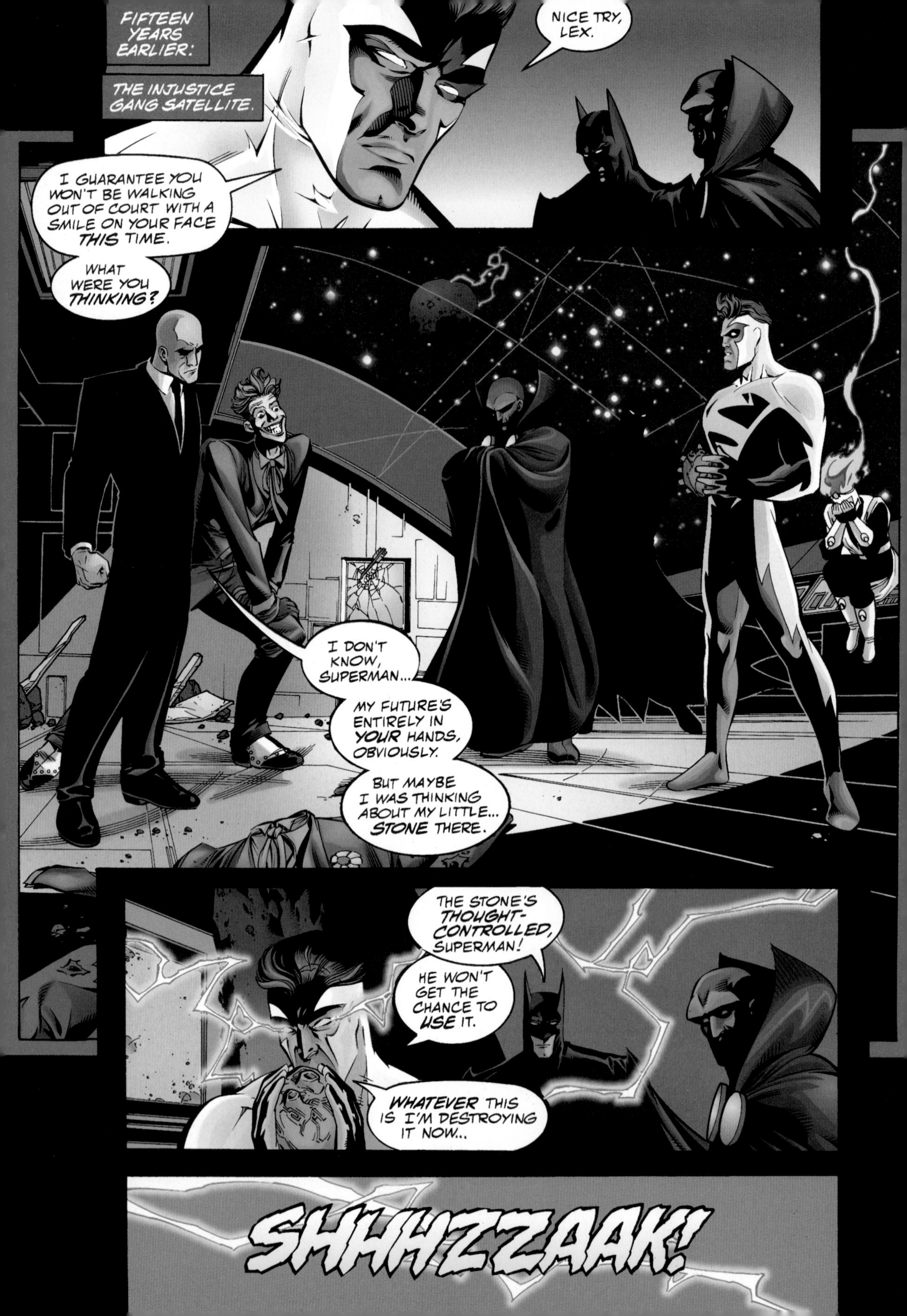
FIFTEEN YEARS EARLIER:
THE INJUSTICE GANG SATELLITE.
NICE TRY, LEX.
I GUARANTEE YOU WON'T BE WALKING OUT OF COURT WITH A SMILE ON YOUR FACE THIS TIME.
WHAT WERE YOU THINKING?
I DON'T KNOW, SUPERMAN...
MY FUTURE'S ENTIRELY IN YOUR HANDS, OBVIOUSLY.
BUT MAYBE I WAS THINKING ABOUT MY LITTLE... STONE THERE.
THE STONE'S THOUGHT-CONTROLLED, SUPERMAN!
HE WON'T GET THE CHANCE TO USE IT.
WHATEVER THIS IS I'M DESTROYING IT NOW...
SHHHZZAAK!

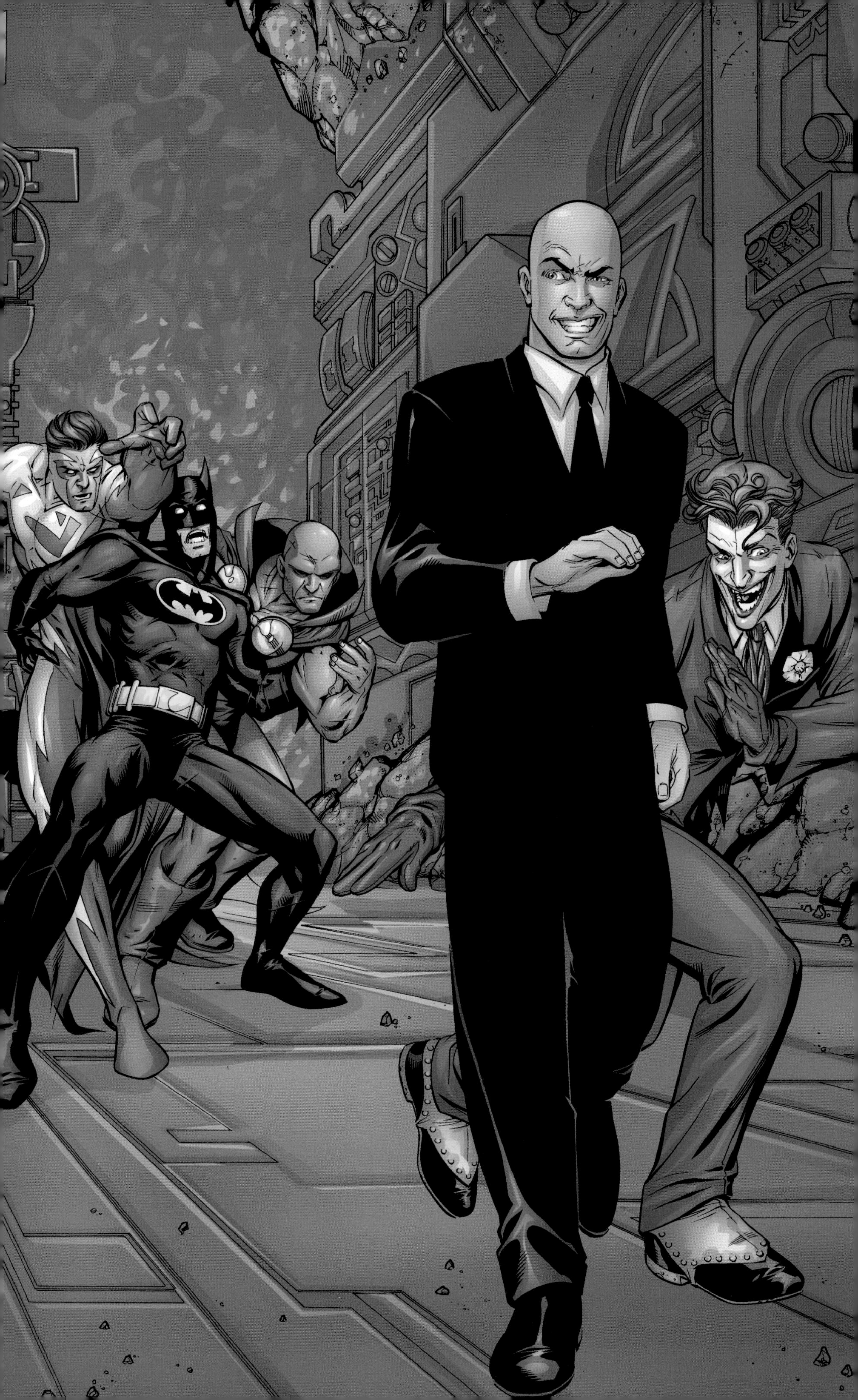

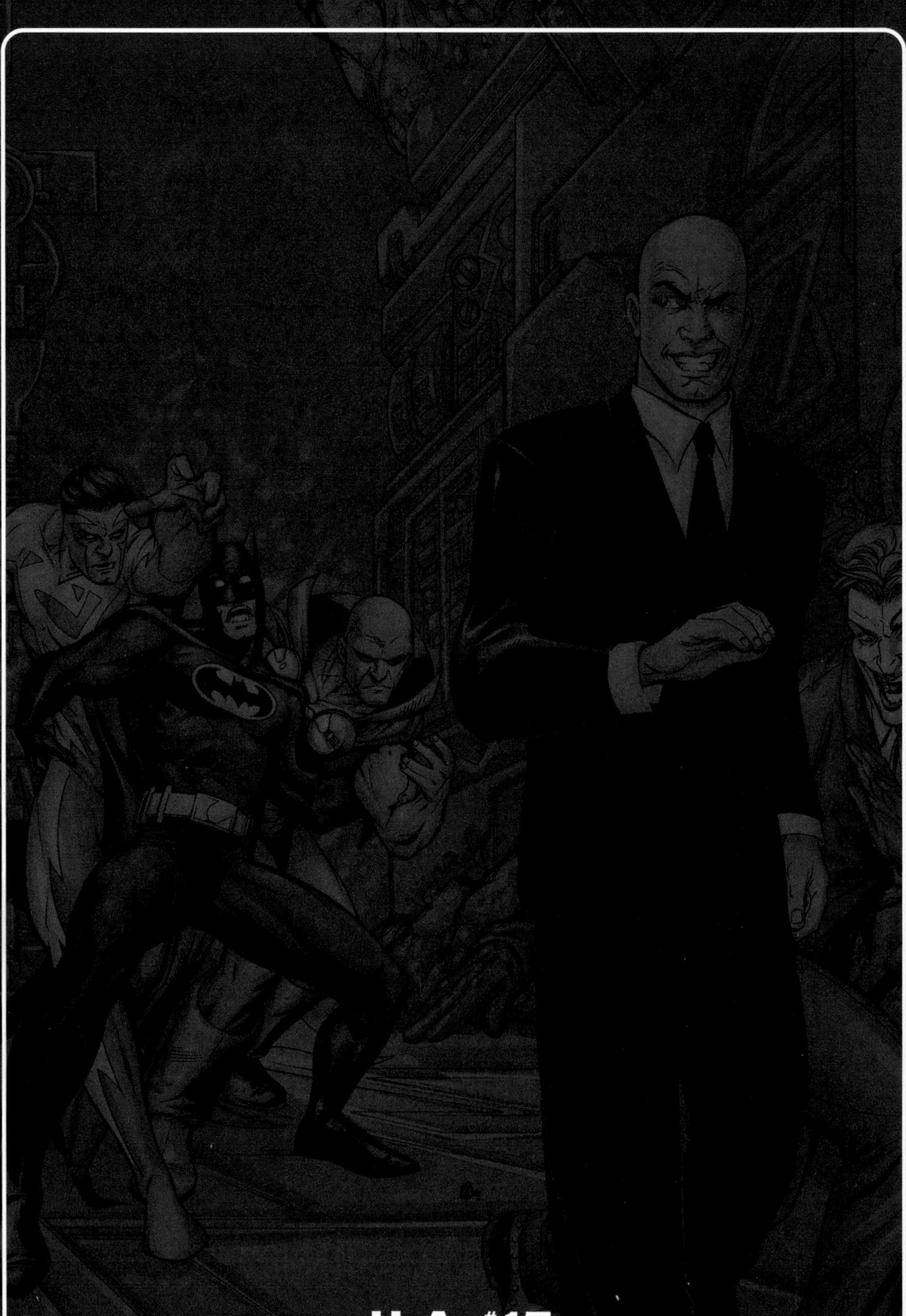

JLA #15

WRITTEN BY GRANT MORRISON

PENCILS BY HOWARD PORTER, GARY FRANK & GREG LAND, WITH INKS BY JOHN DELL & BOB MCLEOD AND COLORS BY PAT GARRAHY

COVER BY PORTER & DELL

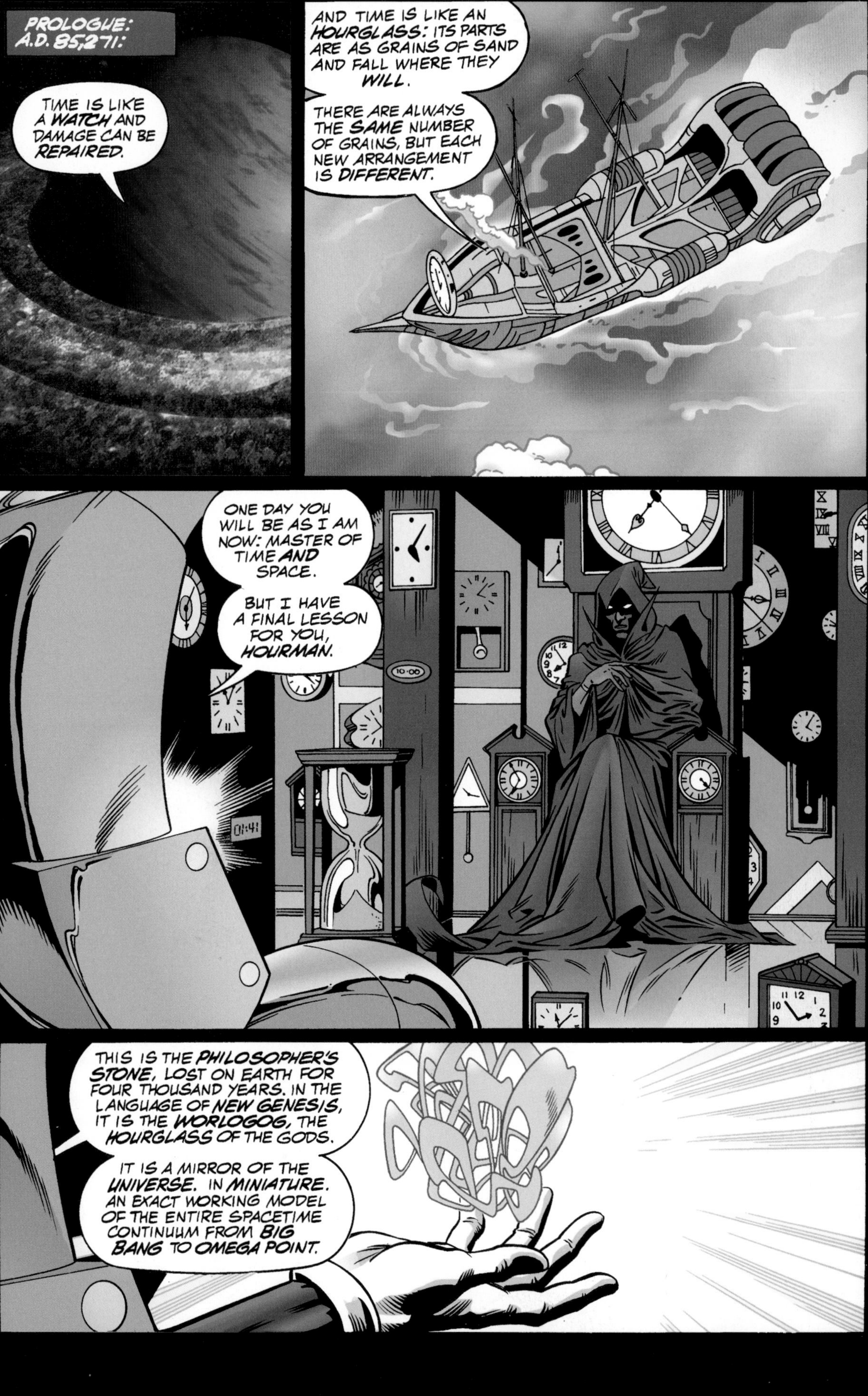
PROLOGUE: A.D. 85,271:
TIME IS LIKE A WATCH AND DAMAGE CAN BE REPAIRED.
AND TIME IS LIKE AN HOURGLASS: ITS PARTS ARE AS GRAINS OF SAND AND FALL WHERE THEY WILL.
THERE ARE ALWAYS THE SAME NUMBER OF GRAINS, BUT EACH NEW ARRANGEMENT IS DIFFERENT.
ONE DAY YOU WILL BE AS I AM NOW: MASTER OF TIME AND SPACE.
BUT I HAVE A FINAL LESSON FOR YOU, HOURMAN.
10:00
01:41
THIS IS THE PHILOSOPHER'S STONE, LOST ON EARTH FOR FOUR THOUSAND YEARS. IN THE LANGUAGE OF NEW GENESIS, IT IS THE WORLOGOG, THE HOURGLASS OF THE GODS.
IT IS A MIRROR OF THE UNIVERSE. IN MINIATURE. AN EXACT WORKING MODEL OF THE ENTIRE SPACETIME CONTINUUM FROM BIG BANG TO OMEGA POINT.

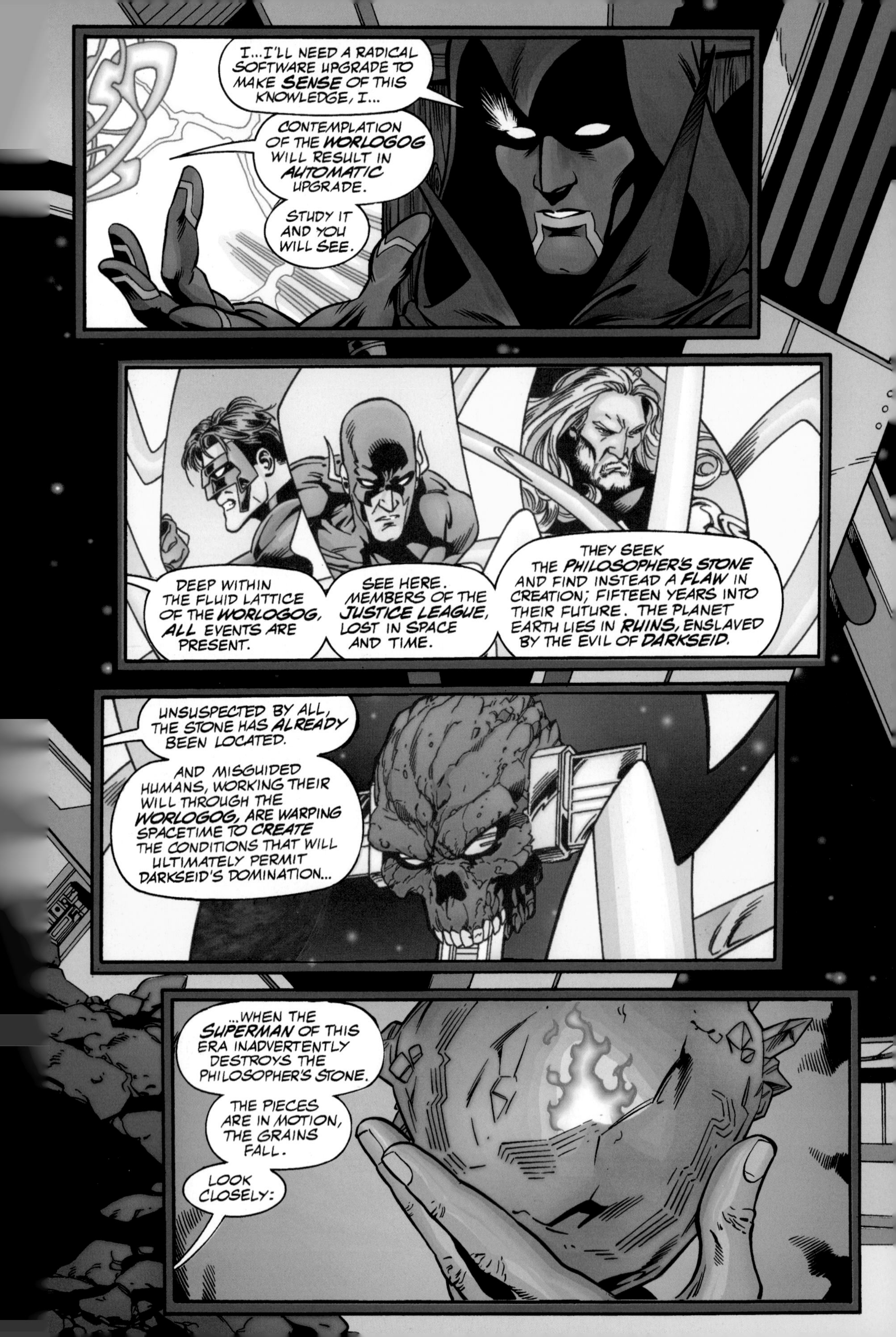
I...I'LL NEED A RADICAL SOFTWARE UPGRADE TO MAKE SENSE OF THIS KNOWLEDGE, I...
CONTEMPLATION OF THE WORLOGOG WILL RESULT IN AUTOMATIC UPGRADE.
STUDY IT AND YOU WILL SEE.
DEEP WITHIN THE FLUID LATTICE OF THE WORLOGOG, ALL EVENTS ARE PRESENT.
SEE HERE. MEMBERS OF THE JUSTICE LEAGUE, LOST IN SPACE AND TIME.
THEY SEEK THE PHILOSOPHER'S STONE AND FIND INSTEAD A FLAW IN CREATION; FIFTEEN YEARS INTO THEIR FUTURE. THE PLANET EARTH LIES IN RUINS, ENSLAVED BY THE EVIL OF DARKSEID.
UNSUSPECTED BY ALL, THE STONE HAS ALREADY BEEN LOCATED.
AND MISGUIDED HUMANS, WORKING THEIR WILL THROUGH THE WORLOGOG, ARE WARPING SPACETIME TO CREATE THE CONDITIONS THAT WILL ULTIMATELY PERMIT DARKSEID'S DOMINATION...
...WHEN THE SUPERMAN OF THIS ERA INADVERTENTLY DESTROYS THE PHILOSOPHER'S STONE.
THE PIECES ARE IN MOTION, THE GRAINS FALL.
LOOK CLOSELY:

ROCK OF AGES PART SIX
STONE OF DESTINY

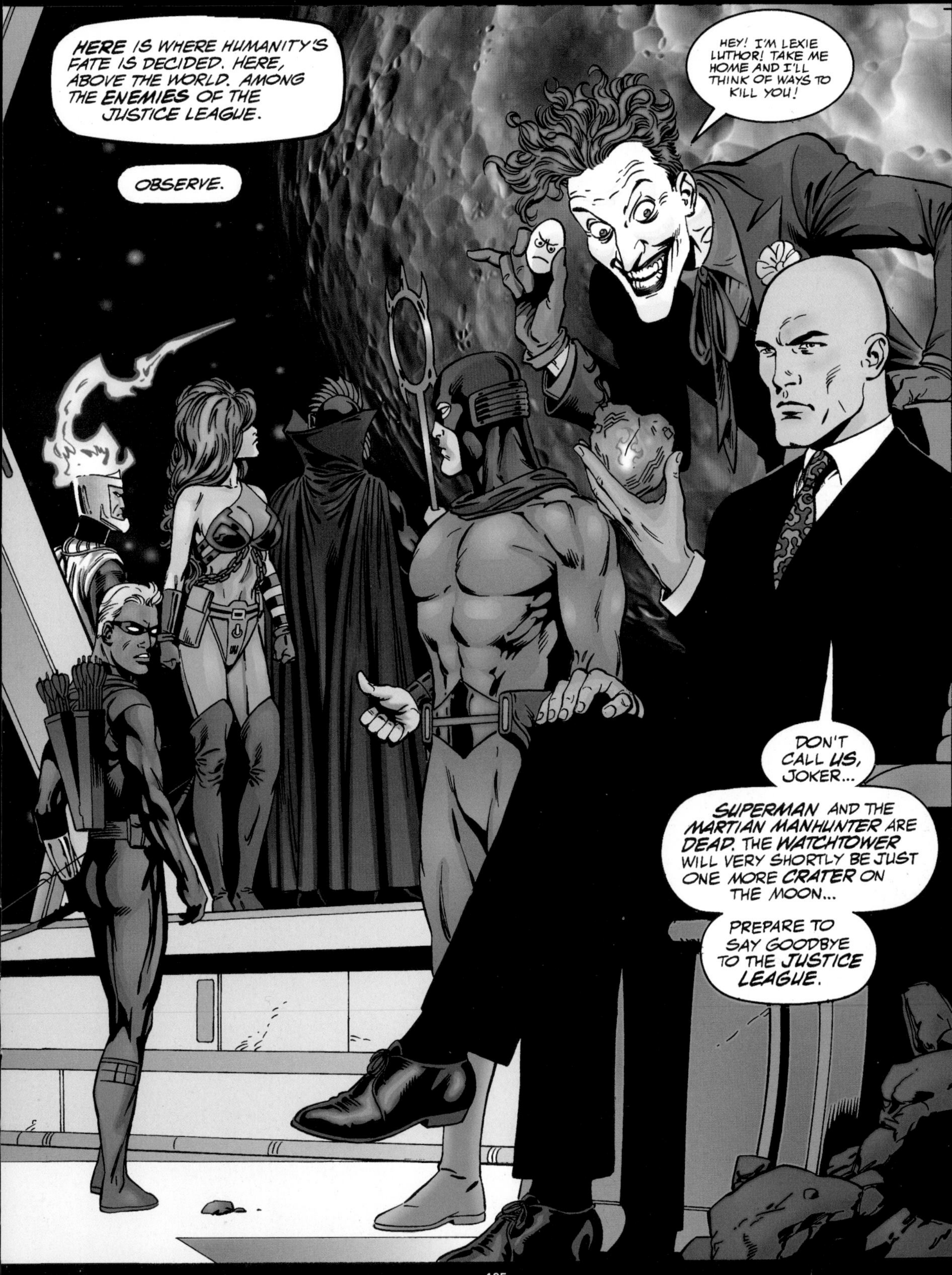
HERE IS WHERE HUMANITY'S FATE IS DECIDED. HERE, ABOVE THE WORLD. AMONG THE ENEMIES OF THE JUSTICE LEAGUE.
OBSERVE.
HEY! I'M LEXIE LUTHOR! TAKE ME HOME AND I'LL THINK OF WAYS TO KILL YOU!
DON'T CALL US, JOKER...
SUPERMAN AND THE MARTIAN MANHUNTER ARE DEAD. THE WATCHTOWER WILL VERY SHORTLY BE JUST ONE MORE CRATER ON THE MOON...
PREPARE TO SAY GOODBYE TO THE JUSTICE LEAGUE.

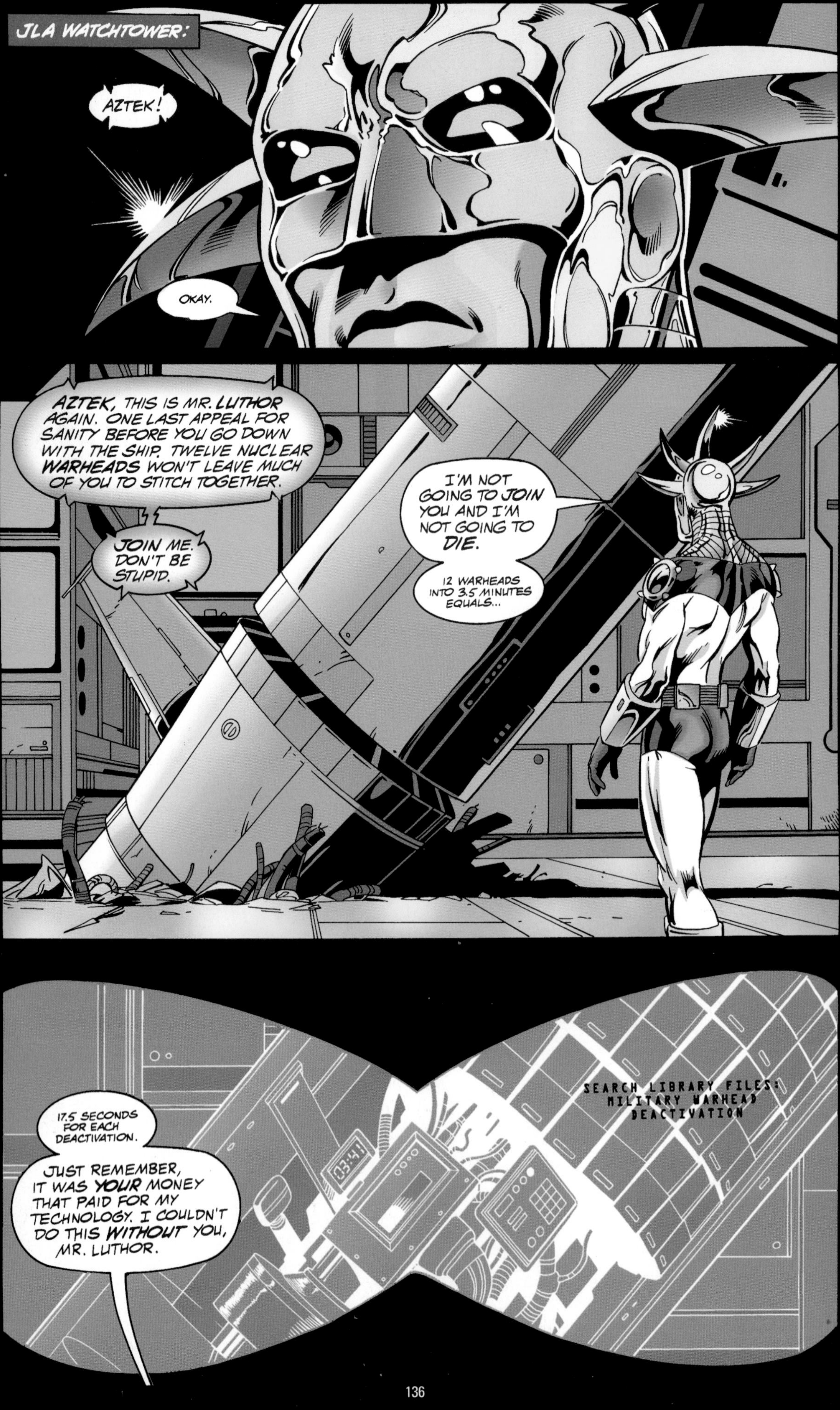
JLA WATCHTOWER:
AZTEK!
OKAY.
AZTEK, THIS IS MR. LUTHOR AGAIN. ONE LAST APPEAL FOR SANITY BEFORE YOU GO DOWN WITH THE SHIP. TWELVE NUCLEAR WARHEADS WON'T LEAVE MUCH OF YOU TO STITCH TOGETHER.
JOIN ME. DON'T BE STUPID.
I'M NOT GOING TO JOIN YOU AND I'M NOT GOING TO DIE.
12 WARHEADS INTO 3.5 MINUTES EQUALS...
SEARCH LIBRARY FILES: MILITARY WARHEAD DEACTIVATION
17.5 SECONDS FOR EACH DEACTIVATION.
JUST REMEMBER, IT WAS YOUR MONEY THAT PAID FOR MY TECHNOLOGY. I COULDN'T DO THIS WITHOUT YOU, MR. LUTHOR.

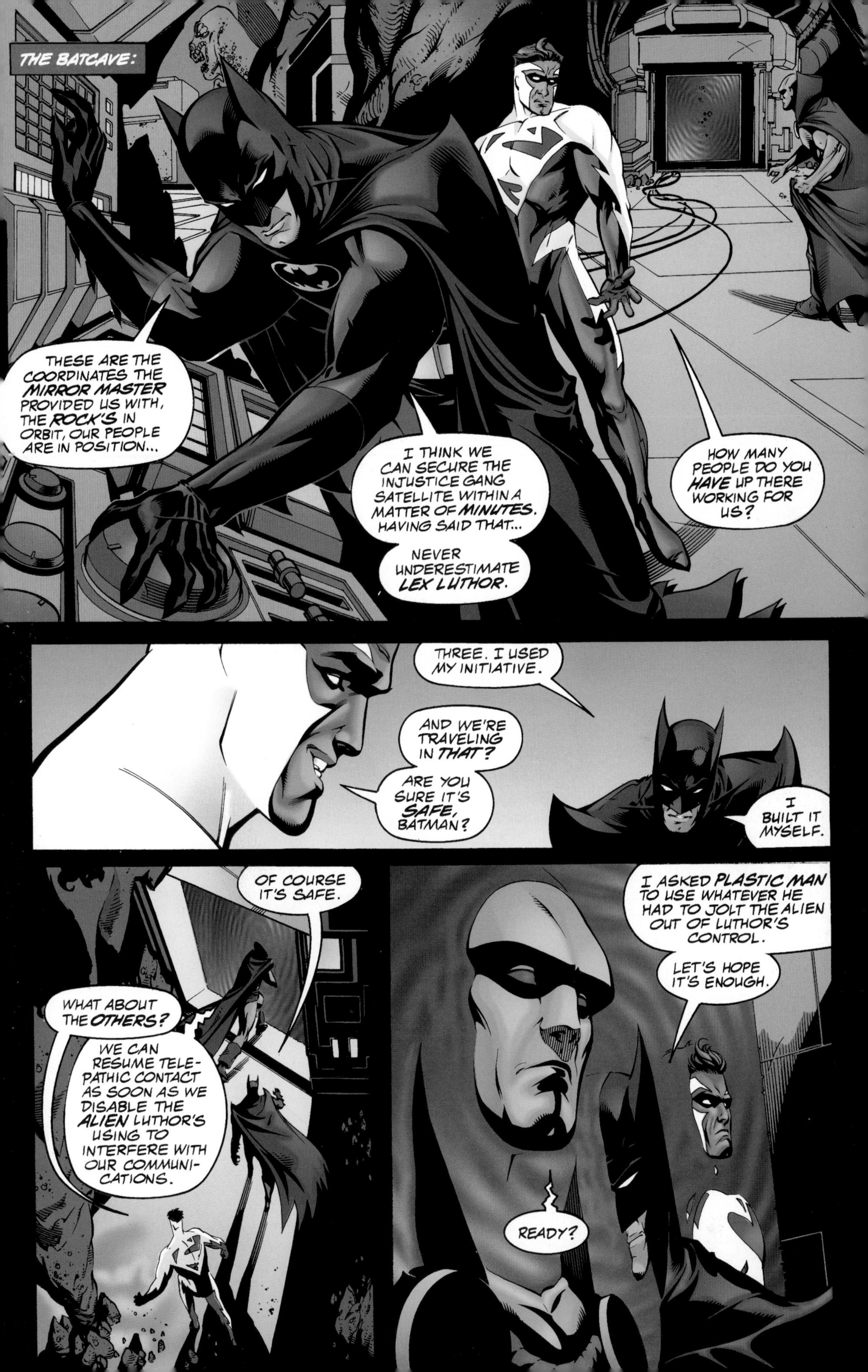
THE BATCAVE:
THESE ARE THE COORDINATES THE MIRROR MASTER PROVIDED US WITH, THE ROCK'S IN ORBIT, OUR PEOPLE ARE IN POSITION...
I THINK WE CAN SECURE THE INJUSTICE GANG SATELLITE WITHIN A MATTER OF MINUTES. HAVING SAID THAT...
NEVER UNDERESTIMATE LEX LUTHOR.
HOW MANY PEOPLE DO YOU HAVE UP THERE WORKING FOR US?
THREE. I USED MY INITIATIVE.
AND WE'RE TRAVELING IN THAT?
ARE YOU SURE IT'S SAFE, BATMAN?
I BUILT IT MYSELF.
OF COURSE IT'S SAFE.
WHAT ABOUT THE OTHERS?
WE CAN RESUME TELE-PATHIC CONTACT AS SOON AS WE DISABLE THE ALIEN LUTHOR'S USING TO INTERFERE WITH OUR COMMUNI-CATIONS.
I ASKED PLASTIC MAN TO USE WHATEVER HE HAD TO JOLT THE ALIEN OUT OF LUTHOR'S CONTROL.
LET'S HOPE IT'S ENOUGH.
READY?

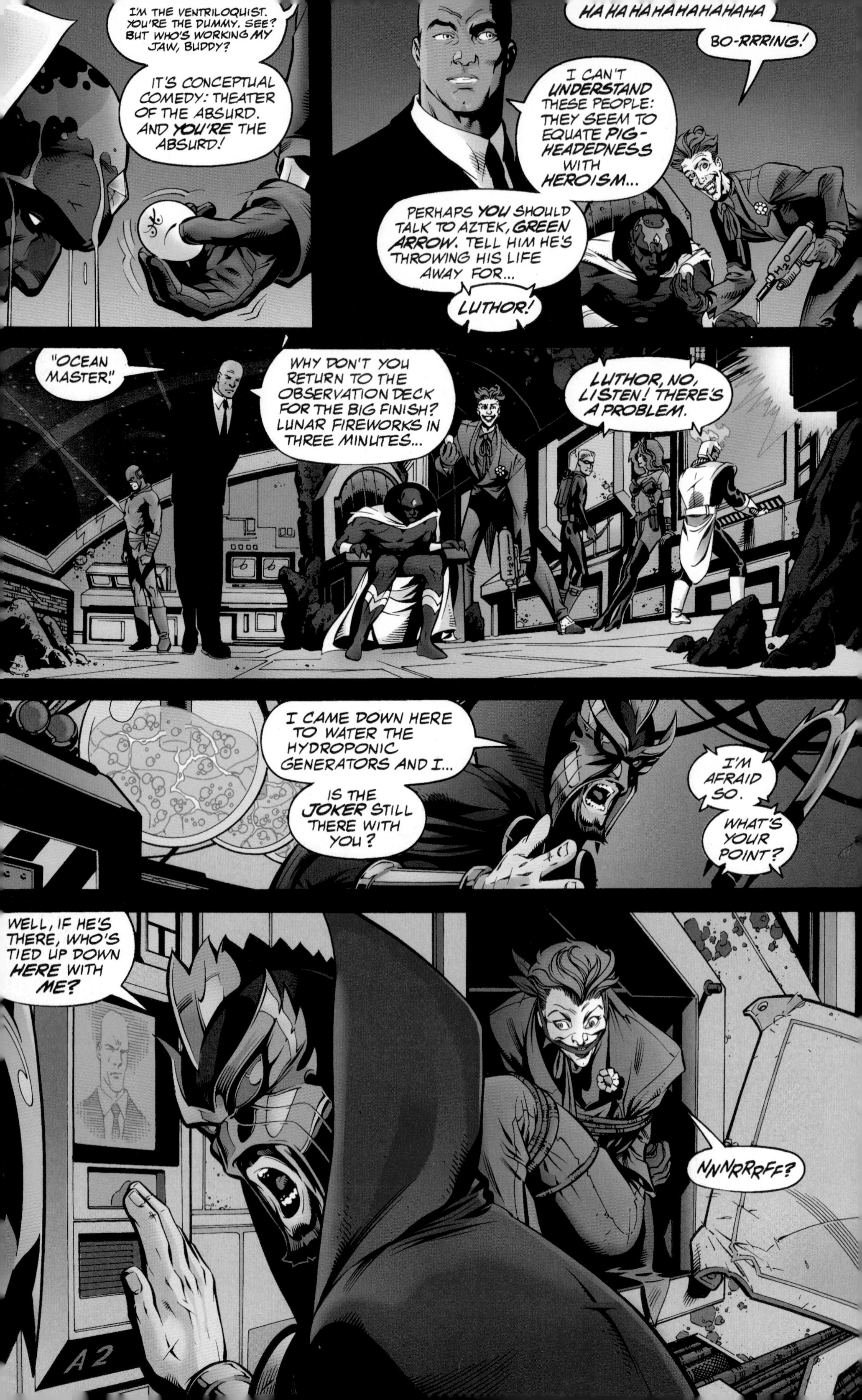
I'M THE VENTRILOQUIST. YOU'RE THE DUMMY. SEE? BUT WHO'S WORKING MY JAW, BUDDY?
IT'S CONCEPTUAL COMEDY: THEATER OF THE ABSURD. AND YOU'RE THE ABSURD!
HA HA HA HA HA HA HA HA HA HA
BO-RRRING!
I CAN'T UNDERSTAND THESE PEOPLE: THEY SEEM TO EQUATE PIG-HEADEDNESS WITH HEROISM...
PERHAPS YOU SHOULD TALK TO AZTEK, GREEN ARROW. TELL HIM HE'S THROWING HIS LIFE AWAY FOR...
LUTHOR!
"OCEAN MASTER."
WHY DON'T YOU RETURN TO THE OBSERVATION DECK FOR THE BIG FINISH? LUNAR FIREWORKS IN THREE MINUTES...
LUTHOR, NO, LISTEN! THERE'S A PROBLEM.
I CAME DOWN HERE TO WATER THE HYDROPONIC GENERATORS AND I...
IS THE JOKER STILL THERE WITH YOU?
I'M AFRAID SO.
WHAT'S YOUR POINT?
WELL, IF HE'S THERE, WHO'S TIED UP DOWN HERE WITH ME?
NNNRRRFF?
A2

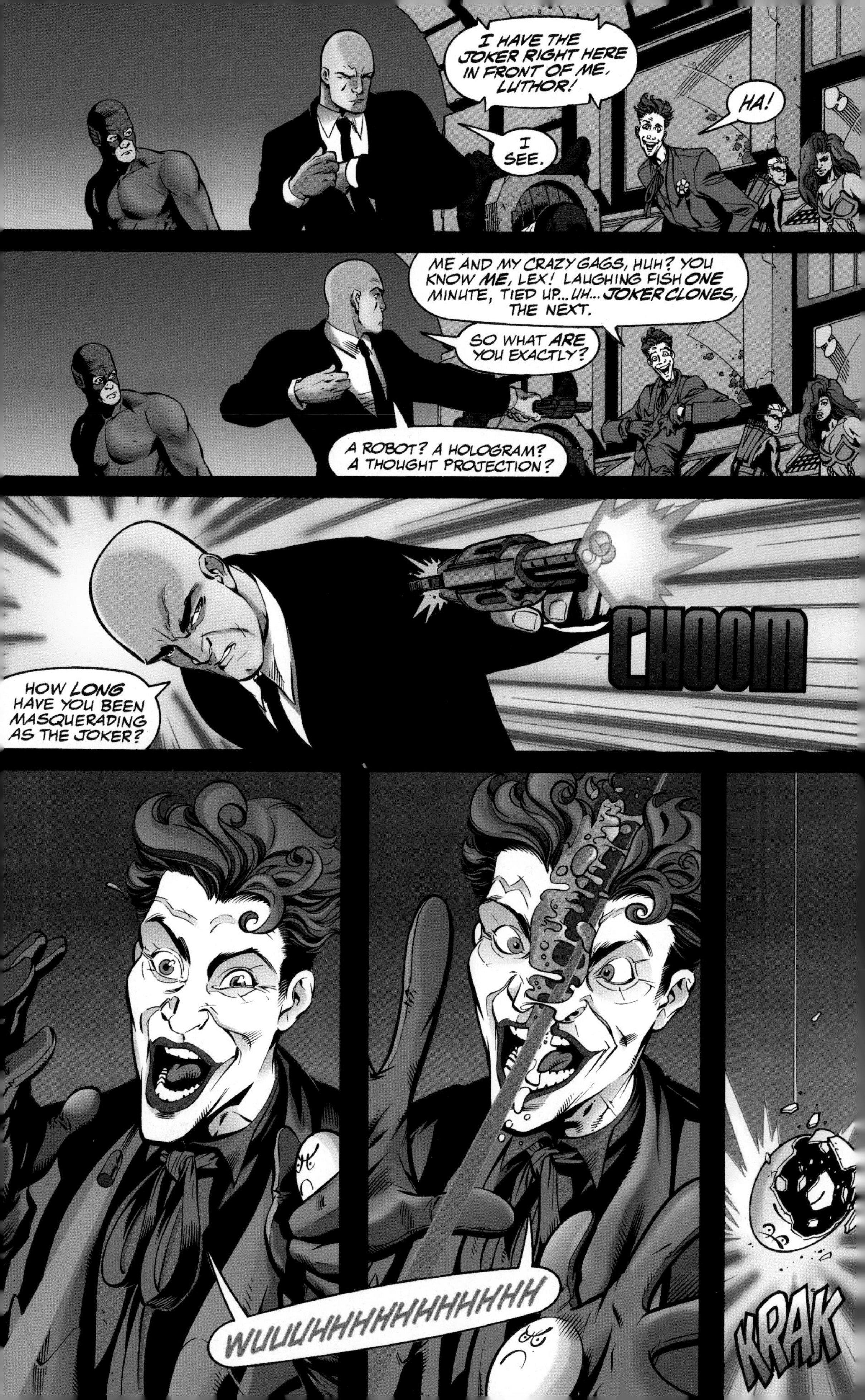
I HAVE THE JOKER RIGHT HERE IN FRONT OF ME, LUTHOR!
I SEE.
HA!
ME AND MY CRAZY GAGS, HUH? YOU KNOW ME, LEX! LAUGHING FISH ONE MINUTE, TIED UP... UH... JOKER CLONES, THE NEXT.
SO WHAT ARE YOU EXACTLY?
A ROBOT? A HOLOGRAM? A THOUGHT PROJECTION?
CHOOM
HOW LONG HAVE YOU BEEN MASQUERADING AS THE JOKER?
WUUUHHHHHHHHHHHH
KRAK

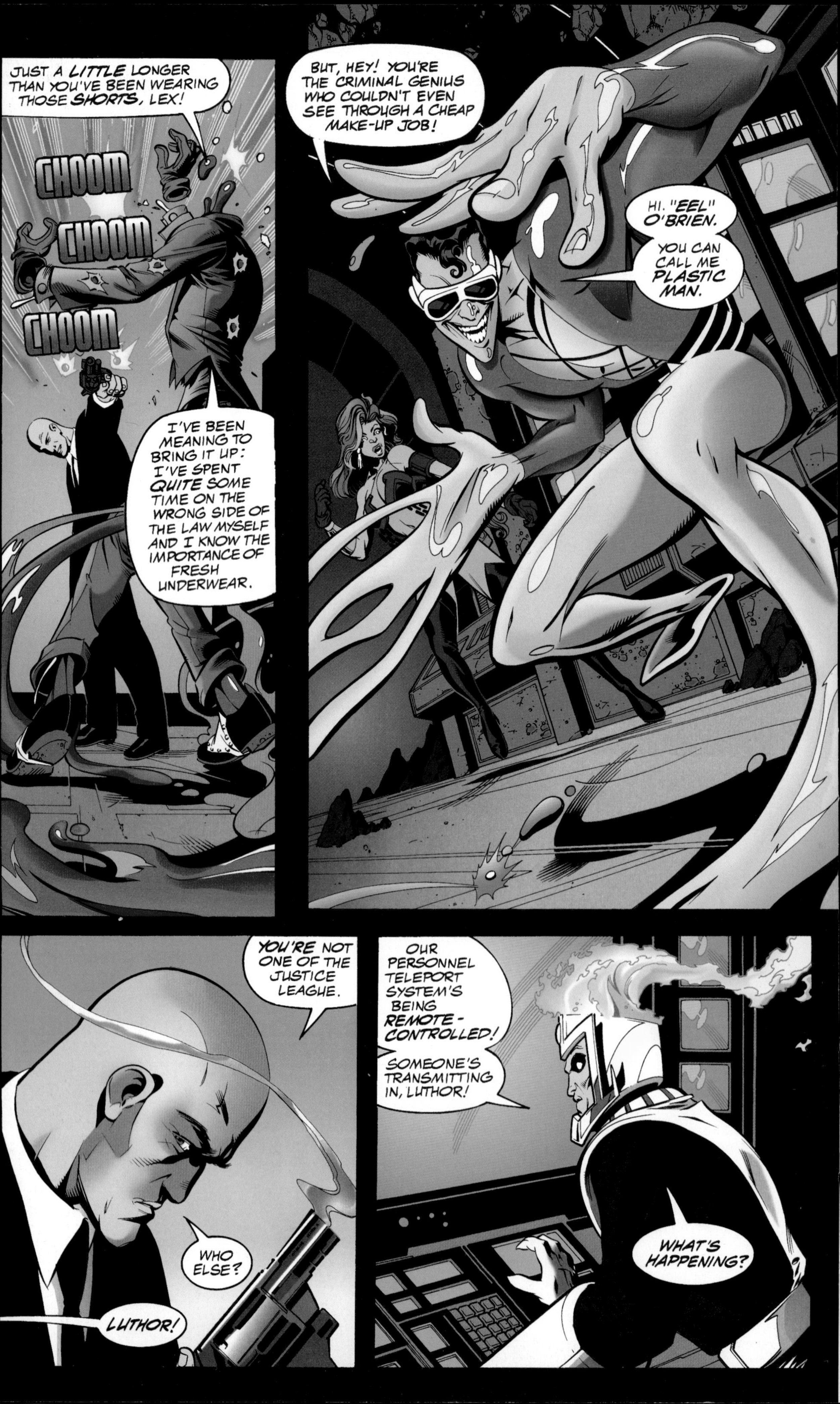
JUST A LITTLE LONGER THAN YOU'VE BEEN WEARING THOSE SHORTS, LEX!
CHOOM
CHOOM
CHOOM
I'VE BEEN MEANING TO BRING IT UP: I'VE SPENT QUITE SOME TIME ON THE WRONG SIDE OF THE LAW MYSELF AND I KNOW THE IMPORTANCE OF FRESH UNDERWEAR.
BUT, HEY! YOU'RE THE CRIMINAL GENIUS WHO COULDN'T EVEN SEE THROUGH A CHEAP MAKE-UP JOB!
HI. "EEL" O'BRIEN.
YOU CAN CALL ME PLASTIC MAN.
YOU'RE NOT ONE OF THE JUSTICE LEAGUE.
WHO ELSE?
LUTHOR!
OUR PERSONNEL TELEPORT SYSTEM'S BEING REMOTE-CONTROLLED!
SOMEONE'S TRANSMITTING IN, LUTHOR!
WHAT'S HAPPENING?

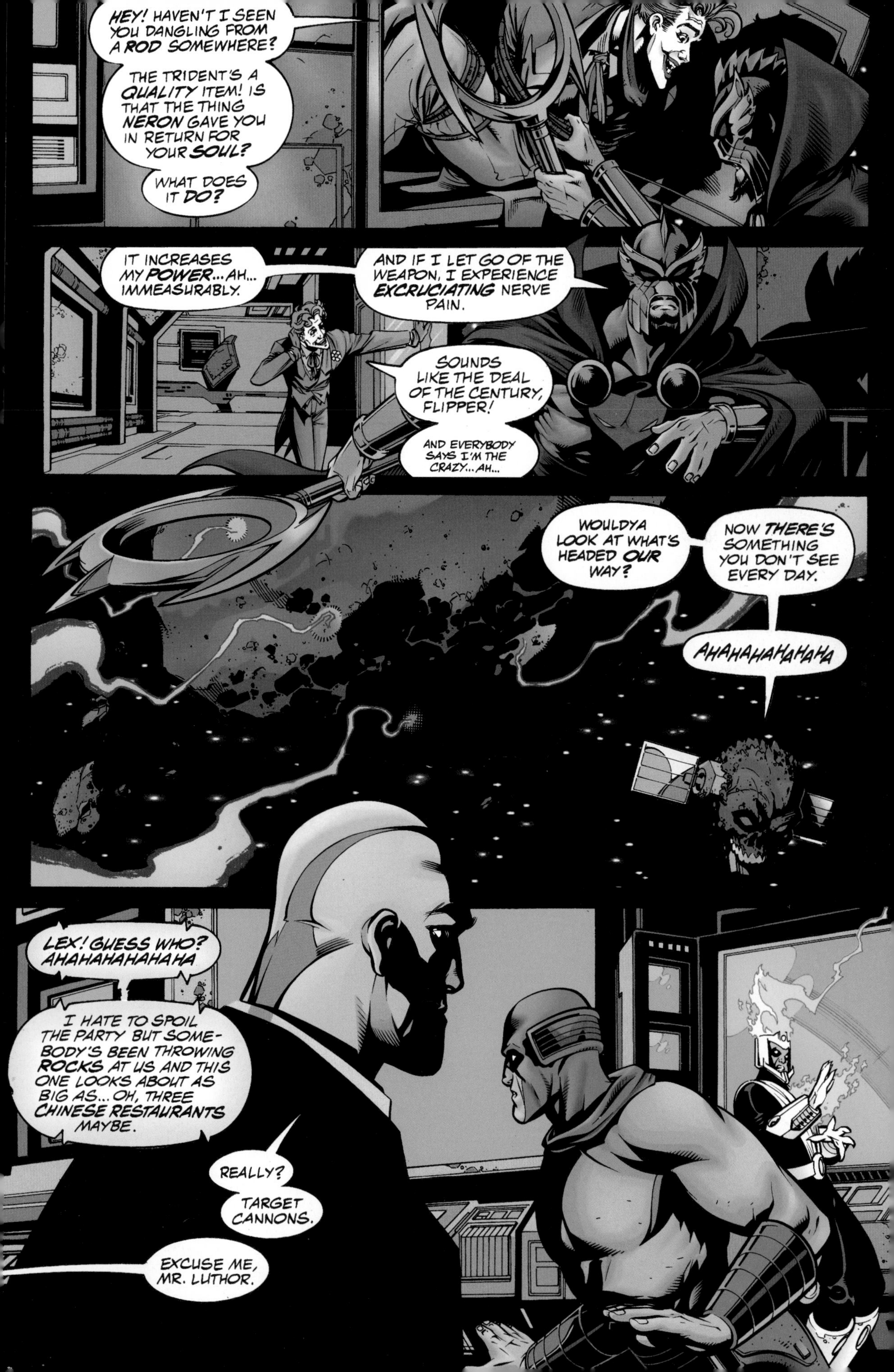

HEY! HAVEN'T I SEEN YOU DANGLING FROM A ROD SOMEWHERE?
THE TRIDENT'S A QUALITY ITEM! IS THAT THE THING NERON GAVE YOU IN RETURN FOR YOUR SOUL?
WHAT DOES IT DO?
IT INCREASES MY POWER... AH... IMMEASURABLY.
AND IF I LET GO OF THE WEAPON, I EXPERIENCE EXCRUCIATING NERVE PAIN.
SOUNDS LIKE THE DEAL OF THE CENTURY, FLIPPER!
AND EVERYBODY SAYS I'M THE CRAZY... AH...
WOULDYA LOOK AT WHAT'S HEADED OUR WAY?
NOW THERE'S SOMETHING YOU DON'T SEE EVERY DAY.
AHAHAHAHAHAHAHA
LEX! GUESS WHO? AHAHAHAHAHAHA
I HATE TO SPOIL THE PARTY BUT SOMEBODY'S BEEN THROWING ROCKS AT US AND THIS ONE LOOKS ABOUT AS BIG AS... OH, THREE CHINESE RESTAURANTS MAYBE.
REALLY?
TARGET CANNONS.
EXCUSE ME, MR. LUTHOR.

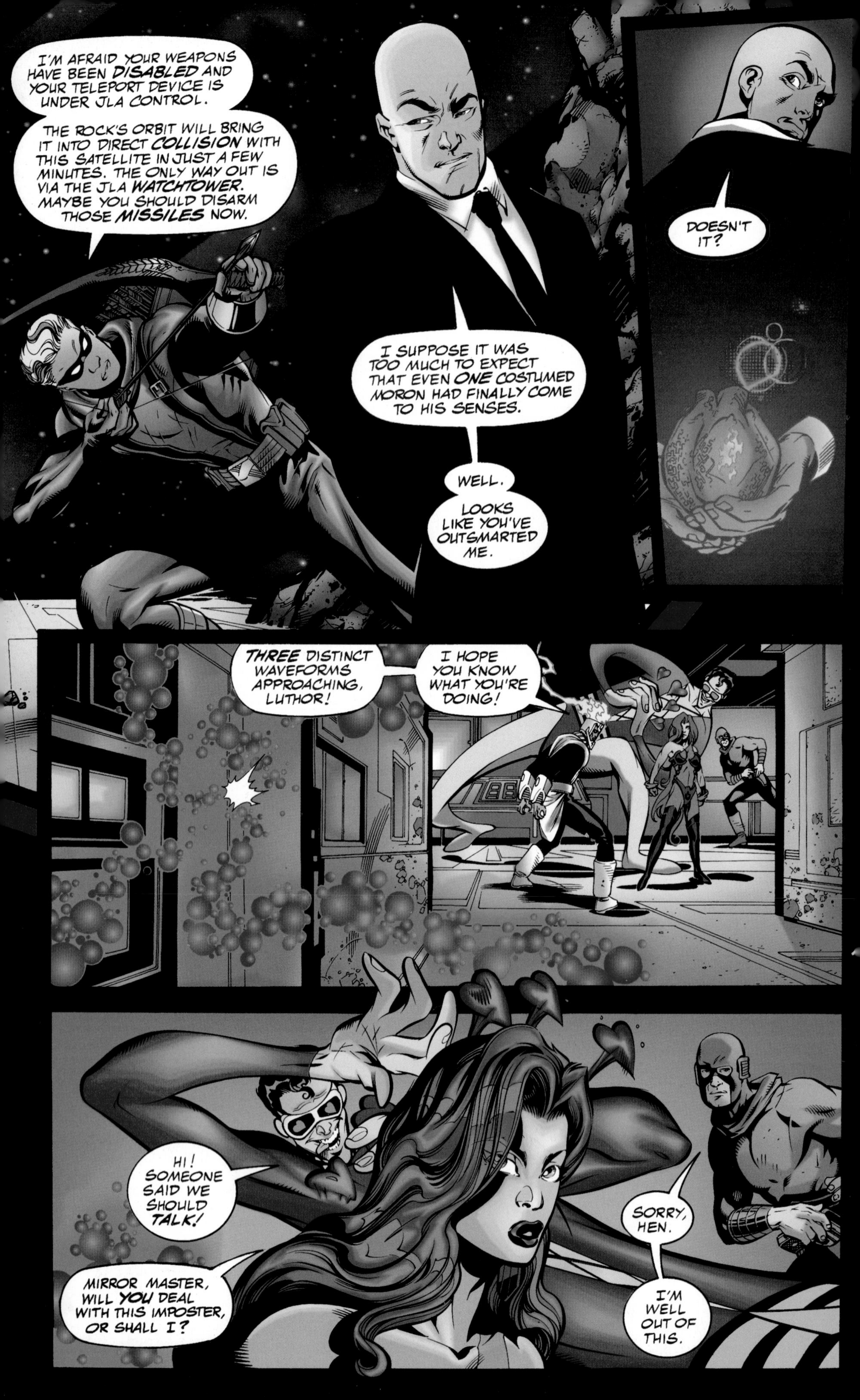
I'M AFRAID YOUR WEAPONS HAVE BEEN DISABLED AND YOUR TELEPORT DEVICE IS UNDER JLA CONTROL.
THE ROCK'S ORBIT WILL BRING IT INTO DIRECT COLLISION WITH THIS SATELLITE IN JUST A FEW MINUTES. THE ONLY WAY OUT IS VIA THE JLA WATCHTOWER. MAYBE YOU SHOULD DISARM THOSE MISSILES NOW.
I SUPPOSE IT WAS TOO MUCH TO EXPECT THAT EVEN ONE COSTUMED MORON HAD FINALLY COME TO HIS SENSES.
WELL.
LOOKS LIKE YOU'VE OUTSMARTED ME.
DOESN'T IT?
THREE DISTINCT WAVEFORMS APPROACHING, LUTHOR!
I HOPE YOU KNOW WHAT YOU'RE DOING!
HI! SOMEONE SAID WE SHOULD TALK!
MIRROR MASTER, WILL YOU DEAL WITH THIS IMPOSTER, OR SHALL I?
SORRY, HEN.
I'M WELL OUT OF THIS.

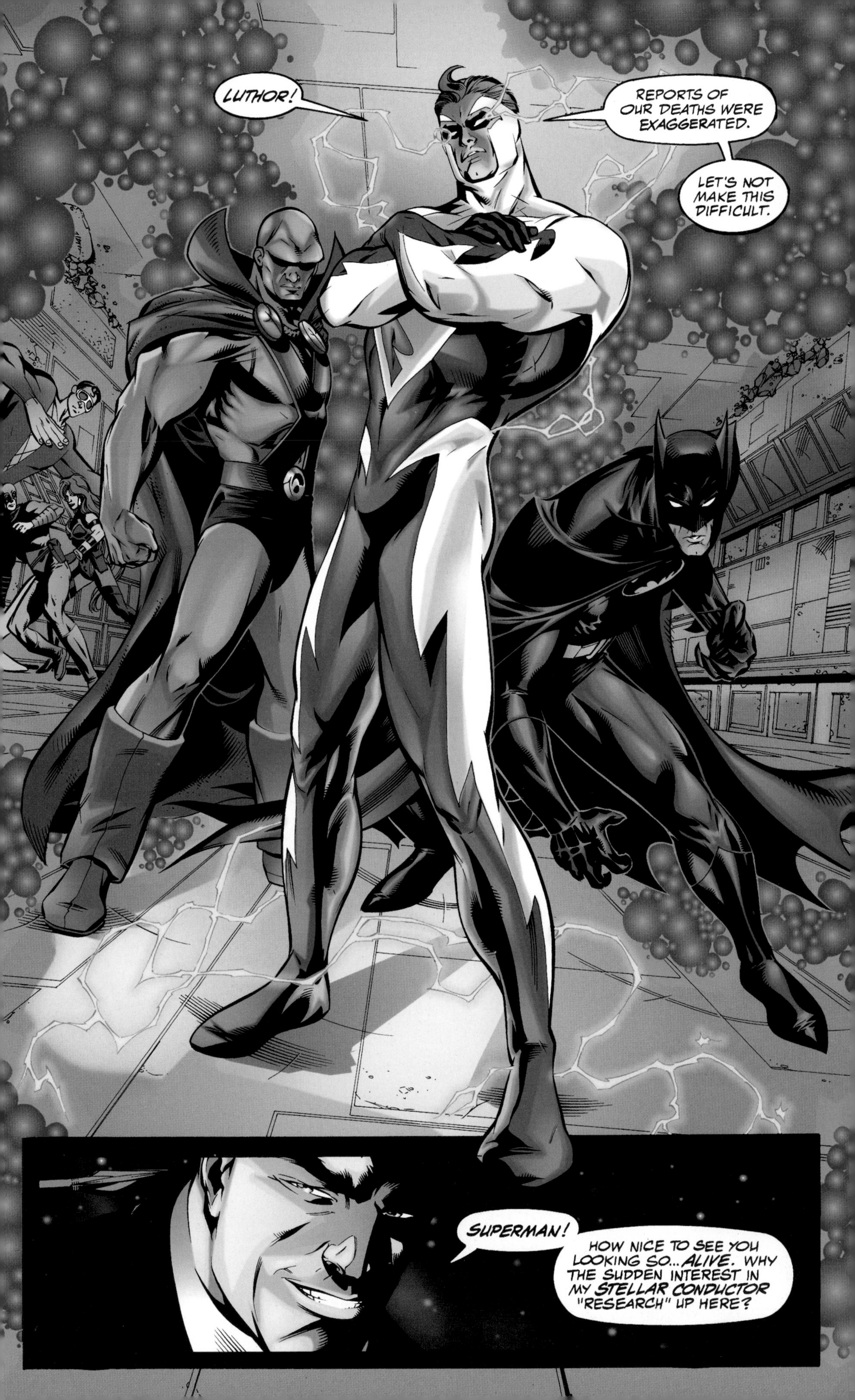
LUTHOR!
REPORTS OF OUR DEATHS WERE EXAGGERATED.
LET'S NOT MAKE THIS DIFFICULT.
SUPERMAN!
HOW NICE TO SEE YOU LOOKING SO... ALIVE. WHY THE SUDDEN INTEREST IN MY STELLAR CONDUCTOR "RESEARCH" UP HERE?

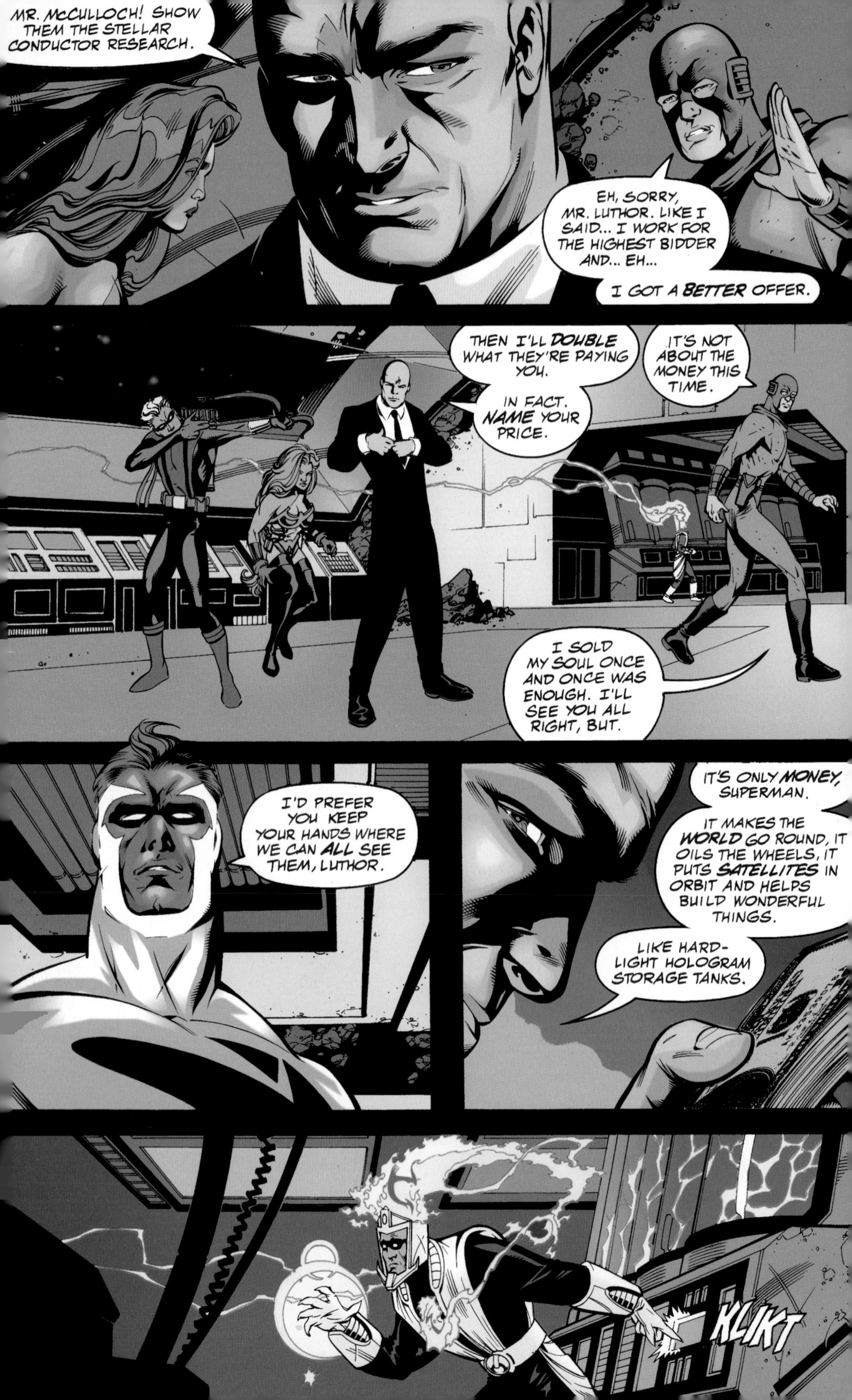
MR. McCULLOCH! SHOW THEM THE STELLAR CONDUCTOR RESEARCH.
EH, SORRY, MR. LUTHOR. LIKE I SAID... I WORK FOR THE HIGHEST BIDDER AND... EH...
I GOT A BETTER OFFER.
THEN I'LL DOUBLE WHAT THEY'RE PAYING YOU.
IN FACT. NAME YOUR PRICE.
IT'S NOT ABOUT THE MONEY THIS TIME.
I SOLD MY SOUL ONCE AND ONCE WAS ENOUGH. I'LL SEE YOU ALL RIGHT, BUT.
I'D PREFER YOU KEEP YOUR HANDS WHERE WE CAN ALL SEE THEM, LUTHOR.
IT'S ONLY MONEY, SUPERMAN.
IT MAKES THE WORLD GO ROUND, IT OILS THE WHEELS, IT PUTS SATELLITES IN ORBIT AND HELPS BUILD WONDERFUL THINGS.
LIKE HARD-LIGHT HOLOGRAM STORAGE TANKS.
KLIKT

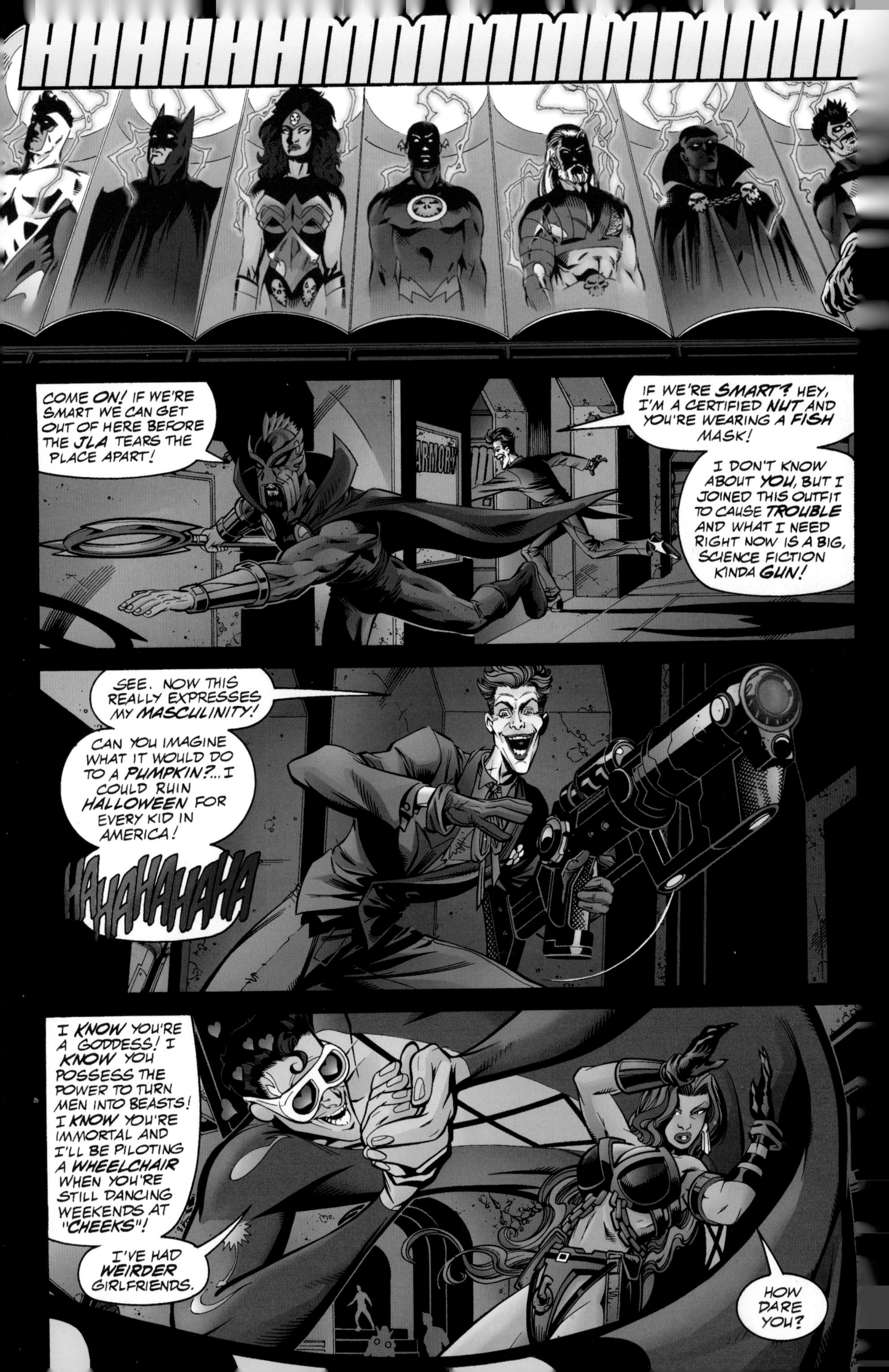
HHHHHHMMMMMMMMMMM
COME ON! IF WE'RE SMART WE CAN GET OUT OF HERE BEFORE THE JLA TEARS THE PLACE APART!
ARMORY
IF WE'RE SMART? HEY, I'M A CERTIFIED NUT AND YOU'RE WEARING A FISH MASK!
I DON'T KNOW ABOUT YOU, BUT I JOINED THIS OUTFIT TO CAUSE TROUBLE AND WHAT I NEED RIGHT NOW IS A BIG, SCIENCE FICTION KINDA GUN!
SEE. NOW THIS REALLY EXPRESSES MY MASCULINITY!
CAN YOU IMAGINE WHAT IT WOULD DO TO A PUMPKIN?...I COULD RUIN HALLOWEEN FOR EVERY KID IN AMERICA!
HAHAHAHAHA
I KNOW YOU'RE A GODDESS! I KNOW YOU POSSESS THE POWER TO TURN MEN INTO BEASTS! I KNOW YOU'RE IMMORTAL AND I'LL BE PILOTING A WHEELCHAIR WHEN YOU'RE STILL DANCING WEEKENDS AT "CHEEKS"!
I'VE HAD WEIRDER GIRLFRIENDS.
HOW DARE YOU?

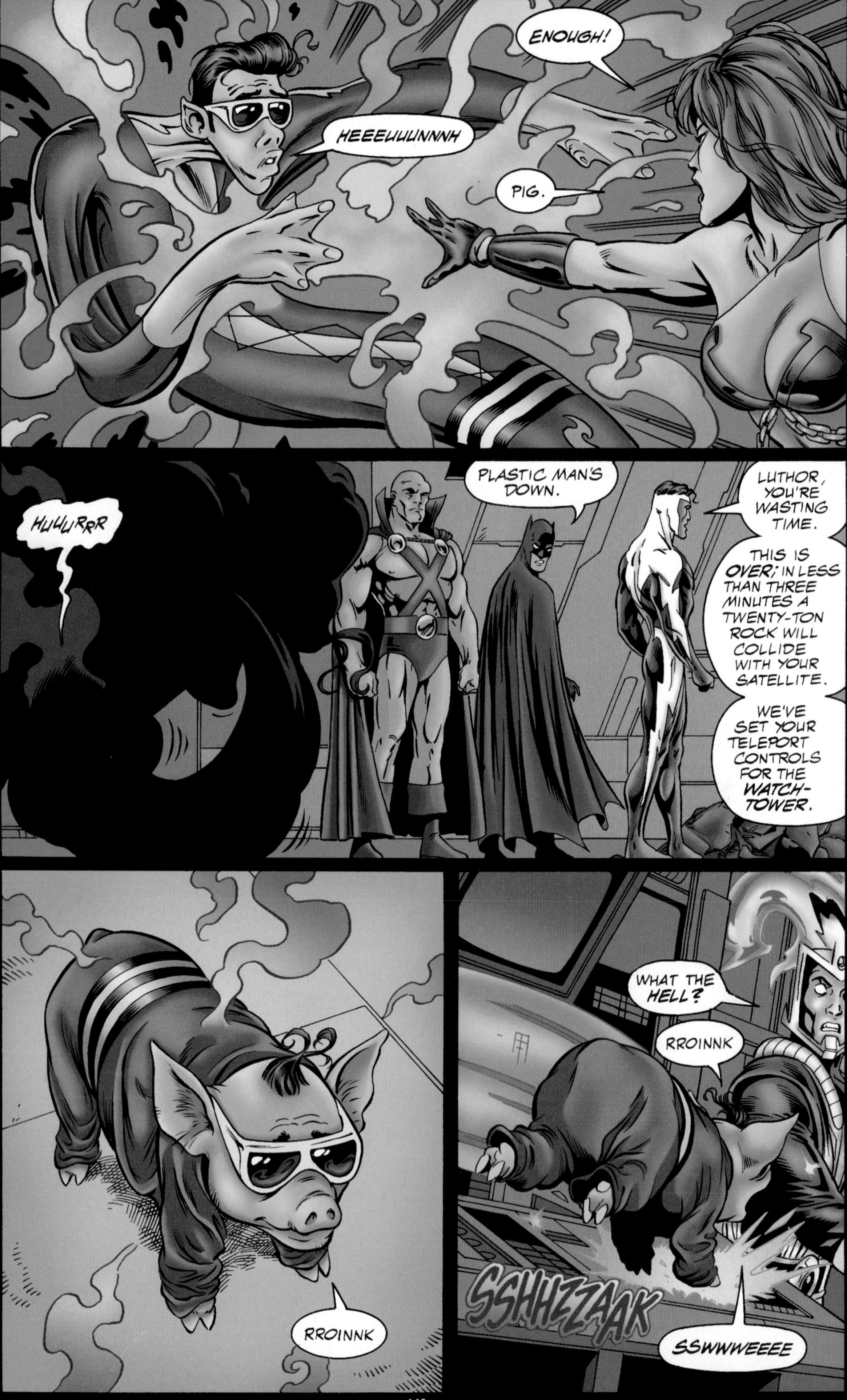

ENOUGH!
HEEEUUUNNNH
PIG.
HUUURRR
PLASTIC MAN'S DOWN.
LUTHOR, YOU'RE WASTING TIME.
THIS IS OVER; IN LESS THAN THREE MINUTES A TWENTY-TON ROCK WILL COLLIDE WITH YOUR SATELLITE.
WE'VE SET YOUR TELEPORT CONTROLS FOR THE WATCHTOWER.
RROINNK
WHAT THE HELL?
RROINNK
SSHHZZAAK
SSWWWEEEE

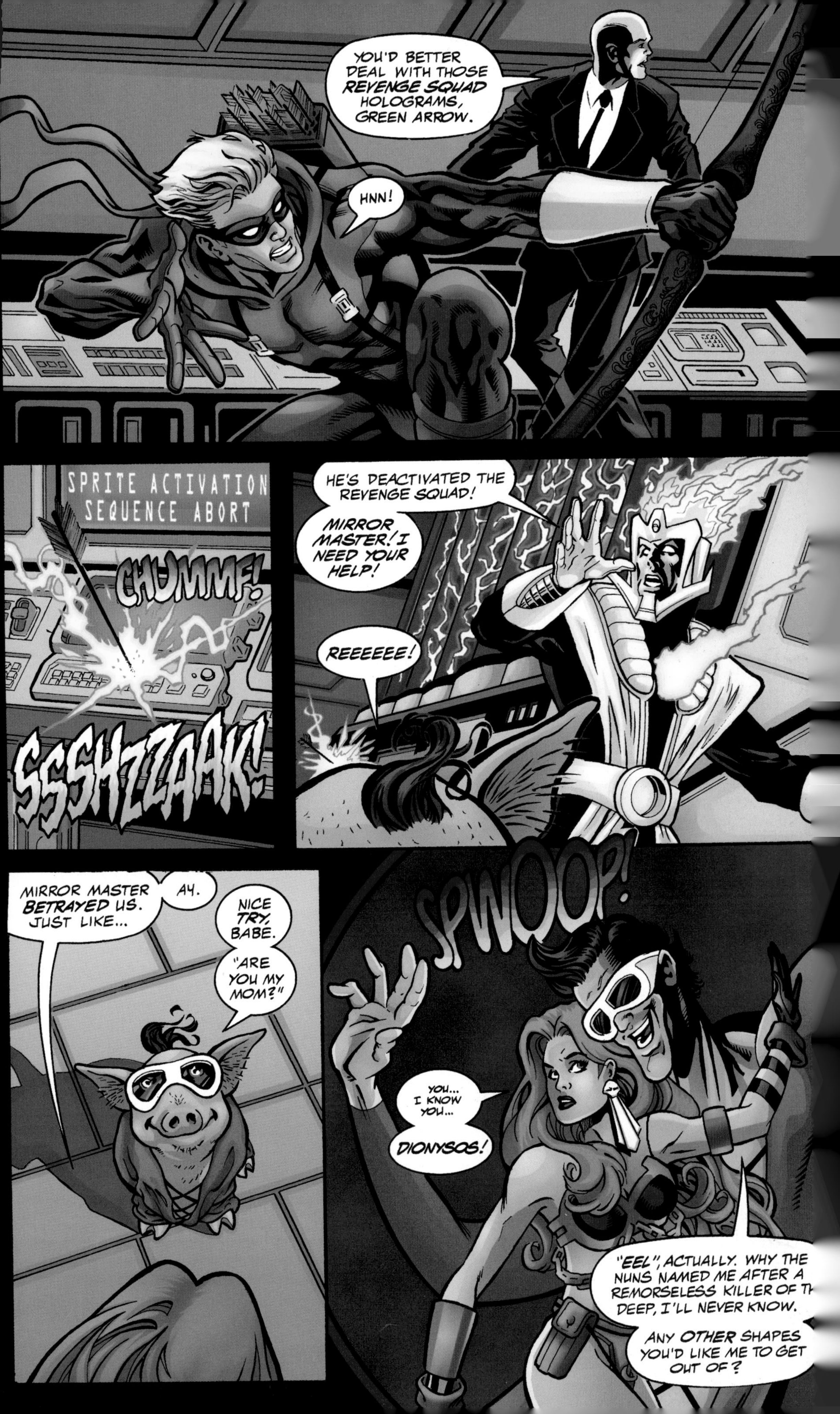
YOU'D BETTER DEAL WITH THOSE REVENGE SQUAD HOLOGRAMS, GREEN ARROW.
HNN!
SPRITE ACTIVATION SEQUENCE ABORT
CHUMMF!
SSSHZZAAK!
HE'S DEACTIVATED THE REVENGE SQUAD!
MIRROR MASTER! I NEED YOUR HELP!
REEEEEE!
MIRROR MASTER BETRAYED US. JUST LIKE...
AY.
NICE TRY, BABE.
"ARE YOU MY MOM?"
SPWOOP!
YOU... I KNOW YOU...
DIONYSOS!
"EEL", ACTUALLY. WHY THE NUNS NAMED ME AFTER A REMORSELESS KILLER OF TH DEEP, I'LL NEVER KNOW.
ANY OTHER SHAPES YOU'D LIKE ME TO GET OUT OF?

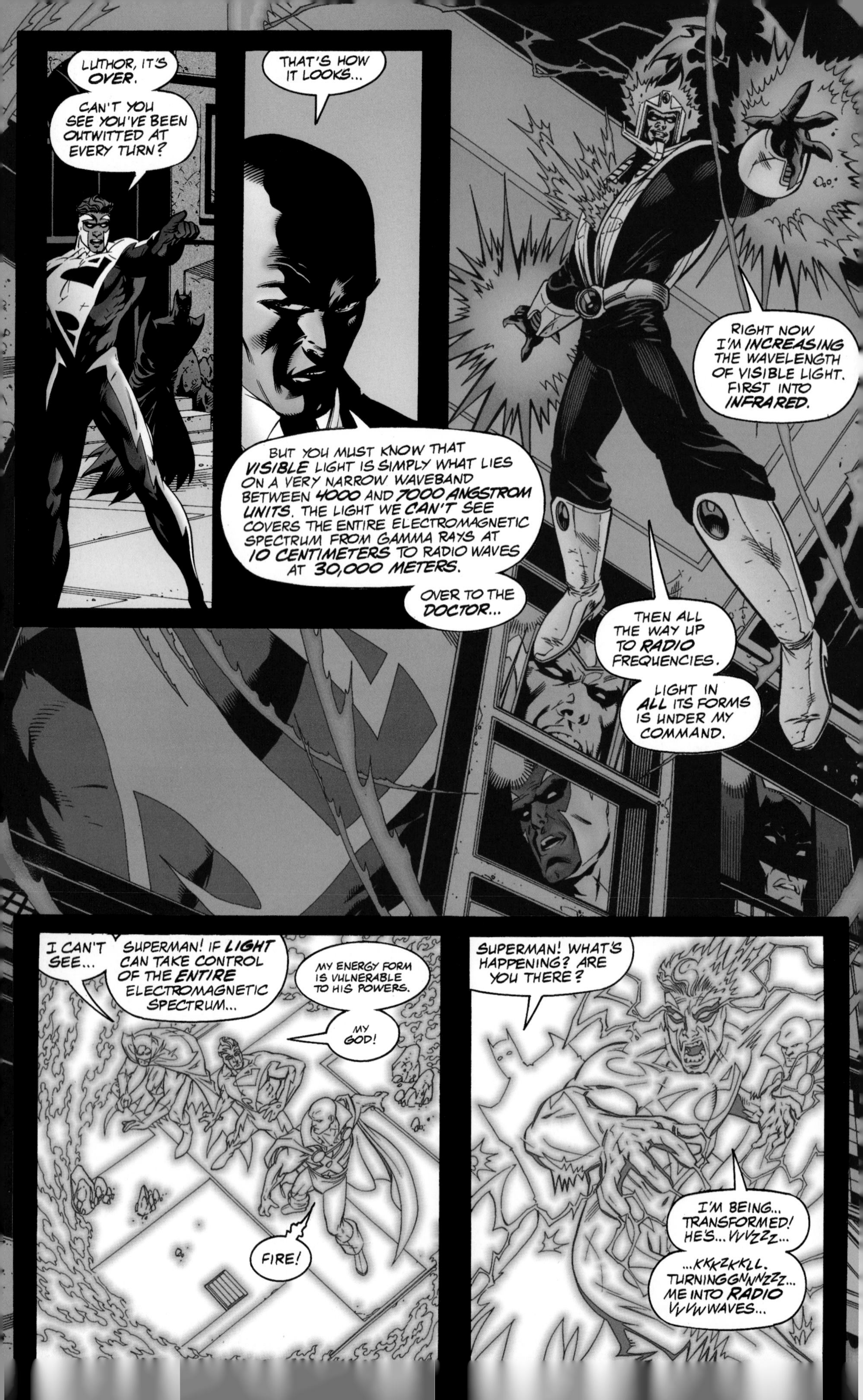
LUTHOR, IT'S OVER.
CAN'T YOU SEE YOU'VE BEEN OUTWITTED AT EVERY TURN?
THAT'S HOW IT LOOKS...
BUT YOU MUST KNOW THAT VISIBLE LIGHT IS SIMPLY WHAT LIES ON A VERY NARROW WAVEBAND BETWEEN 4000 AND 7000 ANGSTROM UNITS. THE LIGHT WE CAN'T SEE COVERS THE ENTIRE ELECTROMAGNETIC SPECTRUM FROM GAMMA RAYS AT 10 CENTIMETERS TO RADIO WAVES AT 30,000 METERS.
OVER TO THE DOCTOR...
RIGHT NOW I'M INCREASING THE WAVELENGTH OF VISIBLE LIGHT. FIRST INTO INFRARED.
THEN ALL THE WAY UP TO RADIO FREQUENCIES.
LIGHT IN ALL ITS FORMS IS UNDER MY COMMAND.
I CAN'T SEE...
SUPERMAN! IF LIGHT CAN TAKE CONTROL OF THE ENTIRE ELECTROMAGNETIC SPECTRUM...
MY ENERGY FORM IS VULNERABLE TO HIS POWERS.
MY GOD!
FIRE!
SUPERMAN! WHAT'S HAPPENING? ARE YOU THERE?
I'M BEING... TRANSFORMED! HE'S...VVVZZZ...
...KKKZKKLL. TURNINGGNNNZZZ... ME INTO RADIO VVVWWAVES...

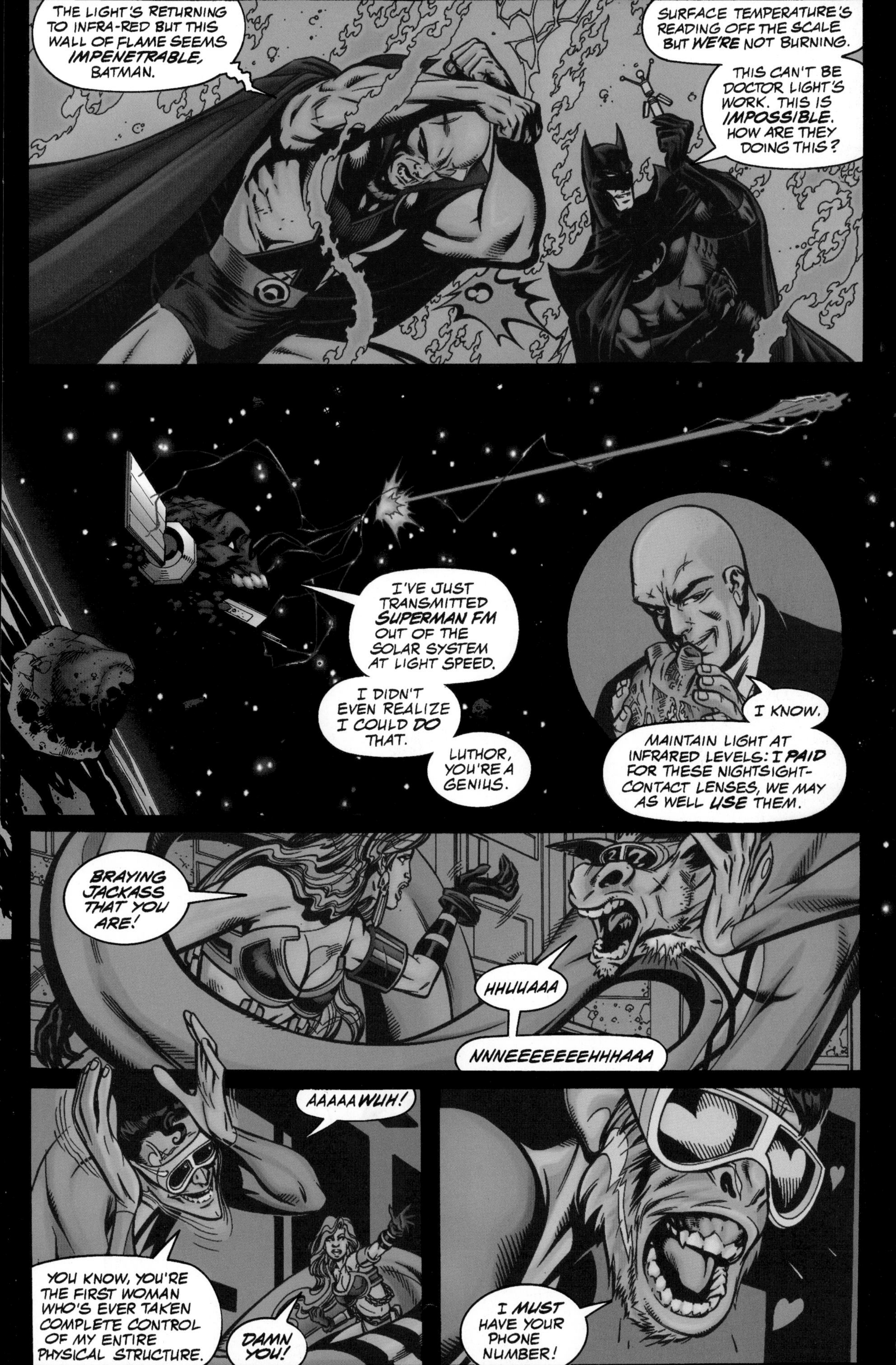
THE LIGHT'S RETURNING TO INFRA-RED BUT THIS WALL OF FLAME SEEMS IMPENETRABLE, BATMAN.
SURFACE TEMPERATURE'S READING OFF THE SCALE BUT WE'RE NOT BURNING.
THIS CAN'T BE DOCTOR LIGHT'S WORK. THIS IS IMPOSSIBLE. HOW ARE THEY DOING THIS?
I'VE JUST TRANSMITTED SUPERMAN FM OUT OF THE SOLAR SYSTEM AT LIGHT SPEED.
I DIDN'T EVEN REALIZE I COULD DO THAT.
LUTHOR, YOU'RE A GENIUS.
I KNOW.
MAINTAIN LIGHT AT INFRARED LEVELS: I PAID FOR THESE NIGHTSIGHT-CONTACT LENSES, WE MAY AS WELL USE THEM.
BRAYING JACKASS THAT YOU ARE!
HHUUAAA
NNNEEEEEEEEHHHAAA
AAAAAWUH!
YOU KNOW, YOU'RE THE FIRST WOMAN WHO'S EVER TAKEN COMPLETE CONTROL OF MY ENTIRE PHYSICAL STRUCTURE.
DAMN YOU!
I MUST HAVE YOUR PHONE NUMBER!

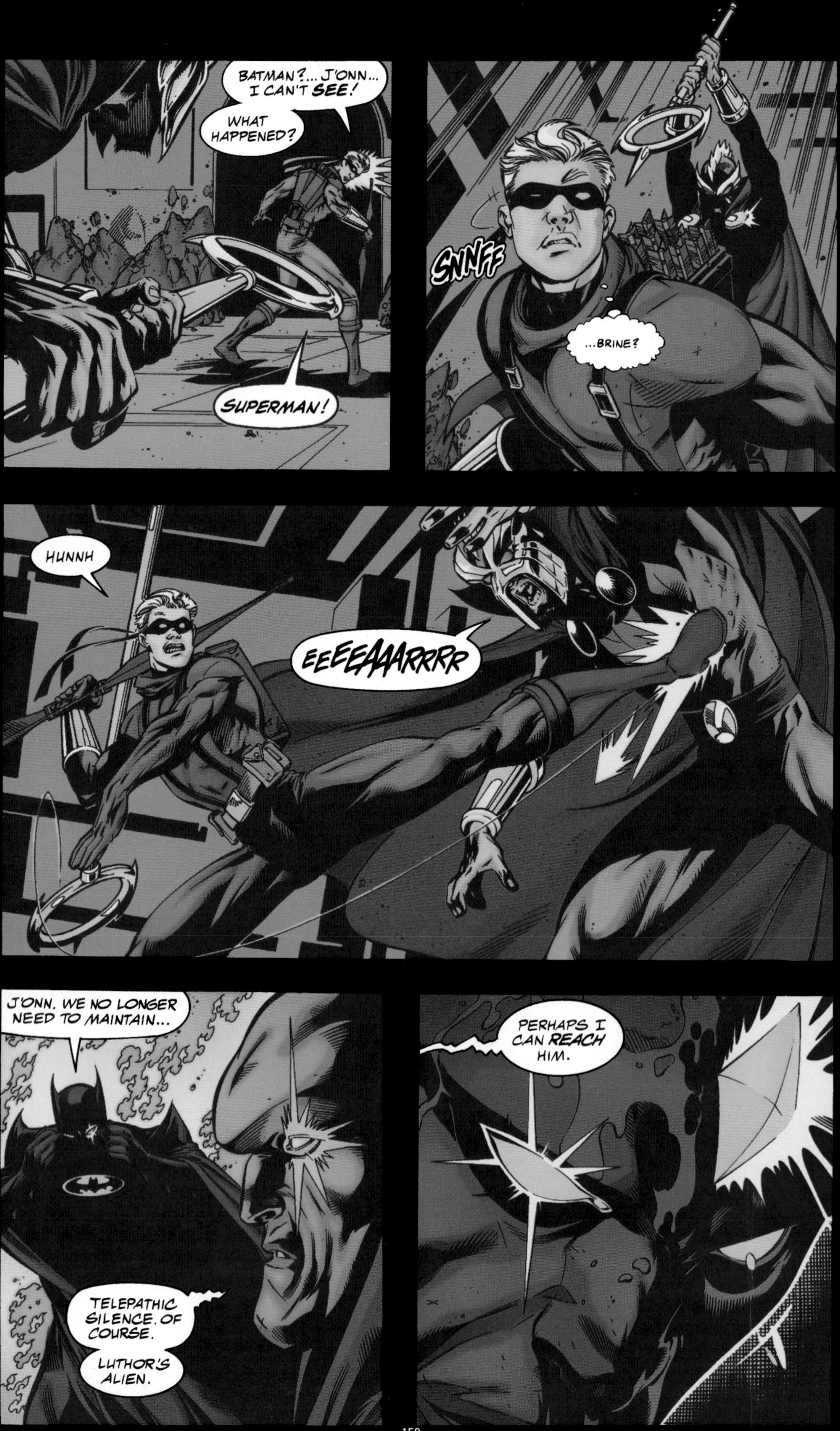
BATMAN?... J'ONN... I CAN'T SEE!
WHAT HAPPENED?
SUPERMAN!
SNNFF
...BRINE?
HUNNH
EEEEAAARRRR
J'ONN. WE NO LONGER NEED TO MAINTAIN...
TELEPATHIC SILENCE. OF COURSE.
LUTHOR'S ALIEN.
PERHAPS I CAN REACH HIM.

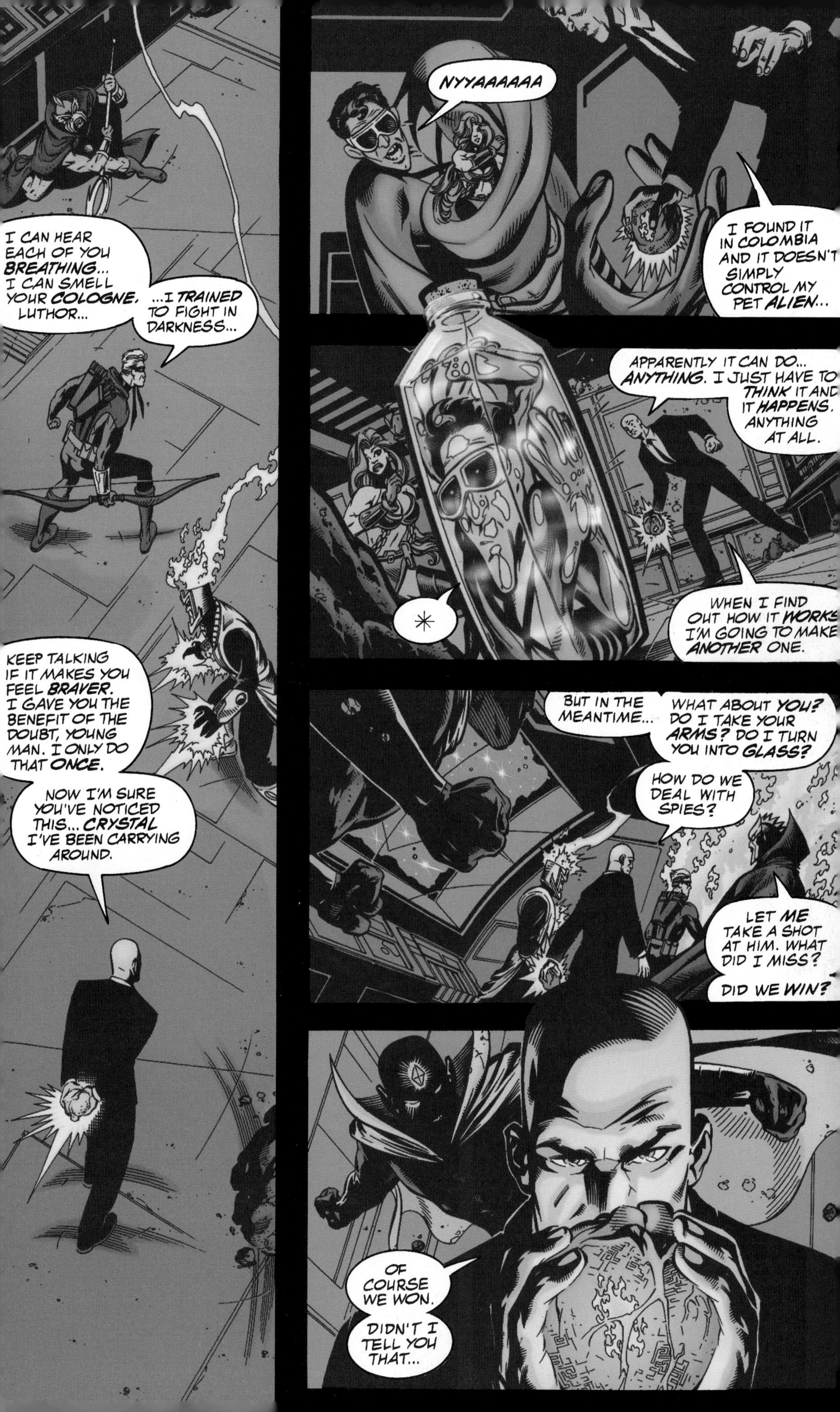
I CAN HEAR EACH OF YOU BREATHING... I CAN SMELL YOUR COLOGNE, LUTHOR...
...I TRAINED TO FIGHT IN DARKNESS...
KEEP TALKING IF IT MAKES YOU FEEL BRAVER. I GAVE YOU THE BENEFIT OF THE DOUBT, YOUNG MAN. I ONLY DO THAT ONCE.
NOW I'M SURE YOU'VE NOTICED THIS... CRYSTAL I'VE BEEN CARRYING AROUND.
NYYAAAAAA
I FOUND IT IN COLOMBIA AND IT DOESN'T SIMPLY CONTROL MY PET ALIEN...
APPARENTLY IT CAN DO... ANYTHING. I JUST HAVE TO THINK IT AND IT HAPPENS. ANYTHING AT ALL.
*
WHEN I FIND OUT HOW IT WORKS I'M GOING TO MAKE ANOTHER ONE.
BUT IN THE MEANTIME...
WHAT ABOUT YOU? DO I TAKE YOUR ARMS? DO I TURN YOU INTO GLASS?
HOW DO WE DEAL WITH SPIES?
LET ME TAKE A SHOT AT HIM. WHAT DID I MISS?
DID WE WIN?
OF COURSE WE WON.
DIDN'T I TELL YOU THAT...

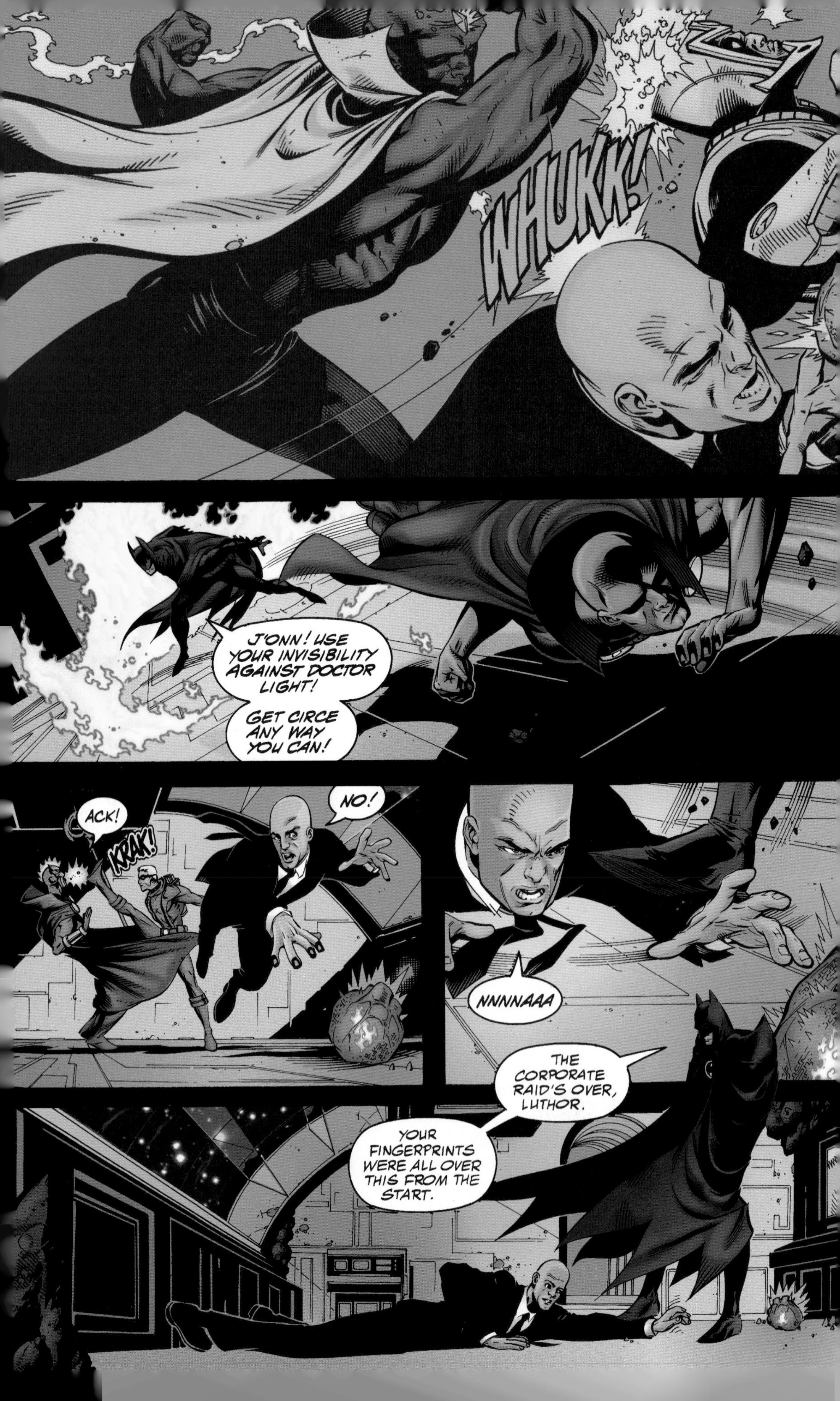
WHUKK!
J'ONN! USE YOUR INVISIBILITY AGAINST DOCTOR LIGHT!
GET CIRCE ANY WAY YOU CAN!
ACK!
KRAK!
NO!
NNNNAAA
THE CORPORATE RAID'S OVER, LUTHOR.
YOUR FINGERPRINTS WERE ALL OVER THIS FROM THE START.

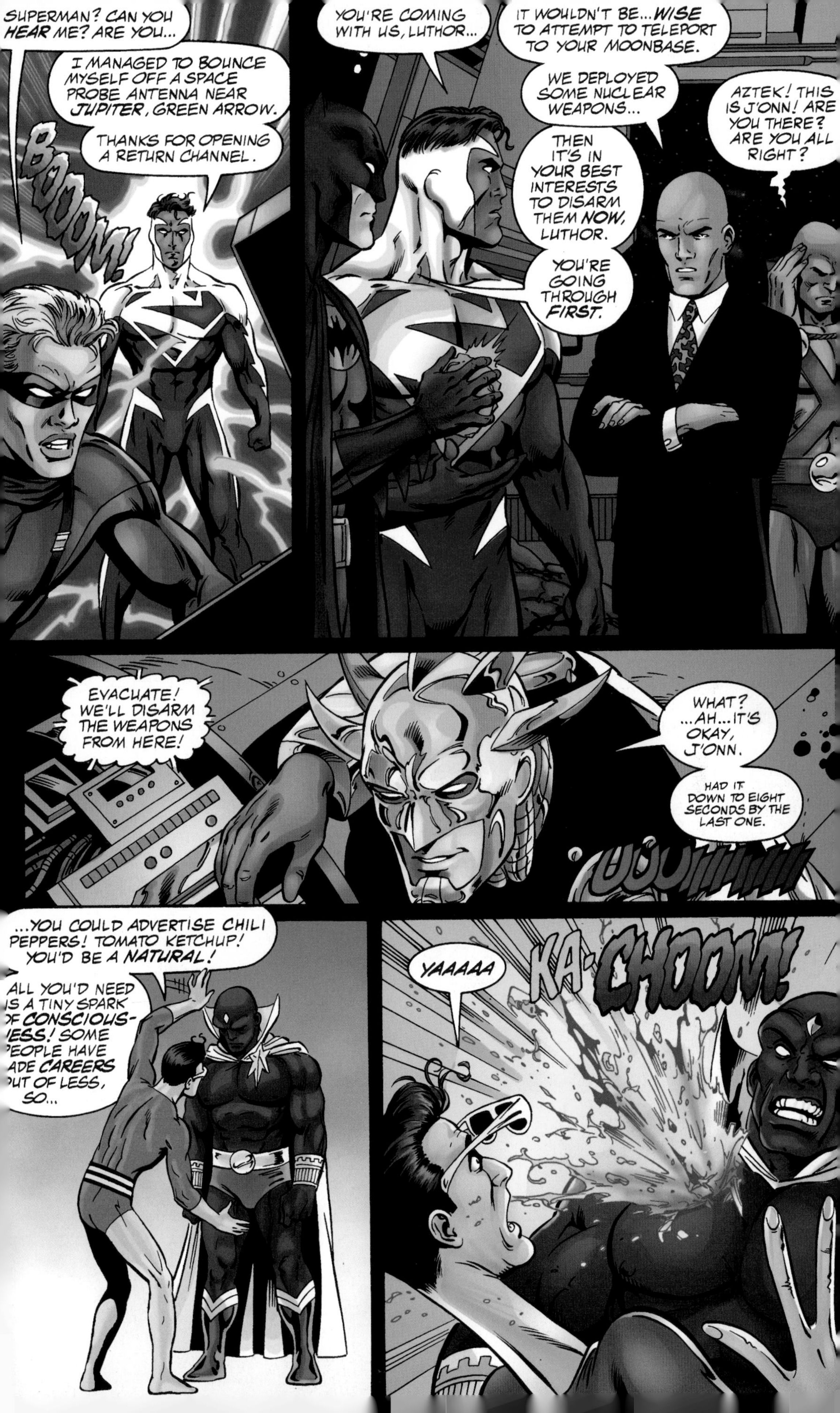
SUPERMAN? CAN YOU HEAR ME? ARE YOU...
I MANAGED TO BOUNCE MYSELF OFF A SPACE PROBE ANTENNA NEAR JUPITER, GREEN ARROW.
THANKS FOR OPENING A RETURN CHANNEL.
BOOOM!
YOU'RE COMING WITH US, LUTHOR...
IT WOULDN'T BE... WISE TO ATTEMPT TO TELEPORT TO YOUR MOONBASE.
WE DEPLOYED SOME NUCLEAR WEAPONS...
THEN IT'S IN YOUR BEST INTERESTS TO DISARM THEM NOW, LUTHOR.
YOU'RE GOING THROUGH FIRST.
AZTEK! THIS IS J'ONN! ARE YOU THERE? ARE YOU ALL RIGHT?
EVACUATE! WE'LL DISARM THE WEAPONS FROM HERE!
WHAT? ...AH... IT'S OKAY, J'ONN.
HAD IT DOWN TO EIGHT SECONDS BY THE LAST ONE.
...YOU COULD ADVERTISE CHILI PEPPERS! TOMATO KETCHUP! YOU'D BE A NATURAL!
ALL YOU'D NEED IS A TINY SPARK OF CONSCIOUSNESS! SOME PEOPLE HAVE MADE CAREERS OUT OF LESS, SO...
YAAAAA
KA-CHOOM!

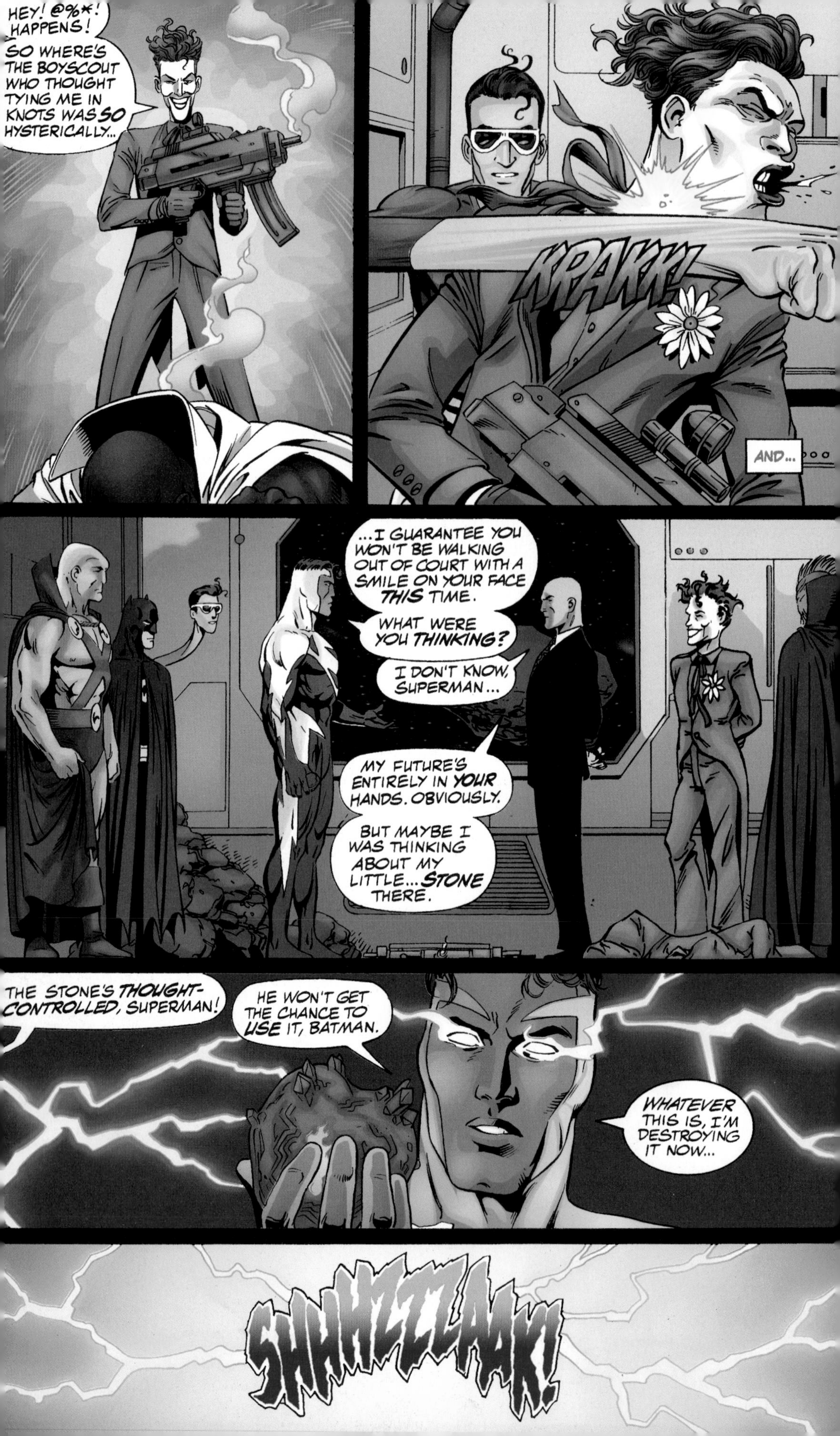
HEY! @%*! HAPPENS!
SO WHERE'S THE BOYSCOUT WHO THOUGHT TYING ME IN KNOTS WAS SO HYSTERICALLY...
KRAKK!
AND...
...I GUARANTEE YOU WON'T BE WALKING OUT OF COURT WITH A SMILE ON YOUR FACE THIS TIME.
WHAT WERE YOU THINKING?
I DON'T KNOW, SUPERMAN...
MY FUTURE'S ENTIRELY IN YOUR HANDS. OBVIOUSLY.
BUT MAYBE I WAS THINKING ABOUT MY LITTLE...STONE THERE.
THE STONE'S THOUGHT-CONTROLLED, SUPERMAN!
HE WON'T GET THE CHANCE TO USE IT, BATMAN.
WHATEVER THIS IS, I'M DESTROYING IT NOW...
SHHZZZAAK!

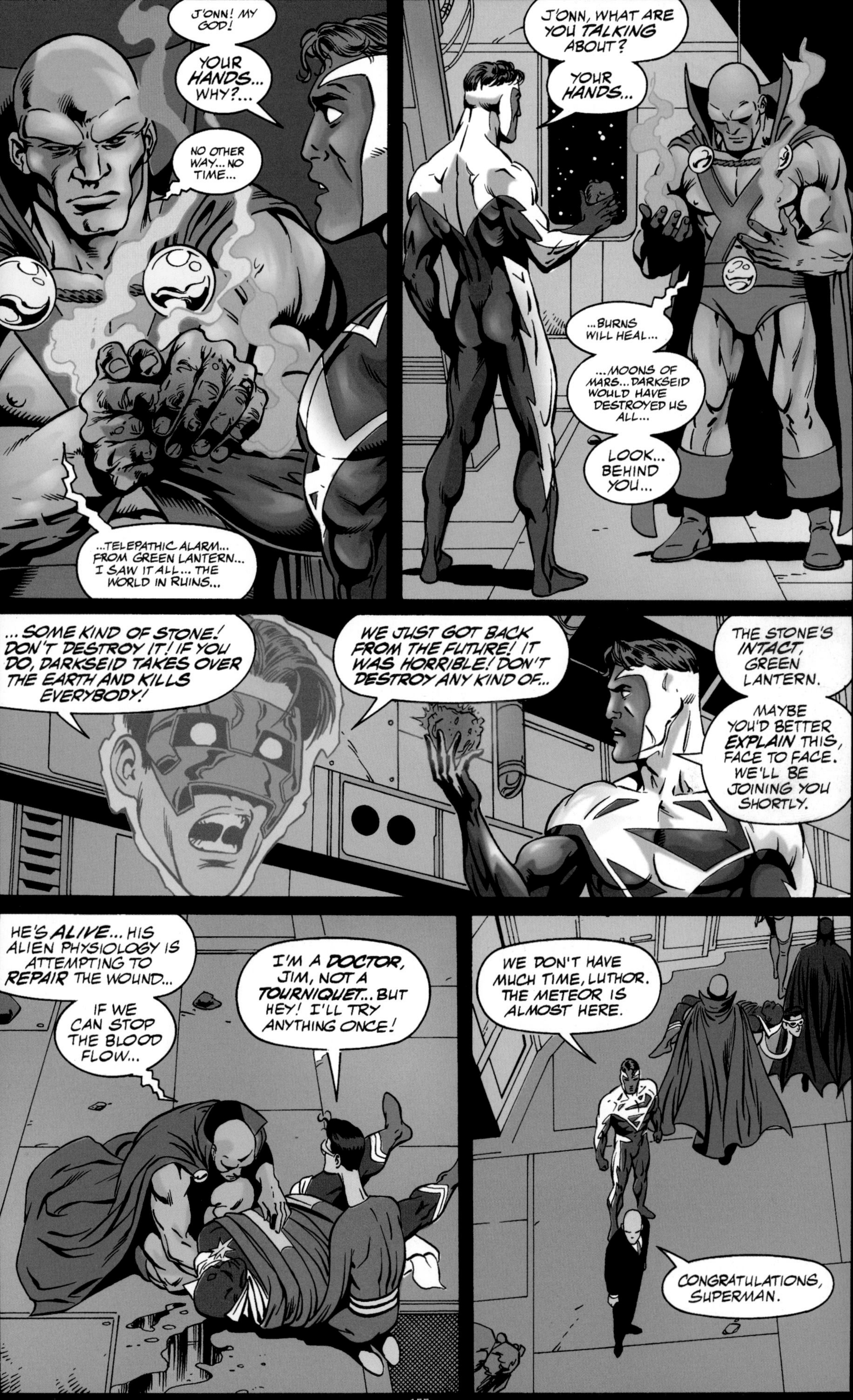
J'ONN! MY GOD!
YOUR HANDS... WHY?...
NO OTHER WAY... NO TIME...
...TELEPATHIC ALARM... FROM GREEN LANTERN... I SAW IT ALL... THE WORLD IN RUINS...
J'ONN, WHAT ARE YOU TALKING ABOUT?
YOUR HANDS...
...BURNS WILL HEAL...
...MOONS OF MARS... DARKSEID WOULD HAVE DESTROYED US ALL...
LOOK... BEHIND YOU...
...SOME KIND OF STONE! DON'T DESTROY IT! IF YOU DO, DARKSEID TAKES OVER THE EARTH AND KILLS EVERYBODY!
WE JUST GOT BACK FROM THE FUTURE! IT WAS HORRIBLE! DON'T DESTROY ANY KIND OF...
THE STONE'S INTACT, GREEN LANTERN.
MAYBE YOU'D BETTER EXPLAIN THIS, FACE TO FACE. WE'LL BE JOINING YOU SHORTLY.
HE'S ALIVE... HIS ALIEN PHYSIOLOGY IS ATTEMPTING TO REPAIR THE WOUND...
IF WE CAN STOP THE BLOOD FLOW...
I'M A DOCTOR, JIM, NOT A TOURNIQUET... BUT HEY! I'LL TRY ANYTHING ONCE!
WE DON'T HAVE MUCH TIME, LUTHOR. THE METEOR IS ALMOST HERE.
CONGRATULATIONS, SUPERMAN.

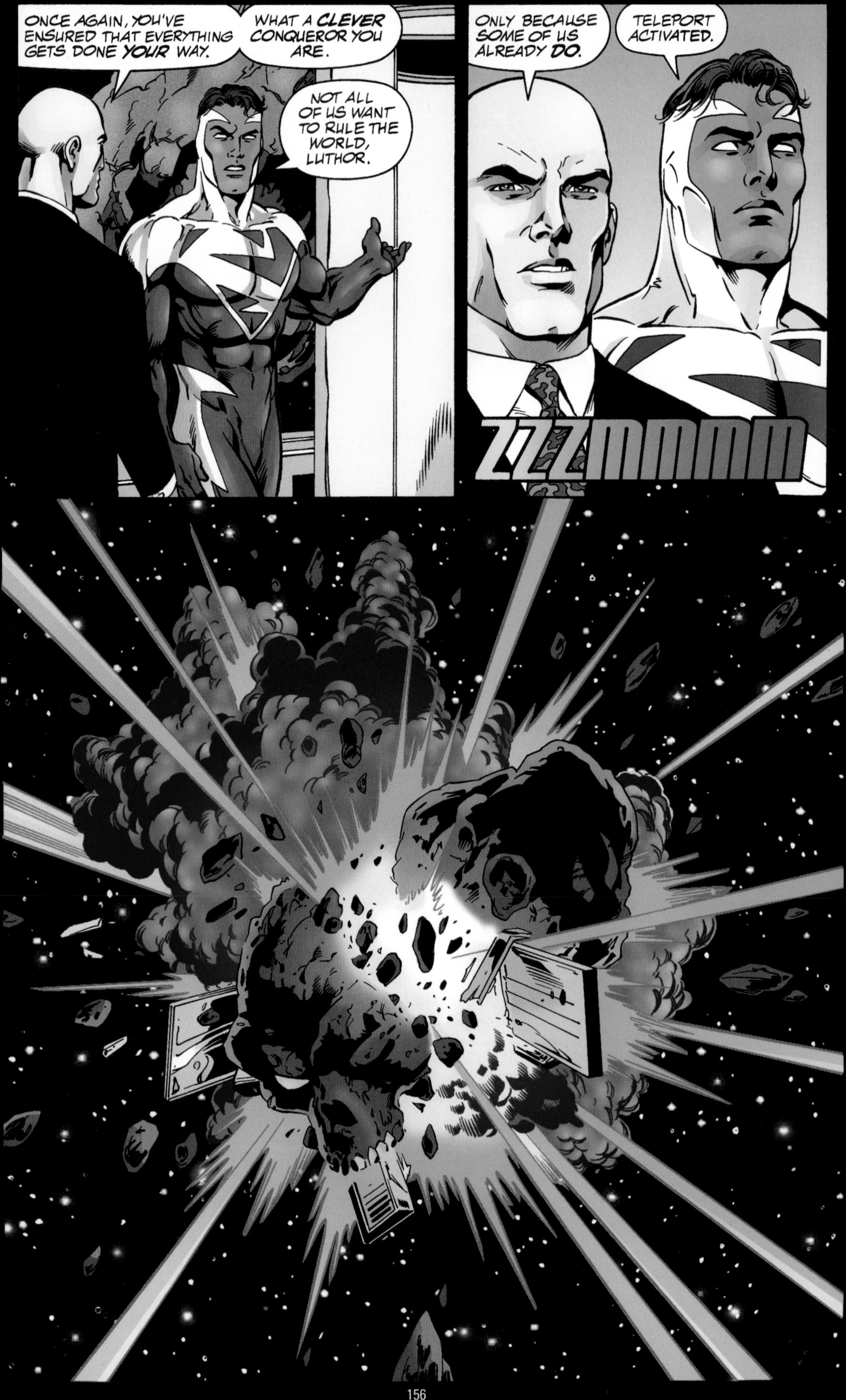
ONCE AGAIN, YOU'VE ENSURED THAT EVERYTHING GETS DONE YOUR WAY.
WHAT A CLEVER CONQUEROR YOU ARE.
NOT ALL OF US WANT TO RULE THE WORLD, LUTHOR.
ONLY BECAUSE SOME OF US ALREADY DO.
TELEPORT ACTIVATED.
ZZZMMMMM

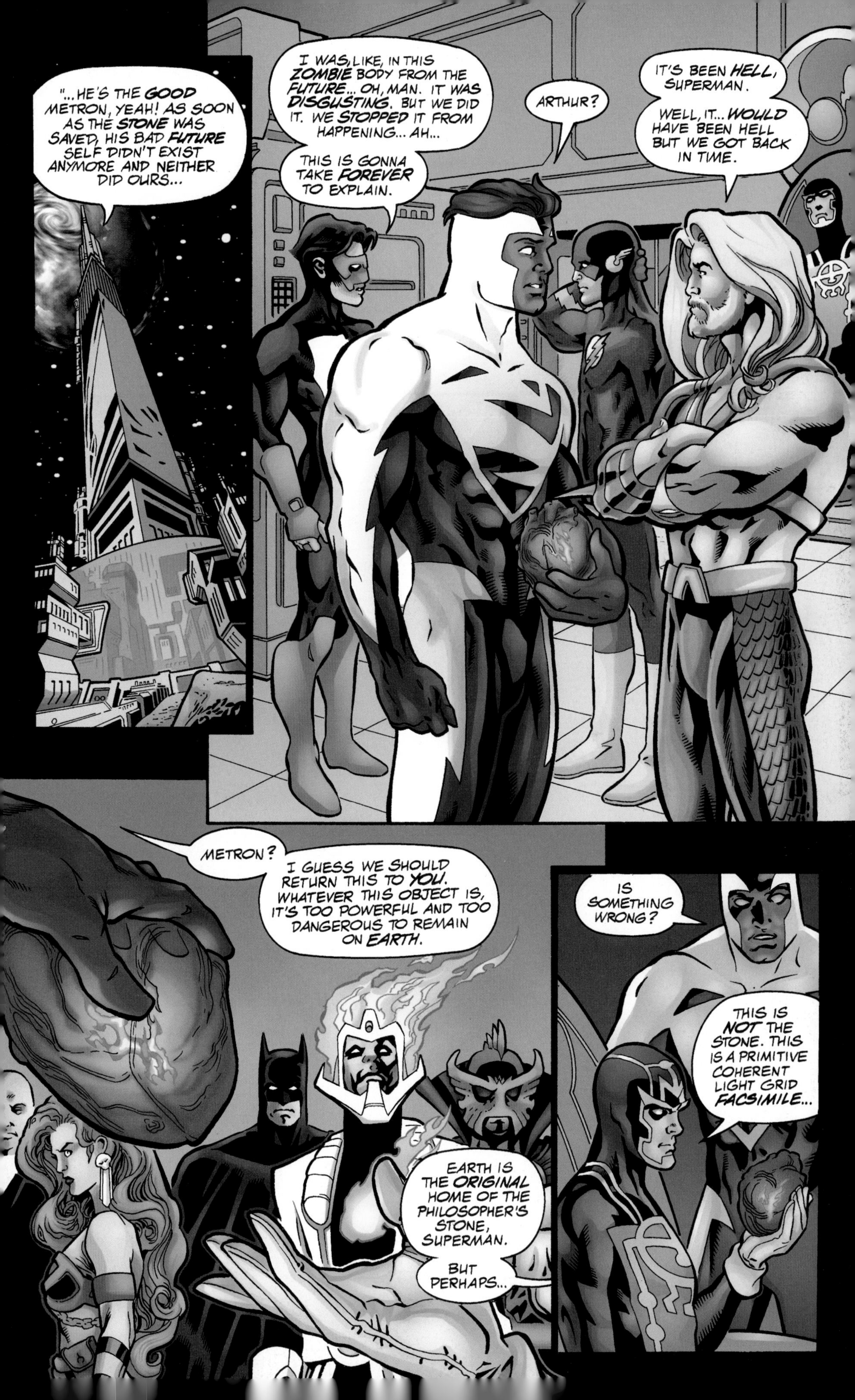
"...HE'S THE GOOD METRON, YEAH! AS SOON AS THE STONE WAS SAVED, HIS BAD FUTURE SELF DIDN'T EXIST ANYMORE AND NEITHER DID OURS...
I WAS, LIKE, IN THIS ZOMBIE BODY FROM THE FUTURE... OH, MAN. IT WAS DISGUSTING. BUT WE DID IT. WE STOPPED IT FROM HAPPENING... AH...
THIS IS GONNA TAKE FOREVER TO EXPLAIN.
ARTHUR?
IT'S BEEN HELL, SUPERMAN.
WELL, IT... WOULD HAVE BEEN HELL BUT WE GOT BACK IN TIME.
METRON?
I GUESS WE SHOULD RETURN THIS TO YOU. WHATEVER THIS OBJECT IS, IT'S TOO POWERFUL AND TOO DANGEROUS TO REMAIN ON EARTH.
EARTH IS THE ORIGINAL HOME OF THE PHILOSOPHER'S STONE, SUPERMAN.
BUT PERHAPS...
IS SOMETHING WRONG?
THIS IS NOT THE STONE. THIS IS A PRIMITIVE COHERENT LIGHT GRID FACSIMILE...

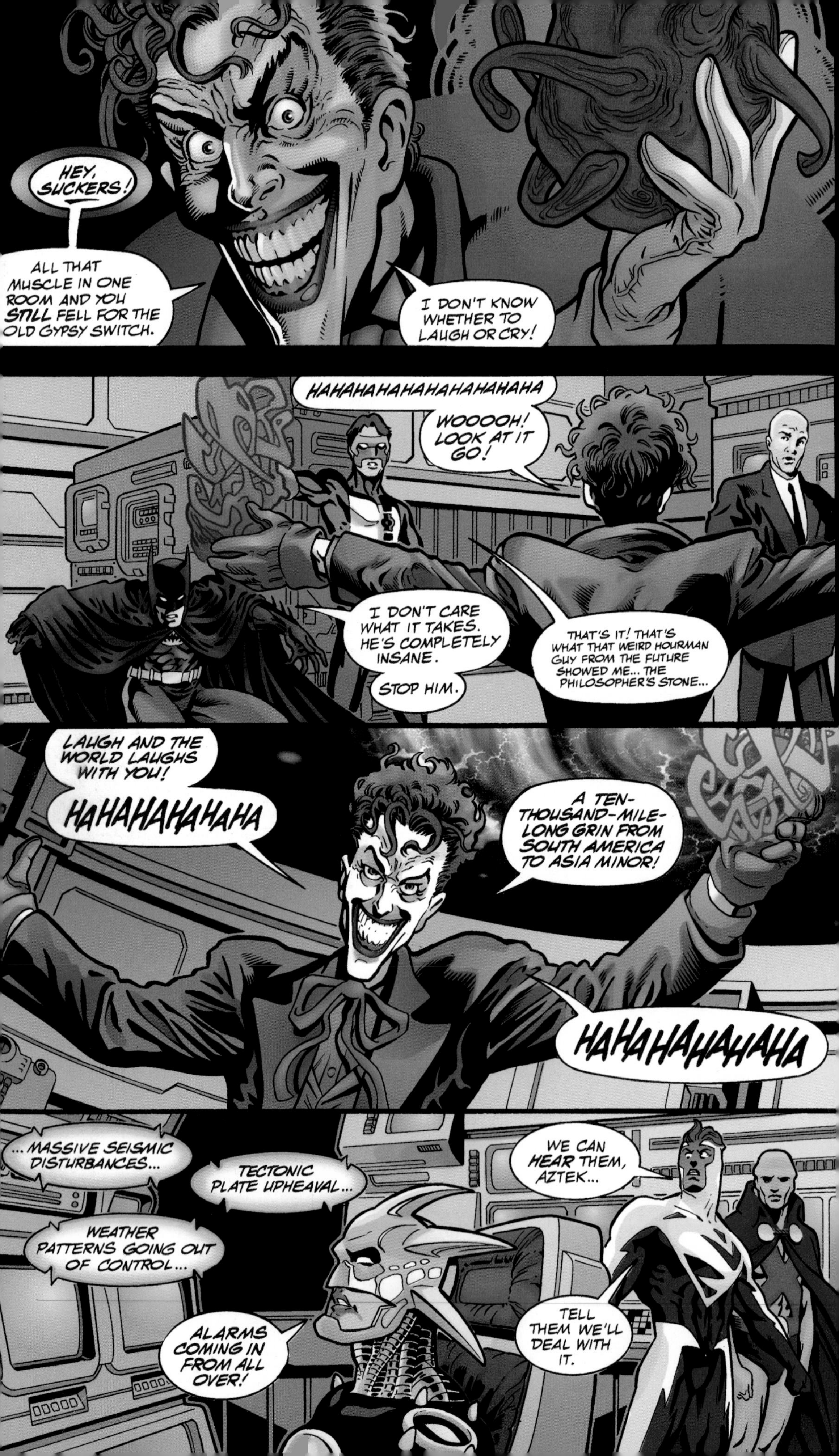
HEY, SUCKERS!
ALL THAT MUSCLE IN ONE ROOM AND YOU STILL FELL FOR THE OLD GYPSY SWITCH.
I DON'T KNOW WHETHER TO LAUGH OR CRY!
HAHAHAHAHAHAHAHAHAHA
WOOOOH! LOOK AT IT GO!
I DON'T CARE WHAT IT TAKES. HE'S COMPLETELY INSANE.
STOP HIM.
THAT'S IT! THAT'S WHAT THAT WEIRD HOURMAN GUY FROM THE FUTURE SHOWED ME... THE PHILOSOPHER'S STONE...
LAUGH AND THE WORLD LAUGHS WITH YOU!
HAHAHAHAHAHA
A TEN-THOUSAND-MILE-LONG GRIN FROM SOUTH AMERICA TO ASIA MINOR!
HAHAHAHAHAHAHA
...MASSIVE SEISMIC DISTURBANCES...
TECTONIC PLATE UPHEAVAL...
WEATHER PATTERNS GOING OUT OF CONTROL...
ALARMS COMING IN FROM ALL OVER!
WE CAN HEAR THEM, AZTEK...
TELL THEM WE'LL DEAL WITH IT.

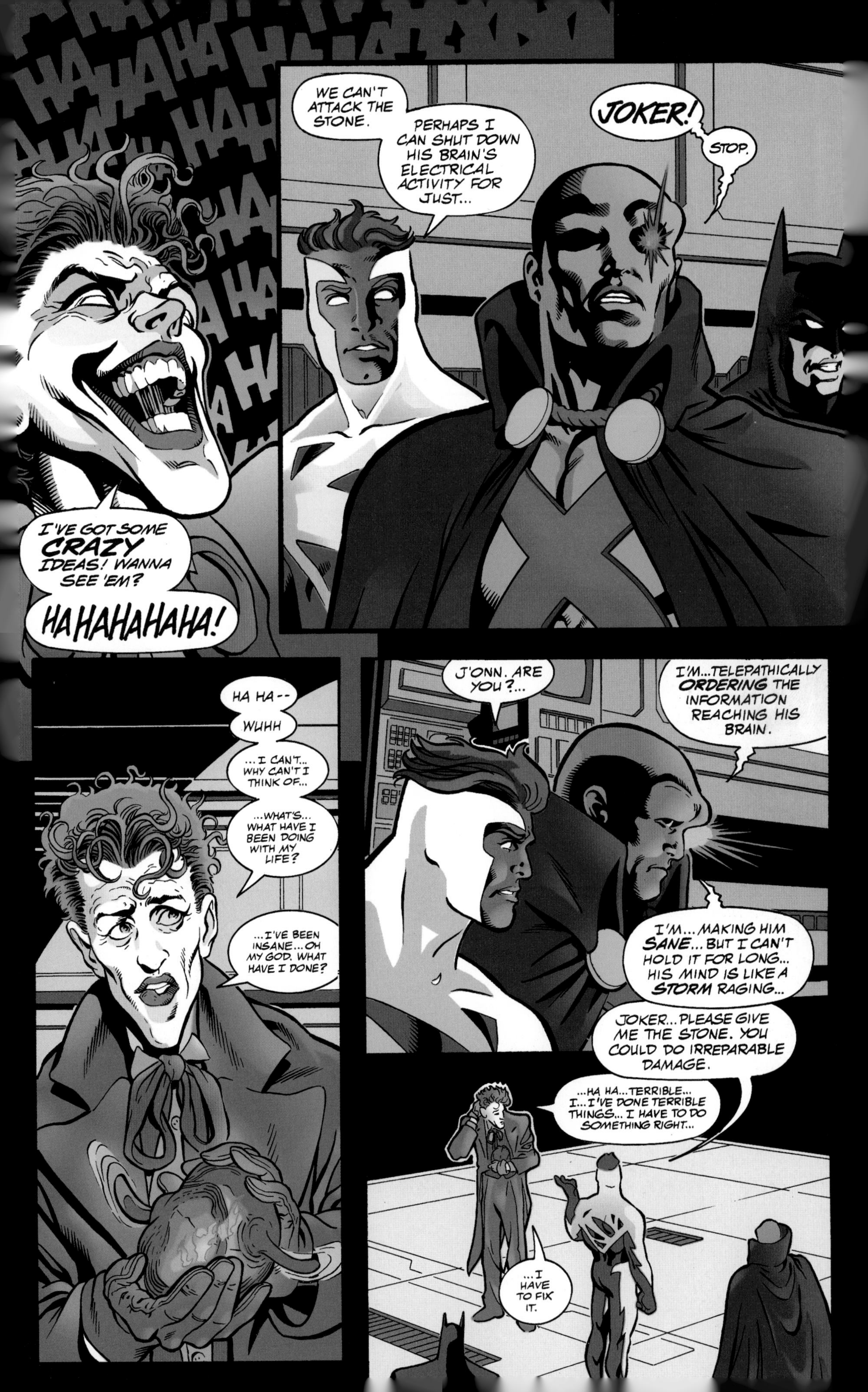
HAHAHAHAHAHAHA
WE CAN'T ATTACK THE STONE.
PERHAPS I CAN SHUT DOWN HIS BRAIN'S ELECTRICAL ACTIVITY FOR JUST...
JOKER!
STOP.
I'VE GOT SOME CRAZY IDEAS! WANNA SEE 'EM?
HAHAHAHAHA!
HA HA--
WUHH
...I CAN'T... WHY CAN'T I THINK OF...
...WHAT'S... WHAT HAVE I BEEN DOING WITH MY LIFE?
...I'VE BEEN INSANE... OH MY GOD. WHAT HAVE I DONE?
J'ONN. ARE YOU?...
I'M...TELEPATHICALLY ORDERING THE INFORMATION REACHING HIS BRAIN.
I'M... MAKING HIM SANE... BUT I CAN'T HOLD IT FOR LONG... HIS MIND IS LIKE A STORM RAGING...
JOKER... PLEASE GIVE ME THE STONE. YOU COULD DO IRREPARABLE DAMAGE.
...HA HA...TERRIBLE... I...I'VE DONE TERRIBLE THINGS... I HAVE TO DO SOMETHING RIGHT...
...I HAVE TO FIX IT.

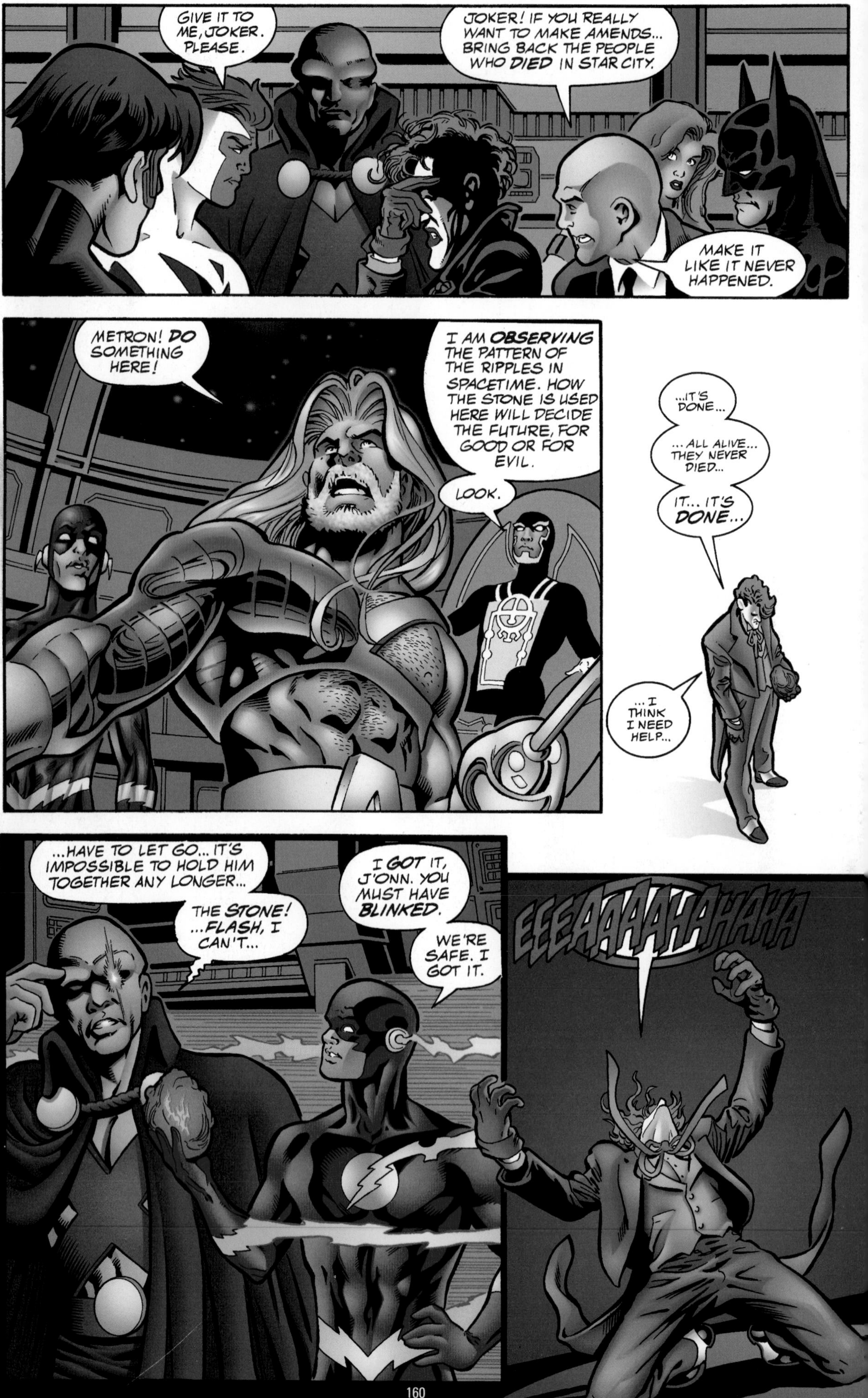
GIVE IT TO ME, JOKER. PLEASE.
JOKER! IF YOU REALLY WANT TO MAKE AMENDS... BRING BACK THE PEOPLE WHO DIED IN STAR CITY.
MAKE IT LIKE IT NEVER HAPPENED.
METRON! DO SOMETHING HERE!
I AM OBSERVING THE PATTERN OF THE RIPPLES IN SPACETIME. HOW THE STONE IS USED HERE WILL DECIDE THE FUTURE, FOR GOOD OR FOR EVIL.
LOOK.
...IT'S DONE...
...ALL ALIVE... THEY NEVER DIED...
IT... IT'S DONE...
...I THINK I NEED HELP...
...HAVE TO LET GO... IT'S IMPOSSIBLE TO HOLD HIM TOGETHER ANY LONGER...
THE STONE! ...FLASH, I CAN'T...
I GOT IT, J'ONN. YOU MUST HAVE BLINKED.
WE'RE SAFE. I GOT IT.
EEEAAAAAHAHAHA

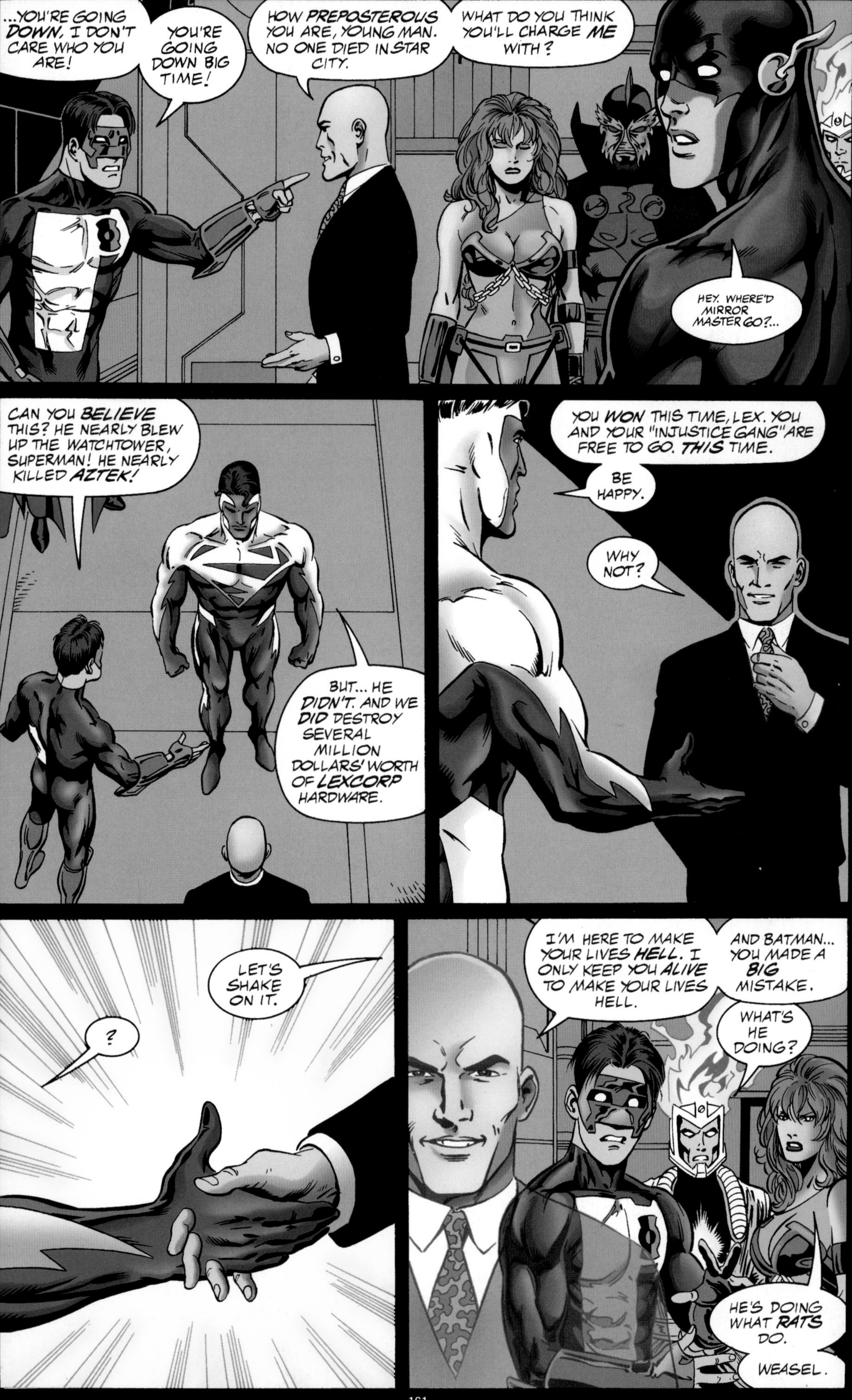
...YOU'RE GOING DOWN. I DON'T CARE WHO YOU ARE!
YOU'RE GOING DOWN BIG TIME!
HOW PREPOSTEROUS YOU ARE, YOUNG MAN. NO ONE DIED IN STAR CITY.
WHAT DO YOU THINK YOU'LL CHARGE ME WITH?
HEY. WHERE'D MIRROR MASTER GO?...
CAN YOU BELIEVE THIS? HE NEARLY BLEW UP THE WATCHTOWER, SUPERMAN! HE NEARLY KILLED AZTEK!
BUT... HE DIDN'T. AND WE DID DESTROY SEVERAL MILLION DOLLARS' WORTH OF LEXCORP HARDWARE.
YOU WON THIS TIME, LEX. YOU AND YOUR "INJUSTICE GANG" ARE FREE TO GO. THIS TIME.
BE HAPPY.
WHY NOT?
LET'S SHAKE ON IT.
?
I'M HERE TO MAKE YOUR LIVES HELL. I ONLY KEEP YOU ALIVE TO MAKE YOUR LIVES HELL.
AND BATMAN... YOU MADE A BIG MISTAKE.
WHAT'S HE DOING?
HE'S DOING WHAT RATS DO.
WEASEL.

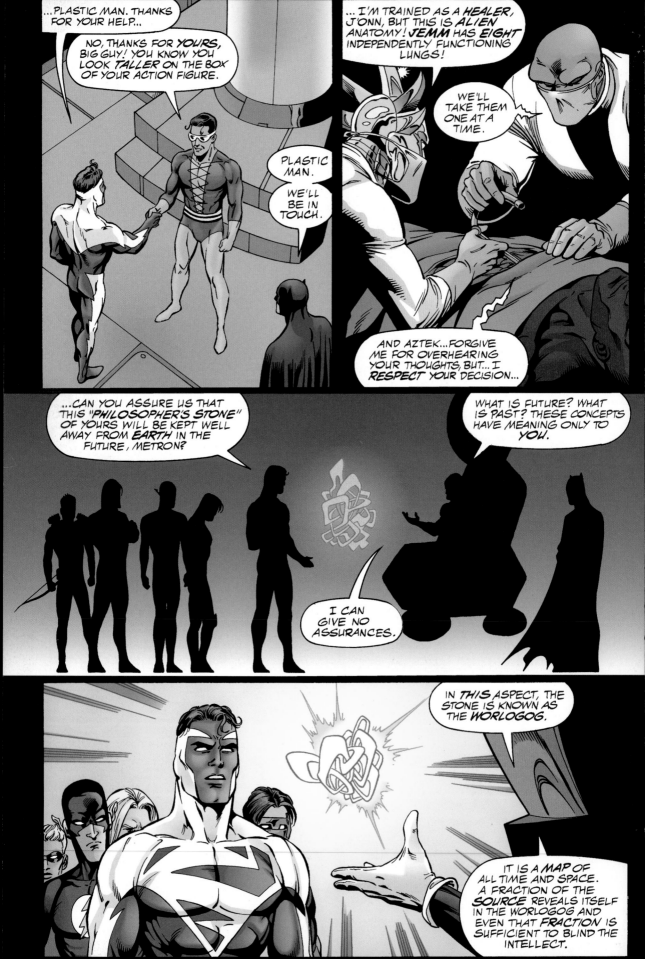

...PLASTIC MAN. THANKS FOR YOUR HELP...

NO, THANKS FOR *YOURS*, BIG GUY! YOU KNOW YOU LOOK *TALLER* ON THE BOX OF YOUR ACTION FIGURE.

PLASTIC MAN.

WE'LL BE IN TOUCH.

... I'M TRAINED AS A *HEALER*, J'ONN, BUT THIS IS *ALIEN ANATOMY!* *JEMM* HAS *EIGHT* INDEPENDENTLY FUNCTIONING LUNGS!

WE'LL TAKE THEM ONE AT A TIME.

AND AZTEK...FORGIVE ME FOR OVERHEARING YOUR THOUGHTS, BUT... I *RESPECT* YOUR DECISION...

...CAN YOU ASSURE US THAT THIS *"PHILOSOPHER'S STONE"* OF YOURS WILL BE KEPT WELL AWAY FROM *EARTH* IN THE FUTURE, METRON?

WHAT IS FUTURE? WHAT IS PAST? THESE CONCEPTS HAVE *MEANING* ONLY TO *YOU.*

I CAN GIVE NO ASSURANCES.

IN *THIS* ASPECT, THE STONE IS KNOWN AS THE *WORLOGOG.*

IT IS A *MAP* OF ALL TIME AND SPACE. A FRACTION OF THE *SOURCE* REVEALS ITSELF IN THE WORLOGOG AND EVEN THAT *FRACTION* IS *SUFFICIENT* TO BLIND THE INTELLECT.

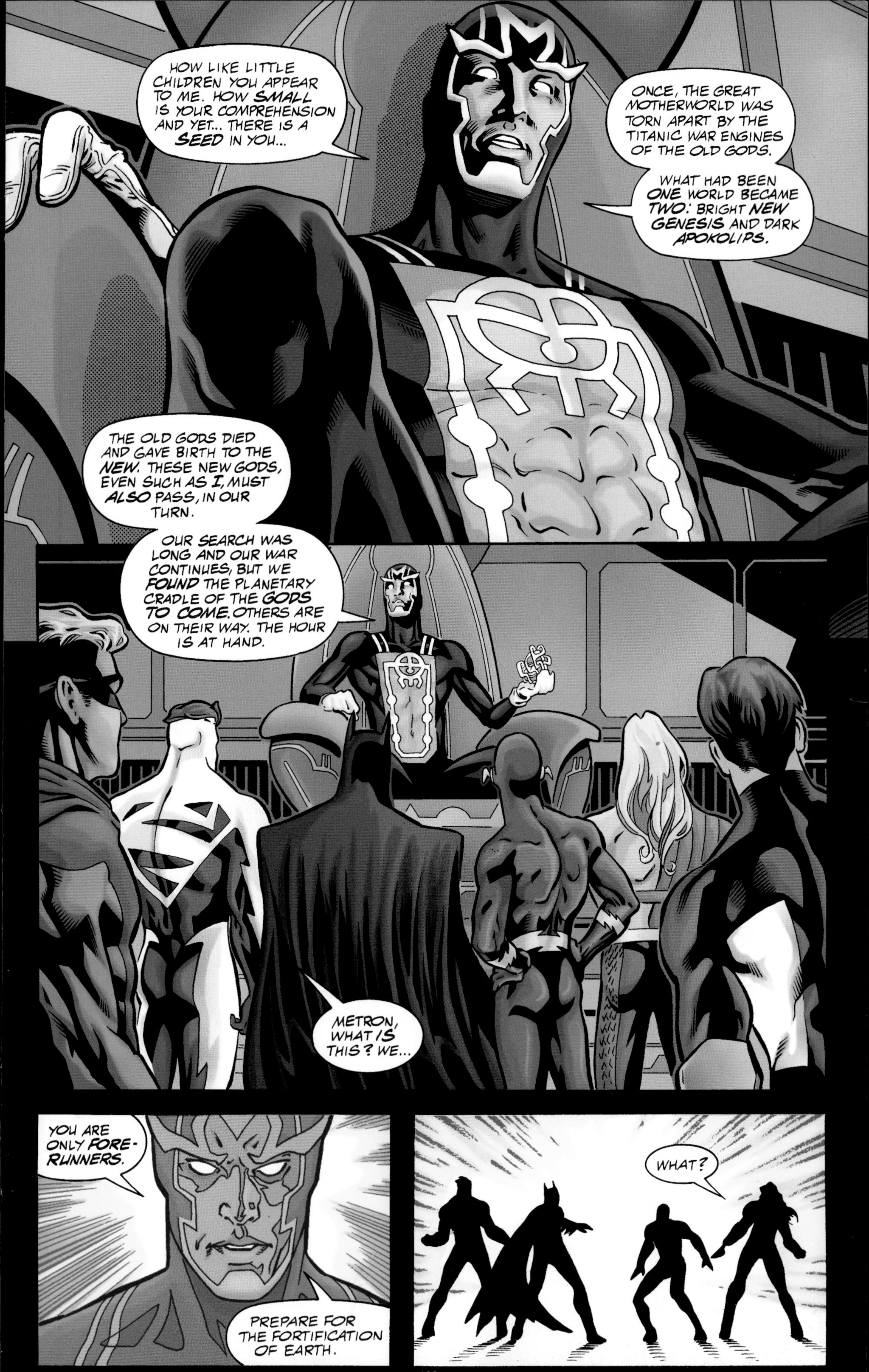
HOW LIKE LITTLE CHILDREN YOU APPEAR TO ME. HOW SMALL IS YOUR COMPREHENSION AND YET... THERE IS A SEED IN YOU...
ONCE, THE GREAT MOTHERWORLD WAS TORN APART BY THE TITANIC WAR ENGINES OF THE OLD GODS.
WHAT HAD BEEN ONE WORLD BECAME TWO: BRIGHT NEW GENESIS AND DARK APOKOLIPS.
THE OLD GODS DIED AND GAVE BIRTH TO THE NEW. THESE NEW GODS, EVEN SUCH AS I, MUST ALSO PASS, IN OUR TURN.
OUR SEARCH WAS LONG AND OUR WAR CONTINUES, BUT WE FOUND THE PLANETARY CRADLE OF THE GODS TO COME. OTHERS ARE ON THEIR WAY. THE HOUR IS AT HAND.
METRON, WHAT IS THIS? WE...
YOU ARE ONLY FORE-RUNNERS.
PREPARE FOR THE FORTIFICATION OF EARTH.
WHAT?

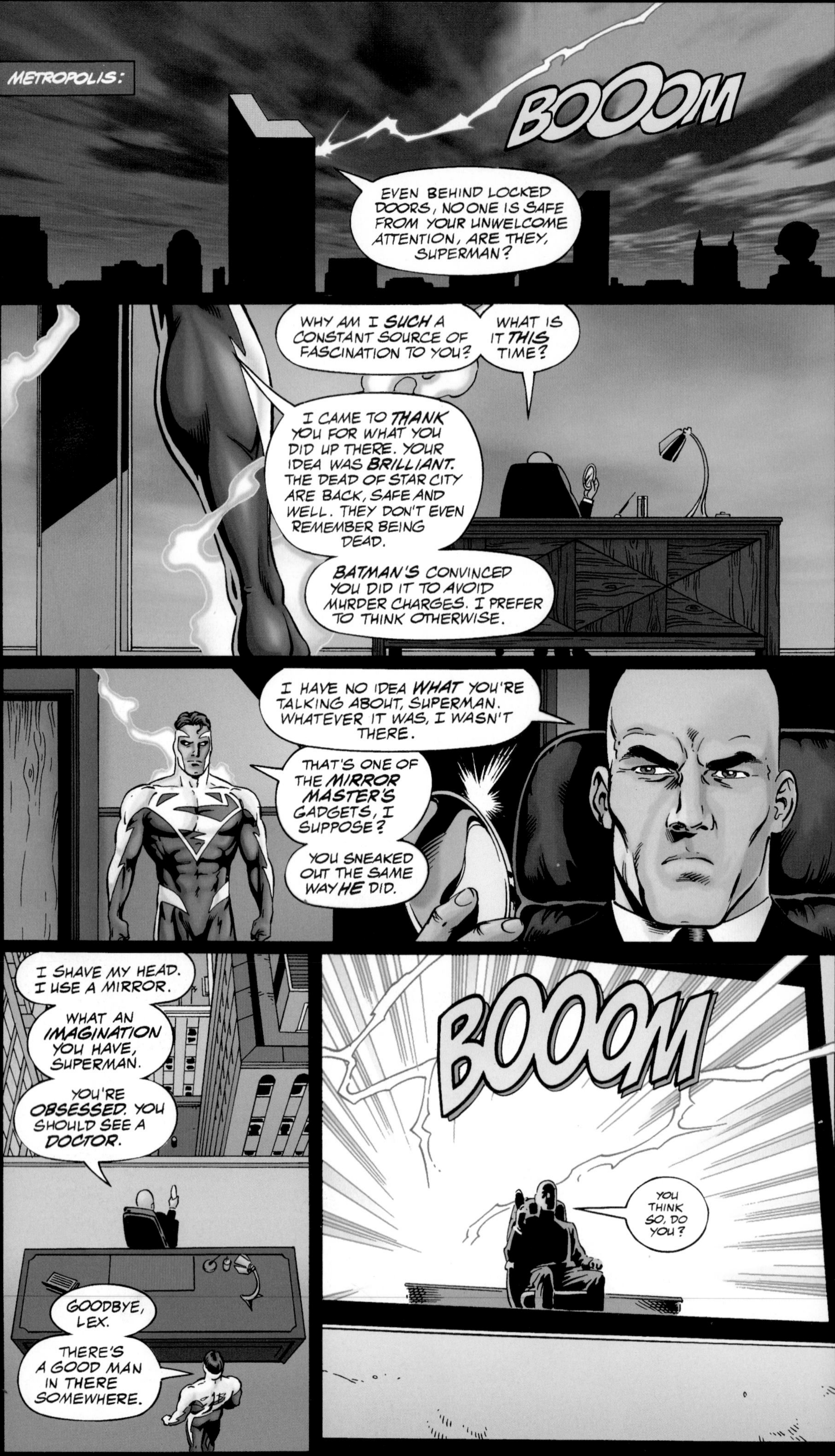
METROPOLIS:
BOOOOM
EVEN BEHIND LOCKED DOORS, NO ONE IS SAFE FROM YOUR UNWELCOME ATTENTION, ARE THEY, SUPERMAN?
WHY AM I SUCH A CONSTANT SOURCE OF FASCINATION TO YOU?
WHAT IS IT THIS TIME?
I CAME TO THANK YOU FOR WHAT YOU DID UP THERE. YOUR IDEA WAS BRILLIANT. THE DEAD OF STAR CITY ARE BACK, SAFE AND WELL. THEY DON'T EVEN REMEMBER BEING DEAD.
BATMAN'S CONVINCED YOU DID IT TO AVOID MURDER CHARGES. I PREFER TO THINK OTHERWISE.
I HAVE NO IDEA WHAT YOU'RE TALKING ABOUT, SUPERMAN. WHATEVER IT WAS, I WASN'T THERE.
THAT'S ONE OF THE MIRROR MASTER'S GADGETS, I SUPPOSE?
YOU SNEAKED OUT THE SAME WAY HE DID.
I SHAVE MY HEAD. I USE A MIRROR.
WHAT AN IMAGINATION YOU HAVE, SUPERMAN.
YOU'RE OBSESSED. YOU SHOULD SEE A DOCTOR.
GOODBYE, LEX.
THERE'S A GOOD MAN IN THERE SOMEWHERE.
BOOOM
YOU THINK SO, DO YOU?

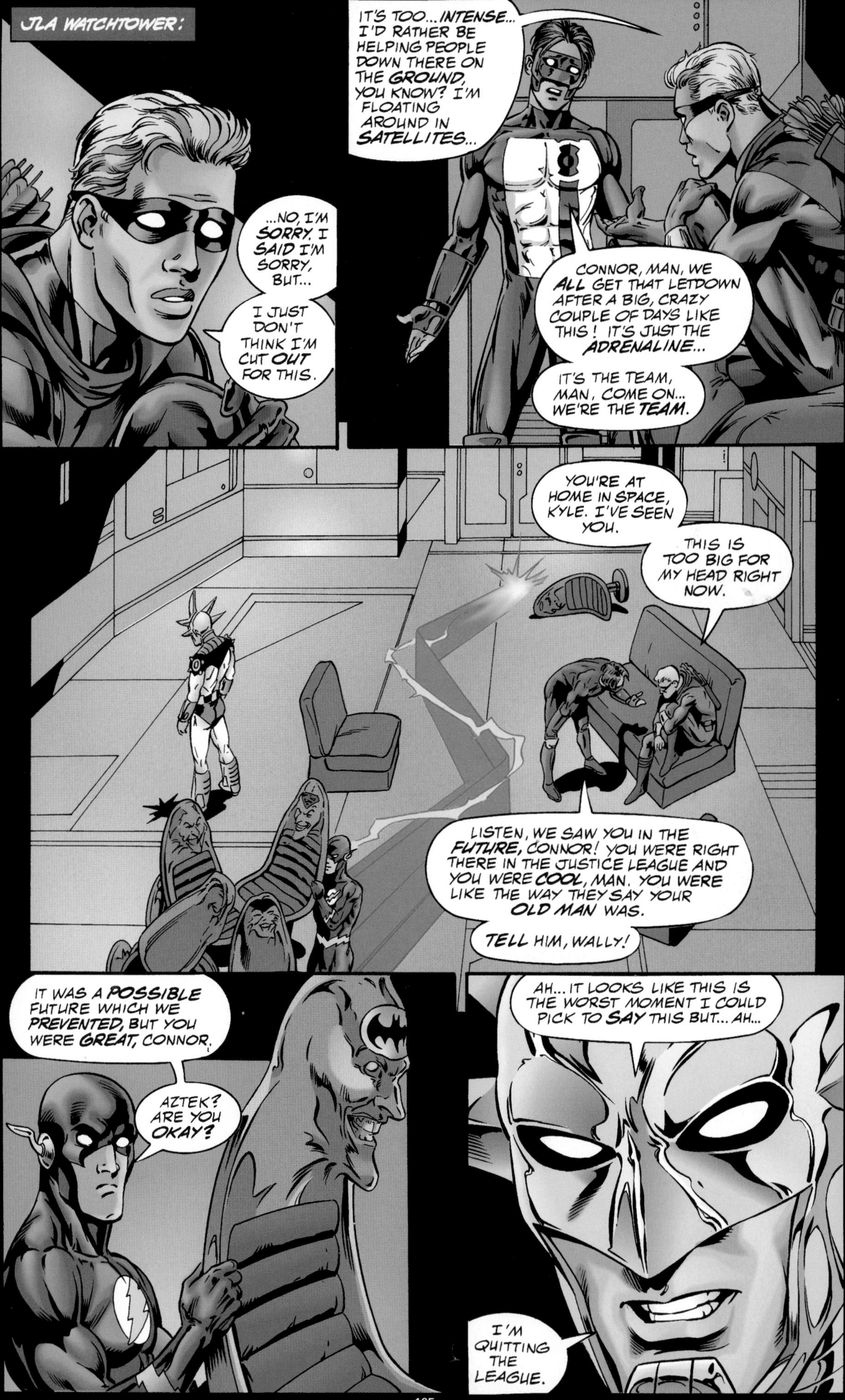
JLA WATCHTOWER:
IT'S TOO... INTENSE... I'D RATHER BE HELPING PEOPLE DOWN THERE ON THE GROUND, YOU KNOW? I'M FLOATING AROUND IN SATELLITES...
...NO, I'M SORRY. I SAID I'M SORRY, BUT...
I JUST DON'T THINK I'M CUT OUT FOR THIS.
CONNOR, MAN, WE ALL GET THAT LETDOWN AFTER A BIG, CRAZY COUPLE OF DAYS LIKE THIS! IT'S JUST THE ADRENALINE...
IT'S THE TEAM, MAN, COME ON... WE'RE THE TEAM.
YOU'RE AT HOME IN SPACE, KYLE. I'VE SEEN YOU.
THIS IS TOO BIG FOR MY HEAD RIGHT NOW.
LISTEN, WE SAW YOU IN THE FUTURE, CONNOR! YOU WERE RIGHT THERE IN THE JUSTICE LEAGUE AND YOU WERE COOL, MAN. YOU WERE LIKE THE WAY THEY SAY YOUR OLD MAN WAS.
TELL HIM, WALLY!
IT WAS A POSSIBLE FUTURE WHICH WE PREVENTED, BUT YOU WERE GREAT, CONNOR.
AZTEK? ARE YOU OKAY?
AH... IT LOOKS LIKE THIS IS THE WORST MOMENT I COULD PICK TO SAY THIS BUT... AH...
I'M QUITTING THE LEAGUE.

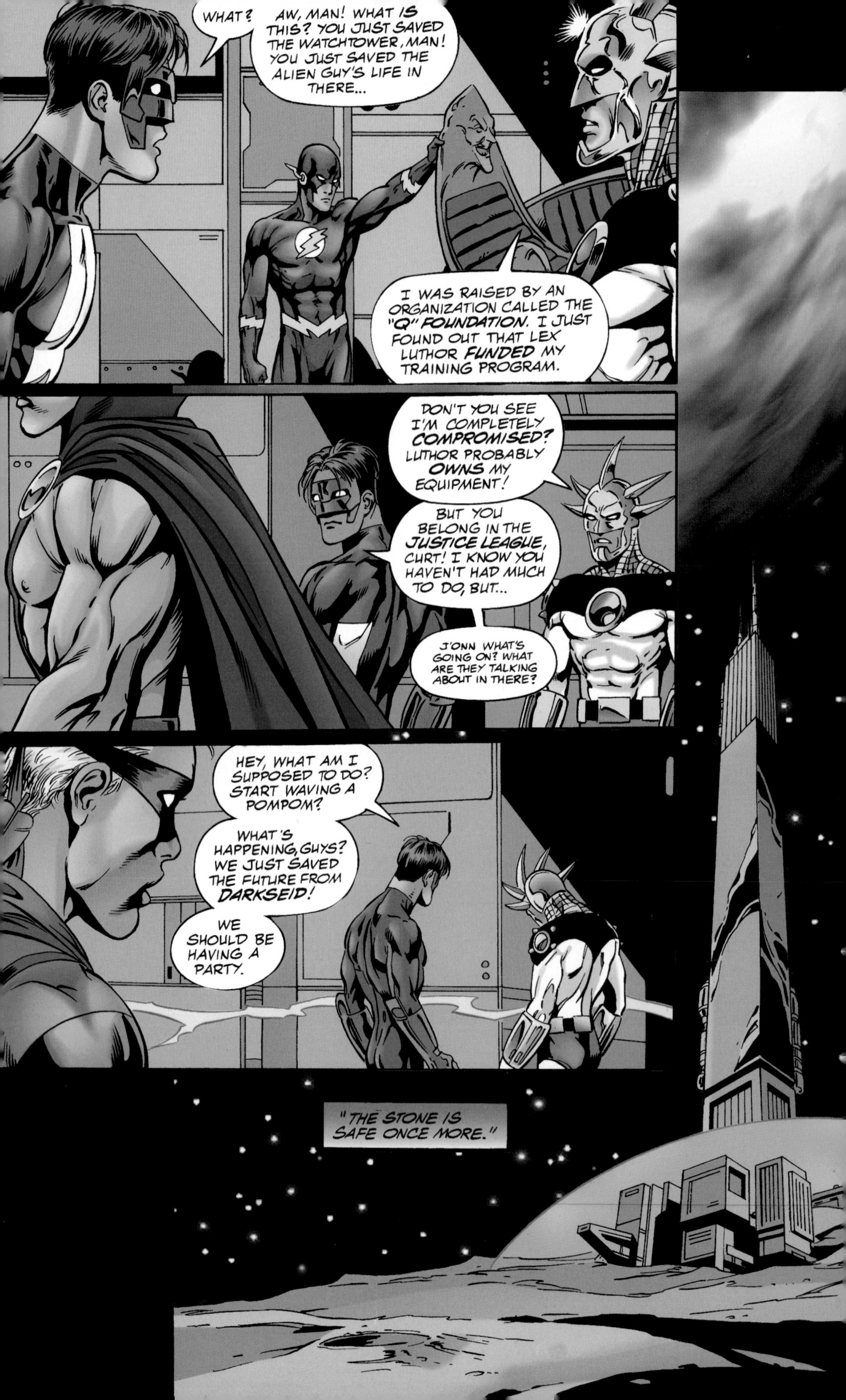
WHAT?
AW, MAN! WHAT IS THIS? YOU JUST SAVED THE WATCHTOWER, MAN! YOU JUST SAVED THE ALIEN GUY'S LIFE IN THERE...
I WAS RAISED BY AN ORGANIZATION CALLED THE "Q" FOUNDATION. I JUST FOUND OUT THAT LEX LUTHOR FUNDED MY TRAINING PROGRAM.
DON'T YOU SEE I'M COMPLETELY COMPROMISED? LUTHOR PROBABLY OWNS MY EQUIPMENT!
BUT YOU BELONG IN THE JUSTICE LEAGUE, CURT! I KNOW YOU HAVEN'T HAD MUCH TO DO, BUT...
J'ONN WHAT'S GOING ON? WHAT ARE THEY TALKING ABOUT IN THERE?
HEY, WHAT AM I SUPPOSED TO DO? START WAVING A POMPOM?
WHAT'S HAPPENING, GUYS? WE JUST SAVED THE FUTURE FROM DARKSEID!
WE SHOULD BE HAVING A PARTY.
"THE STONE IS SAFE ONCE MORE."

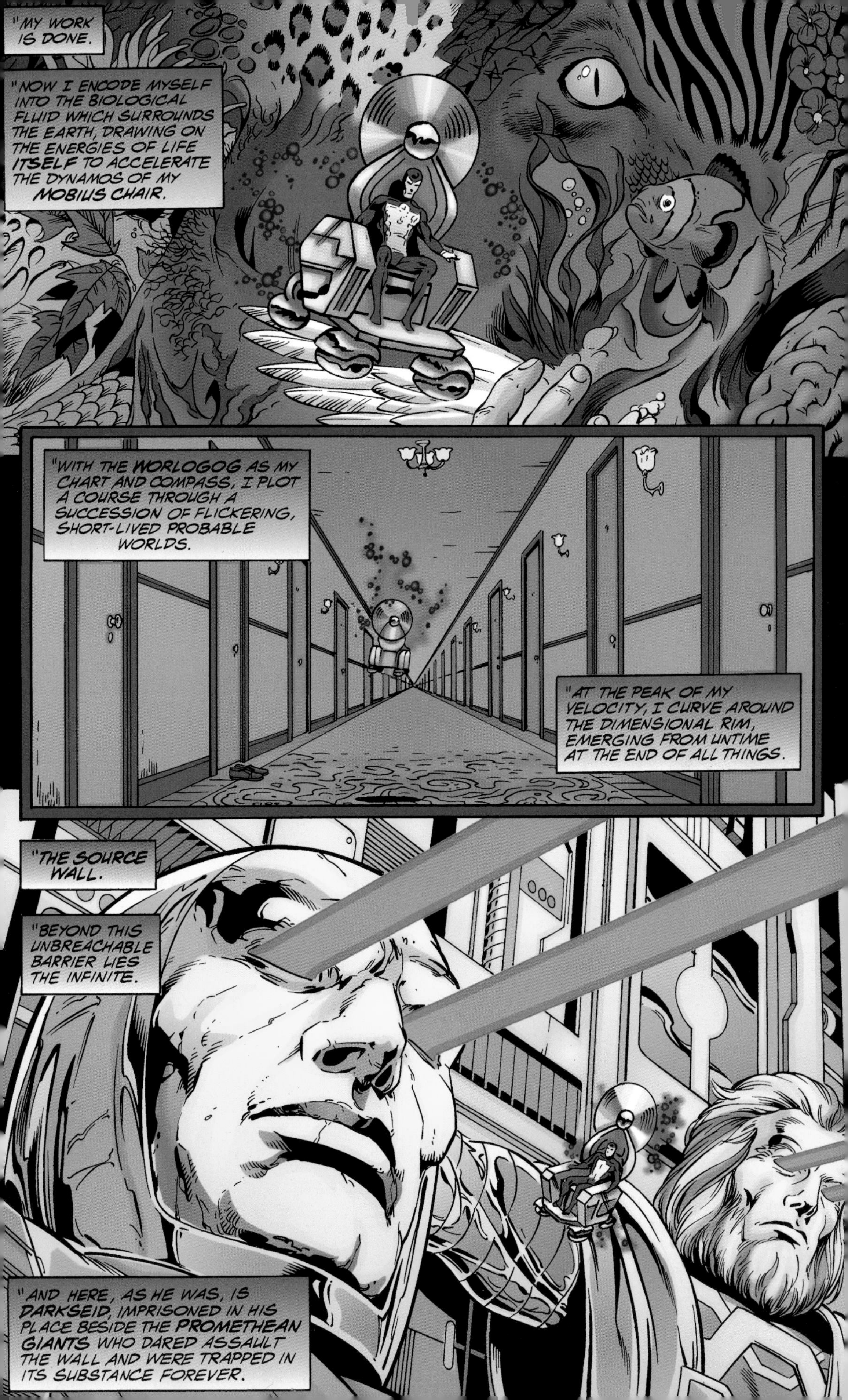
"MY WORK IS DONE.
"NOW I ENCODE MYSELF INTO THE BIOLOGICAL FLUID WHICH SURROUNDS THE EARTH, DRAWING ON THE ENERGIES OF LIFE ITSELF TO ACCELERATE THE DYNAMOS OF MY MOBIUS CHAIR.
"WITH THE WORLOGOG AS MY CHART AND COMPASS, I PLOT A COURSE THROUGH A SUCCESSION OF FLICKERING, SHORT-LIVED PROBABLE WORLDS.
"AT THE PEAK OF MY VELOCITY, I CURVE AROUND THE DIMENSIONAL RIM, EMERGING FROM UNTIME AT THE END OF ALL THINGS.
"THE SOURCE WALL.
"BEYOND THIS UNBREACHABLE BARRIER LIES THE INFINITE.
"AND HERE, AS HE WAS, IS DARKSEID, IMPRISONED IN HIS PLACE BESIDE THE PROMETHEAN GIANTS WHO DARED ASSAULT THE WALL AND WERE TRAPPED IN ITS SUBSTANCE FOREVER.

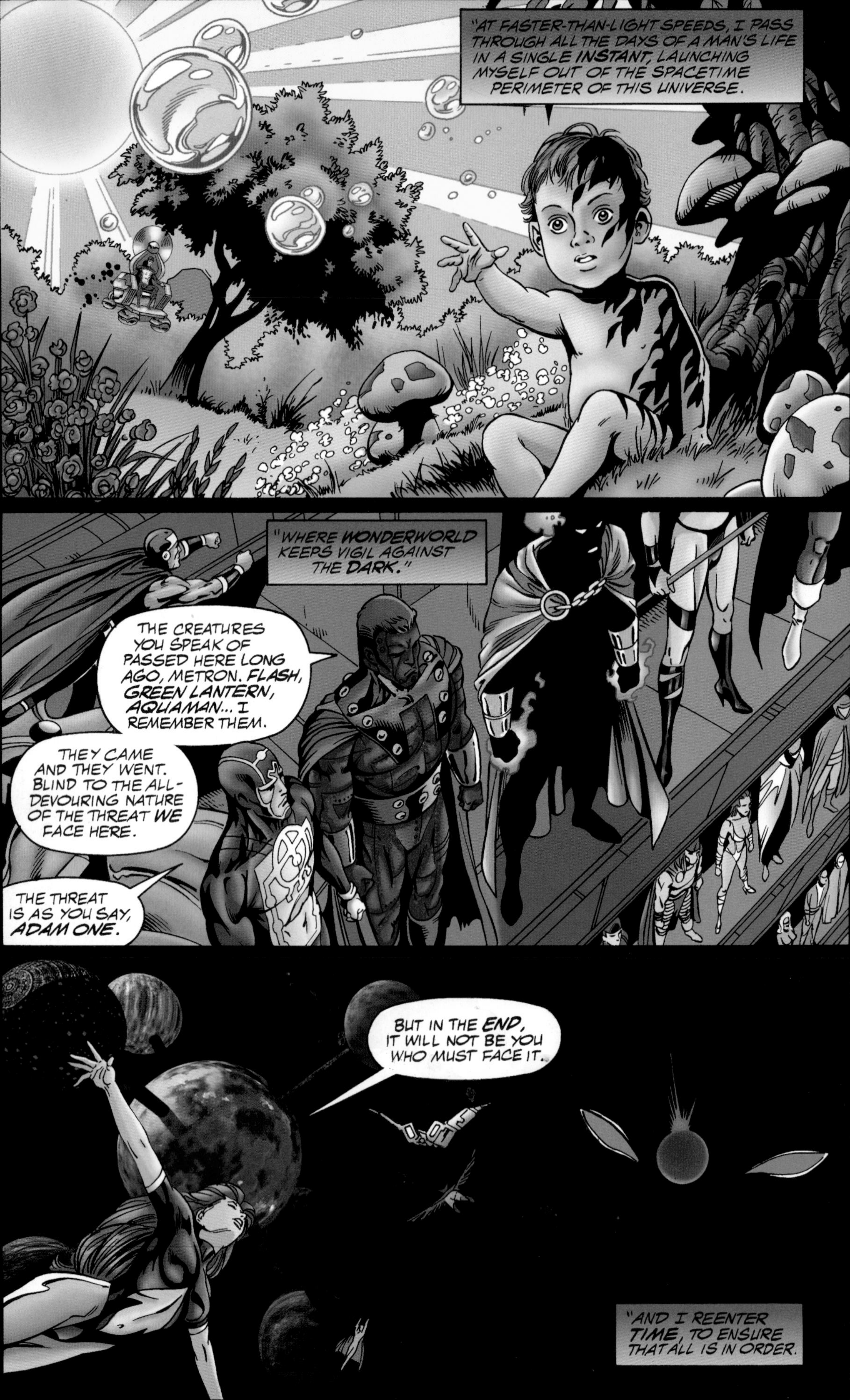
"AT FASTER-THAN-LIGHT SPEEDS, I PASS THROUGH ALL THE DAYS OF A MAN'S LIFE IN A SINGLE INSTANT, LAUNCHING MYSELF OUT OF THE SPACETIME PERIMETER OF THIS UNIVERSE.
"WHERE WONDERWORLD KEEPS VIGIL AGAINST THE DARK."
THE CREATURES YOU SPEAK OF PASSED HERE LONG AGO, METRON. FLASH, GREEN LANTERN, AQUAMAN... I REMEMBER THEM.
THEY CAME AND THEY WENT. BLIND TO THE ALL-DEVOURING NATURE OF THE THREAT WE FACE HERE.
THE THREAT IS AS YOU SAY, ADAM ONE.
BUT IN THE END, IT WILL NOT BE YOU WHO MUST FACE IT.
"AND I REENTER TIME, TO ENSURE THAT ALL IS IN ORDER.

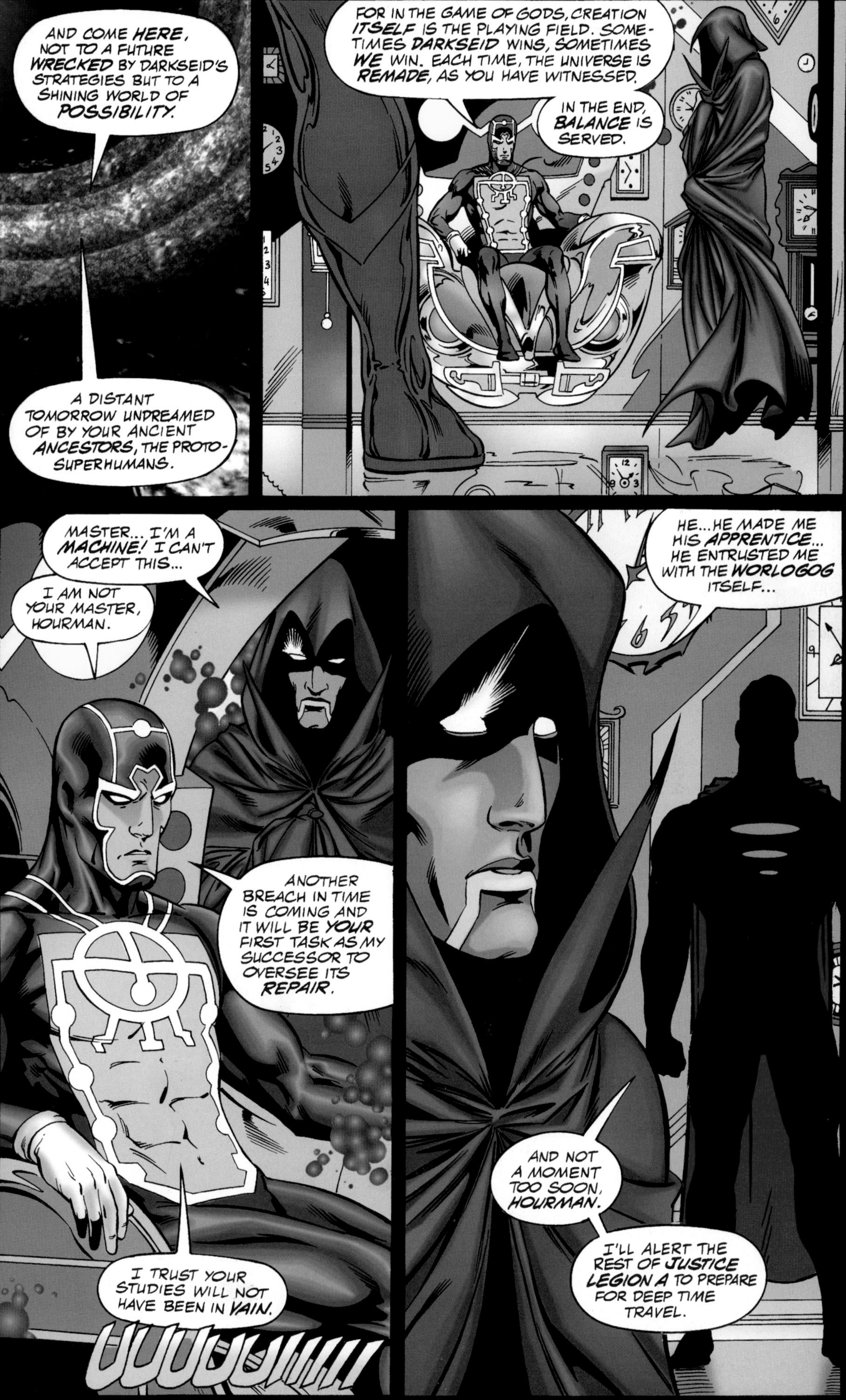

AND COME HERE, NOT TO A FUTURE WRECKED BY DARKSEID'S STRATEGIES BUT TO A SHINING WORLD OF POSSIBILITY.
A DISTANT TOMORROW UNDREAMED OF BY YOUR ANCIENT ANCESTORS, THE PROTO-SUPERHUMANS.
FOR IN THE GAME OF GODS, CREATION ITSELF IS THE PLAYING FIELD. SOMETIMES DARKSEID WINS, SOMETIMES WE WIN. EACH TIME, THE UNIVERSE IS REMADE, AS YOU HAVE WITNESSED.
IN THE END, BALANCE IS SERVED.
MASTER... I'M A MACHINE! I CAN'T ACCEPT THIS...
I AM NOT YOUR MASTER, HOURMAN.
ANOTHER BREACH IN TIME IS COMING AND IT WILL BE YOUR FIRST TASK AS MY SUCCESSOR TO OVERSEE ITS REPAIR.
I TRUST YOUR STUDIES WILL NOT HAVE BEEN IN VAIN.
UUUUUIIIII
HE...HE MADE ME HIS APPRENTICE... HE ENTRUSTED ME WITH THE WORLOGOG ITSELF...
AND NOT A MOMENT TOO SOON, HOURMAN.
I'LL ALERT THE REST OF JUSTICE LEGION A TO PREPARE FOR DEEP TIME TRAVEL.

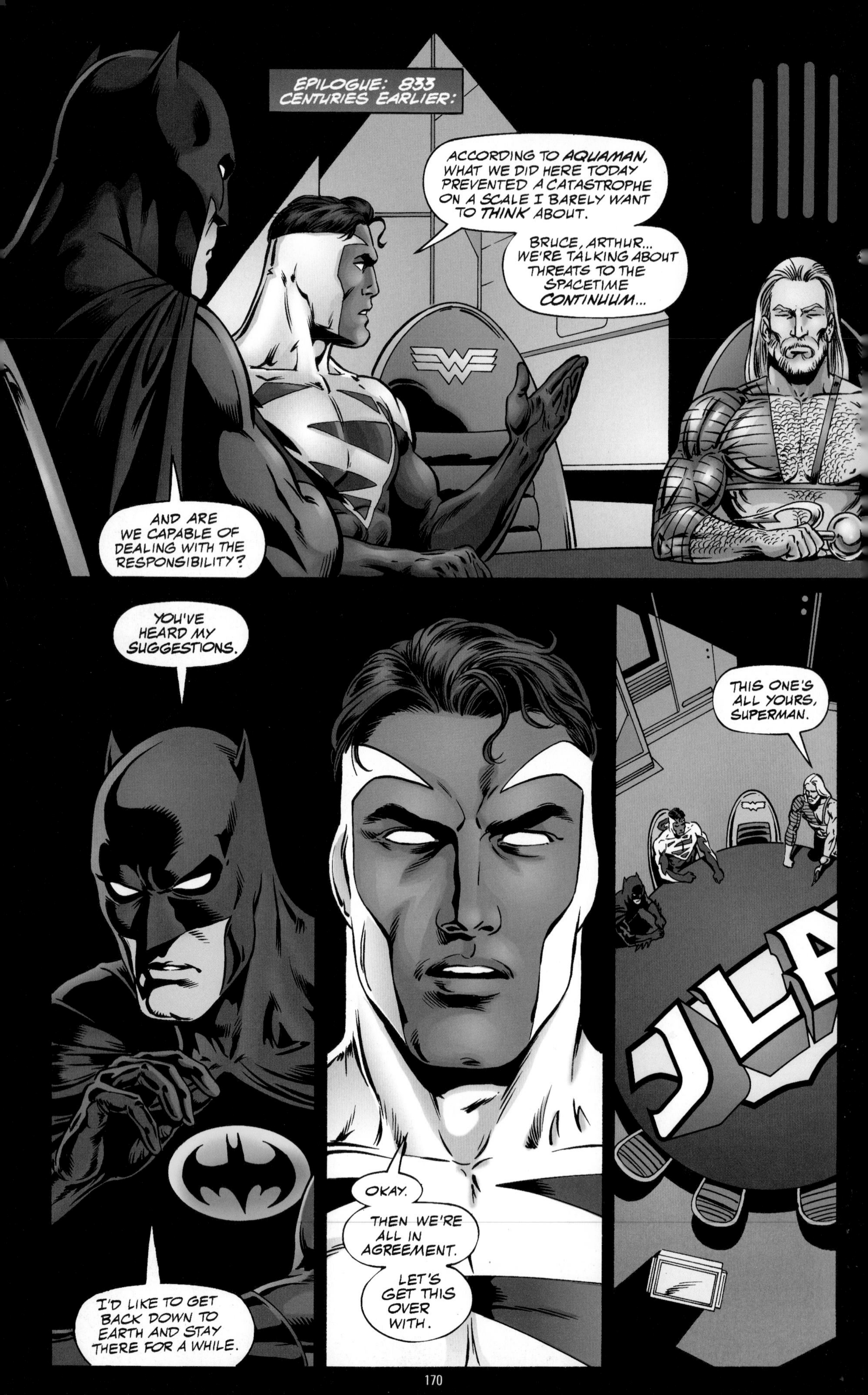
EPILOGUE: 833 CENTURIES EARLIER:
ACCORDING TO AQUAMAN, WHAT WE DID HERE TODAY PREVENTED A CATASTROPHE ON A SCALE I BARELY WANT TO THINK ABOUT.
BRUCE, ARTHUR... WE'RE TALKING ABOUT THREATS TO THE SPACETIME CONTINUUM...
AND ARE WE CAPABLE OF DEALING WITH THE RESPONSIBILITY?
YOU'VE HEARD MY SUGGESTIONS.
I'D LIKE TO GET BACK DOWN TO EARTH AND STAY THERE FOR A WHILE.
OKAY.
THEN WE'RE ALL IN AGREEMENT.
LET'S GET THIS OVER WITH.
THIS ONE'S ALL YOURS, SUPERMAN.
JLA

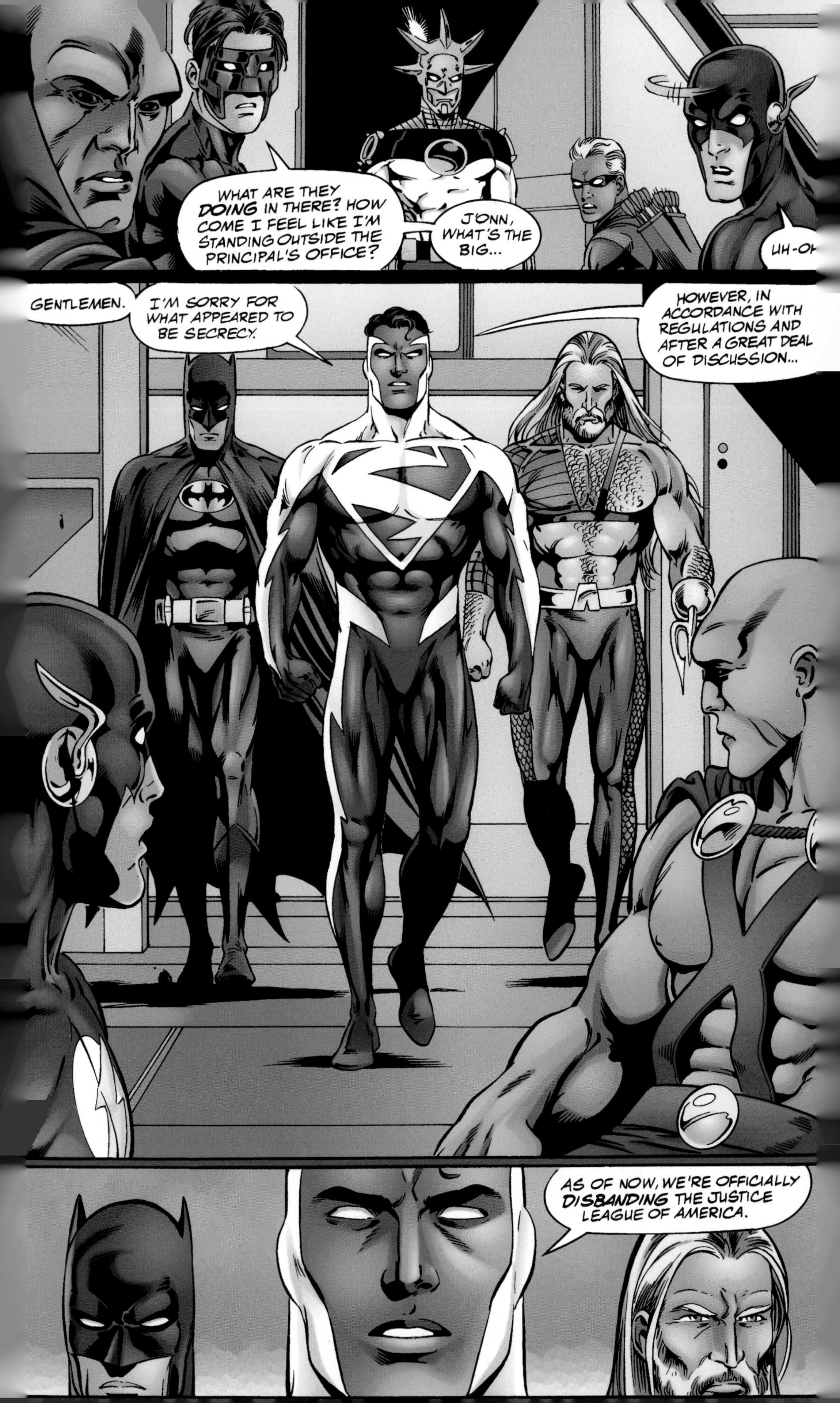
WHAT ARE THEY DOING IN THERE? HOW COME I FEEL LIKE I'M STANDING OUTSIDE THE PRINCIPAL'S OFFICE?
J'ONN, WHAT'S THE BIG...
UH-OH
GENTLEMEN.
I'M SORRY FOR WHAT APPEARED TO BE SECRECY.
HOWEVER, IN ACCORDANCE WITH REGULATIONS AND AFTER A GREAT DEAL OF DISCUSSION...
AS OF NOW, WE'RE OFFICIALLY DISBANDING THE JUSTICE LEAGUE OF AMERICA.

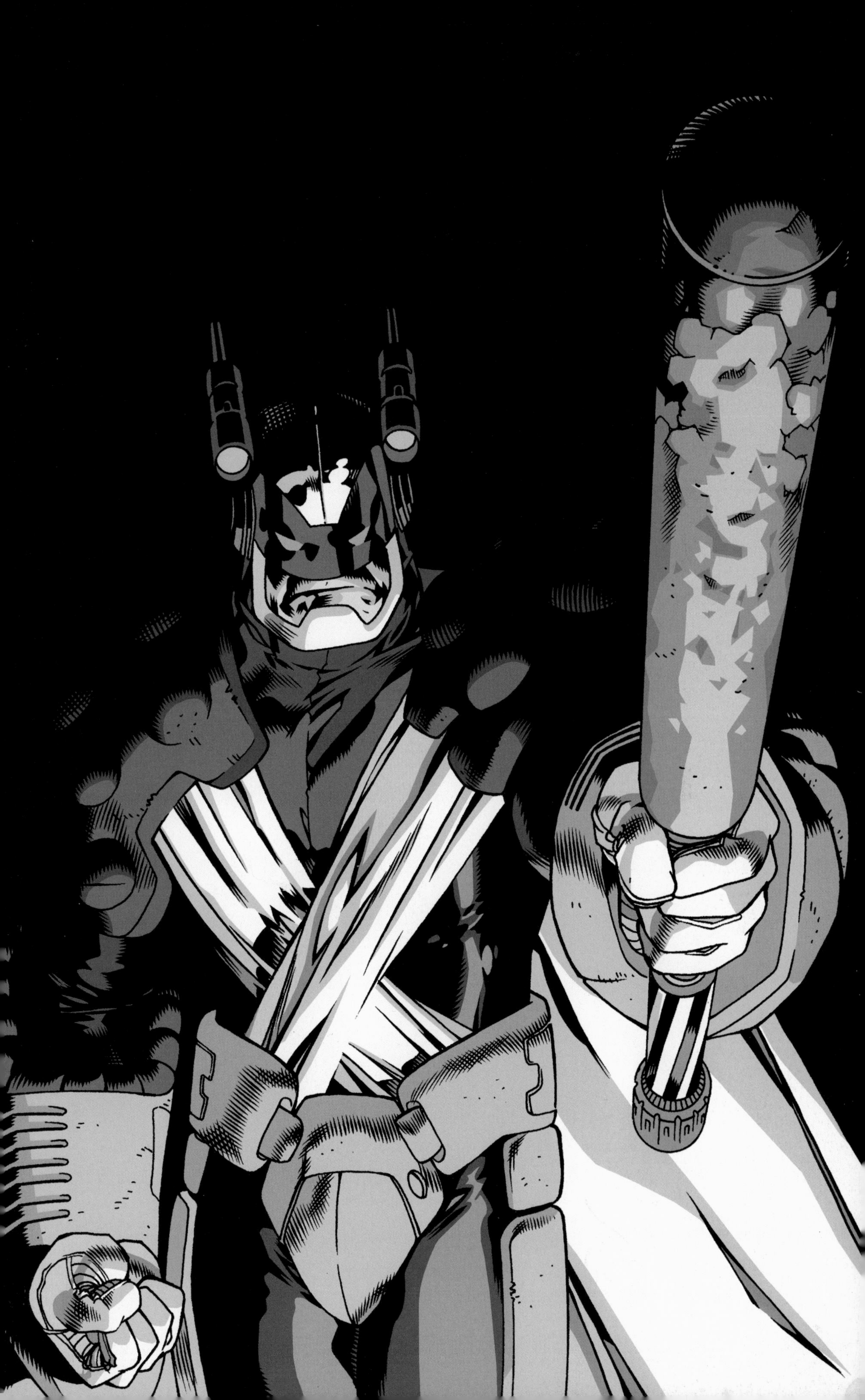

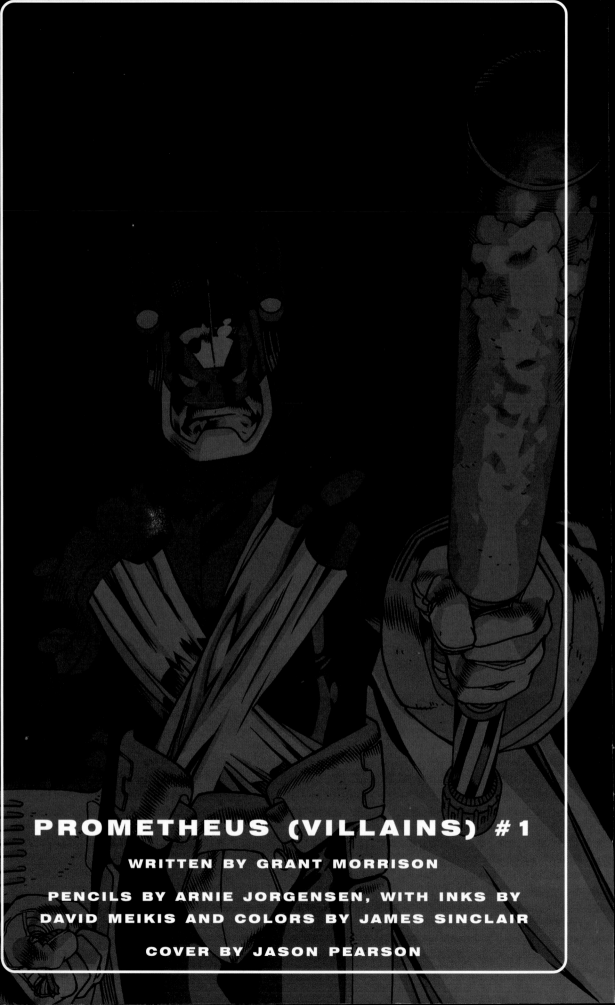

PROMETHEUS (VILLAINS) #1

WRITTEN BY GRANT MORRISON

PENCILS BY ARNIE JORGENSEN, WITH INKS BY
DAVID MEIKIS AND COLORS BY JAMES SINCLAIR

COVER BY JASON PEARSON

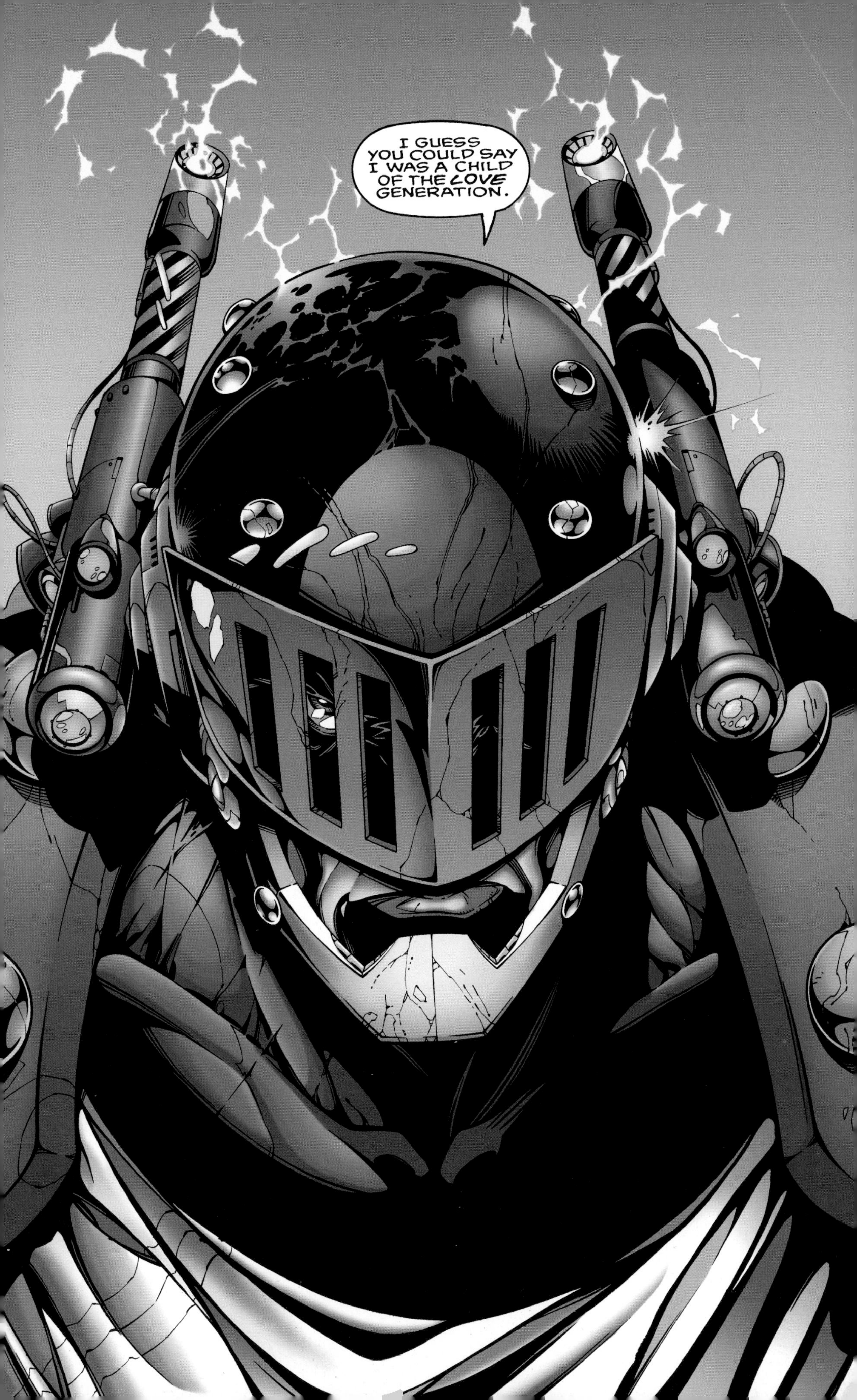
I GUESS YOU COULD SAY I WAS A CHILD OF THE LOVE GENERATION.

THERE WAS A CROOKED MAN

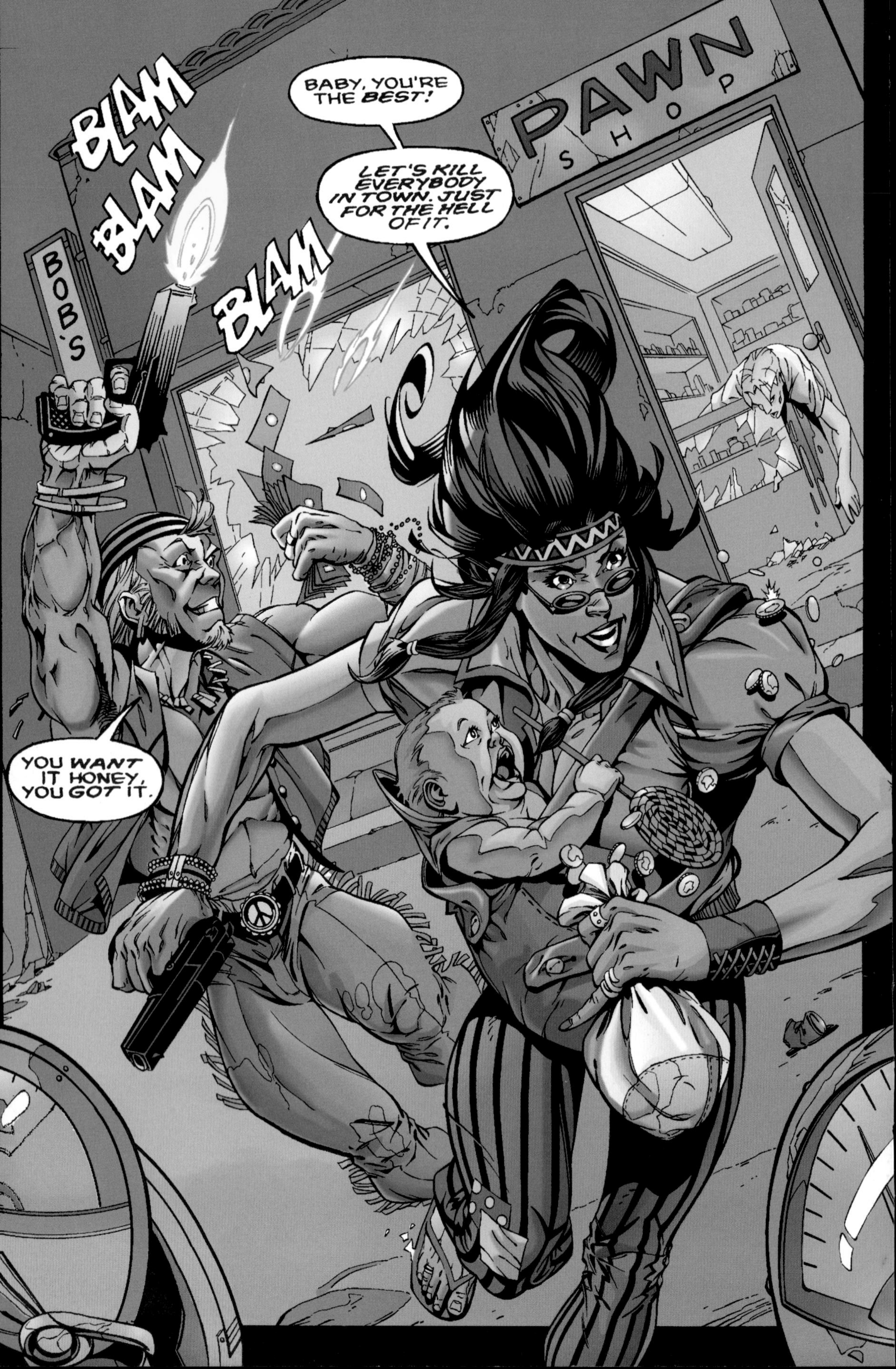

BLAM
BLAM
BLAM
BABY, YOU'RE THE *BEST!*
LET'S KILL EVERYBODY IN TOWN. JUST FOR THE HELL OF IT.
PAWN SHOP
BOB'S
YOU *WANT* IT HONEY, YOU *GOT* IT.

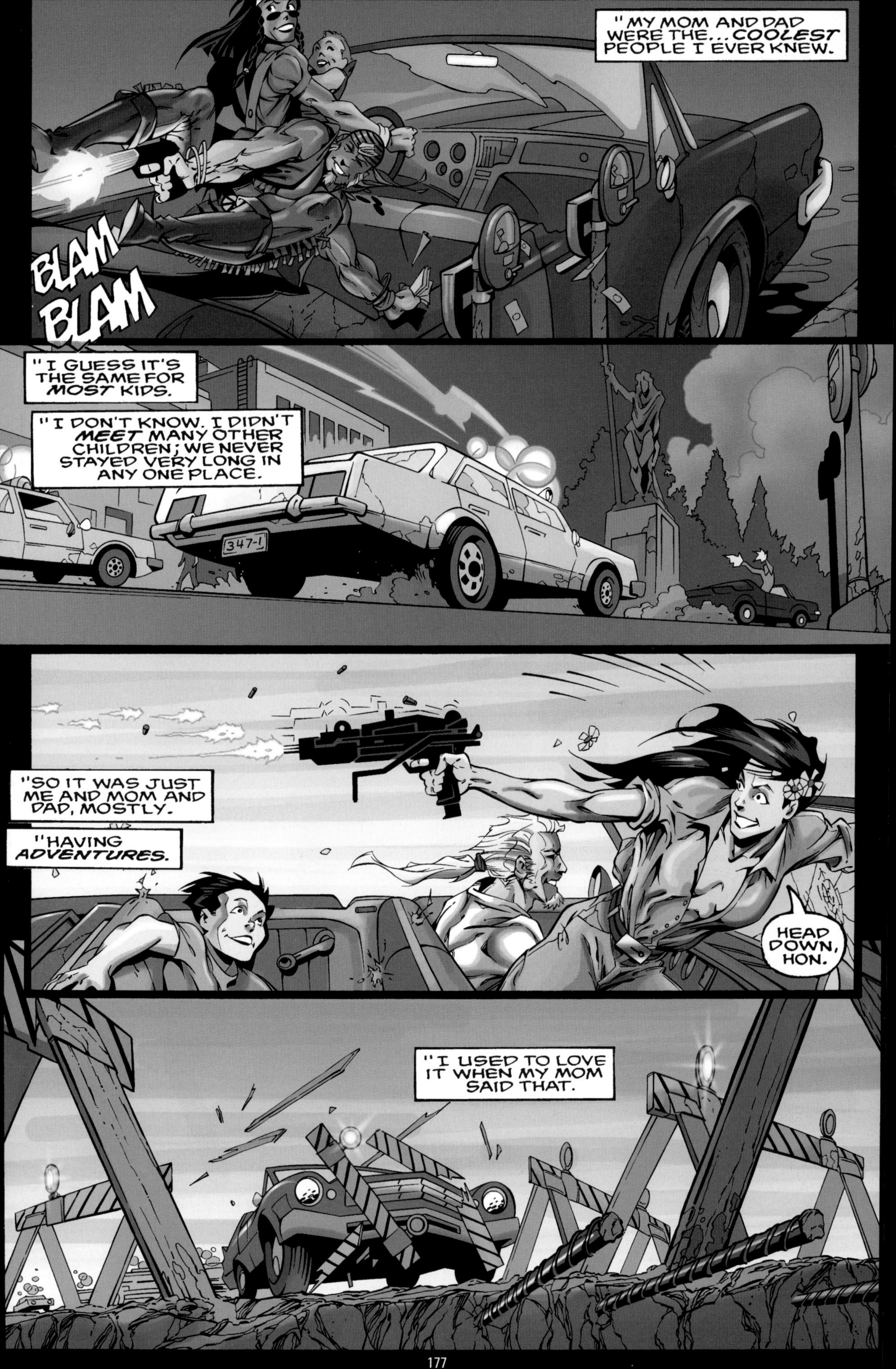
"MY MOM AND DAD WERE THE... COOLEST PEOPLE I EVER KNEW.
BLAM BLAM
"I GUESS IT'S THE SAME FOR MOST KIDS.
"I DON'T KNOW. I DIDN'T MEET MANY OTHER CHILDREN; WE NEVER STAYED VERY LONG IN ANY ONE PLACE.
347-1
"SO IT WAS JUST ME AND MOM AND DAD, MOSTLY.
"HAVING ADVENTURES.
HEAD DOWN, HON.
"I USED TO LOVE IT WHEN MY MOM SAID THAT.

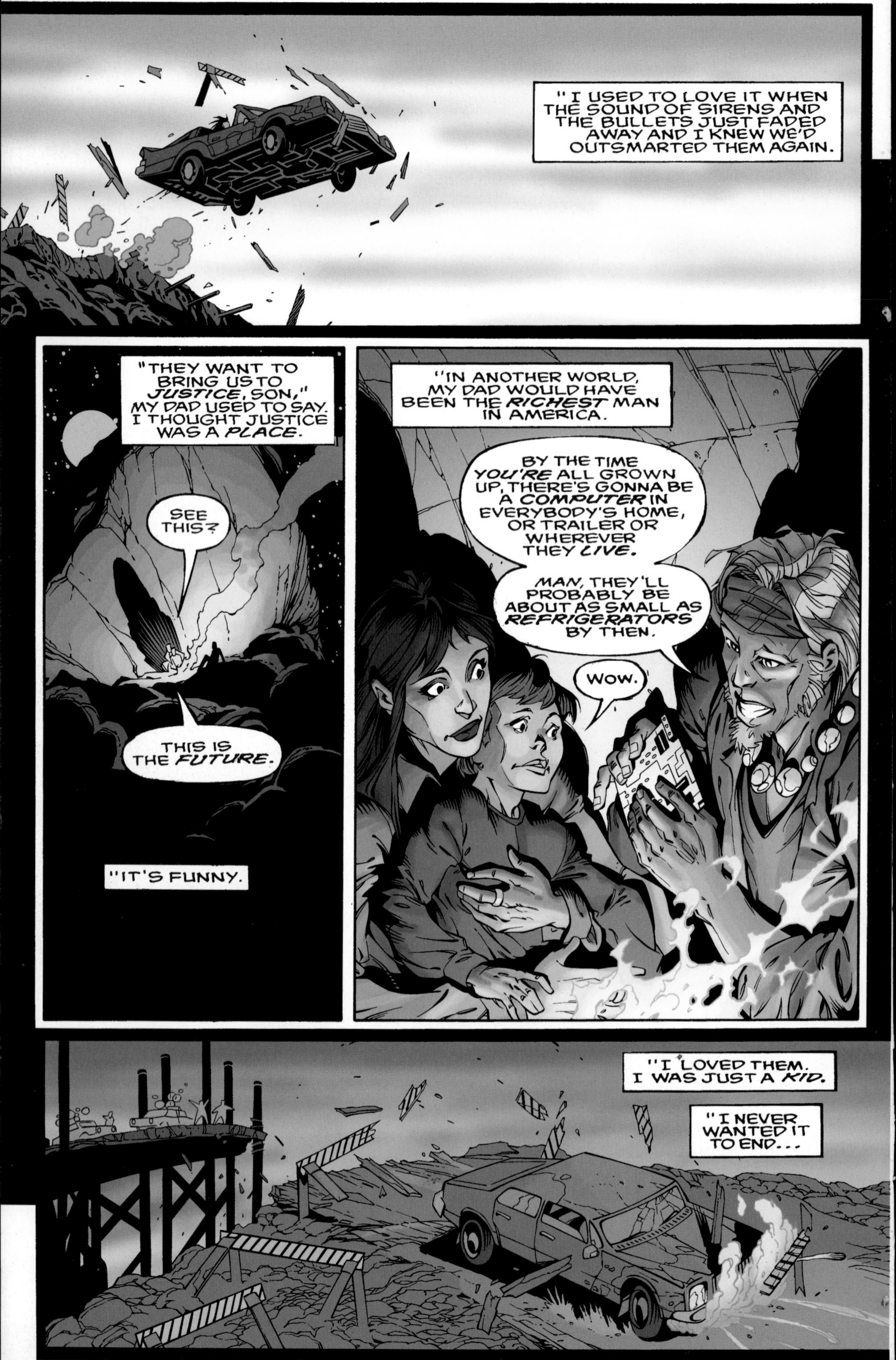
"I USED TO LOVE IT WHEN THE SOUND OF SIRENS AND THE BULLETS JUST FADED AWAY AND I KNEW WE'D OUTSMARTED THEM AGAIN.
"THEY WANT TO BRING US TO JUSTICE, SON," MY DAD USED TO SAY. I THOUGHT JUSTICE WAS A PLACE.
SEE THIS?
THIS IS THE FUTURE.
"IT'S FUNNY.
"IN ANOTHER WORLD, MY DAD WOULD HAVE BEEN THE RICHEST MAN IN AMERICA.
BY THE TIME YOU'RE ALL GROWN UP, THERE'S GONNA BE A COMPUTER IN EVERYBODY'S HOME, OR TRAILER OR WHEREVER THEY LIVE.
MAN, THEY'LL PROBABLY BE ABOUT AS SMALL AS REFRIGERATORS BY THEN.
WOW.
"I LOVED THEM. I WAS JUST A KID.
"I NEVER WANTED IT TO END...

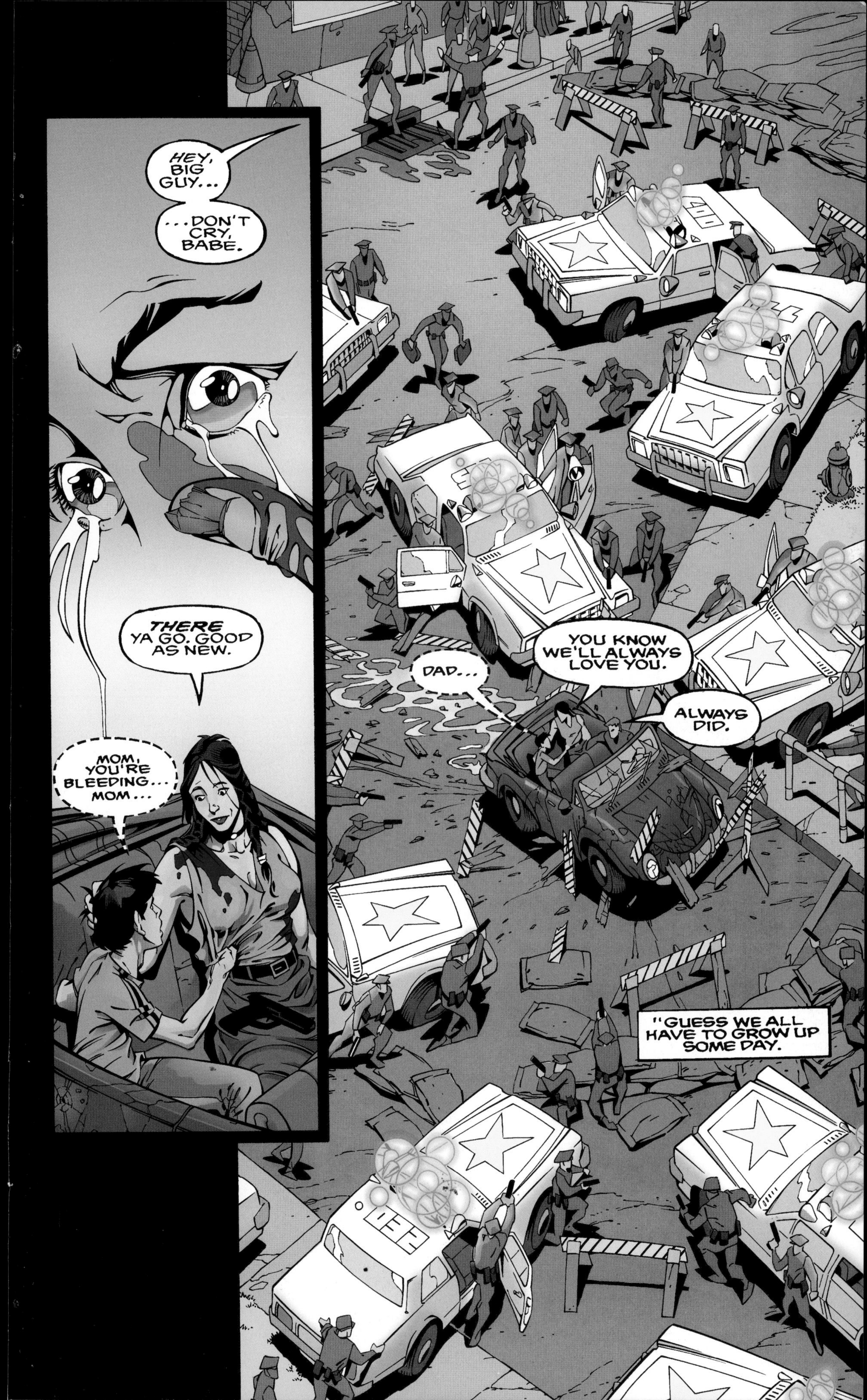
HEY, BIG GUY...
...DON'T CRY, BABE.
THERE YA GO. GOOD AS NEW.
MOM, YOU'RE BLEEDING... MOM...
DAD...
YOU KNOW WE'LL ALWAYS LOVE YOU.
ALWAYS DID.
"GUESS WE ALL HAVE TO GROW UP SOME DAY.

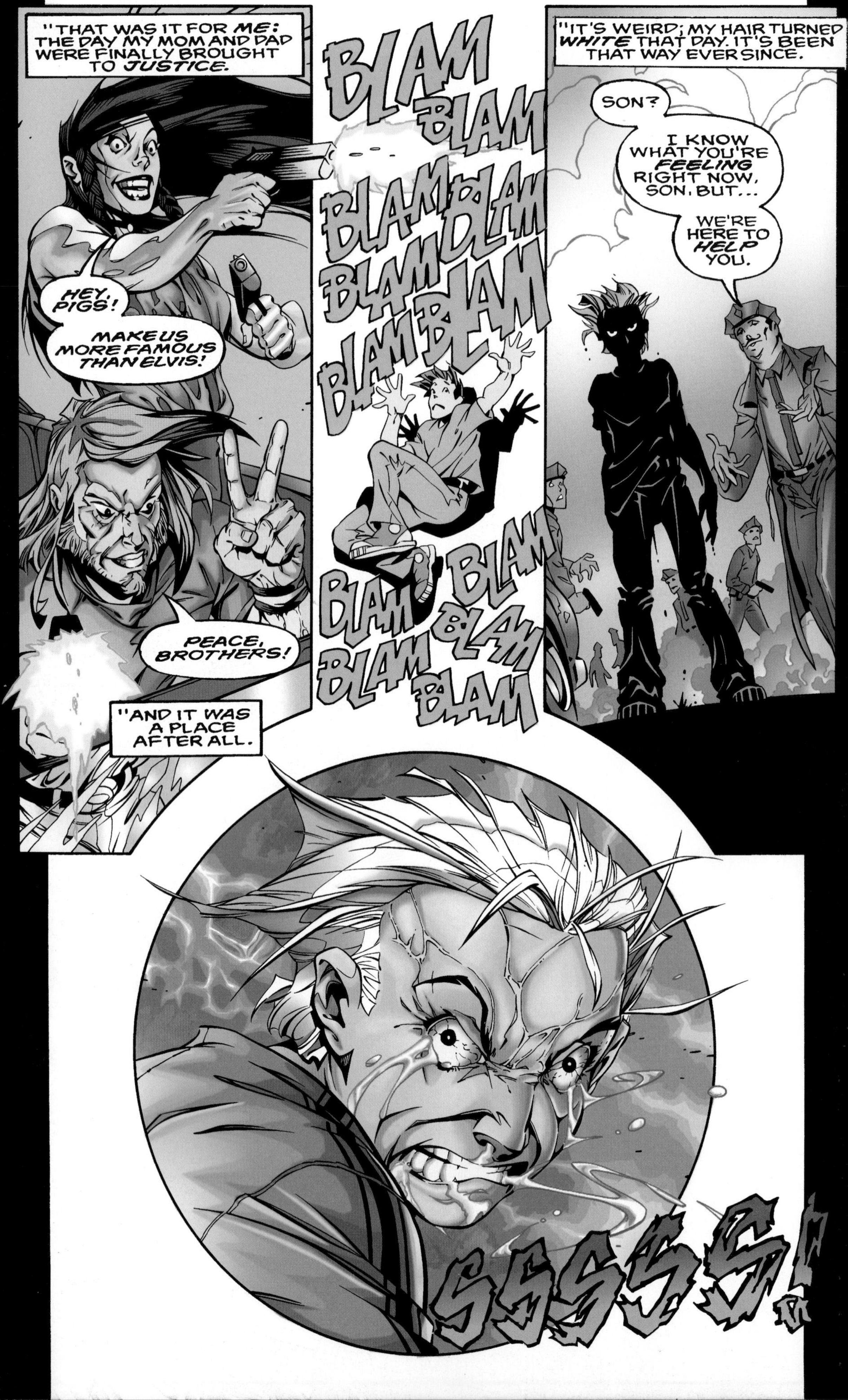
"THAT WAS IT FOR *ME*: THE DAY MY MOM AND DAD WERE FINALLY BROUGHT TO *JUSTICE*.
HEY, PIGS!
MAKE US MORE FAMOUS THAN ELVIS!
PEACE, BROTHERS!
"AND IT WAS A PLACE AFTER ALL.
BLAM BLAM
BLAM BLAM BLAM BLAM
BLAM BLAM
BLAM BLAM BLAM BLAM BLAM
"IT'S WEIRD; MY HAIR TURNED *WHITE* THAT DAY. IT'S BEEN THAT WAY EVER SINCE.
SON?
I KNOW WHAT YOU'RE *FEELING* RIGHT NOW, SON, BUT...
WE'RE HERE TO *HELP* YOU.
SSSSS!

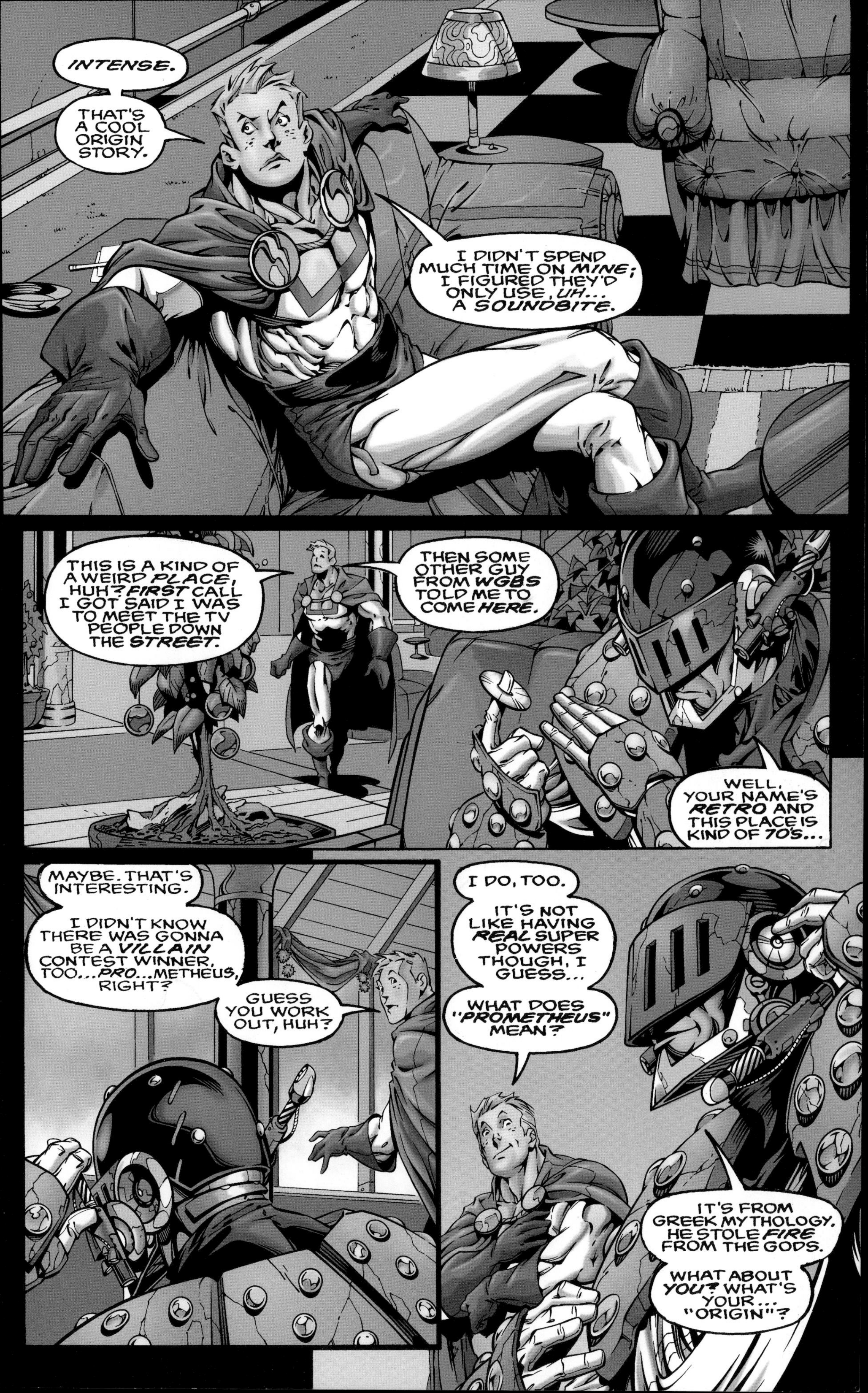
INTENSE.
THAT'S A COOL ORIGIN STORY.
I DIDN'T SPEND MUCH TIME ON MINE; I FIGURED THEY'D ONLY USE, UH... A SOUNDBITE.
THIS IS A KIND OF A WEIRD PLACE, HUH? FIRST CALL I GOT SAID I WAS TO MEET THE TV PEOPLE DOWN THE STREET.
THEN SOME OTHER GUY FROM WGBS TOLD ME TO COME HERE.
WELL, YOUR NAME'S RETRO AND THIS PLACE IS KIND OF 70'S...
MAYBE. THAT'S INTERESTING.
I DIDN'T KNOW THERE WAS GONNA BE A VILLAIN CONTEST WINNER, TOO...PRO...METHEUS, RIGHT?
GUESS YOU WORK OUT, HUH?
I DO, TOO.
IT'S NOT LIKE HAVING REAL SUPER POWERS THOUGH, I GUESS...
WHAT DOES "PROMETHEUS" MEAN?
IT'S FROM GREEK MYTHOLOGY. HE STOLE FIRE FROM THE GODS.
WHAT ABOUT YOU? WHAT'S YOUR... "ORIGIN"?

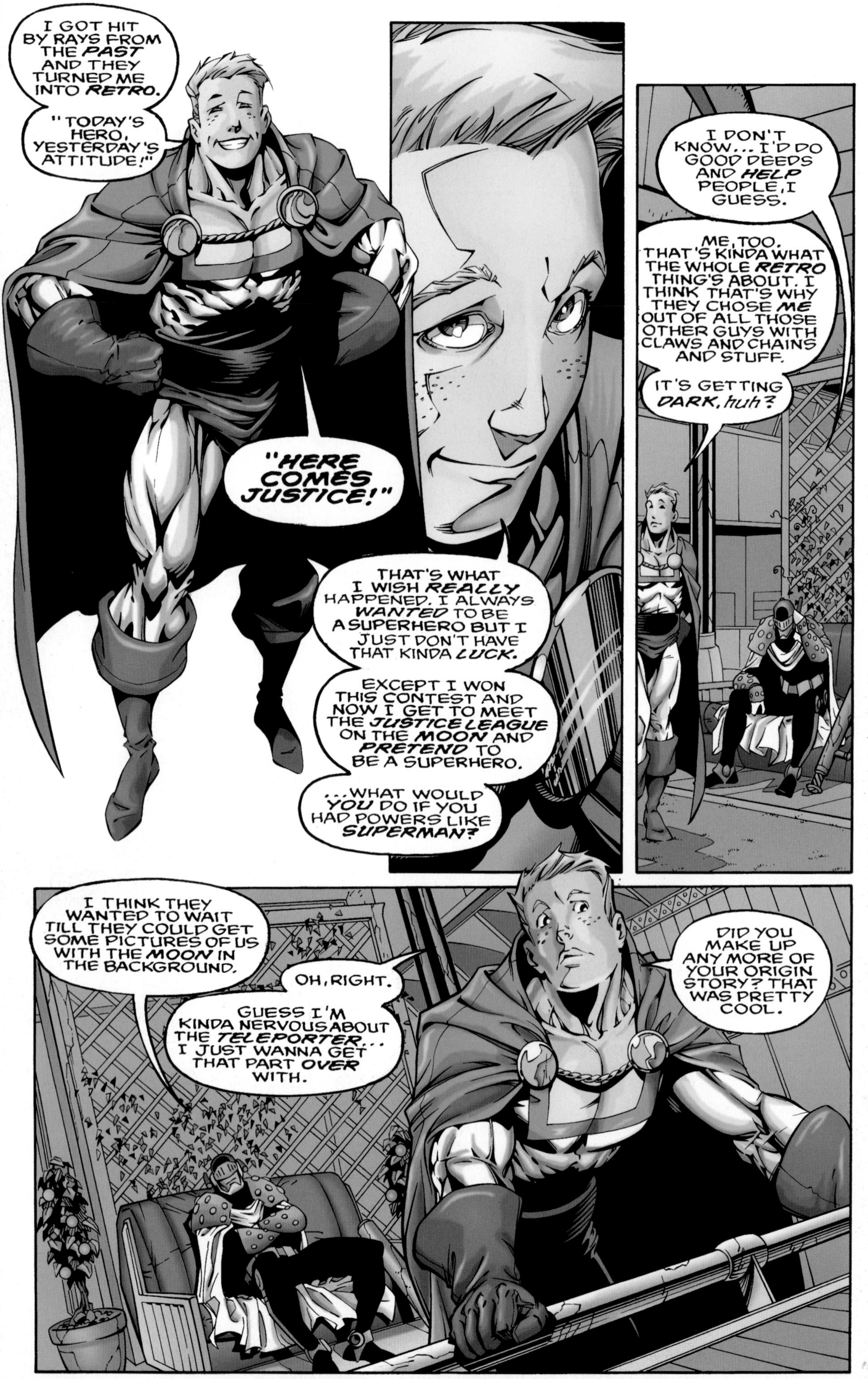

I GOT HIT BY RAYS FROM THE PAST AND THEY TURNED ME INTO RETRO.
"TODAY'S HERO, YESTERDAY'S ATTITUDE!"
"HERE COMES JUSTICE!"
THAT'S WHAT I WISH REALLY HAPPENED. I ALWAYS WANTED TO BE A SUPERHERO BUT I JUST DON'T HAVE THAT KINDA LUCK.
EXCEPT I WON THIS CONTEST AND NOW I GET TO MEET THE JUSTICE LEAGUE ON THE MOON AND PRETEND TO BE A SUPERHERO.
...WHAT WOULD YOU DO IF YOU HAD POWERS LIKE SUPERMAN?
I DON'T KNOW... I'D DO GOOD DEEDS AND HELP PEOPLE, I GUESS.
ME, TOO. THAT'S KINDA WHAT THE WHOLE RETRO THING'S ABOUT. I THINK THAT'S WHY THEY CHOSE ME OUT OF ALL THOSE OTHER GUYS WITH CLAWS AND CHAINS AND STUFF.
IT'S GETTING DARK, huh?
I THINK THEY WANTED TO WAIT TILL THEY COULD GET SOME PICTURES OF US WITH THE MOON IN THE BACKGROUND.
OH, RIGHT.
GUESS I'M KINDA NERVOUS ABOUT THE TELEPORTER... I JUST WANNA GET THAT PART OVER WITH.
DID YOU MAKE UP ANY MORE OF YOUR ORIGIN STORY? THAT WAS PRETTY COOL.

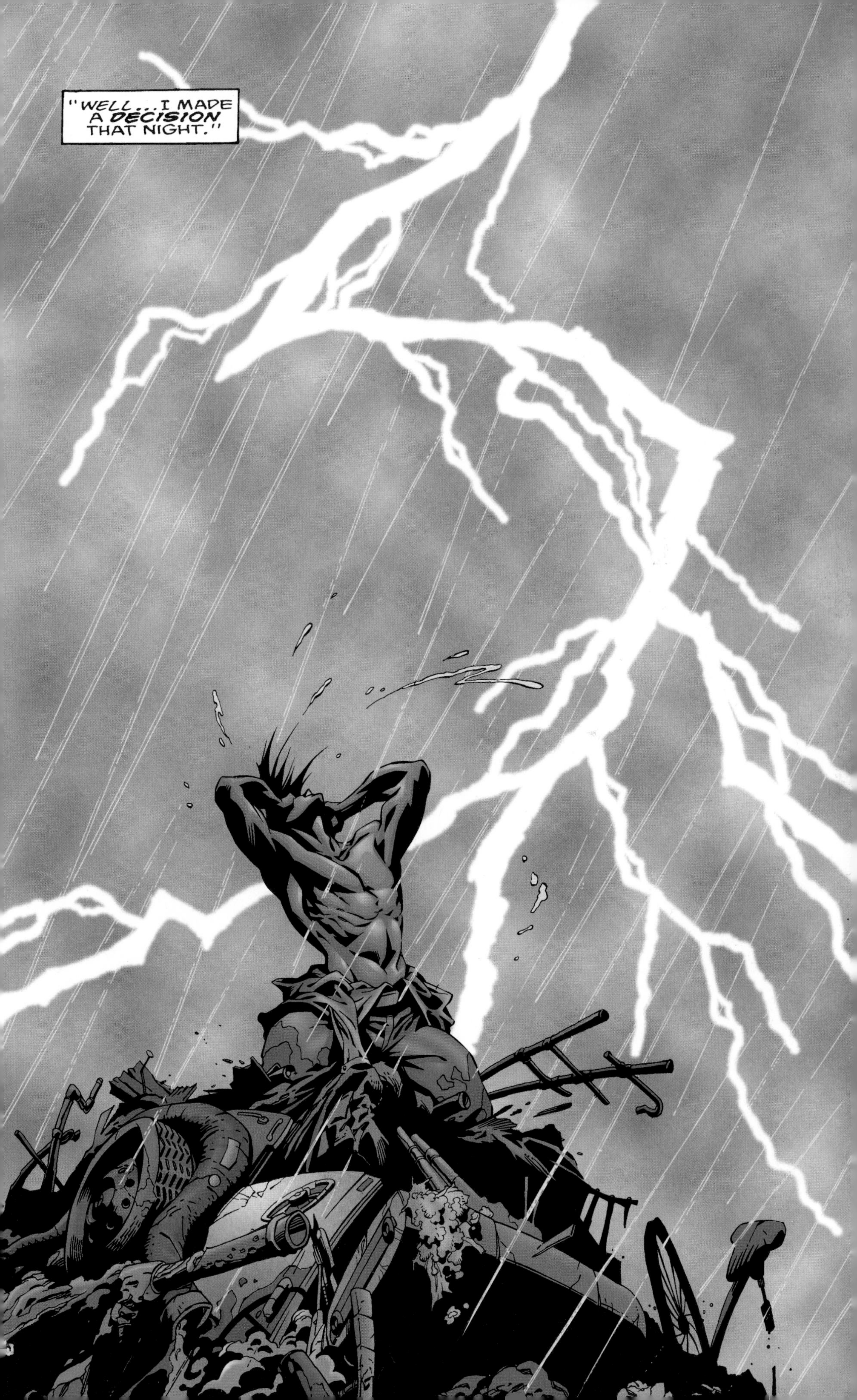
"WELL... I MADE A DECISION THAT NIGHT."

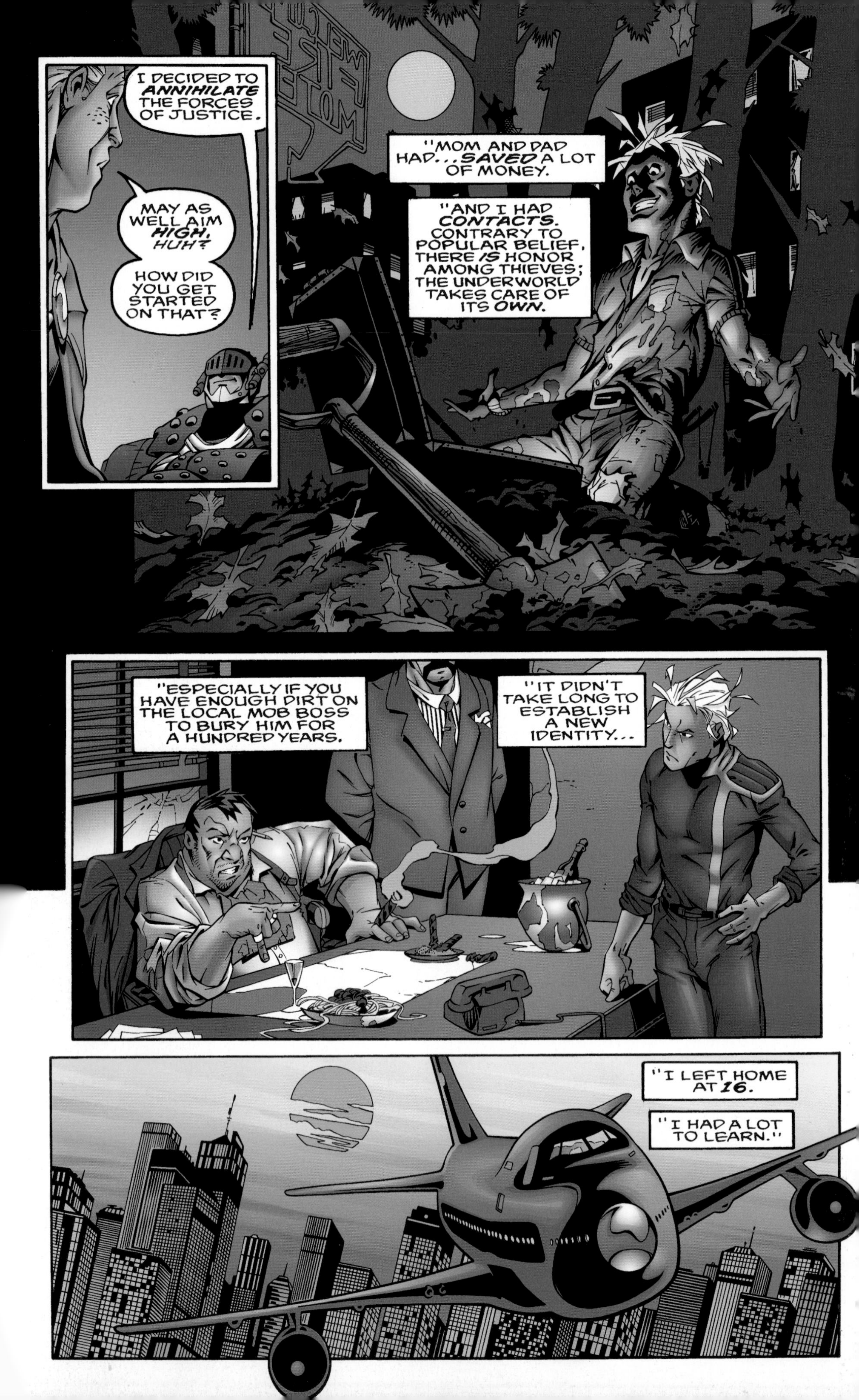
I DECIDED TO ANNIHILATE THE FORCES OF JUSTICE.
MAY AS WELL AIM HIGH, HUH?
HOW DID YOU GET STARTED ON THAT?
"MOM AND DAD HAD... SAVED A LOT OF MONEY.
"AND I HAD CONTACTS. CONTRARY TO POPULAR BELIEF, THERE IS HONOR AMONG THIEVES; THE UNDERWORLD TAKES CARE OF ITS OWN.
"ESPECIALLY IF YOU HAVE ENOUGH DIRT ON THE LOCAL MOB BOSS TO BURY HIM FOR A HUNDRED YEARS.
"IT DIDN'T TAKE LONG TO ESTABLISH A NEW IDENTITY...
"I LEFT HOME AT 16.
"I HAD A LOT TO LEARN."

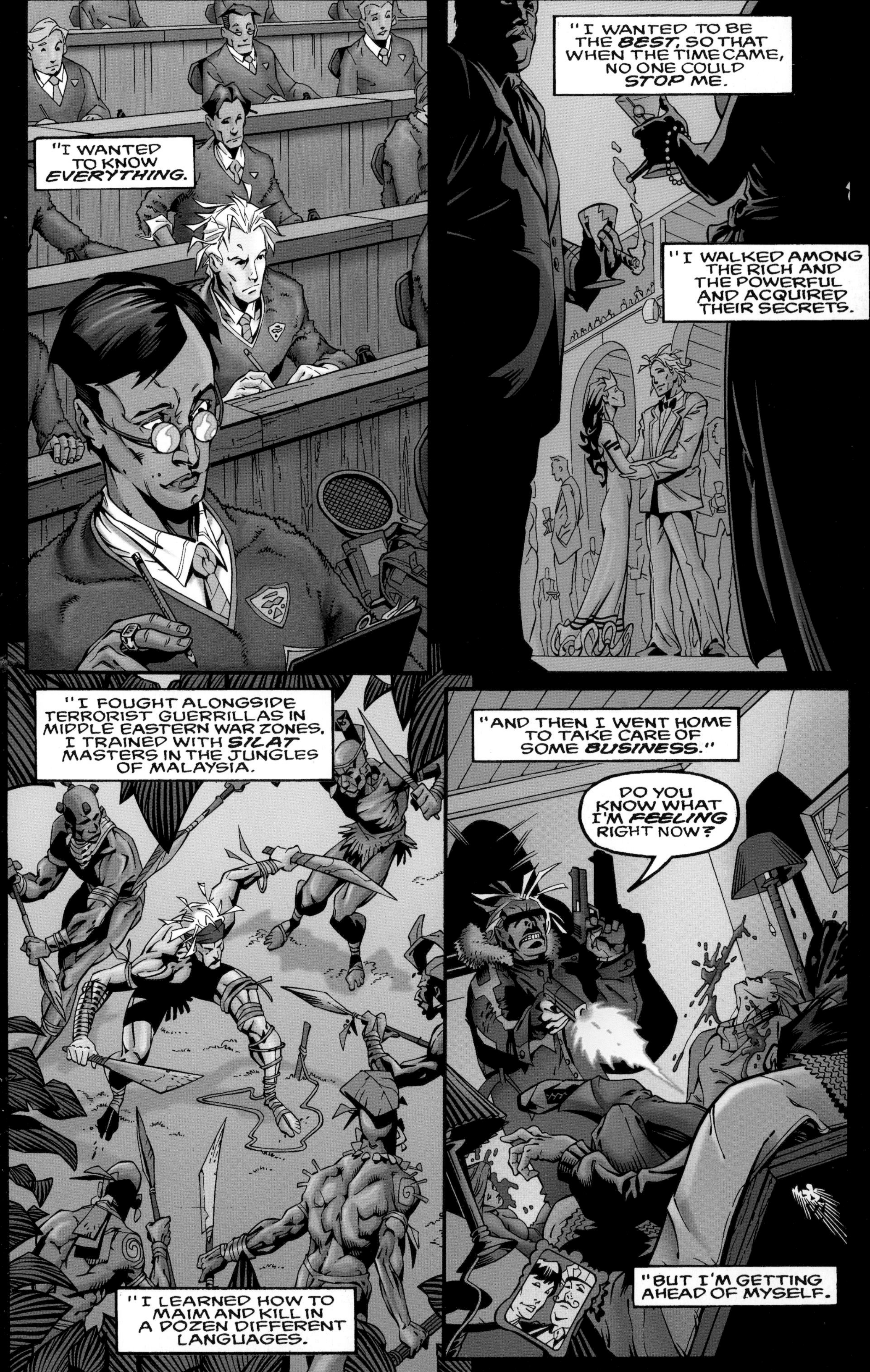
"I WANTED TO KNOW EVERYTHING.
"I WANTED TO BE THE BEST, SO THAT WHEN THE TIME CAME, NO ONE COULD STOP ME.
"I WALKED AMONG THE RICH AND THE POWERFUL AND ACQUIRED THEIR SECRETS.
"I FOUGHT ALONGSIDE TERRORIST GUERRILLAS IN MIDDLE EASTERN WAR ZONES. I TRAINED WITH SILAT MASTERS IN THE JUNGLES OF MALAYSIA.
"I LEARNED HOW TO MAIM AND KILL IN A DOZEN DIFFERENT LANGUAGES.
"AND THEN I WENT HOME TO TAKE CARE OF SOME BUSINESS."
DO YOU KNOW WHAT I'M FEELING RIGHT NOW?
"BUT I'M GETTING AHEAD OF MYSELF.

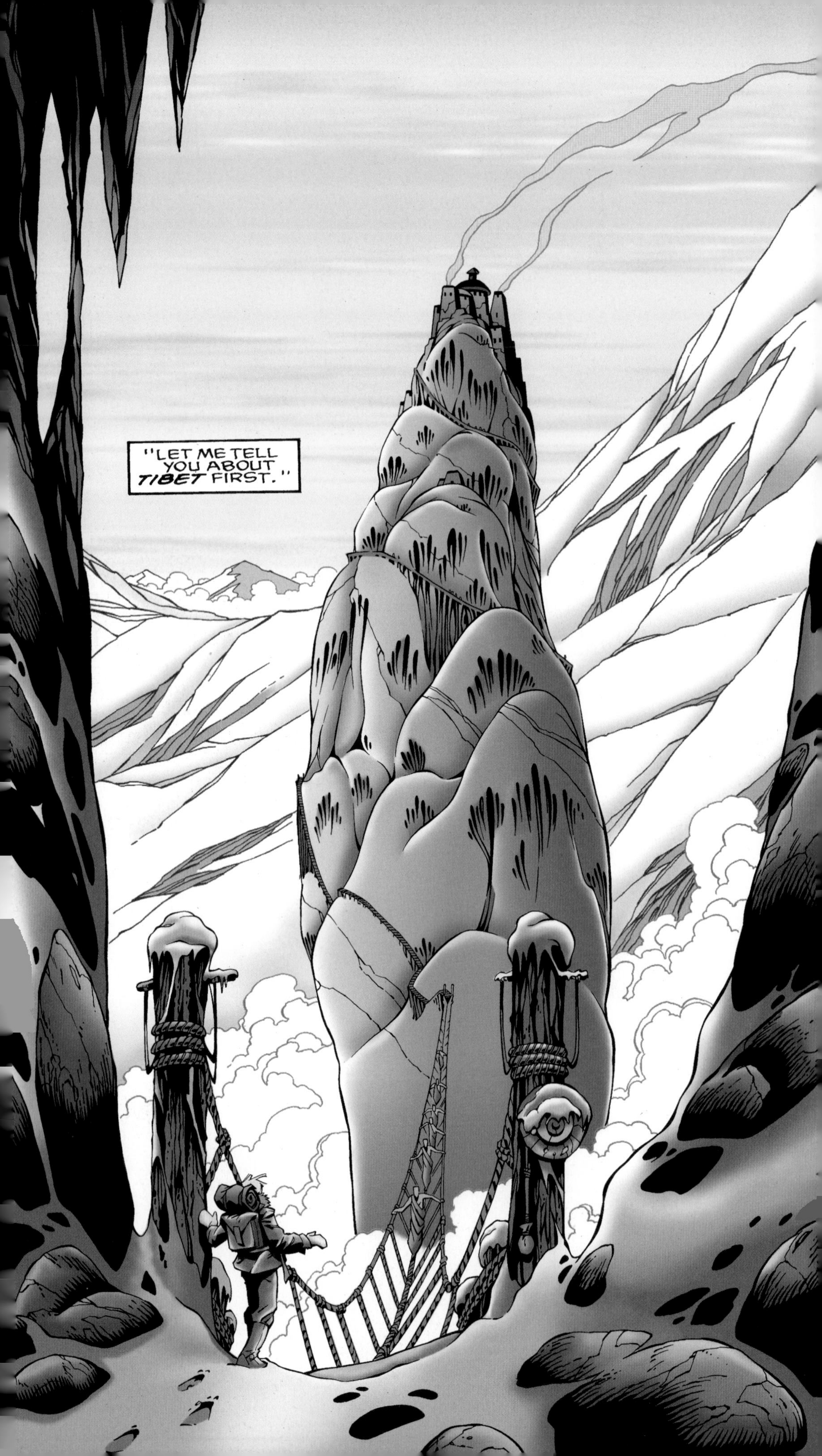
"LET ME TELL YOU ABOUT *TIBET* FIRST."

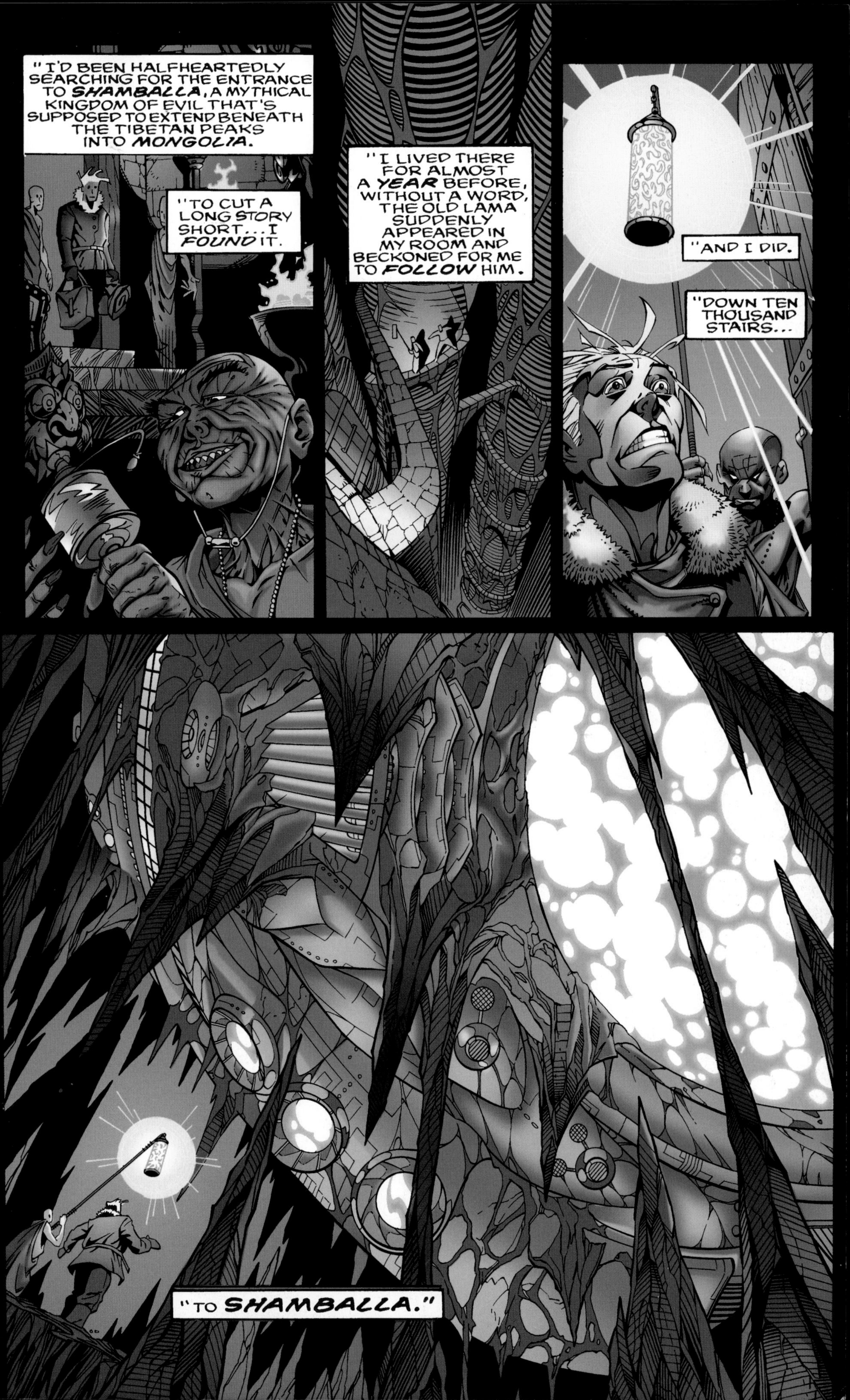
"I'D BEEN HALFHEARTEDLY SEARCHING FOR THE ENTRANCE TO SHAMBALLA, A MYTHICAL KINGDOM OF EVIL THAT'S SUPPOSED TO EXTEND BENEATH THE TIBETAN PEAKS INTO MONGOLIA.
"TO CUT A LONG STORY SHORT... I FOUND IT.
"I LIVED THERE FOR ALMOST A YEAR BEFORE, WITHOUT A WORD, THE OLD LAMA SUDDENLY APPEARED IN MY ROOM AND BECKONED FOR ME TO FOLLOW HIM.
"AND I DID.
"DOWN TEN THOUSAND STAIRS...
"TO SHAMBALLA."

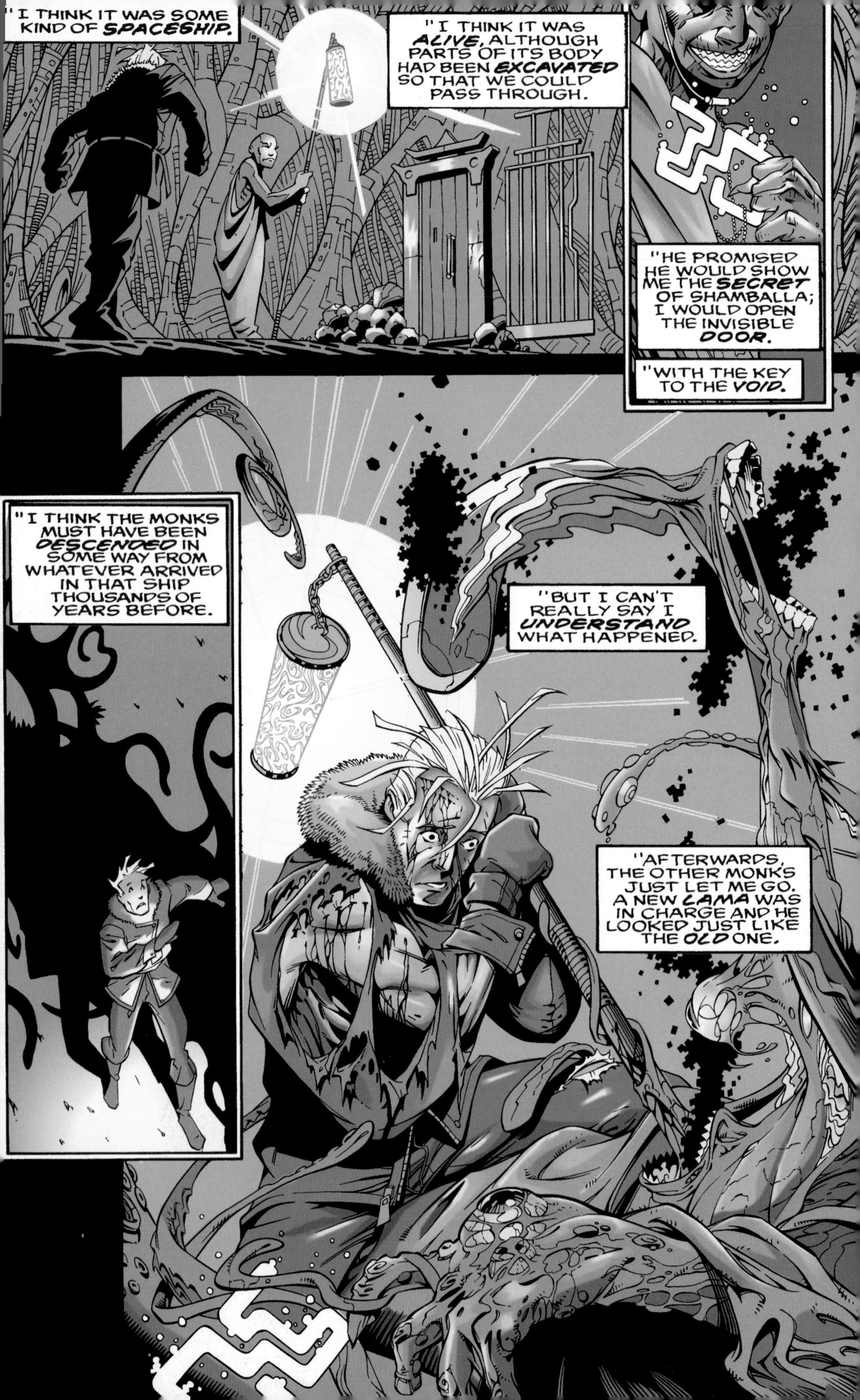
"I THINK IT WAS SOME KIND OF SPACESHIP.
"I THINK IT WAS ALIVE, ALTHOUGH PARTS OF ITS BODY HAD BEEN EXCAVATED SO THAT WE COULD PASS THROUGH.
"HE PROMISED HE WOULD SHOW ME THE SECRET OF SHAMBALLA; I WOULD OPEN THE INVISIBLE DOOR.
"WITH THE KEY TO THE VOID.
"I THINK THE MONKS MUST HAVE BEEN DESCENDED IN SOME WAY FROM WHATEVER ARRIVED IN THAT SHIP THOUSANDS OF YEARS BEFORE.
"BUT I CAN'T REALLY SAY I UNDERSTAND WHAT HAPPENED.
"AFTERWARDS, THE OTHER MONKS JUST LET ME GO. A NEW LAMA WAS IN CHARGE AND HE LOOKED JUST LIKE THE OLD ONE.

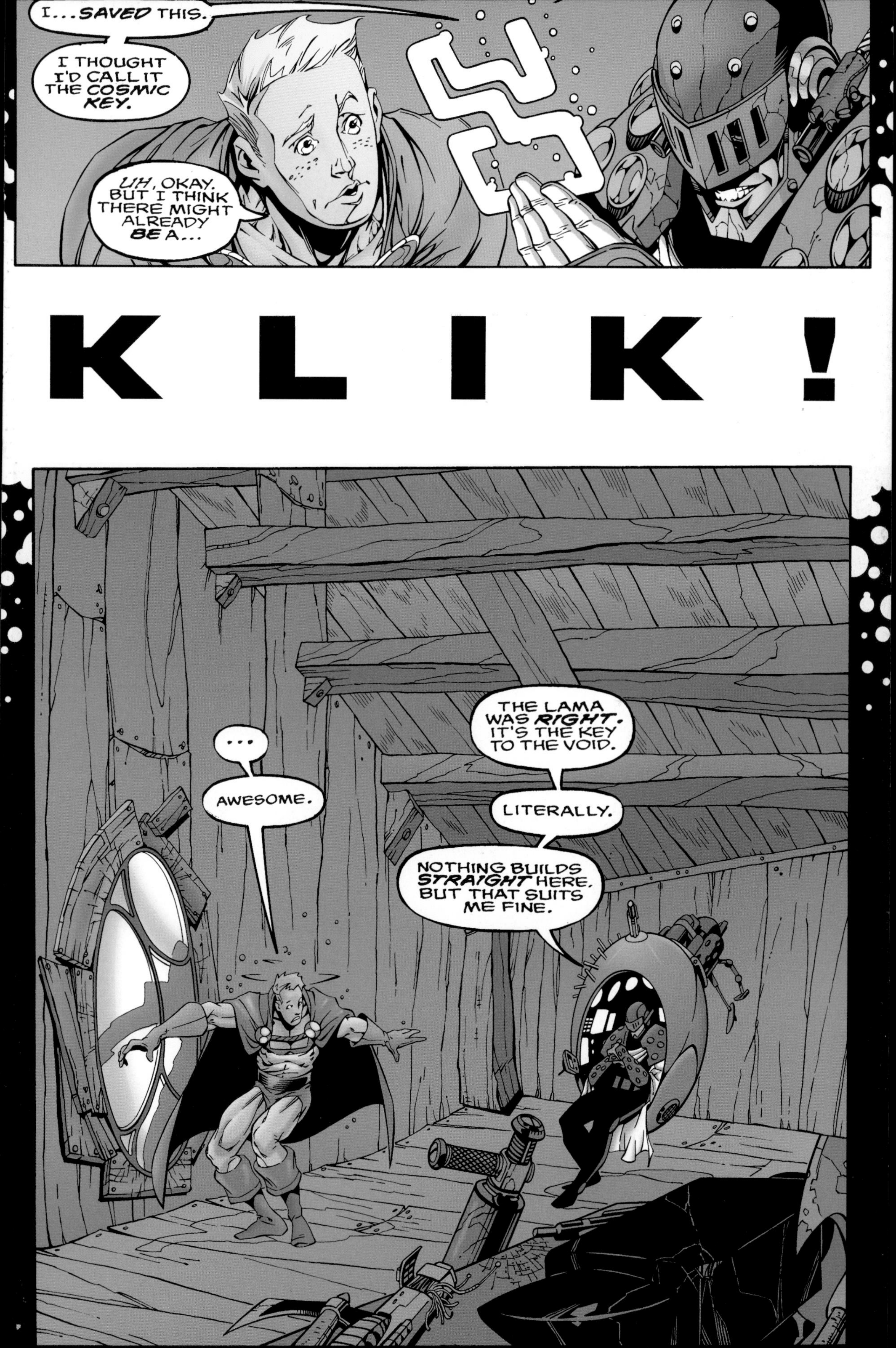
I...SAVED THIS.
I THOUGHT I'D CALL IT THE COSMIC KEY.
UH, OKAY. BUT I THINK THERE MIGHT ALREADY BE A...
KLIK!
THE LAMA WAS RIGHT. IT'S THE KEY TO THE VOID.
...
AWESOME.
LITERALLY.
NOTHING BUILDS STRAIGHT HERE. BUT THAT SUITS ME FINE.

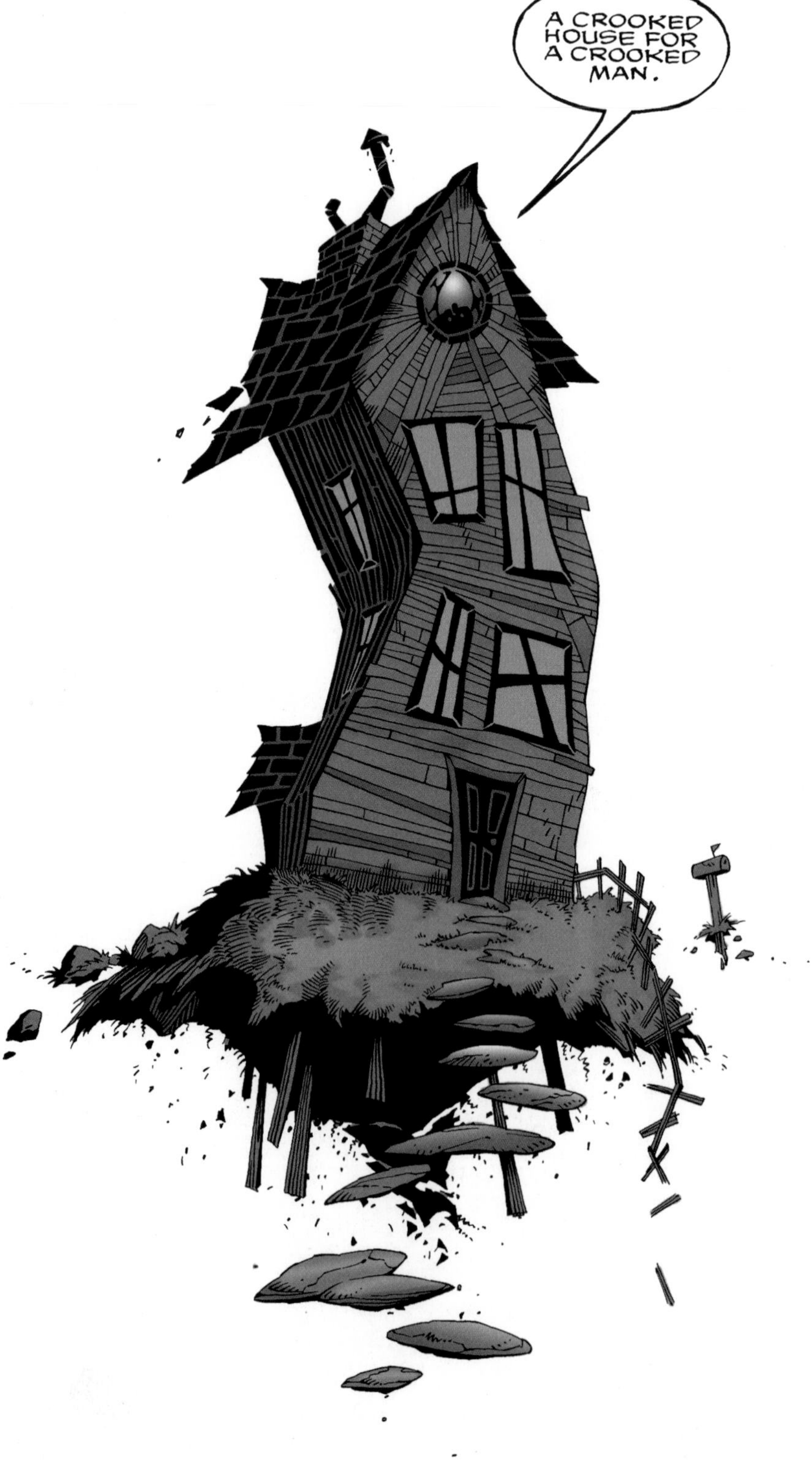
A CROOKED HOUSE FOR A CROOKED MAN.

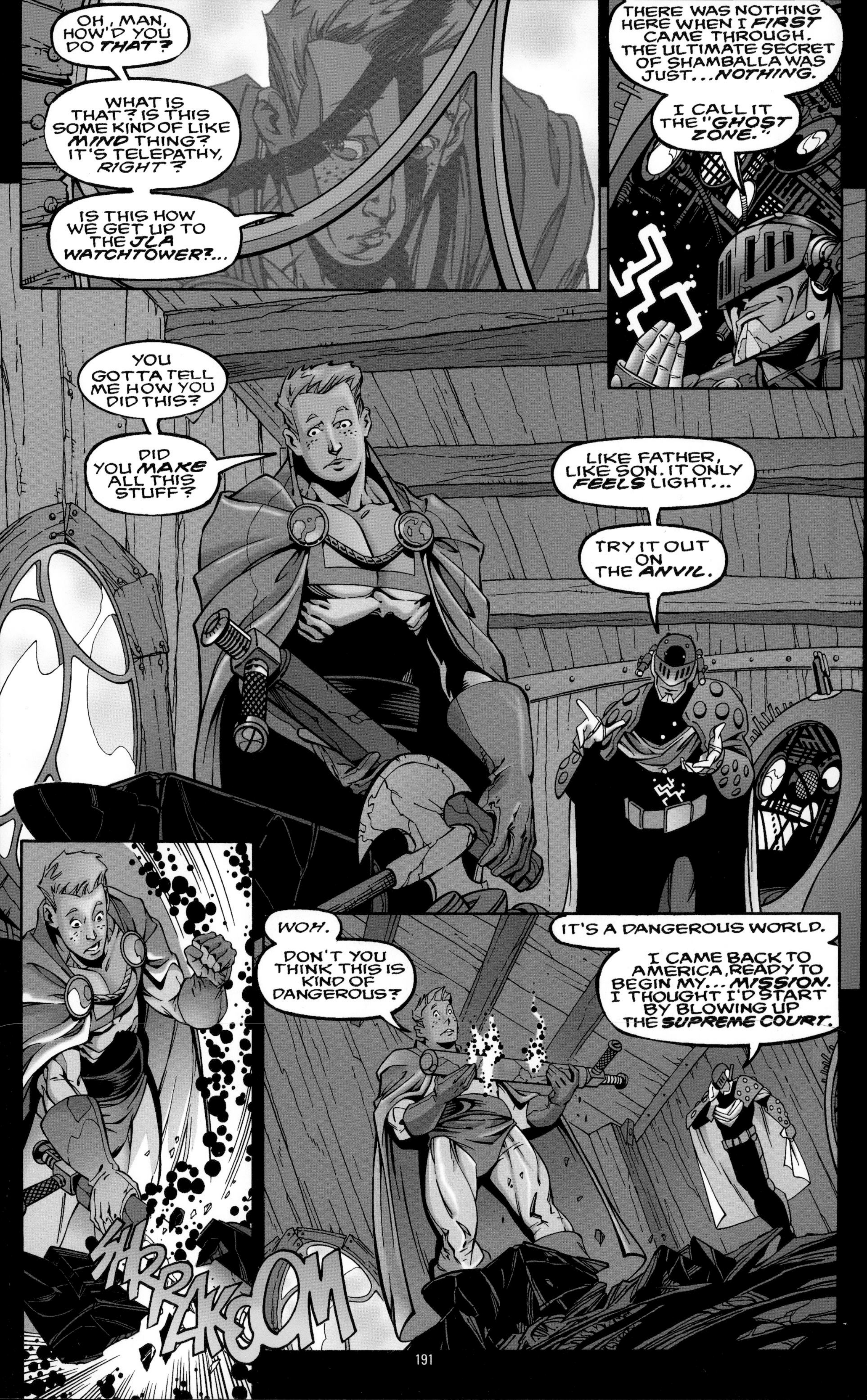

OH, MAN, HOW'D YOU DO *THAT?*
WHAT IS THAT? IS THIS SOME KIND OF LIKE *MIND* THING? IT'S TELEPATHY, *RIGHT?*
IS THIS HOW WE GET UP TO THE *JLA WATCHTOWER?...*
THERE WAS NOTHING HERE WHEN I *FIRST* CAME THROUGH. THE ULTIMATE SECRET OF SHAMBALLA WAS JUST... *NOTHING.*
I CALL IT THE "*GHOST ZONE.*"
YOU GOTTA TELL ME HOW YOU DID THIS?
DID YOU *MAKE* ALL THIS STUFF?
LIKE FATHER, LIKE SON. IT ONLY *FEELS* LIGHT...
TRY IT OUT ON THE *ANVIL.*
SHRRAKOOM
WOH.
DON'T YOU THINK THIS IS KIND OF DANGEROUS?
IT'S A DANGEROUS WORLD.
I CAME BACK TO AMERICA, READY TO BEGIN MY... *MISSION.* I THOUGHT I'D START BY BLOWING UP THE *SUPREME COURT.*

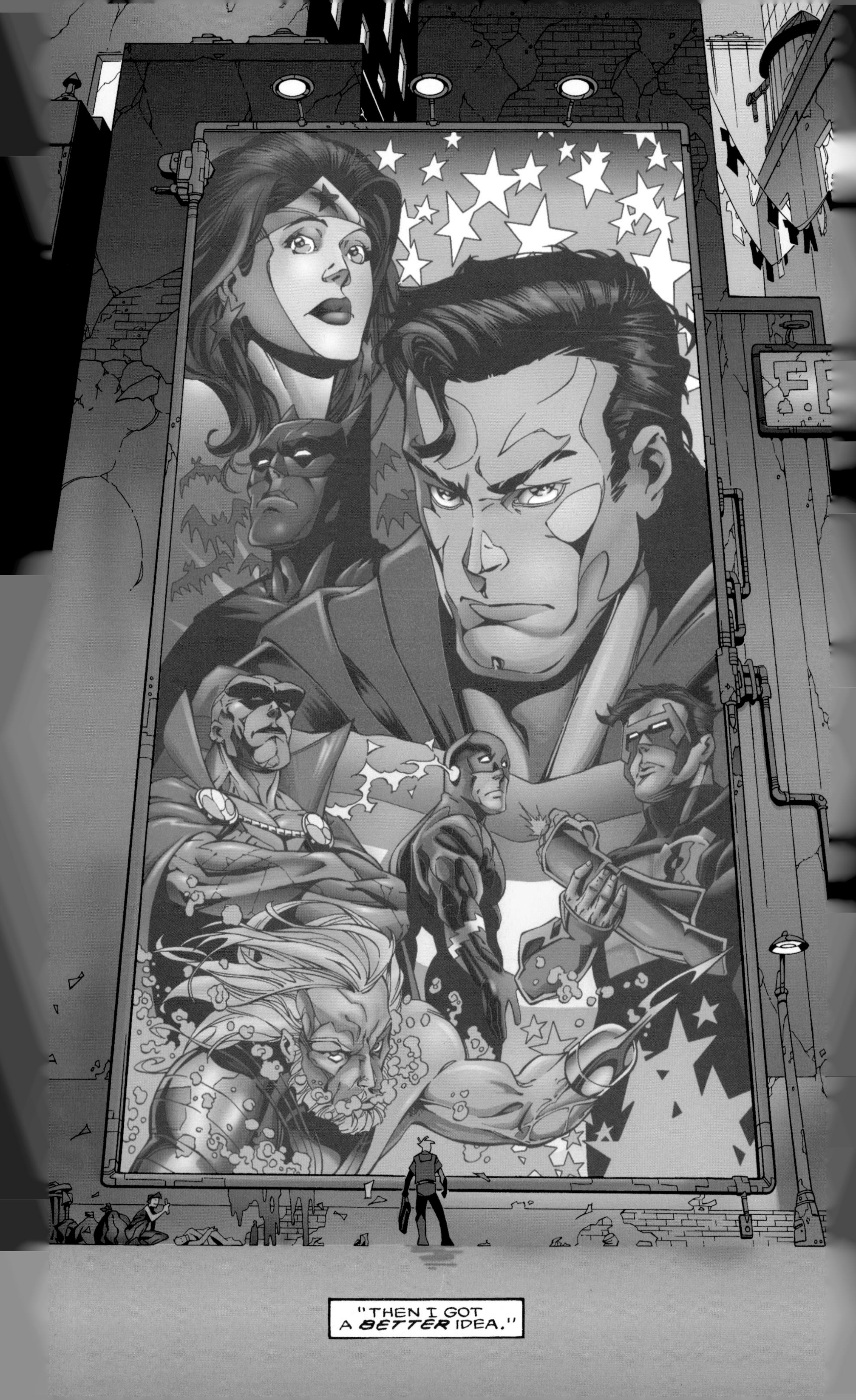
"THEN I GOT A BETTER IDEA."

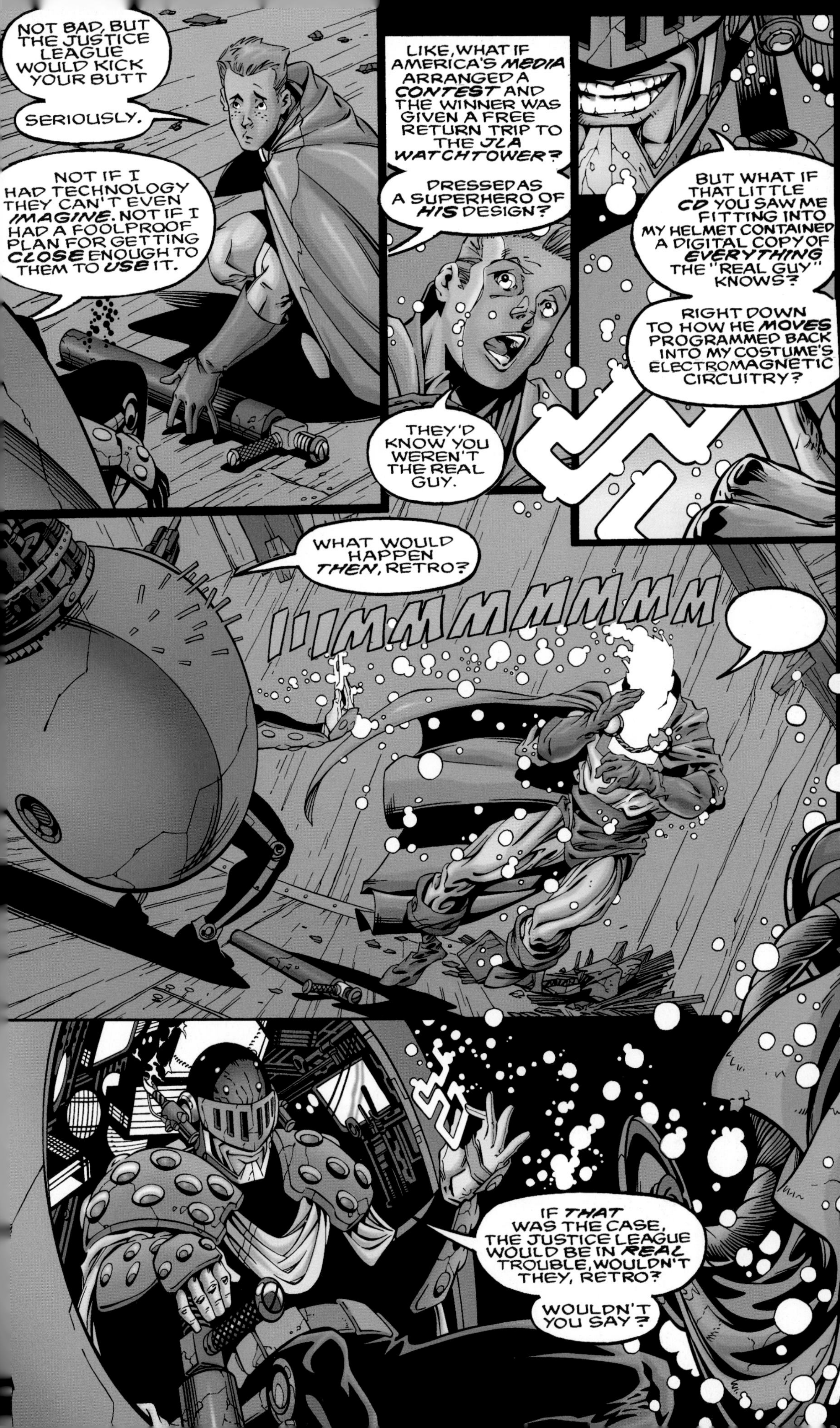
NOT BAD, BUT THE JUSTICE LEAGUE WOULD KICK YOUR BUTT
SERIOUSLY.
NOT IF I HAD TECHNOLOGY THEY CAN'T EVEN IMAGINE. NOT IF I HAD A FOOLPROOF PLAN FOR GETTING CLOSE ENOUGH TO THEM TO USE IT.
LIKE, WHAT IF AMERICA'S MEDIA ARRANGED A CONTEST AND THE WINNER WAS GIVEN A FREE RETURN TRIP TO THE JLA WATCHTOWER?
DRESSED AS A SUPERHERO OF HIS DESIGN?
THEY'D KNOW YOU WEREN'T THE REAL GUY.
BUT WHAT IF THAT LITTLE CD YOU SAW ME FITTING INTO MY HELMET CONTAINED A DIGITAL COPY OF EVERYTHING THE "REAL GUY" KNOWS?
RIGHT DOWN TO HOW HE MOVES PROGRAMMED BACK INTO MY COSTUME'S ELECTROMAGNETIC CIRCUITRY?
WHAT WOULD HAPPEN THEN, RETRO?
IIIMMMMMMMM
IF THAT WAS THE CASE, THE JUSTICE LEAGUE WOULD BE IN REAL TROUBLE, WOULDN'T THEY, RETRO?
WOULDN'T YOU SAY?

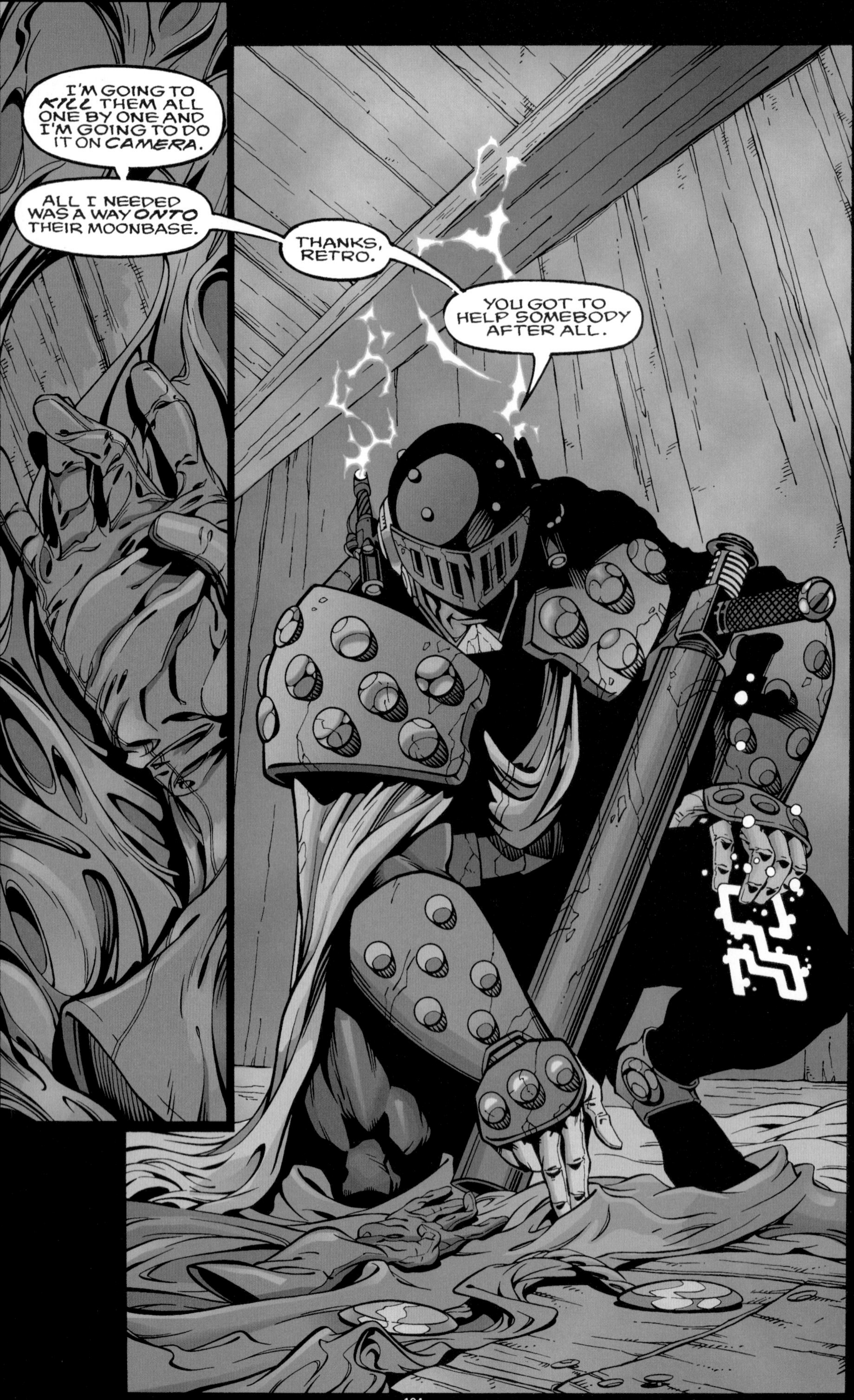
I'M GOING TO KILL THEM ALL ONE BY ONE AND I'M GOING TO DO IT ON CAMERA.
ALL I NEEDED WAS A WAY ONTO THEIR MOONBASE.
THANKS, RETRO.
YOU GOT TO HELP SOMEBODY AFTER ALL.

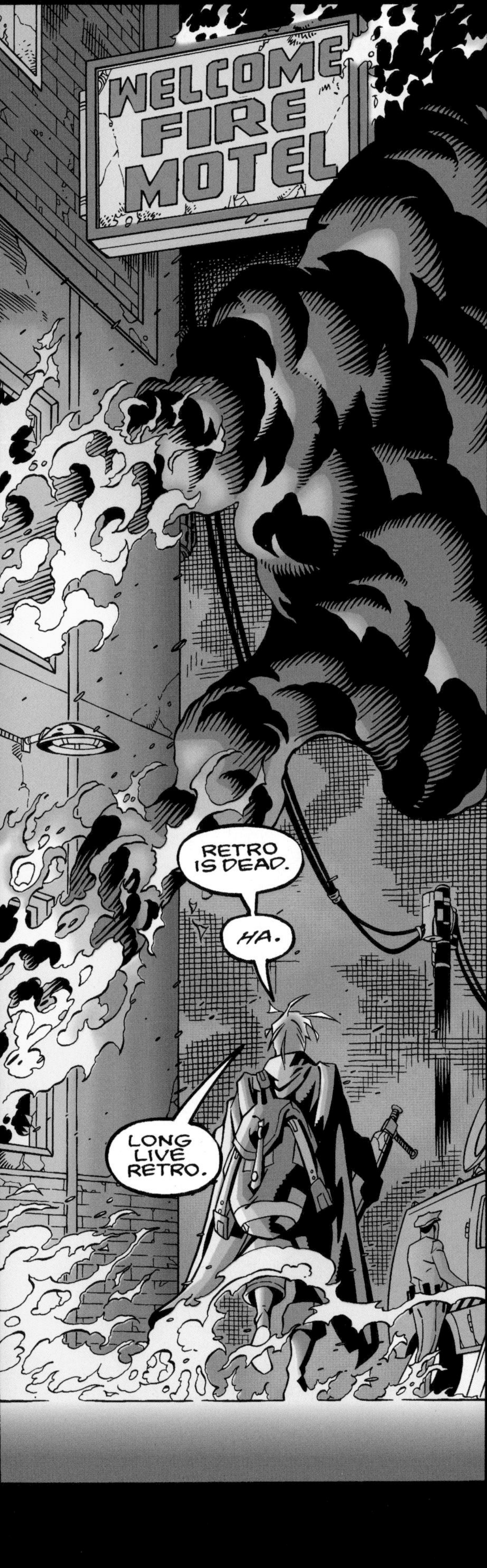
WELCOME FIRE MOTEL
RETRO IS DEAD.
HA.
LONG LIVE RETRO.

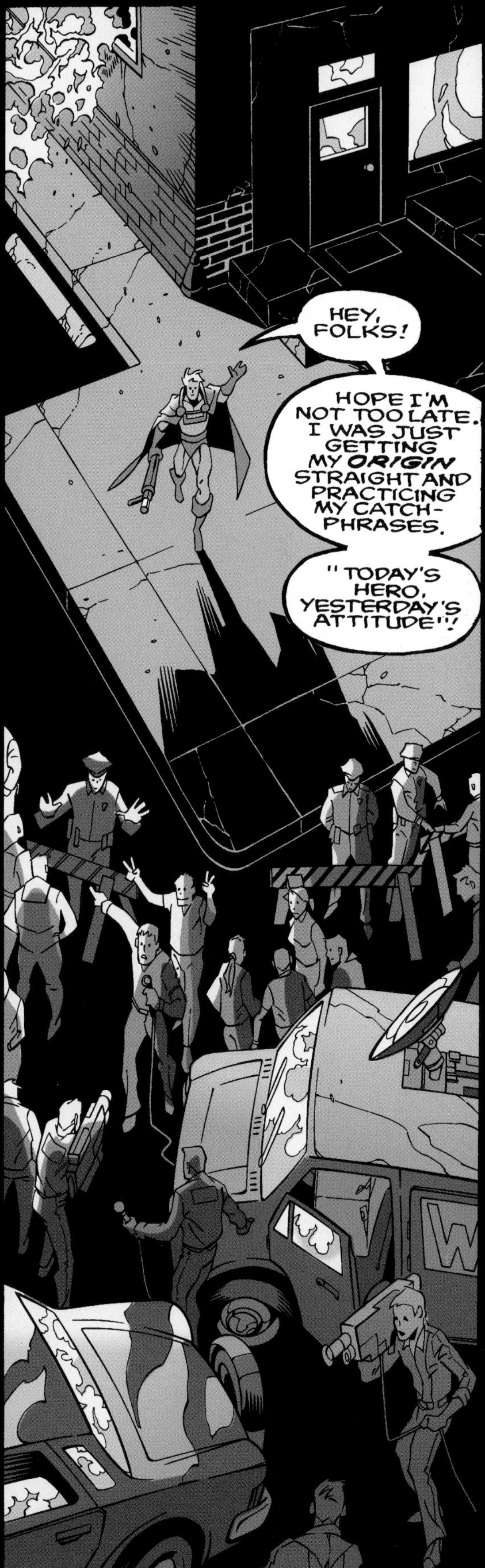
HEY, FOLKS!
HOPE I'M NOT TOO LATE. I WAS JUST GETTING MY ORIGIN STRAIGHT AND PRACTICING MY CATCH-PHRASES.
"TODAY'S HERO, YESTERDAY'S ATTITUDE"!

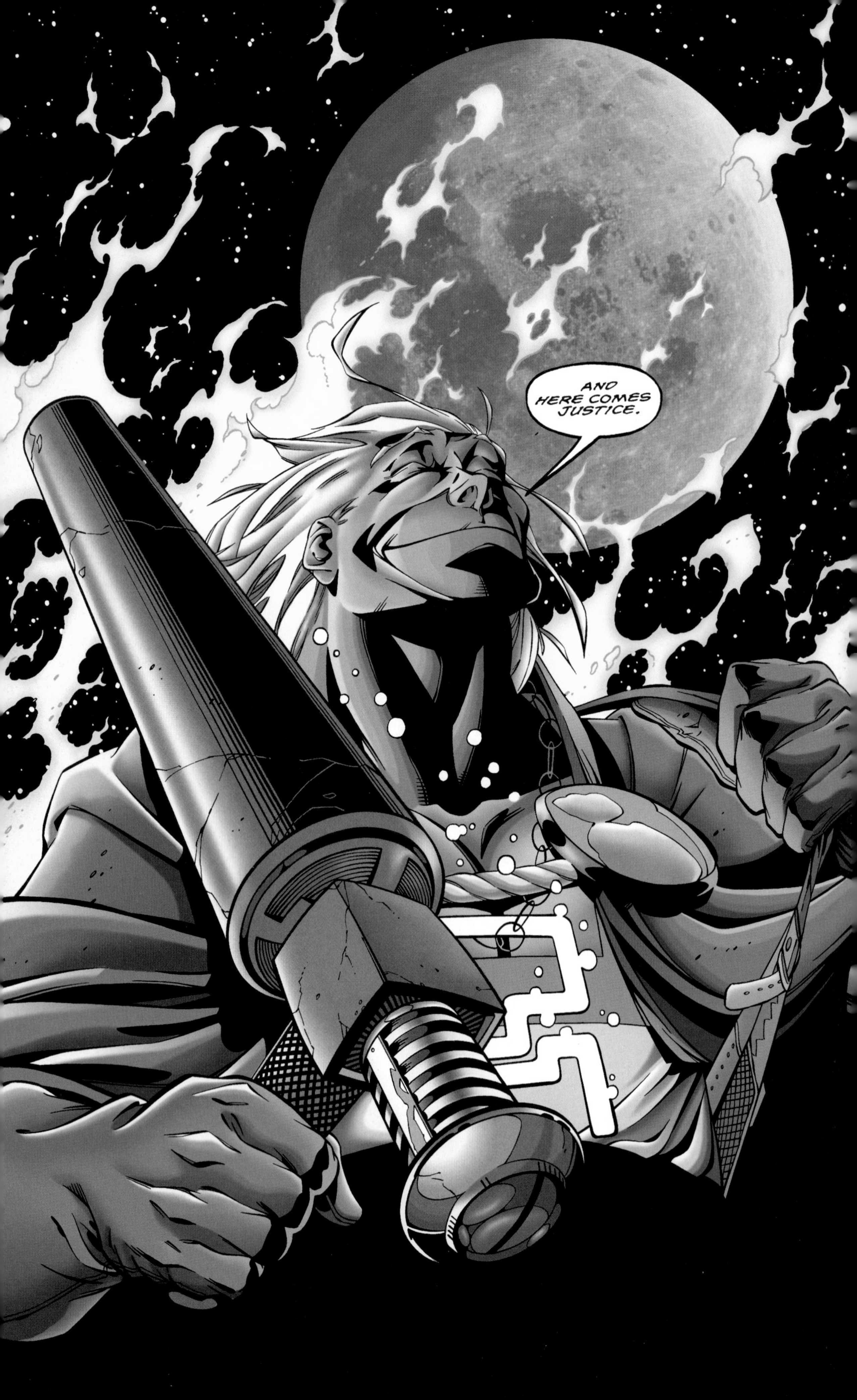
AND HERE COMES JUSTICE.

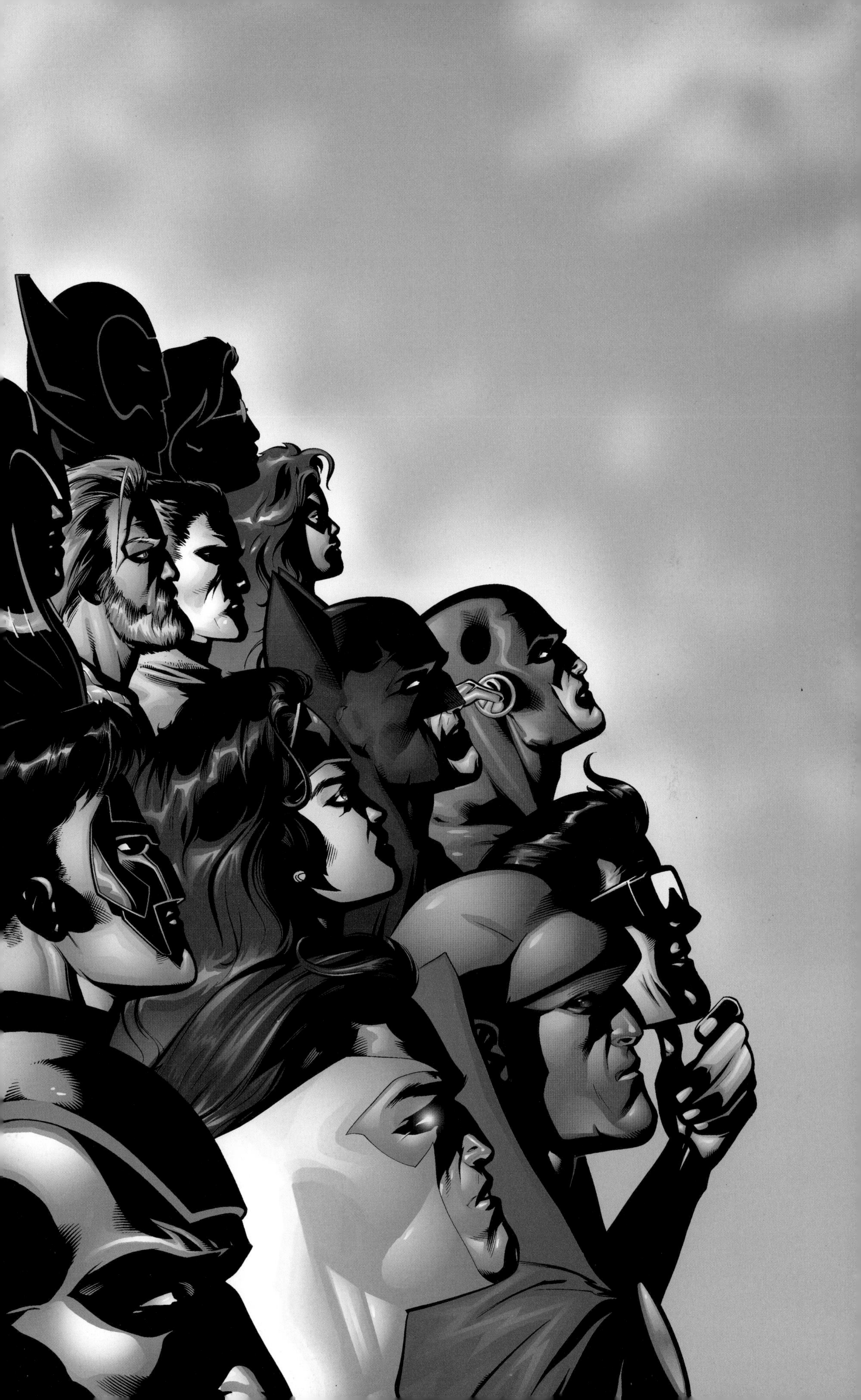

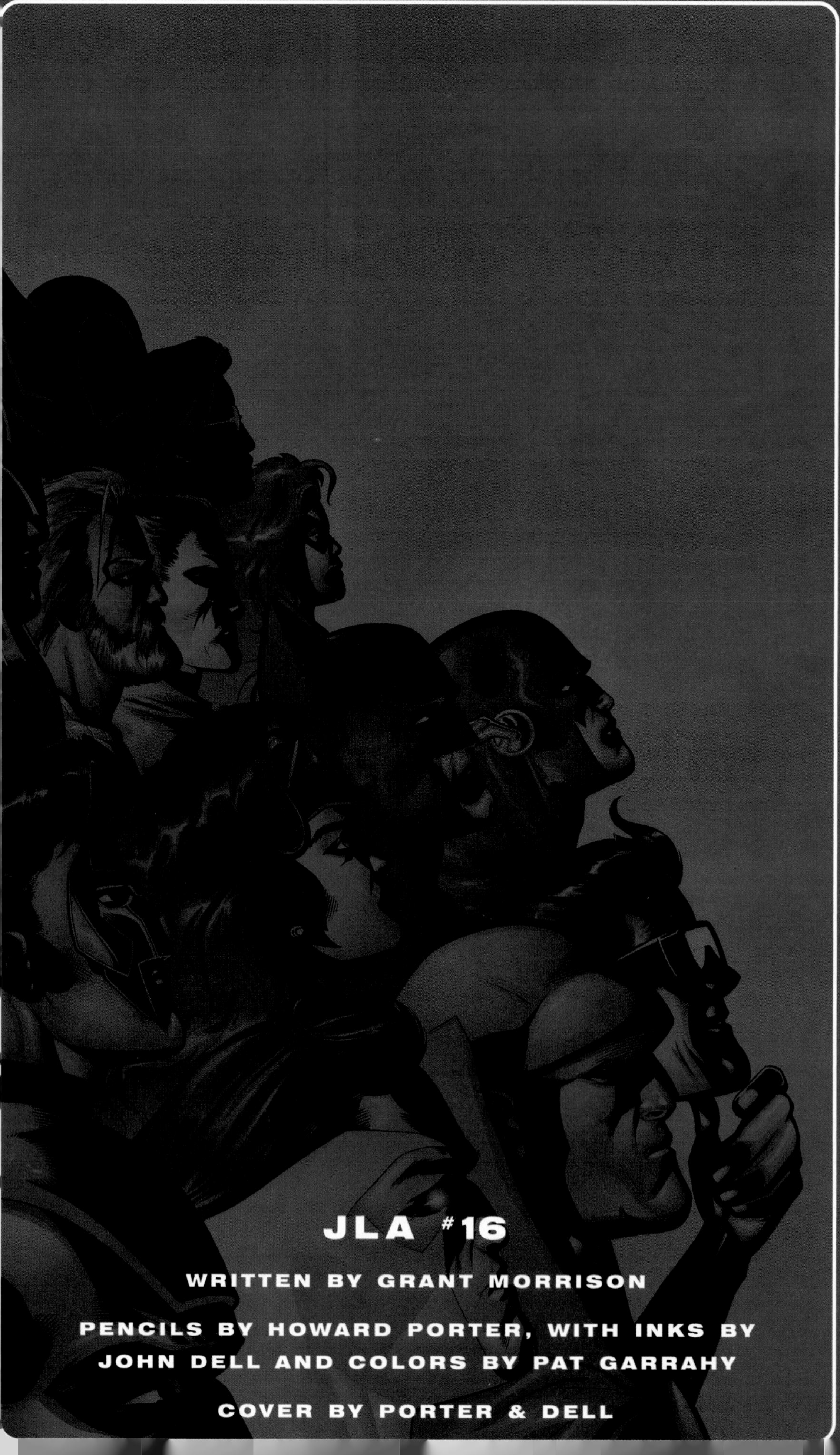

JLA #16

WRITTEN BY GRANT MORRISON

PENCILS BY HOWARD PORTER, WITH INKS BY JOHN DELL AND COLORS BY PAT GARRAHY

COVER BY PORTER & DELL

NEW MEMBERS::

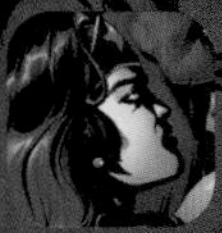

WONDER WOMAN

Diana's mother, Queen Hippolyta, served as the first Wonder Woman during World War II. With Diana currently transformed into the Goddess of Truth, Hippolyta takes her daughter's place in the Justice League.

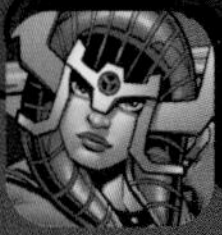

BIG BARDA

Barda was the leader of Darkseid's elite Female Furies battalion until she fell in love with Scott Free — a.k.a. the super-escape artist Mister Miracle — and left to join him on Earth. She was sent by Highfather, the leader of New Genesis, to aid the Justice League and to keep an eye on the unpredictable Orion.

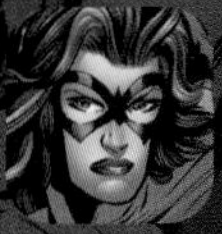

THE HUNTRESS

After losing her own family to organized crime, Helena Bertinelli became the Huntress, exacting her own brand of harsh justice on underworld scumbags. She was brought into the League by Batman in an effort to curb her violent methods and combative attitude.

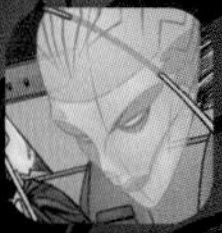

ORACLE

Barbara Gordon once patrolled the streets of Gotham as the masked heroine Batgirl, until a vicious attack by the Joker left her wheelchair-bound. Never one to give up, Barbara created the identity of Oracle, a mysterious freelance information broker who specializes in metahuman activities. She currently serves as Data Central for the JLA.

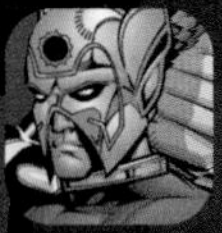

ORION

Orion of the New Gods lives for one thing and one thing alone: combat. The son of Darkseid (the evil lord of the planet Apokolips), Orion possesses a fearsome rage held back only by his sentient Mother Box computer.

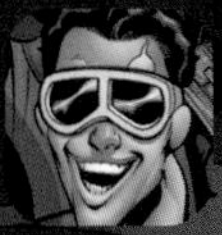

PLASTIC MAN

The League's most versatile and creative member, the shape-changer called Plastic Man serves in the JLA with a dedication and fortitude that often contradict his playful and easygoing demeanor.

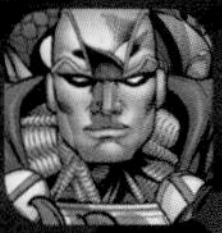

STEEL

A man of strong morals and unshakable ethics, John Henry Irons was saved from certain death by Superman. Inspired by the Man of Steel's example, Irons now uses his greatest creations — a suit of flight-capable armor and a formidable hi-tech hammer — as the hero Steel, the Justice League's resident scientist and techno-artisan.

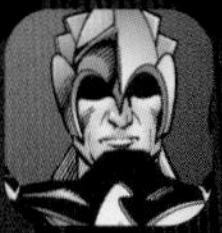

ZAURIEL

A Guardian Angel in Heaven's Eagle Host for over a million years, Zauriel renounced his immortality to serve as Heaven's official champion on Earth. One of the JLA's newest recruits, Zauriel possesses enhanced strength, angel wings, a potent sonic cry and supernatural expertise.

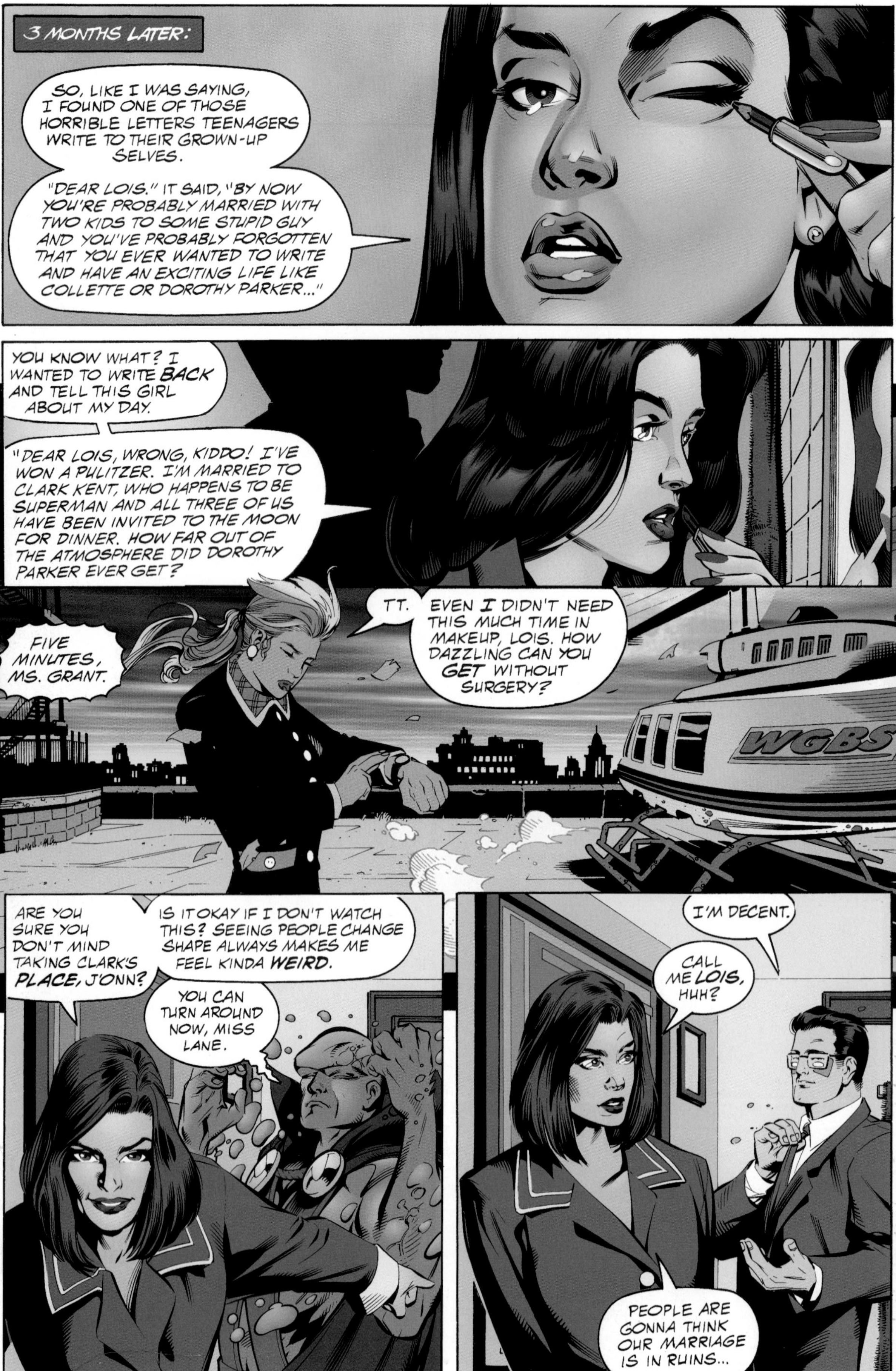
3 MONTHS LATER:
SO, LIKE I WAS SAYING, I FOUND ONE OF THOSE HORRIBLE LETTERS TEENAGERS WRITE TO THEIR GROWN-UP SELVES.
"DEAR LOIS." IT SAID, "BY NOW YOU'RE PROBABLY MARRIED WITH TWO KIDS TO SOME STUPID GUY AND YOU'VE PROBABLY FORGOTTEN THAT YOU EVER WANTED TO WRITE AND HAVE AN EXCITING LIFE LIKE COLLETTE OR DOROTHY PARKER..."
YOU KNOW WHAT? I WANTED TO WRITE BACK AND TELL THIS GIRL ABOUT MY DAY.
"DEAR LOIS, WRONG, KIDDO! I'VE WON A PULITZER. I'M MARRIED TO CLARK KENT, WHO HAPPENS TO BE SUPERMAN AND ALL THREE OF US HAVE BEEN INVITED TO THE MOON FOR DINNER. HOW FAR OUT OF THE ATMOSPHERE DID DOROTHY PARKER EVER GET?
FIVE MINUTES, MS. GRANT.
TT.
EVEN I DIDN'T NEED THIS MUCH TIME IN MAKEUP, LOIS. HOW DAZZLING CAN YOU GET WITHOUT SURGERY?
WGBS
ARE YOU SURE YOU DON'T MIND TAKING CLARK'S PLACE, J'ONN?
IS IT OKAY IF I DON'T WATCH THIS? SEEING PEOPLE CHANGE SHAPE ALWAYS MAKES ME FEEL KINDA WEIRD.
YOU CAN TURN AROUND NOW, MISS LANE.
I'M DECENT.
CALL ME LOIS, HUH?
PEOPLE ARE GONNA THINK OUR MARRIAGE IS IN RUINS...

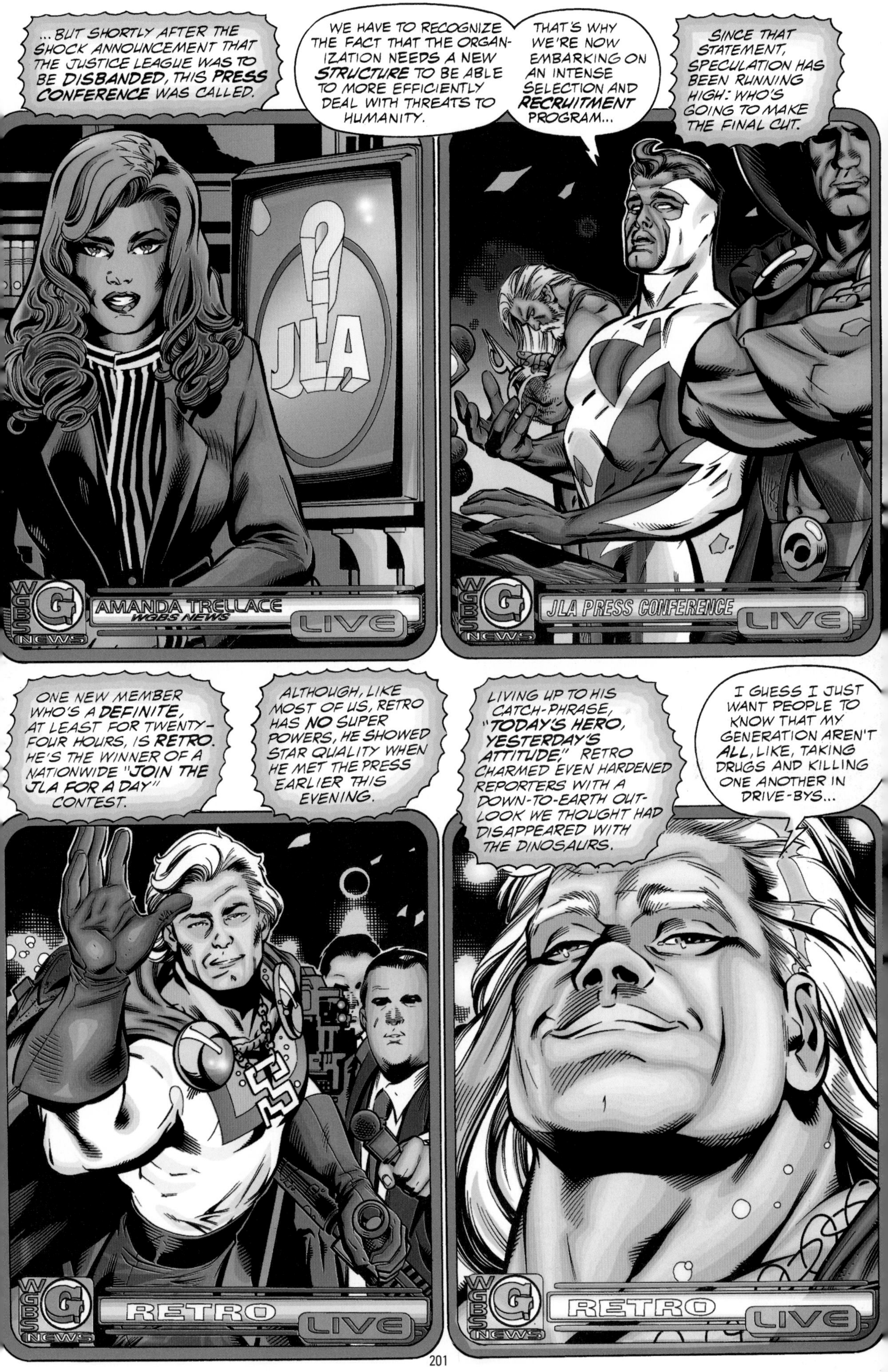
...BUT SHORTLY AFTER THE SHOCK ANNOUNCEMENT THAT THE JUSTICE LEAGUE WAS TO BE DISBANDED, THIS PRESS CONFERENCE WAS CALLED.
WE HAVE TO RECOGNIZE THE FACT THAT THE ORGANIZATION NEEDS A NEW STRUCTURE TO BE ABLE TO MORE EFFICIENTLY DEAL WITH THREATS TO HUMANITY.
THAT'S WHY WE'RE NOW EMBARKING ON AN INTENSE SELECTION AND RECRUITMENT PROGRAM...
SINCE THAT STATEMENT, SPECULATION HAS BEEN RUNNING HIGH: WHO'S GOING TO MAKE THE FINAL CUT.
JLA
WGBS NEWS
AMANDA TRELLACE
WGBS NEWS
LIVE
WGBS NEWS
JLA PRESS CONFERENCE
LIVE
ONE NEW MEMBER WHO'S A DEFINITE, AT LEAST FOR TWENTY-FOUR HOURS, IS RETRO. HE'S THE WINNER OF A NATIONWIDE "JOIN THE JLA FOR A DAY" CONTEST.
ALTHOUGH, LIKE MOST OF US, RETRO HAS NO SUPER POWERS, HE SHOWED STAR QUALITY WHEN HE MET THE PRESS EARLIER THIS EVENING.
LIVING UP TO HIS CATCH-PHRASE, "TODAY'S HERO, YESTERDAY'S ATTITUDE," RETRO CHARMED EVEN HARDENED REPORTERS WITH A DOWN-TO-EARTH OUTLOOK WE THOUGHT HAD DISAPPEARED WITH THE DINOSAURS.
I GUESS I JUST WANT PEOPLE TO KNOW THAT MY GENERATION AREN'T ALL, LIKE, TAKING DRUGS AND KILLING ONE ANOTHER IN DRIVE-BYS...
WGBS NEWS
RETRO
LIVE
WGBS NEWS
RETRO
LIVE

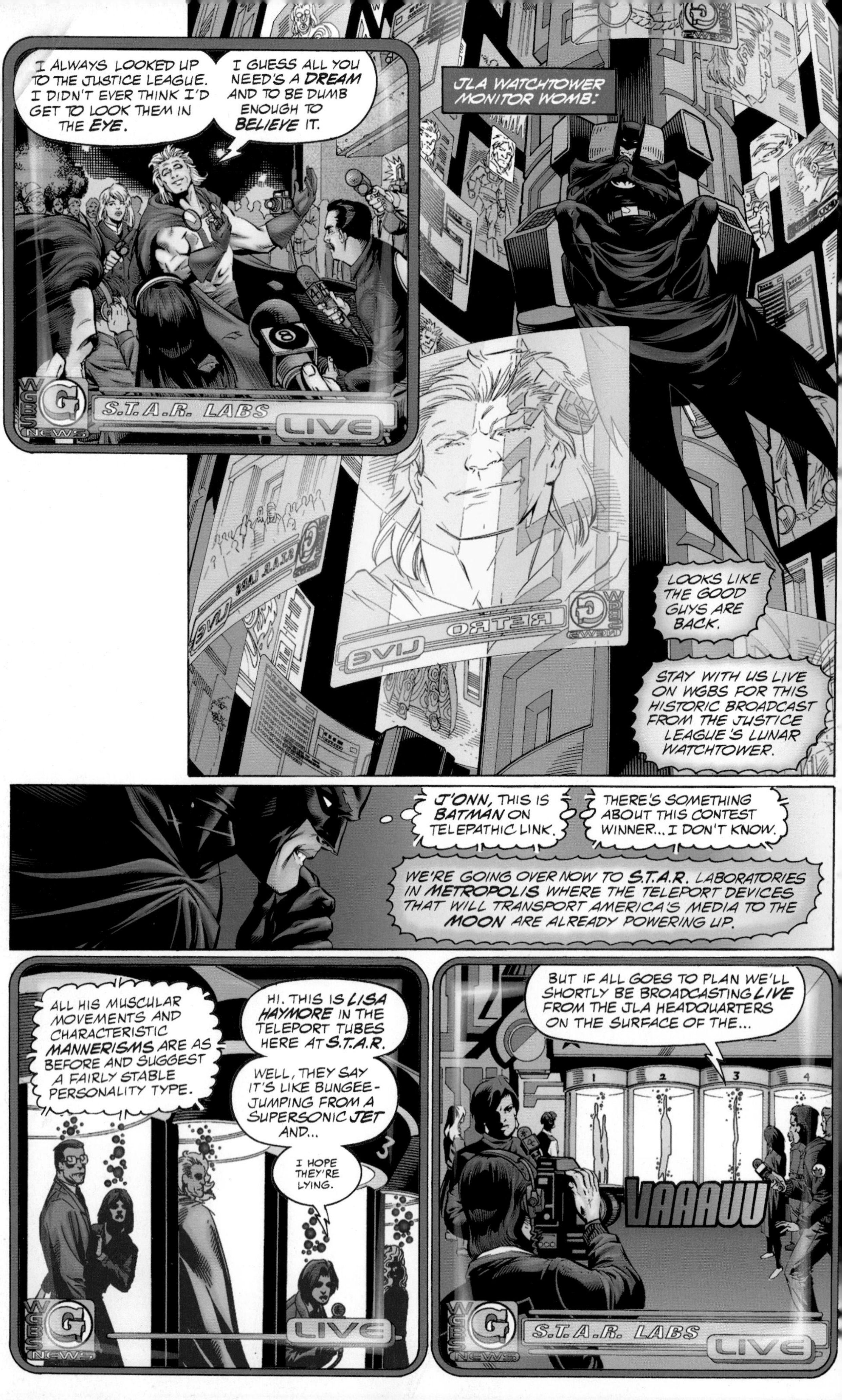
I ALWAYS LOOKED UP TO THE JUSTICE LEAGUE. I DIDN'T EVER THINK I'D GET TO LOOK THEM IN THE EYE.
I GUESS ALL YOU NEED'S A DREAM AND TO BE DUMB ENOUGH TO BELIEVE IT.
S.T.A.R. LABS
LIVE
JLA WATCHTOWER MONITOR WOMB:
RETRO
LIVE
LOOKS LIKE THE GOOD GUYS ARE BACK.
STAY WITH US LIVE ON WGBS FOR THIS HISTORIC BROADCAST FROM THE JUSTICE LEAGUE'S LUNAR WATCHTOWER.
J'ONN, THIS IS BATMAN ON TELEPATHIC LINK.
THERE'S SOMETHING ABOUT THIS CONTEST WINNER... I DON'T KNOW.
WE'RE GOING OVER NOW TO S.T.A.R. LABORATORIES IN METROPOLIS WHERE THE TELEPORT DEVICES THAT WILL TRANSPORT AMERICA'S MEDIA TO THE MOON ARE ALREADY POWERING UP.
ALL HIS MUSCULAR MOVEMENTS AND CHARACTERISTIC MANNERISMS ARE AS BEFORE AND SUGGEST A FAIRLY STABLE PERSONALITY TYPE.
HI. THIS IS LISA HAYMORE IN THE TELEPORT TUBES HERE AT S.T.A.R.
WELL, THEY SAY IT'S LIKE BUNGEE-JUMPING FROM A SUPERSONIC JET AND...
I HOPE THEY'RE LYING.
LIVE
BUT IF ALL GOES TO PLAN WE'LL SHORTLY BE BROADCASTING LIVE FROM THE JLA HEADQUARTERS ON THE SURFACE OF THE...
VAAAUU
S.T.A.R. LABS
LIVE

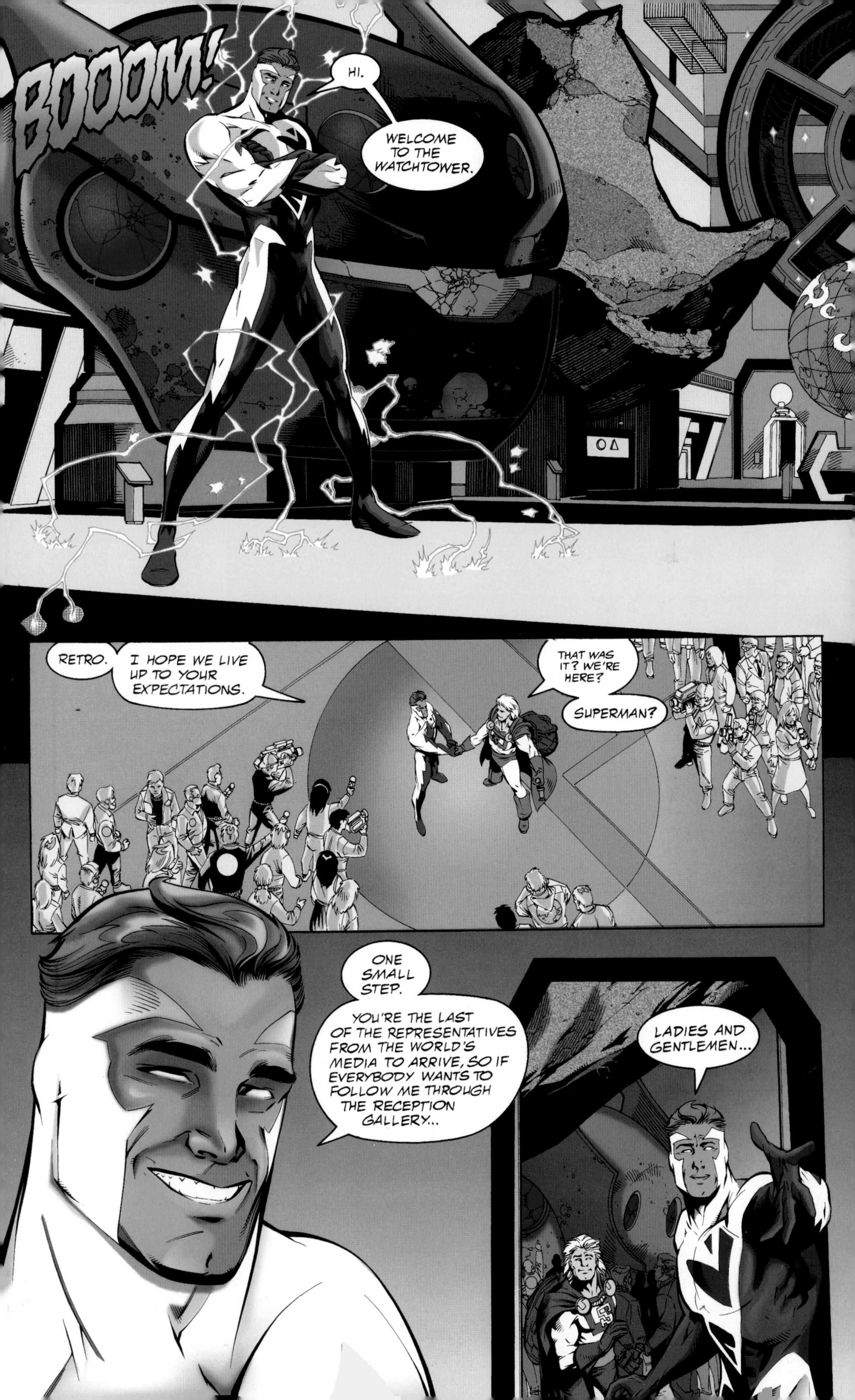
BOOOM!
HI.
WELCOME TO THE WATCHTOWER.
RETRO.
I HOPE WE LIVE UP TO YOUR EXPECTATIONS.
THAT WAS IT? WE'RE HERE?
SUPERMAN?
ONE SMALL STEP.
YOU'RE THE LAST OF THE REPRESENTATIVES FROM THE WORLD'S MEDIA TO ARRIVE, SO IF EVERYBODY WANTS TO FOLLOW ME THROUGH THE RECEPTION GALLERY...
LADIES AND GENTLEMEN...

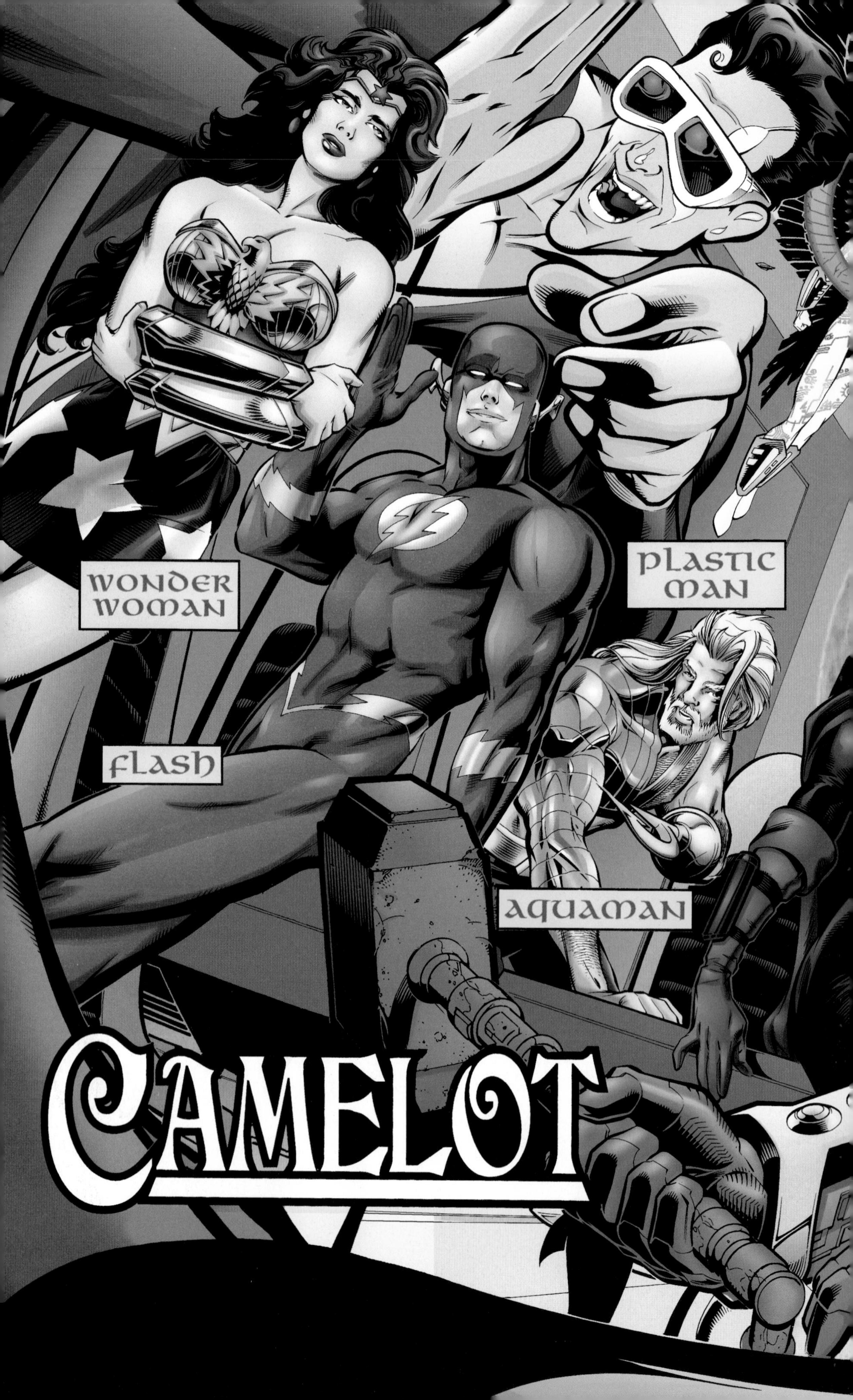
WONDER WOMAN
PLASTIC MAN
FLASH
AQUAMAN
CAMELOT

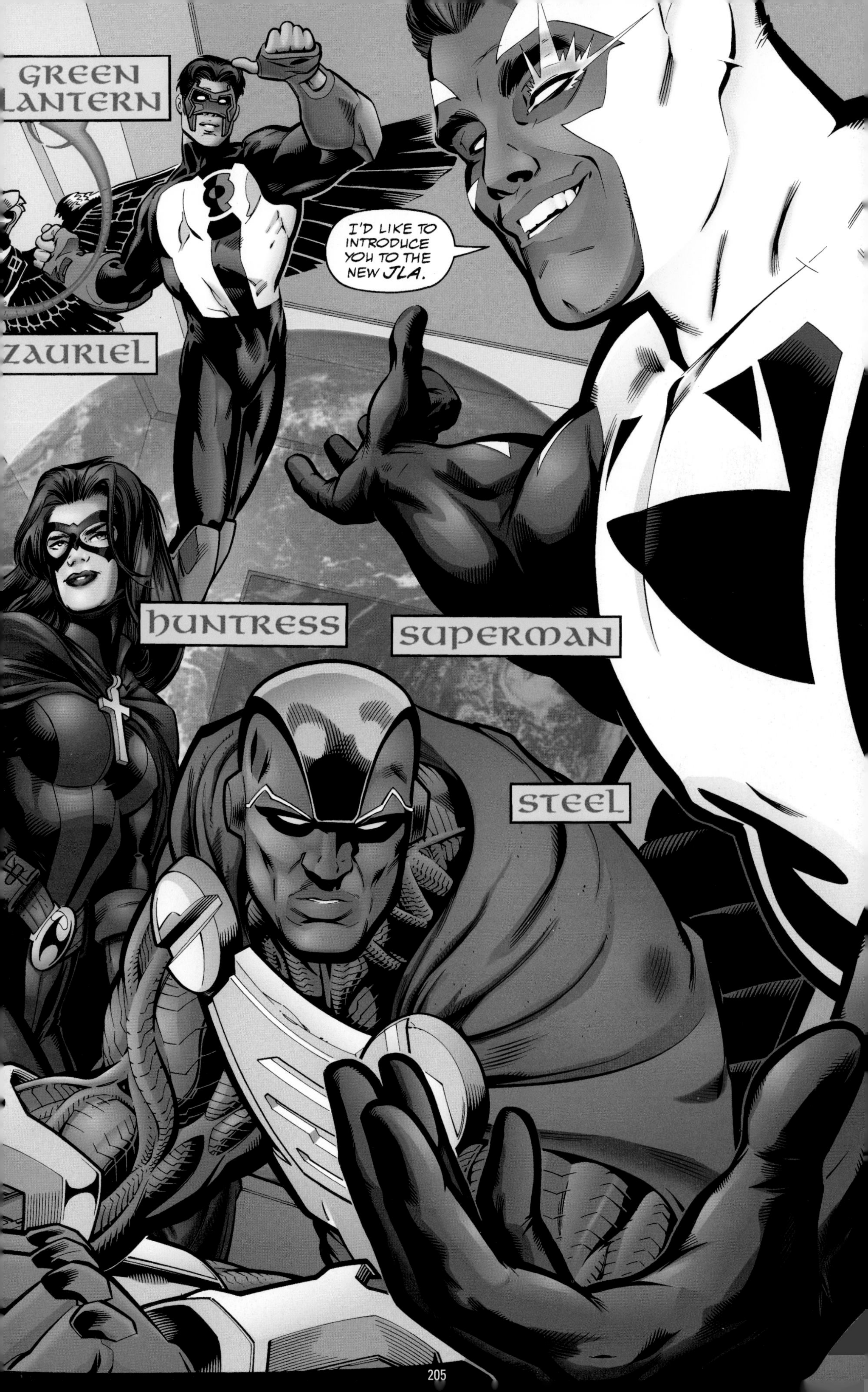

GREEN LANTERN
ZAURIEL
I'D LIKE TO INTRODUCE YOU TO THE NEW JLA.
HUNTRESS
SUPERMAN
STEEL

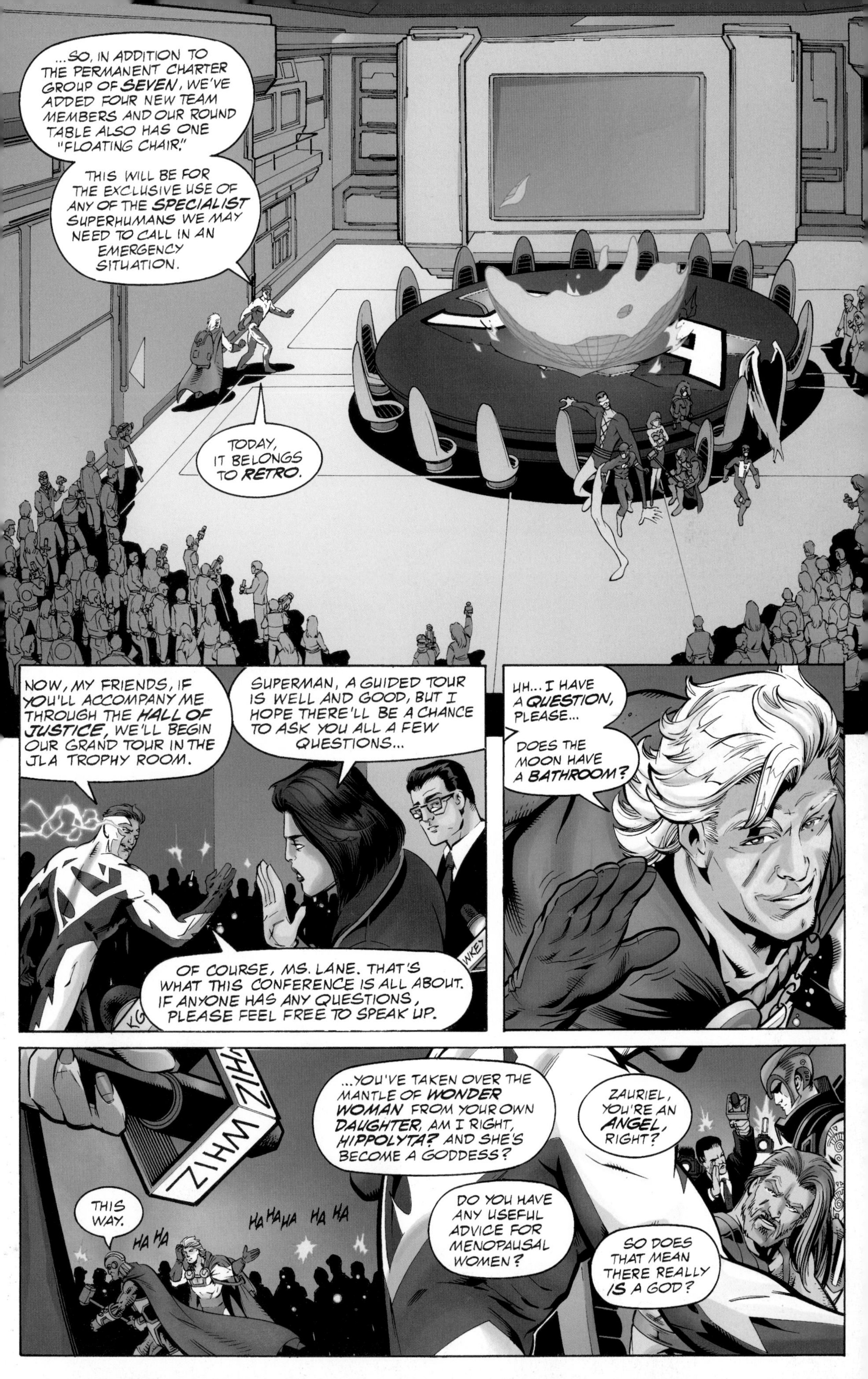
...SO, IN ADDITION TO THE PERMANENT CHARTER GROUP OF SEVEN, WE'VE ADDED FOUR NEW TEAM MEMBERS AND OUR ROUND TABLE ALSO HAS ONE "FLOATING CHAIR."
THIS WILL BE FOR THE EXCLUSIVE USE OF ANY OF THE SPECIALIST SUPERHUMANS WE MAY NEED TO CALL IN AN EMERGENCY SITUATION.
TODAY, IT BELONGS TO RETRO.
NOW, MY FRIENDS, IF YOU'LL ACCOMPANY ME THROUGH THE HALL OF JUSTICE, WE'LL BEGIN OUR GRAND TOUR IN THE JLA TROPHY ROOM.
SUPERMAN, A GUIDED TOUR IS WELL AND GOOD, BUT I HOPE THERE'LL BE A CHANCE TO ASK YOU ALL A FEW QUESTIONS...
OF COURSE, MS. LANE. THAT'S WHAT THIS CONFERENCE IS ALL ABOUT. IF ANYONE HAS ANY QUESTIONS, PLEASE FEEL FREE TO SPEAK UP.
UH... I HAVE A QUESTION, PLEASE...
DOES THE MOON HAVE A BATHROOM?
WHIZ
THIS WAY.
HA HA
HA HA HA HA HA
...YOU'VE TAKEN OVER THE MANTLE OF WONDER WOMAN FROM YOUR OWN DAUGHTER, AM I RIGHT, HIPPOLYTA? AND SHE'S BECOME A GODDESS?
DO YOU HAVE ANY USEFUL ADVICE FOR MENOPAUSAL WOMEN?
ZAURIEL, YOU'RE AN ANGEL, RIGHT?
SO DOES THAT MEAN THERE REALLY IS A GOD?

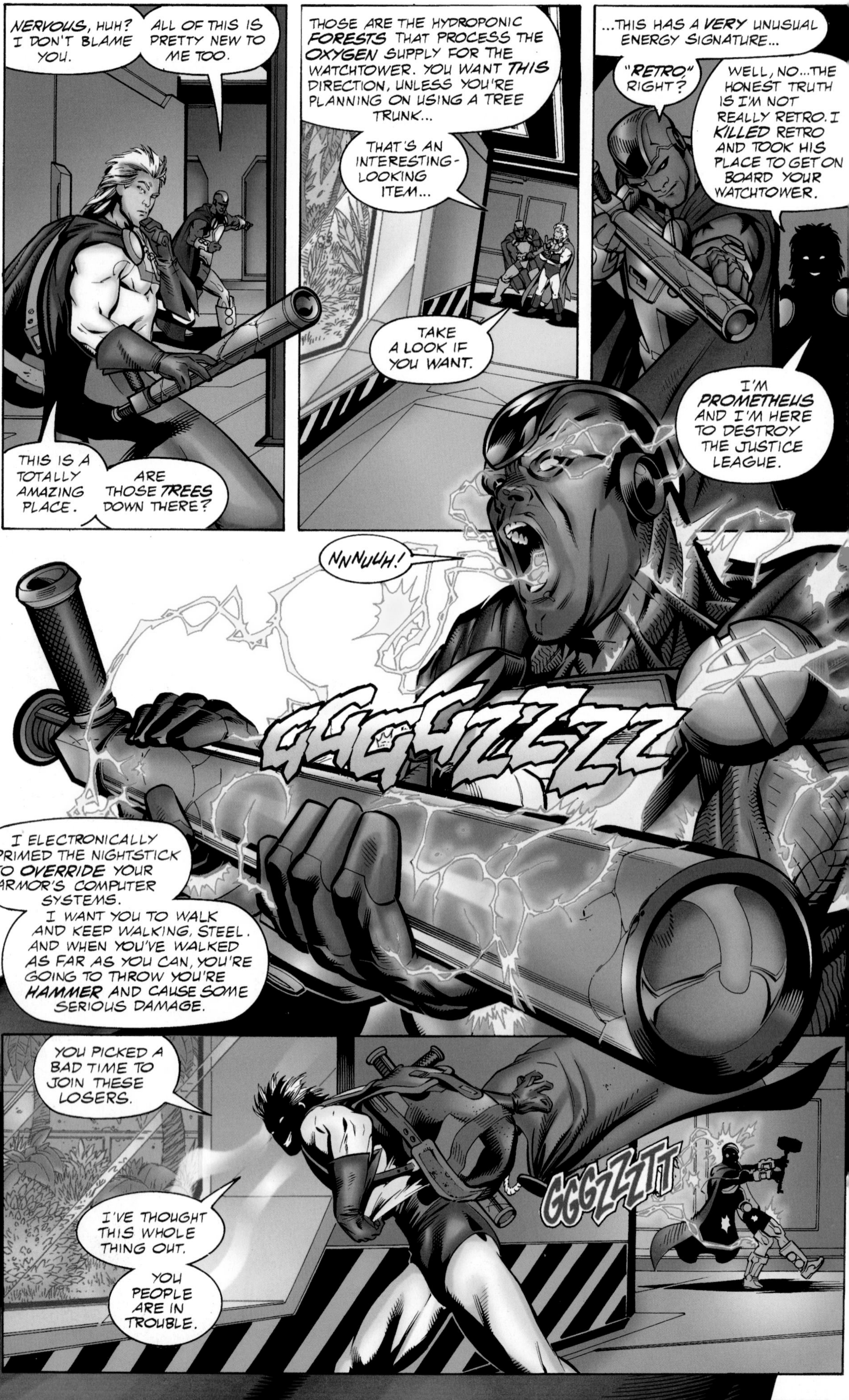
NERVOUS, HUH? I DON'T BLAME YOU.
ALL OF THIS IS PRETTY NEW TO ME TOO.
THIS IS A TOTALLY AMAZING PLACE.
ARE THOSE TREES DOWN THERE?
THOSE ARE THE HYDROPONIC FORESTS THAT PROCESS THE OXYGEN SUPPLY FOR THE WATCHTOWER. YOU WANT THIS DIRECTION, UNLESS YOU'RE PLANNING ON USING A TREE TRUNK...
THAT'S AN INTERESTING-LOOKING ITEM...
TAKE A LOOK IF YOU WANT.
...THIS HAS A VERY UNUSUAL ENERGY SIGNATURE...
"RETRO," RIGHT?
WELL, NO...THE HONEST TRUTH IS I'M NOT REALLY RETRO. I KILLED RETRO AND TOOK HIS PLACE TO GET ON BOARD YOUR WATCHTOWER.
I'M PROMETHEUS AND I'M HERE TO DESTROY THE JUSTICE LEAGUE.
NNNUUH!
GGGZZZZZ
I ELECTRONICALLY PRIMED THE NIGHTSTICK TO OVERRIDE YOUR ARMOR'S COMPUTER SYSTEMS.
I WANT YOU TO WALK AND KEEP WALKING, STEEL. AND WHEN YOU'VE WALKED AS FAR AS YOU CAN, YOU'RE GOING TO THROW YOU'RE HAMMER AND CAUSE SOME SERIOUS DAMAGE.
YOU PICKED A BAD TIME TO JOIN THESE LOSERS.
I'VE THOUGHT THIS WHOLE THING OUT.
YOU PEOPLE ARE IN TROUBLE.
GGGZZZTT

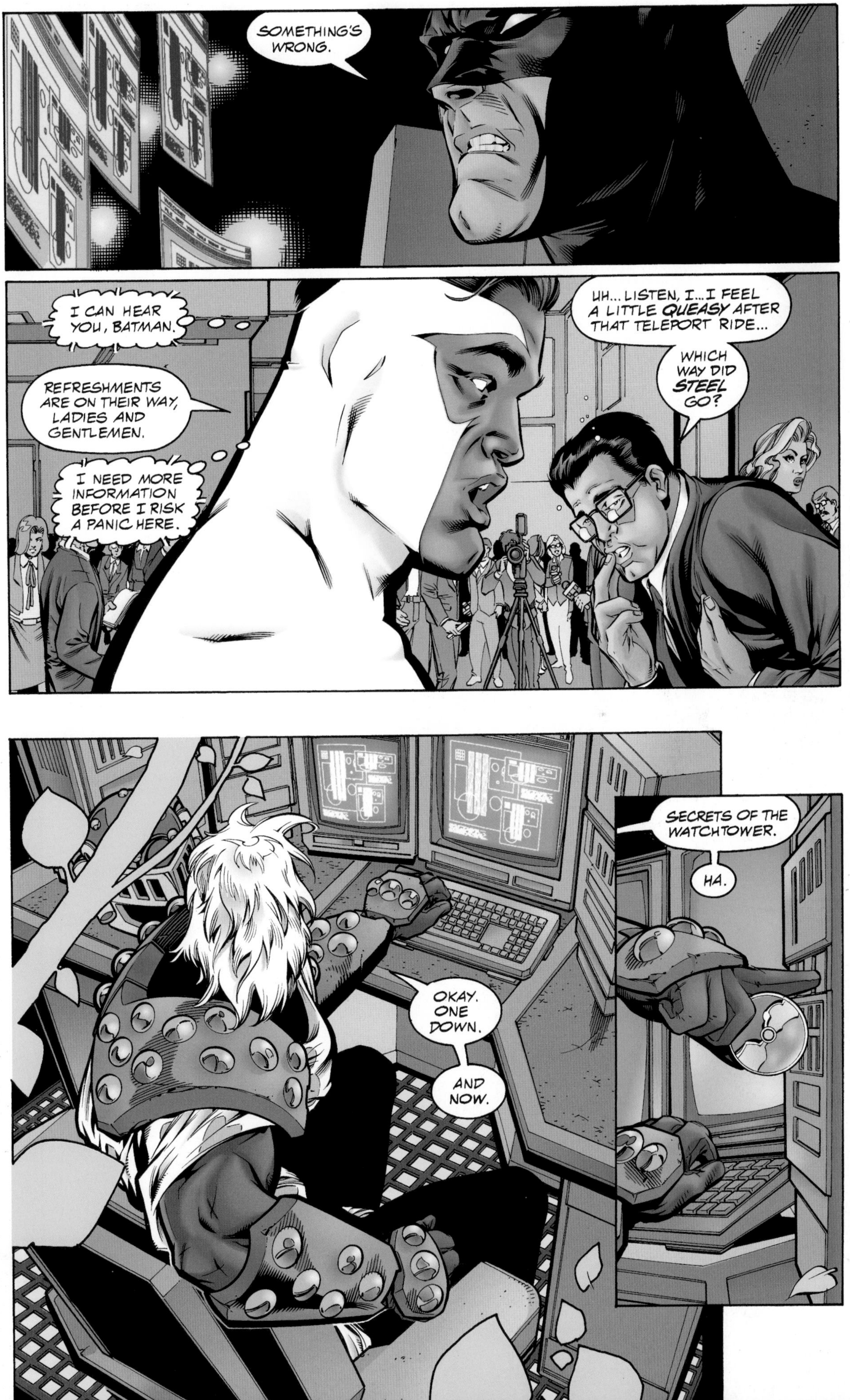

SOMETHING'S WRONG.
I CAN HEAR YOU, BATMAN.
UH... LISTEN, I...I FEEL A LITTLE QUEASY AFTER THAT TELEPORT RIDE...
WHICH WAY DID STEEL GO?
REFRESHMENTS ARE ON THEIR WAY, LADIES AND GENTLEMEN.
I NEED MORE INFORMATION BEFORE I RISK A PANIC HERE.
OKAY. ONE DOWN.
AND NOW.
SECRETS OF THE WATCHTOWER.
HA.

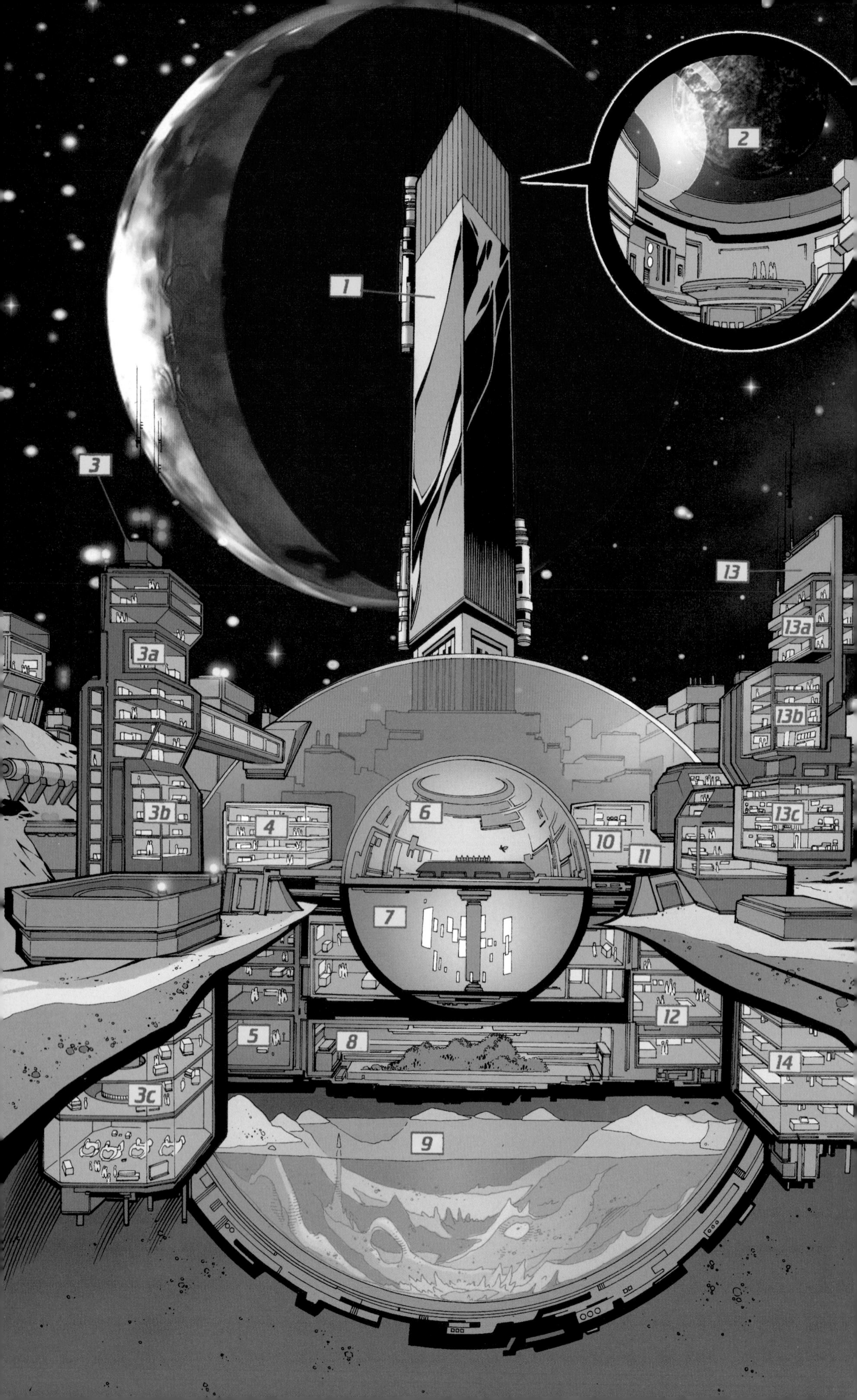
1
2
3
3a
3b
3c
4
5
6
7
8
9
10
11
12
13
13a
13b
13c
14

MAIN VIEW

1 Solar Tower
2 Observation deck
3 Laboratory building
4 Armory
5 Steel's workshop
6 Hall of Justice
7 Monitor Womb
8 Hydroponic forests
9 Aquaman deep water tanks (connected via tunnels to surface pool)
10 Teleporters
11 Reception
12 Secure facility
13 Living quarters
14 Bulk teleport hangar

EXTERIOR STRUCTURES:

3a Research lab
3b Medical lab
3c Martian Jumpship shuttle hangar
13a Lounge
13b Kitchen
13c Dining area

CROSS-SECTION:

15 Engineering control
16 Trophy room
17 Villain gallery
18 Games/Recreation/Simulators
19 Gymnasium/saunas
20 Pool (connected to deep water tank)
21 Park
22 Private teleporters
23 Air control
24 Tunnels to shuttle bay
25 Stairs to lower levels

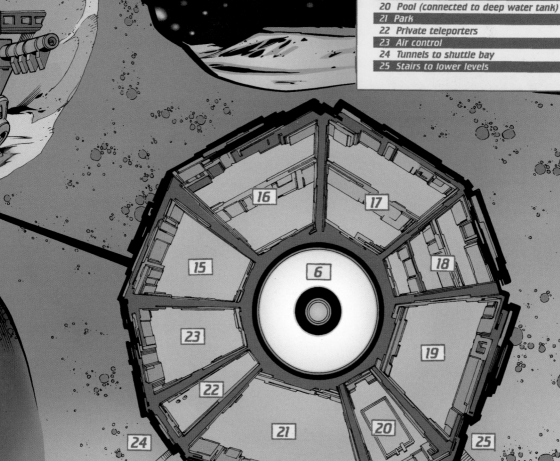

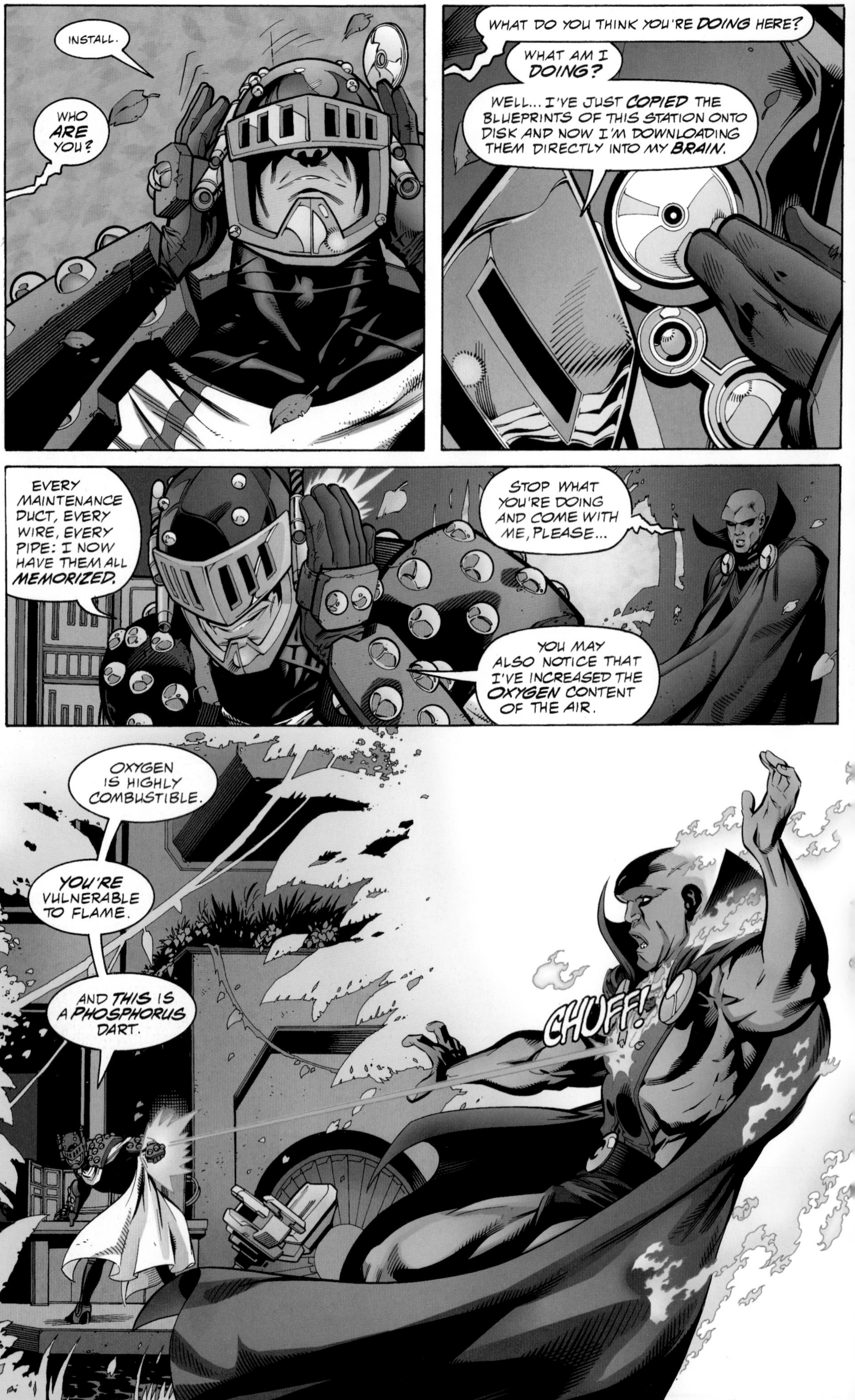

INSTALL.
WHO ARE YOU?
WHAT DO YOU THINK YOU'RE DOING HERE?
WHAT AM I DOING?
WELL... I'VE JUST COPIED THE BLUEPRINTS OF THIS STATION ONTO DISK AND NOW I'M DOWNLOADING THEM DIRECTLY INTO MY BRAIN.
EVERY MAINTENANCE DUCT, EVERY WIRE, EVERY PIPE: I NOW HAVE THEM ALL MEMORIZED.
STOP WHAT YOU'RE DOING AND COME WITH ME, PLEASE...
YOU MAY ALSO NOTICE THAT I'VE INCREASED THE OXYGEN CONTENT OF THE AIR.
OXYGEN IS HIGHLY COMBUSTIBLE.
YOU'RE VULNERABLE TO FLAME.
AND THIS IS A PHOSPHORUS DART.
CHUFF!

SHWWUFF

UUUGGHHH

AND **WHILE** YOU'RE VULNERABLE...

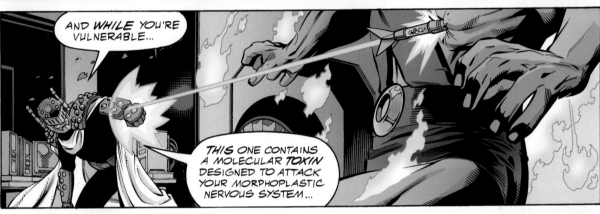

THIS ONE CONTAINS A MOLECULAR **TOXIN** DESIGNED TO ATTACK YOUR MORPHOPLASTIC NERVOUS SYSTEM...

WHAT'S HAPPENING TO MUHHHHH

COMPLETE SPASTIC **PARALYSIS.** YOU NO LONGER HAVE ANY **CONTROL** OVER YOUR PHYSICAL STRUCTURE.

IT SHOULD ONLY LAST ABOUT AN HOUR. MUCH LONGER THAN I'M GOING TO **NEED.**

UULLBBB

UNTIL THEN YOU'RE THE MOST POWERFUL PUDDLE OF GOO ALIVE.

SCOURGE OF THE UNDERWORLD!

HA!

TWO DOWN.

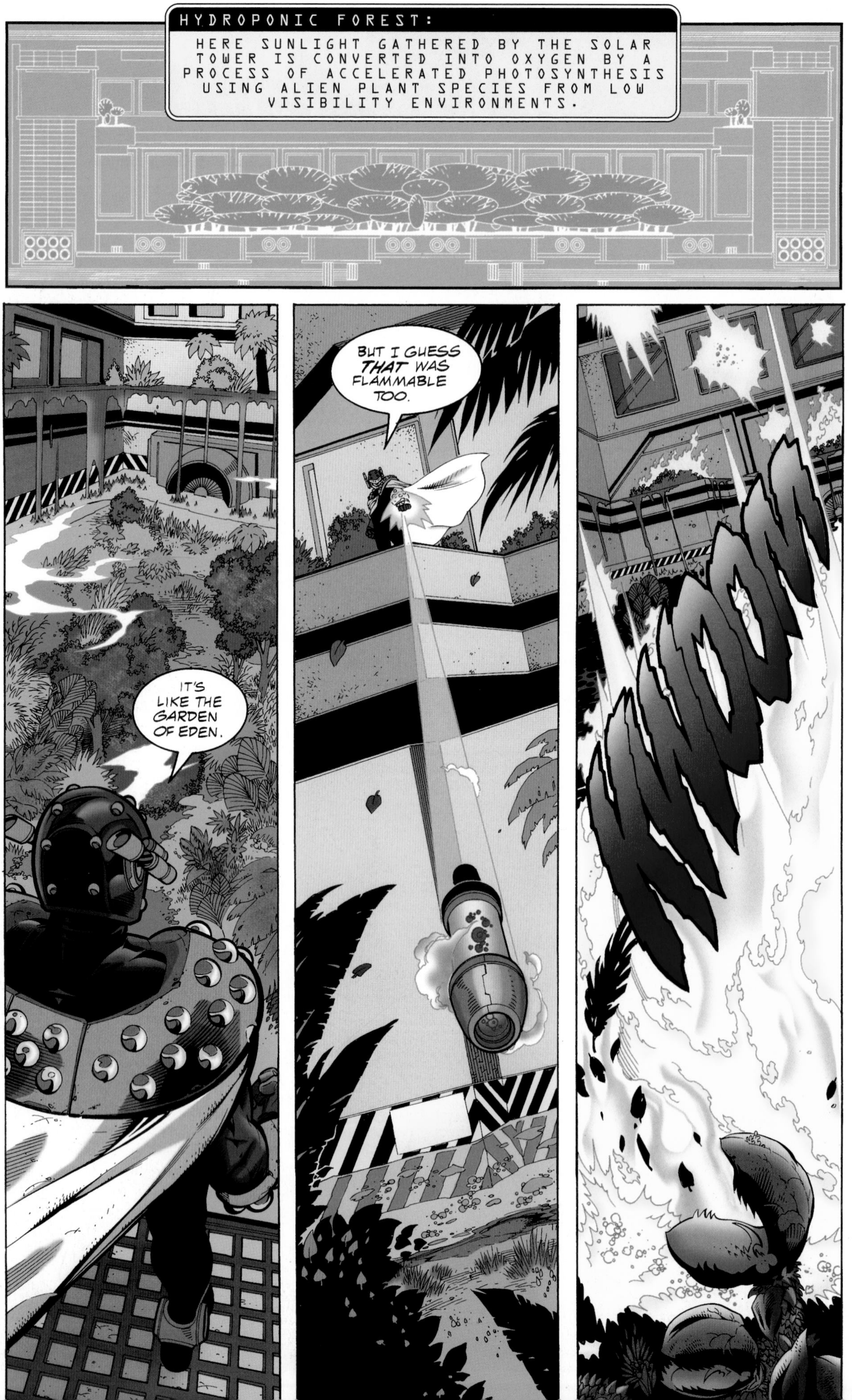
HYDROPONIC FOREST:
HERE SUNLIGHT GATHERED BY THE SOLAR TOWER IS CONVERTED INTO OXYGEN BY A PROCESS OF ACCELERATED PHOTOSYNTHESIS USING ALIEN PLANT SPECIES FROM LOW VISIBILITY ENVIRONMENTS.
IT'S LIKE THE GARDEN OF EDEN.
BUT I GUESS THAT WAS FLAMMABLE TOO.
WHOOM

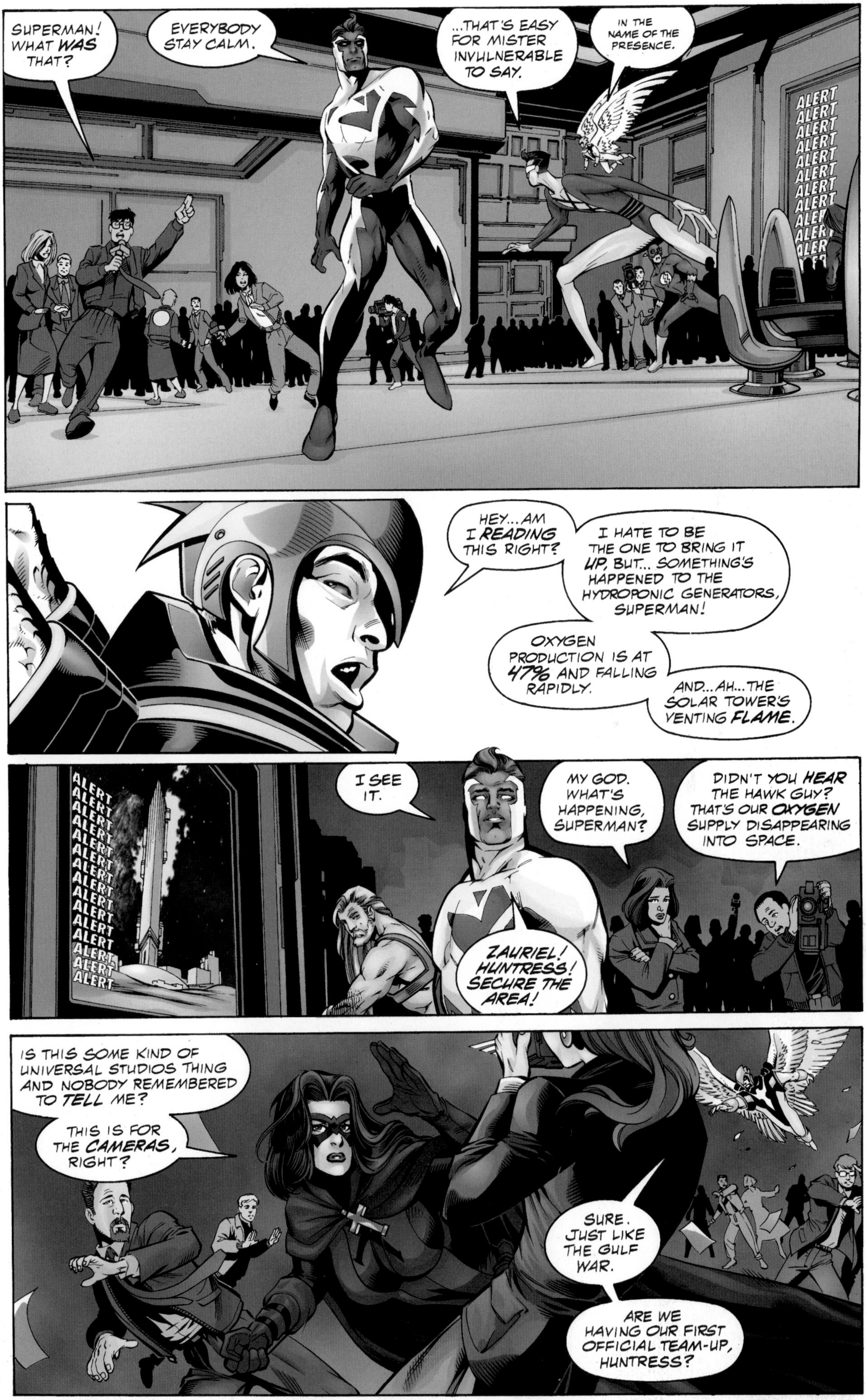
SUPERMAN! WHAT WAS THAT?
EVERYBODY STAY CALM.
...THAT'S EASY FOR MISTER INVULNERABLE TO SAY.
IN THE NAME OF THE PRESENCE.
ALERT ALERT ALERT ALERT ALERT ALERT ALERT ALERT ALERT ALERT ALERT ALERT ALERT
HEY... AM I READING THIS RIGHT?
I HATE TO BE THE ONE TO BRING IT UP, BUT... SOMETHING'S HAPPENED TO THE HYDROPONIC GENERATORS, SUPERMAN!
OXYGEN PRODUCTION IS AT 47% AND FALLING RAPIDLY.
AND...AH...THE SOLAR TOWER'S VENTING FLAME.
ALERT ALERT ALERT ALERT ALERT ALERT ALERT ALERT ALERT ALERT ALERT ALERT ALERT ALERT ALERT ALERT
I SEE IT.
MY GOD. WHAT'S HAPPENING, SUPERMAN?
DIDN'T YOU HEAR THE HAWK GUY? THAT'S OUR OXYGEN SUPPLY DISAPPEARING INTO SPACE.
ZAURIEL! HUNTRESS! SECURE THE AREA!
IS THIS SOME KIND OF UNIVERSAL STUDIOS THING AND NOBODY REMEMBERED TO TELL ME?
THIS IS FOR THE CAMERAS, RIGHT?
SURE. JUST LIKE THE GULF WAR.
ARE WE HAVING OUR FIRST OFFICIAL TEAM-UP, HUNTRESS?

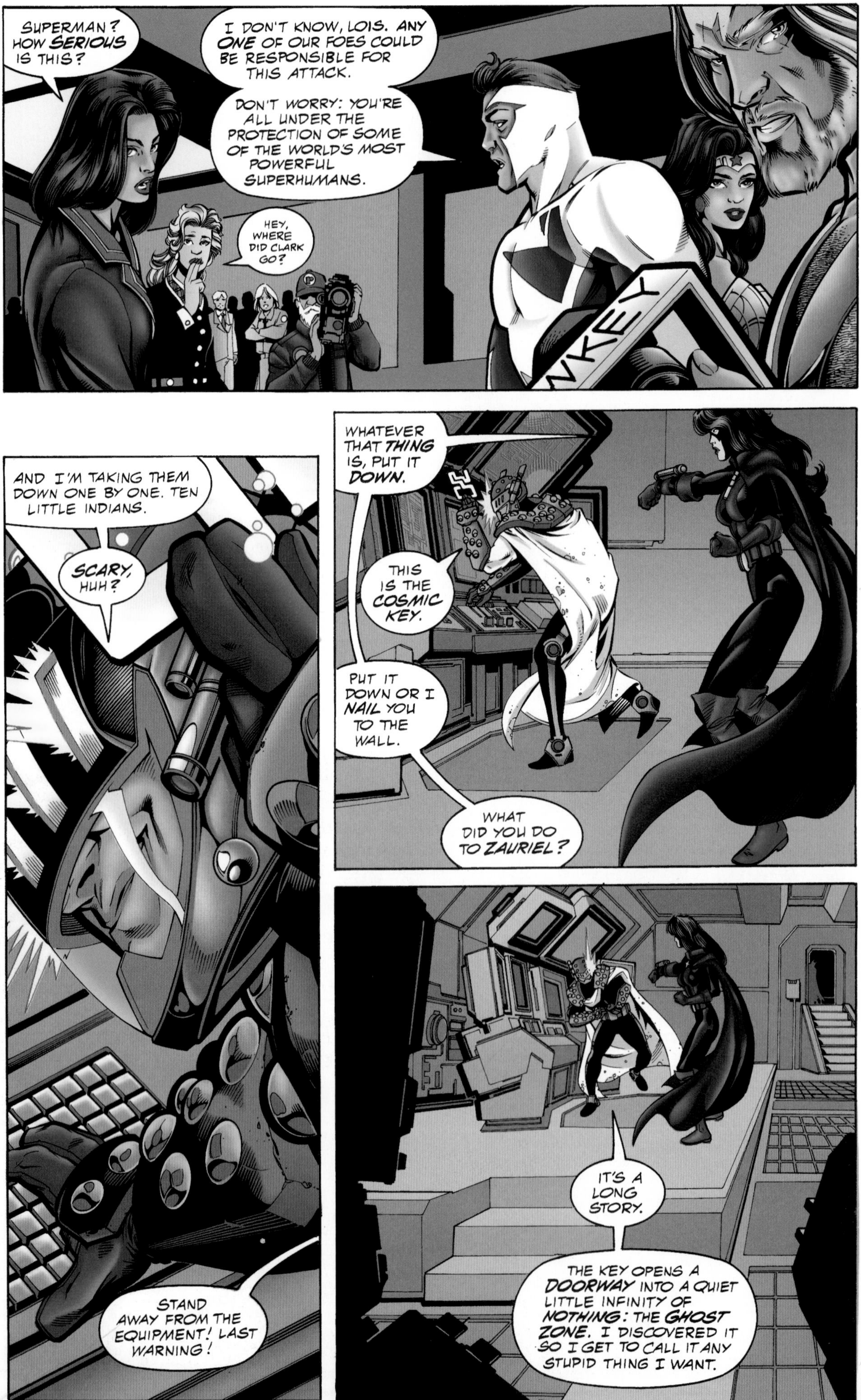
SUPERMAN? HOW SERIOUS IS THIS?
I DON'T KNOW, LOIS. ANY ONE OF OUR FOES COULD BE RESPONSIBLE FOR THIS ATTACK.
DON'T WORRY: YOU'RE ALL UNDER THE PROTECTION OF SOME OF THE WORLD'S MOST POWERFUL SUPERHUMANS.
HEY, WHERE DID CLARK GO?
AND I'M TAKING THEM DOWN ONE BY ONE. TEN LITTLE INDIANS.
SCARY, HUH?
STAND AWAY FROM THE EQUIPMENT! LAST WARNING!
WHATEVER THAT THING IS, PUT IT DOWN.
THIS IS THE COSMIC KEY.
PUT IT DOWN OR I NAIL YOU TO THE WALL.
WHAT DID YOU DO TO ZAURIEL?
IT'S A LONG STORY.
THE KEY OPENS A DOORWAY INTO A QUIET LITTLE INFINITY OF NOTHING: THE GHOST ZONE. I DISCOVERED IT SO I GET TO CALL IT ANY STUPID THING I WANT.

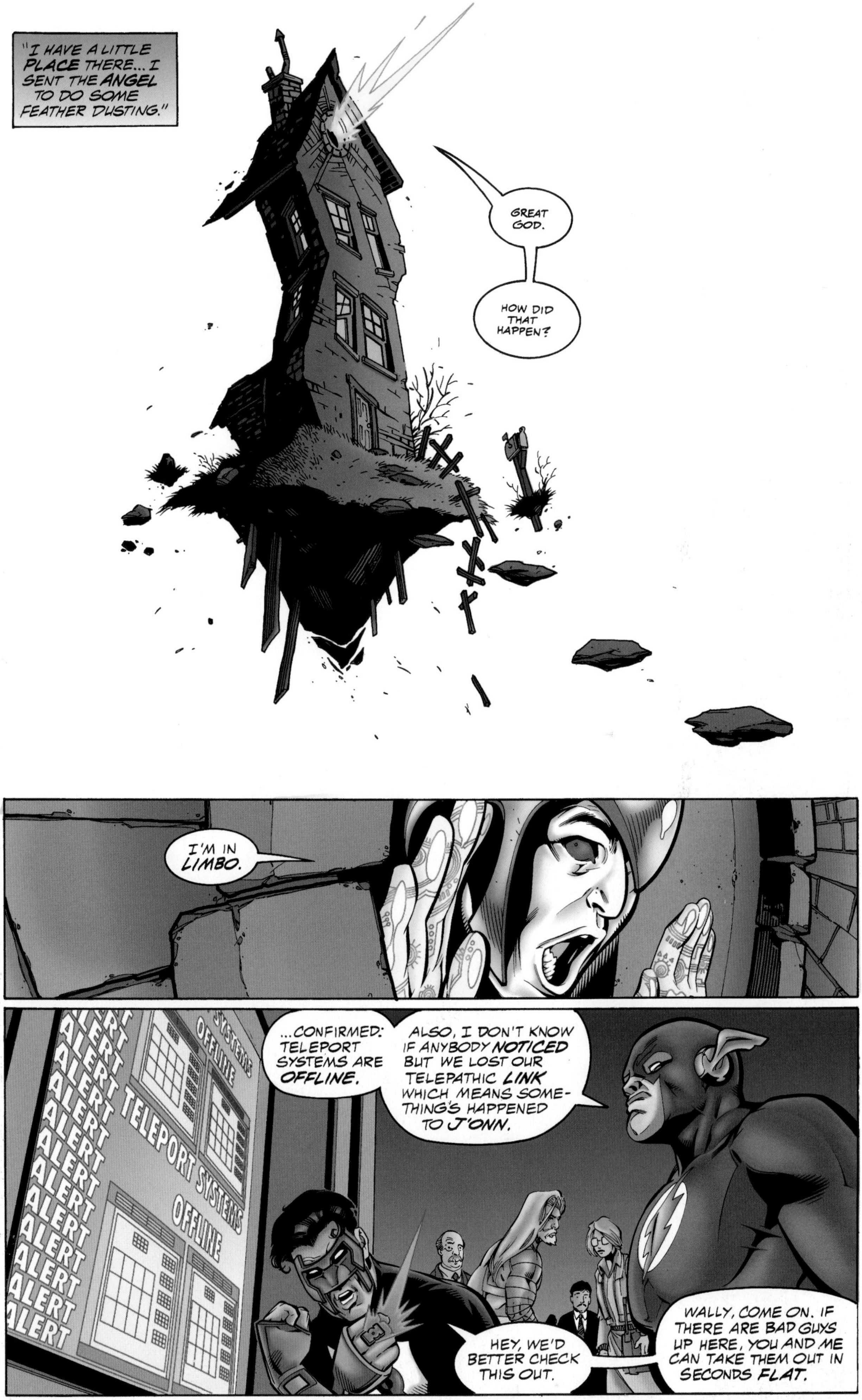
"I HAVE A LITTLE PLACE THERE... I SENT THE ANGEL TO DO SOME FEATHER DUSTING."
GREAT GOD.
HOW DID THAT HAPPEN?
I'M IN LIMBO.
...CONFIRMED: TELEPORT SYSTEMS ARE OFFLINE.
ALSO, I DON'T KNOW IF ANYBODY NOTICED BUT WE LOST OUR TELEPATHIC LINK WHICH MEANS SOMETHING'S HAPPENED TO J'ONN.
ALERT
TELEPORT SYSTEMS
OFFLINE
HEY, WE'D BETTER CHECK THIS OUT.
WALLY, COME ON. IF THERE ARE BAD GUYS UP HERE, YOU AND ME CAN TAKE THEM OUT IN SECONDS FLAT.

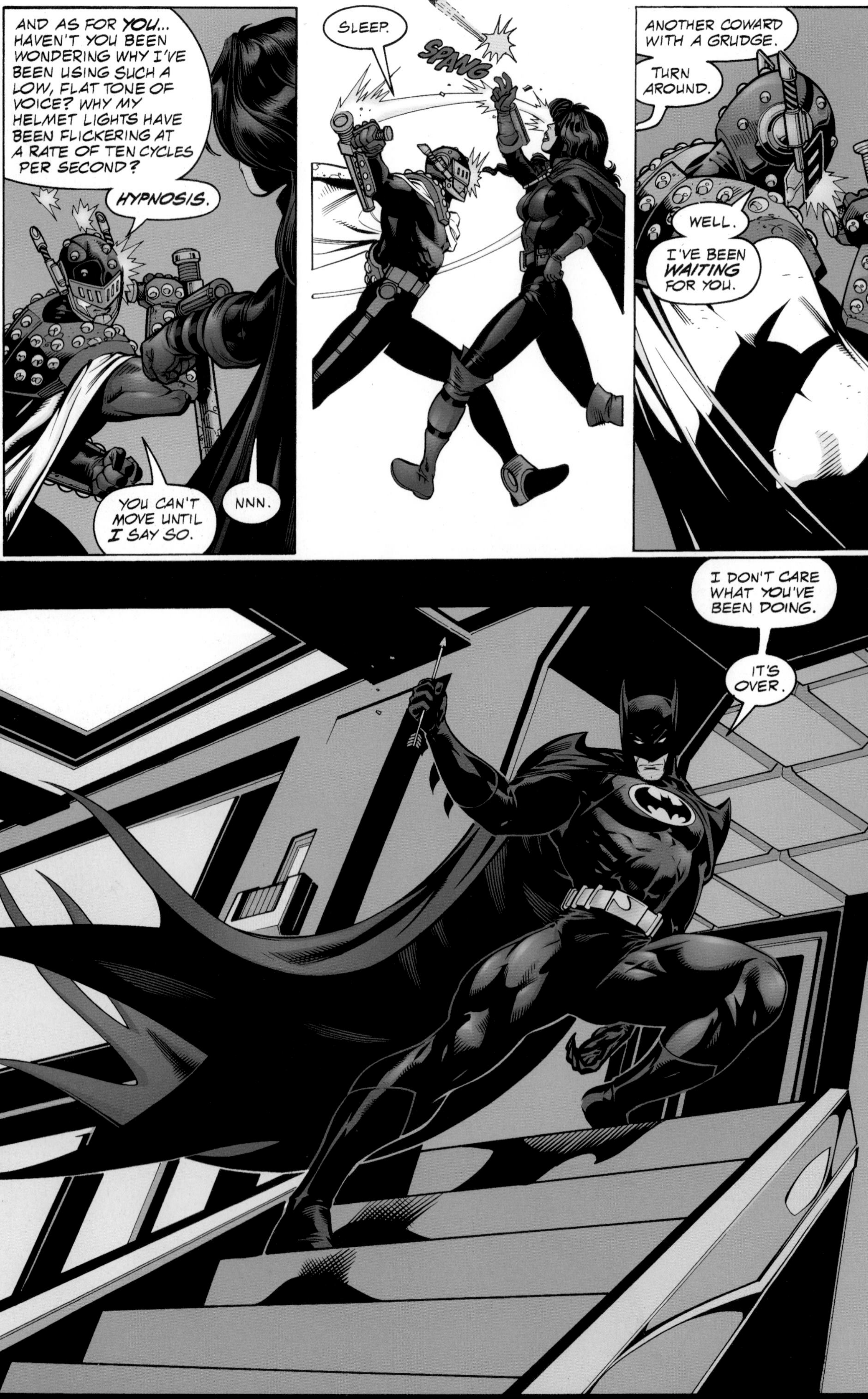
AND AS FOR YOU... HAVEN'T YOU BEEN WONDERING WHY I'VE BEEN USING SUCH A LOW, FLAT TONE OF VOICE? WHY MY HELMET LIGHTS HAVE BEEN FLICKERING AT A RATE OF TEN CYCLES PER SECOND?
HYPNOSIS.
YOU CAN'T MOVE UNTIL I SAY SO.
NNN.
SLEEP.
SPANG
ANOTHER COWARD WITH A GRUDGE.
TURN AROUND.
WELL.
I'VE BEEN WAITING FOR YOU.
I DON'T CARE WHAT YOU'VE BEEN DOING.
IT'S OVER.

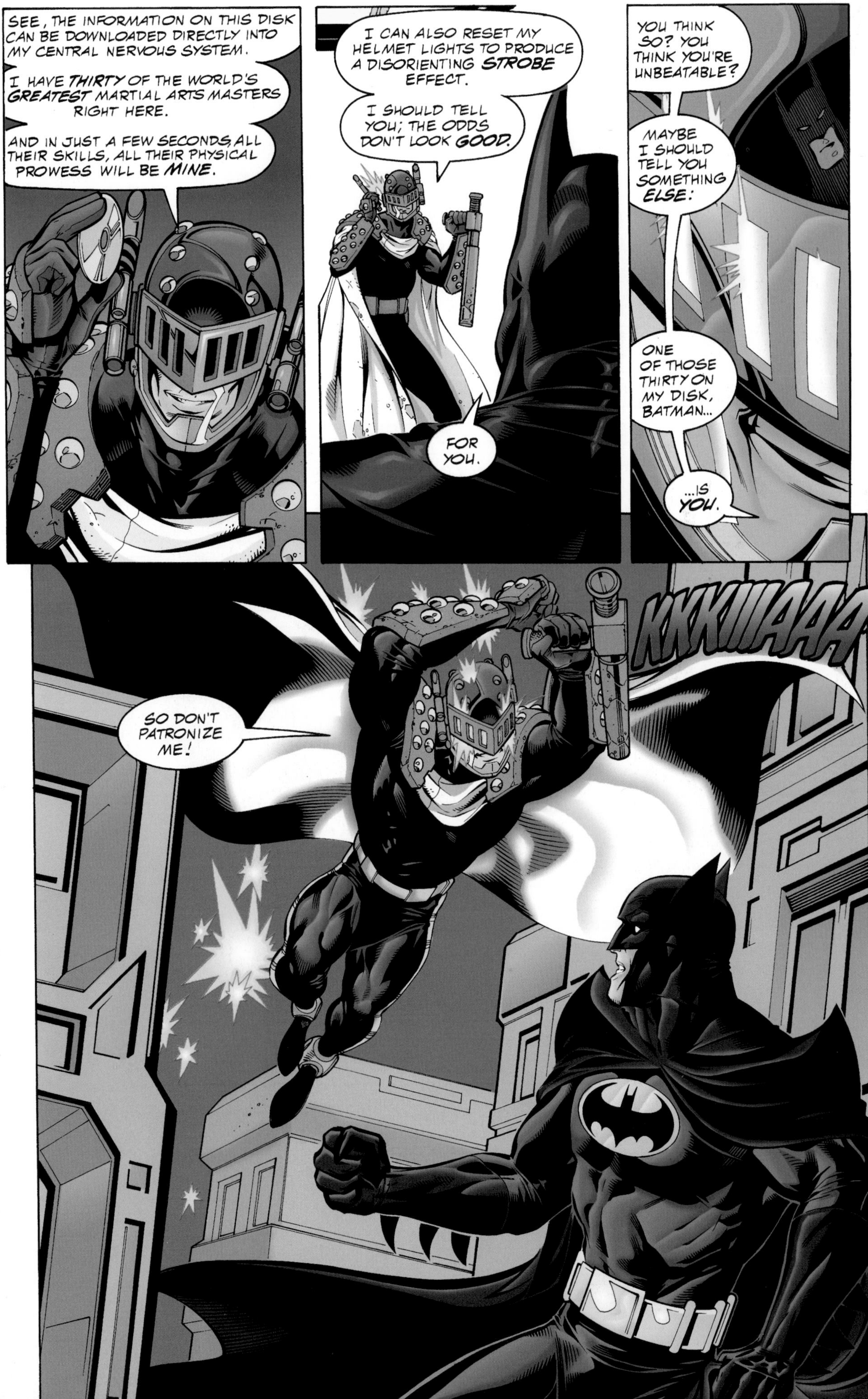
SEE, THE INFORMATION ON THIS DISK CAN BE DOWNLOADED DIRECTLY INTO MY CENTRAL NERVOUS SYSTEM.
I HAVE THIRTY OF THE WORLD'S GREATEST MARTIAL ARTS MASTERS RIGHT HERE.
AND IN JUST A FEW SECONDS, ALL THEIR SKILLS, ALL THEIR PHYSICAL PROWESS WILL BE MINE.
I CAN ALSO RESET MY HELMET LIGHTS TO PRODUCE A DISORIENTING STROBE EFFECT.
I SHOULD TELL YOU; THE ODDS DON'T LOOK GOOD.
FOR YOU.
YOU THINK SO? YOU THINK YOU'RE UNBEATABLE?
MAYBE I SHOULD TELL YOU SOMETHING ELSE:
ONE OF THOSE THIRTY ON MY DISK, BATMAN...
...IS YOU.
KKKIIIAAAA
SO DON'T PATRONIZE ME!

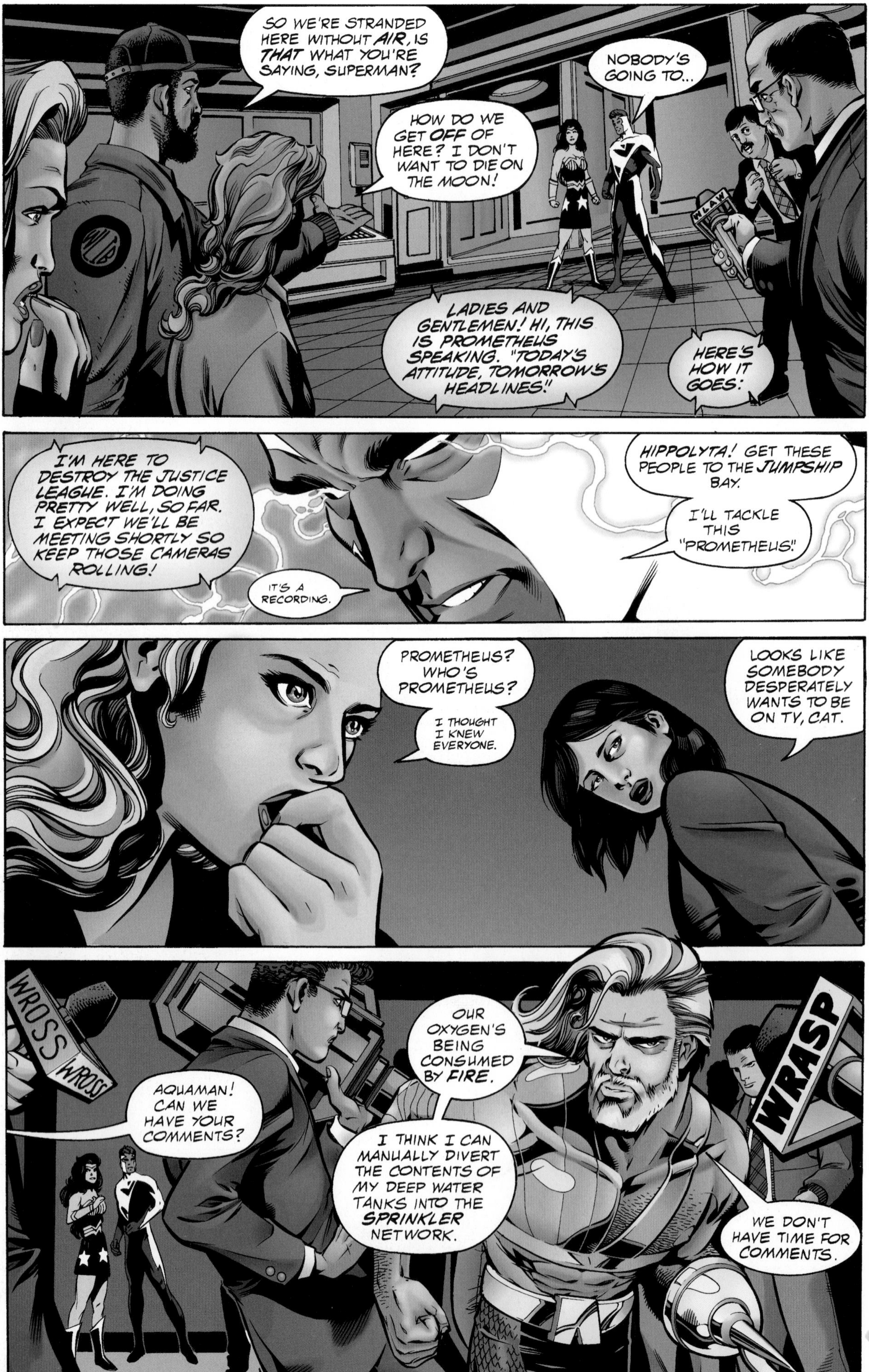
SO WE'RE STRANDED HERE WITHOUT AIR, IS THAT WHAT YOU'RE SAYING, SUPERMAN?
HOW DO WE GET OFF OF HERE? I DON'T WANT TO DIE ON THE MOON!
NOBODY'S GOING TO...
WLAW
LADIES AND GENTLEMEN! HI, THIS IS PROMETHEUS SPEAKING. "TODAY'S ATTITUDE, TOMORROW'S HEADLINES!"
HERE'S HOW IT GOES:
I'M HERE TO DESTROY THE JUSTICE LEAGUE. I'M DOING PRETTY WELL, SO FAR. I EXPECT WE'LL BE MEETING SHORTLY SO KEEP THOSE CAMERAS ROLLING!
IT'S A RECORDING.
HIPPOLYTA! GET THESE PEOPLE TO THE JUMPSHIP BAY.
I'LL TACKLE THIS "PROMETHEUS!"
PROMETHEUS? WHO'S PROMETHEUS?
I THOUGHT I KNEW EVERYONE.
LOOKS LIKE SOMEBODY DESPERATELY WANTS TO BE ON TV, CAT.
WROSS
WROSS
WRASP
OUR OXYGEN'S BEING CONSUMED BY FIRE.
AQUAMAN! CAN WE HAVE YOUR COMMENTS?
I THINK I CAN MANUALLY DIVERT THE CONTENTS OF MY DEEP WATER TANKS INTO THE SPRINKLER NETWORK.
WE DON'T HAVE TIME FOR COMMENTS.

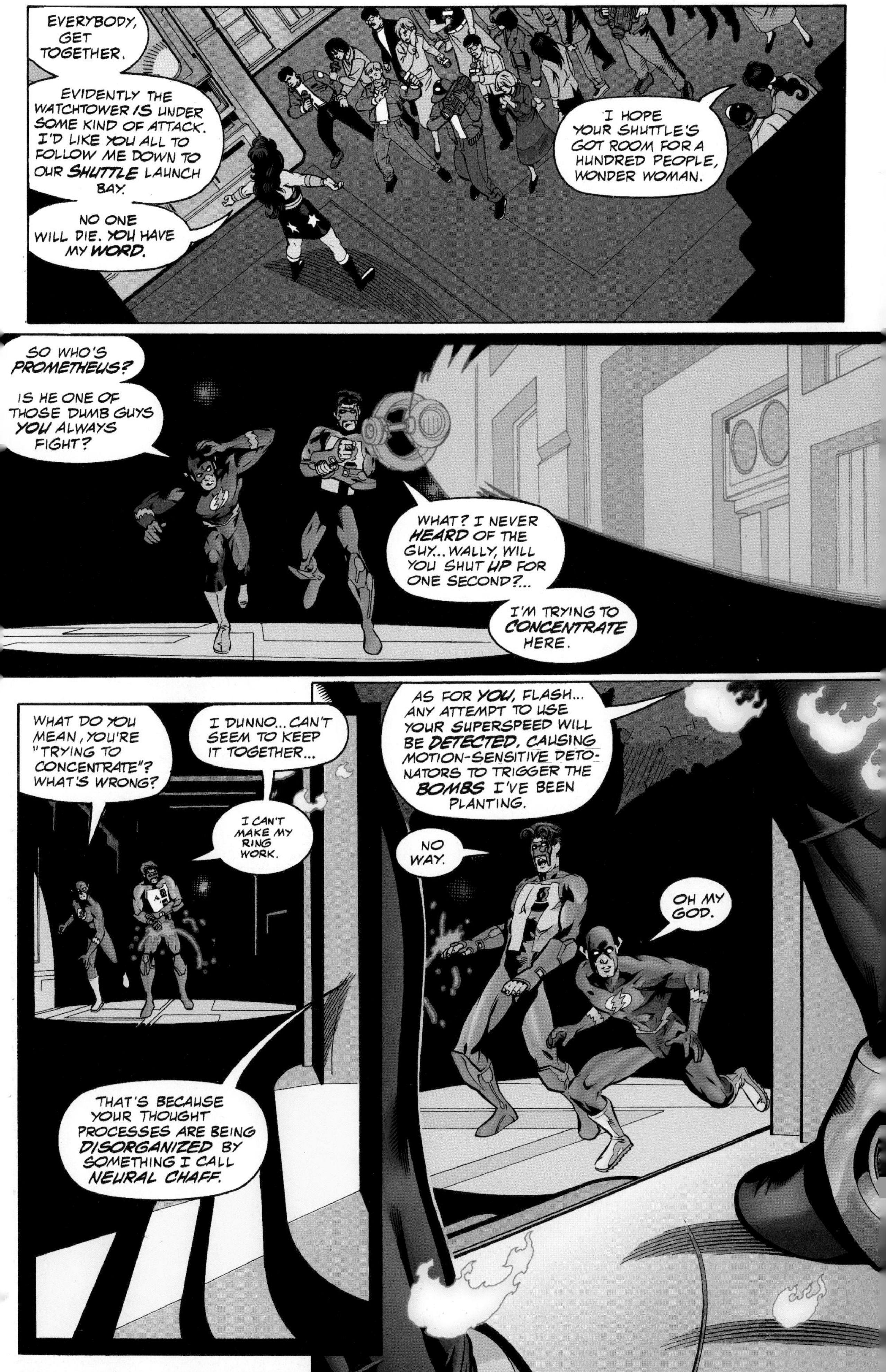
EVERYBODY, GET TOGETHER.
EVIDENTLY THE WATCHTOWER IS UNDER SOME KIND OF ATTACK. I'D LIKE YOU ALL TO FOLLOW ME DOWN TO OUR SHUTTLE LAUNCH BAY.
NO ONE WILL DIE. YOU HAVE MY WORD.
I HOPE YOUR SHUTTLE'S GOT ROOM FOR A HUNDRED PEOPLE, WONDER WOMAN.
SO WHO'S PROMETHEUS?
IS HE ONE OF THOSE DUMB GUYS YOU ALWAYS FIGHT?
WHAT? I NEVER HEARD OF THE GUY... WALLY, WILL YOU SHUT UP FOR ONE SECOND?...
I'M TRYING TO CONCENTRATE HERE.
WHAT DO YOU MEAN, YOU'RE "TRYING TO CONCENTRATE"? WHAT'S WRONG?
I DUNNO... CAN'T SEEM TO KEEP IT TOGETHER...
I CAN'T MAKE MY RING WORK.
THAT'S BECAUSE YOUR THOUGHT PROCESSES ARE BEING DISORGANIZED BY SOMETHING I CALL NEURAL CHAFF.
AS FOR YOU, FLASH... ANY ATTEMPT TO USE YOUR SUPERSPEED WILL BE DETECTED, CAUSING MOTION-SENSITIVE DETONATORS TO TRIGGER THE BOMBS I'VE BEEN PLANTING.
NO WAY.
OH MY GOD.

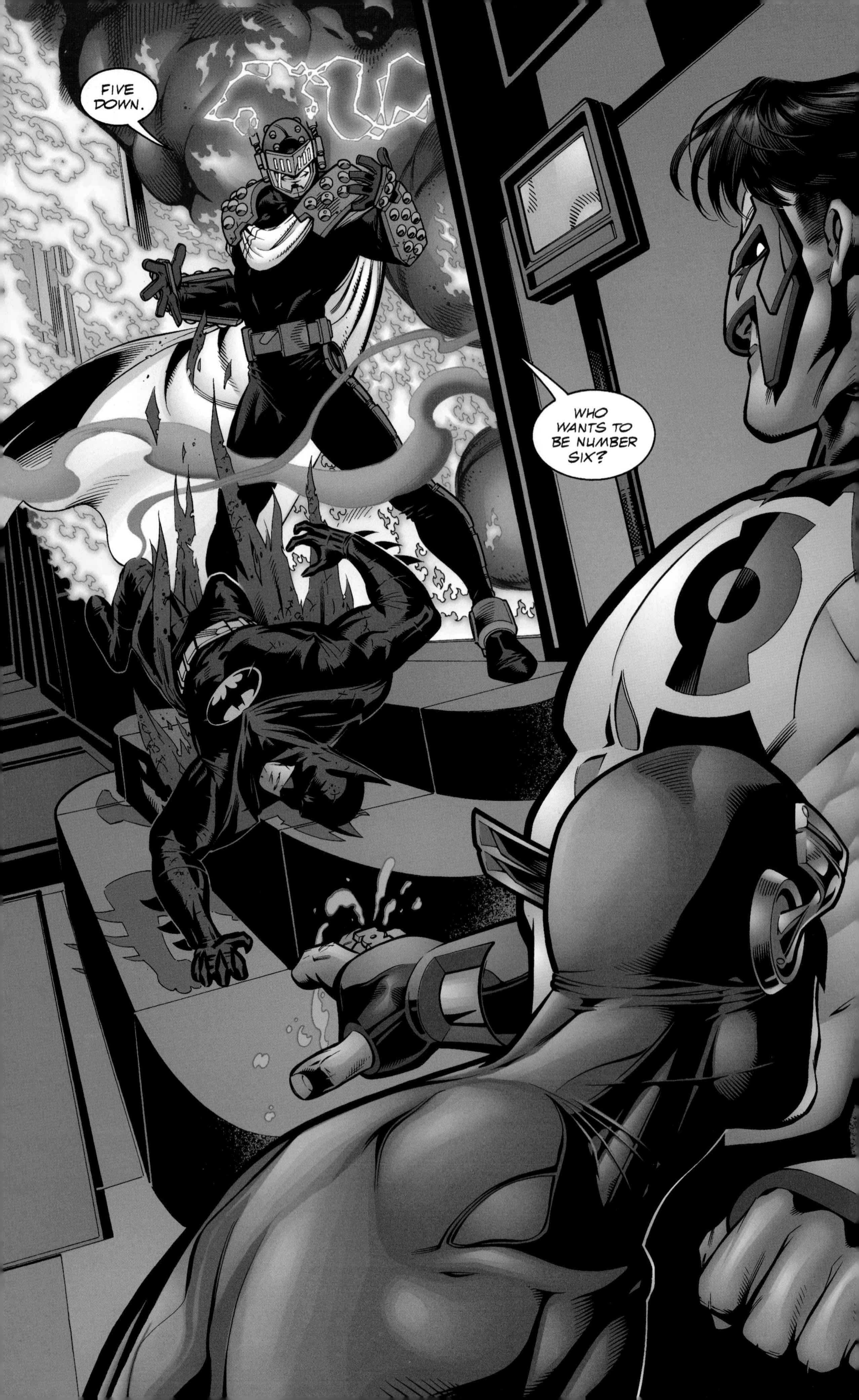
FIVE DOWN.
WHO WANTS TO BE NUMBER SIX?

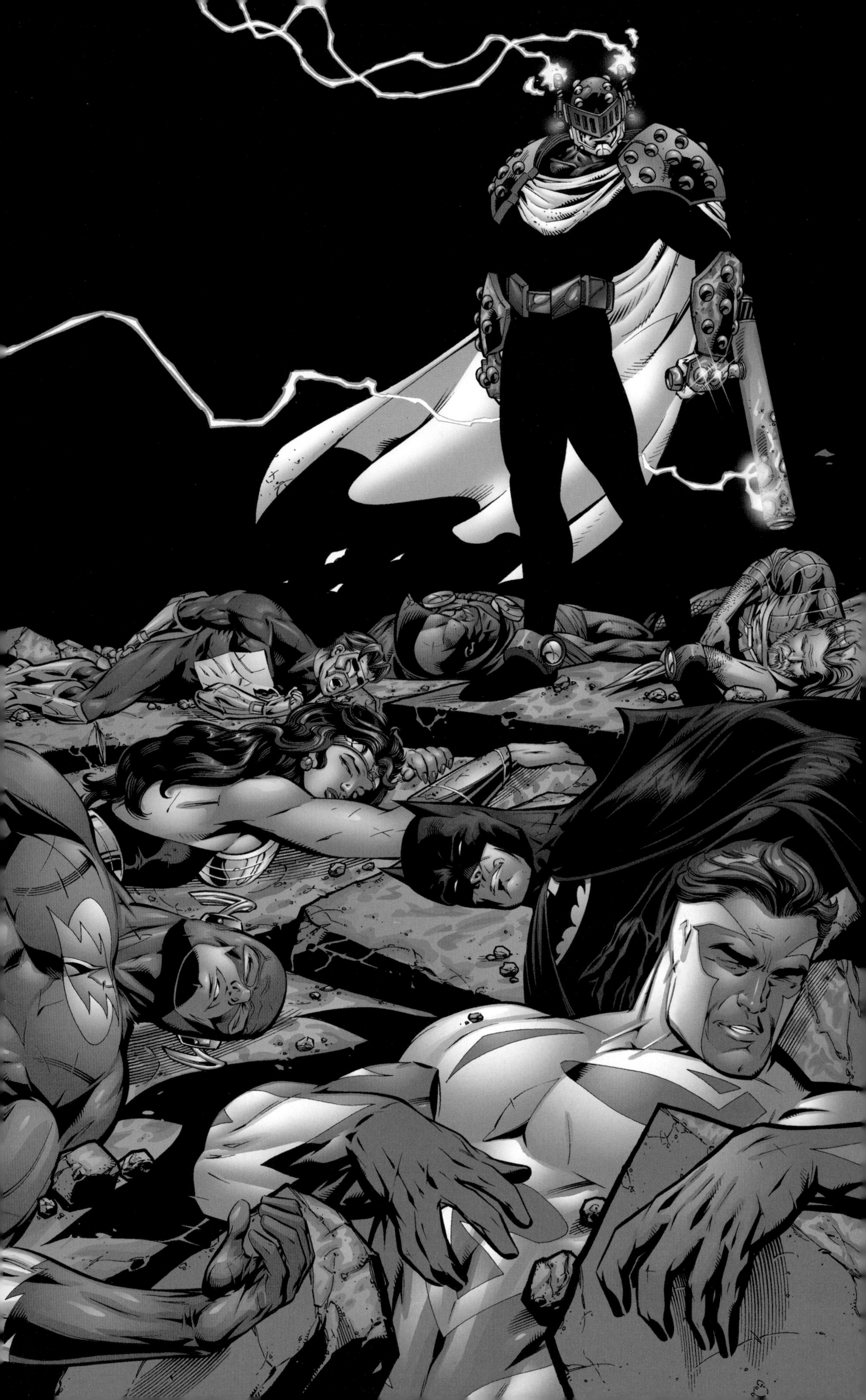

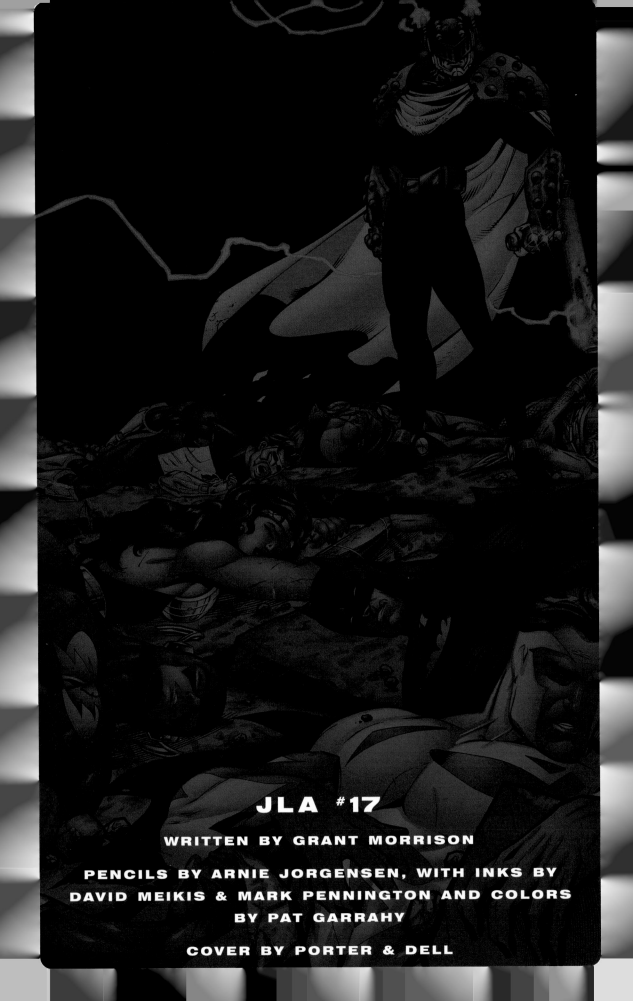

JLA #17

WRITTEN BY GRANT MORRISON

PENCILS BY ARNIE JORGENSEN, WITH INKS BY
DAVID MEIKIS & MARK PENNINGTON AND COLORS
BY PAT GARRAHY

COVER BY PORTER & DELL

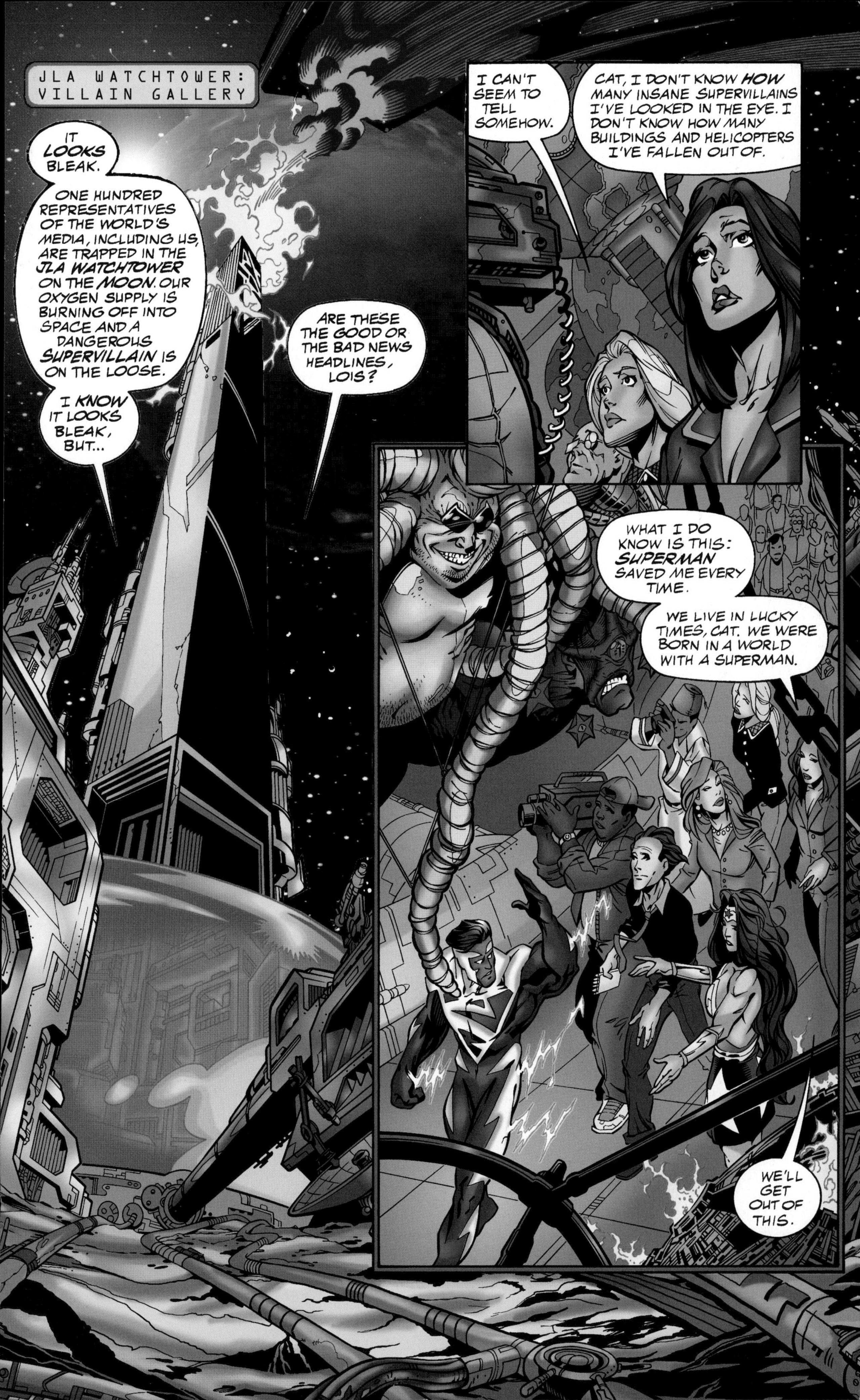
JLA WATCHTOWER: VILLAIN GALLERY
IT LOOKS BLEAK.
ONE HUNDRED REPRESENTATIVES OF THE WORLD'S MEDIA, INCLUDING US, ARE TRAPPED IN THE JLA WATCHTOWER ON THE MOON. OUR OXYGEN SUPPLY IS BURNING OFF INTO SPACE AND A DANGEROUS SUPERVILLAIN IS ON THE LOOSE.
I KNOW IT LOOKS BLEAK, BUT...
ARE THESE THE GOOD OR THE BAD NEWS HEADLINES, LOIS?
I CAN'T SEEM TO TELL SOMEHOW.
CAT, I DON'T KNOW HOW MANY INSANE SUPERVILLAINS I'VE LOOKED IN THE EYE. I DON'T KNOW HOW MANY BUILDINGS AND HELICOPTERS I'VE FALLEN OUT OF.
WHAT I DO KNOW IS THIS: SUPERMAN SAVED ME EVERY TIME.
WE LIVE IN LUCKY TIMES, CAT. WE WERE BORN IN A WORLD WITH A SUPERMAN.
WE'LL GET OUT OF THIS.

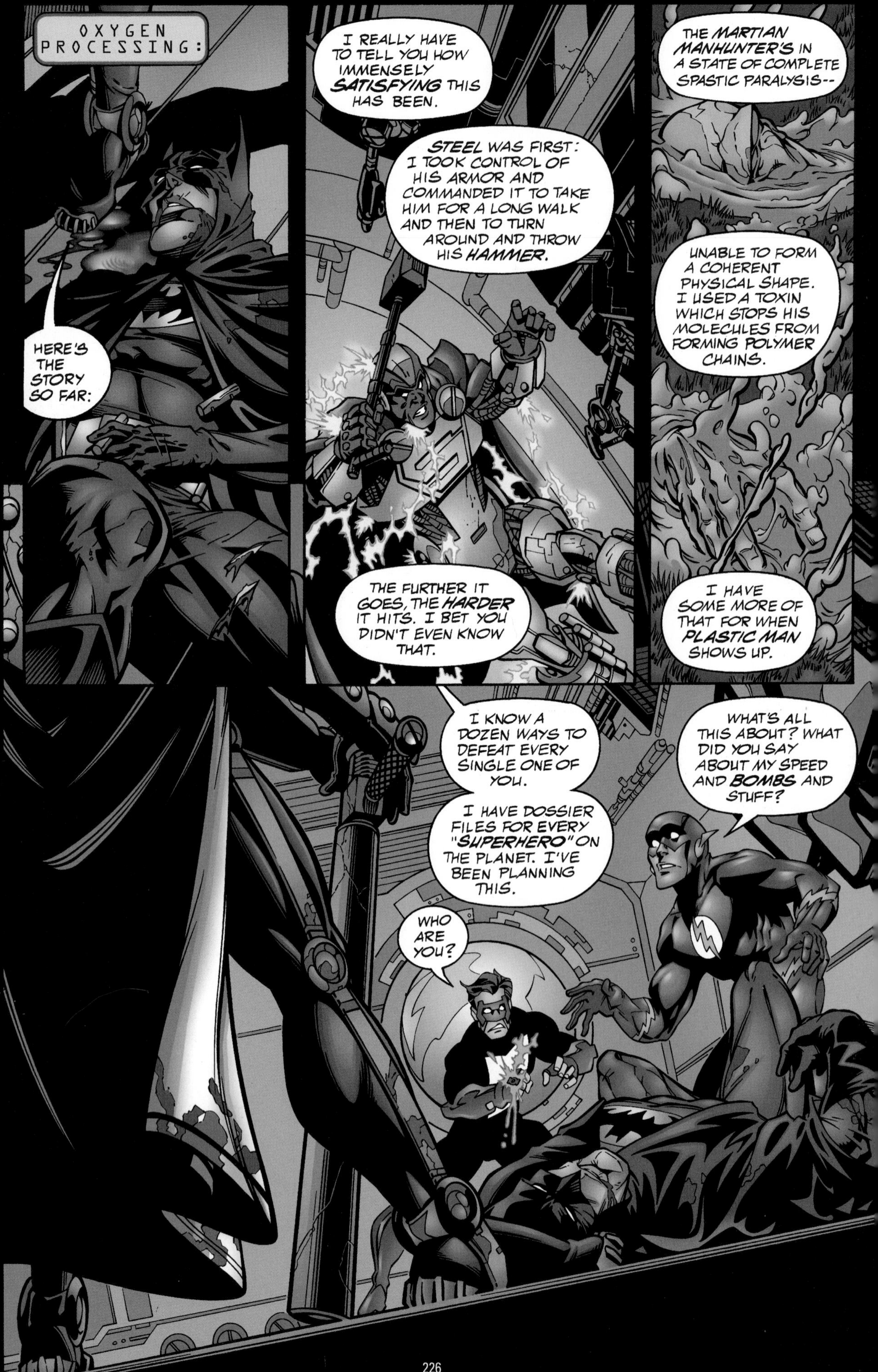
OXYGEN PROCESSING:
HERE'S THE STORY SO FAR:
I REALLY HAVE TO TELL YOU HOW IMMENSELY SATISFYING THIS HAS BEEN.
STEEL WAS FIRST: I TOOK CONTROL OF HIS ARMOR AND COMMANDED IT TO TAKE HIM FOR A LONG WALK AND THEN TO TURN AROUND AND THROW HIS HAMMER.
THE FURTHER IT GOES, THE HARDER IT HITS. I BET YOU DIDN'T EVEN KNOW THAT.
THE MARTIAN MANHUNTER'S IN A STATE OF COMPLETE SPASTIC PARALYSIS--
UNABLE TO FORM A COHERENT PHYSICAL SHAPE. I USED A TOXIN WHICH STOPS HIS MOLECULES FROM FORMING POLYMER CHAINS.
I HAVE SOME MORE OF THAT FOR WHEN PLASTIC MAN SHOWS UP.
I KNOW A DOZEN WAYS TO DEFEAT EVERY SINGLE ONE OF YOU.
I HAVE DOSSIER FILES FOR EVERY "SUPERHERO" ON THE PLANET. I'VE BEEN PLANNING THIS.
WHAT'S ALL THIS ABOUT? WHAT DID YOU SAY ABOUT MY SPEED AND BOMBS AND STUFF?
WHO ARE YOU?

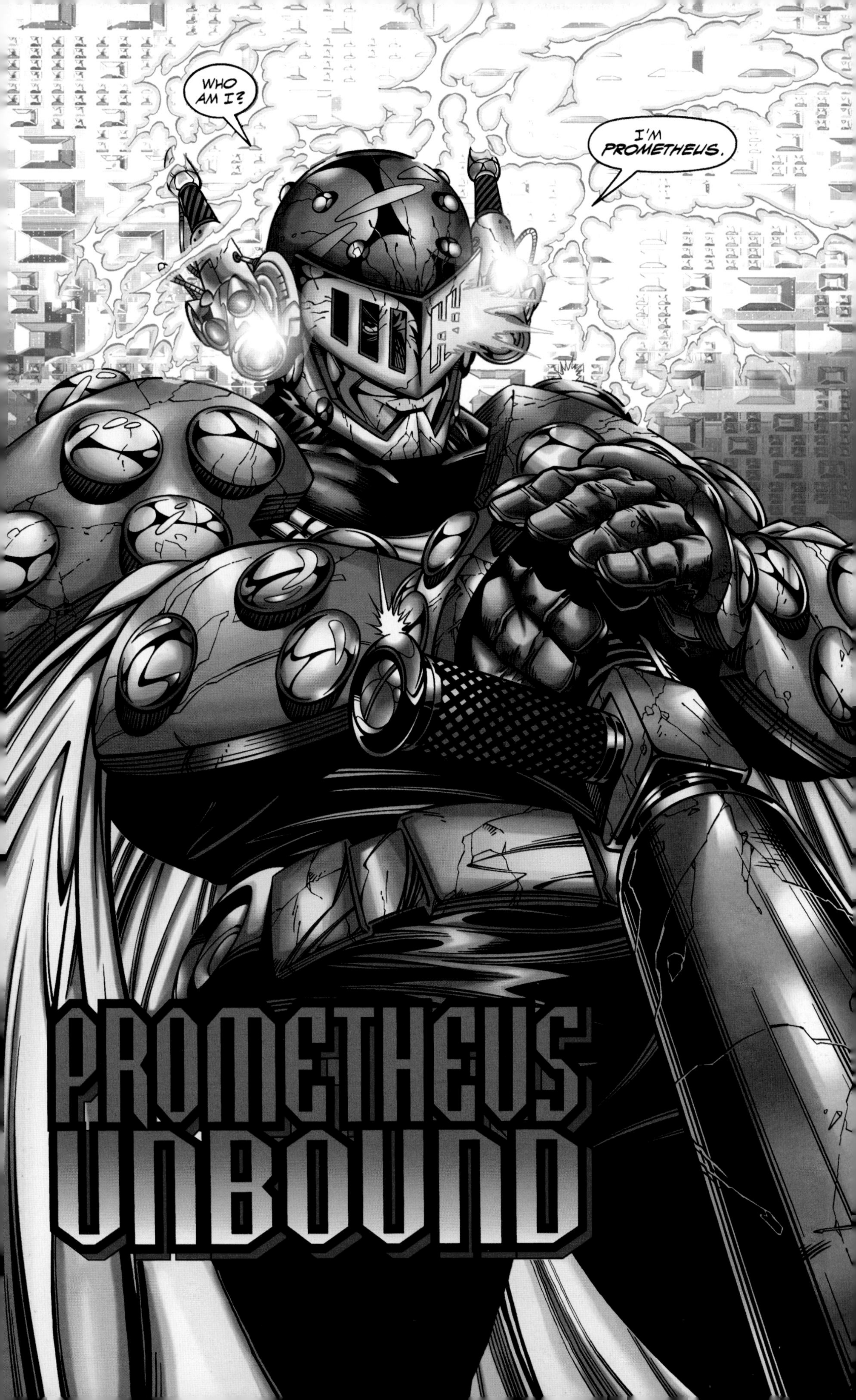
WHO AM I?
I'M PROMETHEUS.
PROMETHEUS UNBOUND

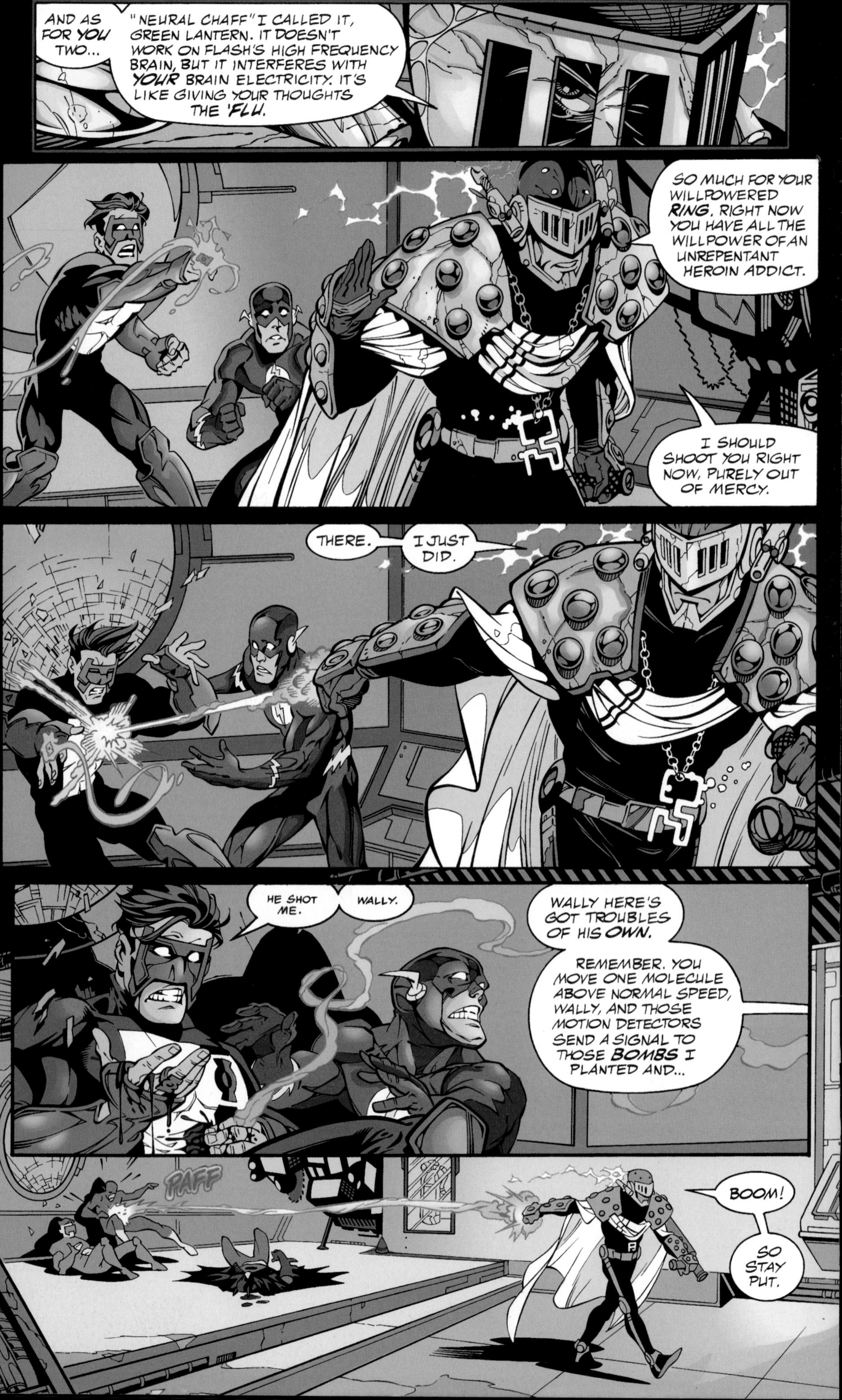
AND AS FOR YOU TWO...
"NEURAL CHAFF" I CALLED IT, GREEN LANTERN. IT DOESN'T WORK ON FLASH'S HIGH FREQUENCY BRAIN, BUT IT INTERFERES WITH YOUR BRAIN ELECTRICITY. IT'S LIKE GIVING YOUR THOUGHTS THE 'FLU.
SO MUCH FOR YOUR WILLPOWERED RING. RIGHT NOW YOU HAVE ALL THE WILLPOWER OF AN UNREPENTANT HEROIN ADDICT.
I SHOULD SHOOT YOU RIGHT NOW, PURELY OUT OF MERCY.
THERE.
I JUST DID.
HE SHOT ME.
WALLY.
WALLY HERE'S GOT TROUBLES OF HIS OWN.
REMEMBER. YOU MOVE ONE MOLECULE ABOVE NORMAL SPEED, WALLY, AND THOSE MOTION DETECTORS SEND A SIGNAL TO THOSE BOMBS I PLANTED AND...
PAFF
BOOM!
SO STAY PUT.

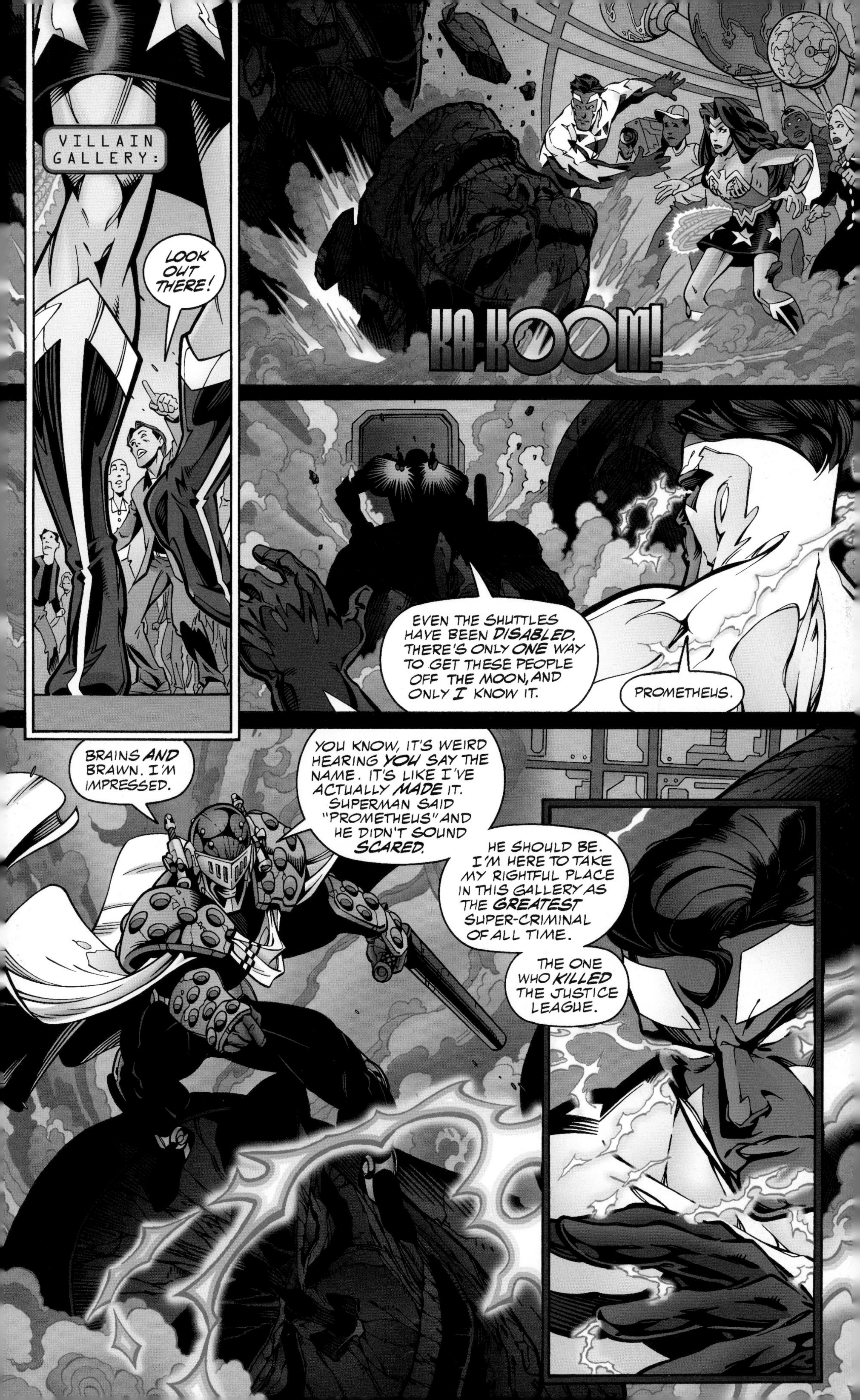
VILLAIN GALLERY:
LOOK OUT THERE!
KA-KOOM!
EVEN THE SHUTTLES HAVE BEEN DISABLED. THERE'S ONLY ONE WAY TO GET THESE PEOPLE OFF THE MOON, AND ONLY I KNOW IT.
PROMETHEUS.
BRAINS AND BRAWN. I'M IMPRESSED.
YOU KNOW, IT'S WEIRD HEARING YOU SAY THE NAME. IT'S LIKE I'VE ACTUALLY MADE IT. SUPERMAN SAID "PROMETHEUS" AND HE DIDN'T SOUND SCARED.
HE SHOULD BE. I'M HERE TO TAKE MY RIGHTFUL PLACE IN THIS GALLERY AS THE GREATEST SUPER-CRIMINAL OF ALL TIME.
THE ONE WHO KILLED THE JUSTICE LEAGUE.

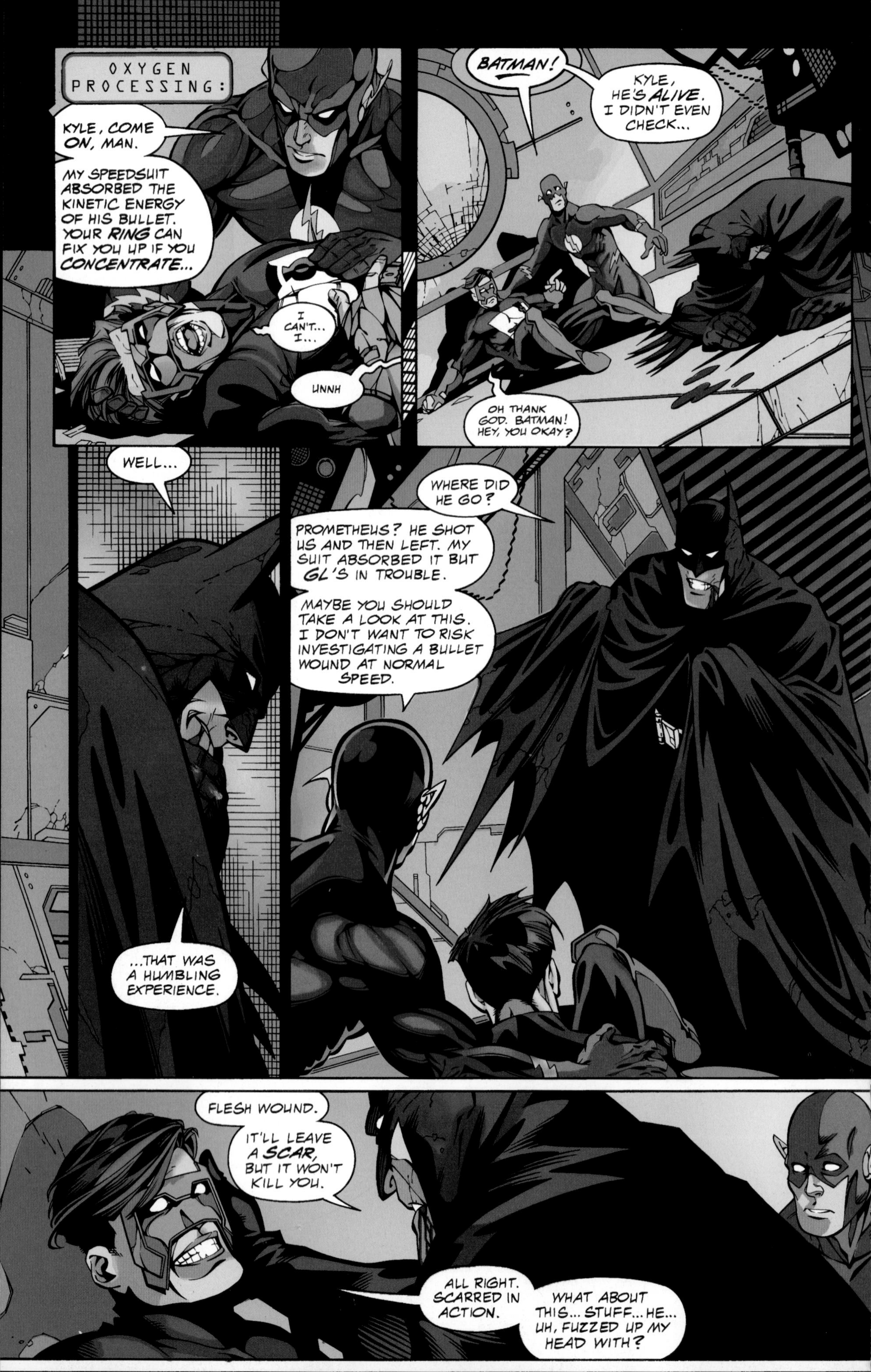

OXYGEN PROCESSING:
KYLE, COME ON, MAN.
MY SPEEDSUIT ABSORBED THE KINETIC ENERGY OF HIS BULLET. YOUR RING CAN FIX YOU UP IF YOU CONCENTRATE...
I CAN'T... I...
UNNH
BATMAN!
KYLE, HE'S ALIVE. I DIDN'T EVEN CHECK...
OH THANK GOD. BATMAN! HEY, YOU OKAY?
WELL...
...THAT WAS A HUMBLING EXPERIENCE.
WHERE DID HE GO?
PROMETHEUS? HE SHOT US AND THEN LEFT. MY SUIT ABSORBED IT BUT GL'S IN TROUBLE.
MAYBE YOU SHOULD TAKE A LOOK AT THIS. I DON'T WANT TO RISK INVESTIGATING A BULLET WOUND AT NORMAL SPEED.
FLESH WOUND.
IT'LL LEAVE A SCAR, BUT IT WON'T KILL YOU.
ALL RIGHT. SCARRED IN ACTION.
WHAT ABOUT THIS... STUFF... HE... UH, FUZZED UP MY HEAD WITH?

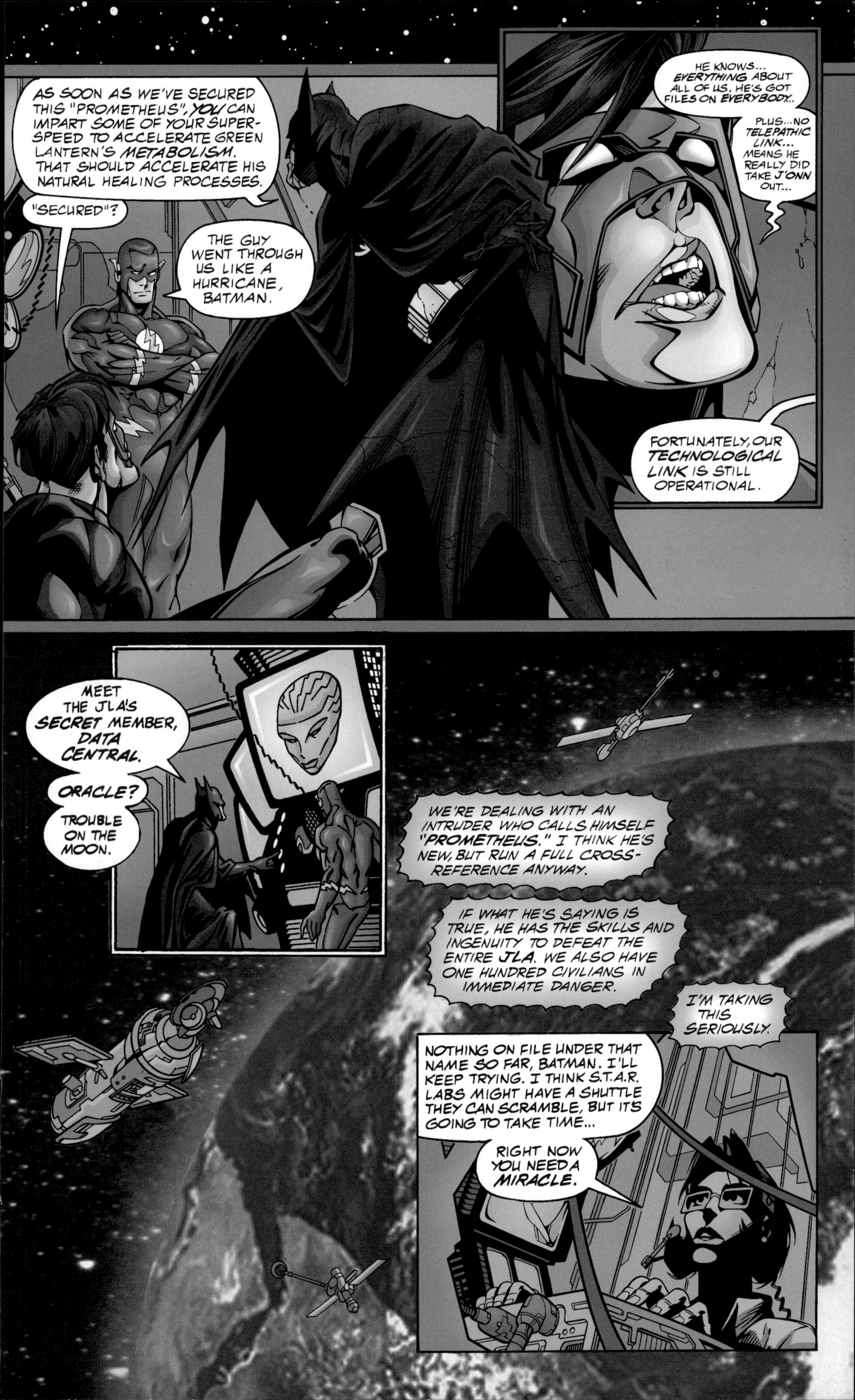
AS SOON AS WE'VE SECURED THIS "PROMETHEUS", YOU CAN IMPART SOME OF YOUR SUPER-SPEED TO ACCELERATE GREEN LANTERN'S METABOLISM. THAT SHOULD ACCELERATE HIS NATURAL HEALING PROCESSES.
"SECURED"?
THE GUY WENT THROUGH US LIKE A HURRICANE, BATMAN.
HE KNOWS... EVERYTHING ABOUT ALL OF US. HE'S GOT FILES ON EVERYBODY..
PLUS...NO TELEPATHIC LINK... MEANS HE REALLY DID TAKE J'ONN OUT...
FORTUNATELY, OUR TECHNOLOGICAL LINK IS STILL OPERATIONAL.
MEET THE JLA'S SECRET MEMBER, DATA CENTRAL.
ORACLE?
TROUBLE ON THE MOON.
WE'RE DEALING WITH AN INTRUDER WHO CALLS HIMSELF "PROMETHEUS." I THINK HE'S NEW, BUT RUN A FULL CROSS-REFERENCE ANYWAY.
IF WHAT HE'S SAYING IS TRUE, HE HAS THE SKILLS AND INGENUITY TO DEFEAT THE ENTIRE JLA. WE ALSO HAVE ONE HUNDRED CIVILIANS IN IMMEDIATE DANGER.
I'M TAKING THIS SERIOUSLY.
NOTHING ON FILE UNDER THAT NAME SO FAR, BATMAN. I'LL KEEP TRYING. I THINK S.T.A.R. LABS MIGHT HAVE A SHUTTLE THEY CAN SCRAMBLE, BUT IT'S GOING TO TAKE TIME...
RIGHT NOW YOU NEED A MIRACLE.

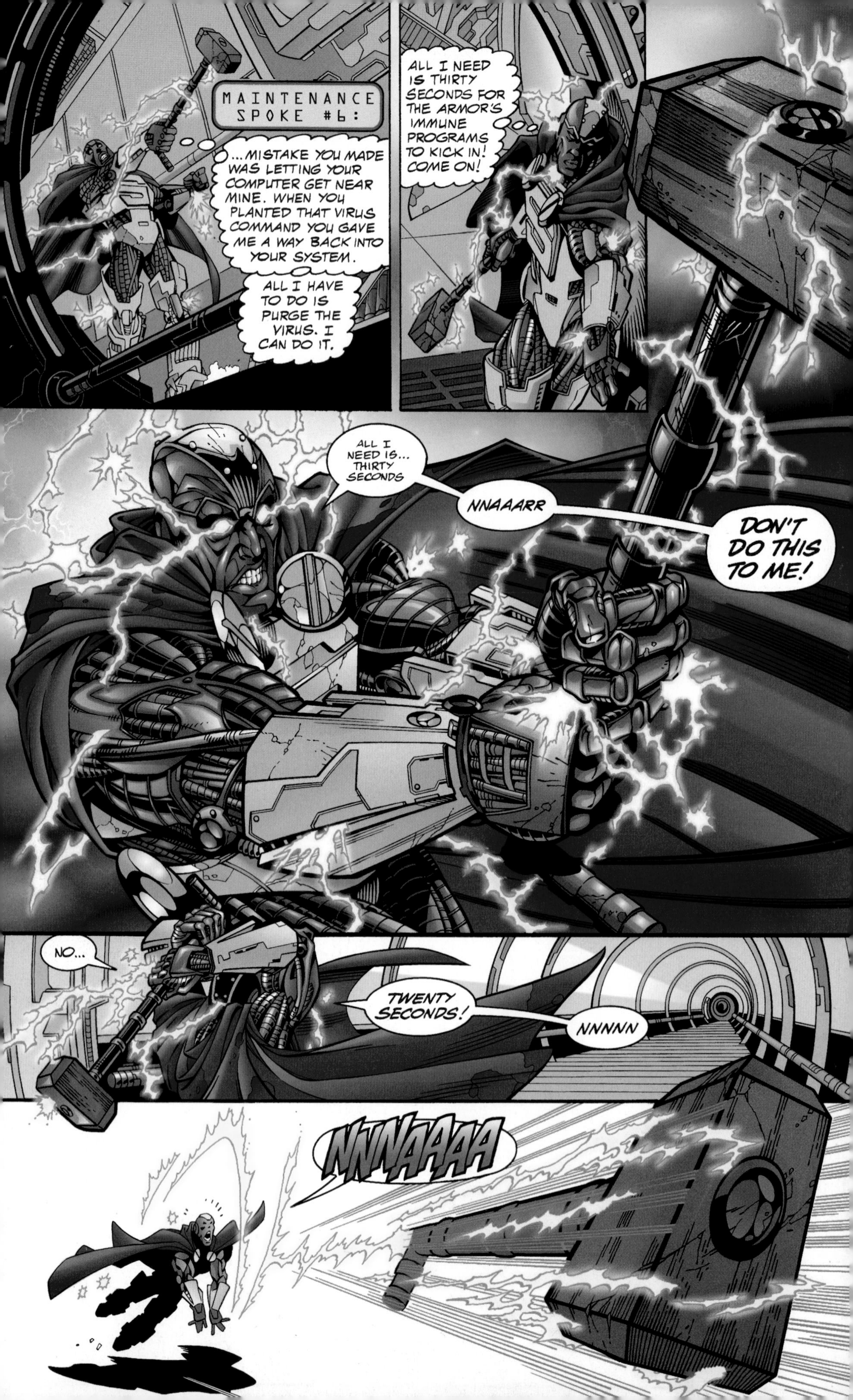
MAINTENANCE SPOKE #6:
...MISTAKE YOU MADE WAS LETTING YOUR COMPUTER GET NEAR MINE. WHEN YOU PLANTED THAT VIRUS COMMAND YOU GAVE ME A WAY BACK INTO YOUR SYSTEM.
ALL I HAVE TO DO IS PURGE THE VIRUS. I CAN DO IT.
ALL I NEED IS THIRTY SECONDS FOR THE ARMOR'S IMMUNE PROGRAMS TO KICK IN! COME ON!
ALL I NEED IS... THIRTY SECONDS
NNAAARR
DON'T DO THIS TO ME!
NO...
TWENTY SECONDS!
NNNNN
NNNAAAA

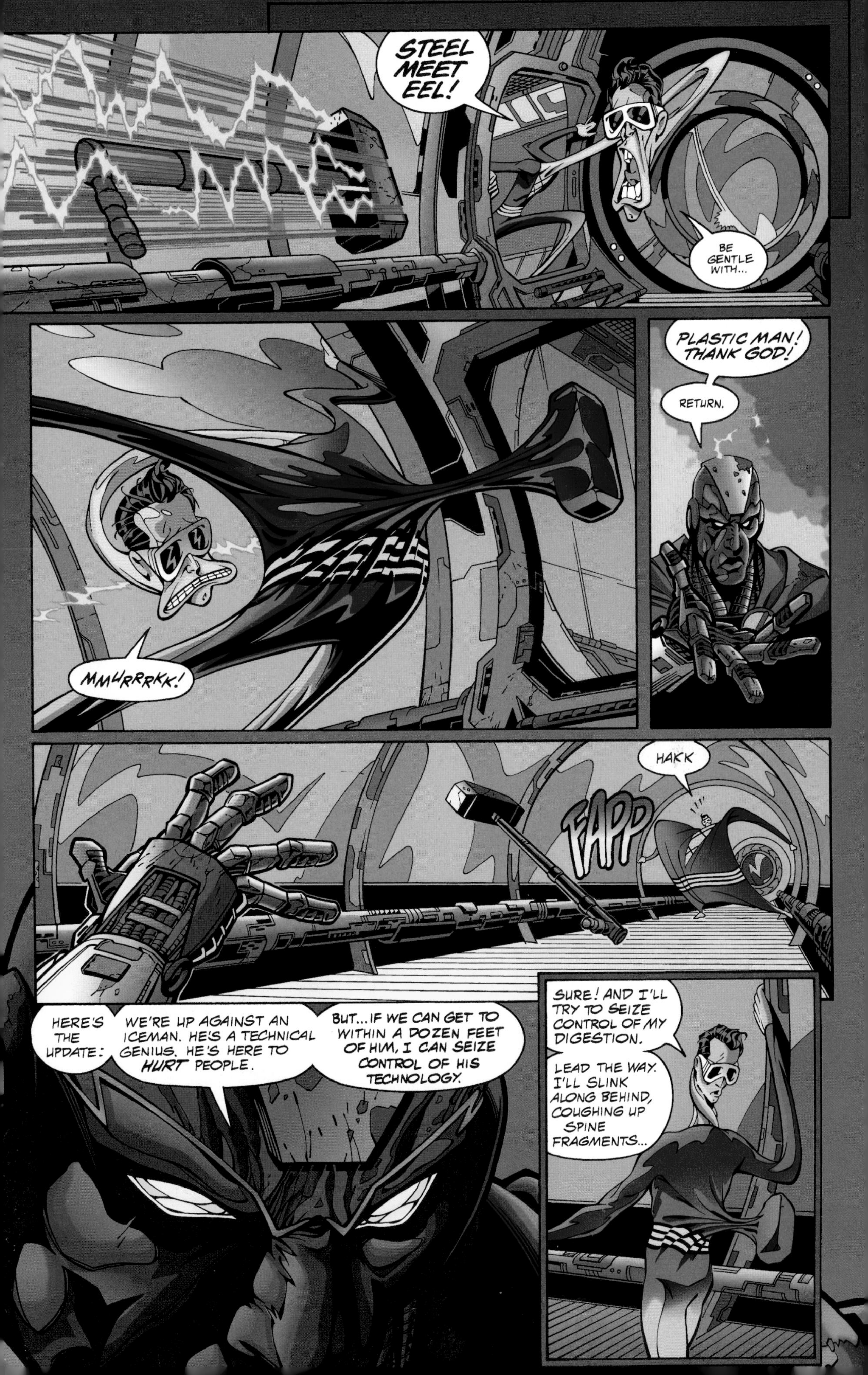
STEEL MEET EEL!
BE GENTLE WITH...
MMURRRKK!
PLASTIC MAN! THANK GOD!
RETURN.
HAKK
FAPP
HERE'S THE UPDATE:
WE'RE UP AGAINST AN ICEMAN. HE'S A TECHNICAL GENIUS. HE'S HERE TO HURT PEOPLE.
BUT...IF WE CAN GET TO WITHIN A DOZEN FEET OF HIM, I CAN SEIZE CONTROL OF HIS TECHNOLOGY.
SURE! AND I'LL TRY TO SEIZE CONTROL OF MY DIGESTION.
LEAD THE WAY. I'LL SLINK ALONG BEHIND, COUGHING UP SPINE FRAGMENTS...

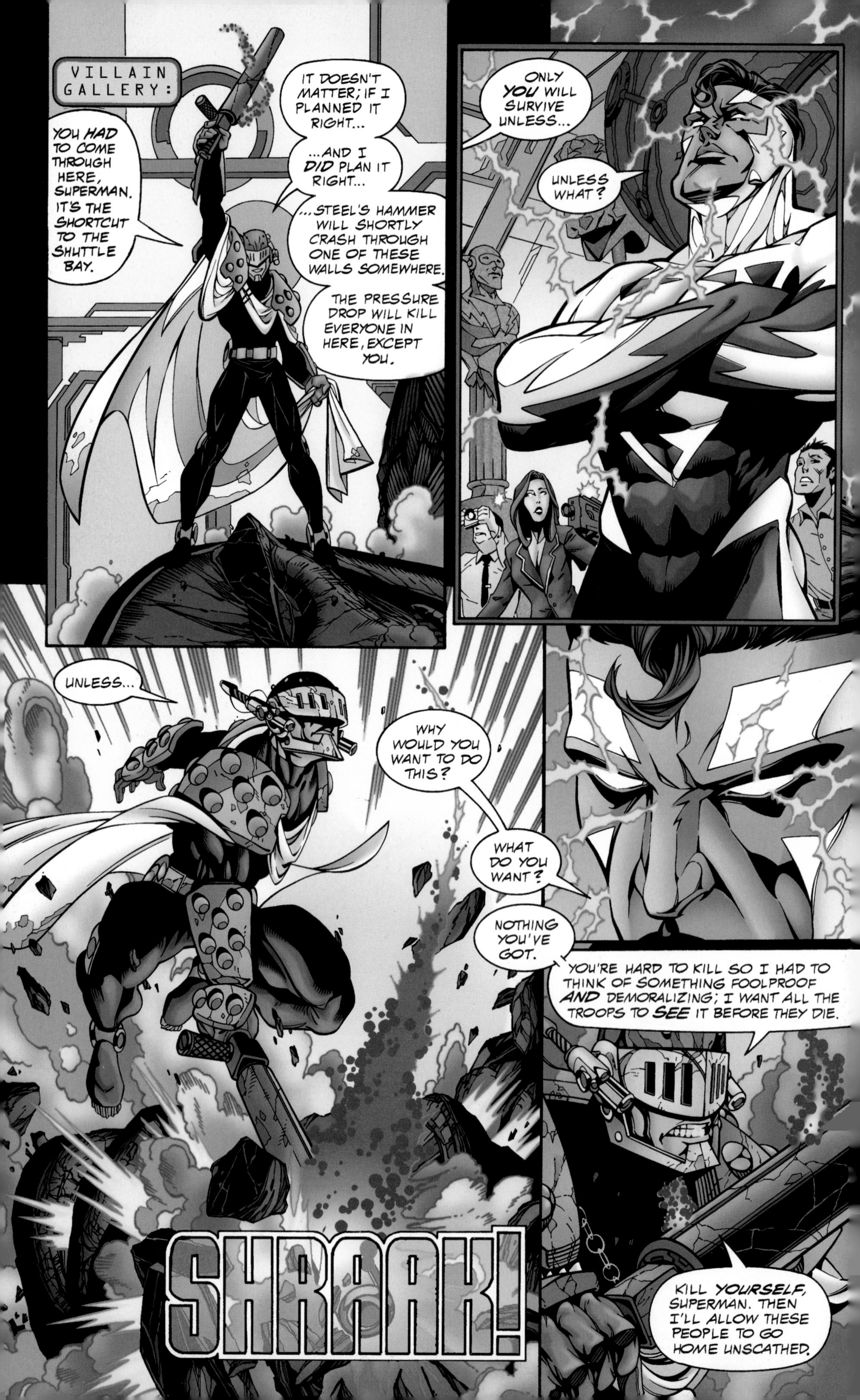
VILLAIN GALLERY:
YOU HAD TO COME THROUGH HERE, SUPERMAN. IT'S THE SHORTCUT TO THE SHUTTLE BAY.
IT DOESN'T MATTER; IF I PLANNED IT RIGHT...
...AND I DID PLAN IT RIGHT...
...STEEL'S HAMMER WILL SHORTLY CRASH THROUGH ONE OF THESE WALLS SOMEWHERE.
THE PRESSURE DROP WILL KILL EVERYONE IN HERE, EXCEPT YOU.
ONLY YOU WILL SURVIVE UNLESS...
UNLESS WHAT?
UNLESS...
WHY WOULD YOU WANT TO DO THIS?
WHAT DO YOU WANT?
NOTHING YOU'VE GOT.
YOU'RE HARD TO KILL SO I HAD TO THINK OF SOMETHING FOOLPROOF AND DEMORALIZING; I WANT ALL THE TROOPS TO SEE IT BEFORE THEY DIE.
SHRAAK!
KILL YOURSELF, SUPERMAN. THEN I'LL ALLOW THESE PEOPLE TO GO HOME UNSCATHED.

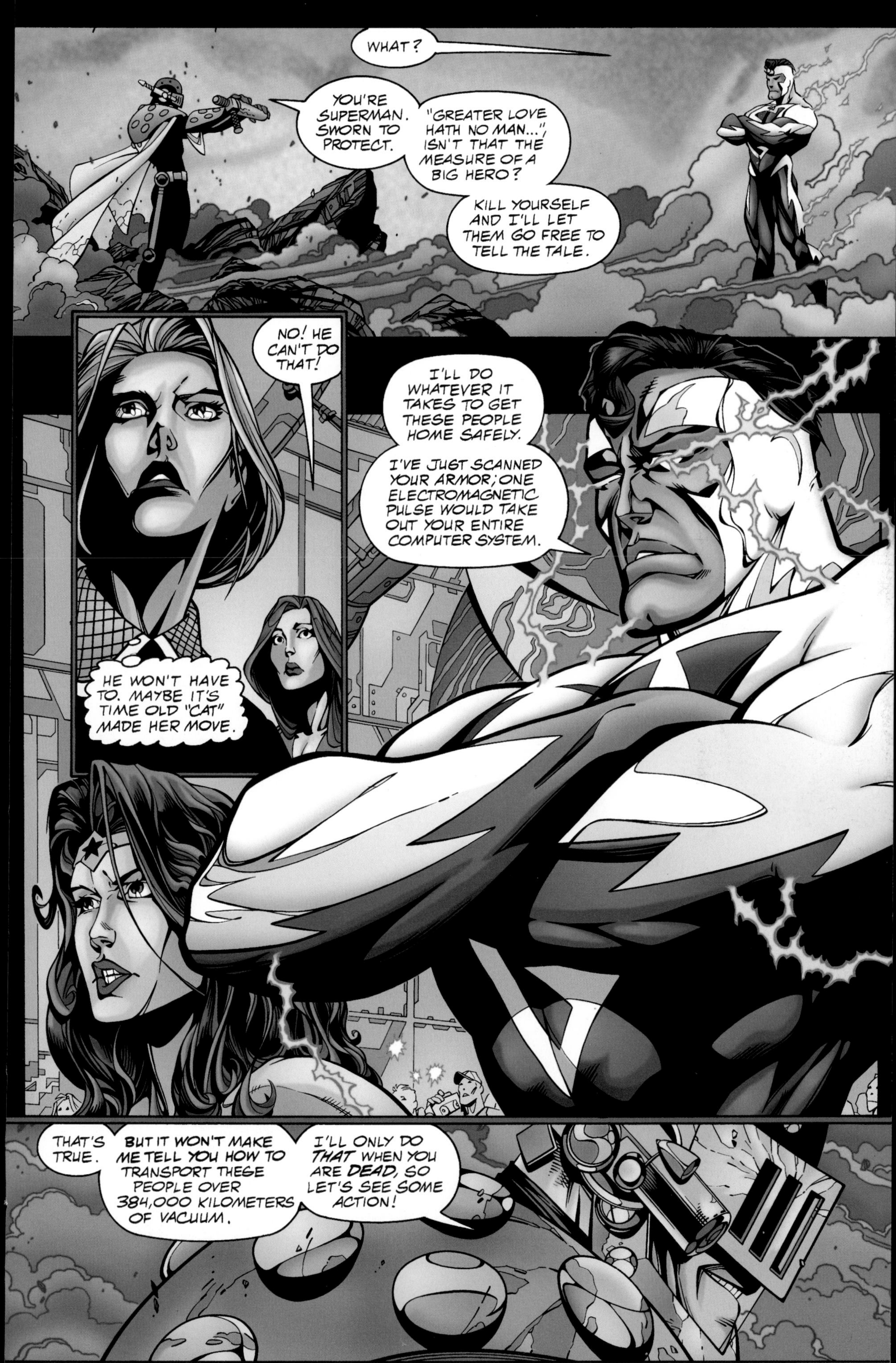
WHAT?
YOU'RE SUPERMAN. SWORN TO PROTECT.
"GREATER LOVE HATH NO MAN...", ISN'T THAT THE MEASURE OF A BIG HERO?
KILL YOURSELF AND I'LL LET THEM GO FREE TO TELL THE TALE.
NO! HE CAN'T DO THAT!
I'LL DO WHATEVER IT TAKES TO GET THESE PEOPLE HOME SAFELY.
I'VE JUST SCANNED YOUR ARMOR; ONE ELECTROMAGNETIC PULSE WOULD TAKE OUT YOUR ENTIRE COMPUTER SYSTEM.
HE WON'T HAVE TO. MAYBE IT'S TIME OLD "CAT" MADE HER MOVE.
THAT'S TRUE.
BUT IT WON'T MAKE ME TELL YOU HOW TO TRANSPORT THESE PEOPLE OVER 384,000 KILOMETERS OF VACUUM.
I'LL ONLY DO THAT WHEN YOU ARE DEAD, SO LET'S SEE SOME ACTION!

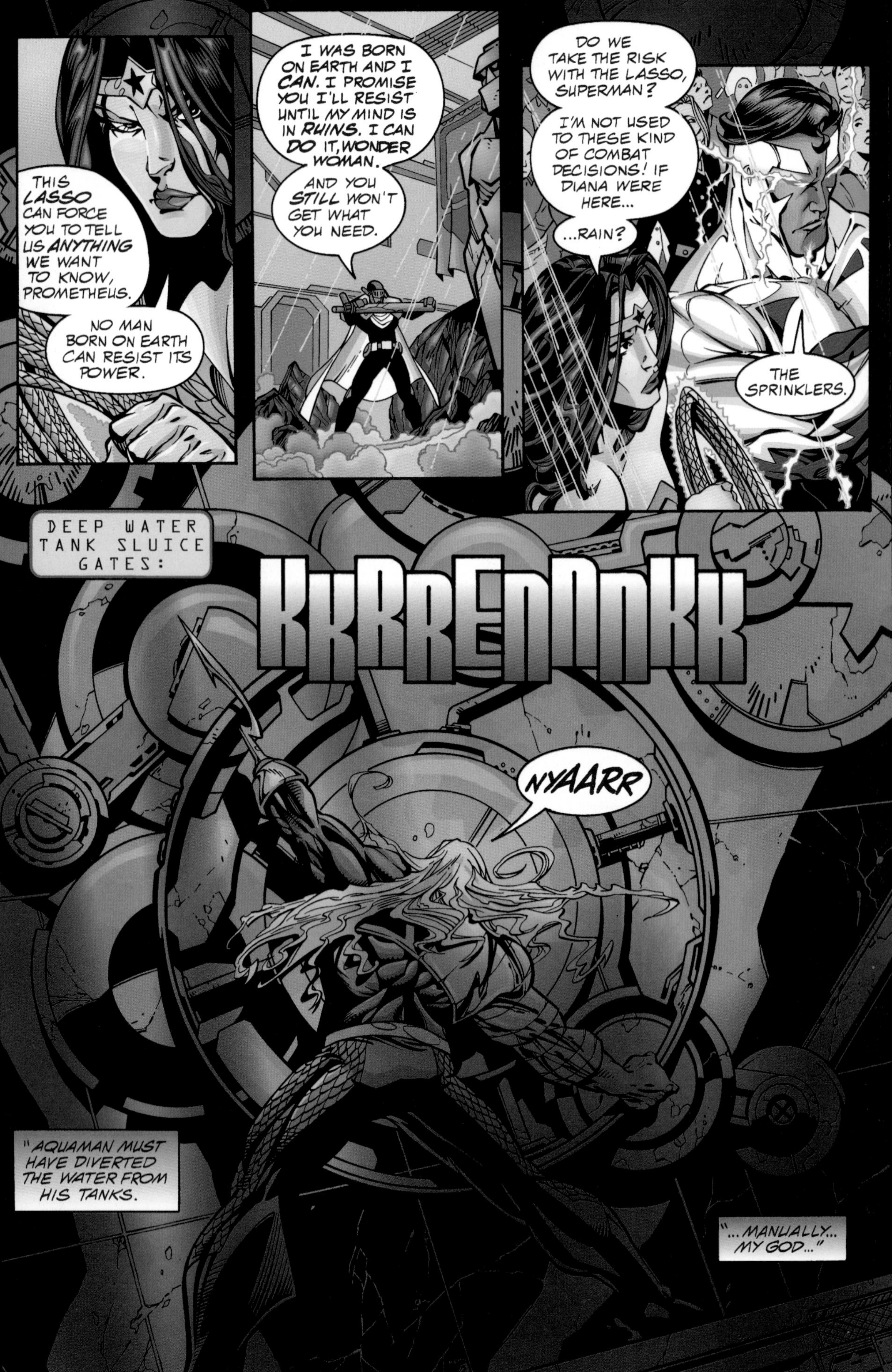
THIS LASSO CAN FORCE YOU TO TELL US ANYTHING WE WANT TO KNOW, PROMETHEUS.
NO MAN BORN ON EARTH CAN RESIST ITS POWER.
I WAS BORN ON EARTH AND I CAN. I PROMISE YOU I'LL RESIST UNTIL MY MIND IS IN RUINS. I CAN DO IT, WONDER WOMAN.
AND YOU STILL WON'T GET WHAT YOU NEED.
DO WE TAKE THE RISK WITH THE LASSO, SUPERMAN?
I'M NOT USED TO THESE KIND OF COMBAT DECISIONS! IF DIANA WERE HERE...
...RAIN?
THE SPRINKLERS.
DEEP WATER TANK SLUICE GATES:
KKRRENNNKK
NYAARR
"AQUAMAN MUST HAVE DIVERTED THE WATER FROM HIS TANKS.
"...MANUALLY... MY GOD..."

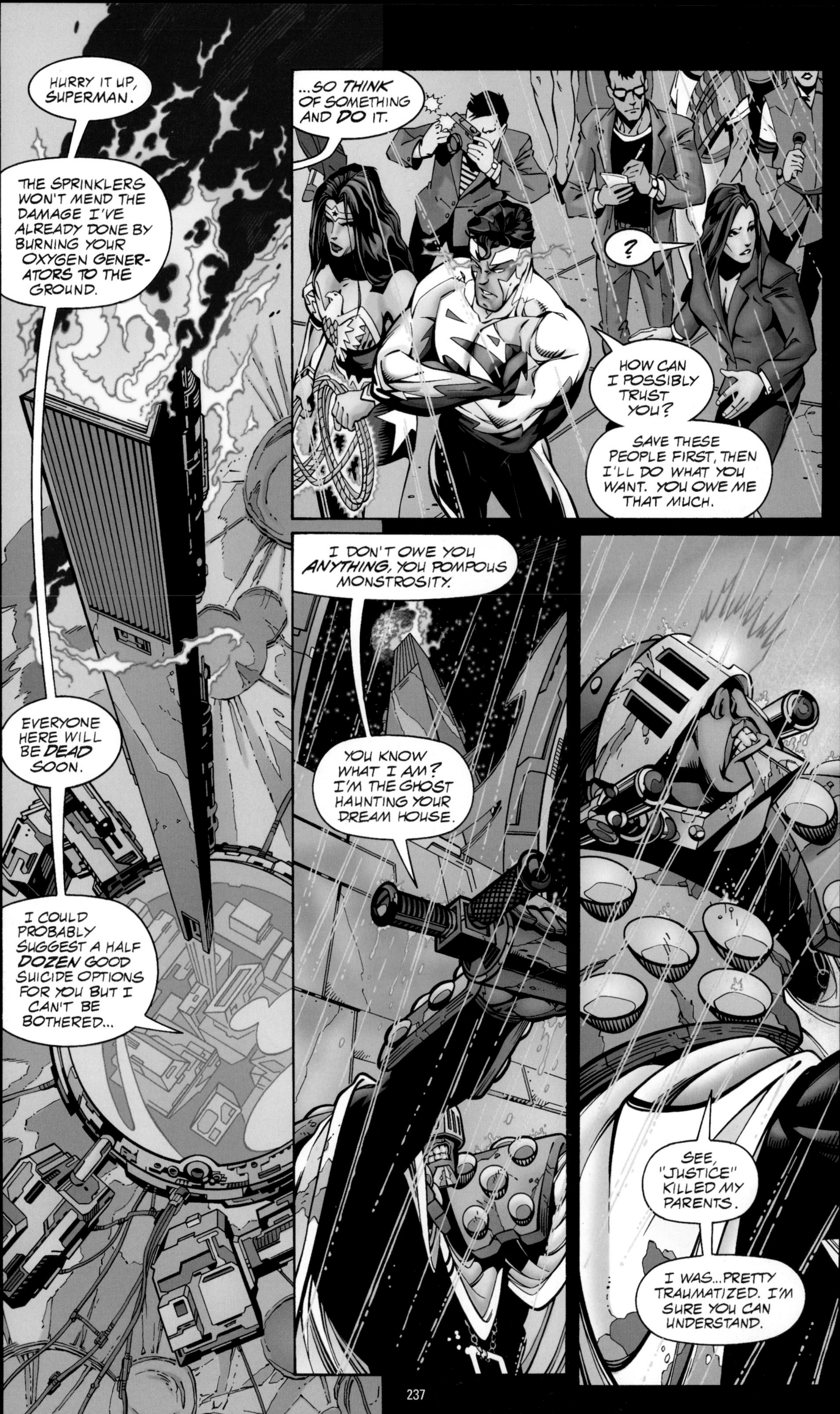
HURRY IT UP, SUPERMAN.
THE SPRINKLERS WON'T MEND THE DAMAGE I'VE ALREADY DONE BY BURNING YOUR OXYGEN GENERATORS TO THE GROUND.
EVERYONE HERE WILL BE DEAD SOON.
I COULD PROBABLY SUGGEST A HALF DOZEN GOOD SUICIDE OPTIONS FOR YOU BUT I CAN'T BE BOTHERED...
...SO THINK OF SOMETHING AND DO IT.
?
HOW CAN I POSSIBLY TRUST YOU?
SAVE THESE PEOPLE FIRST, THEN I'LL DO WHAT YOU WANT. YOU OWE ME THAT MUCH.
I DON'T OWE YOU ANYTHING, YOU POMPOUS MONSTROSITY.
YOU KNOW WHAT I AM? I'M THE GHOST HAUNTING YOUR DREAM HOUSE.
SEE, "JUSTICE" KILLED MY PARENTS.
I WAS...PRETTY TRAUMATIZED. I'M SURE YOU CAN UNDERSTAND.

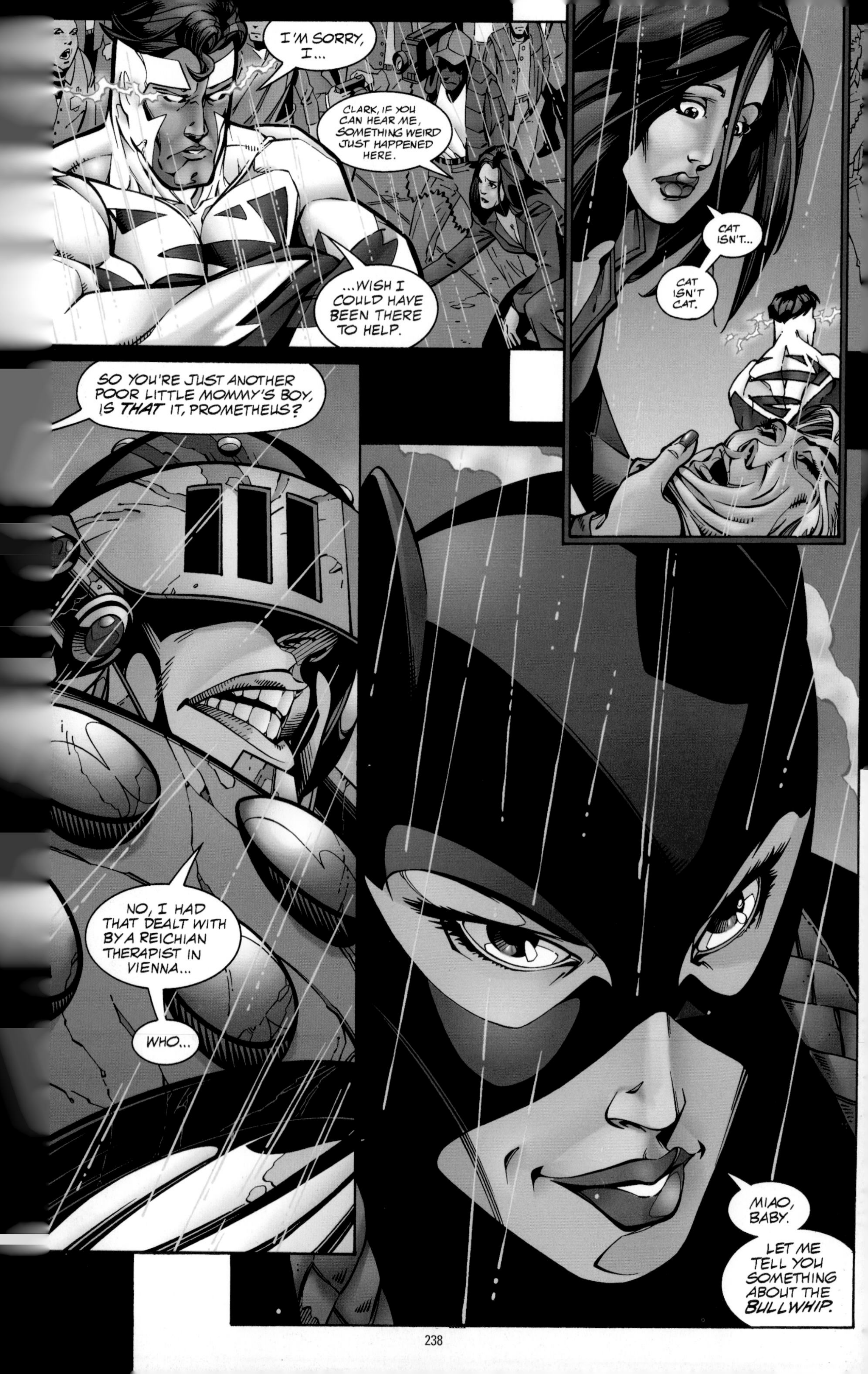
I'M SORRY, I...
CLARK, IF YOU CAN HEAR ME, SOMETHING WEIRD JUST HAPPENED HERE.
...WISH I COULD HAVE BEEN THERE TO HELP.
CAT ISN'T...
CAT ISN'T CAT.
SO YOU'RE JUST ANOTHER POOR LITTLE MOMMY'S BOY, IS *THAT* IT, PROMETHEUS?
NO, I HAD THAT DEALT WITH BY A REICHIAN THERAPIST IN VIENNA...
WHO...
MIAO, BABY.
LET ME TELL YOU SOMETHING ABOUT THE *BULLWHIP*.

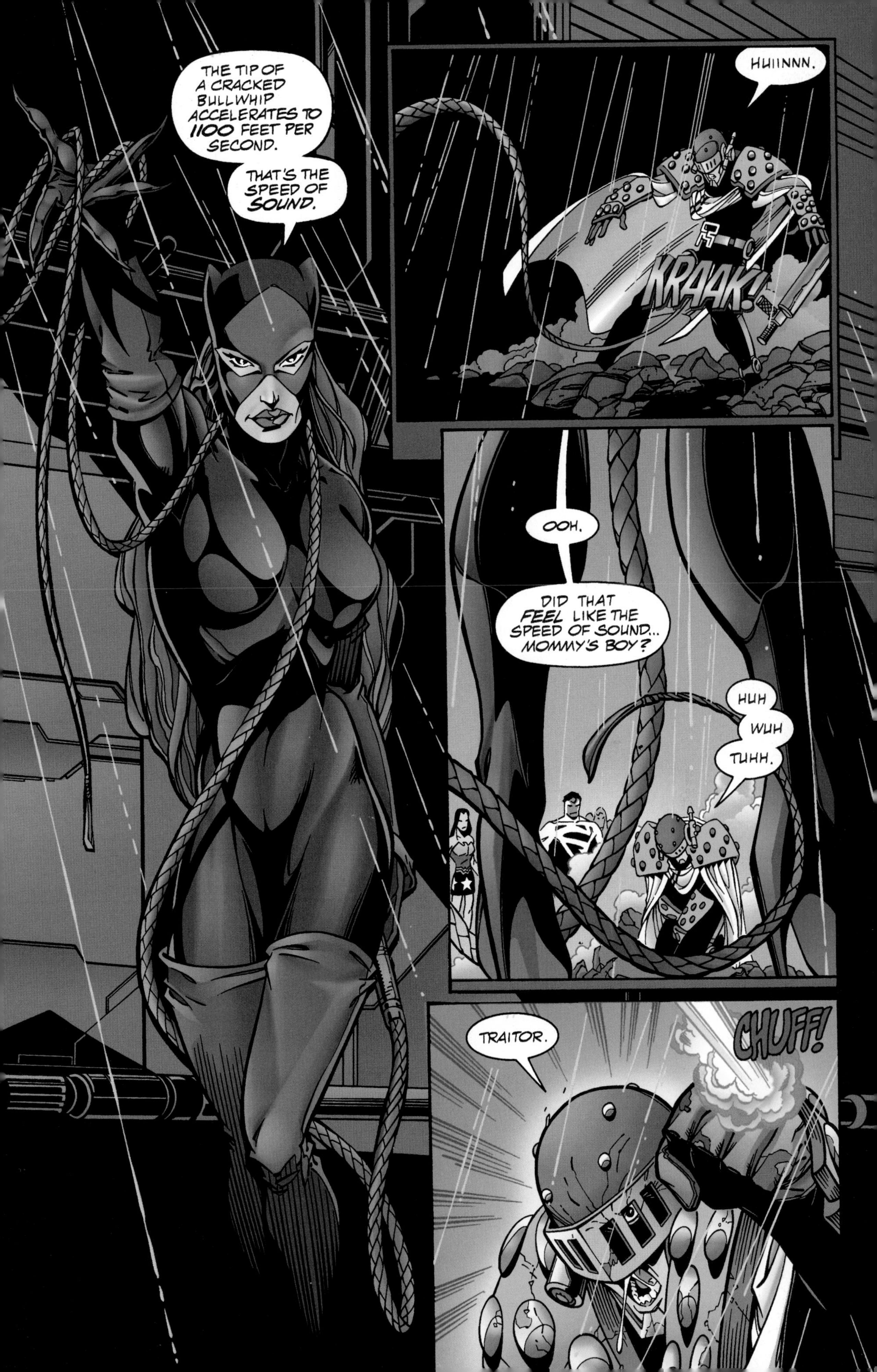
THE TIP OF A CRACKED BULLWHIP ACCELERATES TO 1100 FEET PER SECOND.
THAT'S THE SPEED OF SOUND.
HUIINNN.
KRAAK!
OOH.
DID THAT FEEL LIKE THE SPEED OF SOUND... MOMMY'S BOY?
HUH WUH TUHH.
TRAITOR.
CHUFF!

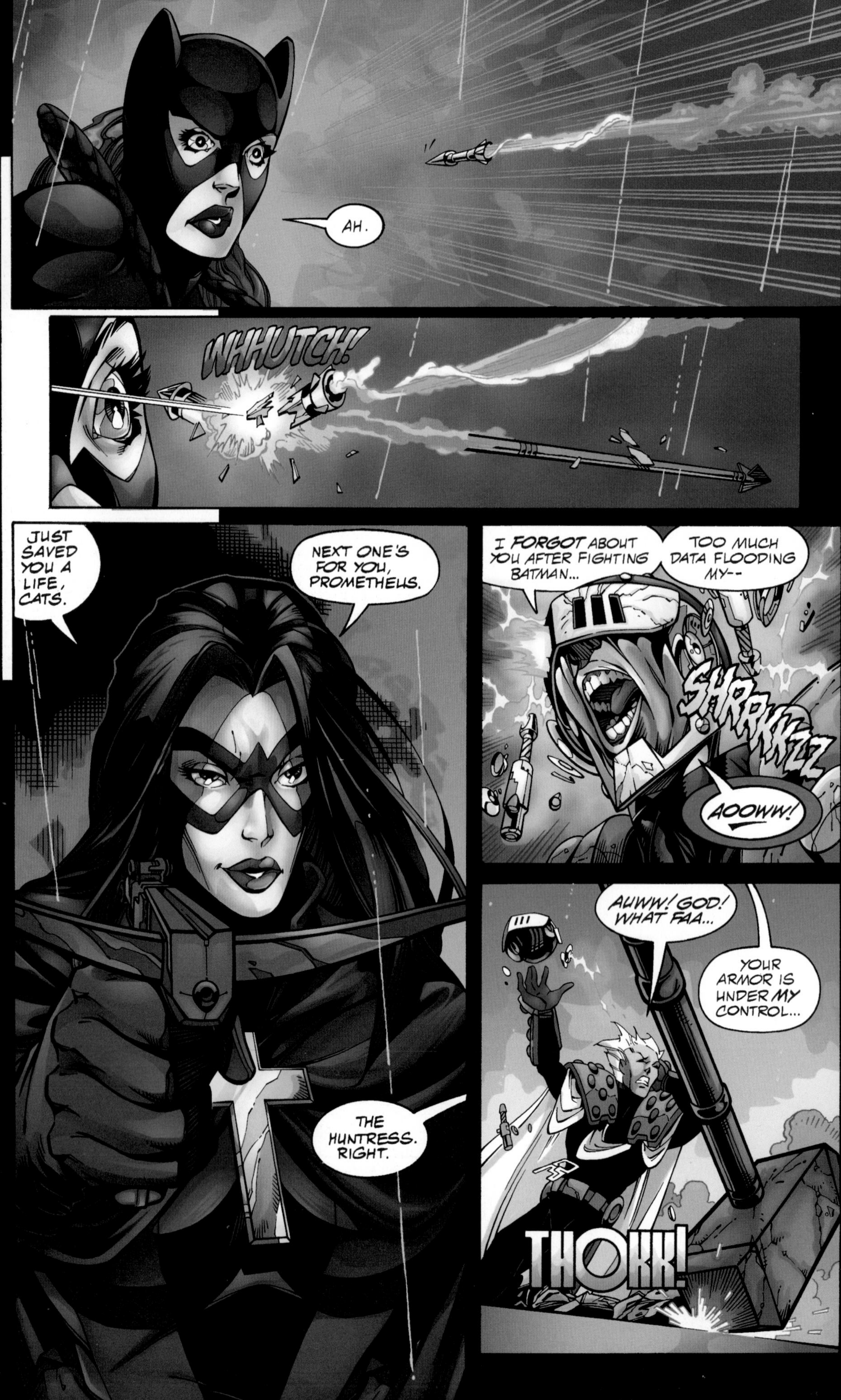
AH.
WHHUTCH!
JUST SAVED YOU A LIFE, CATS.
NEXT ONE'S FOR YOU, PROMETHEUS.
THE HUNTRESS. RIGHT.
I FORGOT ABOUT YOU AFTER FIGHTING BATMAN...
TOO MUCH DATA FLOODING MY--
SHRRKKZZ
AOOWW!
AUWW! GOD! WHAT FAA...
YOUR ARMOR IS UNDER MY CONTROL...
THOKK!

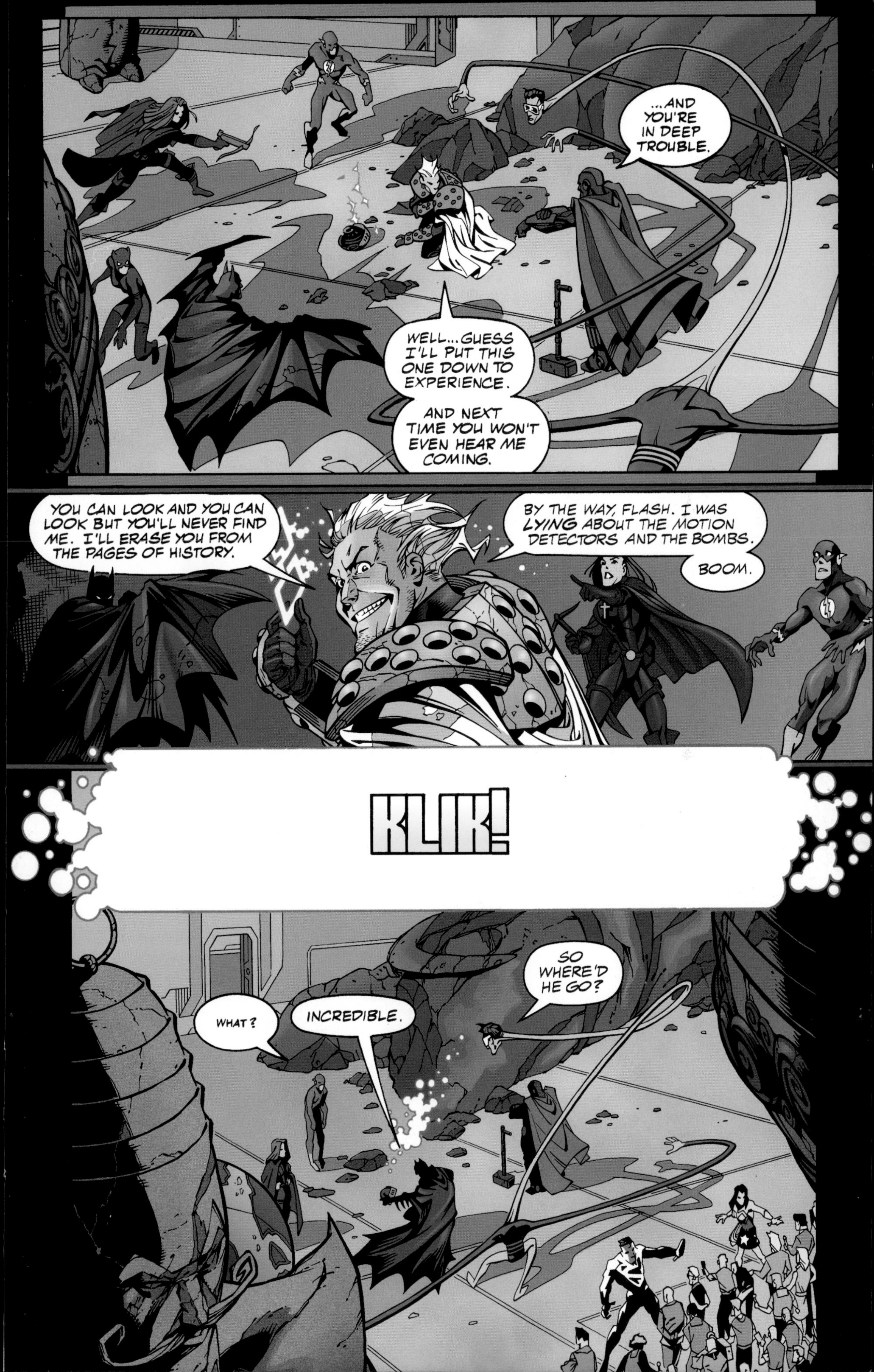
...AND YOU'RE IN DEEP TROUBLE.
WELL...GUESS I'LL PUT THIS ONE DOWN TO EXPERIENCE.
AND NEXT TIME YOU WON'T EVEN HEAR ME COMING.
YOU CAN LOOK AND YOU CAN LOOK BUT YOU'LL NEVER FIND ME. I'LL ERASE YOU FROM THE PAGES OF HISTORY.
BY THE WAY, FLASH. I WAS LYING ABOUT THE MOTION DETECTORS AND THE BOMBS.
BOOM.
KLIK!
WHAT?
INCREDIBLE.
SO WHERE'D HE GO?

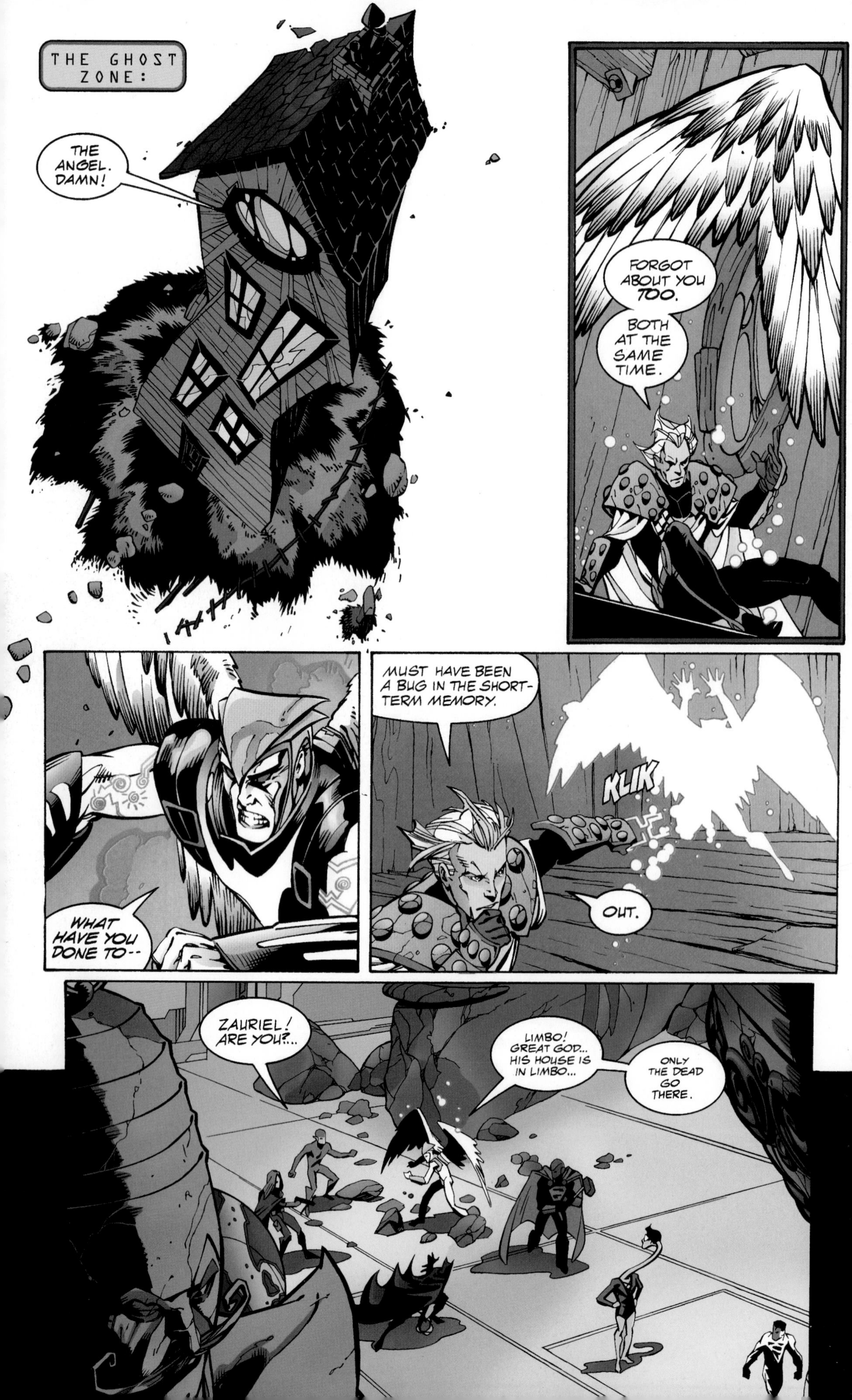
THE GHOST ZONE:
THE ANGEL. DAMN!
FORGOT ABOUT YOU TOO.
BOTH AT THE SAME TIME.
WHAT HAVE YOU DONE TO--
MUST HAVE BEEN A BUG IN THE SHORT-TERM MEMORY.
KLIK
OUT.
ZAURIEL! ARE YOU?...
LIMBO! GREAT GOD... HIS HOUSE IS IN LIMBO...
ONLY THE DEAD GO THERE.

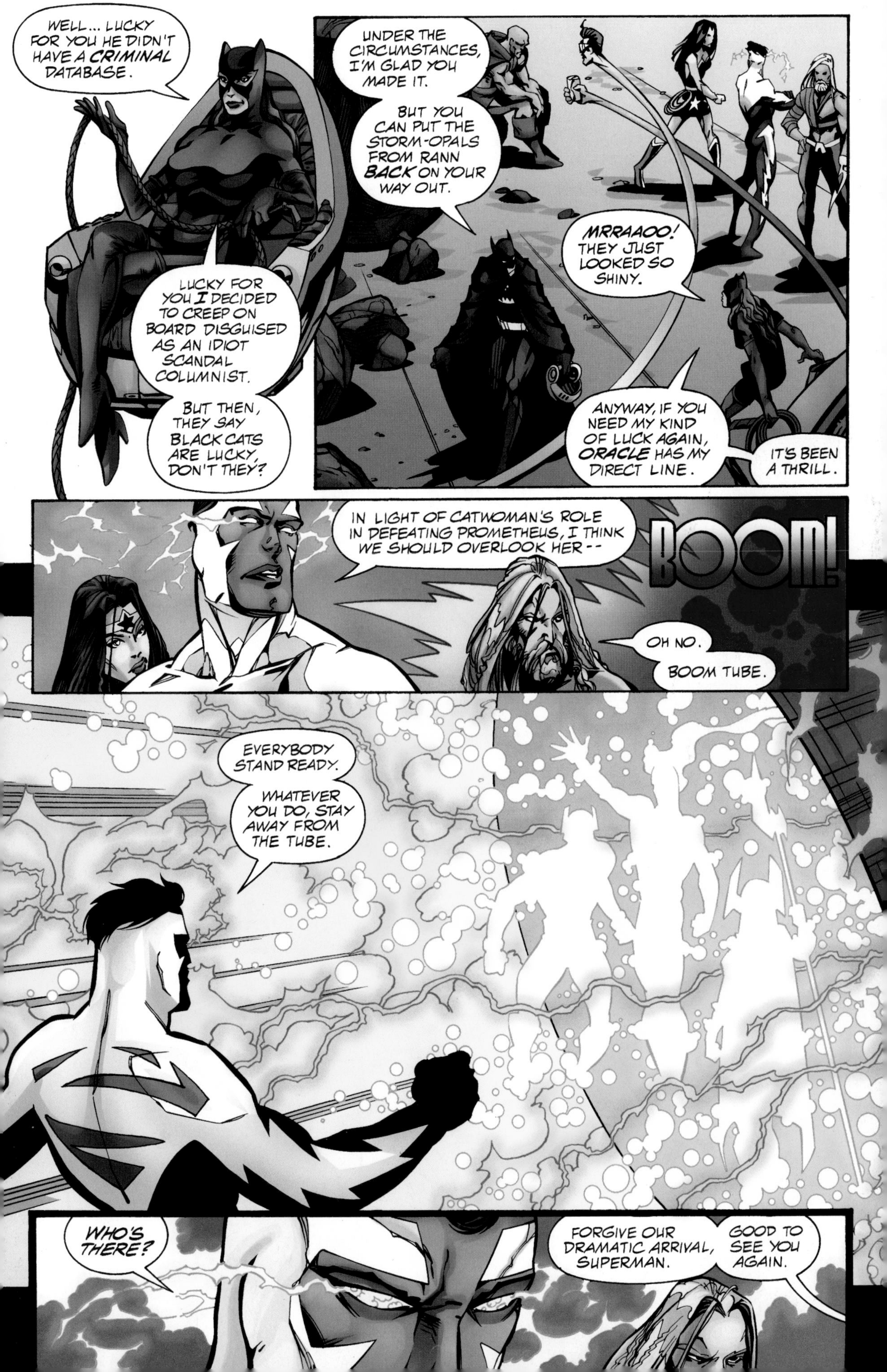
WELL... LUCKY FOR YOU HE DIDN'T HAVE A CRIMINAL DATABASE.
UNDER THE CIRCUMSTANCES, I'M GLAD YOU MADE IT.
BUT YOU CAN PUT THE STORM-OPALS FROM RANN BACK ON YOUR WAY OUT.
LUCKY FOR YOU I DECIDED TO CREEP ON BOARD DISGUISED AS AN IDIOT SCANDAL COLUMNIST.
BUT THEN, THEY SAY BLACK CATS ARE LUCKY, DON'T THEY?
MRRAAOO! THEY JUST LOOKED SO SHINY.
ANYWAY, IF YOU NEED MY KIND OF LUCK AGAIN, ORACLE HAS MY DIRECT LINE.
IT'S BEEN A THRILL.
IN LIGHT OF CATWOMAN'S ROLE IN DEFEATING PROMETHEUS, I THINK WE SHOULD OVERLOOK HER--
BOOM!
OH NO.
BOOM TUBE.
EVERYBODY STAND READY.
WHATEVER YOU DO, STAY AWAY FROM THE TUBE.
WHO'S THERE?
FORGIVE OUR DRAMATIC ARRIVAL, SUPERMAN.
GOOD TO SEE YOU AGAIN.

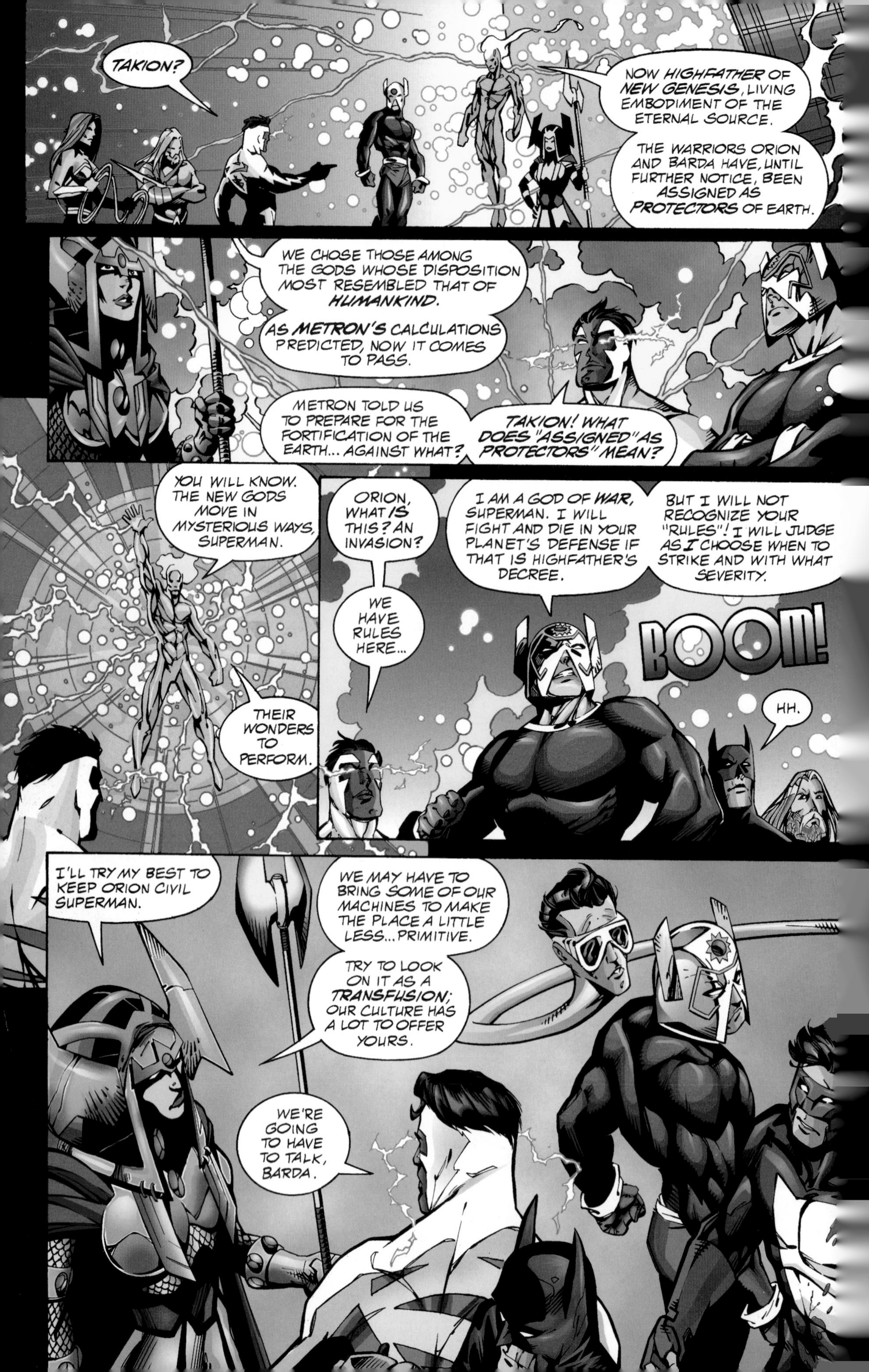
TAKION?
NOW HIGHFATHER OF NEW GENESIS, LIVING EMBODIMENT OF THE ETERNAL SOURCE.
THE WARRIORS ORION AND BARDA HAVE, UNTIL FURTHER NOTICE, BEEN ASSIGNED AS PROTECTORS OF EARTH.
WE CHOSE THOSE AMONG THE GODS WHOSE DISPOSITION MOST RESEMBLED THAT OF HUMANKIND.
AS METRON'S CALCULATIONS PREDICTED, NOW IT COMES TO PASS.
METRON TOLD US TO PREPARE FOR THE FORTIFICATION OF THE EARTH... AGAINST WHAT?
TAKION! WHAT DOES "ASSIGNED" AS PROTECTORS" MEAN?
YOU WILL KNOW. THE NEW GODS MOVE IN MYSTERIOUS WAYS, SUPERMAN.
THEIR WONDERS TO PERFORM.
ORION, WHAT IS THIS? AN INVASION?
WE HAVE RULES HERE...
I AM A GOD OF WAR, SUPERMAN. I WILL FIGHT AND DIE IN YOUR PLANET'S DEFENSE IF THAT IS HIGHFATHER'S DECREE.
BUT I WILL NOT RECOGNIZE YOUR "RULES"! I WILL JUDGE AS I CHOOSE WHEN TO STRIKE AND WITH WHAT SEVERITY.
BOOM!
HH.
I'LL TRY MY BEST TO KEEP ORION CIVIL SUPERMAN.
WE MAY HAVE TO BRING SOME OF OUR MACHINES TO MAKE THE PLACE A LITTLE LESS... PRIMITIVE.
TRY TO LOOK ON IT AS A TRANSFUSION; OUR CULTURE HAS A LOT TO OFFER YOURS.
WE'RE GOING TO HAVE TO TALK, BARDA.

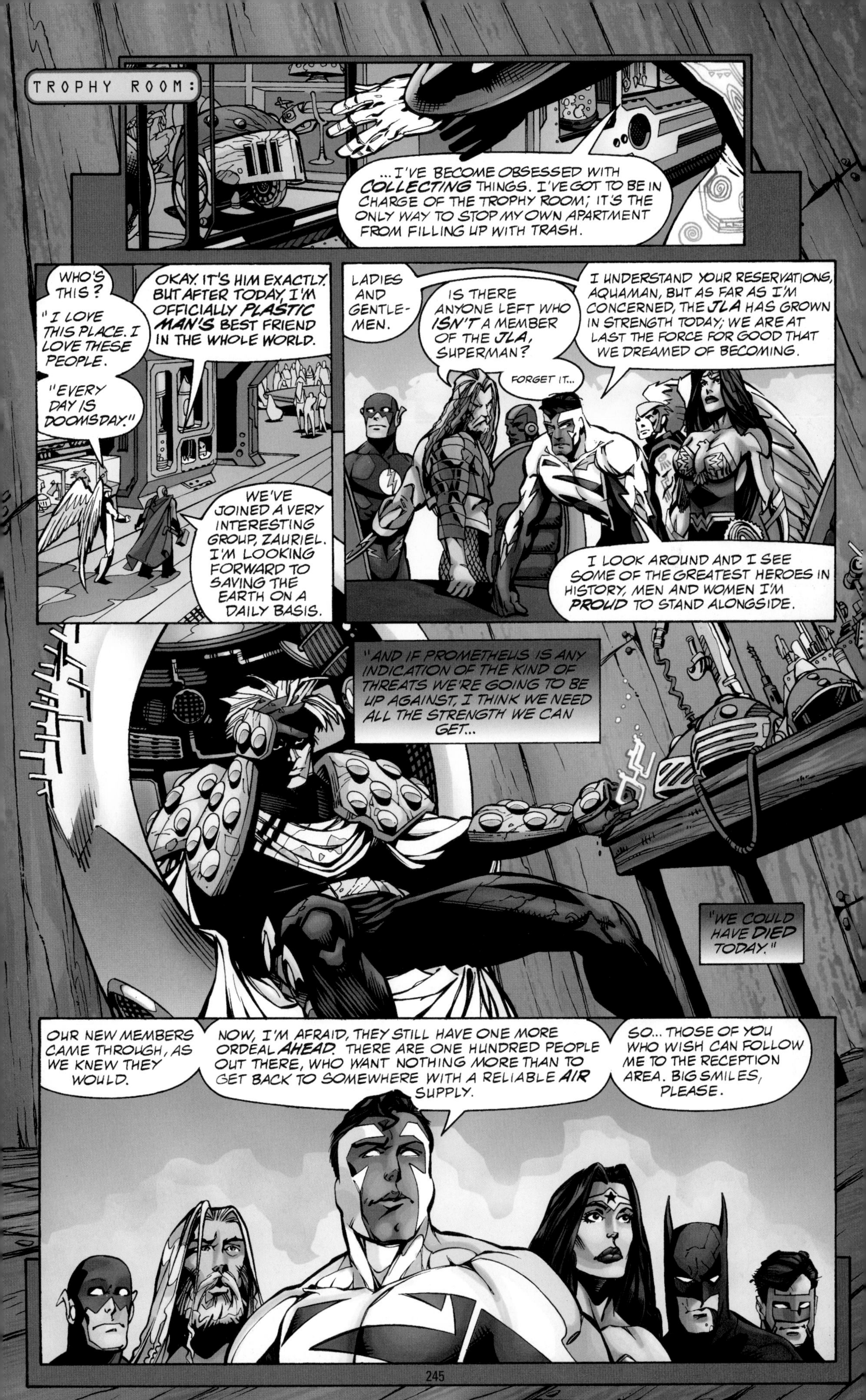
TROPHY ROOM:
...I'VE BECOME OBSESSED WITH COLLECTING THINGS. I'VE GOT TO BE IN CHARGE OF THE TROPHY ROOM; IT'S THE ONLY WAY TO STOP MY OWN APARTMENT FROM FILLING UP WITH TRASH.
WHO'S THIS?
"I LOVE THIS PLACE. I LOVE THESE PEOPLE.
"EVERY DAY IS DOOMSDAY."
OKAY. IT'S HIM EXACTLY. BUT AFTER TODAY, I'M OFFICIALLY PLASTIC MAN'S BEST FRIEND IN THE WHOLE WORLD.
WE'VE JOINED A VERY INTERESTING GROUP, ZAURIEL. I'M LOOKING FORWARD TO SAVING THE EARTH ON A DAILY BASIS.
LADIES AND GENTLE-MEN.
IS THERE ANYONE LEFT WHO ISN'T A MEMBER OF THE JLA, SUPERMAN?
FORGET IT...
I UNDERSTAND YOUR RESERVATIONS, AQUAMAN, BUT AS FAR AS I'M CONCERNED, THE JLA HAS GROWN IN STRENGTH TODAY; WE ARE AT LAST THE FORCE FOR GOOD THAT WE DREAMED OF BECOMING.
I LOOK AROUND AND I SEE SOME OF THE GREATEST HEROES IN HISTORY, MEN AND WOMEN I'M PROUD TO STAND ALONGSIDE.
"AND IF PROMETHEUS IS ANY INDICATION OF THE KIND OF THREATS WE'RE GOING TO BE UP AGAINST, I THINK WE NEED ALL THE STRENGTH WE CAN GET...
"WE COULD HAVE DIED TODAY."
OUR NEW MEMBERS CAME THROUGH, AS WE KNEW THEY WOULD.
NOW, I'M AFRAID, THEY STILL HAVE ONE MORE ORDEAL AHEAD. THERE ARE ONE HUNDRED PEOPLE OUT THERE, WHO WANT NOTHING MORE THAN TO GET BACK TO SOMEWHERE WITH A RELIABLE AIR SUPPLY.
SO... THOSE OF YOU WHO WISH CAN FOLLOW ME TO THE RECEPTION AREA. BIG SMILES, PLEASE.

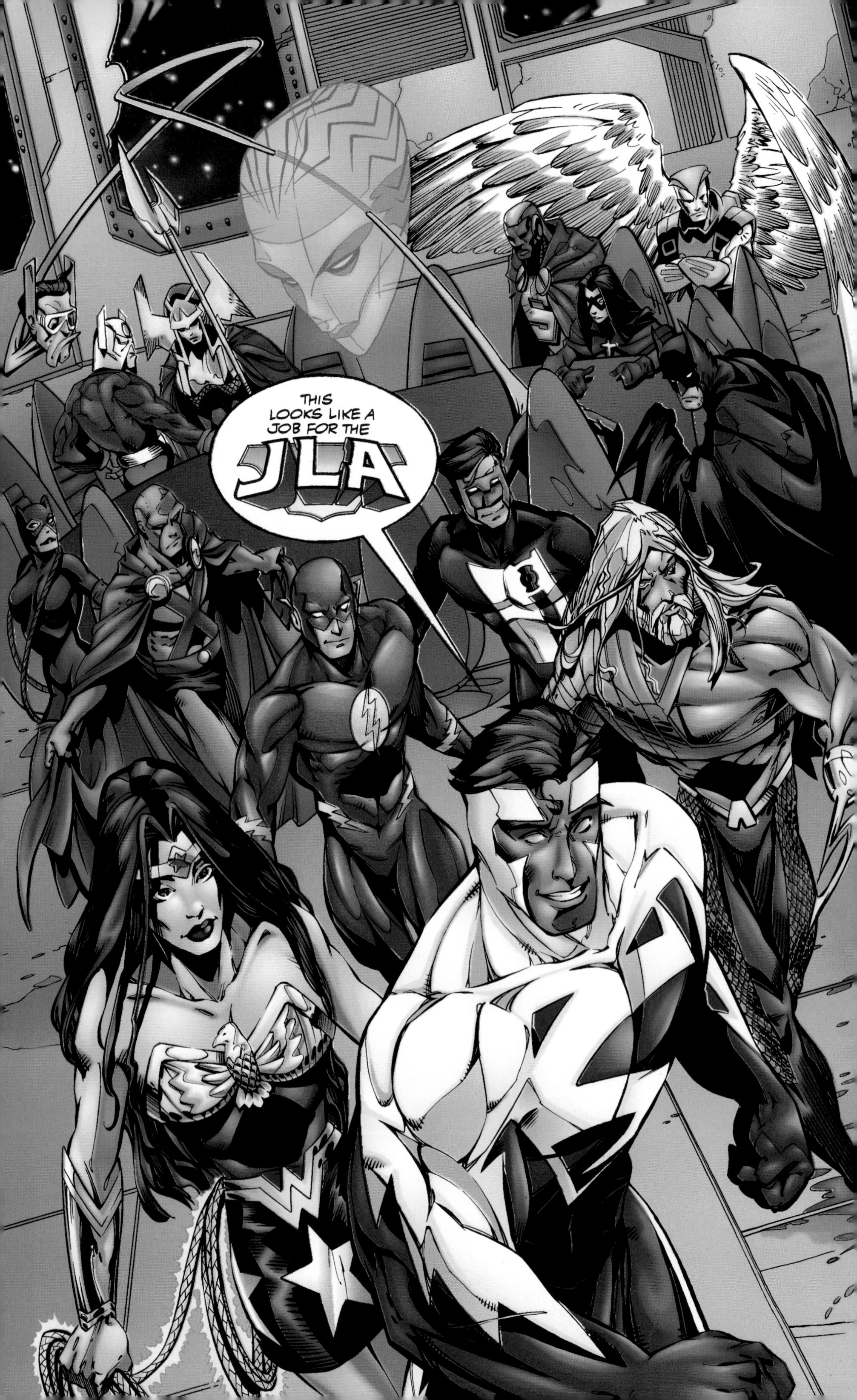
THIS LOOKS LIKE A JOB FOR THE JLA

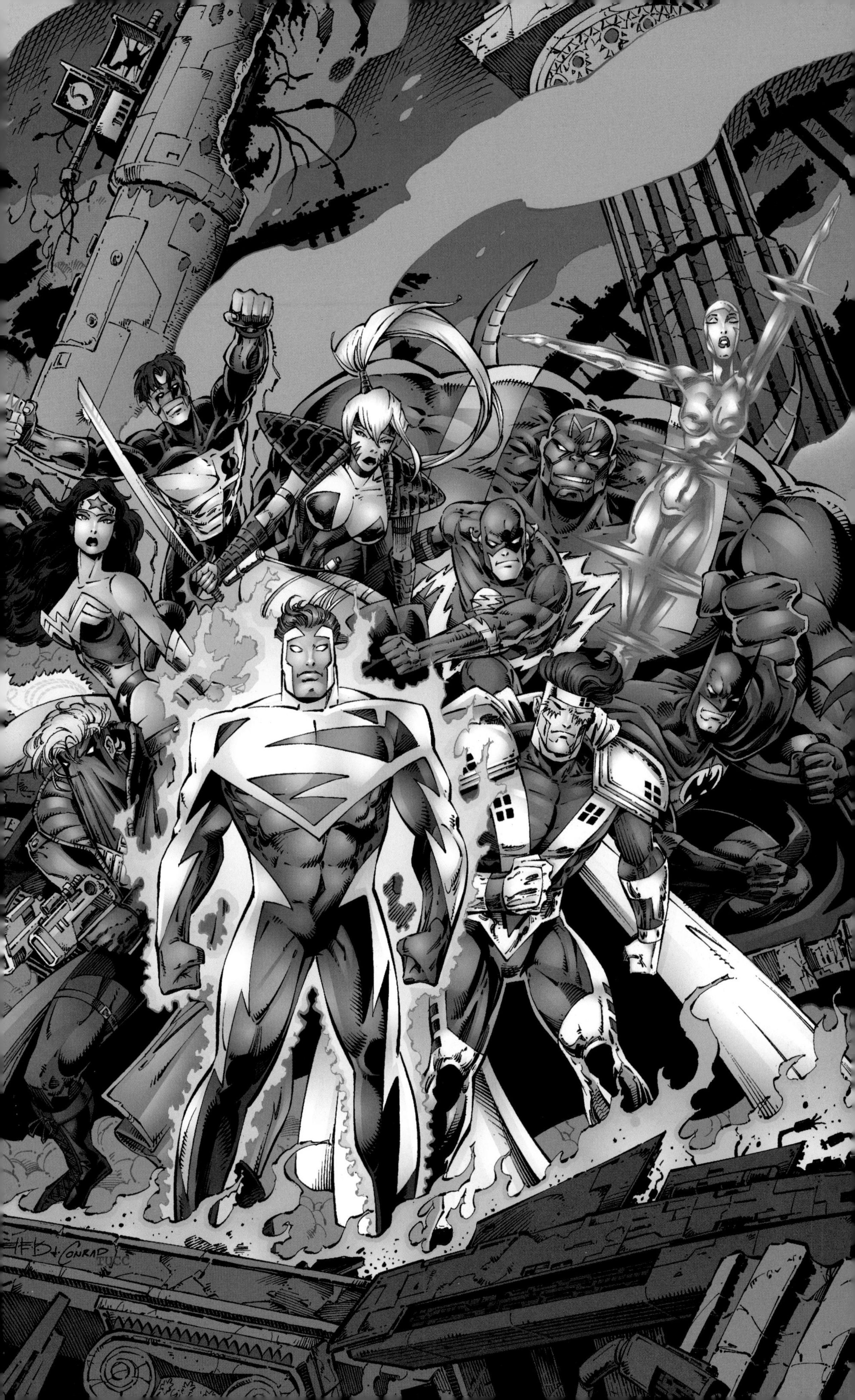

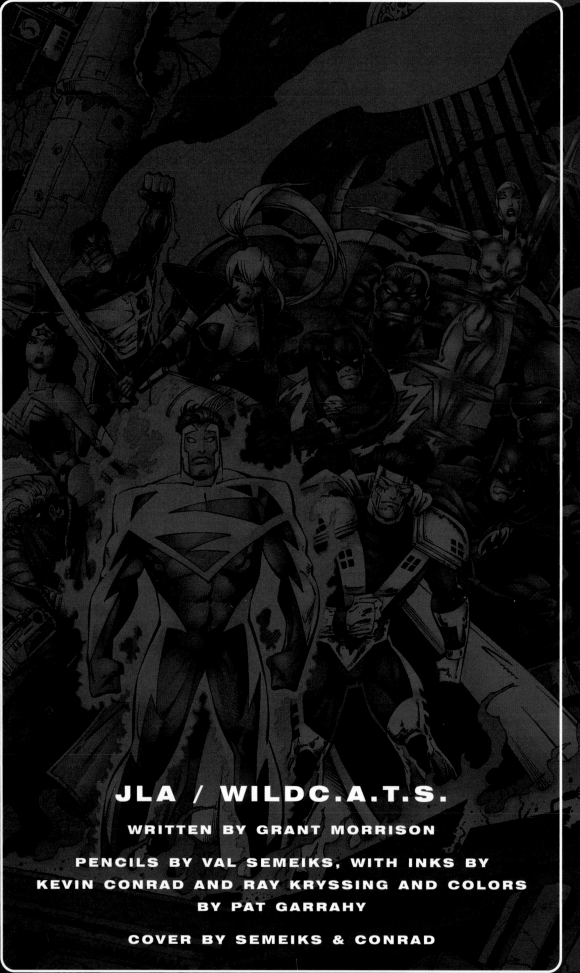

JLA / WILDC.A.T.S.

WRITTEN BY GRANT MORRISON

PENCILS BY VAL SEMEIKS, WITH INKS BY KEVIN CONRAD AND RAY KRYSSING AND COLORS BY PAT GARRAHY

COVER BY SEMEIKS & CONRAD

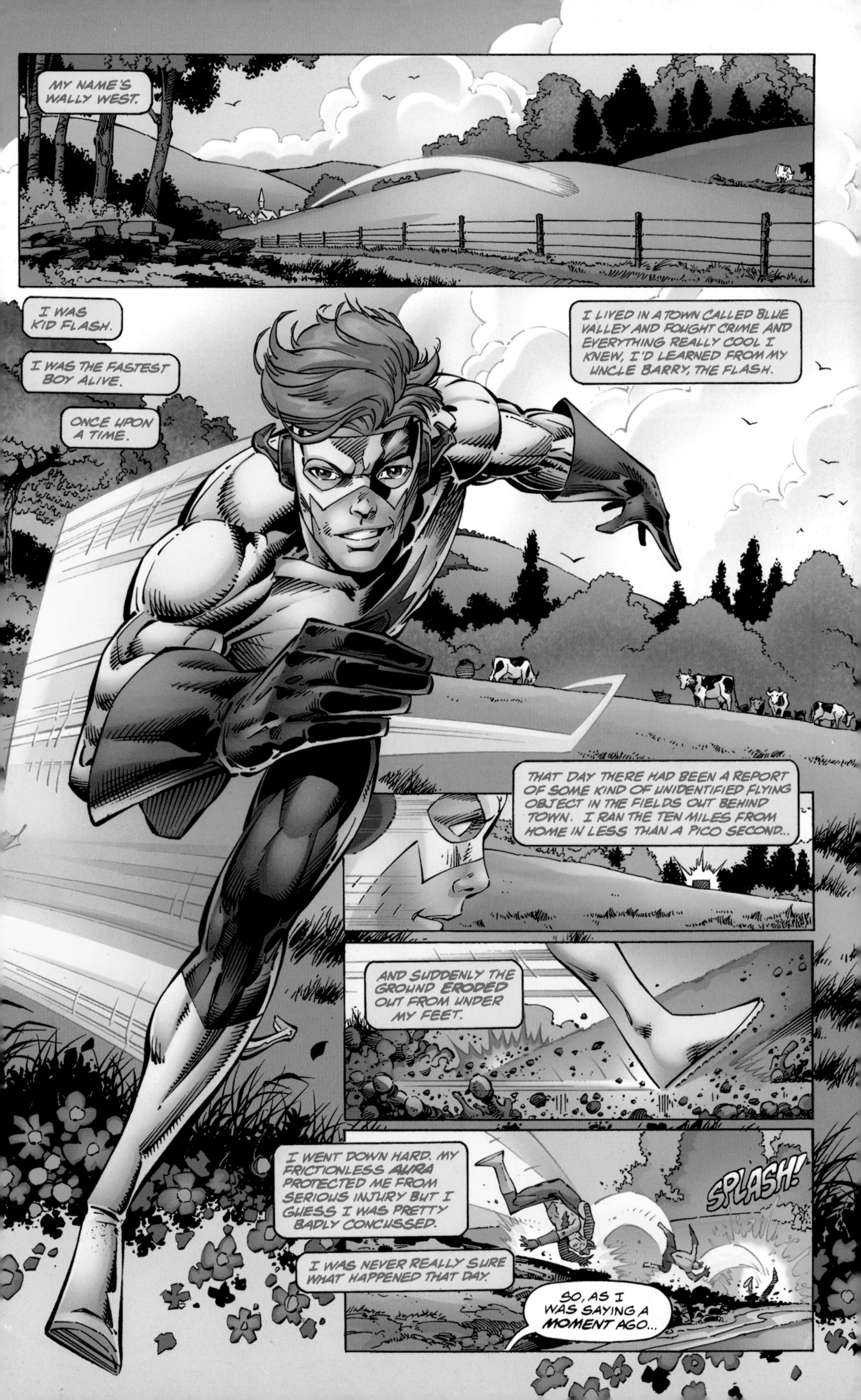

MY NAME'S WALLY WEST.
I WAS KID FLASH.
I WAS THE FASTEST BOY ALIVE.
ONCE UPON A TIME.
I LIVED IN A TOWN CALLED BLUE VALLEY AND FOUGHT CRIME AND EVERYTHING REALLY COOL I KNEW, I'D LEARNED FROM MY UNCLE BARRY, THE FLASH.
THAT DAY THERE HAD BEEN A REPORT OF SOME KIND OF UNIDENTIFIED FLYING OBJECT IN THE FIELDS OUT BEHIND TOWN. I RAN THE TEN MILES FROM HOME IN LESS THAN A PICO SECOND...
AND SUDDENLY THE GROUND ERODED OUT FROM UNDER MY FEET.
I WENT DOWN HARD. MY FRICTIONLESS AURA PROTECTED ME FROM SERIOUS INJURY BUT I GUESS I WAS PRETTY BADLY CONCUSSED.
I WAS NEVER REALLY SURE WHAT HAPPENED THAT DAY.
SPLASH!
SO, AS I WAS SAYING A MOMENT AGO...

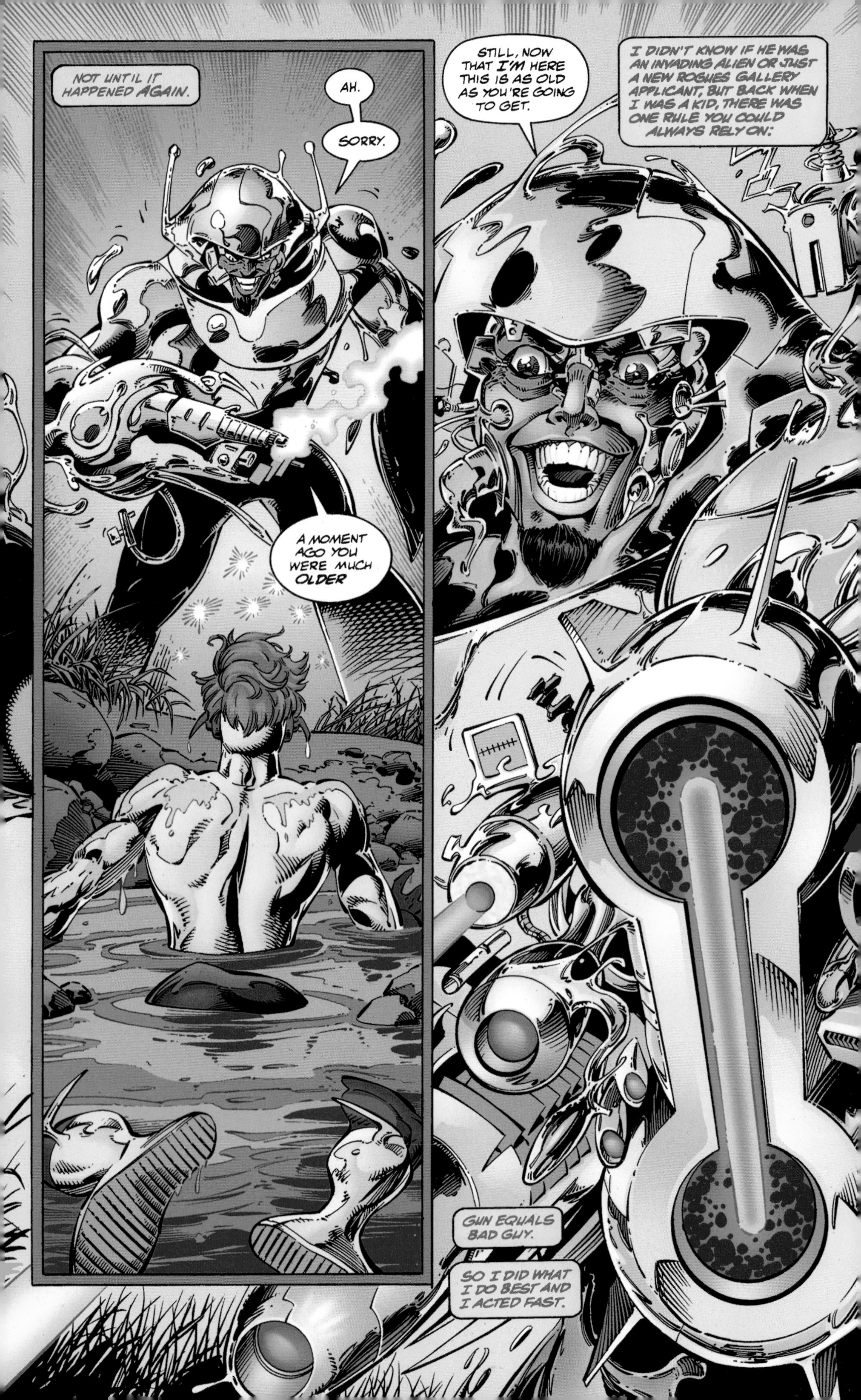
NOT UNTIL IT HAPPENED AGAIN.
AH.
SORRY.
A MOMENT AGO YOU WERE MUCH OLDER
STILL, NOW THAT I'M HERE THIS IS AS OLD AS YOU'RE GOING TO GET.
I DIDN'T KNOW IF HE WAS AN INVADING ALIEN OR JUST A NEW ROGUES GALLERY APPLICANT, BUT BACK WHEN I WAS A KID, THERE WAS ONE RULE YOU COULD ALWAYS RELY ON:
GUN EQUALS BAD GUY.
SO I DID WHAT I DO BEST AND I ACTED FAST.

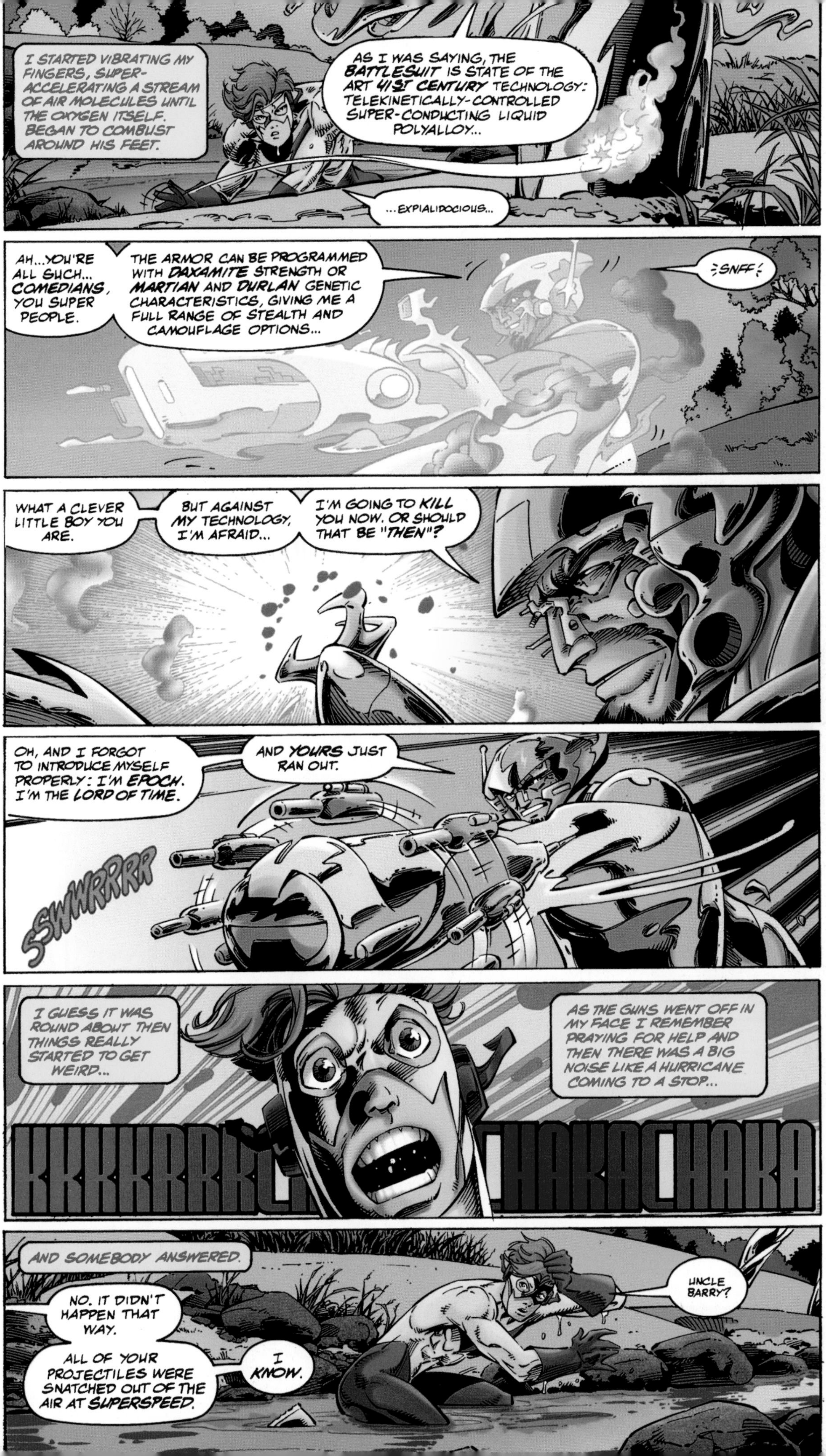

I STARTED VIBRATING MY FINGERS, SUPER-ACCELERATING A STREAM OF AIR MOLECULES UNTIL THE OXYGEN ITSELF BEGAN TO COMBUST AROUND HIS FEET.
AS I WAS SAYING, THE BATTLESUIT IS STATE OF THE ART 41ST CENTURY TECHNOLOGY: TELEKINETICALLY-CONTROLLED SUPER-CONDUCTING LIQUID POLYALLOY...
...EXPIALIDOCIOUS...
AH...YOU'RE ALL SUCH... COMEDIANS, YOU SUPER PEOPLE.
THE ARMOR CAN BE PROGRAMMED WITH DAXAMITE STRENGTH OR MARTIAN AND DURLAN GENETIC CHARACTERISTICS, GIVING ME A FULL RANGE OF STEALTH AND CAMOUFLAGE OPTIONS...
SNFF
WHAT A CLEVER LITTLE BOY YOU ARE.
BUT AGAINST MY TECHNOLOGY, I'M AFRAID...
I'M GOING TO KILL YOU NOW. OR SHOULD THAT BE "THEN"?
OH, AND I FORGOT TO INTRODUCE MYSELF PROPERLY: I'M EPOCH. I'M THE LORD OF TIME.
AND YOURS JUST RAN OUT.
SSWWRRRP
I GUESS IT WAS ROUND ABOUT THEN THINGS REALLY STARTED TO GET WEIRD...
AS THE GUNS WENT OFF IN MY FACE I REMEMBER PRAYING FOR HELP AND THEN THERE WAS A BIG NOISE LIKE A HURRICANE COMING TO A STOP...
KKKKRRRK
CHAKACHAKA
AND SOMEBODY ANSWERED.
UNCLE BARRY?
NO. IT DIDN'T HAPPEN THAT WAY.
ALL OF YOUR PROJECTILES WERE SNATCHED OUT OF THE AIR AT SUPERSPEED.
I KNOW.

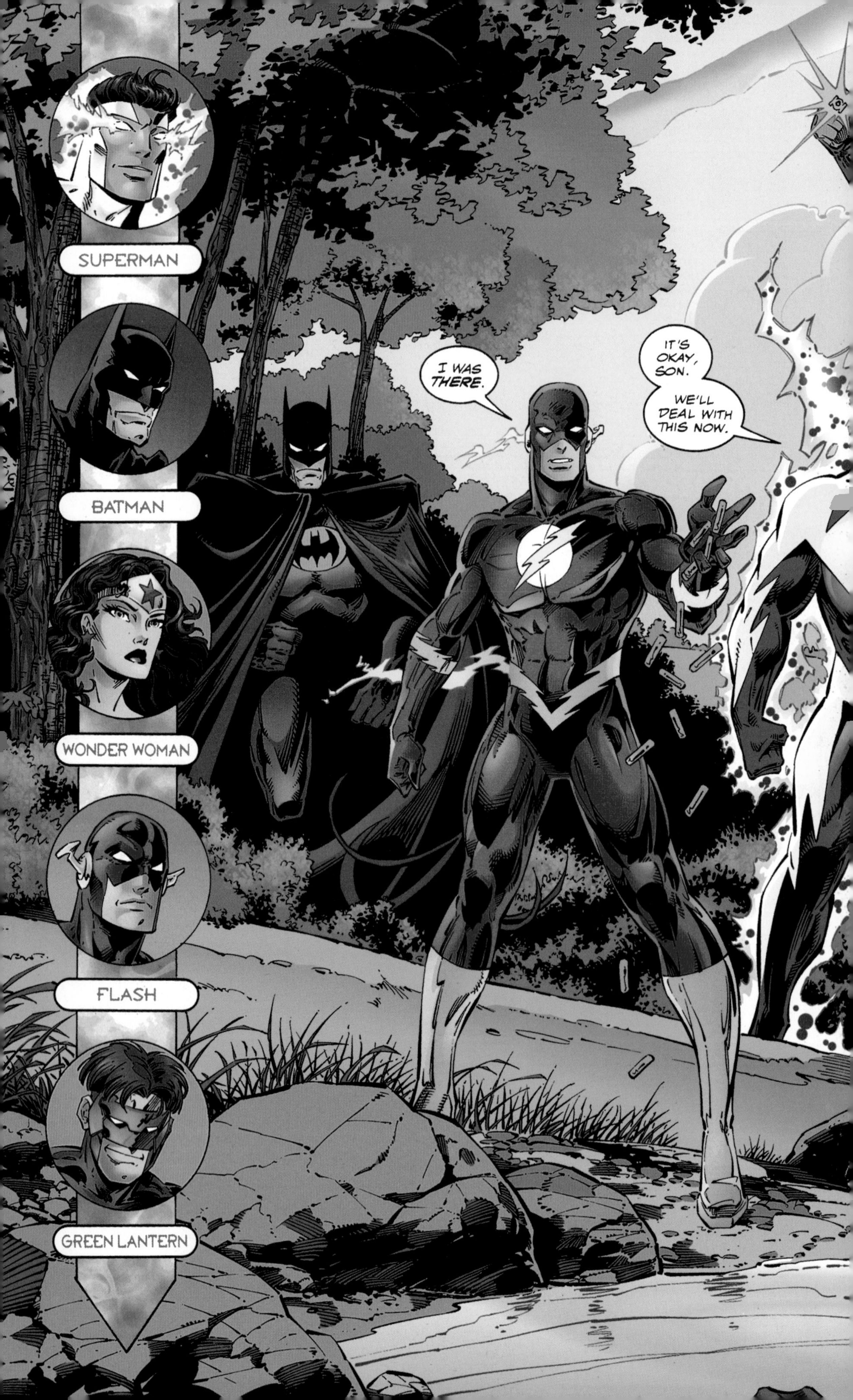
SUPERMAN
BATMAN
WONDER WOMAN
FLASH
GREEN LANTERN
I WAS THERE.
IT'S OKAY, SON.
WE'LL DEAL WITH THIS NOW.

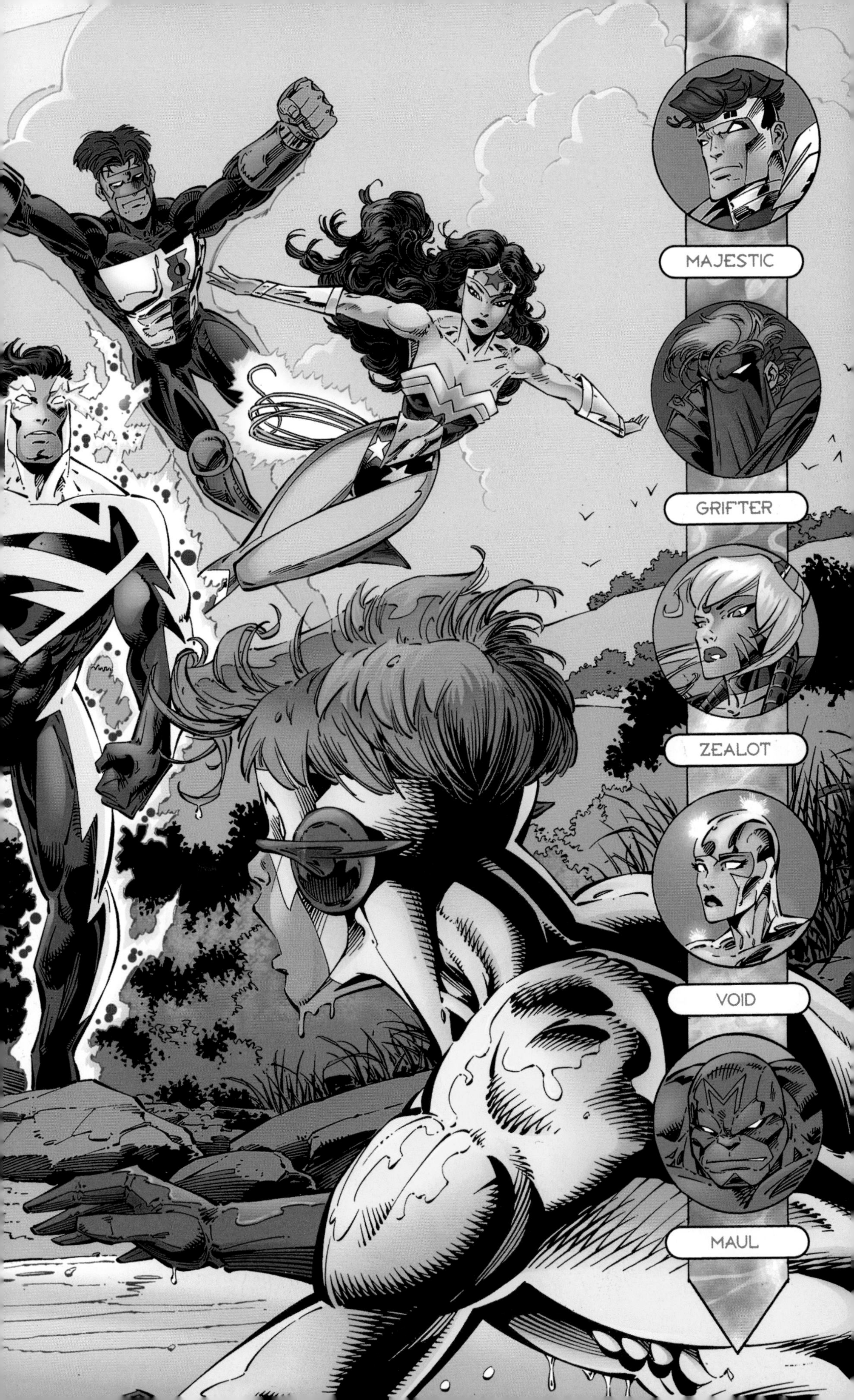

MAJESTIC
GRIFTER
ZEALOT
VOID
MAUL

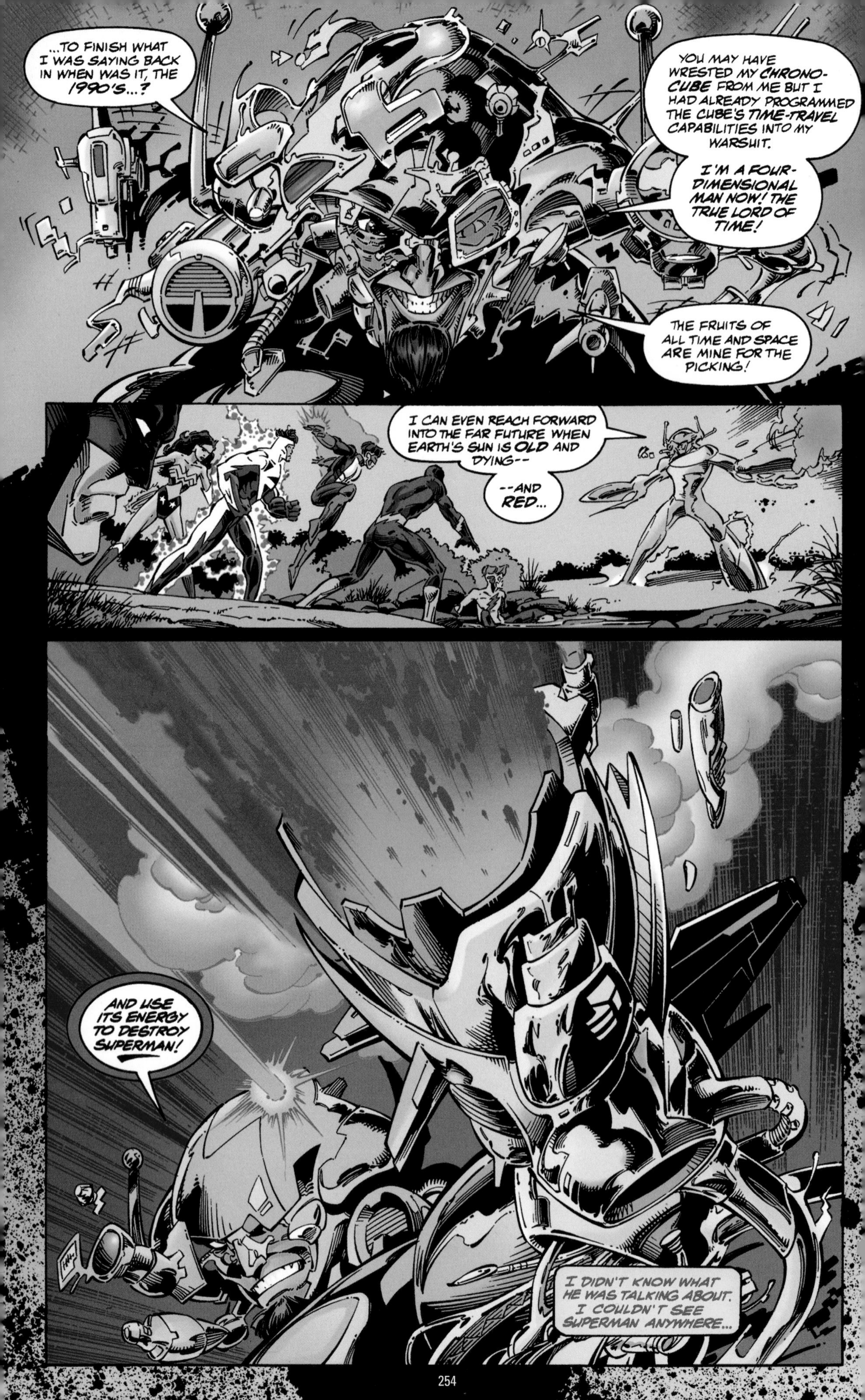
...TO FINISH WHAT I WAS SAYING BACK IN WHEN WAS IT, THE 1990'S...?
YOU MAY HAVE WRESTED MY CHRONO-CUBE FROM ME BUT I HAD ALREADY PROGRAMMED THE CUBE'S TIME-TRAVEL CAPABILITIES INTO MY WARSUIT.
I'M A FOUR-DIMENSIONAL MAN NOW! THE TRUE LORD OF TIME!
THE FRUITS OF ALL TIME AND SPACE ARE MINE FOR THE PICKING!
I CAN EVEN REACH FORWARD INTO THE FAR FUTURE WHEN EARTH'S SUN IS OLD AND DYING--
--AND RED...
AND USE ITS ENERGY TO DESTROY SUPERMAN!
I DIDN'T KNOW WHAT HE WAS TALKING ABOUT. I COULDN'T SEE SUPERMAN ANYWHERE...

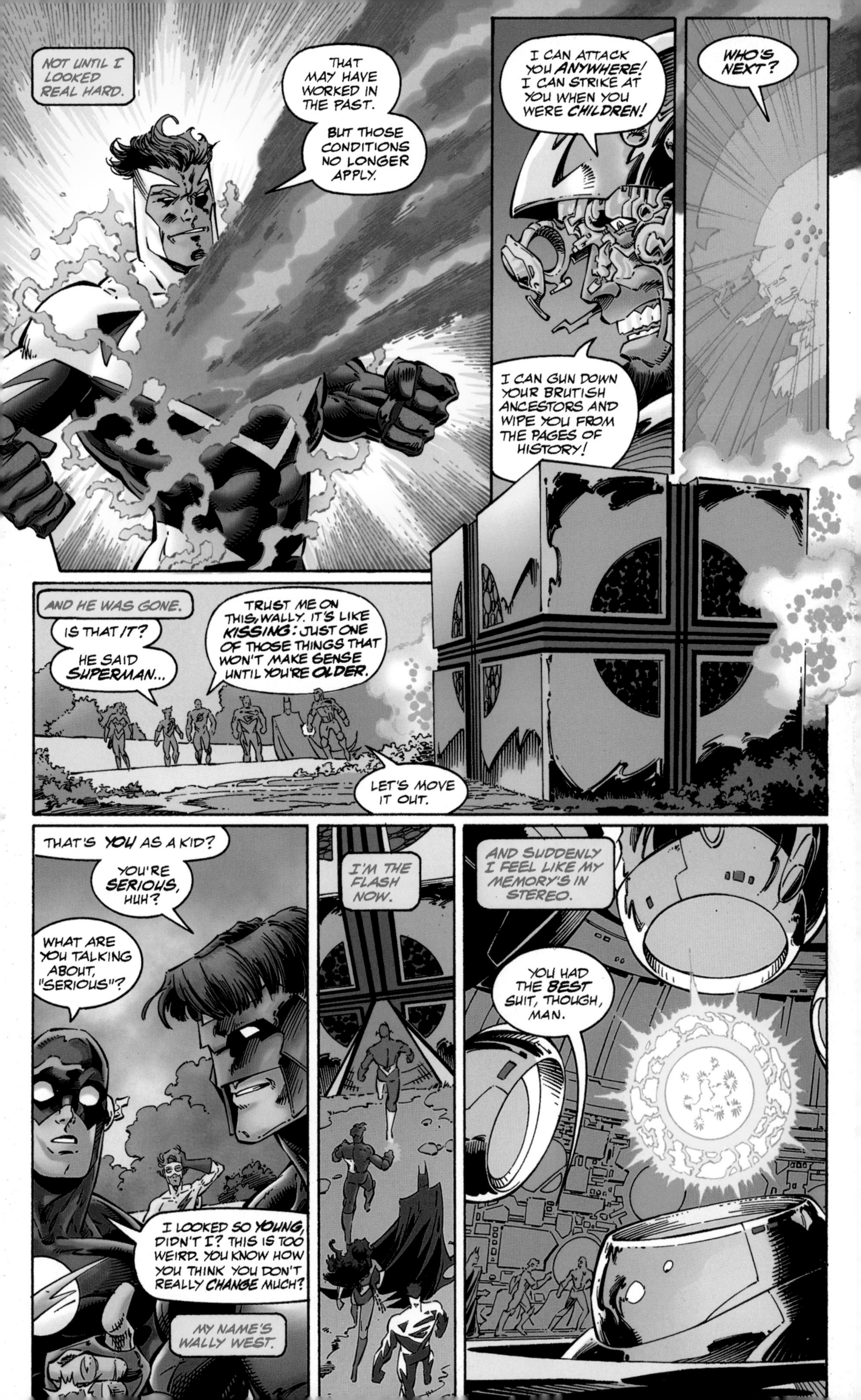
NOT UNTIL I LOOKED REAL HARD.
THAT MAY HAVE WORKED IN THE PAST.
BUT THOSE CONDITIONS NO LONGER APPLY.
I CAN ATTACK YOU ANYWHERE! I CAN STRIKE AT YOU WHEN YOU WERE CHILDREN!
I CAN GUN DOWN YOUR BRUTISH ANCESTORS AND WIPE YOU FROM THE PAGES OF HISTORY!
WHO'S NEXT?
AND HE WAS GONE.
IS THAT IT?
HE SAID SUPERMAN...
TRUST ME ON THIS, WALLY. IT'S LIKE KISSING: JUST ONE OF THOSE THINGS THAT WON'T MAKE SENSE UNTIL YOU'RE OLDER.
LET'S MOVE IT OUT.
THAT'S YOU AS A KID?
YOU'RE SERIOUS, HUH?
WHAT ARE YOU TALKING ABOUT, "SERIOUS"?
I LOOKED SO YOUNG, DIDN'T I? THIS IS TOO WEIRD. YOU KNOW HOW YOU THINK YOU DON'T REALLY CHANGE MUCH?
MY NAME'S WALLY WEST.
I'M THE FLASH NOW.
AND SUDDENLY I FEEL LIKE MY MEMORY'S IN STEREO.
YOU HAD THE BEST SUIT, THOUGH, MAN.

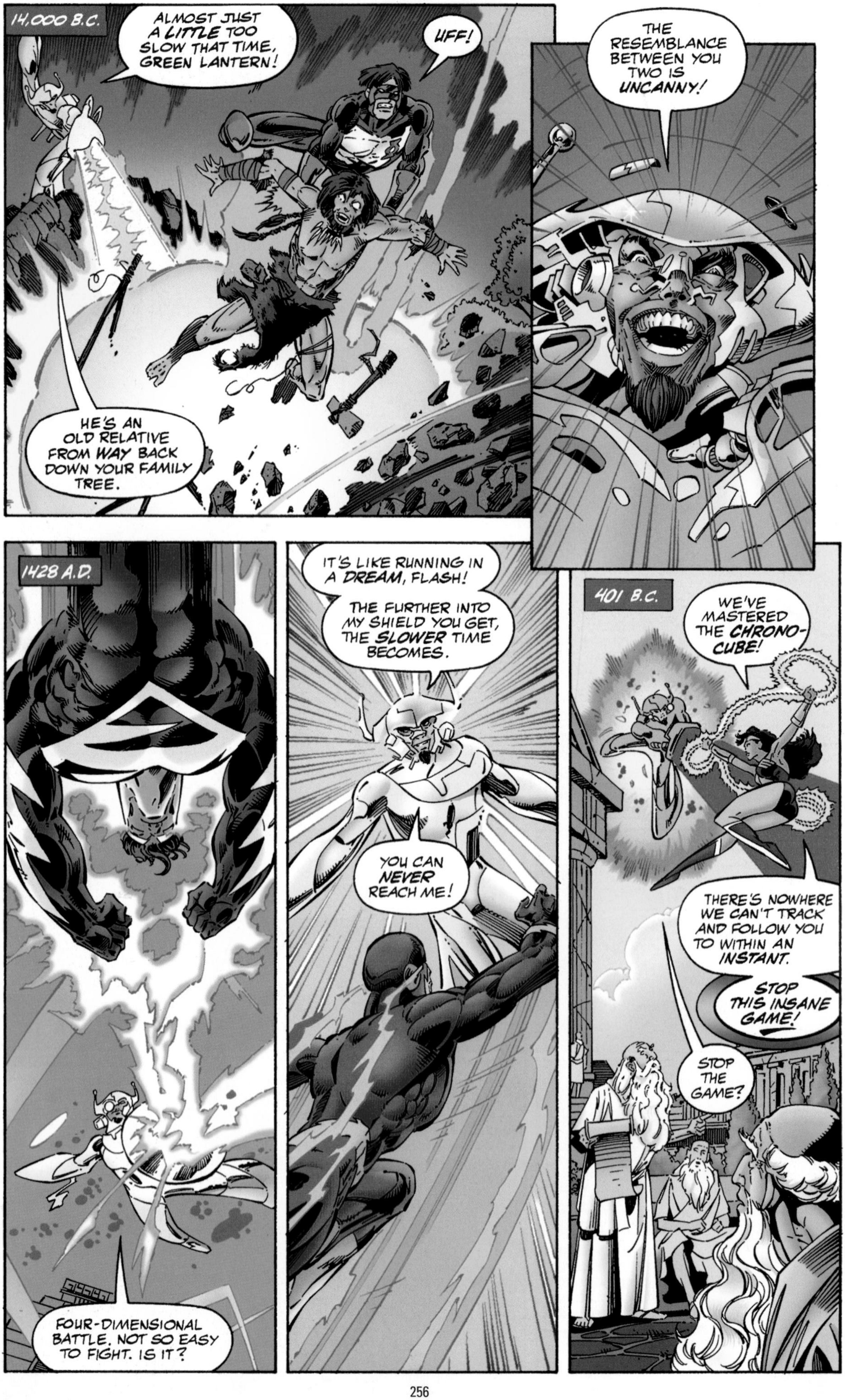
14,000 B.C.
ALMOST JUST A LITTLE TOO SLOW THAT TIME, GREEN LANTERN!
UFF!
HE'S AN OLD RELATIVE FROM WAY BACK DOWN YOUR FAMILY TREE.
THE RESEMBLANCE BETWEEN YOU TWO IS UNCANNY!
1428 A.D.
FOUR-DIMENSIONAL BATTLE. NOT SO EASY TO FIGHT. IS IT?
IT'S LIKE RUNNING IN A DREAM, FLASH!
THE FURTHER INTO MY SHIELD YOU GET, THE SLOWER TIME BECOMES.
YOU CAN NEVER REACH ME!
401 B.C.
WE'VE MASTERED THE CHRONO-CUBE!
THERE'S NOWHERE WE CAN'T TRACK AND FOLLOW YOU TO WITHIN AN INSTANT.
STOP THIS INSANE GAME!
STOP THE GAME?

THE GAME HAS ONLY BEGUN!

2016 A.D.

THIS IS *INSANE.*

AND HIS ARMOR'S *MUTATING* RAPIDLY. WE MUST STOP HIM *SOON.*

WHAT DOES "SOON" MEAN NOW?

WE NEED TO LEARN *TACTICAL* MANEUVERS...

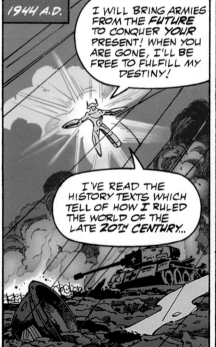

1944 A.D.

I WILL BRING ARMIES FROM THE *FUTURE* TO CONQUER *YOUR* PRESENT! WHEN YOU ARE GONE, I'LL BE FREE TO FULFILL MY *DESTINY!*

I'VE READ THE HISTORY TEXTS WHICH TELL OF HOW *I* RULED THE WORLD OF THE LATE *20TH* CENTURY...

WE'RE RIGHT BEHIND YOU FOR AS LONG AS IT TAKES.

WE CAN MATCH YOUR EVERY MOVE. YOU CAN'T *WIN.*

DON'T YOU *UNDERSTAND?!* I ALREADY *HAVE.*

ONE LAST MOVE, SUPERMAN.

CHECKMATE.

HHUUOIIIII

257

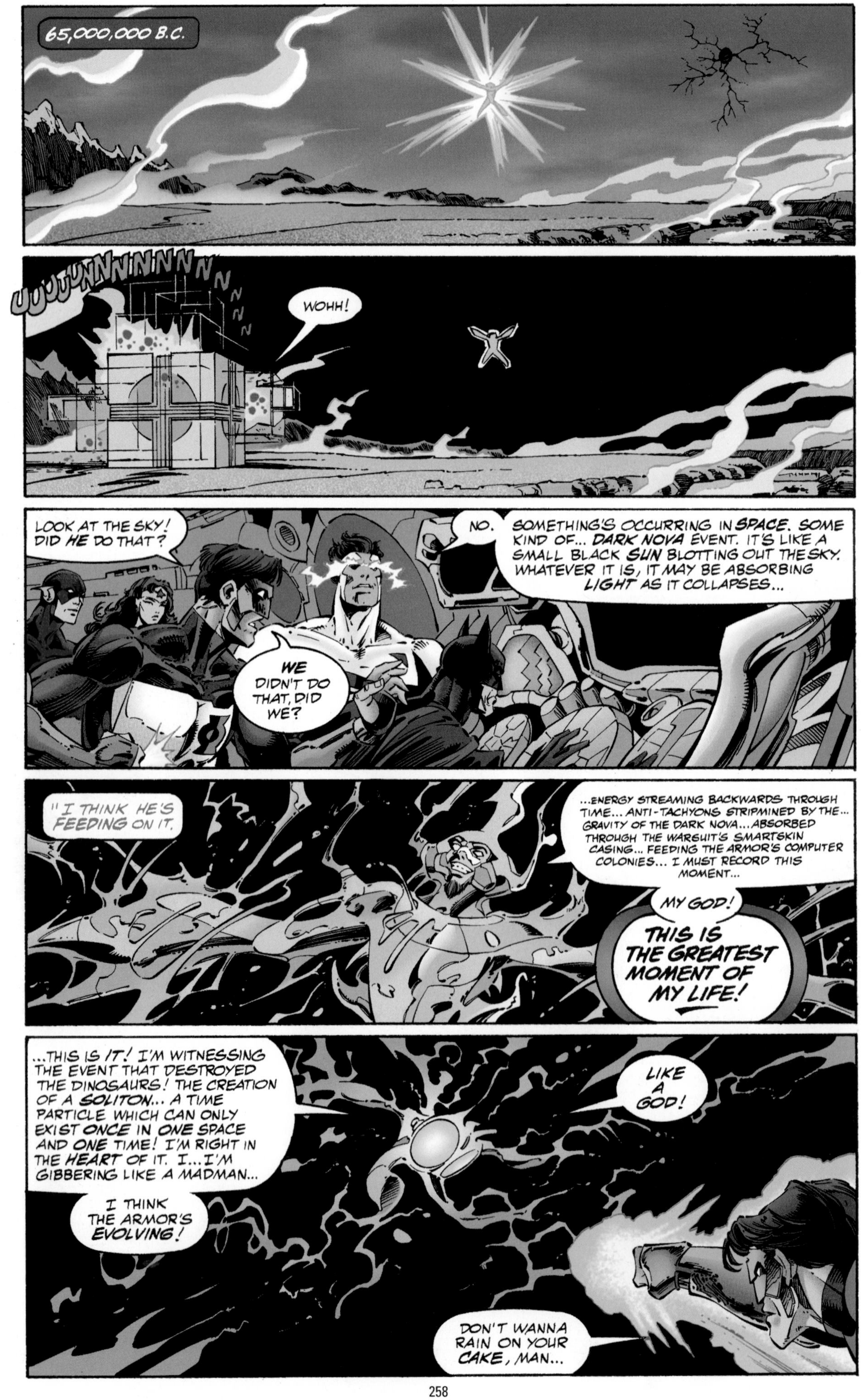

65,000,000 B.C.
UUUUNNNNNNNNNNNNNN
WOHH!
LOOK AT THE SKY! DID HE DO THAT?
NO.
SOMETHING'S OCCURRING IN SPACE. SOME KIND OF... DARK NOVA EVENT. IT'S LIKE A SMALL BLACK SUN BLOTTING OUT THE SKY. WHATEVER IT IS, IT MAY BE ABSORBING LIGHT AS IT COLLAPSES...
WE DIDN'T DO THAT, DID WE?
"I THINK HE'S FEEDING ON IT.
...ENERGY STREAMING BACKWARDS THROUGH TIME... ANTI-TACHYONS STRIPMINED BY THE... GRAVITY OF THE DARK NOVA... ABSORBED THROUGH THE WARSUIT'S SMARTSKIN CASING... FEEDING THE ARMOR'S COMPUTER COLONIES... I MUST RECORD THIS MOMENT...
MY GOD!
THIS IS THE GREATEST MOMENT OF MY LIFE!
...THIS IS IT! I'M WITNESSING THE EVENT THAT DESTROYED THE DINOSAURS! THE CREATION OF A SOLITON... A TIME PARTICLE WHICH CAN ONLY EXIST ONCE IN ONE SPACE AND ONE TIME! I'M RIGHT IN THE HEART OF IT. I... I'M GIBBERING LIKE A MADMAN...
LIKE A GOD!
I THINK THE ARMOR'S EVOLVING!
DON'T WANNA RAIN ON YOUR CAKE, MAN...

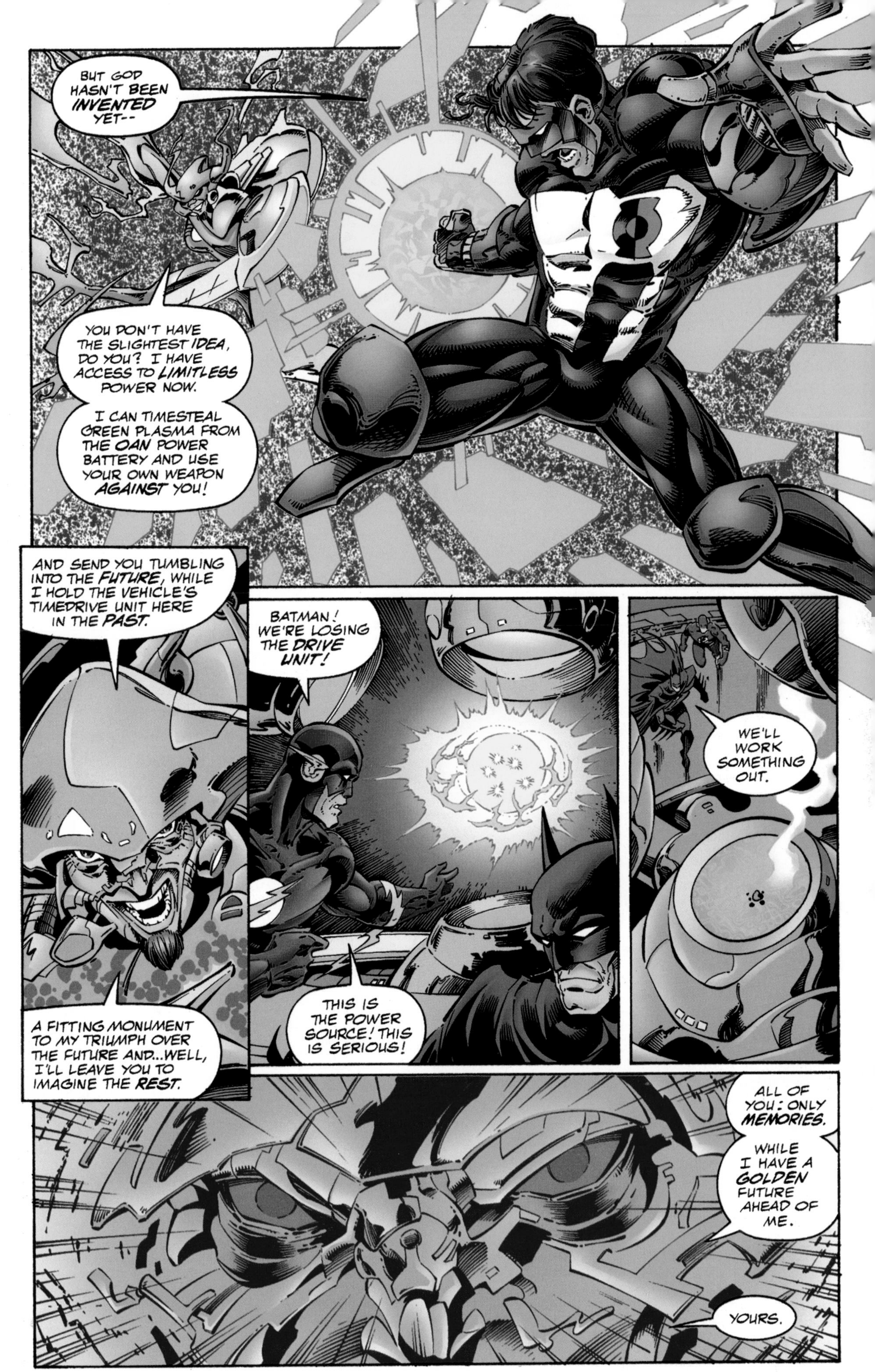
BUT GOD HASN'T BEEN INVENTED YET--
YOU DON'T HAVE THE SLIGHTEST IDEA, DO YOU? I HAVE ACCESS TO LIMITLESS POWER NOW.
I CAN TIMESTEAL GREEN PLASMA FROM THE OAN POWER BATTERY AND USE YOUR OWN WEAPON AGAINST YOU!
AND SEND YOU TUMBLING INTO THE FUTURE, WHILE I HOLD THE VEHICLE'S TIMEDRIVE UNIT HERE IN THE PAST.
A FITTING MONUMENT TO MY TRIUMPH OVER THE FUTURE AND...WELL, I'LL LEAVE YOU TO IMAGINE THE REST.
BATMAN! WE'RE LOSING THE DRIVE UNIT!
THIS IS THE POWER SOURCE! THIS IS SERIOUS!
WE'LL WORK SOMETHING OUT.
ALL OF YOU: ONLY MEMORIES.
WHILE I HAVE A GOLDEN FUTURE AHEAD OF ME.
YOURS.

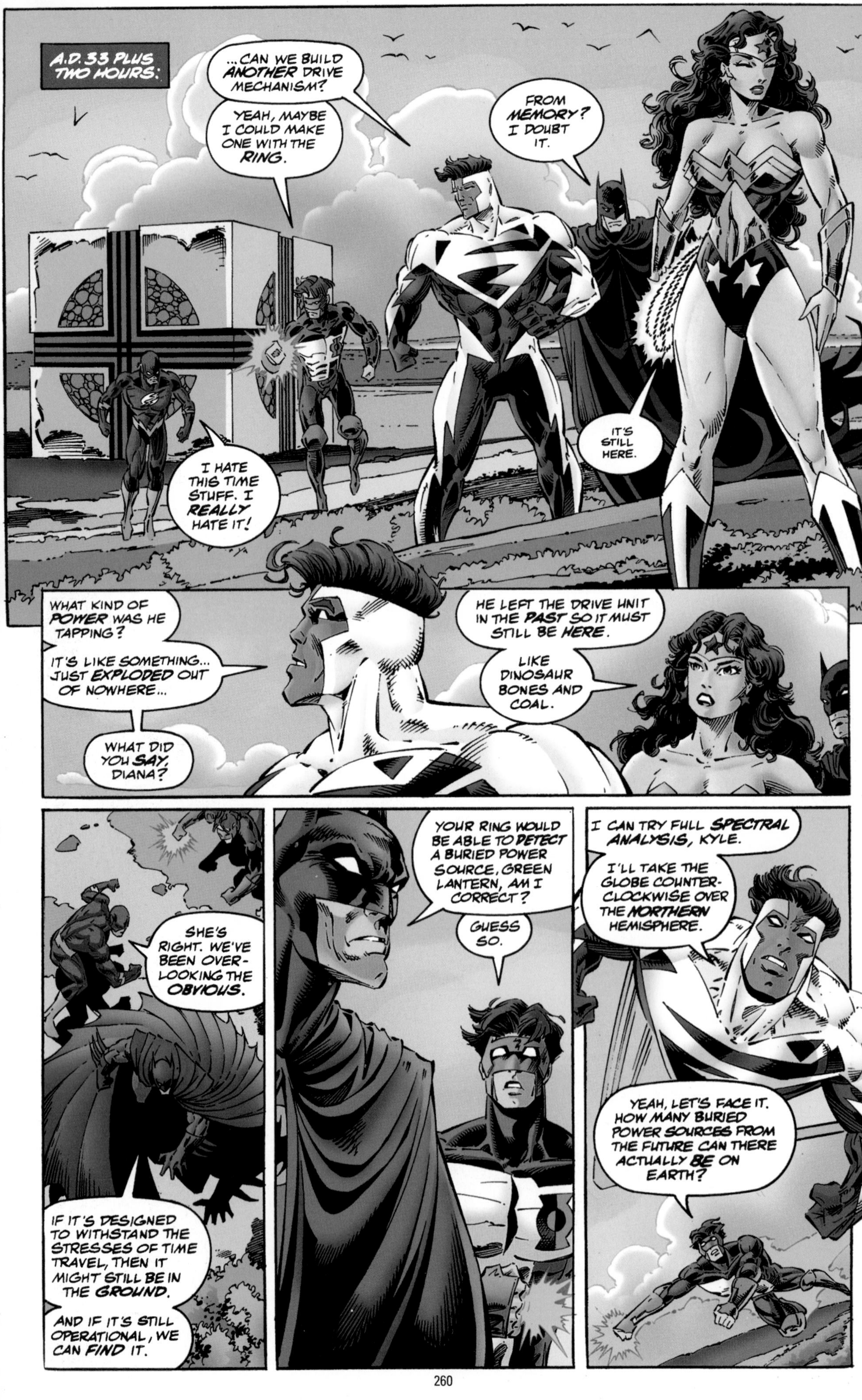
A.D. 33 PLUS TWO HOURS:
...CAN WE BUILD ANOTHER DRIVE MECHANISM?
YEAH, MAYBE I COULD MAKE ONE WITH THE RING.
FROM MEMORY? I DOUBT IT.
I HATE THIS TIME STUFF. I REALLY HATE IT!
IT'S STILL HERE.
WHAT KIND OF POWER WAS HE TAPPING?
IT'S LIKE SOMETHING... JUST EXPLODED OUT OF NOWHERE...
WHAT DID YOU SAY, DIANA?
HE LEFT THE DRIVE UNIT IN THE PAST SO IT MUST STILL BE HERE.
LIKE DINOSAUR BONES AND COAL.
SHE'S RIGHT. WE'VE BEEN OVER-LOOKING THE OBVIOUS.
IF IT'S DESIGNED TO WITHSTAND THE STRESSES OF TIME TRAVEL, THEN IT MIGHT STILL BE IN THE GROUND.
AND IF IT'S STILL OPERATIONAL, WE CAN FIND IT.
YOUR RING WOULD BE ABLE TO DETECT A BURIED POWER SOURCE, GREEN LANTERN, AM I CORRECT?
GUESS SO.
I CAN TRY FULL SPECTRAL ANALYSIS, KYLE.
I'LL TAKE THE GLOBE COUNTER-CLOCKWISE OVER THE NORTHERN HEMISPHERE.
YEAH, LET'S FACE IT. HOW MANY BURIED POWER SOURCES FROM THE FUTURE CAN THERE ACTUALLY BE ON EARTH?

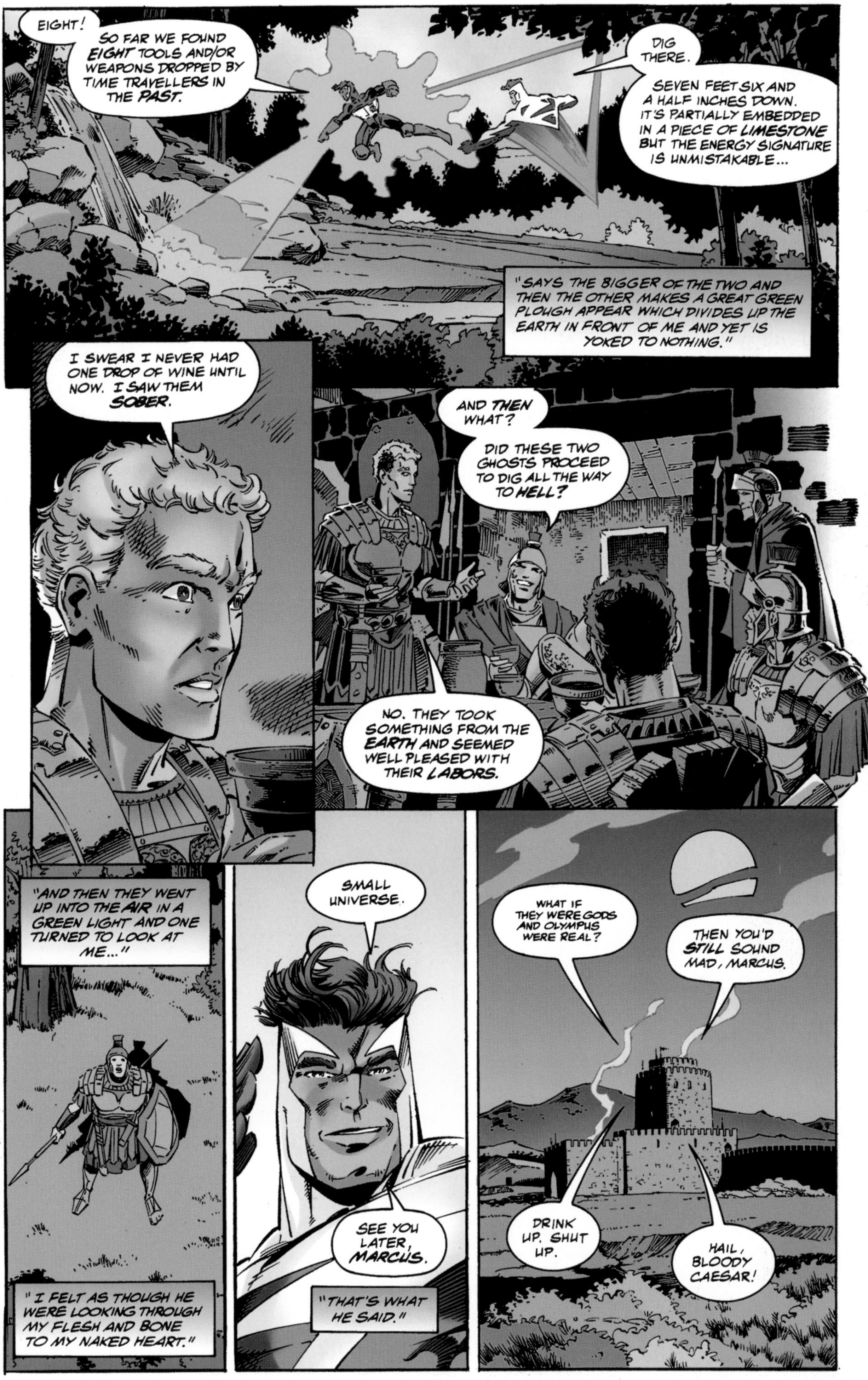
EIGHT!
SO FAR WE FOUND EIGHT TOOLS AND/OR WEAPONS DROPPED BY TIME TRAVELLERS IN THE PAST.
DIG THERE.
SEVEN FEET SIX AND A HALF INCHES DOWN. IT'S PARTIALLY EMBEDDED IN A PIECE OF LIMESTONE BUT THE ENERGY SIGNATURE IS UNMISTAKABLE...
"SAYS THE BIGGER OF THE TWO AND THEN THE OTHER MAKES A GREAT GREEN PLOUGH APPEAR WHICH DIVIDES UP THE EARTH IN FRONT OF ME AND YET IS YOKED TO NOTHING."
I SWEAR I NEVER HAD ONE DROP OF WINE UNTIL NOW. I SAW THEM SOBER.
AND THEN WHAT?
DID THESE TWO GHOSTS PROCEED TO DIG ALL THE WAY TO HELL?
NO. THEY TOOK SOMETHING FROM THE EARTH AND SEEMED WELL PLEASED WITH THEIR LABORS.
"AND THEN THEY WENT UP INTO THE AIR IN A GREEN LIGHT AND ONE TURNED TO LOOK AT ME..."
"I FELT AS THOUGH HE WERE LOOKING THROUGH MY FLESH AND BONE TO MY NAKED HEART."
SMALL UNIVERSE.
SEE YOU LATER, MARCUS.
"THAT'S WHAT HE SAID."
WHAT IF THEY WERE GODS AND OLYMPUS WERE REAL?
THEN YOU'D STILL SOUND MAD, MARCUS.
DRINK UP. SHUT UP.
HAIL, BLOODY CAESAR!

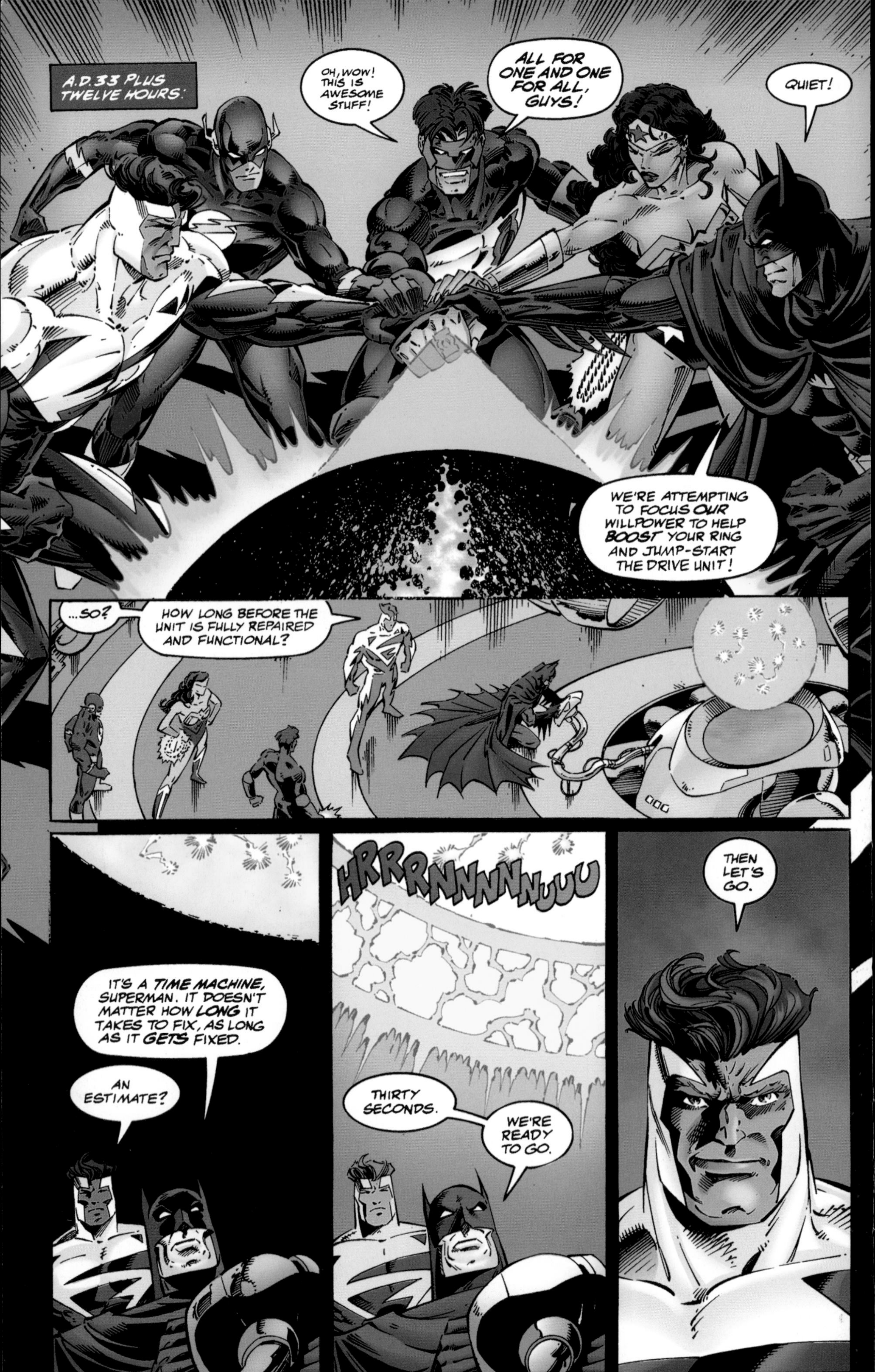
A.D. 33 PLUS TWELVE HOURS:
OH, WOW! THIS IS AWESOME STUFF!
ALL FOR ONE AND ONE FOR ALL, GUYS!
QUIET!
WE'RE ATTEMPTING TO FOCUS OUR WILLPOWER TO HELP BOOST YOUR RING AND JUMP-START THE DRIVE UNIT!
...SO?
HOW LONG BEFORE THE UNIT IS FULLY REPAIRED AND FUNCTIONAL?
IT'S A TIME MACHINE, SUPERMAN. IT DOESN'T MATTER HOW LONG IT TAKES TO FIX, AS LONG AS IT GETS FIXED.
AN ESTIMATE?
HRRRNNNNNNUUU
THIRTY SECONDS.
WE'RE READY TO GO.
THEN LET'S GO.

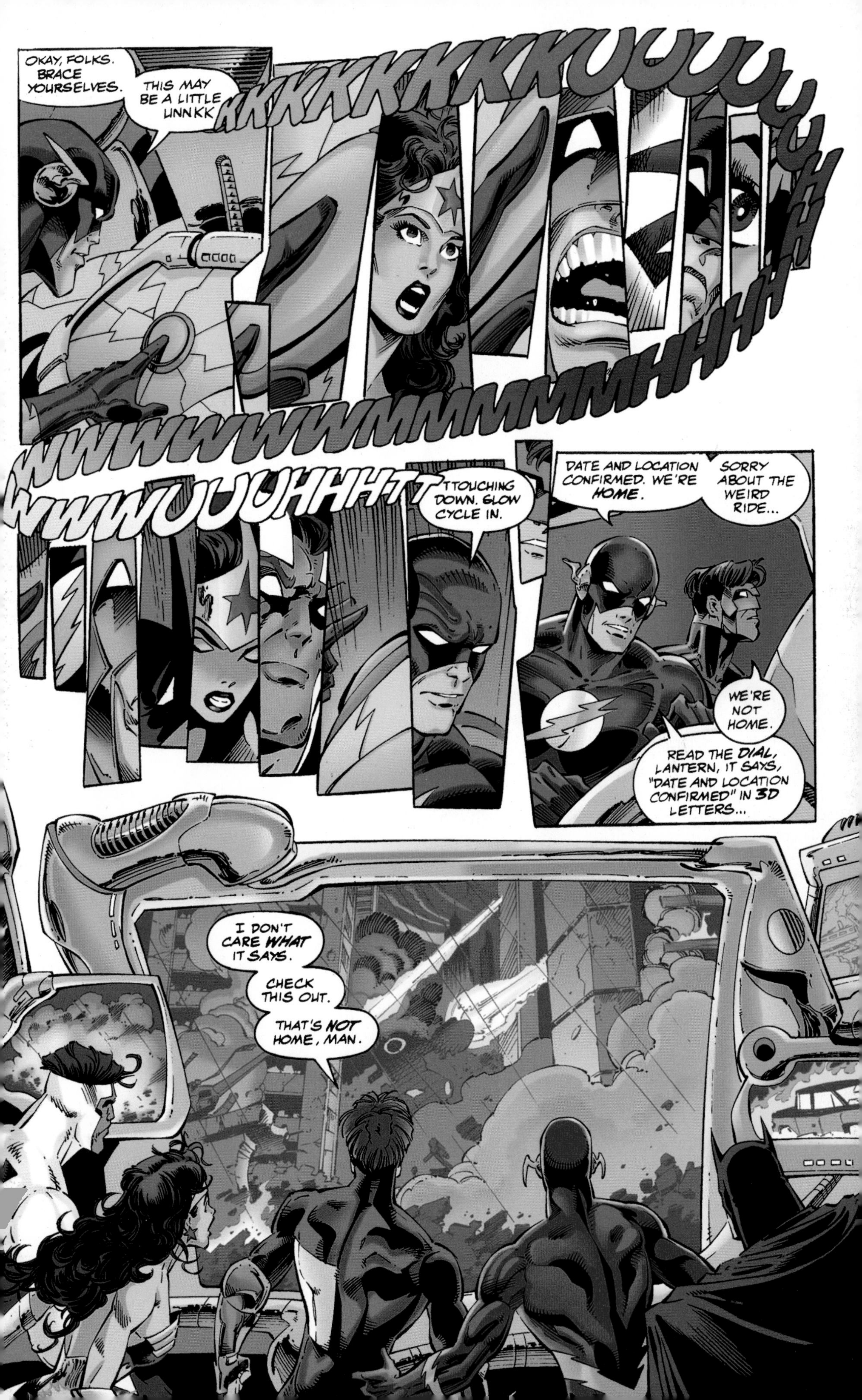
OKAY, FOLKS. BRACE YOURSELVES.
THIS MAY BE A LITTLE UNNKK
KKKKKKKKKUUUUUUUUHHHHHHHHMMMMMMMMWWWWWWWW
WWWWUUUUHHHTT
TTOUCHING DOWN. SLOW CYCLE IN.
DATE AND LOCATION CONFIRMED. WE'RE HOME.
SORRY ABOUT THE WEIRD RIDE...
WE'RE NOT HOME.
READ THE DIAL, LANTERN, IT SAYS, "DATE AND LOCATION CONFIRMED" IN 3D LETTERS...
I DON'T CARE WHAT IT SAYS.
CHECK THIS OUT.
THAT'S NOT HOME, MAN.

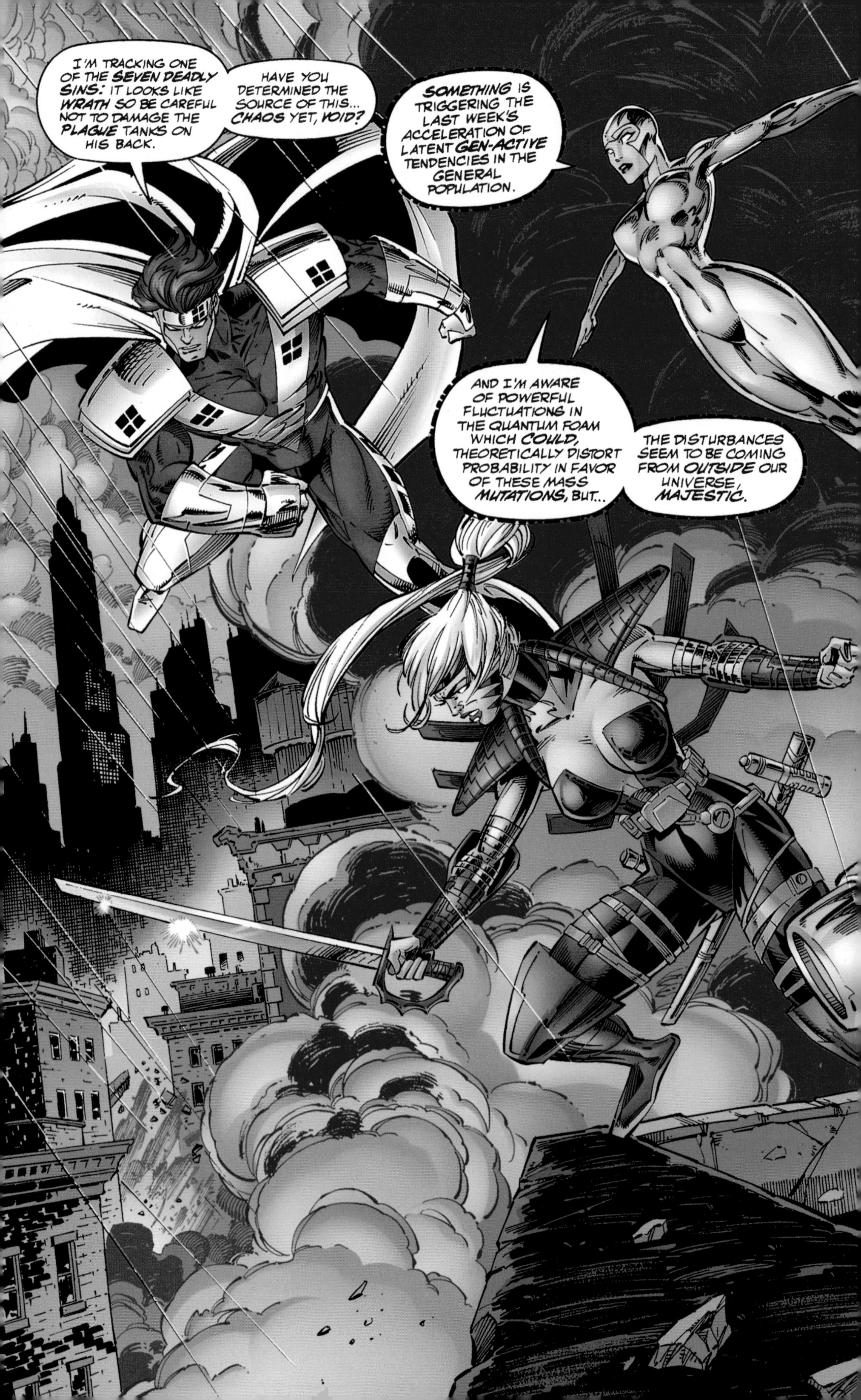
I'M TRACKING ONE OF THE SEVEN DEADLY SINS: IT LOOKS LIKE WRATH SO BE CAREFUL NOT TO DAMAGE THE PLAGUE TANKS ON HIS BACK.
HAVE YOU DETERMINED THE SOURCE OF THIS... CHAOS YET, VOID?
SOMETHING IS TRIGGERING THE LAST WEEK'S ACCELERATION OF LATENT GEN-ACTIVE TENDENCIES IN THE GENERAL POPULATION.
AND I'M AWARE OF POWERFUL FLUCTUATIONS IN THE QUANTUM FOAM WHICH COULD, THEORETICALLY DISTORT PROBABILITY IN FAVOR OF THESE MASS MUTATIONS, BUT...
THE DISTURBANCES SEEM TO BE COMING FROM OUTSIDE OUR UNIVERSE, MAJESTIC.

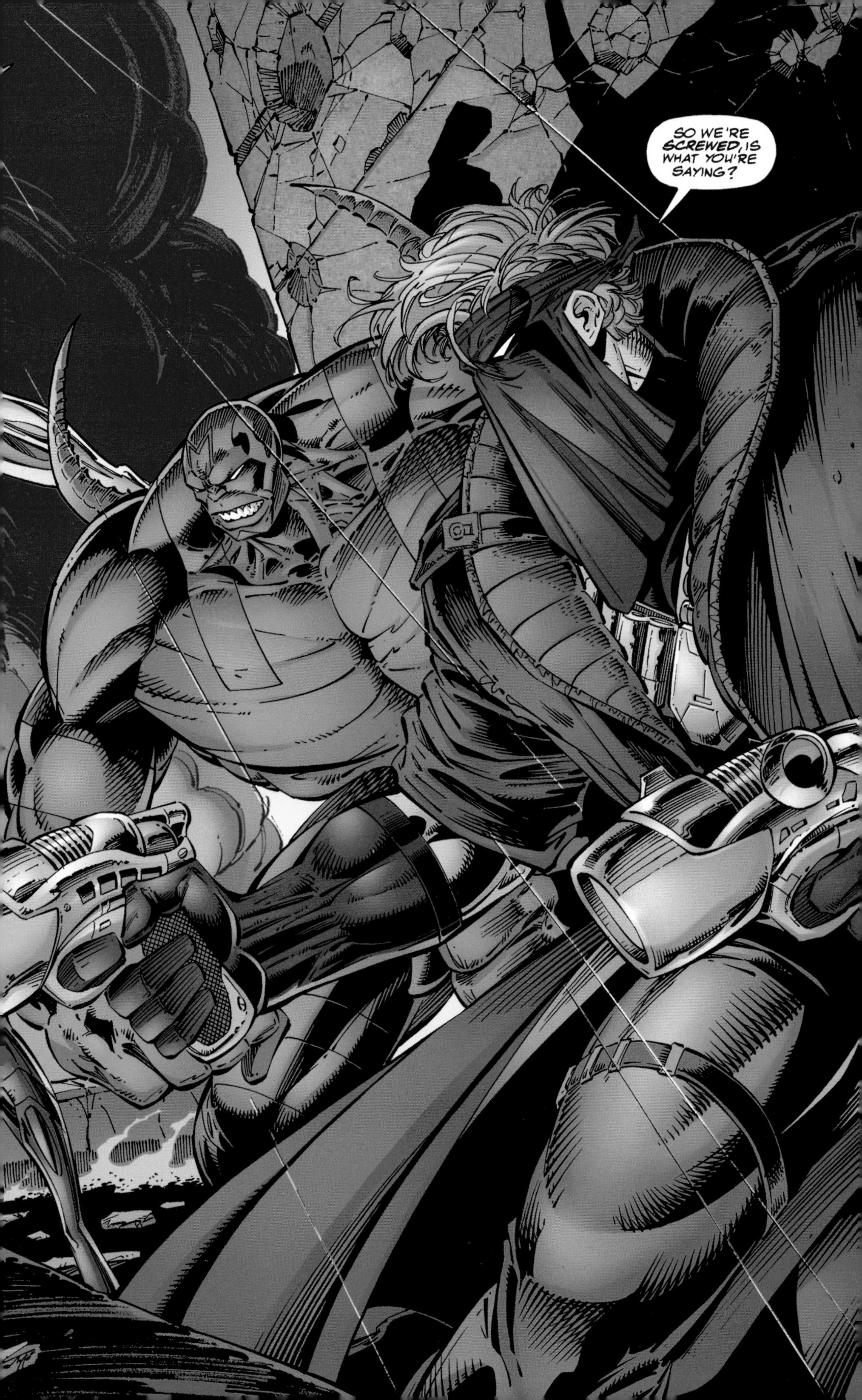
SO WE'RE SCREWED, IS WHAT YOU'RE SAYING?

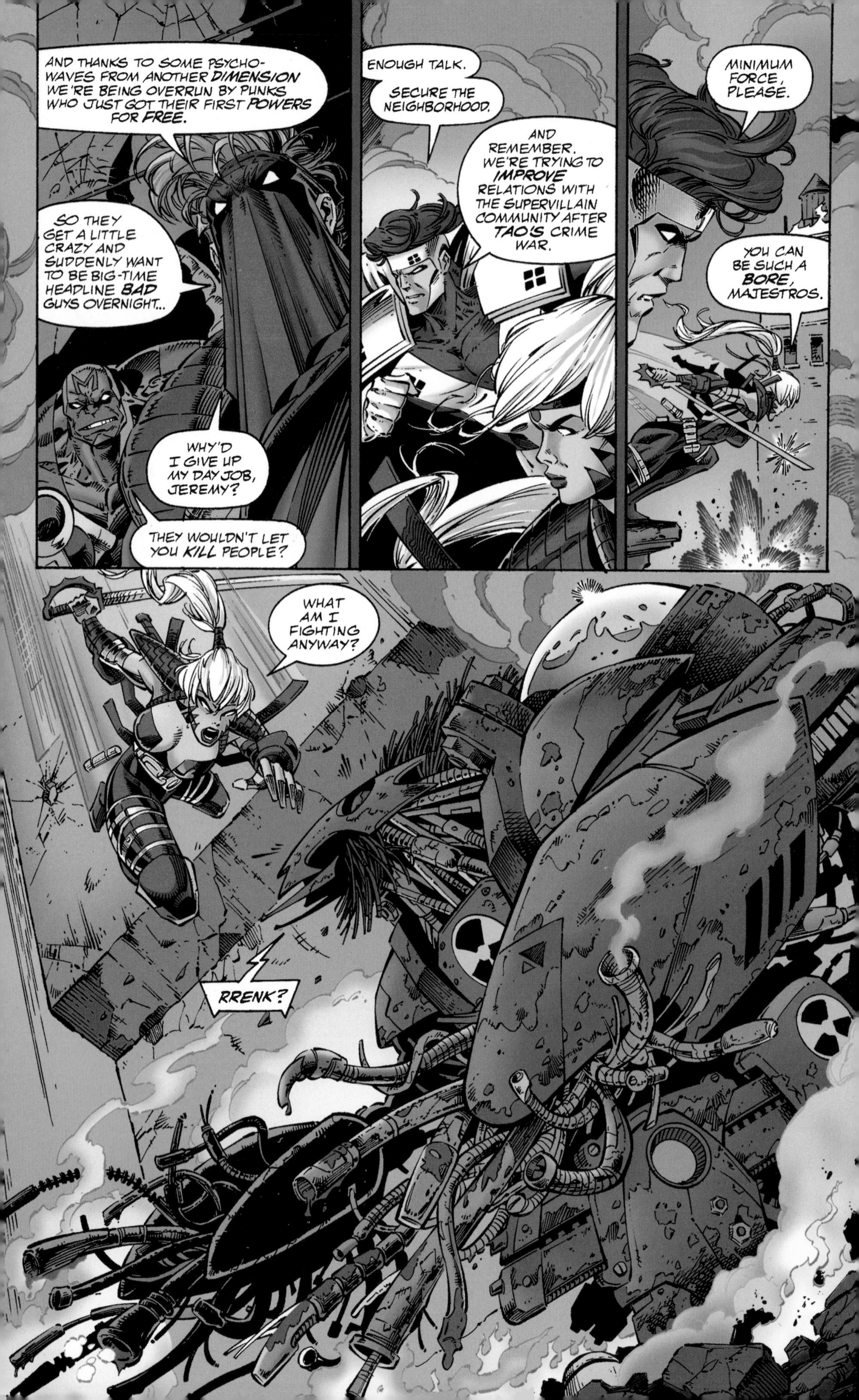
AND THANKS TO SOME PSYCHO-WAVES FROM ANOTHER DIMENSION WE'RE BEING OVERRUN BY PUNKS WHO JUST GOT THEIR FIRST POWERS FOR FREE.
SO THEY GET A LITTLE CRAZY AND SUDDENLY WANT TO BE BIG-TIME HEADLINE BAD GUYS OVERNIGHT...
WHY'D I GIVE UP MY DAY JOB, JEREMY?
THEY WOULDN'T LET YOU KILL PEOPLE?
ENOUGH TALK.
SECURE THE NEIGHBORHOOD.
AND REMEMBER. WE'RE TRYING TO IMPROVE RELATIONS WITH THE SUPERVILLAIN COMMUNITY AFTER TAO'S CRIME WAR.
MINIMUM FORCE, PLEASE.
YOU CAN BE SUCH A BORE, MAJESTROS.
WHAT AM I FIGHTING ANYWAY?
RRENK?

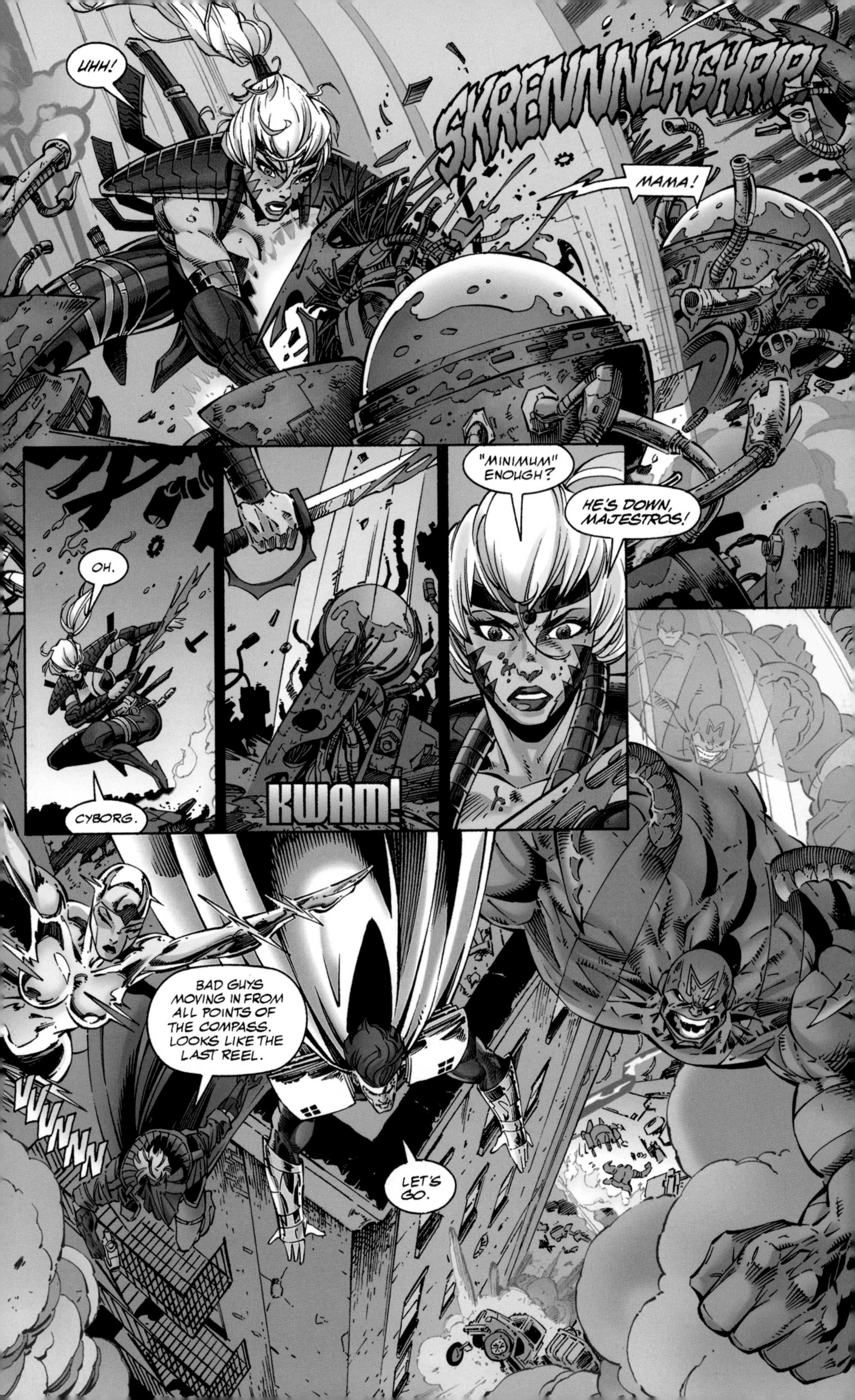
UHH!
SKRENNNCHSHRIP!
MAMA!
OH.
CYBORG.
KWAM!
"MINIMUM" ENOUGH?
HE'S DOWN, MAJESTROS!
BAD GUYS MOVING IN FROM ALL POINTS OF THE COMPASS. LOOKS LIKE THE LAST REEL.
VVUNNN
LET'S GO.

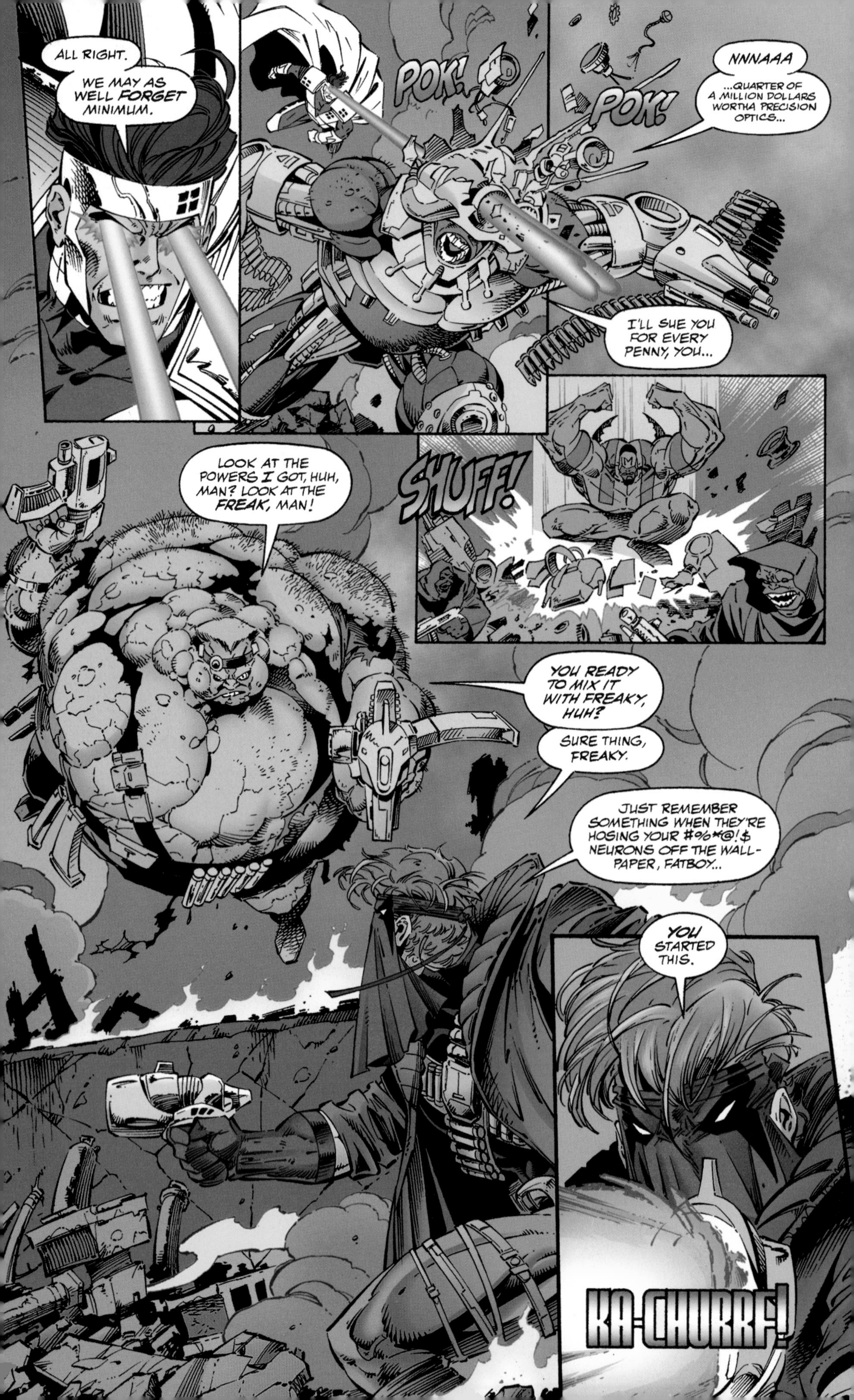

ALL RIGHT.
WE MAY AS WELL FORGET MINIMUM.
POK!
POK!
NNNAAA
...QUARTER OF A MILLION DOLLARS WORTHA PRECISION OPTICS...
I'LL SUE YOU FOR EVERY PENNY, YOU...
SHUFF!
LOOK AT THE POWERS I GOT, HUH, MAN? LOOK AT THE FREAK, MAN!
YOU READY TO MIX IT WITH FREAKY, HUH?
SURE THING, FREAKY.
JUST REMEMBER SOMETHING WHEN THEY'RE HOSING YOUR #%*@!$ NEURONS OFF THE WALL-PAPER, FATBOY...
YOU STARTED THIS.
KA-CHURRF!

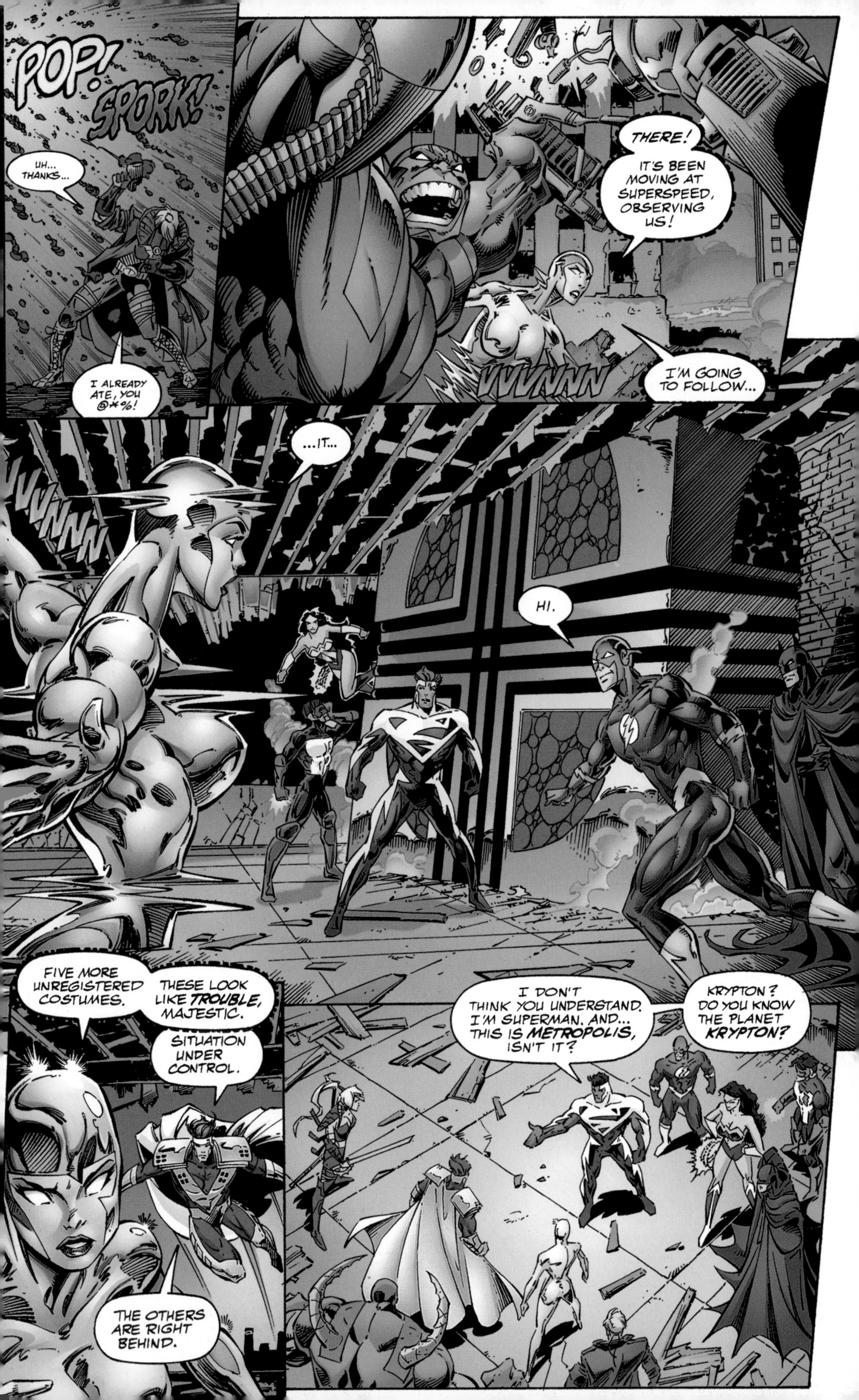
POP!
SPORK!
UH... THANKS...
I ALREADY ATE, YOU @*%!
THERE!
IT'S BEEN MOVING AT SUPERSPEED, OBSERVING US!
VVVNNNN
I'M GOING TO FOLLOW...
...IT...
VVVNNNN
HI.
FIVE MORE UNREGISTERED COSTUMES.
THESE LOOK LIKE TROUBLE, MAJESTIC.
SITUATION UNDER CONTROL.
THE OTHERS ARE RIGHT BEHIND.
I DON'T THINK YOU UNDERSTAND. I'M SUPERMAN. AND... THIS IS METROPOLIS, ISN'T IT?
KRYPTON? DO YOU KNOW THE PLANET KRYPTON?

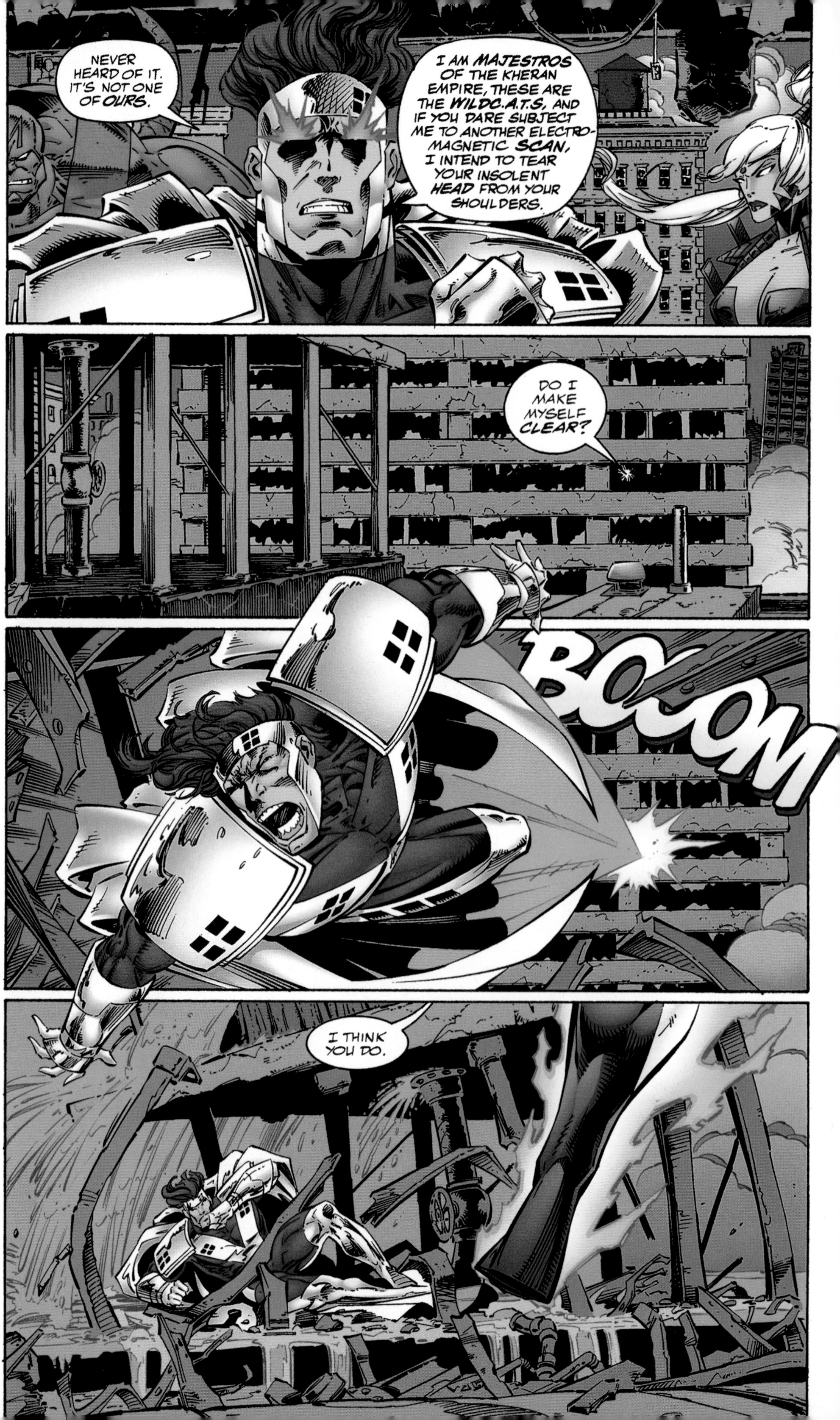
NEVER HEARD OF IT. IT'S NOT ONE OF OURS.
I AM MAJESTROS OF THE KHERAN EMPIRE, THESE ARE THE WILDC.A.T.S, AND IF YOU DARE SUBJECT ME TO ANOTHER ELECTRO-MAGNETIC SCAN, I INTEND TO TEAR YOUR INSOLENT HEAD FROM YOUR SHOULDERS.
DO I MAKE MYSELF CLEAR?
BOOOM
I THINK YOU DO.

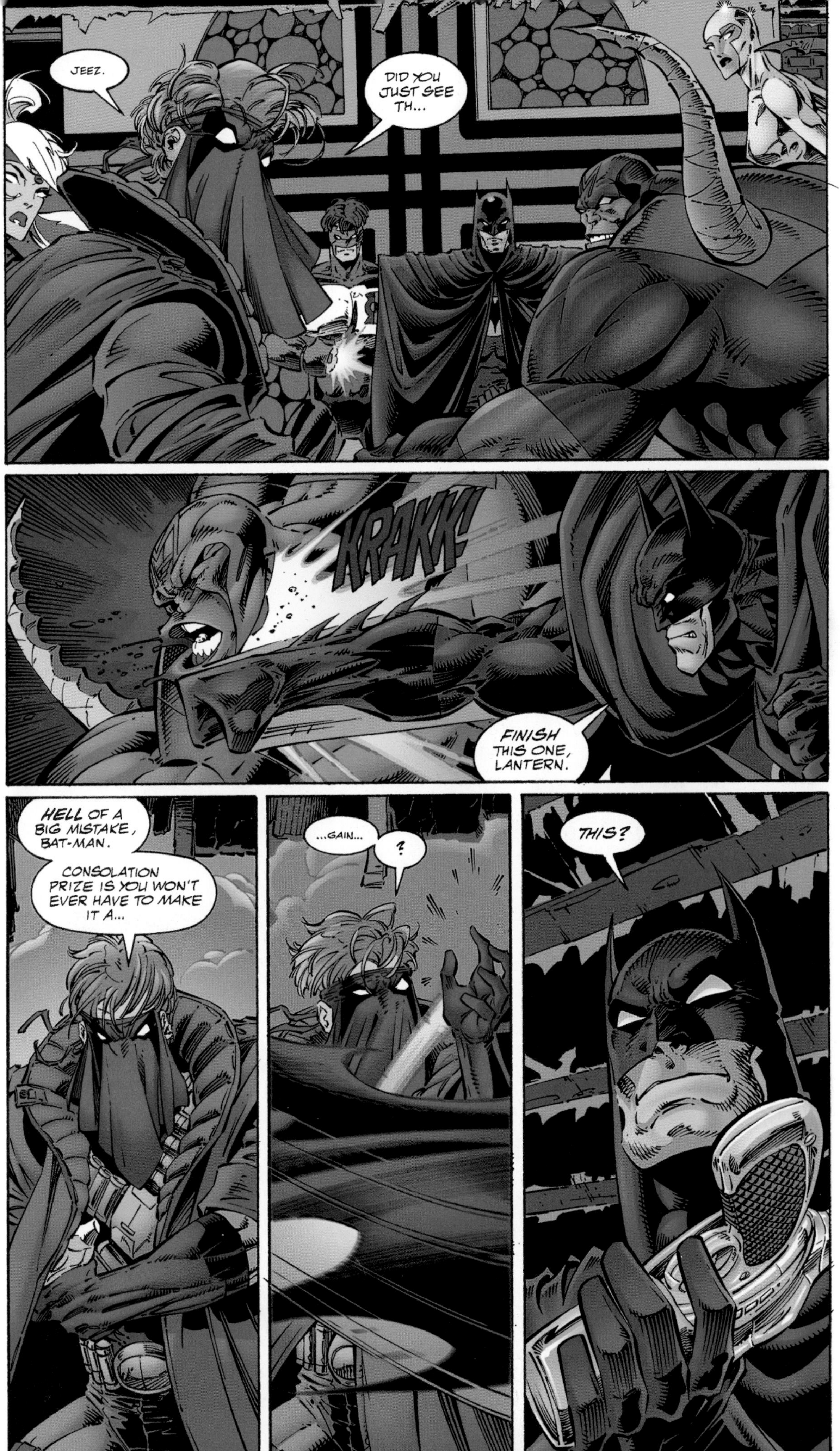
JEEZ.
DID YOU JUST SEE TH...
KRAKK!
FINISH THIS ONE, LANTERN.
HELL OF A BIG MISTAKE, BAT-MAN.
CONSOLATION PRIZE IS YOU WON'T EVER HAVE TO MAKE IT A...
...GAIN...
?
THIS?

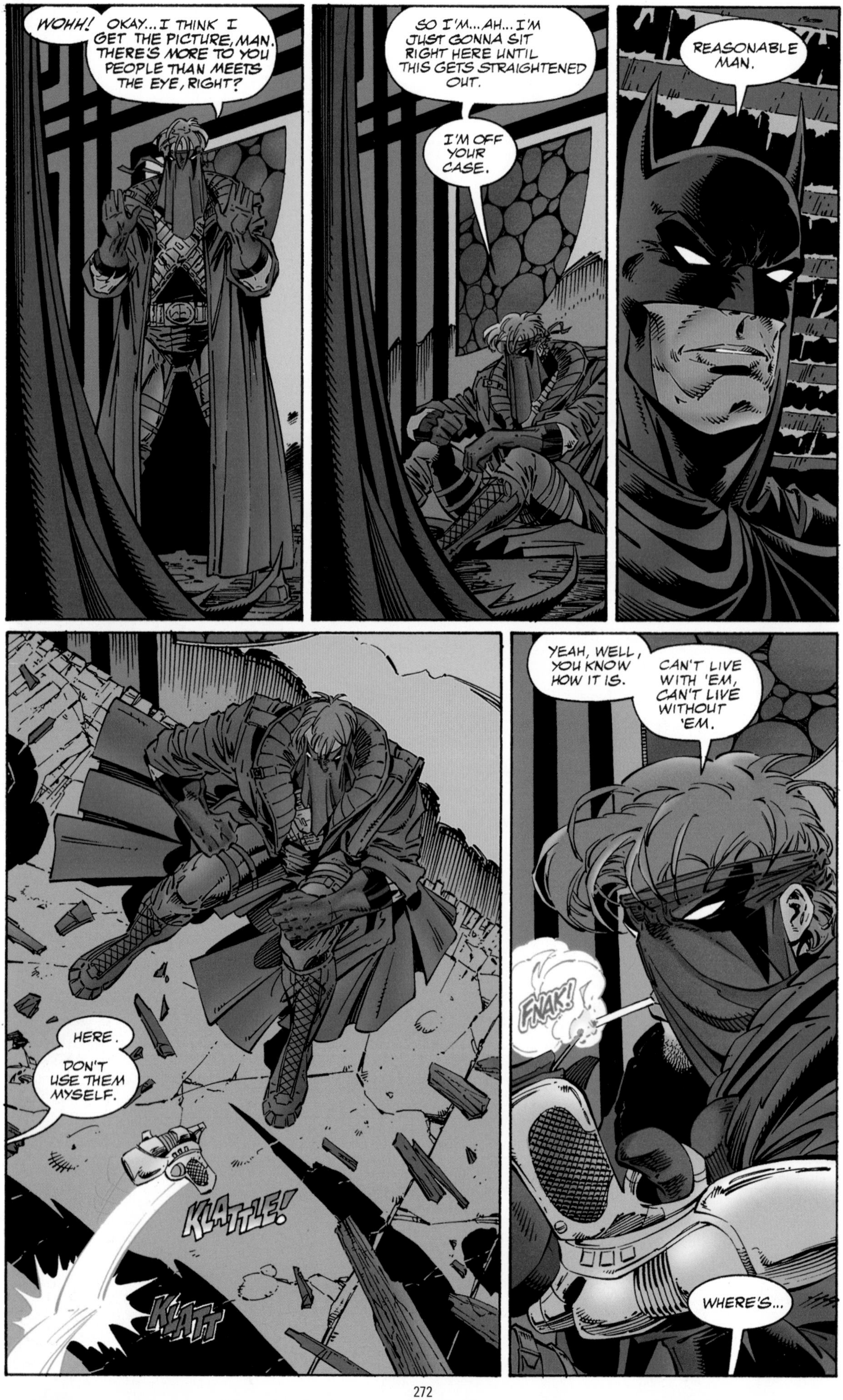
WOHH!
OKAY... I THINK I GET THE PICTURE, MAN. THERE'S MORE TO YOU PEOPLE THAN MEETS THE EYE, RIGHT?
SO I'M... AH... I'M JUST GONNA SIT RIGHT HERE UNTIL THIS GETS STRAIGHTENED OUT.
I'M OFF YOUR CASE.
REASONABLE MAN.
HERE.
DON'T USE THEM MYSELF.
KLATTLE!
KLATT
YEAH, WELL, YOU KNOW HOW IT IS.
CAN'T LIVE WITH 'EM, CAN'T LIVE WITHOUT 'EM.
FNAK!
WHERE'S...

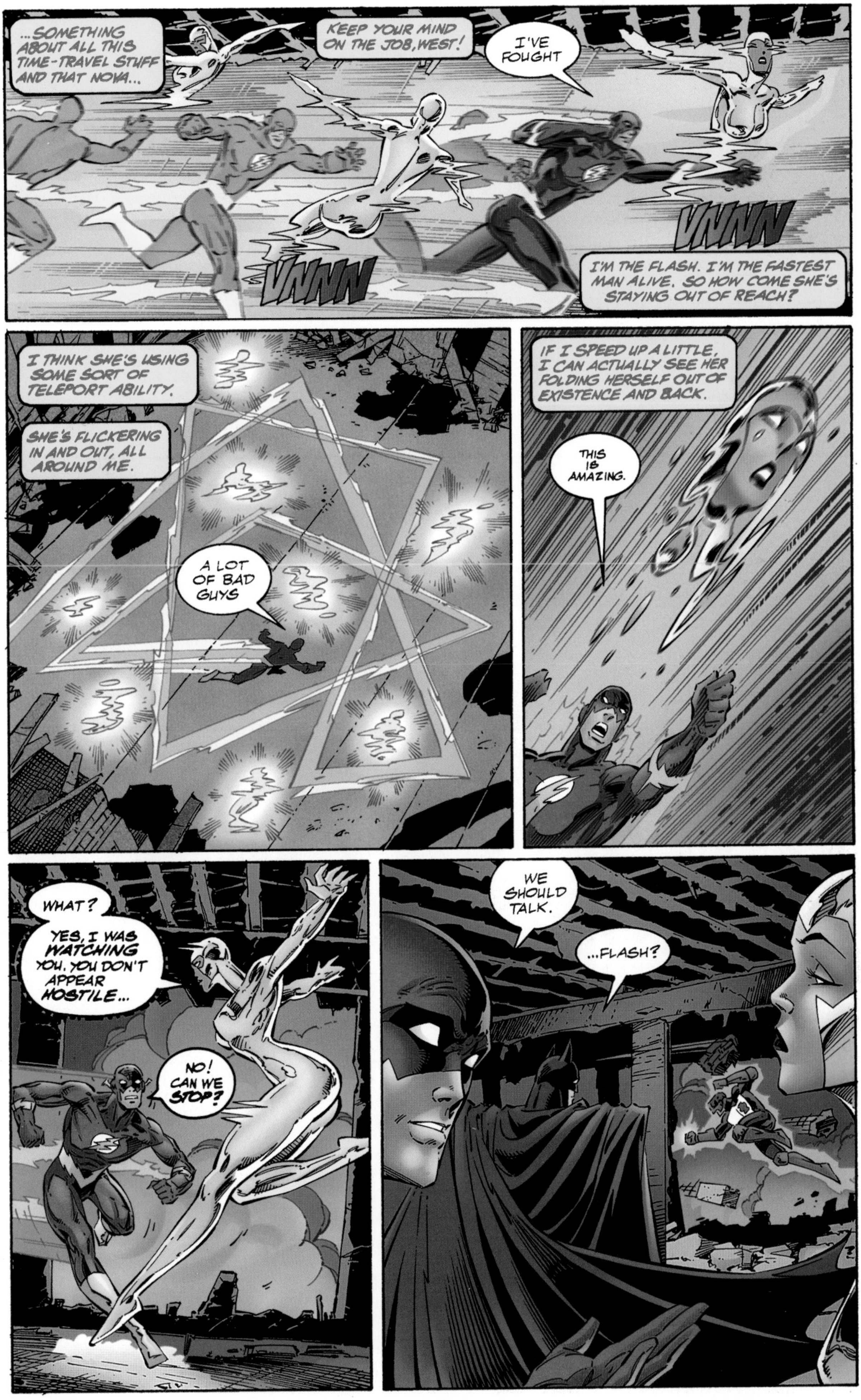
...SOMETHING ABOUT ALL THIS TIME-TRAVEL STUFF AND THAT NOVA...
KEEP YOUR MIND ON THE JOB, WEST!
I'VE FOUGHT
VNNN
VNNN
I'M THE FLASH. I'M THE FASTEST MAN ALIVE. SO HOW COME SHE'S STAYING OUT OF REACH?
I THINK SHE'S USING SOME SORT OF TELEPORT ABILITY.
SHE'S FLICKERING IN AND OUT, ALL AROUND ME.
A LOT OF BAD GUYS
IF I SPEED UP A LITTLE, I CAN ACTUALLY SEE HER FOLDING HERSELF OUT OF EXISTENCE AND BACK.
THIS IS AMAZING.
WHAT?
YES, I WAS WATCHING YOU. YOU DON'T APPEAR HOSTILE...
NO! CAN WE STOP?
WE SHOULD TALK.
...FLASH?

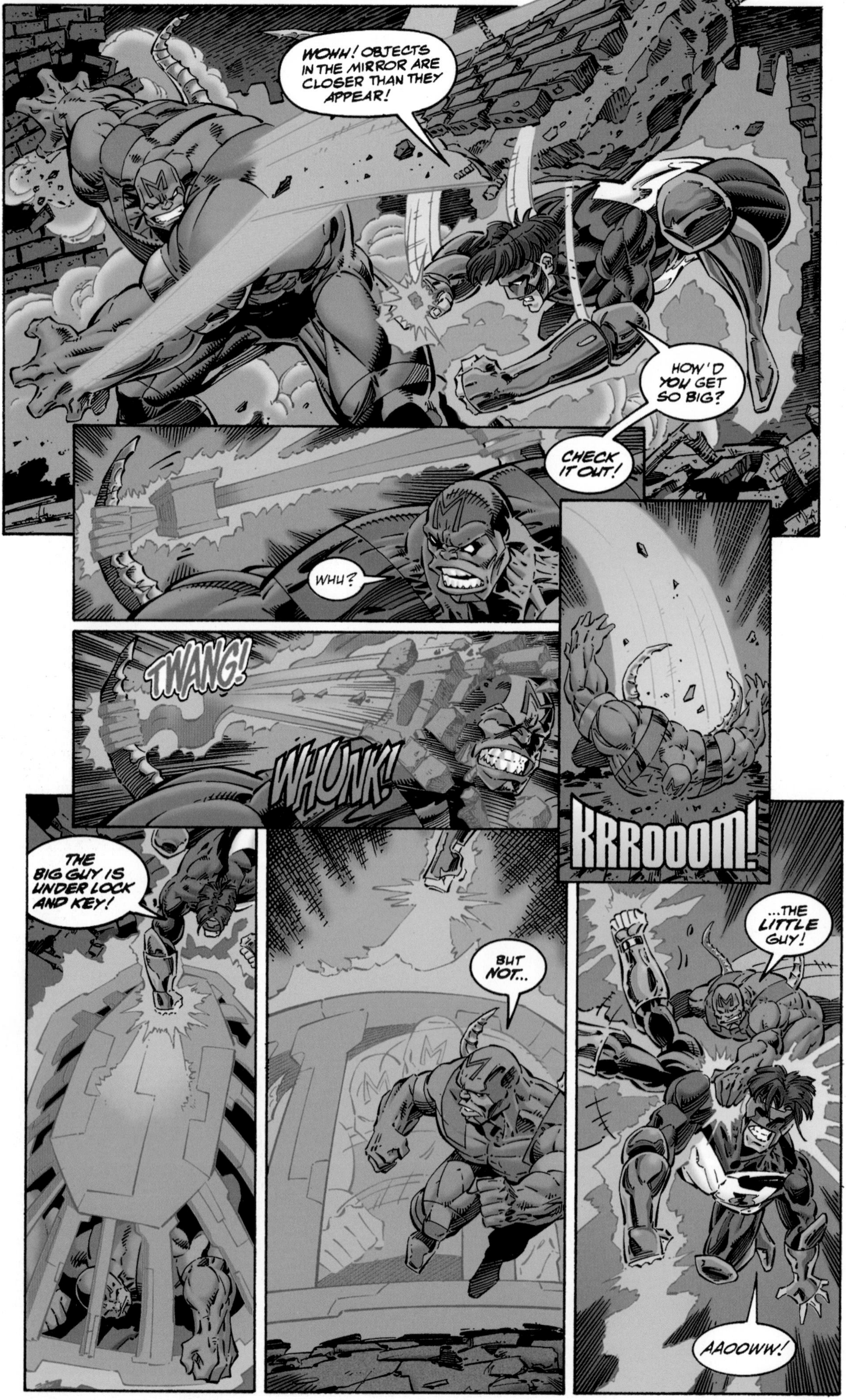
WOHH! OBJECTS IN THE MIRROR ARE CLOSER THAN THEY APPEAR!
HOW'D YOU GET SO BIG?
CHECK IT OUT!
WHU?
TWANG!
WHUNK!
KRROOOM!
THE BIG GUY IS UNDER LOCK AND KEY!
BUT NOT...
...THE LITTLE GUY!
AAOOWW!

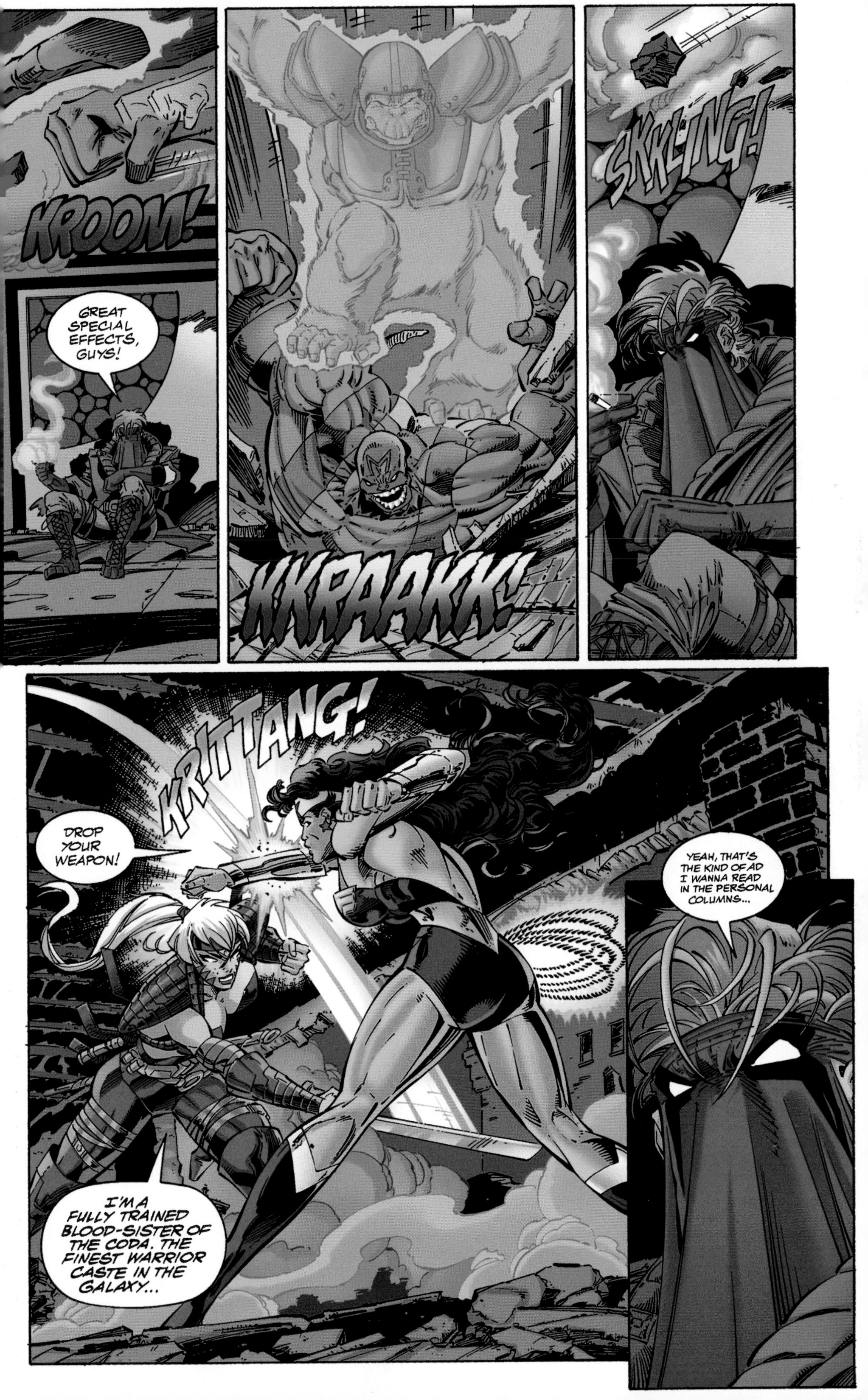
KROOM!
GREAT SPECIAL EFFECTS, GUYS!
KKRAAKK!
SKKLING!
KRITTANG!
DROP YOUR WEAPON!
I'M A FULLY TRAINED BLOOD-SISTER OF THE CODA. THE FINEST WARRIOR CASTE IN THE GALAXY...
YEAH, THAT'S THE KIND OF AD I WANNA READ IN THE PERSONAL COLUMNS...

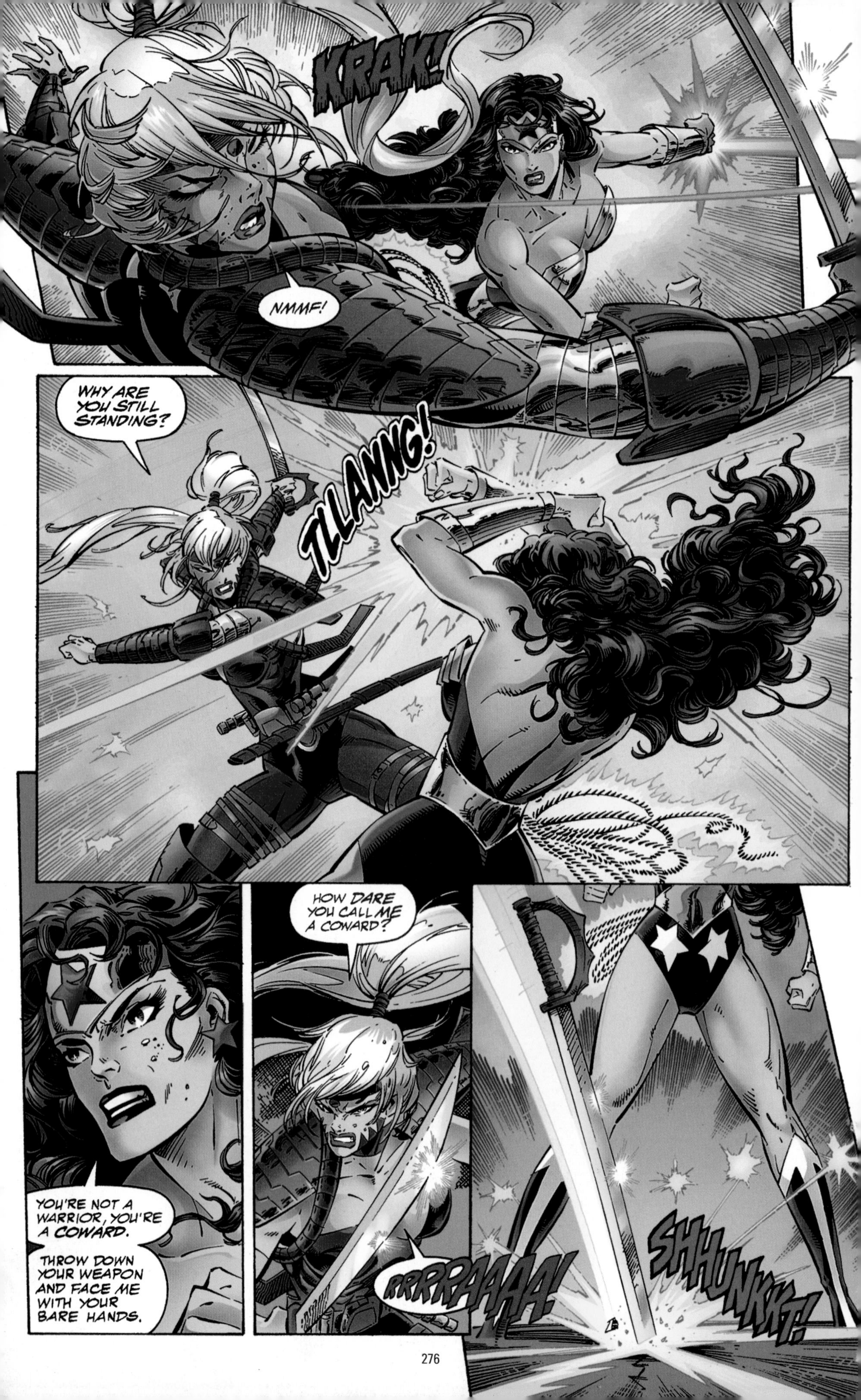
KRAK!
NMMF!
WHY ARE YOU STILL STANDING?
TLLANNG!
YOU'RE NOT A WARRIOR, YOU'RE A COWARD.
THROW DOWN YOUR WEAPON AND FACE ME WITH YOUR BARE HANDS.
HOW DARE YOU CALL ME A COWARD?
RRRRAAAA!
SHHUNKKT!

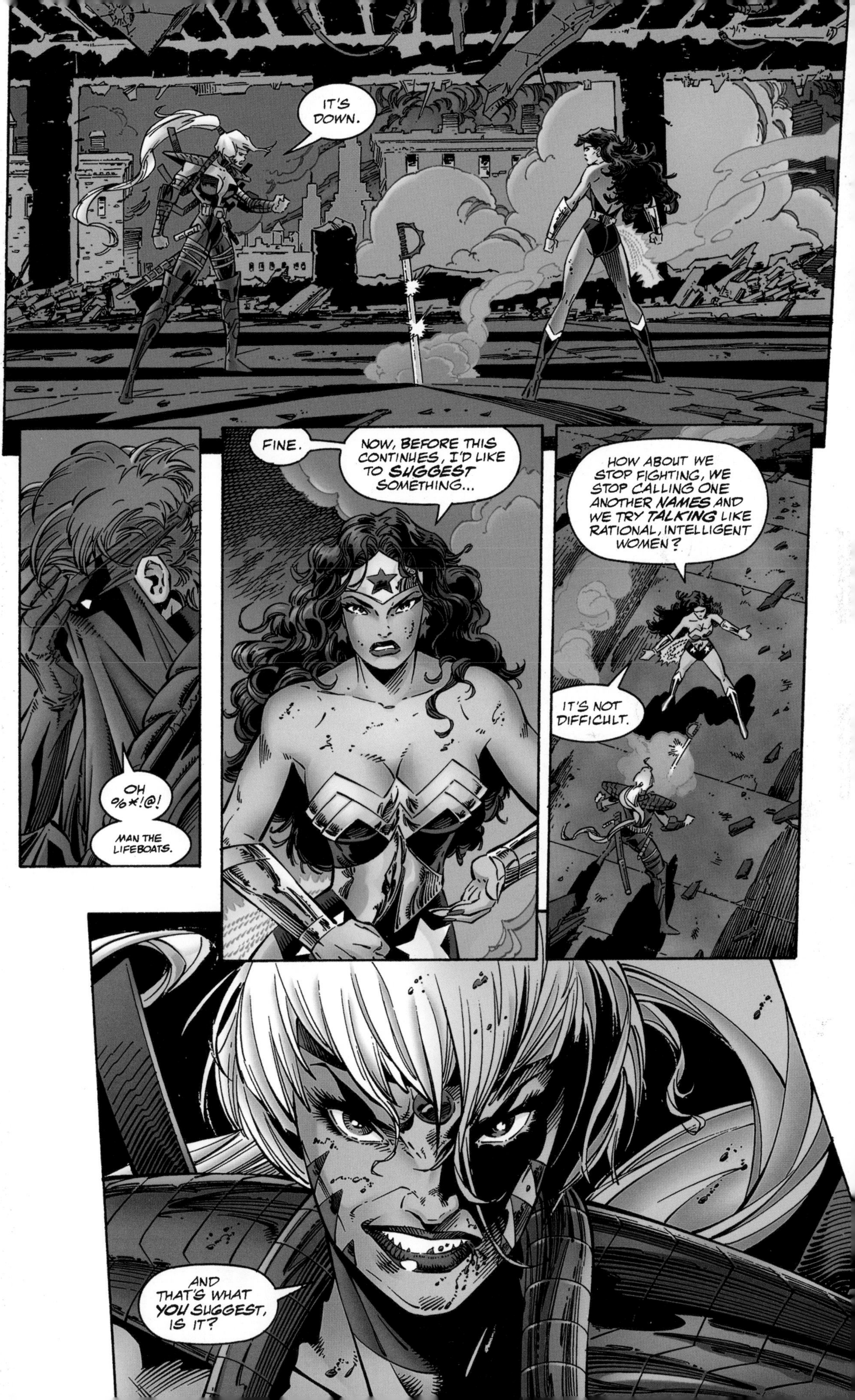

IT'S DOWN.
OH %*!@!
MAN THE LIFEBOATS.
FINE.
NOW, BEFORE THIS CONTINUES, I'D LIKE TO SUGGEST SOMETHING...
HOW ABOUT WE STOP FIGHTING, WE STOP CALLING ONE ANOTHER NAMES AND WE TRY TALKING LIKE RATIONAL, INTELLIGENT WOMEN?
IT'S NOT DIFFICULT.
AND THAT'S WHAT YOU SUGGEST, IS IT?

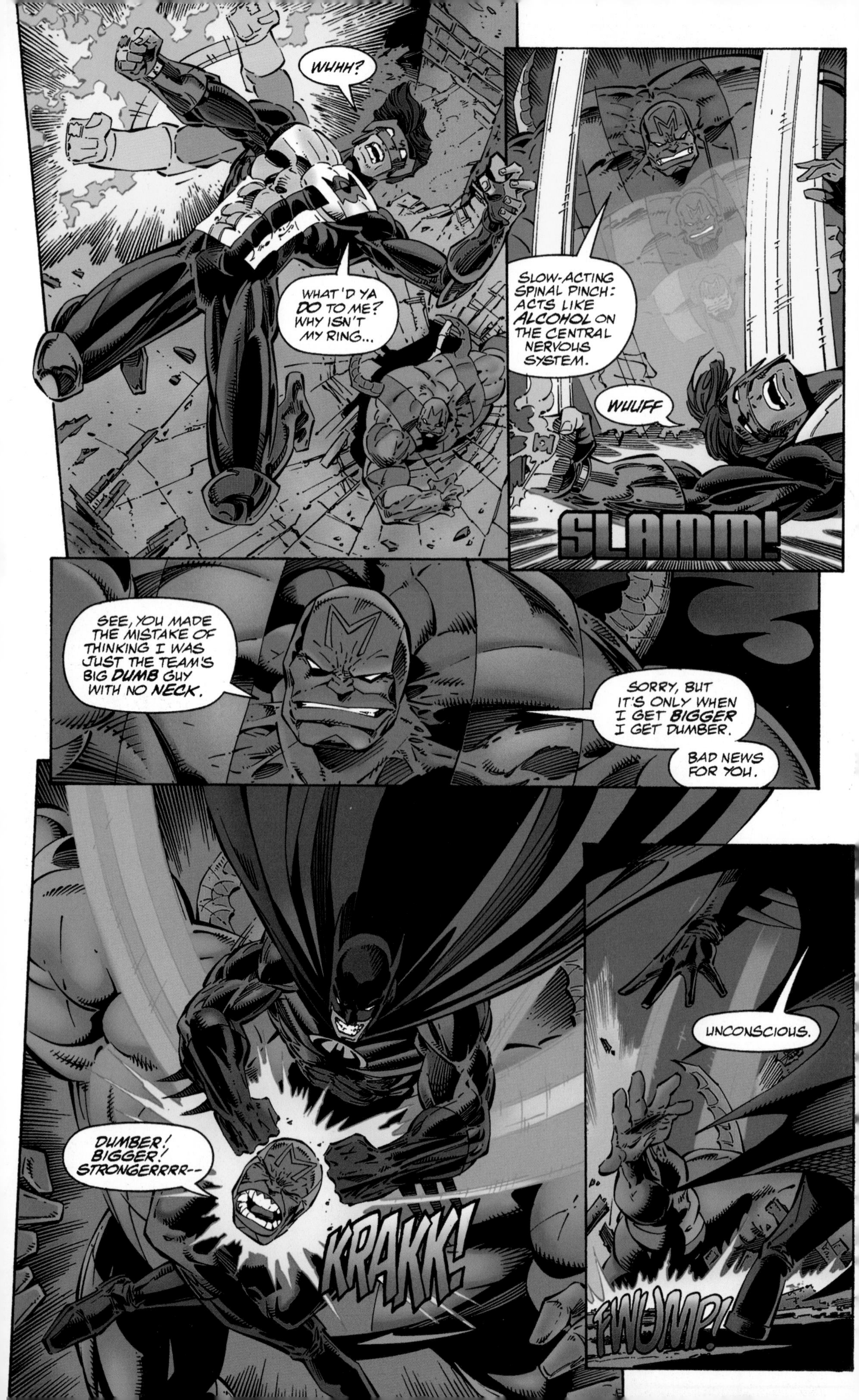
WUHH?
WHAT'D YA DO TO ME? WHY ISN'T MY RING...
SLOW-ACTING SPINAL PINCH: ACTS LIKE ALCOHOL ON THE CENTRAL NERVOUS SYSTEM.
WUUFF
SLAMM!
SEE, YOU MADE THE MISTAKE OF THINKING I WAS JUST THE TEAM'S BIG DUMB GUY WITH NO NECK.
SORRY, BUT IT'S ONLY WHEN I GET BIGGER I GET DUMBER.
BAD NEWS FOR YOU.
DUMBER! BIGGER! STRONGERRRR--
KRAKK!
UNCONSCIOUS.
FWUMP!

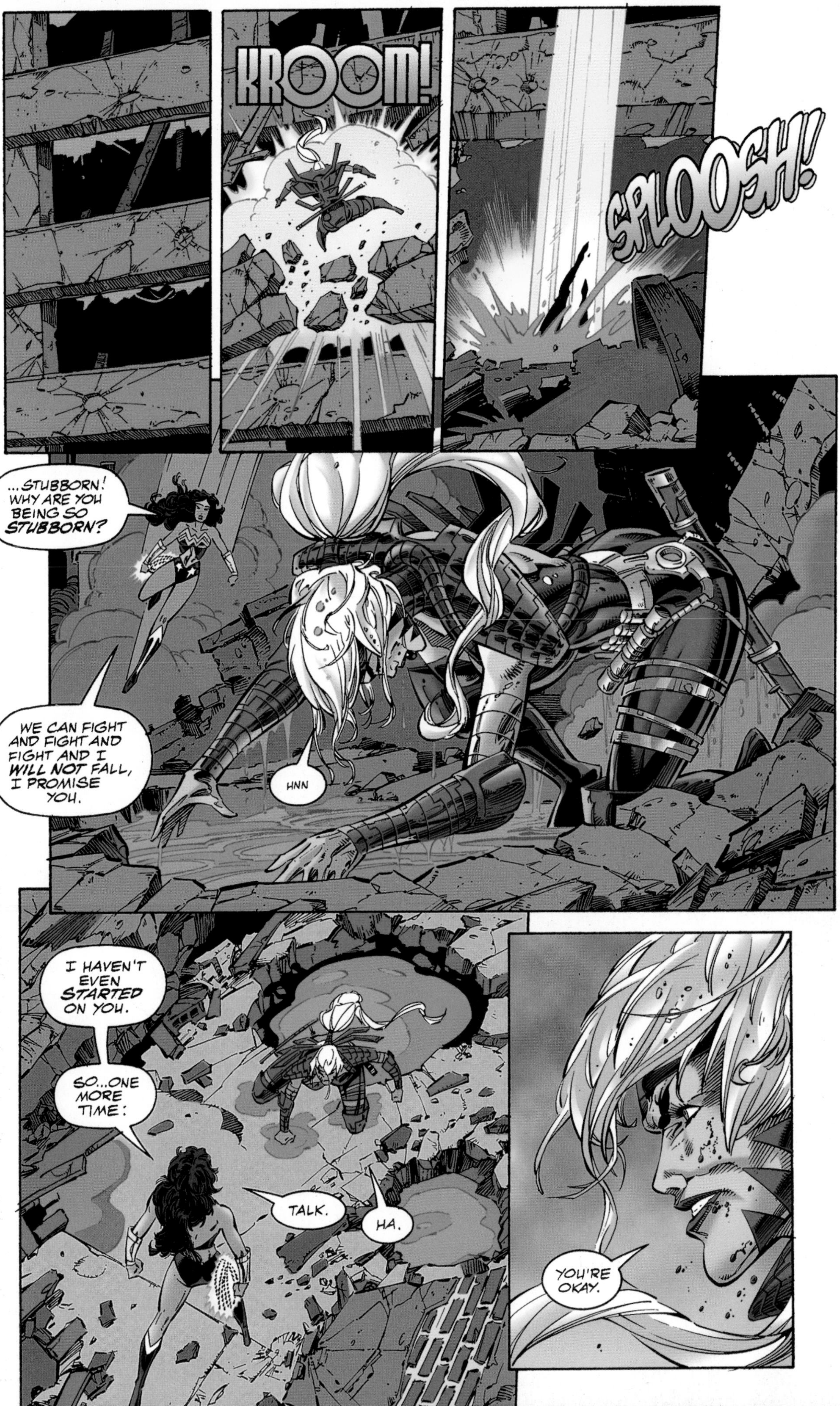
KROOM!
SPLOOSH!!
...STUBBORN! WHY ARE YOU BEING SO STUBBORN?
WE CAN FIGHT AND FIGHT AND FIGHT AND I WILL NOT FALL, I PROMISE YOU.
HNN
I HAVEN'T EVEN STARTED ON YOU.
SO...ONE MORE TIME:
TALK.
HA.
YOU'RE OKAY.

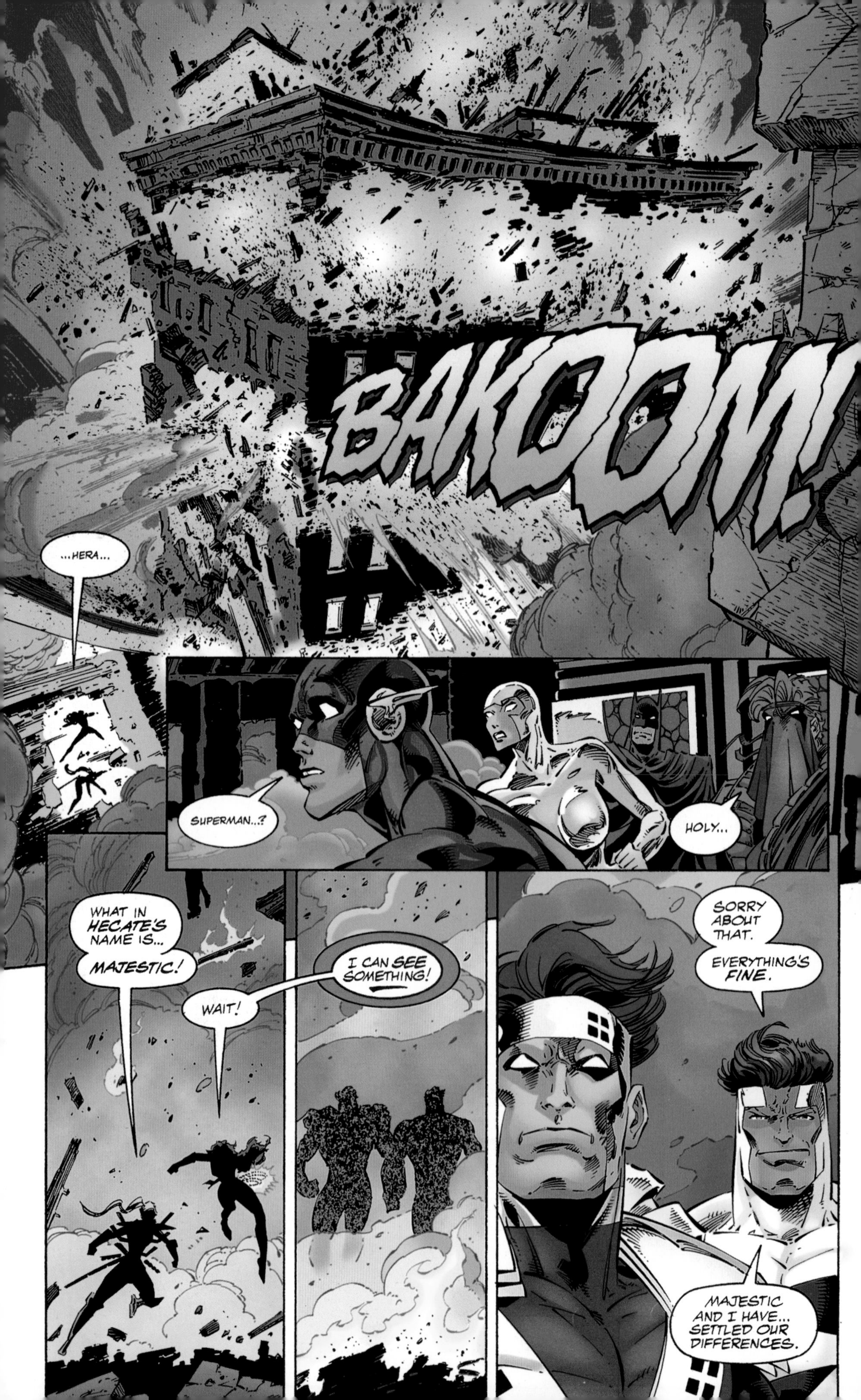
BAKOOM!
...HERA...
SUPERMAN...?
HOLY...
WHAT IN HECATE'S NAME IS...
MAJESTIC!
WAIT!
I CAN SEE SOMETHING!
SORRY ABOUT THAT.
EVERYTHING'S FINE.
MAJESTIC AND I HAVE... SETTLED OUR DIFFERENCES.

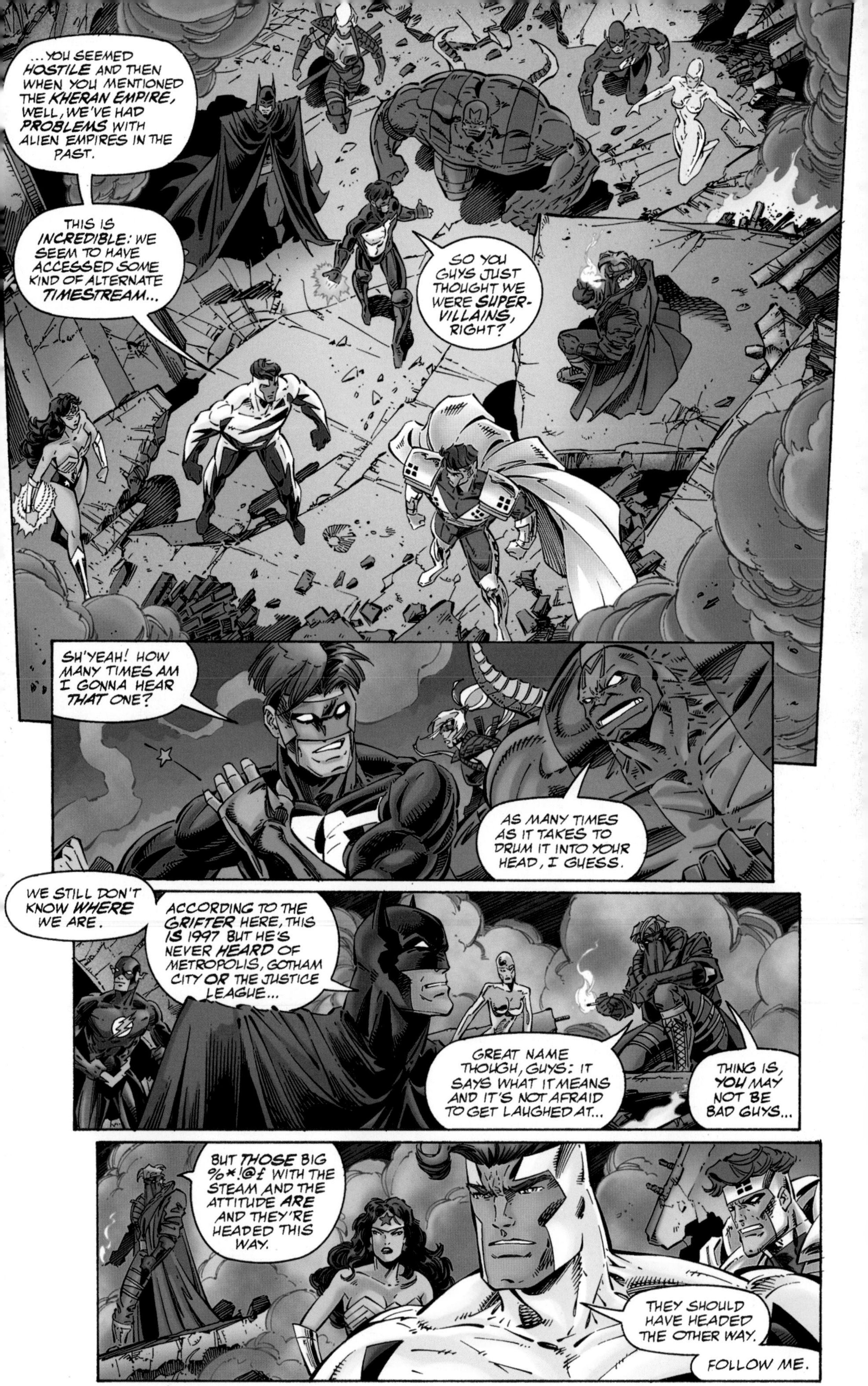
...YOU SEEMED HOSTILE AND THEN WHEN YOU MENTIONED THE KHERAN EMPIRE, WELL, WE'VE HAD PROBLEMS WITH ALIEN EMPIRES IN THE PAST.
THIS IS INCREDIBLE: WE SEEM TO HAVE ACCESSED SOME KIND OF ALTERNATE TIMESTREAM...
SO YOU GUYS JUST THOUGHT WE WERE SUPER-VILLAINS, RIGHT?
SH'YEAH! HOW MANY TIMES AM I GONNA HEAR THAT ONE?
AS MANY TIMES AS IT TAKES TO DRUM IT INTO YOUR HEAD, I GUESS.
WE STILL DON'T KNOW WHERE WE ARE.
ACCORDING TO THE GRIFTER HERE, THIS IS 1997 BUT HE'S NEVER HEARD OF METROPOLIS, GOTHAM CITY OR THE JUSTICE LEAGUE...
GREAT NAME THOUGH, GUYS: IT SAYS WHAT IT MEANS AND IT'S NOT AFRAID TO GET LAUGHED AT...
THING IS, YOU MAY NOT BE BAD GUYS...
BUT THOSE BIG %*!@£ WITH THE STEAM AND THE ATTITUDE ARE AND THEY'RE HEADED THIS WAY.
THEY SHOULD HAVE HEADED THE OTHER WAY.
FOLLOW ME.

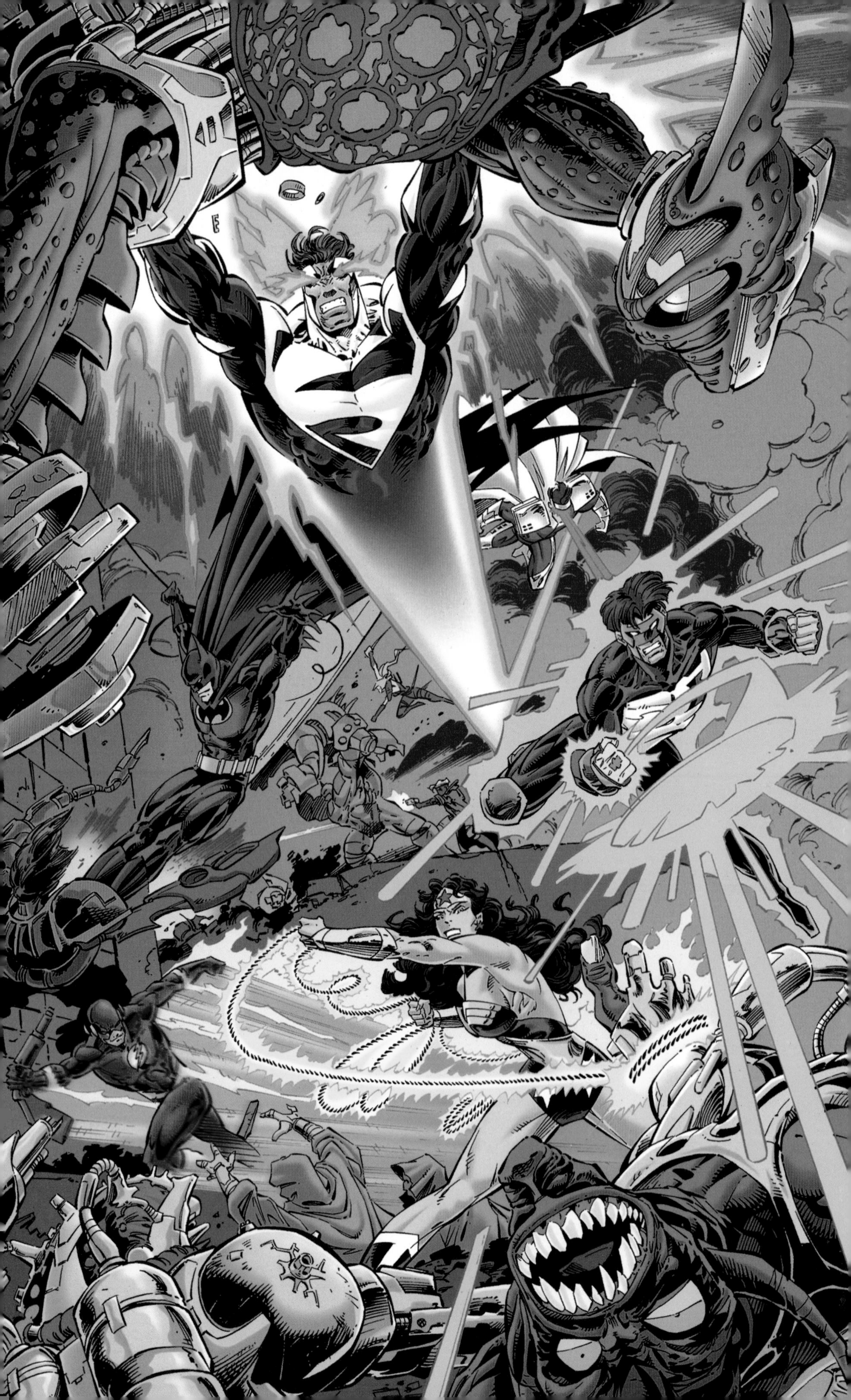

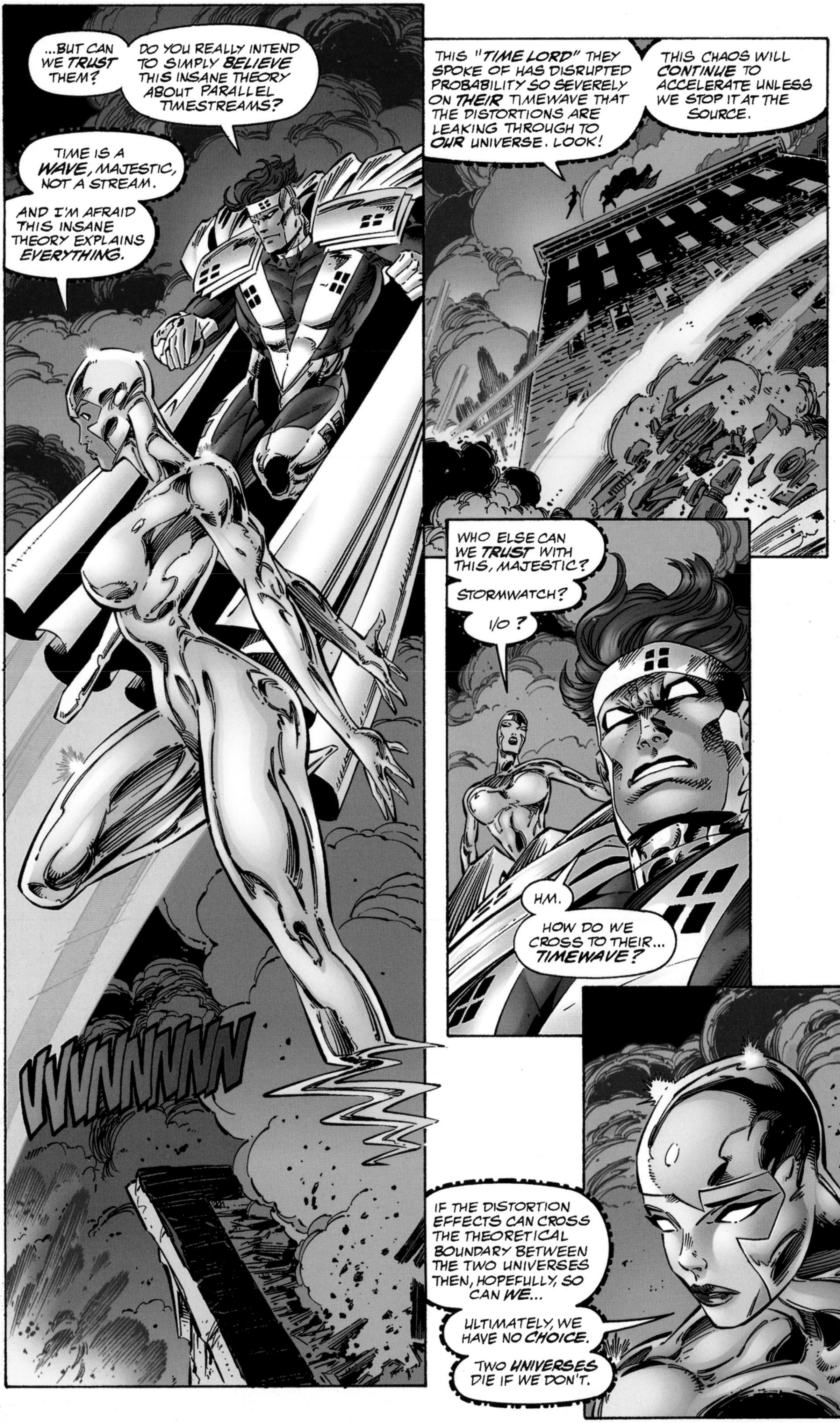
...BUT CAN WE TRUST THEM?
DO YOU REALLY INTEND TO SIMPLY BELIEVE THIS INSANE THEORY ABOUT PARALLEL TIMESTREAMS?
TIME IS A WAVE, MAJESTIC, NOT A STREAM.
AND I'M AFRAID THIS INSANE THEORY EXPLAINS EVERYTHING.
VVVNNNNNN
THIS "TIME LORD" THEY SPOKE OF HAS DISRUPTED PROBABILITY SO SEVERELY ON THEIR TIMEWAVE THAT THE DISTORTIONS ARE LEAKING THROUGH TO OUR UNIVERSE. LOOK!
THIS CHAOS WILL CONTINUE TO ACCELERATE UNLESS WE STOP IT AT THE SOURCE.
WHO ELSE CAN WE TRUST WITH THIS, MAJESTIC?
STORMWATCH?
I/O?
HM.
HOW DO WE CROSS TO THEIR... TIMEWAVE?
IF THE DISTORTION EFFECTS CAN CROSS THE THEORETICAL BOUNDARY BETWEEN THE TWO UNIVERSES THEN, HOPEFULLY, SO CAN WE...
ULTIMATELY, WE HAVE NO CHOICE.
TWO UNIVERSES DIE IF WE DON'T.

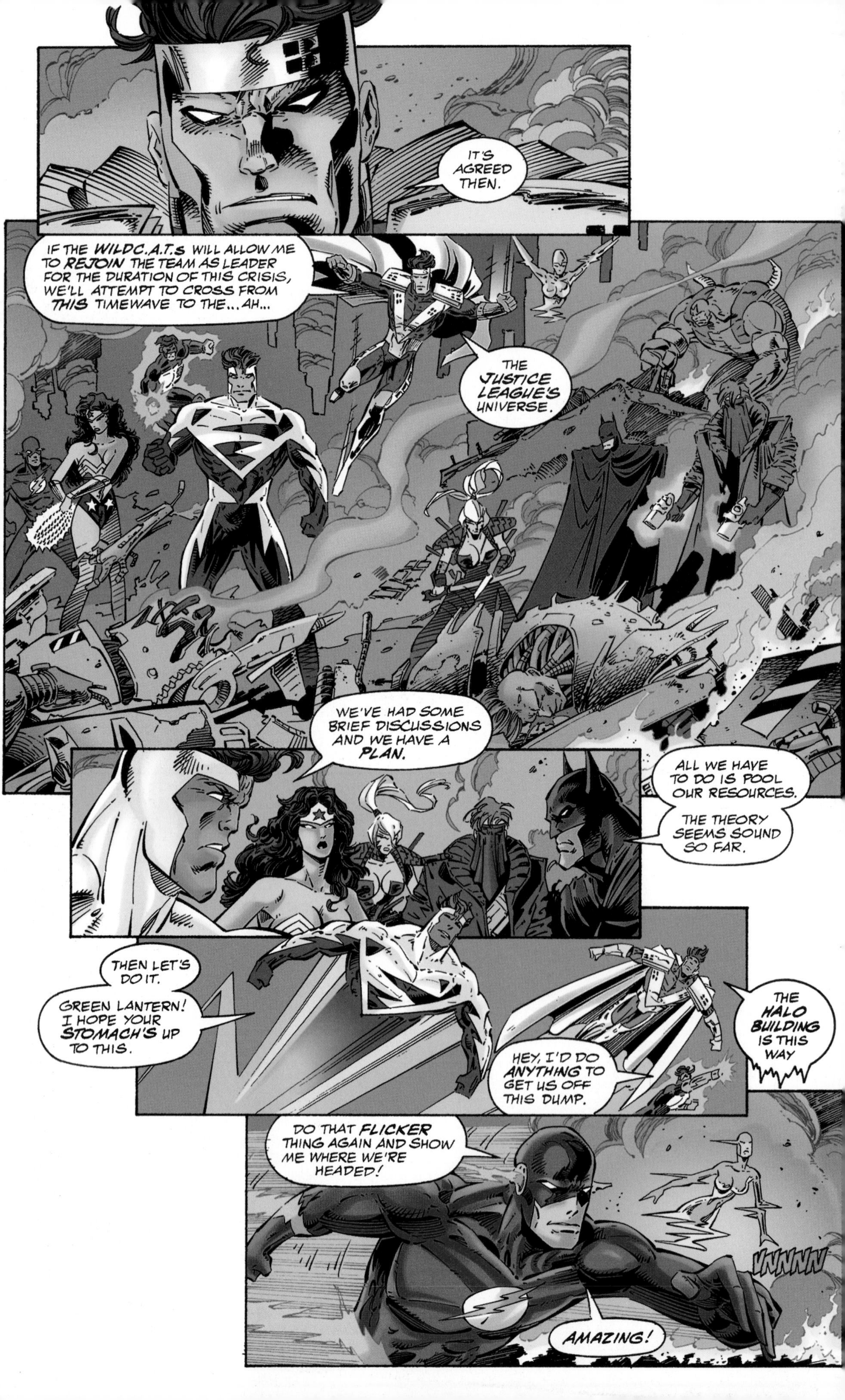
IT'S AGREED THEN.
IF THE WILDC.A.T.s WILL ALLOW ME TO REJOIN THE TEAM AS LEADER FOR THE DURATION OF THIS CRISIS, WE'LL ATTEMPT TO CROSS FROM THIS TIMEWAVE TO THE... AH...
THE JUSTICE LEAGUE'S UNIVERSE.
WE'VE HAD SOME BRIEF DISCUSSIONS AND WE HAVE A PLAN.
ALL WE HAVE TO DO IS POOL OUR RESOURCES.
THE THEORY SEEMS SOUND SO FAR.
THEN LET'S DO IT.
GREEN LANTERN! I HOPE YOUR STOMACH'S UP TO THIS.
HEY, I'D DO ANYTHING TO GET US OFF THIS DUMP.
THE HALO BUILDING IS THIS WAY
DO THAT FLICKER THING AGAIN AND SHOW ME WHERE WE'RE HEADED!
VNNNN
AMAZING!

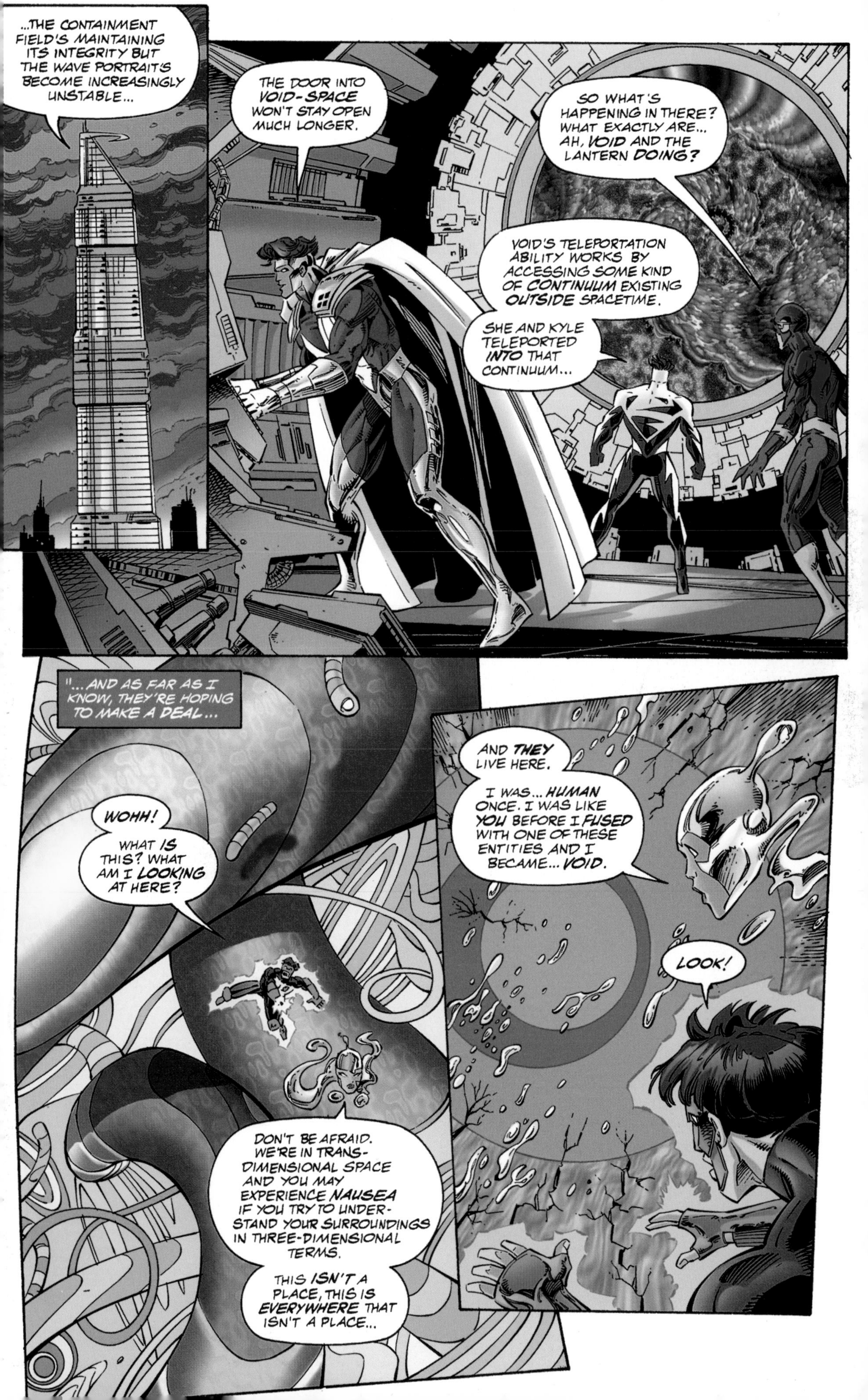

...THE CONTAINMENT FIELD'S MAINTAINING ITS INTEGRITY BUT THE WAVE PORTRAITS BECOME INCREASINGLY UNSTABLE...
THE DOOR INTO VOID-SPACE WON'T STAY OPEN MUCH LONGER.
SO WHAT'S HAPPENING IN THERE? WHAT EXACTLY ARE... AH, VOID AND THE LANTERN DOING?
VOID'S TELEPORTATION ABILITY WORKS BY ACCESSING SOME KIND OF CONTINUUM EXISTING OUTSIDE SPACETIME.
SHE AND KYLE TELEPORTED INTO THAT CONTINUUM...
"...AND AS FAR AS I KNOW, THEY'RE HOPING TO MAKE A DEAL...
WOHH!
WHAT IS THIS? WHAT AM I LOOKING AT HERE?
DON'T BE AFRAID. WE'RE IN TRANS-DIMENSIONAL SPACE AND YOU MAY EXPERIENCE NAUSEA IF YOU TRY TO UNDER-STAND YOUR SURROUNDINGS IN THREE-DIMENSIONAL TERMS.
THIS ISN'T A PLACE, THIS IS EVERYWHERE THAT ISN'T A PLACE...
AND THEY LIVE HERE.
I WAS... HUMAN ONCE. I WAS LIKE YOU BEFORE I FUSED WITH ONE OF THESE ENTITIES AND I BECAME... VOID.
LOOK!

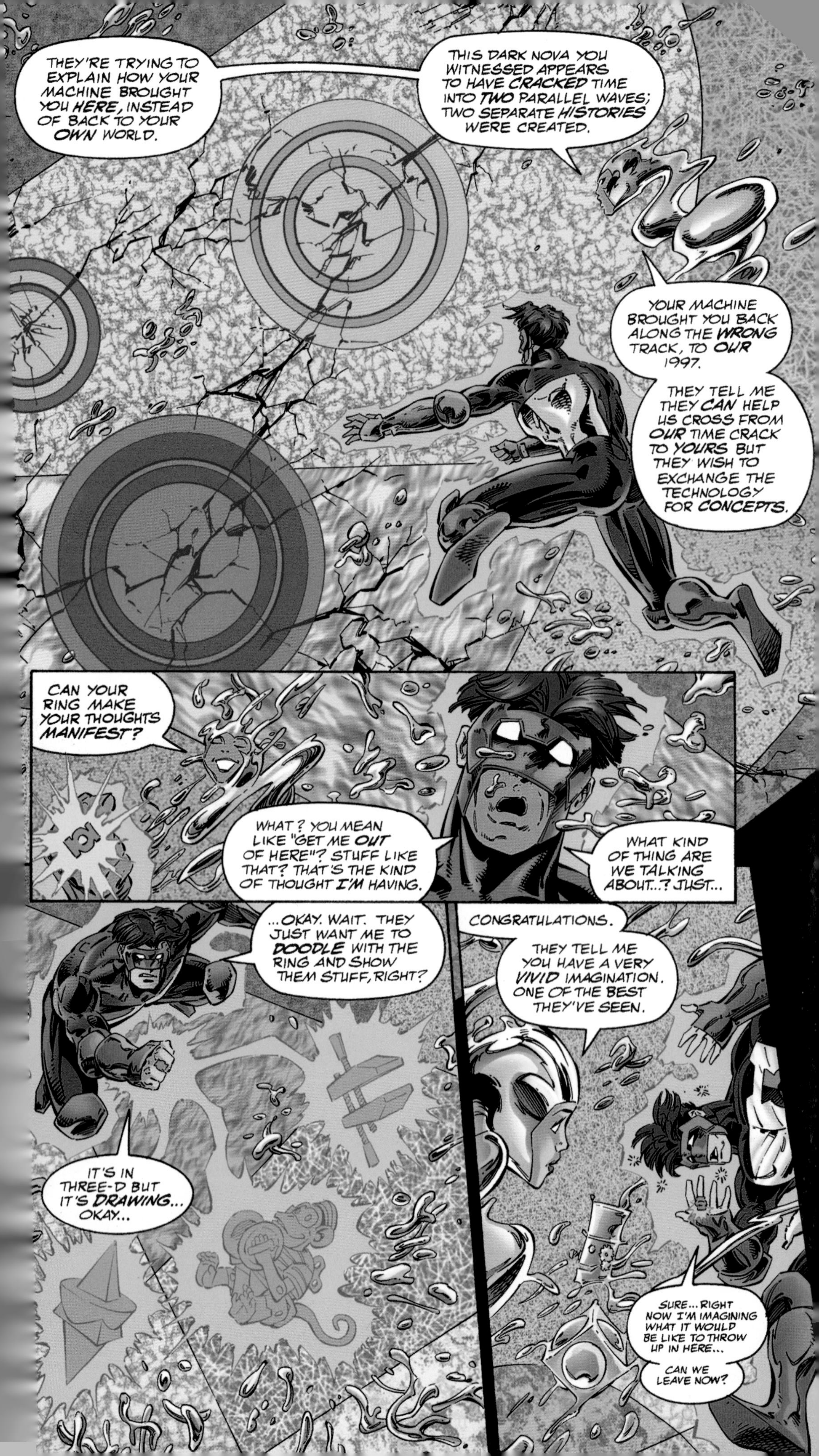
THEY'RE TRYING TO EXPLAIN HOW YOUR MACHINE BROUGHT YOU HERE, INSTEAD OF BACK TO YOUR OWN WORLD.
THIS DARK NOVA YOU WITNESSED APPEARS TO HAVE CRACKED TIME INTO TWO PARALLEL WAVES; TWO SEPARATE HISTORIES WERE CREATED.
YOUR MACHINE BROUGHT YOU BACK ALONG THE WRONG TRACK, TO OUR 1997.
THEY TELL ME THEY CAN HELP US CROSS FROM OUR TIME CRACK TO YOURS BUT THEY WISH TO EXCHANGE THE TECHNOLOGY FOR CONCEPTS.
CAN YOUR RING MAKE YOUR THOUGHTS MANIFEST?
WHAT? YOU MEAN LIKE "GET ME OUT OF HERE"? STUFF LIKE THAT? THAT'S THE KIND OF THOUGHT I'M HAVING.
WHAT KIND OF THING ARE WE TALKING ABOUT...? JUST...
...OKAY. WAIT. THEY JUST WANT ME TO DOODLE WITH THE RING AND SHOW THEM STUFF, RIGHT?
IT'S IN THREE-D BUT IT'S DRAWING... OKAY...
CONGRATULATIONS.
THEY TELL ME YOU HAVE A VERY VIVID IMAGINATION. ONE OF THE BEST THEY'VE SEEN.
SURE... RIGHT NOW I'M IMAGINING WHAT IT WOULD BE LIKE TO THROW UP IN HERE...
CAN WE LEAVE NOW?

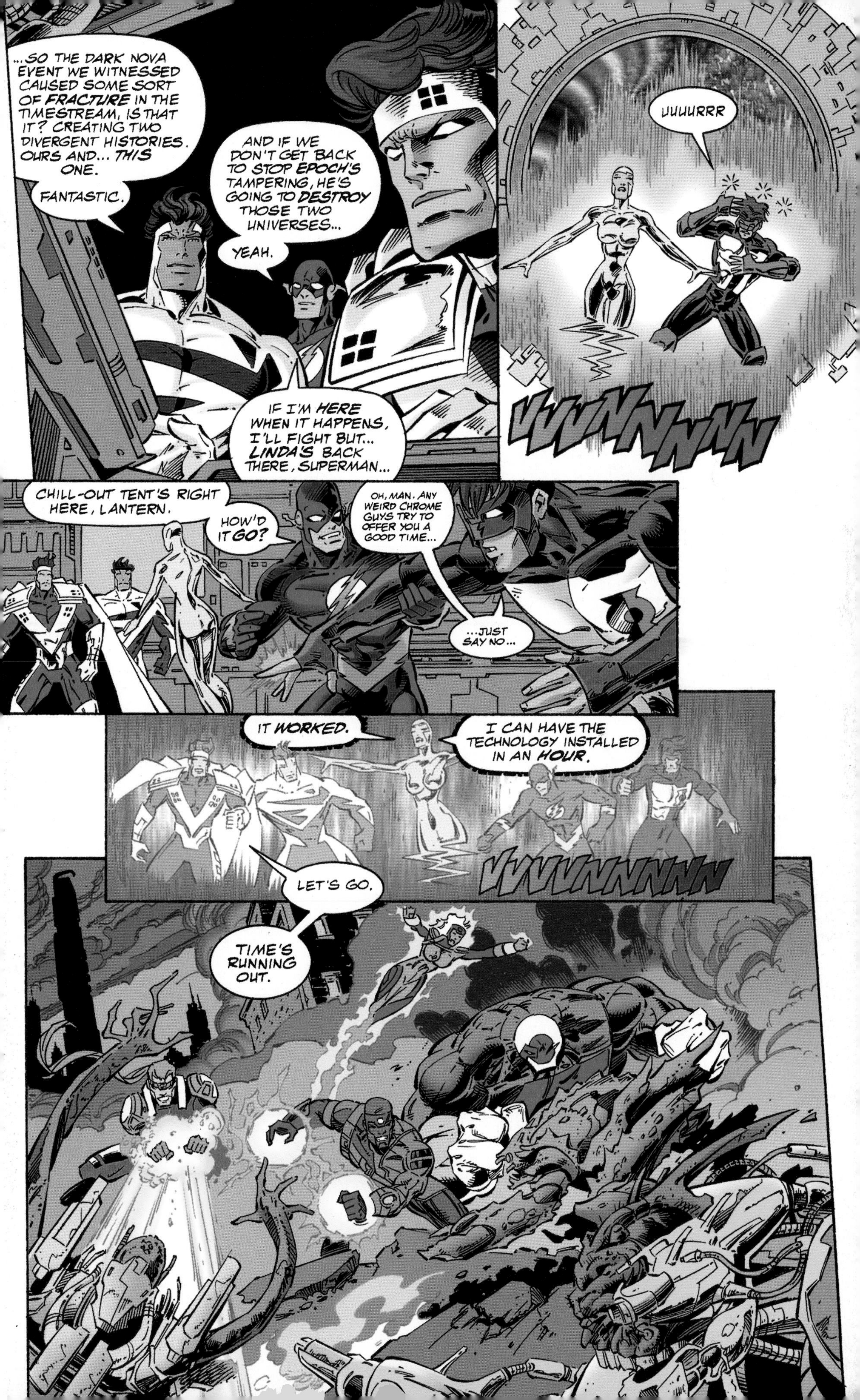
...SO THE DARK NOVA EVENT WE WITNESSED CAUSED SOME SORT OF FRACTURE IN THE TIMESTREAM, IS THAT IT? CREATING TWO DIVERGENT HISTORIES. OURS AND... THIS ONE.
FANTASTIC.
AND IF WE DON'T GET BACK TO STOP EPOCH'S TAMPERING, HE'S GOING TO DESTROY THOSE TWO UNIVERSES...
YEAH.
IF I'M HERE WHEN IT HAPPENS, I'LL FIGHT BUT... LINDA'S BACK THERE, SUPERMAN...
UUUURRR
VVVVNNNNN
CHILL-OUT TENT'S RIGHT HERE, LANTERN.
HOW'D IT GO?
OH, MAN. ANY WEIRD CHROME GUYS TRY TO OFFER YOU A GOOD TIME...
...JUST SAY NO...
IT WORKED.
I CAN HAVE THE TECHNOLOGY INSTALLED IN AN HOUR.
VVVVNNNNNN
LET'S GO.
TIME'S RUNNING OUT.

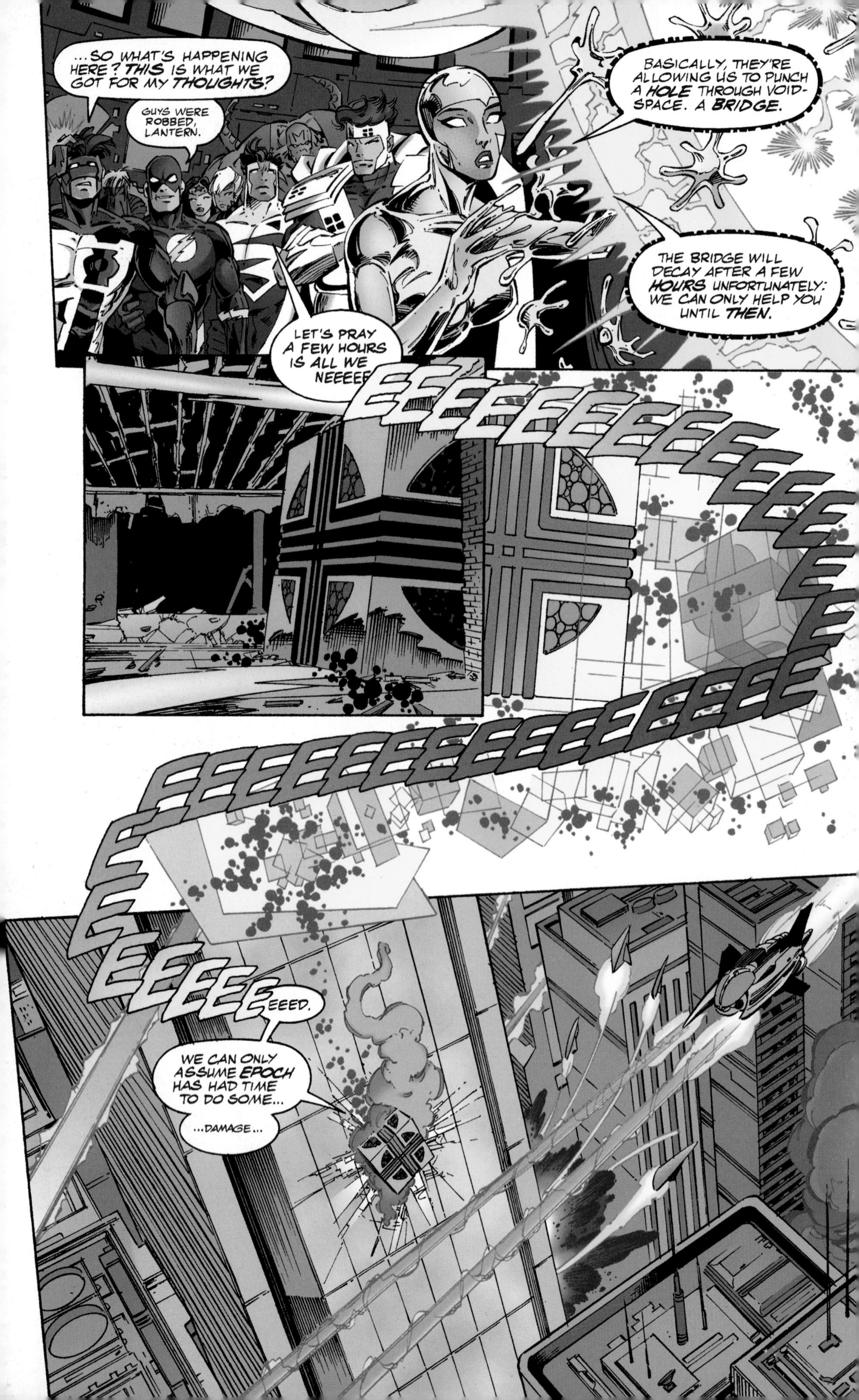
...SO WHAT'S HAPPENING HERE? THIS IS WHAT WE GOT FOR MY THOUGHTS?
GUYS WERE ROBBED, LANTERN.
BASICALLY, THEY'RE ALLOWING US TO PUNCH A HOLE THROUGH VOID-SPACE. A BRIDGE.
THE BRIDGE WILL DECAY AFTER A FEW HOURS UNFORTUNATELY: WE CAN ONLY HELP YOU UNTIL THEN.
LET'S PRAY A FEW HOURS IS ALL WE NEEEEE
EEEED.
WE CAN ONLY ASSUME EPOCH HAS HAD TIME TO DO SOME...
...DAMAGE...

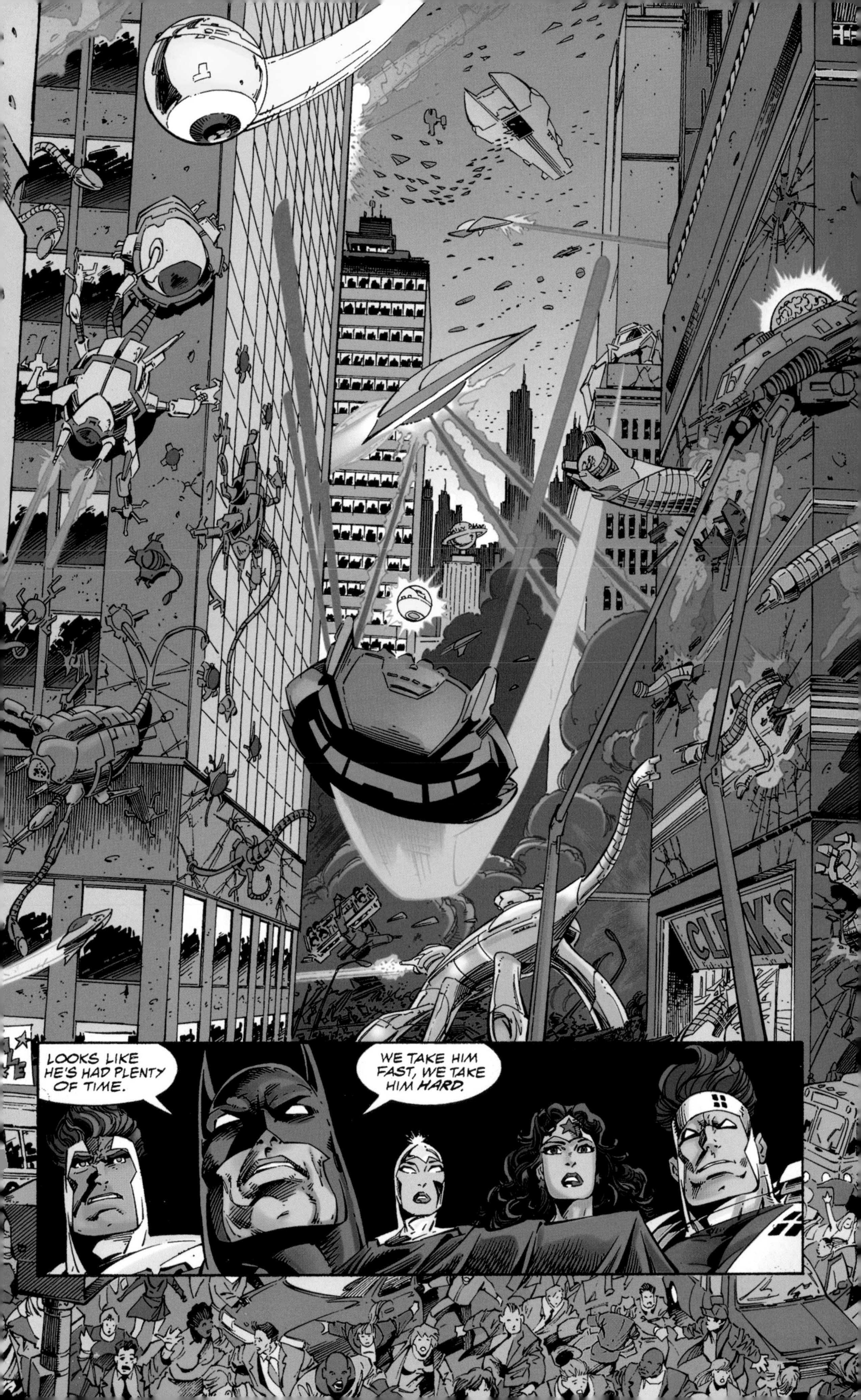
LOOKS LIKE HE'S HAD PLENTY OF TIME.
WE TAKE HIM FAST, WE TAKE HIM HARD.

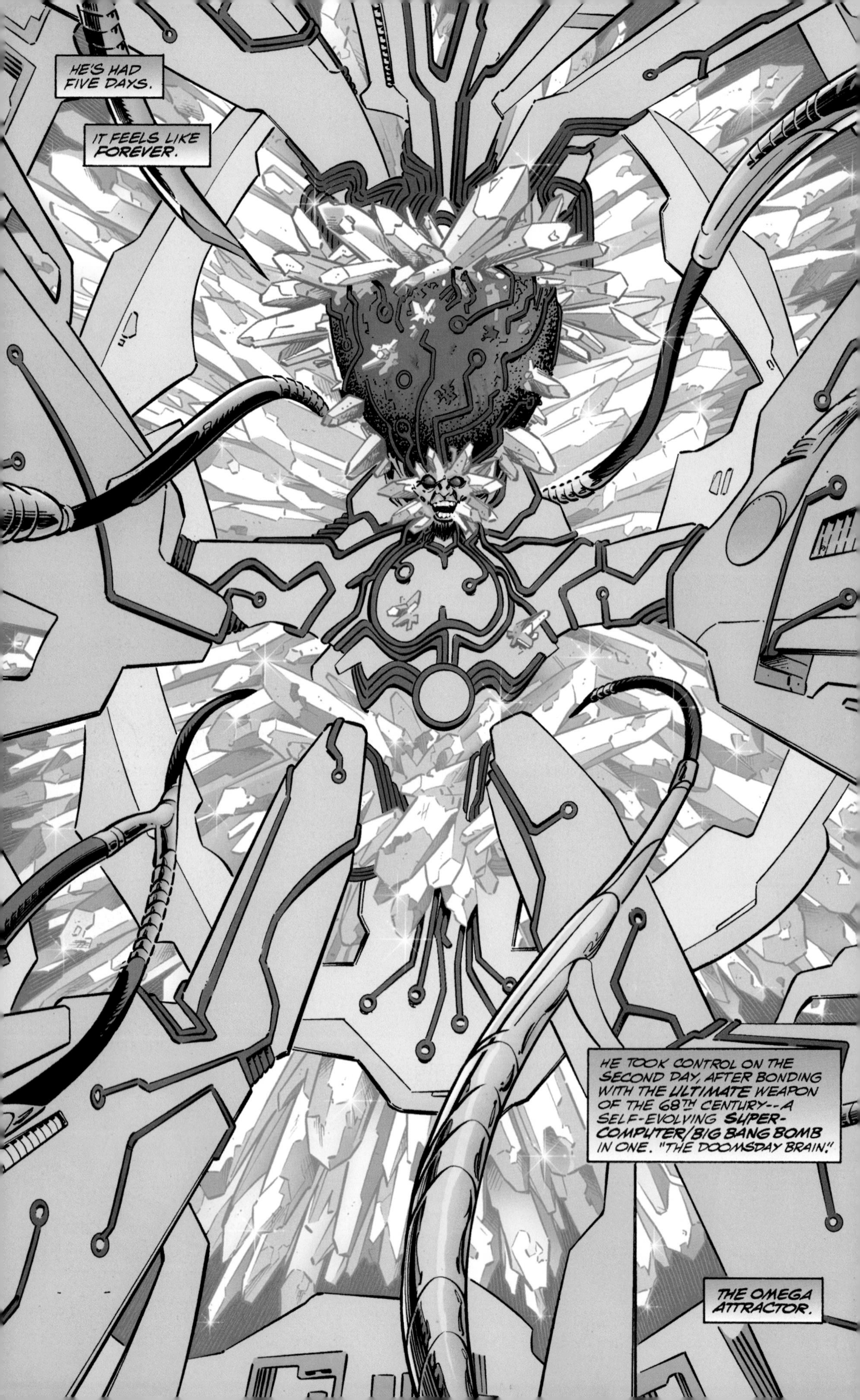
HE'S HAD FIVE DAYS.
IT FEELS LIKE FOREVER.
HE TOOK CONTROL ON THE SECOND DAY, AFTER BONDING WITH THE ULTIMATE WEAPON OF THE 68TH CENTURY--A SELF-EVOLVING SUPER-COMPUTER/BIG BANG BOMB IN ONE. "THE DOOMSDAY BRAIN."
THE OMEGA ATTRACTOR.

NOW HE CAN'T TELL WHERE HE *ENDS* AND IT *BEGINS.*

EVERYTHING IS THE OMEGA ATTRACTOR.

HIS THOUGHTS ARE *ENORMOUS* NOW.

BIG ENOUGH TO REACH EFFORTLESSLY ACROSS SPACE AND TIME. BIG ENOUGH TO COMMAND THE LEGIONS OF THE *FUTURE* AND SUBDUE THE EARTH.

INTELLIGENT CLOUD SURVEILLANCE SYSTEMS FROM THE 22ND CENTURY, RELEASE SHOWERS OF MIND-SOFTENING *RAIN* OVER THE EASTERN SEABOARD OF THE USA.

GARGOYLE-TROOPS FROM THE 98TH CENTURY GOTHIC IMPERIUM OF *NEO-PANGEA* HAUNT THE SPIRES OF *MOSCOW.*

THE SCALE OF HIS *PLANS* GROWS GRANDER EVERY HOUR AS HIS MIND OUTRACES *ALL* LIMITS.

28TH CENTURY *MACROSUITS* PROWL THE PACIFIC RIM.

ALL OF IT UNDER *HIS* CONTROL.

HE INTENDS NOW TO CONVERT THE ENTIRE EARTH INTO A VAST TIME-TRAVELING *ENGINE* POWERED BY ITS HUMAN SLAVE POPULATION.

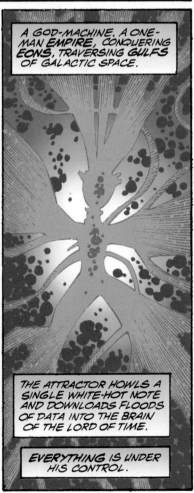

A GOD-MACHINE. A ONE-MAN *EMPIRE,* CONQUERING *EONS,* TRAVERSING *GULFS* OF GALACTIC SPACE.

THE ATTRACTOR HOWLS A SINGLE WHITE-HOT NOTE AND DOWNLOADS FLOODS OF DATA INTO THE BRAIN OF THE LORD OF TIME.

EVERYTHING IS UNDER HIS CONTROL.

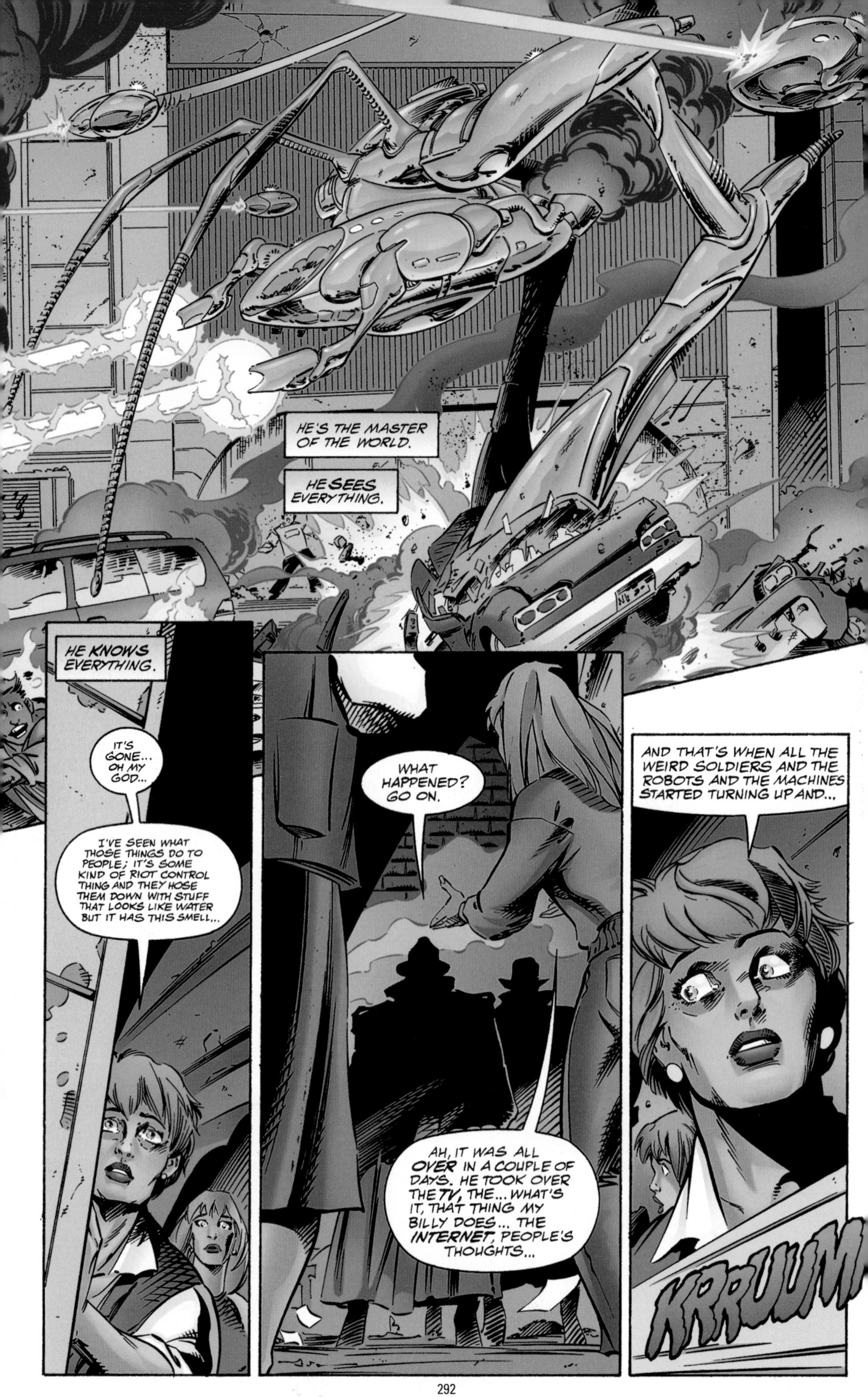
HE'S THE MASTER OF THE WORLD.
HE SEES EVERYTHING.
HE KNOWS EVERYTHING.
IT'S GONE... OH MY GOD...
I'VE SEEN WHAT THOSE THINGS DO TO PEOPLE; IT'S SOME KIND OF RIOT CONTROL THING AND THEY HOSE THEM DOWN WITH STUFF THAT LOOKS LIKE WATER BUT IT HAS THIS SMELL...
WHAT HAPPENED? GO ON.
AH, IT WAS ALL OVER IN A COUPLE OF DAYS. HE TOOK OVER THE TV, THE... WHAT'S IT, THAT THING MY BILLY DOES... THE INTERNET, PEOPLE'S THOUGHTS...
AND THAT'S WHEN ALL THE WEIRD SOLDIERS AND THE ROBOTS AND THE MACHINES STARTED TURNING UP AND...
KRRUUM

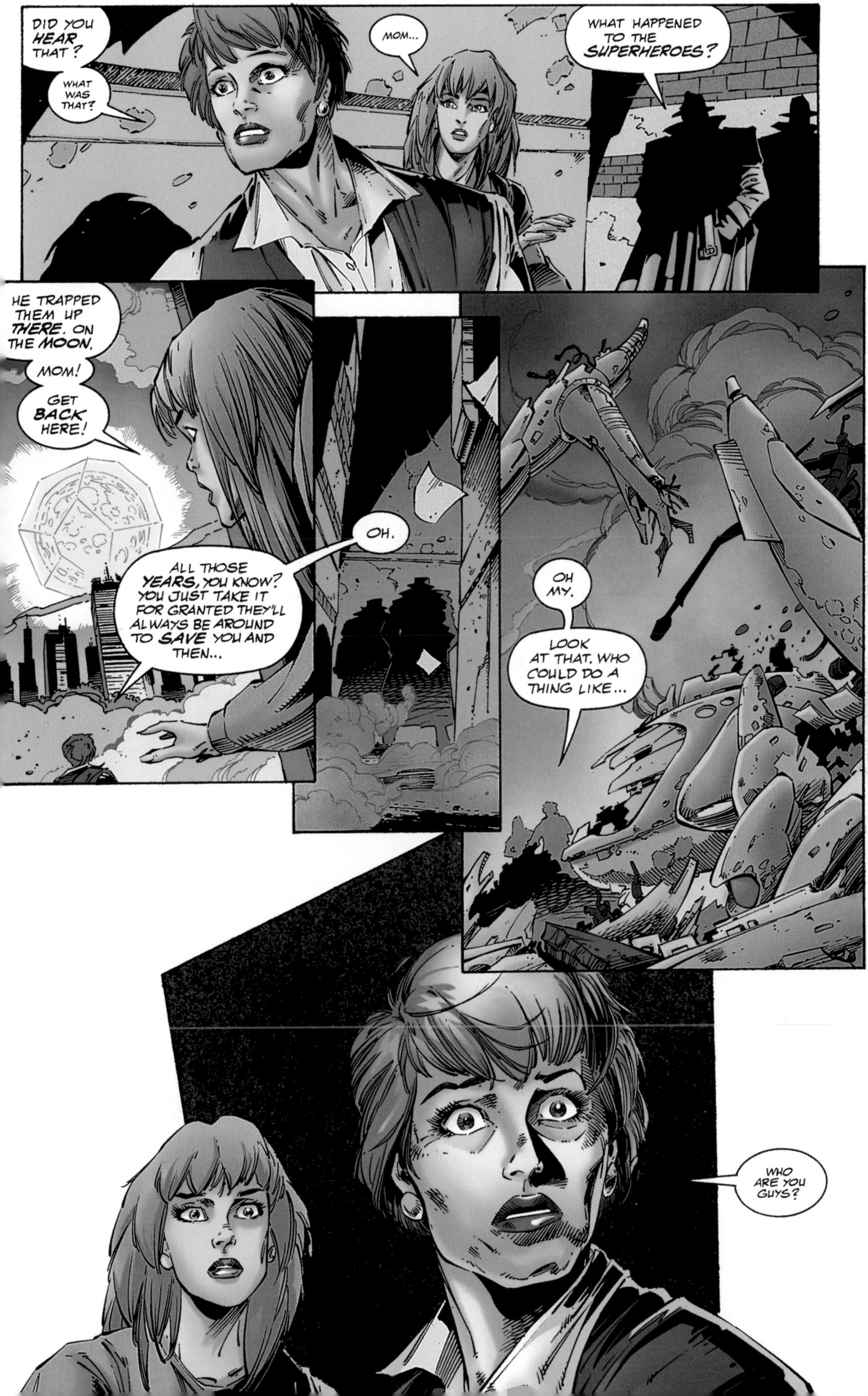
DID YOU HEAR THAT?
WHAT WAS THAT?
MOM...
WHAT HAPPENED TO THE SUPERHEROES?
HE TRAPPED THEM UP THERE. ON THE MOON.
MOM!
GET BACK HERE!
ALL THOSE YEARS, YOU KNOW? YOU JUST TAKE IT FOR GRANTED THEY'LL ALWAYS BE AROUND TO SAVE YOU AND THEN...
OH.
OH MY.
LOOK AT THAT. WHO COULD DO A THING LIKE...
WHO ARE YOU GUYS?

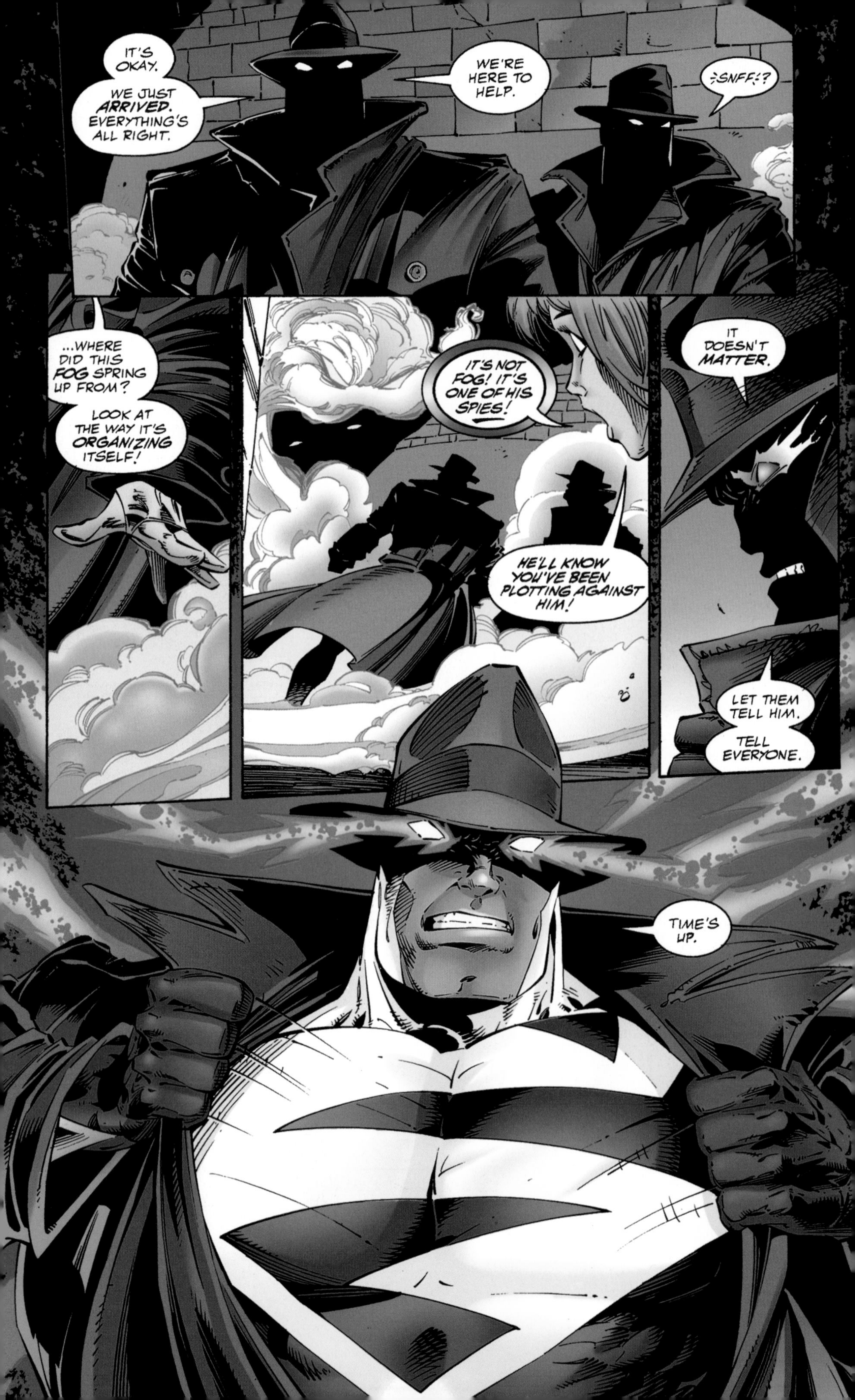
IT'S OKAY.
WE JUST ARRIVED. EVERYTHING'S ALL RIGHT.
WE'RE HERE TO HELP.
SNFF?
...WHERE DID THIS FOG SPRING UP FROM?
LOOK AT THE WAY IT'S ORGANIZING ITSELF!
IT'S NOT FOG! IT'S ONE OF HIS SPIES!
HE'LL KNOW YOU'VE BEEN PLOTTING AGAINST HIM!
IT DOESN'T MATTER.
LET THEM TELL HIM.
TELL EVERYONE.
TIME'S UP.

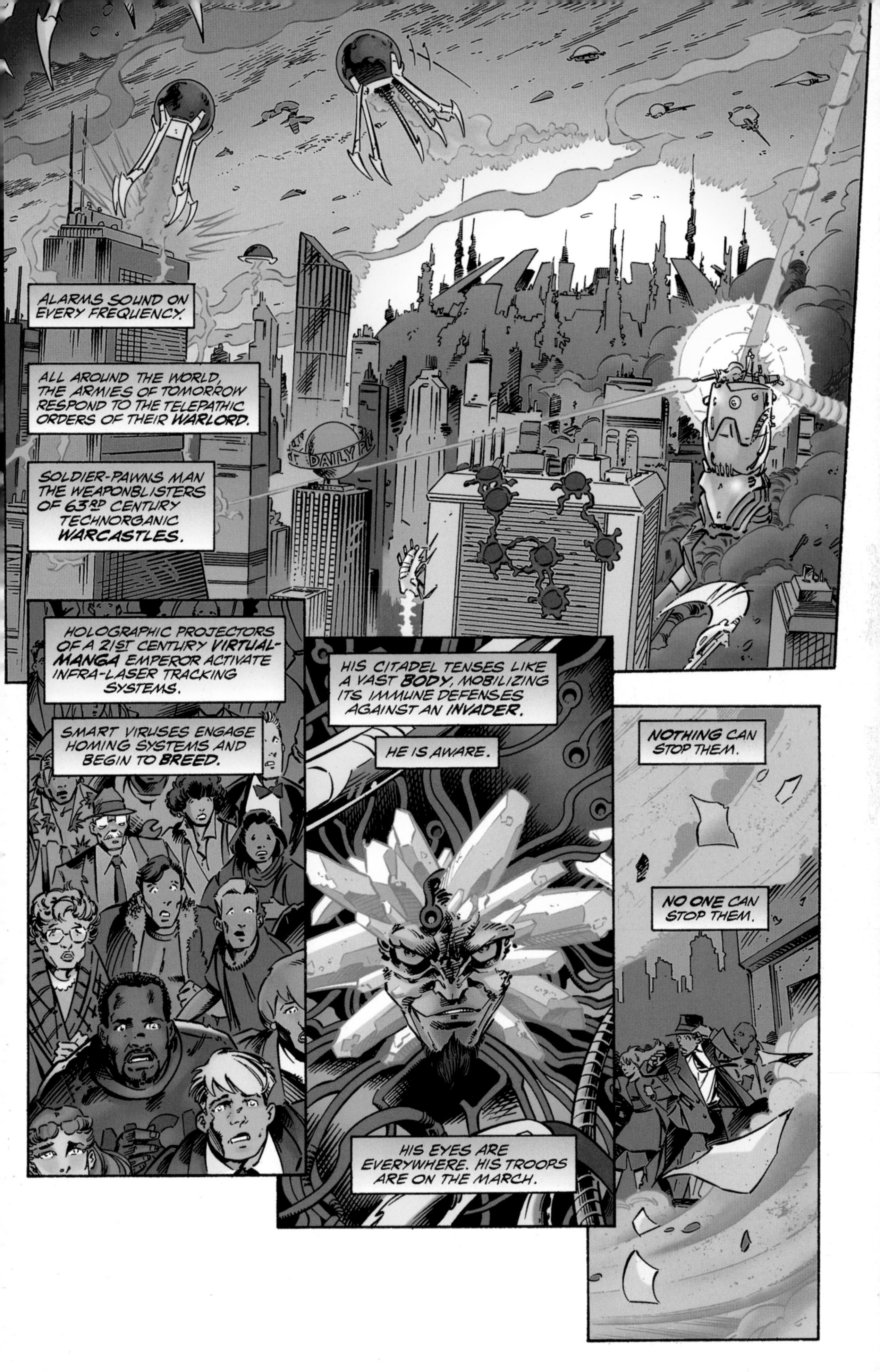
ALARMS SOUND ON EVERY FREQUENCY.
ALL AROUND THE WORLD, THE ARMIES OF TOMORROW RESPOND TO THE TELEPATHIC ORDERS OF THEIR WARLORD.
SOLDIER-PAWNS MAN THE WEAPONBLISTERS OF 63RD CENTURY TECHNORGANIC WARCASTLES.
HOLOGRAPHIC PROJECTORS OF A 21ST CENTURY VIRTUAL-MANGA EMPEROR ACTIVATE INFRA-LASER TRACKING SYSTEMS.
SMART VIRUSES ENGAGE HOMING SYSTEMS AND BEGIN TO BREED.
HIS CITADEL TENSES LIKE A VAST BODY, MOBILIZING ITS IMMUNE DEFENSES AGAINST AN INVADER.
HE IS AWARE.
HIS EYES ARE EVERYWHERE. HIS TROOPS ARE ON THE MARCH.
NOTHING CAN STOP THEM.
NO ONE CAN STOP THEM.

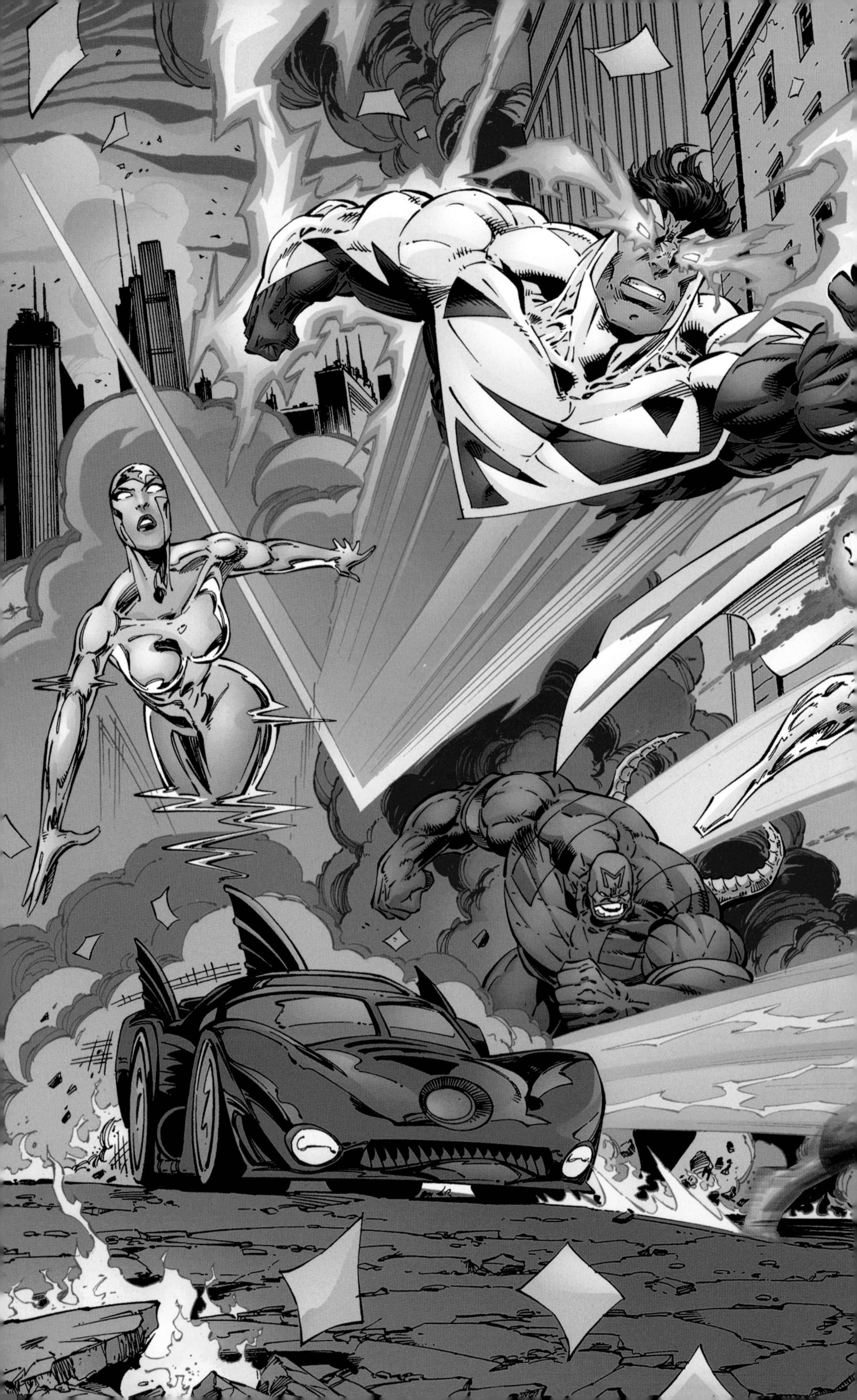

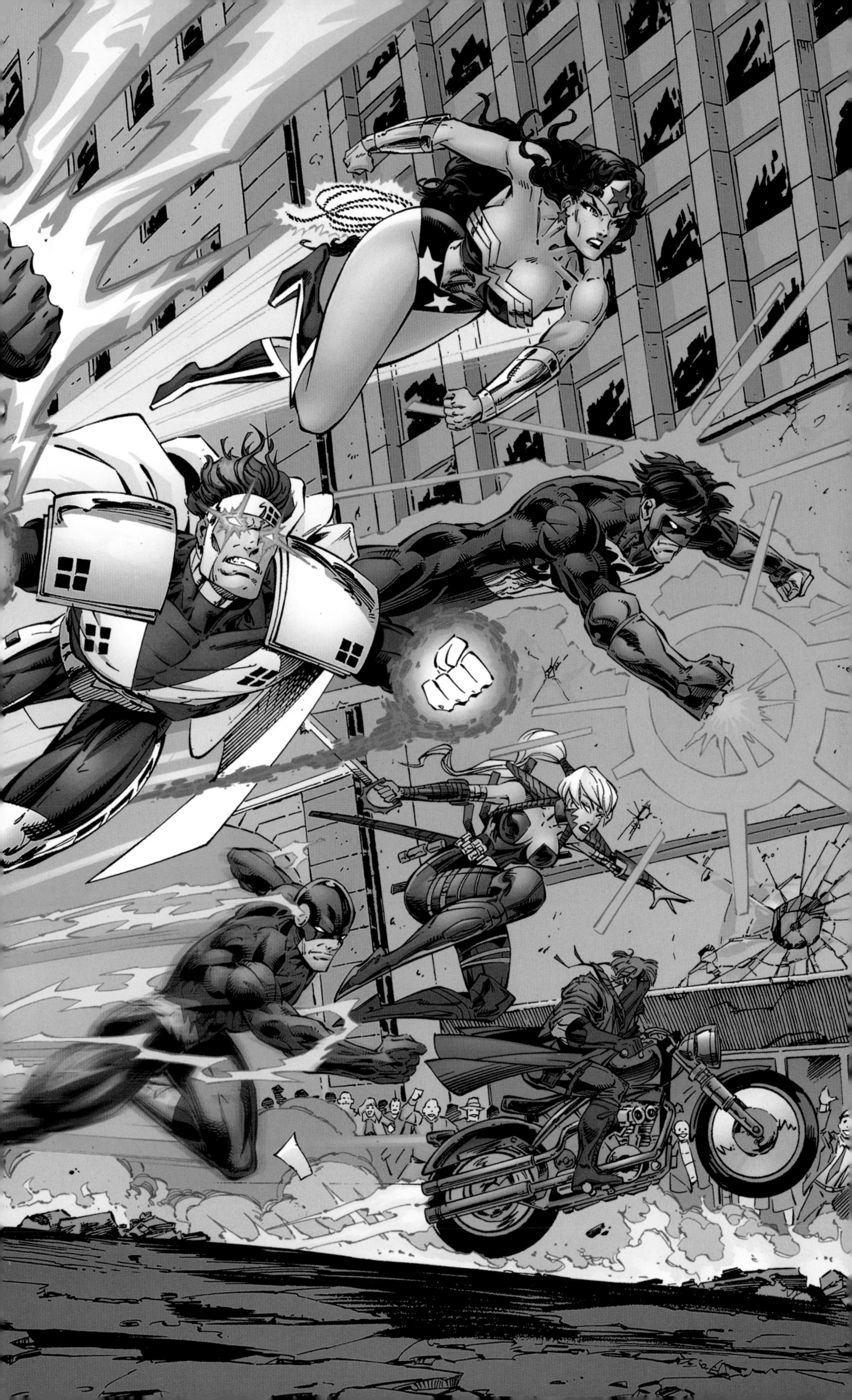

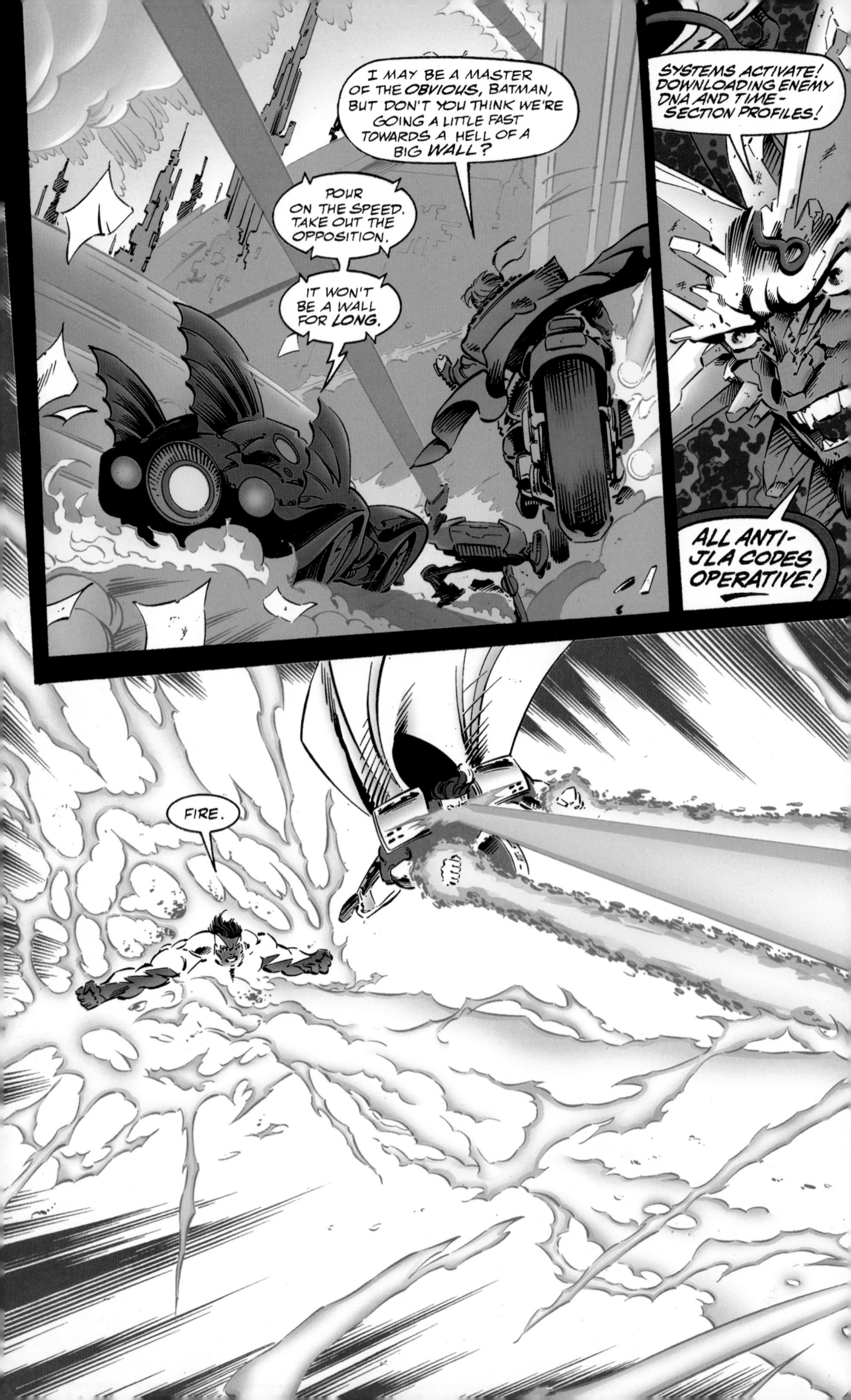
I MAY BE A MASTER OF THE OBVIOUS, BATMAN, BUT DON'T YOU THINK WE'RE GOING A LITTLE FAST TOWARDS A HELL OF A BIG WALL?
POUR ON THE SPEED. TAKE OUT THE OPPOSITION.
IT WON'T BE A WALL FOR LONG.
SYSTEMS ACTIVATE! DOWNLOADING ENEMY DNA AND TIME-SECTION PROFILES!
ALL ANTI-JLA CODES OPERATIVE!
FIRE.

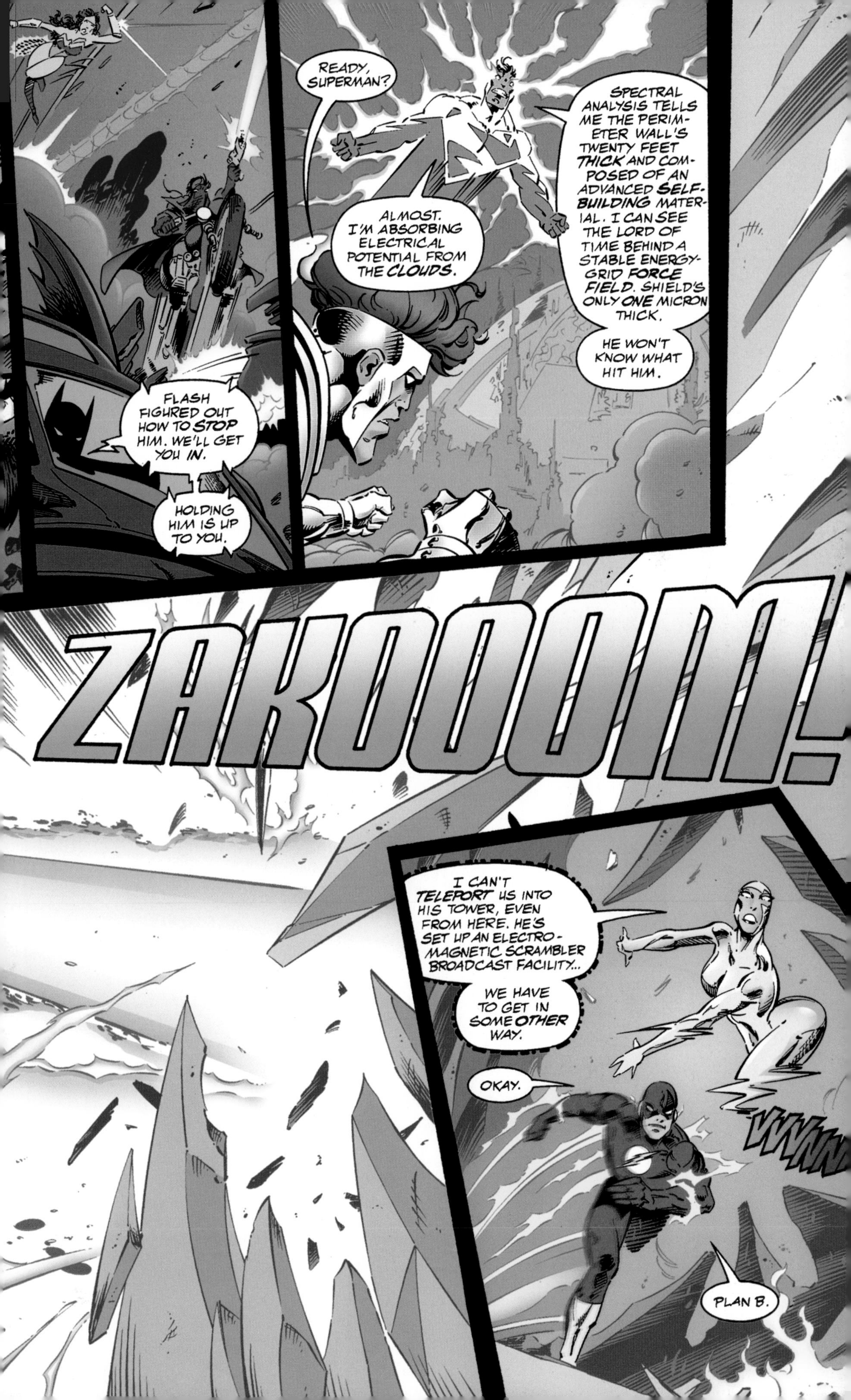
FLASH FIGURED OUT HOW TO STOP HIM. WE'LL GET YOU IN.
HOLDING HIM IS UP TO YOU.
READY, SUPERMAN?
ALMOST. I'M ABSORBING ELECTRICAL POTENTIAL FROM THE CLOUDS.
SPECTRAL ANALYSIS TELLS ME THE PERIMETER WALL'S TWENTY FEET THICK AND COMPOSED OF AN ADVANCED SELF-BUILDING MATERIAL. I CAN SEE THE LORD OF TIME BEHIND A STABLE ENERGY-GRID FORCE FIELD. SHIELD'S ONLY ONE MICRON THICK.
HE WON'T KNOW WHAT HIT HIM.
ZAKOOOM!
I CAN'T TELEPORT US INTO HIS TOWER, EVEN FROM HERE. HE'S SET UP AN ELECTRO-MAGNETIC SCRAMBLER BROADCAST FACILITY...
WE HAVE TO GET IN SOME OTHER WAY.
OKAY.
VVVNN
PLAN B.

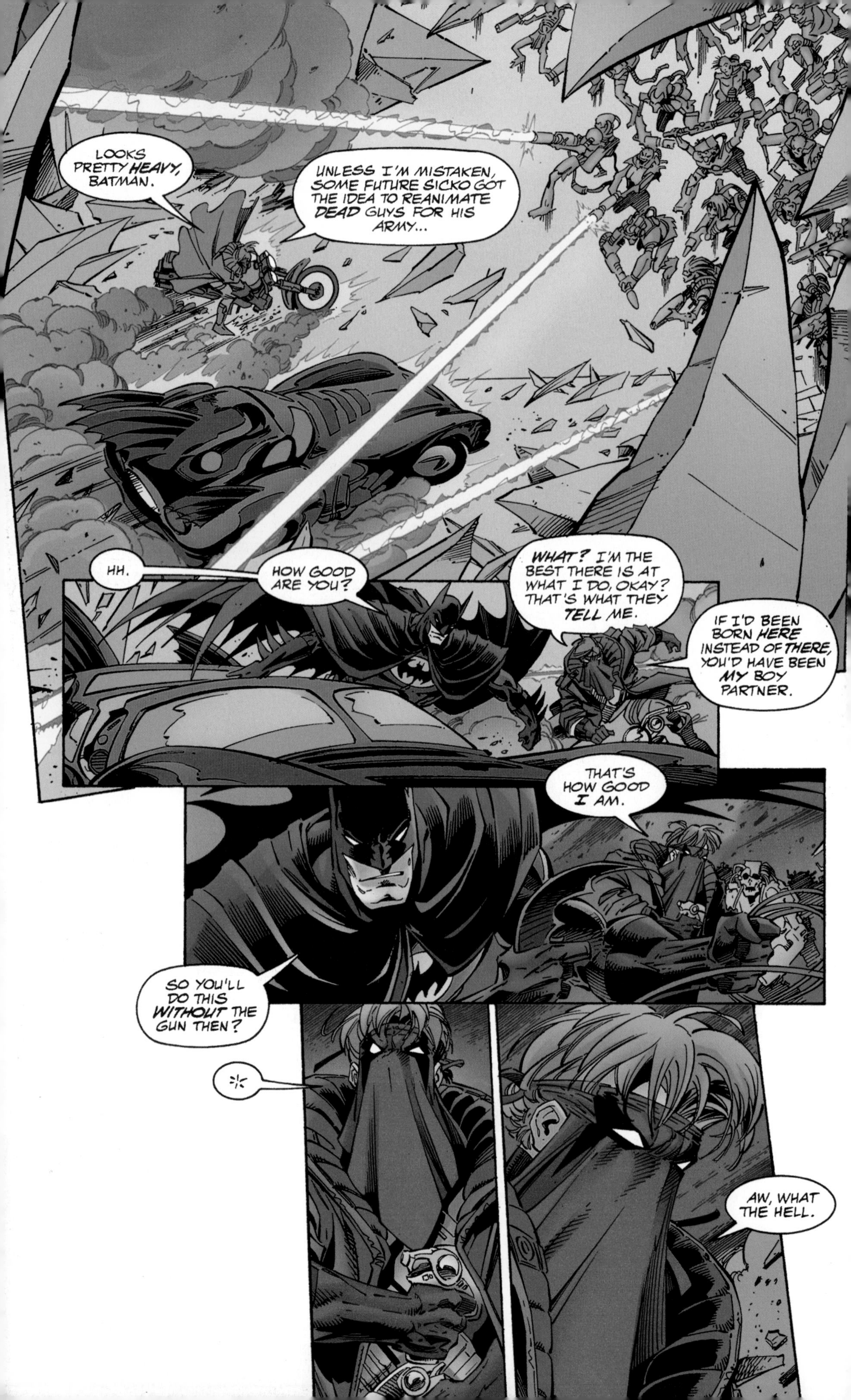
LOOKS PRETTY HEAVY, BATMAN.
UNLESS I'M MISTAKEN, SOME FUTURE SICKO GOT THE IDEA TO REANIMATE DEAD GUYS FOR HIS ARMY...
HH.
HOW GOOD ARE YOU?
WHAT? I'M THE BEST THERE IS AT WHAT I DO, OKAY? THAT'S WHAT THEY TELL ME.
IF I'D BEEN BORN HERE INSTEAD OF THERE, YOU'D HAVE BEEN MY BOY PARTNER.
THAT'S HOW GOOD I AM.
SO YOU'LL DO THIS WITHOUT THE GUN THEN?
AW, WHAT THE HELL.

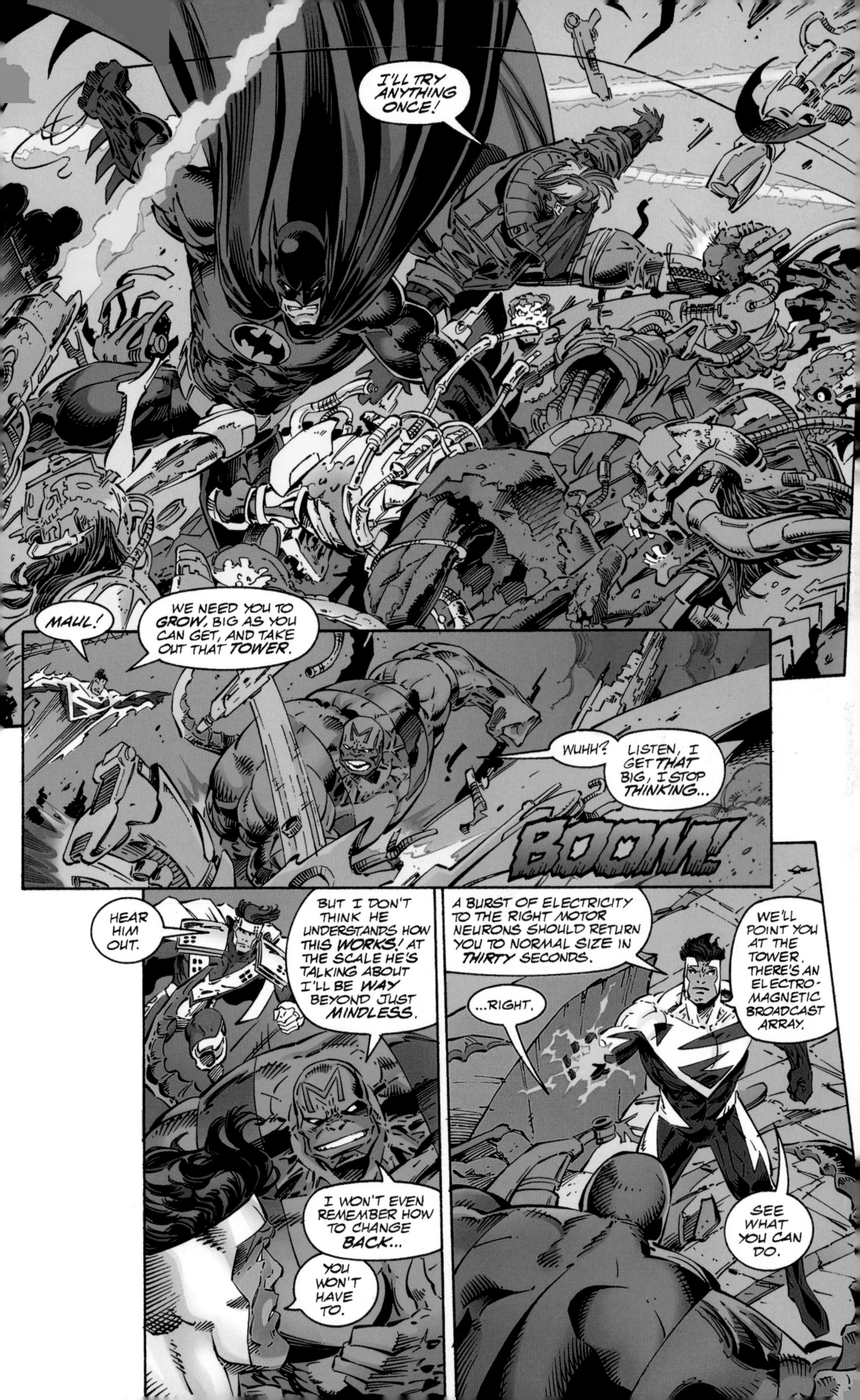
I'LL TRY ANYTHING ONCE!
MAUL!
WE NEED YOU TO GROW, BIG AS YOU CAN GET, AND TAKE OUT THAT TOWER.
WUHH?
LISTEN, I GET THAT BIG, I STOP THINKING...
BOOM!
HEAR HIM OUT.
BUT I DON'T THINK HE UNDERSTANDS HOW THIS WORKS! AT THE SCALE HE'S TALKING ABOUT I'LL BE WAY BEYOND JUST MINDLESS.
I WON'T EVEN REMEMBER HOW TO CHANGE BACK...
YOU WON'T HAVE TO.
A BURST OF ELECTRICITY TO THE RIGHT MOTOR NEURONS SHOULD RETURN YOU TO NORMAL SIZE IN THIRTY SECONDS.
...RIGHT.
WE'LL POINT YOU AT THE TOWER. THERE'S AN ELECTRO-MAGNETIC BROADCAST ARRAY.
SEE WHAT YOU CAN DO.

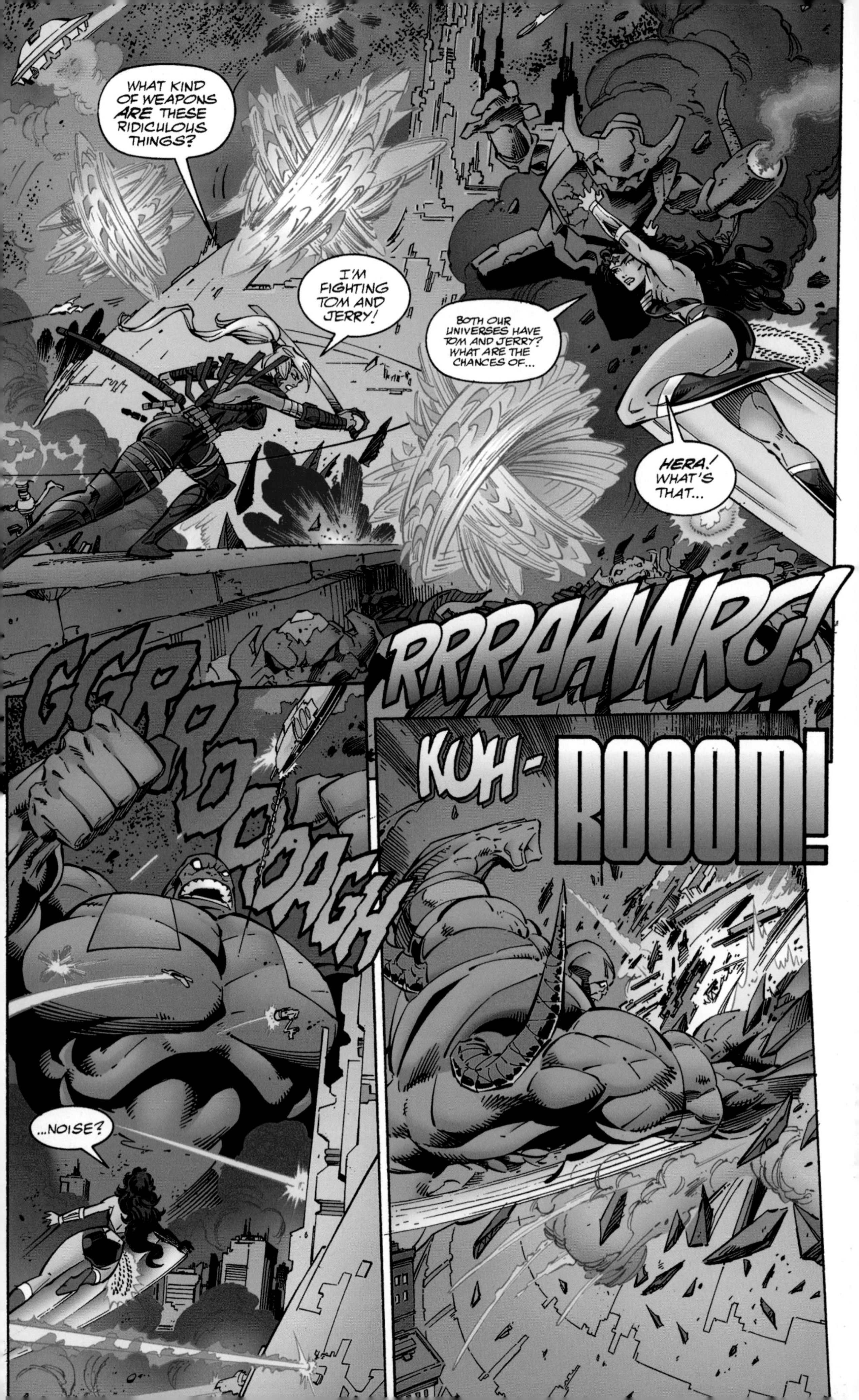
WHAT KIND OF WEAPONS ARE THESE RIDICULOUS THINGS?
I'M FIGHTING TOM AND JERRY!
BOTH OUR UNIVERSES HAVE TOM AND JERRY? WHAT ARE THE CHANCES OF...
HERA! WHAT'S THAT...
GGROOOAGH
RRRAAWRG!
KUH-ROOOM!
...NOISE?

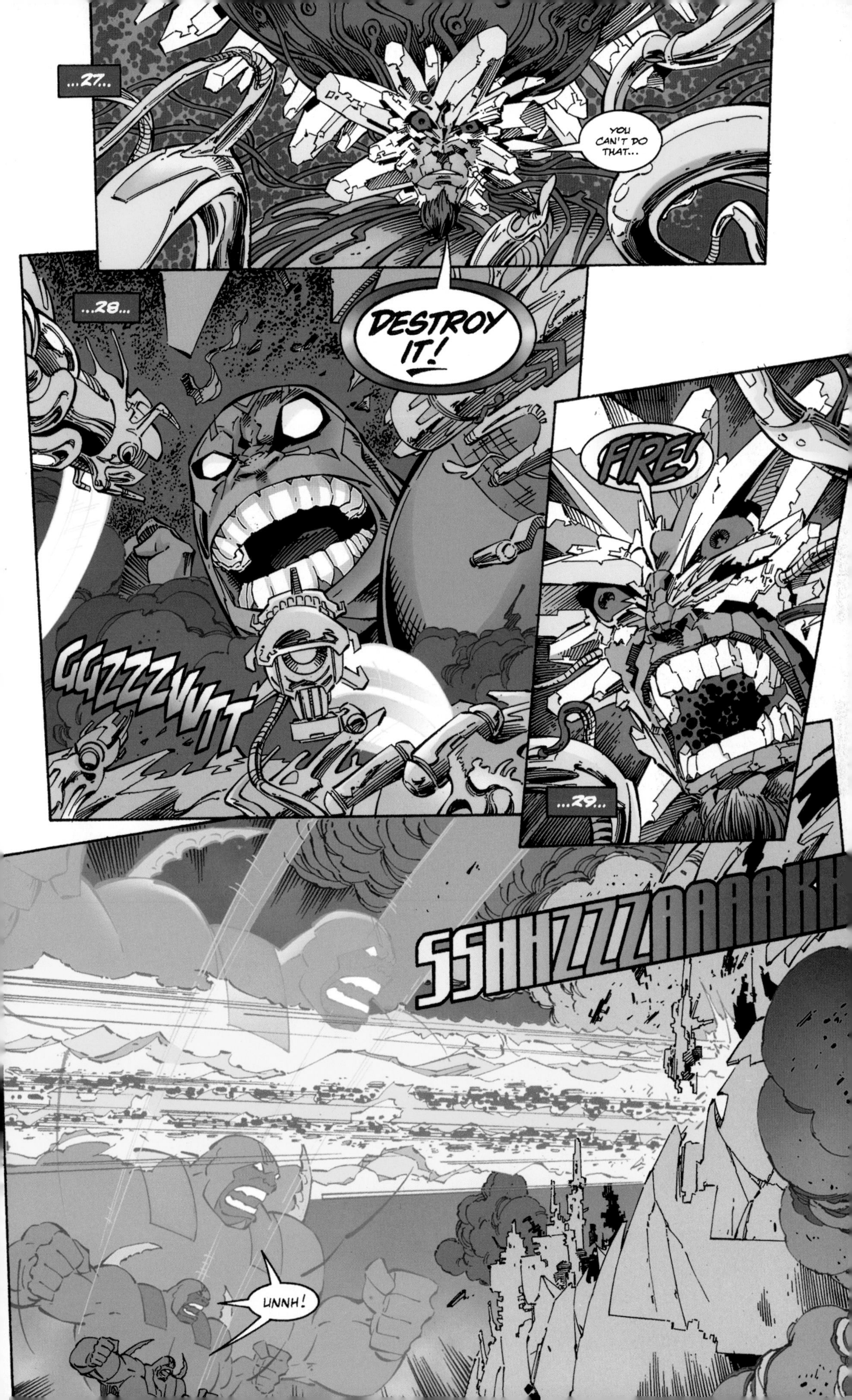
...27...
YOU CAN'T DO THAT...
...28...
DESTROY IT!
GGZZZVUTT
FIRE!
...29...
SSHZZZAAAAKH
UNNH!

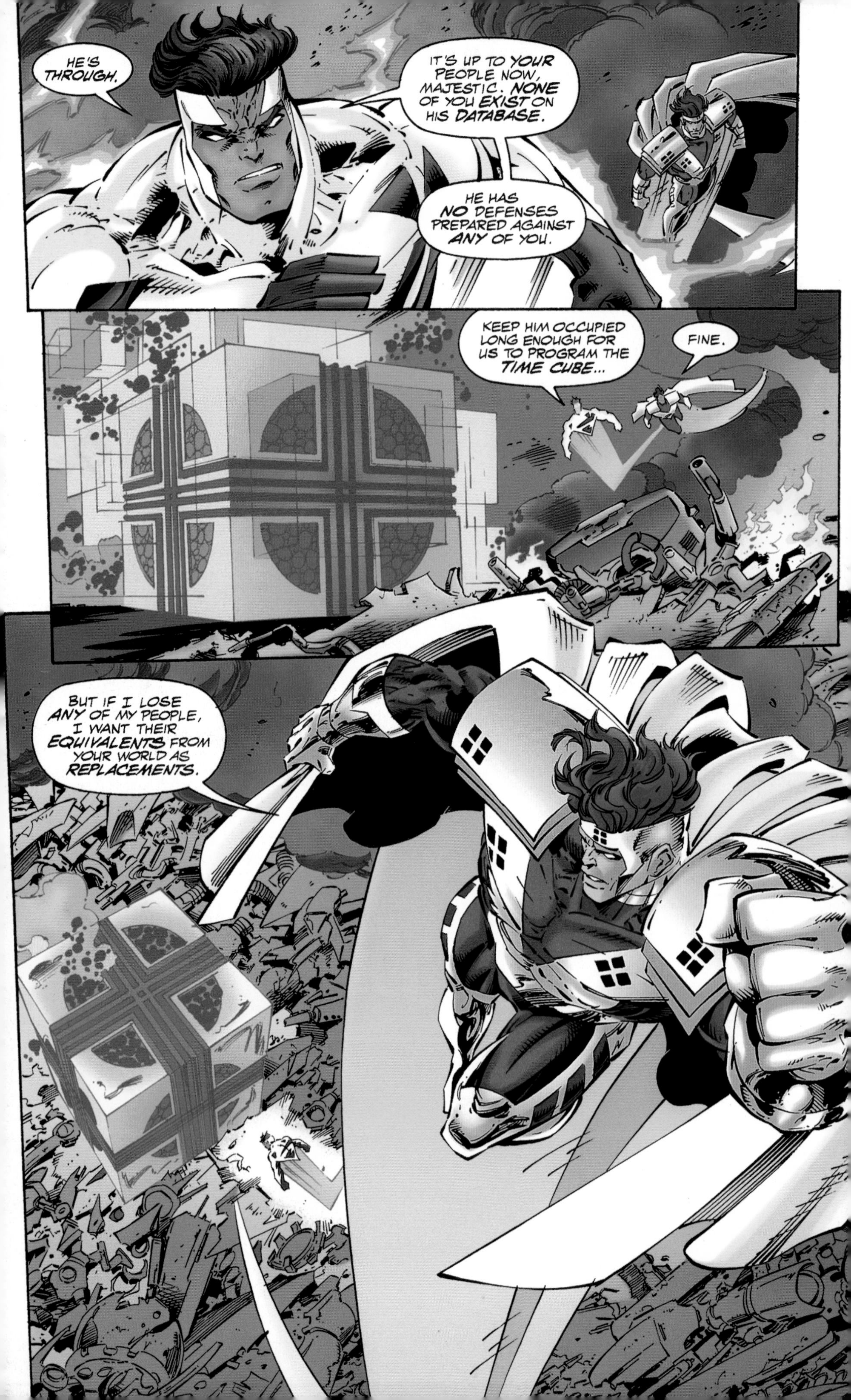
HE'S THROUGH.
IT'S UP TO YOUR PEOPLE NOW, MAJESTIC. NONE OF YOU EXIST ON HIS DATABASE.
HE HAS NO DEFENSES PREPARED AGAINST ANY OF YOU.
KEEP HIM OCCUPIED LONG ENOUGH FOR US TO PROGRAM THE TIME CUBE...
FINE.
BUT IF I LOSE ANY OF MY PEOPLE, I WANT THEIR EQUIVALENTS FROM YOUR WORLD AS REPLACEMENTS.

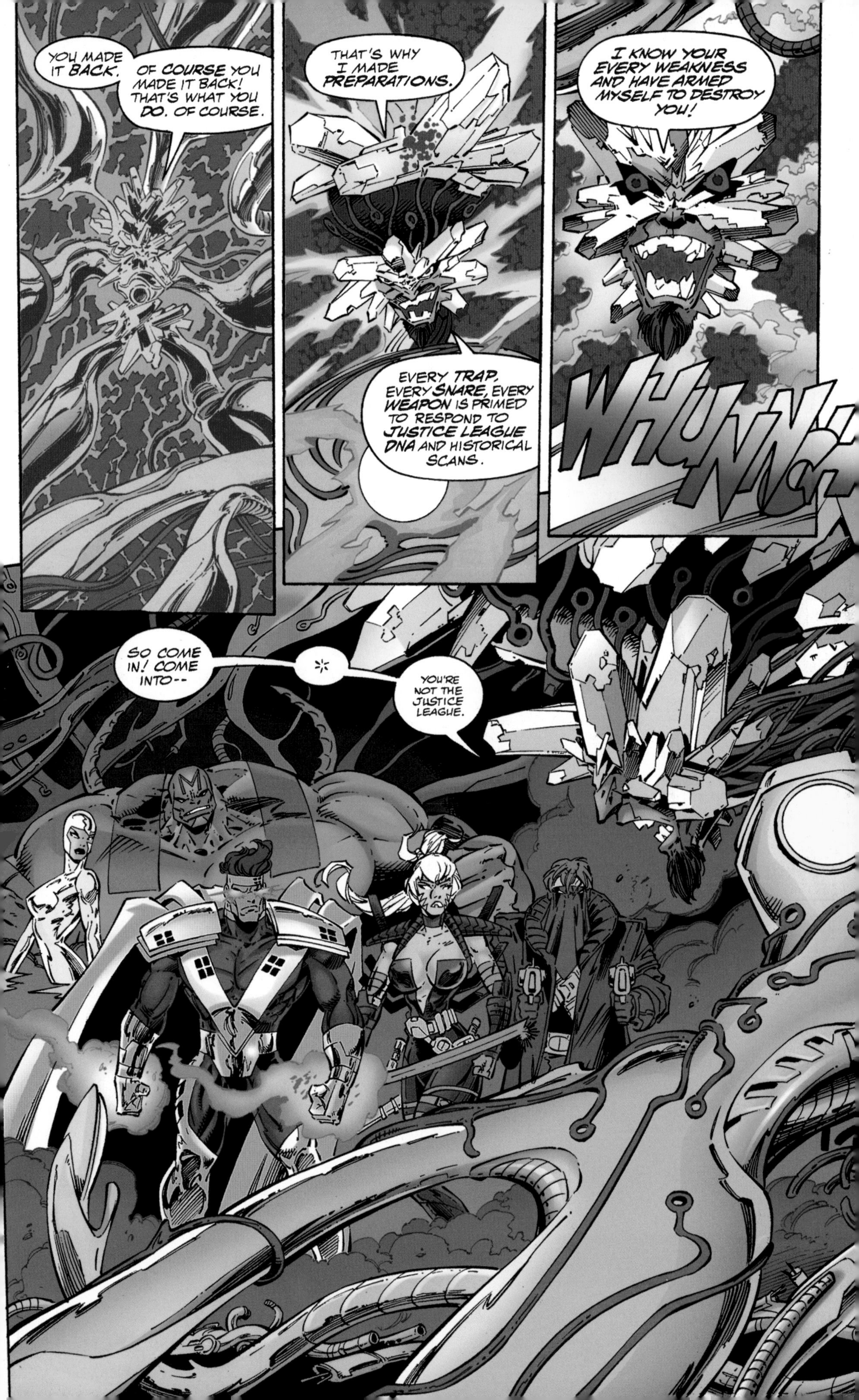

YOU MADE IT BACK.
OF COURSE YOU MADE IT BACK! THAT'S WHAT YOU DO. OF COURSE.
THAT'S WHY I MADE PREPARATIONS.
EVERY TRAP, EVERY SNARE, EVERY WEAPON IS PRIMED TO RESPOND TO JUSTICE LEAGUE DNA AND HISTORICAL SCANS.
I KNOW YOUR EVERY WEAKNESS AND HAVE ARMED MYSELF TO DESTROY YOU!
WHUNNNCH
SO COME IN! COME INTO--
YOU'RE NOT THE JUSTICE LEAGUE.

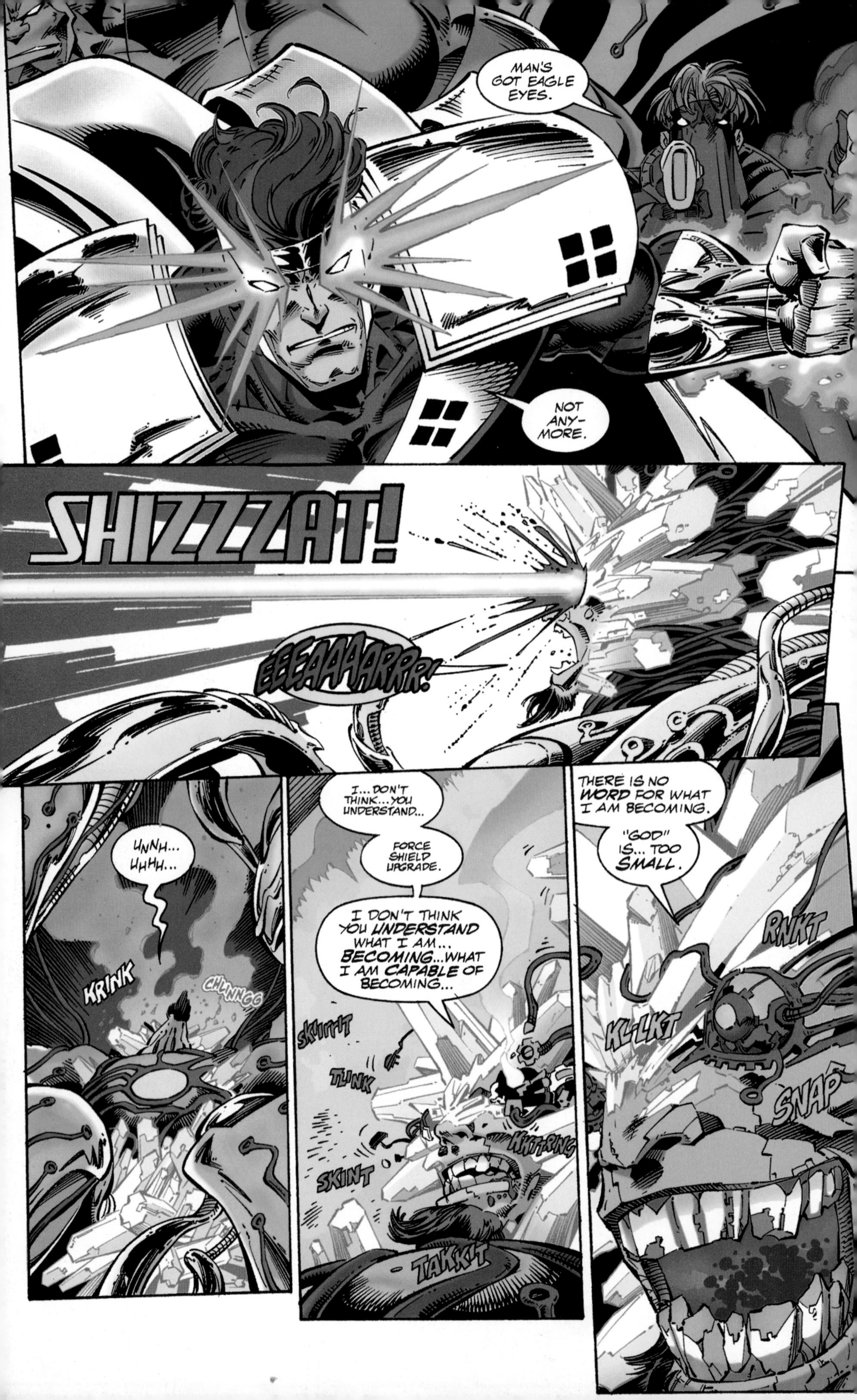

MAN'S GOT EAGLE EYES.
NOT ANY-MORE.
SHIZZZAT!
EEEAAAAARRR!
UNNH... UHHH...
KRINK
CHUNNGG
I... DON'T THINK... YOU UNDERSTAND...
FORCE SHIELD UPGRADE.
I DON'T THINK YOU UNDERSTAND WHAT I AM... BECOMING...WHAT I AM CAPABLE OF BECOMING...
SKIRRT
TUNK
SKINT
TAKK'T
THERE IS NO WORD FOR WHAT I AM BECOMING.
"GOD" IS... TOO SMALL.
RNKT
KL-LKT
SNAP

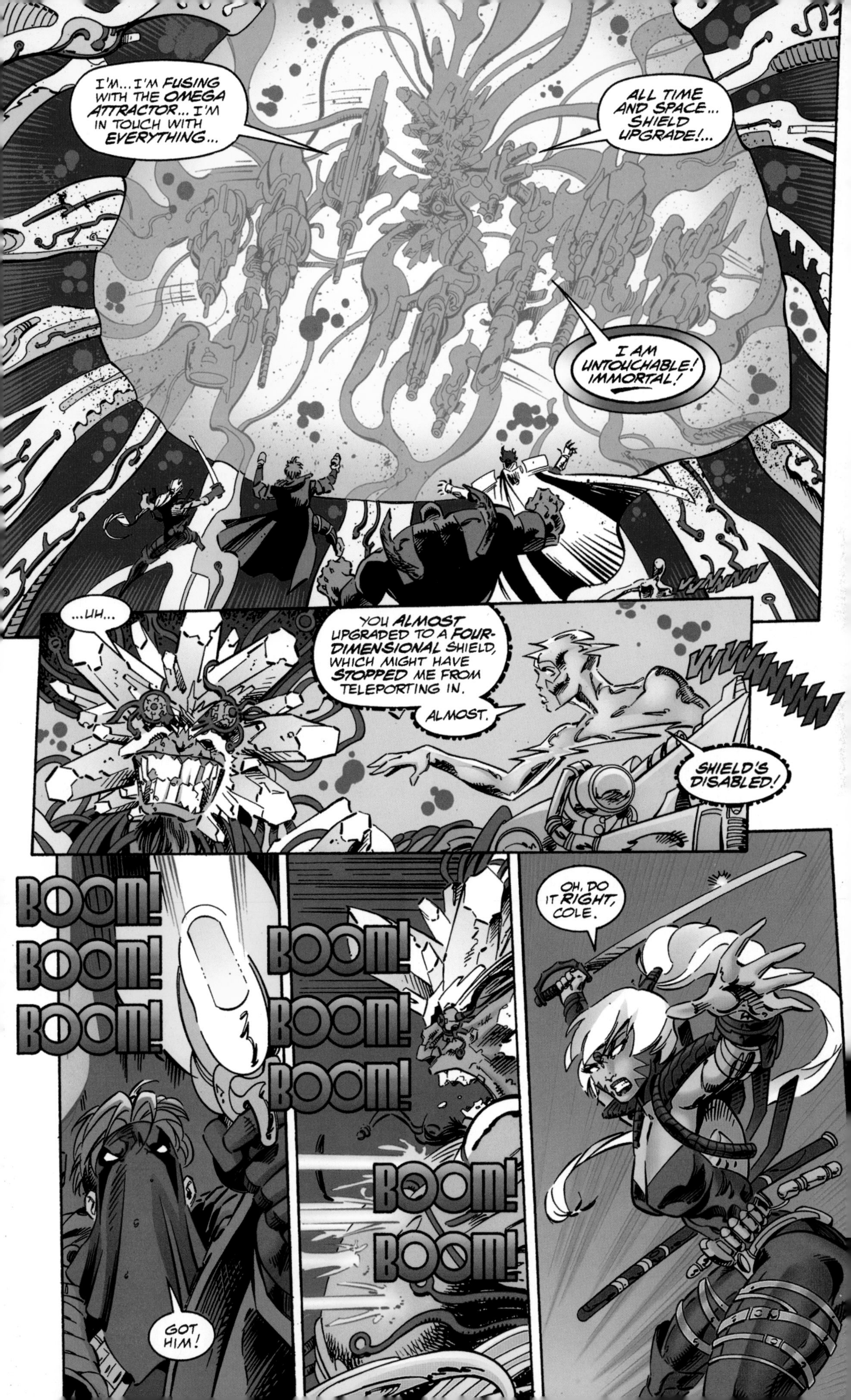
I'M... I'M FUSING WITH THE OMEGA ATTRACTOR... I'M IN TOUCH WITH EVERYTHING...
ALL TIME AND SPACE... SHIELD UPGRADE!...
I AM UNTOUCHABLE! IMMORTAL!
VVNNNN
...UH...
YOU ALMOST UPGRADED TO A FOUR-DIMENSIONAL SHIELD, WHICH MIGHT HAVE STOPPED ME FROM TELEPORTING IN.
ALMOST.
VVVVNNNNNNN
SHIELD'S DISABLED!
BOOM! BOOM! BOOM!
GOT HIM!
BOOM! BOOM! BOOM!
BOOM! BOOM!
OH, DO IT RIGHT, COLE.

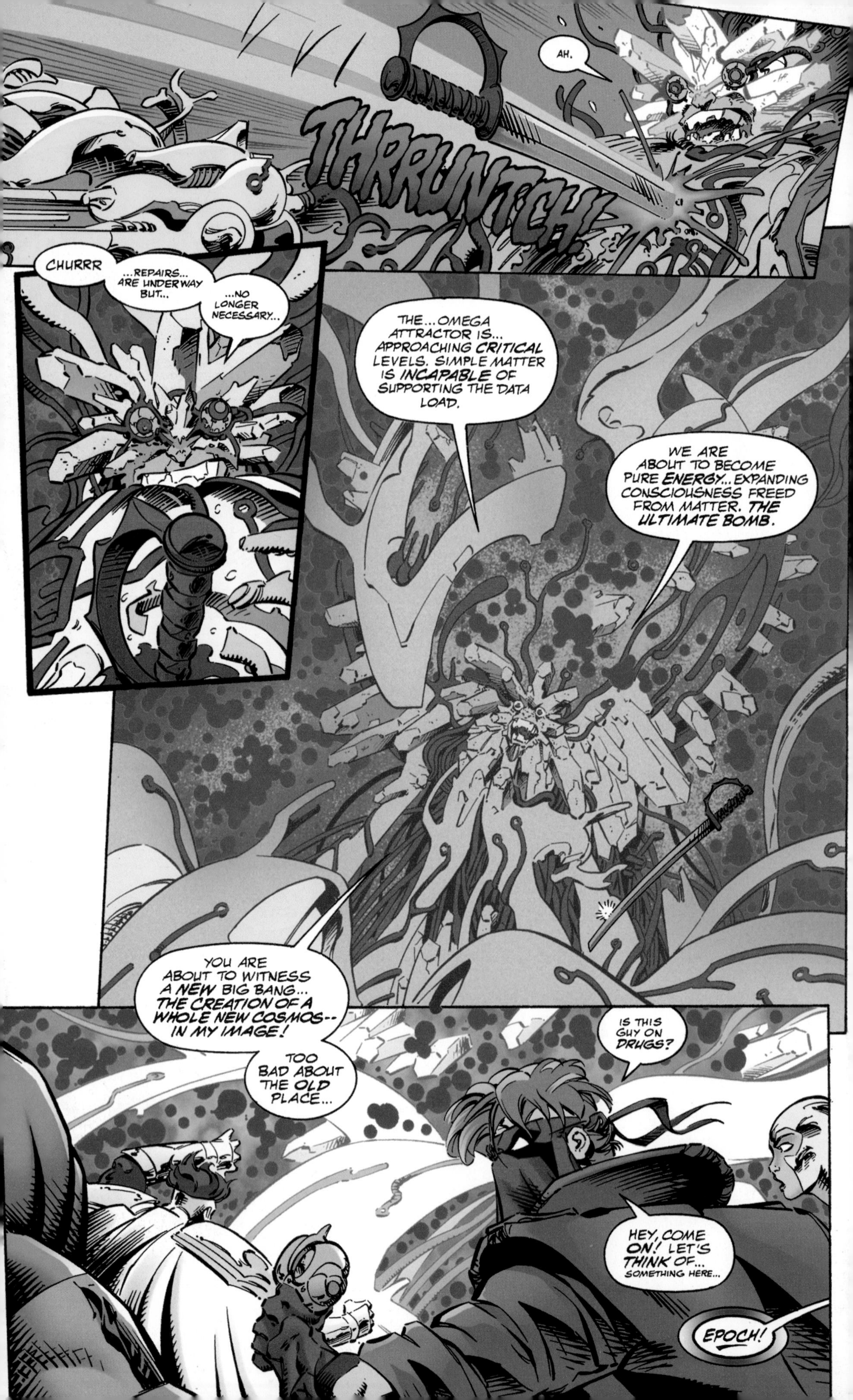
AH.
THRRUNTCH!
CHURRR
...REPAIRS... ARE UNDERWAY BUT...
...NO LONGER NECESSARY...
THE...OMEGA ATTRACTOR IS... APPROACHING CRITICAL LEVELS. SIMPLE MATTER IS INCAPABLE OF SUPPORTING THE DATA LOAD.
WE ARE ABOUT TO BECOME PURE ENERGY... EXPANDING CONSCIOUSNESS FREED FROM MATTER. THE ULTIMATE BOMB.
YOU ARE ABOUT TO WITNESS A NEW BIG BANG... THE CREATION OF A WHOLE NEW COSMOS-- IN MY IMAGE!
TOO BAD ABOUT THE OLD PLACE...
IS THIS GUY ON DRUGS?
HEY, COME ON! LET'S THINK OF... SOMETHING HERE...
EPOCH!

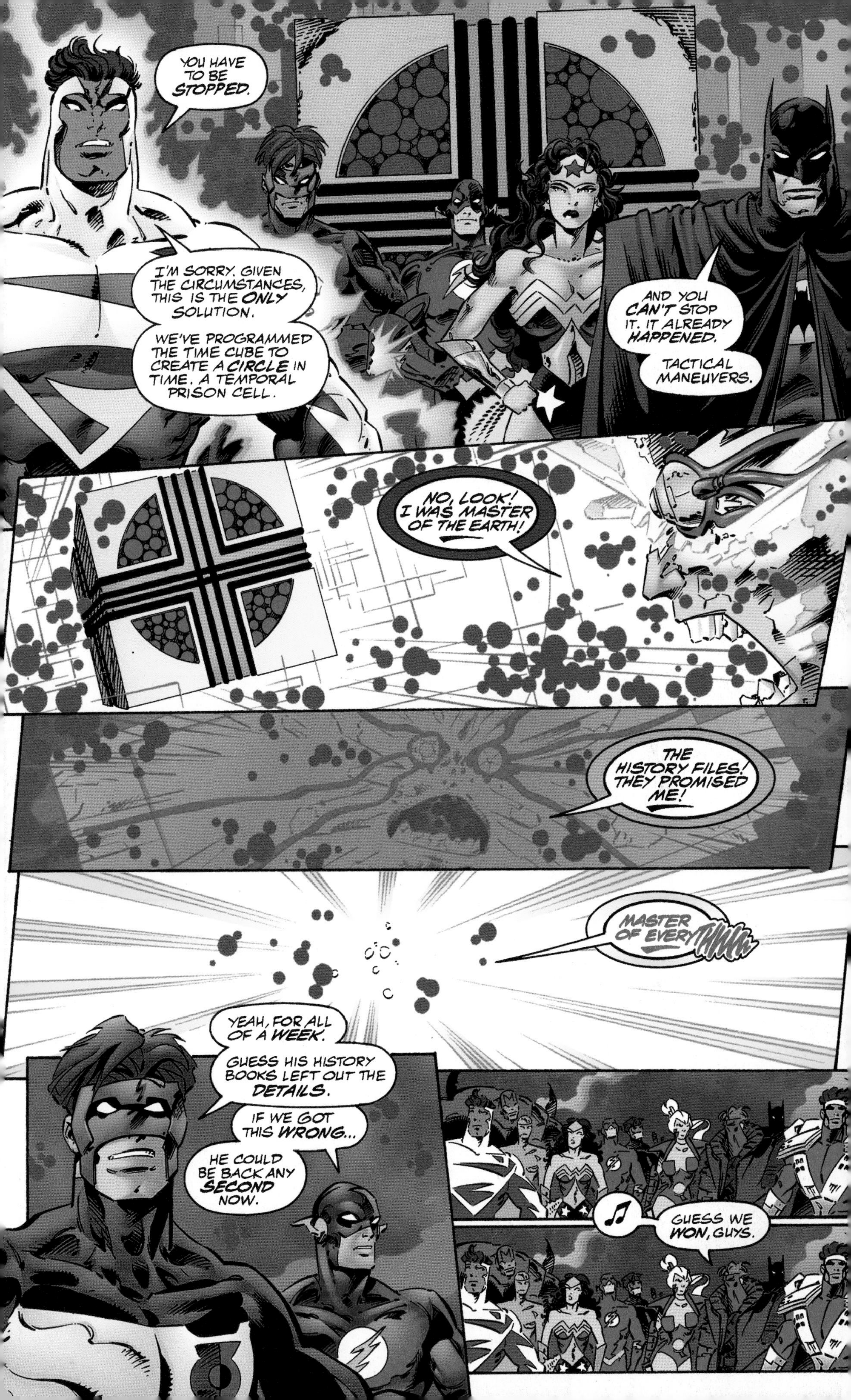

YOU HAVE TO BE STOPPED.
I'M SORRY. GIVEN THE CIRCUMSTANCES, THIS IS THE ONLY SOLUTION.
WE'VE PROGRAMMED THE TIME CUBE TO CREATE A CIRCLE IN TIME. A TEMPORAL PRISON CELL.
AND YOU CAN'T STOP IT. IT ALREADY HAPPENED.
TACTICAL MANEUVERS.
NO, LOOK! I WAS MASTER OF THE EARTH!
THE HISTORY FILES! THEY PROMISED ME!
MASTER OF EVERYTHHHH
YEAH, FOR ALL OF A WEEK.
GUESS HIS HISTORY BOOKS LEFT OUT THE DETAILS.
IF WE GOT THIS WRONG...
HE COULD BE BACK ANY SECOND NOW.
♪
GUESS WE WON, GUYS.

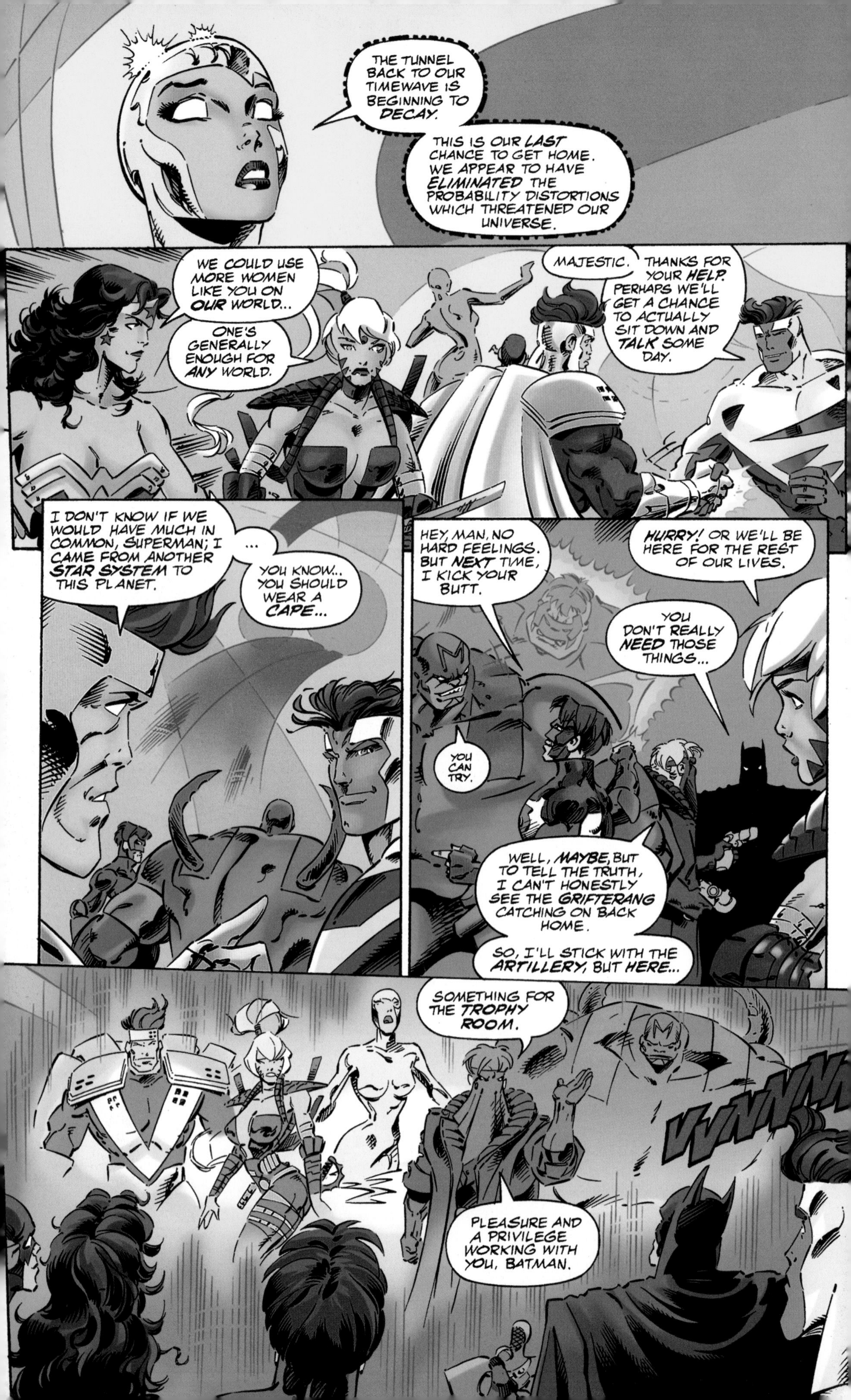
THE TUNNEL BACK TO OUR TIMEWAVE IS BEGINNING TO DECAY.
THIS IS OUR LAST CHANCE TO GET HOME. WE APPEAR TO HAVE ELIMINATED THE PROBABILITY DISTORTIONS WHICH THREATENED OUR UNIVERSE.
WE COULD USE MORE WOMEN LIKE YOU ON OUR WORLD...
ONE'S GENERALLY ENOUGH FOR ANY WORLD.
MAJESTIC.
THANKS FOR YOUR HELP. PERHAPS WE'LL GET A CHANCE TO ACTUALLY SIT DOWN AND TALK SOME DAY.
I DON'T KNOW IF WE WOULD HAVE MUCH IN COMMON, SUPERMAN; I CAME FROM ANOTHER STAR SYSTEM TO THIS PLANET.
...
YOU KNOW... YOU SHOULD WEAR A CAPE...
HEY, MAN, NO HARD FEELINGS. BUT NEXT TIME, I KICK YOUR BUTT.
HURRY! OR WE'LL BE HERE FOR THE REST OF OUR LIVES.
YOU DON'T REALLY NEED THOSE THINGS...
YOU CAN TRY.
WELL, MAYBE, BUT TO TELL THE TRUTH, I CAN'T HONESTLY SEE THE GRIFTERANG CATCHING ON BACK HOME.
SO, I'LL STICK WITH THE ARTILLERY, BUT HERE...
SOMETHING FOR THE TROPHY ROOM.
VVNNN
PLEASURE AND A PRIVILEGE WORKING WITH YOU, BATMAN.

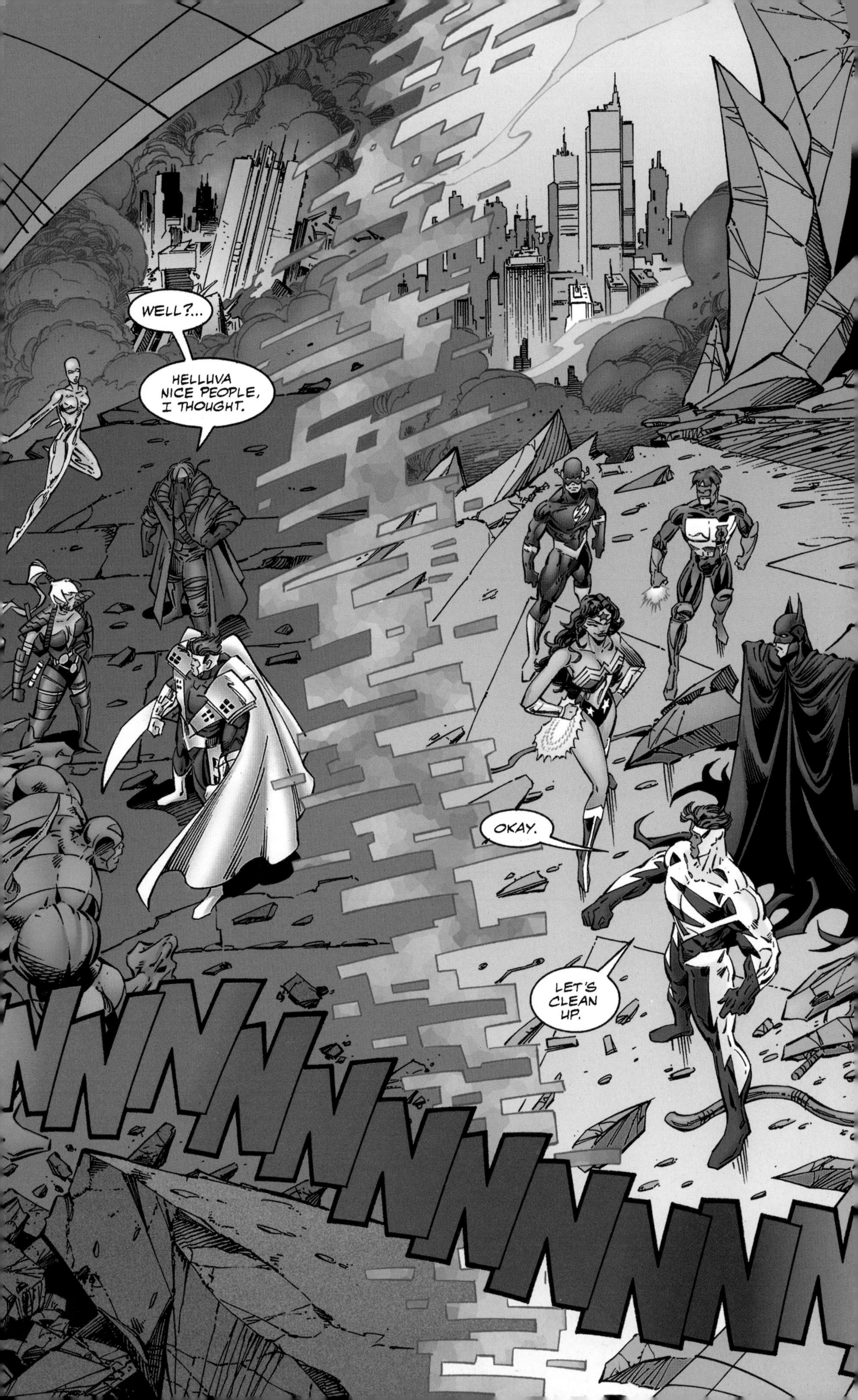
WELL?...
HELLUVA NICE PEOPLE, I THOUGHT.
OKAY.
LET'S CLEAN UP.
NNNNNNNNNNNNNNNNN

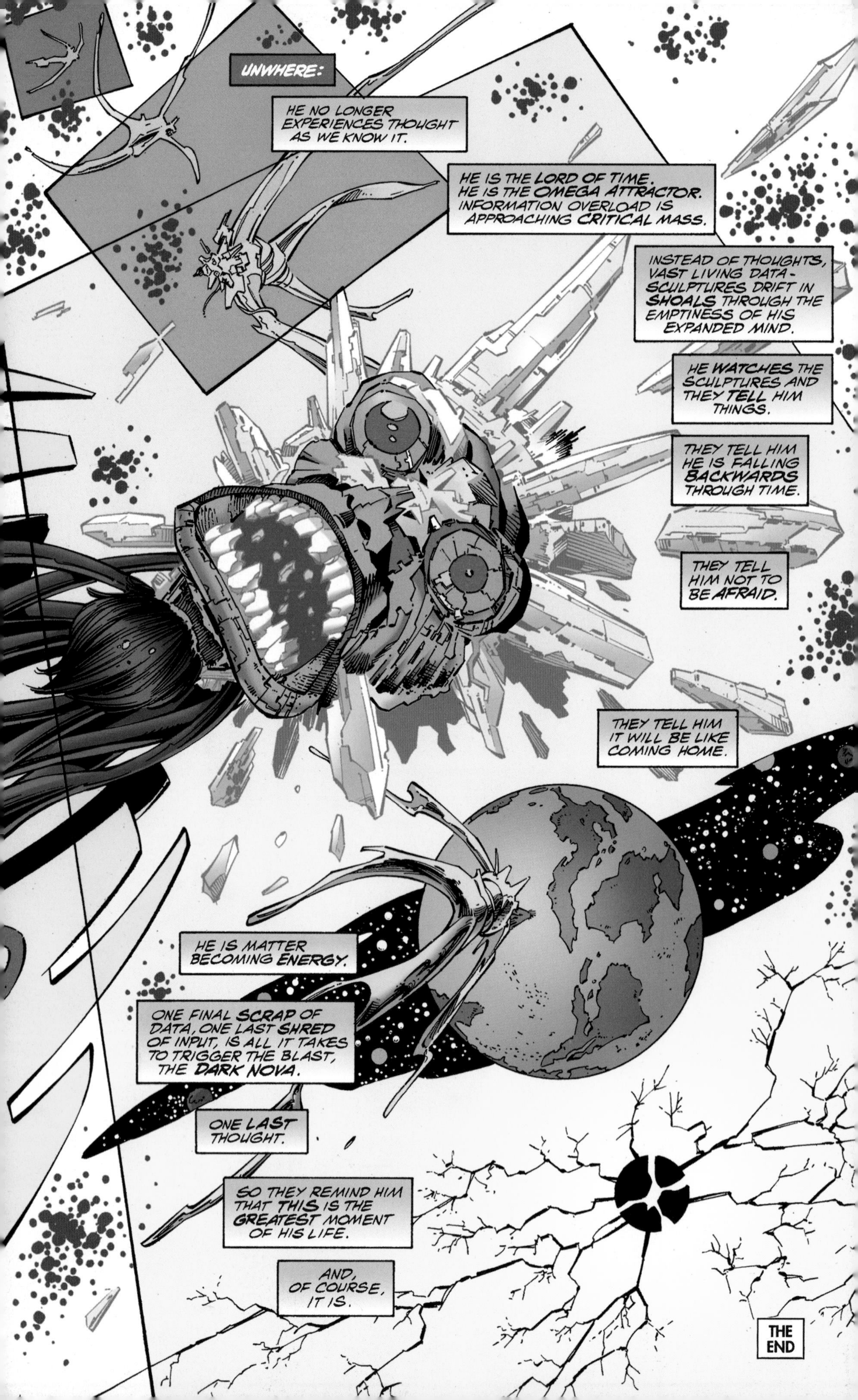
UNWHERE:
HE NO LONGER EXPERIENCES THOUGHT AS WE KNOW IT.
HE IS THE LORD OF TIME. HE IS THE OMEGA ATTRACTOR. INFORMATION OVERLOAD IS APPROACHING CRITICAL MASS.
INSTEAD OF THOUGHTS, VAST LIVING DATA-SCULPTURES DRIFT IN SHOALS THROUGH THE EMPTINESS OF HIS EXPANDED MIND.
HE WATCHES THE SCULPTURES AND THEY TELL HIM THINGS.
THEY TELL HIM HE IS FALLING BACKWARDS THROUGH TIME.
THEY TELL HIM NOT TO BE AFRAID.
THEY TELL HIM IT WILL BE LIKE COMING HOME.
HE IS MATTER BECOMING ENERGY.
ONE FINAL SCRAP OF DATA, ONE LAST SHRED OF INPUT, IS ALL IT TAKES TO TRIGGER THE BLAST, THE DARK NOVA.
ONE LAST THOUGHT.
SO THEY REMIND HIM THAT THIS IS THE GREATEST MOMENT OF HIS LIFE.
AND, OF COURSE, IT IS.
THE END

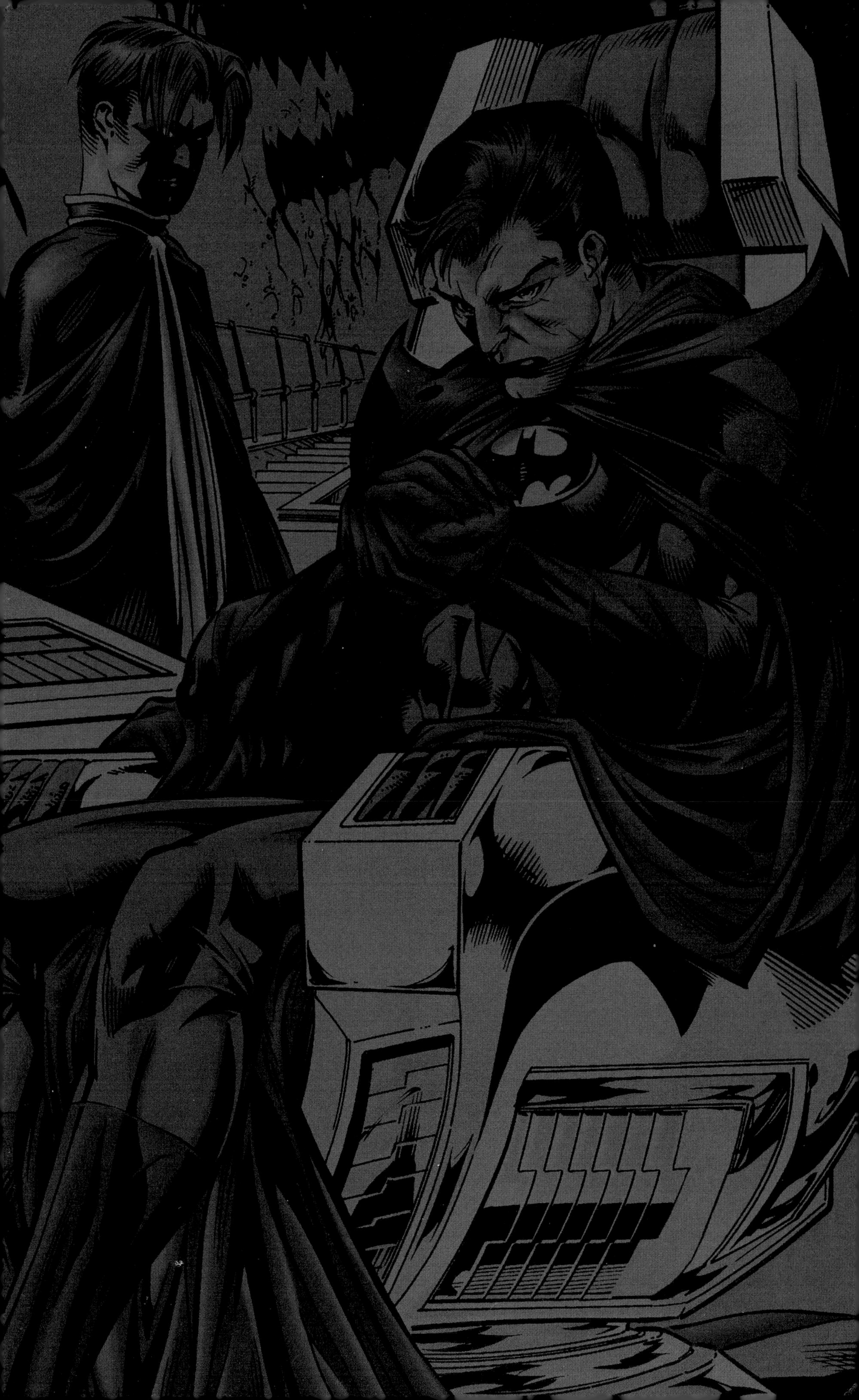

COVER ART TO
JLA: ROCK OF AGES
TRADE PAPERBACK
BY HOWARD PORTER WITH LEE LOUGHRIDGE

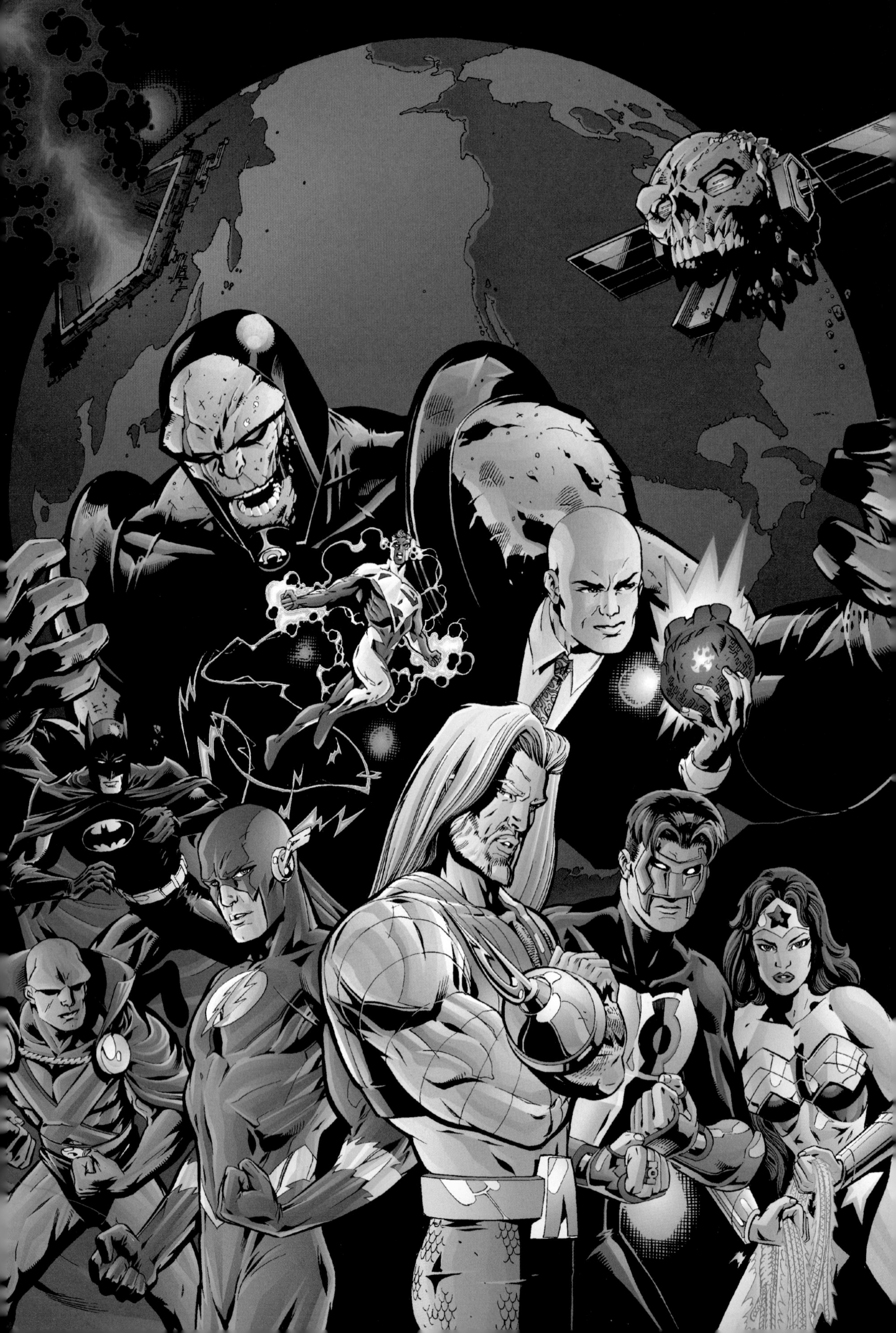

COVER ART TO
JLA: STRENGTH IN NUMBERS
TRADE PAPERBACK
BY HOWARD PORTER & JOHN DELL WITH PAT GARRAHY

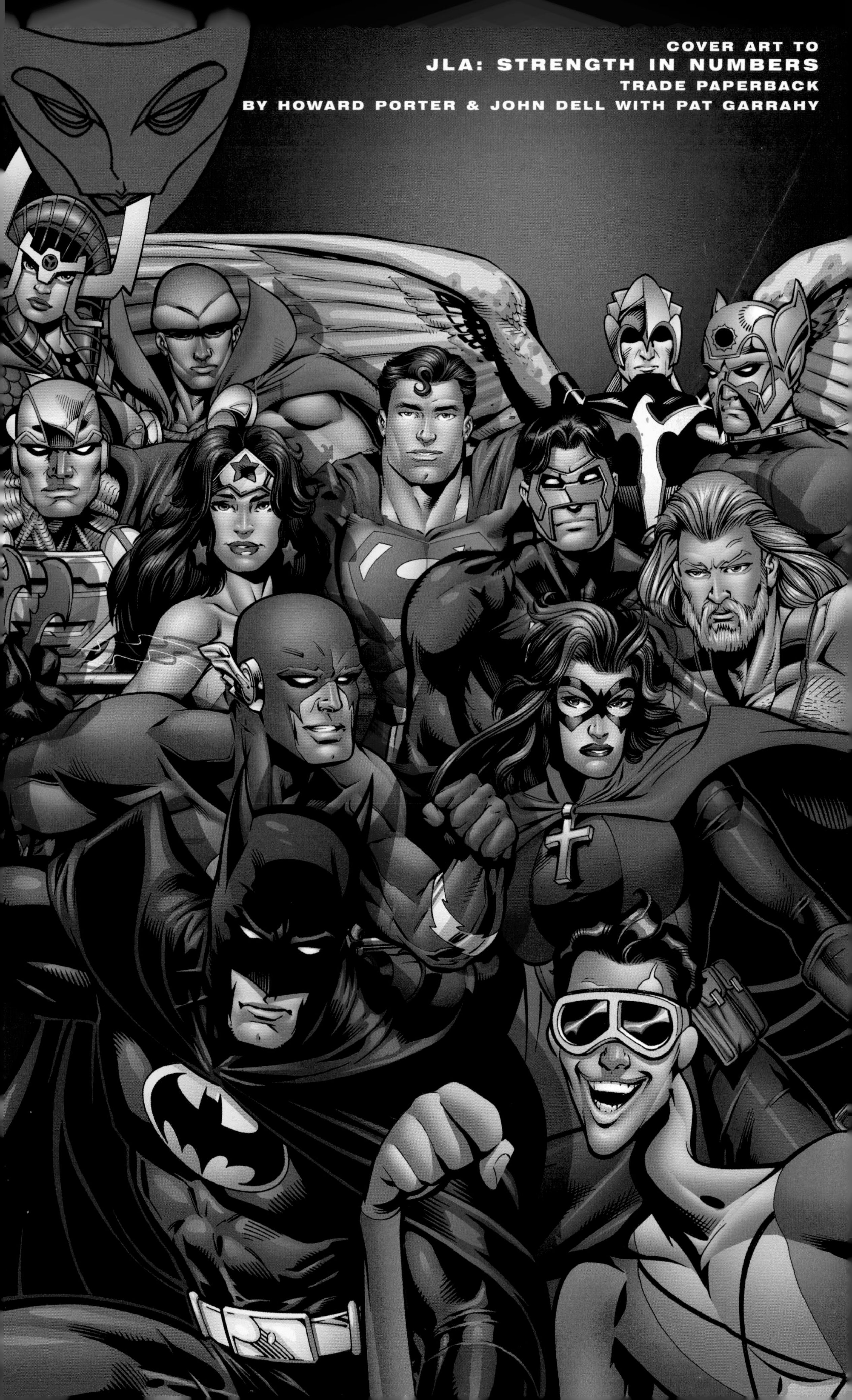

SOMETHING
VERY LIKE
THIS!
GOLD + SILVER

Lights
swim
under
glass
gauntlet

WRITER GRANT MORRISON OFTEN SKETCHES
DESIGNS FOR NEW CHARACTERS FOR
ARTISTS TO THEN FOLLOW. FOR JLA,
HE PROVIDED THE INITIAL VISUAL CONCEPTS
FOR THE WINGED HERO ZAURIEL,
AS WELL AS NEW VILLAIN PROMETHEUS.

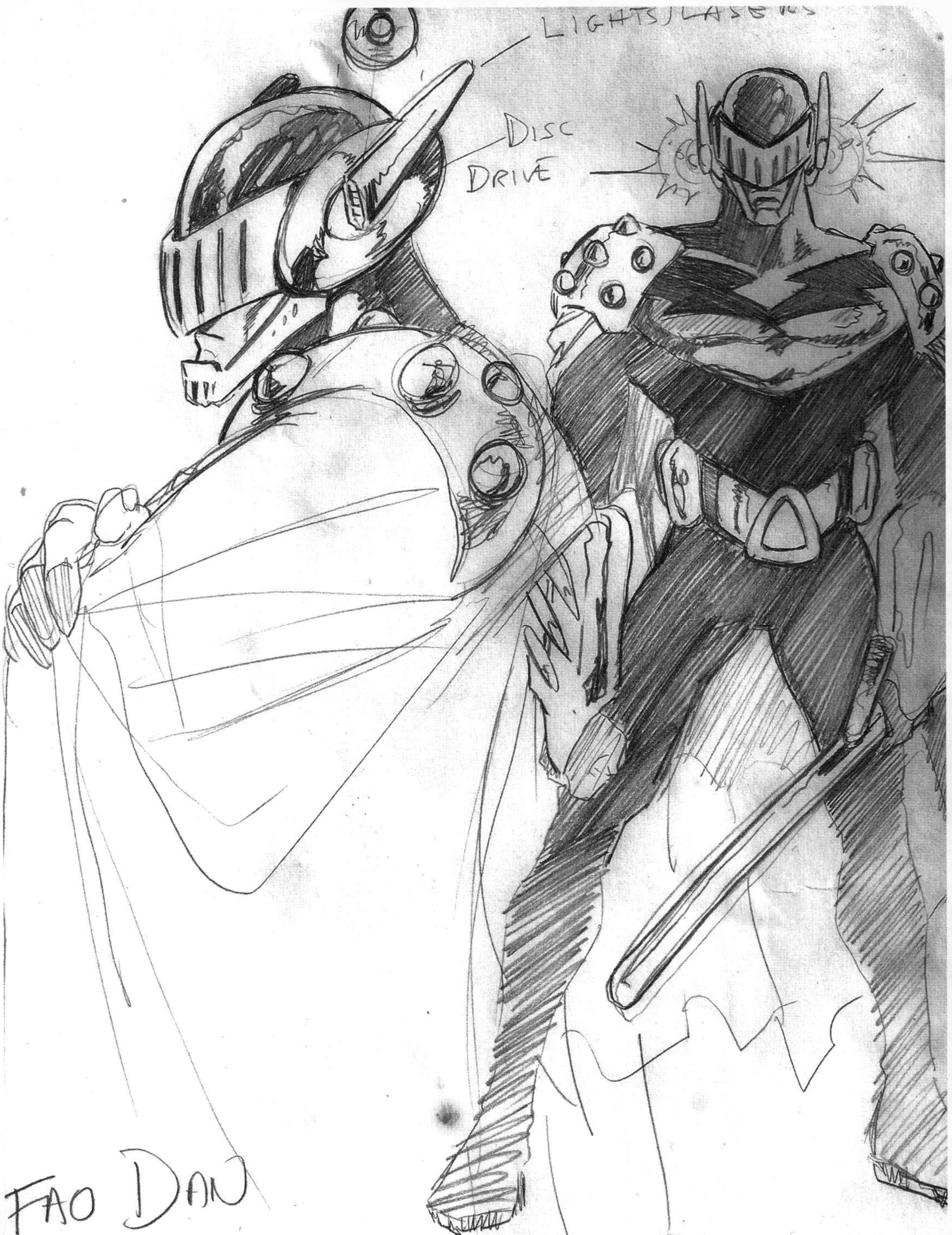
LIGHTS/LASERS
DISC
DRIVE
FAO DAN
RASPLER
PROMETHEUS
POLICE-STYLE
BATON
SOMETHING
LIKE THIS...

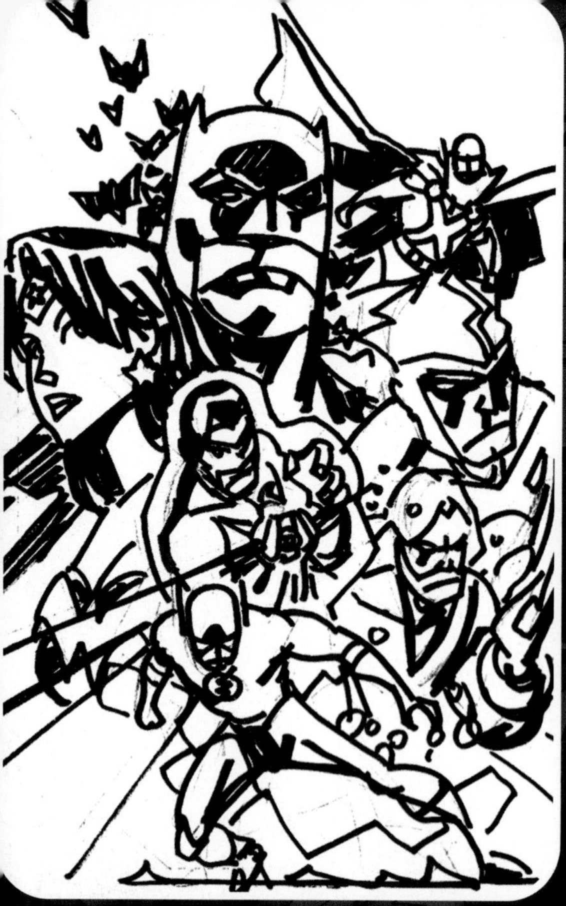

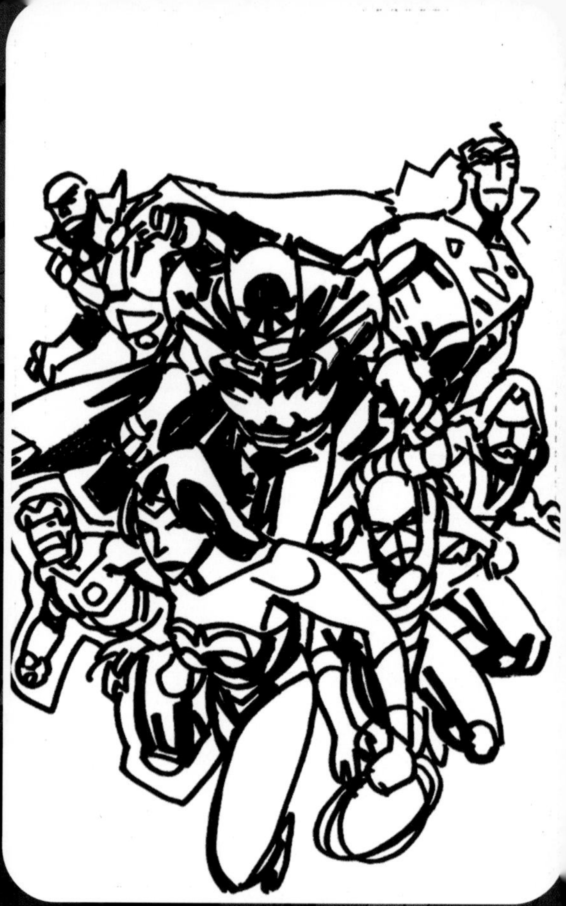

PENCILLER HOWARD PORTER PROVIDED THREE DIFFERENT COVER CONCEPTS FOR THIS COLLECTION. ALL THREE SKETCHES WERE GREAT, BUT SINCE A "CHARGING"-TYPE IMAGE WAS USED FOR THE COVER OF THE PREVIOUS VOLUME, THE DECISION WAS TO GO WITH THE THIRD IMAGE FOR SOMETHING DIFFERENT.

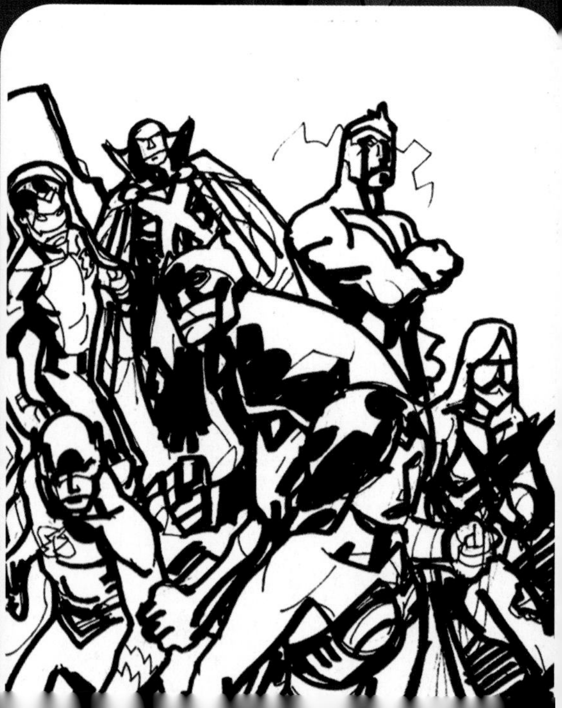

PINUP BY JOHN DELANEY, HOWARD PORTER & JOHN DELL

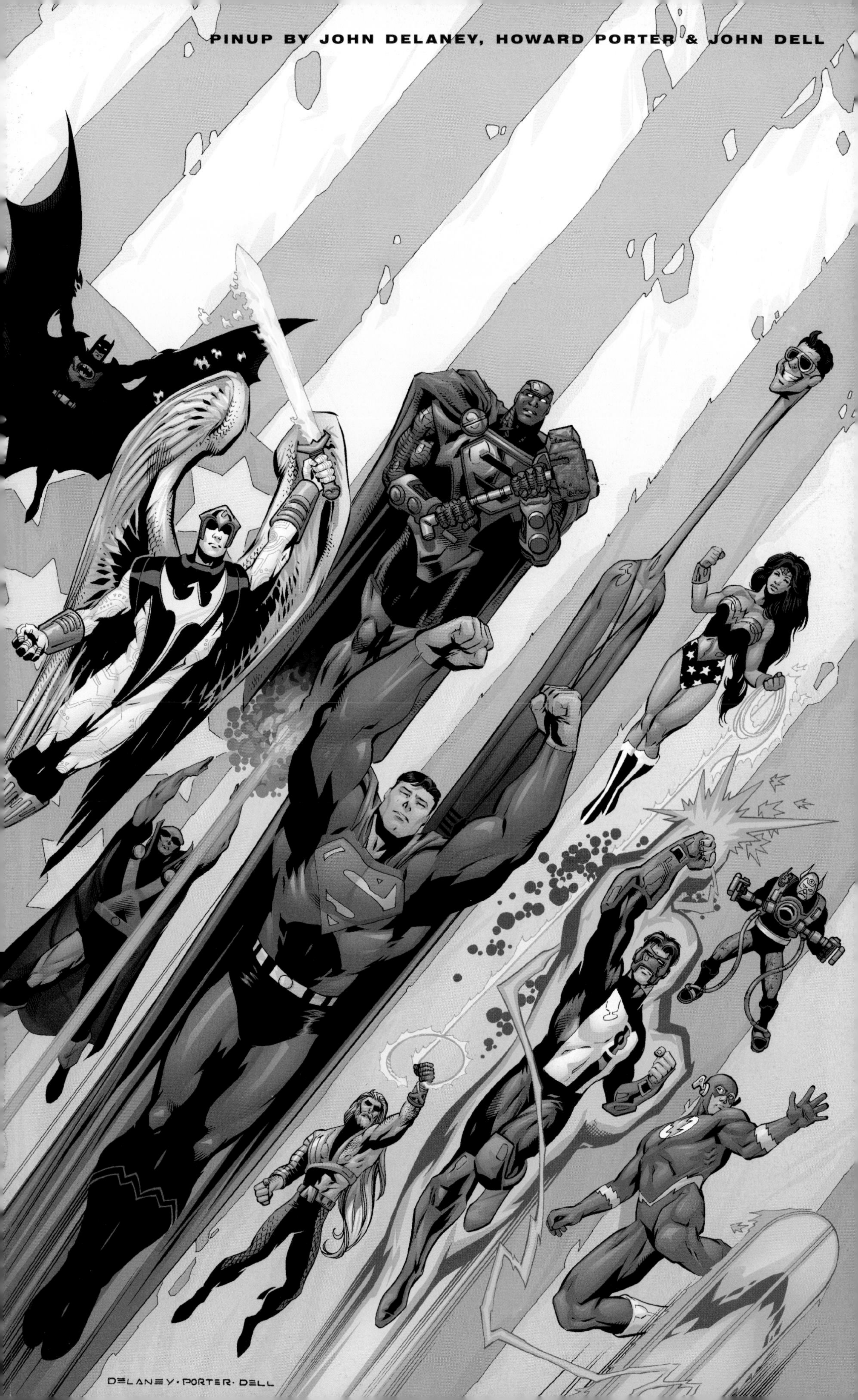
DELANEY · PORTER · DELL

GRANT MORRISON Grant Morrison has been working at DC Comics for over 20 years, starting his US career with acclaimed runs on ANIMAL MAN and DOOM PATROL. Since then he has written best selling titles JLA, BATMAN and *New X-Men*, as well as his subversive creator-owned titles such as THE INVISIBLES, SEAGUY, THE FILTH, and WE3. He has been hard at work helping to reinvent the DC Universe in titles such as the Eisner Award-winning ALL-STAR SUPERMAN, FINAL CRISIS, and BATMAN AND ROBIN.

In his secret identity, he is a "counterculture" spokesperson, a musician, an award-winning playwright and a chaos magician. He lives and works between LA and his homes in Scotland.

HOWARD PORTER Howard Porter started in the comics industry as an inking assistant, but soon graduated to being a penciller — where his first major work was on DC Comics' THE RAY series written by Christopher Priest. Shortly after, he pencilled DC's 1995 crossover event UNDERWORLD UNLEASHED written by Mark Waid, followed by the re-launching of JLA with writer Grant Morrison.

After a short break from illustrating, Porter came back to comics to reunite with Waid on Marvel's *Fantastic Four* series, before returning to DC with a run on THE FLASH with writer Geoff Johns. Most recently, Porter teamed up with Judd Winick on THE TRAILS OF SHAZAM! and TITANS.

VAL SEMEIKS Val has been illustrating comics for over twenty years, starting with monthly work on *Conan The Barbarian* for Marvel. He then moved on to DC Comics, with long runs on THE DEMON and LOBO (both with writer Alan Grant), DC ONE MILLION (with Grant Morrison), as well as work on such titles as JLA: INCARNATIONS (with John Ostrander), SUPERMAN'S NEMESIS: LEX LUTHOR (with David Michelinie), and BATMAN: LEGENDS OF THE DARK KNIGHT (with Dwayne McDuffie).

JLA

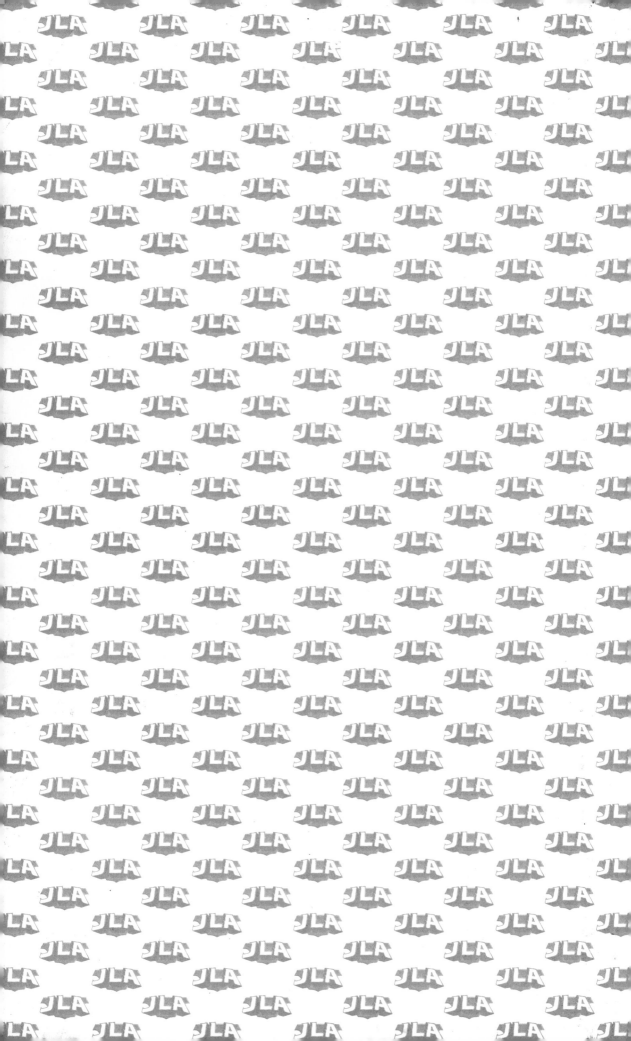